June 10–12, 2015
London, UK

I0028737

**Association for
Computing Machinery**

Advancing Computing as a Science & Profession

SIGSIM-PADS'15

Proceedings of the 3rd ACM Conference on

SIGSIM-Principles of Advanced Discrete Simulation

Sponsored by:
ACM SIGSIM

Association for Computing Machinery

Advancing Computing as a Science & Profession

ISBN: 978-1-4503-3583-6 (Digital)

ISBN: 978-1-4503-3870-7 (Print)

Additional copies may be ordered prepaid from:

ACM Order Department
PO Box 30777
New York, NY 10087-0777, USA

Phone: 1-800-342-6626 (USA and Canada)
+1-212-626-0500 (Global)
Fax: +1-212-944-1318
E-mail: acmhelp@acm.org
Hours of Operation: 8:30 am – 4:30 pm ET

Printed in the USA

Message from the Conference Chairs

Welcome to the 3rd ACM SIGSIM-PADS conference on Principles of Advanced Discrete Simulation. Modeling & simulation is at the heat of nearly all science and engineering disciplines, and conferences such as SIGSIM-PADS are key to reporting advances in critical simulation methods and important application domains. Every paper author or attendee in ACM SIGSIM-PADS helps to advance the state of the art in critical simulation methodologies and applications.

This year the conference is hosted by the University of Westminster in the thriving metropolis of London. We have an excellent program to offer our attendees this year. All papers submitted to the conference were rigorously reviewed with most papers receiving 3 referee reports and follow on discussion. We thank the program committee and additional referees for their diligent efforts to provide timely, critical reviews and feedback to the authors. This process resulted in a total of 60 submissions: 24 were accepted as full papers and 3 were initially accepted as work-in-progress (WIP) papers. A number of authors who were initially rejected were given the opportunity to submit WIP papers. A further 8 WIP papers were subsequently accepted. The PhD Colloquium has 9 students taking part. We expect the fine tradition of high-quality papers and presentations will continue this year.

The best paper candidates for this year are:

FatTreeSim: Modeling a Large-scale Fat-Tree Network for HPC Systems and Data Centers Using Parallel and Discrete Event Simulation by Ning Liu, Adnan Haider, Xian-He Sun and Dong Jin

Exploring the Relationship between Adherence to Treatment and Viral Load through a New Discrete Simulation Model of HIV Infectivity by Ela Rana, Philippe Giabbanelli, Naga Balabhadrapathruni, Xiaoyu Li and Vijay Mago

A Virtual Time System for Linux-container-based Emulation of Software-defined Networks by Jiaqi Yan and Dong Jin

The winner will be announced at the conference and will be mentioned in the Chair's message for the 2016 conference.

We are pleased to confirm that the 2015 SIGSIM-PADS best paper award went to:

GPU-Assisted Hybrid Network Traffic Model by Jason Liu, Yuan Liu, Zhihui Du and Ting Li

Congratulations to Jason, Yuan, Zhihui, and Ting on this well-deserved award!

We would like to thank the hard working SIGSIM-PADS program committee for their diligent (and on time!) reviewing. We would also like to thank the other members of the organizing committee:

Professor Steffen Strassburger (TU Ilmenau) (Publicity Chair)

Dr Anastasia Anagnostou (Brunel University London) (Registration Chair)

Dr David Bell (Brunel University London) (PhD Colloquium Chair)

Dr Tamas Kiss (University of Westminster (Local Chair)

Finally, we would like to thank our two keynotes, Professor Georgios Theodoropoulos and Professor Peter Kacsuk, for their stimulating presentations, Professor Adrian Johnstone (Royal Holloway) for a special session on Babbage's Language of Thought, Professor Paul Fishwick, the current chair of ACM SIGSIM, for his support and enthusiasm and Professor Osman Balci for his excellent ACM SIGSIM PADS website (and instantaneous response to any requests!)

London is an exciting place to visit. We hope that both the conference and your visit will renew old friendships, give you the opportunity to make new friends and, above all, inspire you to push the boundaries of our exciting discipline!

Simon J E Taylor
ACM SIGSIM-PADS'15
General Chair
Brunel University London, UK

Navonil Mustafee
ACM SIGSIM-PADS'15
Program Co-Chair
University of Exeter, UK

Young-Jun Son
ACM SIGSIM-PADS'15
Program Co-Chair
University of Arizona, USA

Table of Contents

Session: Distributed Simulation IV
Session Chair: Jonatan Lindén *(Uppsala University)*

Session: Network Applications
Session Chair: Wentong Cai *(Nanyang Technological University)*

Session: Traffic Applications
Session Chair: Young-Jun Son *(University of Arizona)*

ACM SIGSIM-PADS 2015 Conference Organization

General Chair: Simon J. E. Taylor *(Brunel University London, UK)*

Program Chairs: Navonil Mustafee *(University of Exeter, UK)*
Young-Jun Son *(University of Arizona, USA)*

Proceedings Chairs: Simon J. E. Taylor *(Brunel University London, UK)*
Navonil Mustafee *(University of Exeter, UK)*
Young-Jun Son *(University of Arizona, USA)*

Local Chair: Tamas Kiss *(University of Westminster, UK)*

Publicity Chair: Steffen Strassburger *(Technical University of Ilmenau, Germany)*

Treasurer & Registration Chair: Anastasia Anagnostou *(Brunel University London, UK)*

PhD Colloquium Chair: David Bell *(Brunel University London, UK)*

Steering Committee Chair: George Riley *(Georgia Institute of Technology, USA)*

Steering Committee: Osman Balci *(Virginia Tech, USA)*
Paul Fishwick *(The University of Texas at Dallas, USA)*
Richard M. Fujimoto *(Georgia Institute of Technology, USA)*
John A. (Drew) Hamilton, Jr. *(Mississippi State University, USA)*
Jason Liu *(Florida International University, USA)*
David M. Nicol *(University of Illinois at Urbana-Champaign, USA)*

Program Committee: Khaldoon Al-Zoubi *(Blackberry, Canada)*
Michele Amoretti *(Università degli Studi di Parma, Italy)*
Anastasia Anagnostous *(Brunel University London, UK)*
Osman Balci *(Virginia Tech, USA)*
Fernando J. Barros *(University of Coimbra, Portugal)*
Wengtong Cai *(Nanyang Technological University, Singapore)*
Christopher D. Carothers *(Rensselaer Polytechnic Institute, USA)*
Rodrigo Castro *(University of Buenos Aires, Argentina)*
Olivier Dalle *(INRIA/University of Nice Sophia-Antipolis, France)*
Andrea D'Ambrogio *(University of Rome "Tor Vergata", Italy)*
Umut Durak *(Roketsan Inc. System Simulations, Turkey)*
Roland Ewald *(University of Rostock, Germany)*
Tony Field *(Imperial College, UK)*
Paul Fishwick *(The University of Texas at Dallas, USA)*
Richard M. Fujimoto *(Georgia Tech, USA)*
Drew Hamilton *(Mississippi State University, USA)*
J David Hill *(Blaise Pascal University, France)*
Jan Himmelspach *(University of Rostock, Germany)*

Program Committee (continued):

Xiaolin Hu *(Georgia State University, USA)*
Shafagh Jafer *(University of Milwaukee, USA)*
David R. Jefferson *(Lawrence Livermore National Lab, USA)*
Cameron Kiddle *(University of Calgary, Canada)*
Franziska Klügl *(Orebro University, Sweden)*
Sunil Kothari *(Hewlett Packard Development Company, L.P., USA)*
Hillel Kugler *(Microsoft Research, UK)*
Sunil Kothari *(Hewlett Packard Development Company, L.P., USA)*
Hillel Kugler *(Microsoft Research, UK)*
Jason Liu *(Florida International University, USA)*
Qi Liu *(GE Global Research, USA)*
Emilio P. Mancini *(INRIA Sophia-Antipolis, France)*
Mohammad Moallemi *(Carleton University, Canada)*
David M. Nicol *(University of Illinois at Urbana-Champaign, USA)*
Libero Nigro *(University of Calabria, Italy)*
James Nutaro *(Oak Ridge National Lab, USA)*
Francesco Quaglia *(University of Rome "La Sapienza", Italy)*
Martin Quinson *(Université de Lorraine, France)*
Ernie Page *(MITRE Corp., USA)*
Kalyan S. Perumalla *(Oak Ridge National Lab, USA)*
George F. Riley *(Georgia Tech, USA)*
José L. Risco-Martín *(Universidad Complutense de Madrid, Spain)*
Hessam S. Sarjoughian *(Arizona State University, USA)*
Thomas Schulze *(University of Magdeburg, Germany)*
Mamadou D. Seck *(TU Delft, Netherlands)*
Steffen Straßburger *(TU Ilmenau, Germany)*
Claudia Szabo *(University of Adelaide, Australia)*
Simon J E Taylor *(Brunel University London, UK)*
Andreas Tolk *(Old Dominion University, USA)*
Mamadou K. Traoré *(Blaise Pascal University, France)*
Carl Tropper *(McGill University, Canada)*
Bruno Tuffin *(INRIA, France)*
Charles Turnitsa *(Columbus State University, USA)*
Adelinde M. Uhrmacher *(University of Rostock, Germany)*
Brian Unger *(University of Calgary, Canada)*
Kurt Vanmechelen *(University of Antwerp, Belgium)*
Philip A. Wilsey *(University of Cincinnati, USA)*
Yiping Yao *(National University of Defense Technology, China)*
Levent Yilmaz *(Auburn University, USA)*
Enver Yücesan *(INSEAD, France)*

Sponsor:

ix

Keynote Talk

Simulation in the Era of Big Data: Trends and Challenges

Georgios Theodoropoulos
Institute of Advanced Research Computing
Durham University
United Kingdom
theogeorgios@gmail.com

ABSTRACT

The emergence of extreme scale computing systems and the data explosion have presented an unprecedented opportunity for the analysis of systems at a rapidly increasing scale, complexity and granularity. This paradigm shift calls for an intermingling of "what-if" and data analytics approaches, however the worlds of Simulation and Big Data have so far been largely separate. The talk will focus on the interplay between simulation, data and emerging computational platforms, identifying gaps and opportunities and discussing some concrete examples of interacting scalable data infrastructures and agent-based simulations.

Categories and Subject Descriptors

I.6.0 [**Simulation and Modelling**]: General

General Terms

Algorithms.

Keywords

Simulation, Big Data, Exascale, Agent-based models

SIGSIM-PADS'15, June 10–12, 2015, London, UK.
ACM 978-1-4503-3583-6/15/06.
http://dx.doi.org/10.1145/2769458.2769484

Knowledge Discovery in Manufacturing Simulations

Niclas Feldkamp, Soeren Bergmann, Steffen Strassburger
Ilmenau University of Technology
P.O. Box 100565
D-98684 Ilmenau
+49 3677 - 69 4050
{niclas.feldkamp, soeren.bergmann, steffen.strassburger}@tu-ilmenau.de

ABSTRACT

Discrete event simulation studies in a manufacturing context are a powerful instrument when modeling and evaluating processes of various industries. Usually simulation experts conduct simulation experiments for a predetermined system specification by manually varying parameters through educated assumptions and according to a prior defined goal. Moreover, simulation experts try to reduce complexity and number of simulation runs by excluding parameters that they consider as not influential regarding the simulation project scope. On the other hand, today's world of big data technology enables us to handle huge amounts of data. We therefore investigate the potential benefits of designing large scale experiments with a much broader coverage of possible system behavior. In this paper, we propose an approach for applying data mining methods on simulation data in combination with suitable visualization methods in order to uncover relationships in model behavior to discover knowledge that otherwise would have remained hidden. For a prototypical demonstration we used a clustering algorithm to divide large amounts of simulation output datasets into groups of similar performance values and depict those groups through visualizations to conduct a visual investigation process of the simulation data.

Categories and Subject Descriptors

I.6.6. [**Simulation and Modeling**]: Simulation Output Analysis

Keywords

Simulation, data farming, data mining, visual analytics, knowledge discovery.

1. INTRODUCTION

According to Law, one of the biggest pitfalls while conducting a simulation study is the absence of a clearly outlined project scope [9]. Reversely, a simulation always has to have a clearly defined goal. In context of a manufacturing system, a goal to achieve through simulation might be answering questions like "which scheduling strategy performs best" or "what size does this

SIGSIM-PADS '15, June 10 - 12, 2015, London, United Kingdom
© 2015 ACM. ISBN 978-1-4503-3583-6/15/06…$15.00
DOI: http://dx.doi.org/10.1145/2769458.2769468

buffer need". As a side effect of this approach, one does not have to model aspects of the system that are not influential to answering the proposed questions.

Analyzing discrete event manufacturing simulations is usually performed by looking at a few distinct parameters according to the simulation project scope. An optimization is not conducted by a simulation itself, but rather through execution of multiple simulation runs. In order to reduce complexity and number of runs, the input parameters of each single run have to be varied cleverly, eventually assisted by mathematic optimization procedures.

The simulation analyst usually takes an educated guess based on his experience which parameters might be influential on the project scope and therefore time and effort is invested in experimenting with these focus parameters in a fixed system configuration environment. Kleijnen et al. refer to this as the trial-and-error approach to finding a good solution and argue that simulation analysts should spend more time in analyzing than building the model [7].

While this generally accepted way of conducting manufacturing simulations is best practice when it comes to meet a specific, predetermined goal, we can learn rather less about the systems behavior in general. In this paper, we propose a somewhat different approach, which is analyzing the whole range of possible model behavior without a specific goal in order to eventually uncover interesting relations that prior were unknown.

On a database level, this process is referred to as "knowledge discovery in databases [2]. In the work presented here we aim to adapt this process to manufacturing simulations. If we want to look at the whole bandwidth or at least the biggest part of possible systems behavior, we have to conduct a massive number of experiments. Arising amounts of data can be kept under control through cleverly designed input spaces. This approach is similar to the *data farming* metaphor, which means one should let grow the simulation output efficiently through large-scale designed experiments in order to discovery surprises and potential options [5, 12].

That way we support decision making in a manufacturing context that may lead to more outside-of-the-box solutions that eventually the analyst did not think of before.

Certainly this approach will produce much more output data than a traditional, project-goal centric simulation study. This viewpoint of conducting manufacturing simulations is driven by technical evolution as well. In today's world of cheap commodity hardware clusters and distributed, lightweight databases, minimizing experimental effort is not a primary concern and handling large amounts of data has become a lot easier than thirty years ago when discrete-event simulations became viable for factory planning and entrepreneurial decision making. If we take a look at the term *big data*, Sanchez argues that big data was always there because it is whatever pushes against the limits of currently available technology [12].

In order to support the analysis of hundreds of thousands or maybe millions of simulation records we investigate on the application of data mining methods alongside suitable visual representations that allow to quickly overview large amounts of simulation data. Simulation modeling is partly a creative process and the definition of what is interesting and potentially useful may depend on the analyst's subjective viewpoint. Therefore, our approach provides a semi-automatic analysis through intuitive visual representations of mining results to make use of the human ability to quickly identify patterns and relations in visual arrangements.

The remainder of this paper is structured as follows. Section 2 introduces the process for knowledge discovery in databases (KDD). In Section 3 we adapt this process for the knowledge discovery in manufacturing simulations. Section 4 presents a small case study illustrating the application of this process. Section 5 summarizes our findings and discusses future work.

2. KDD AND DATA MINING
2.1 The KDD Process
Originally, knowledge discovery in databases means making sense of data. To be specific, this refers to data collections that are too big to manually review each and every single record. Possible input sources are for example structured data or data warehouses, graphs or data streams and sequences [15].

Fayyad et al. describe a process of multiple steps to ultimately transform low level data into useful knowledge, which can be seen in Figure 1. The KDD process is highly interactive with many decisions made by the user and some steps may have to be iteratively repeated.

KDD is a semi-automatic process because the user is ultimately responsible for interpretation and evaluation of mining results. This is especially true when it comes to evaluating if the gained knowledge is potentially useful. This process' main effort is transforming data into forms of representation that are more useful like abstractions, summaries or more compact mappings. Therefore the data mining step is essential. Data mining basically means applying algorithms over the data that are able to extract patterns based on statistical measurements and machine learning [2]. The data mining toolset offers a broad range of methods like for example clustering, regression or classification.

In this work, we investigated the application of clustering methods. In general, clustering means grouping a set of objects into subsets (clusters), so that objects within the same cluster are very similar to each other but have low similarity to objects outside the cluster. For our purpose we used the K-means clustering algorithm. K-means separates n objects into k clusters, whereas every object has to belong to the cluster with the nearest mean in similarity and every cluster has to contain at least one object. The similarity is called *distance*, which is the measurement level to express how similar two objects are. The most common method to determine the distance between two objects is the *Euclidian distance* shown in Equation 1.

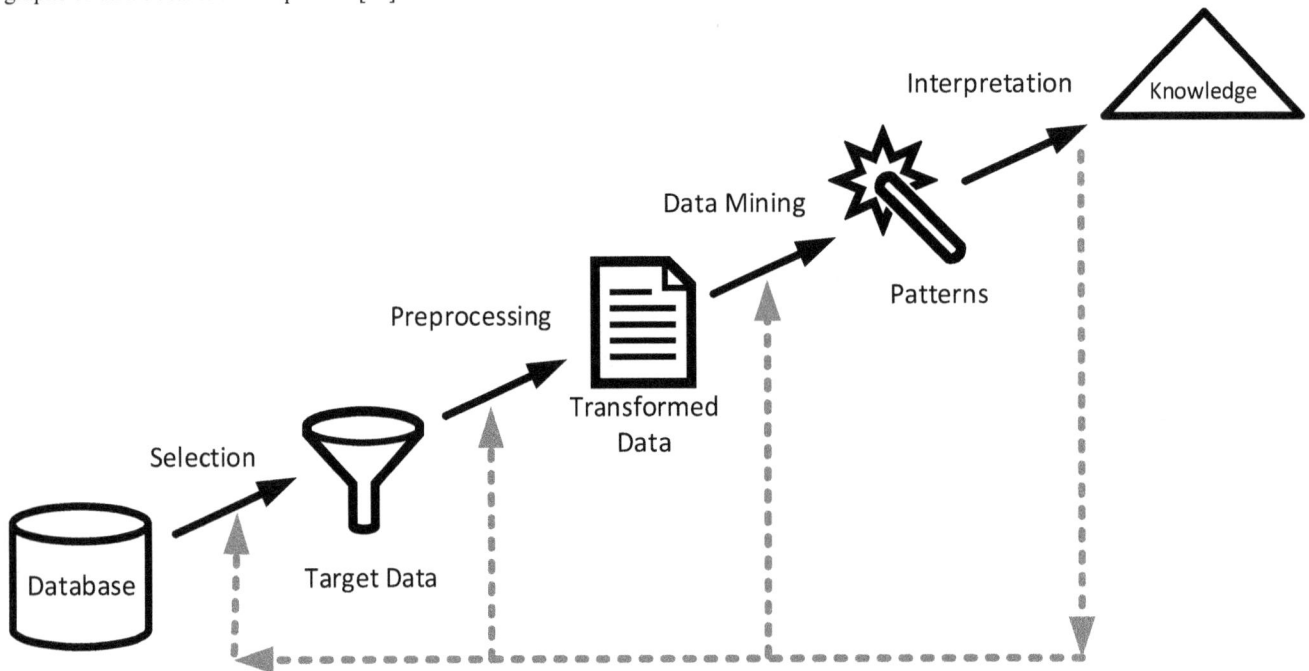

Figure 1. Overview of the steps that compose the KDD process. Adapted from [2].

$$d(i, j) = \sqrt{(x_{i1} - x_{j1})^2 + (x_{i2} - x_{j2})^2 + \cdots + (x_{in} - x_{jn})^2}$$

Equation 1: Euclidian distance between an object pair with n dimensions

A good clustering is achieved when the sum of squared distances of objects in a cluster to their cluster center are minimized and distances between cluster centers are maximized [3].

2.2 Visual Analytics

Visualizing results is an important tool when an interpretation of data is needed. Suitable visualizations can utilize the human ability to recognize patterns and coherence. This is also referred to as *visual reasoning*, which is the science of synthesizing information from massive datasets in order to provide understandable assessments that can be used effectively for communication action and decision making [13].

Since this is in turn in conformity with the general perception of sense and purpose of simulations, our approach aims to combine both research disciplines. Certainly visual analytics is only then a reasonable tool when datasets become big enough, respectively are too big to manually review each observation individually.

A proper visual analysis should show the important, big picture first, and uncover details on demand. The visual analytics process is furthermore conducted through a frequent shift between visual and computational analysis of data [6], which makes it a semi-automatic process.

Among others, main benefits of visual analytics are increasing cognitive resources by expanding human working memory, reducing time exposure by representing large amounts of data in a small space and promoting recognition of patterns as well as exploring relationships that otherwise remain hidden or at least were more difficult to find [13].

3. KNOWLEDGE DISCOVERY IN MANUFACTURING SIMULATION

Revisiting simulation experiments, on an abstracted level a simulation model can be seen as a black box that transforms input data into result (output) data. In a manufacturing context, the input data are adjustable system variables like intervals, buffer sizes or scheduling strategies. Result data on the other hand is composed of the system's performance indicators like throughput times or machine utilization.

Looking at the KDD-Process shown in Figure 1, knowledge discovery in a simulation begins at data transformation. We are in total control of data creation since the simulation analyst defines the experiments. Therefore we don't have to deal with faulty or incomplete data on a technical or database level and can skip the selection and preprocessing step.

This is in line with the definition of data farming. If we take a look at the term big data, it is described as having three dimensions, volume, velocity, and variety, and all these dimensions are increasing at a very high rate [8].

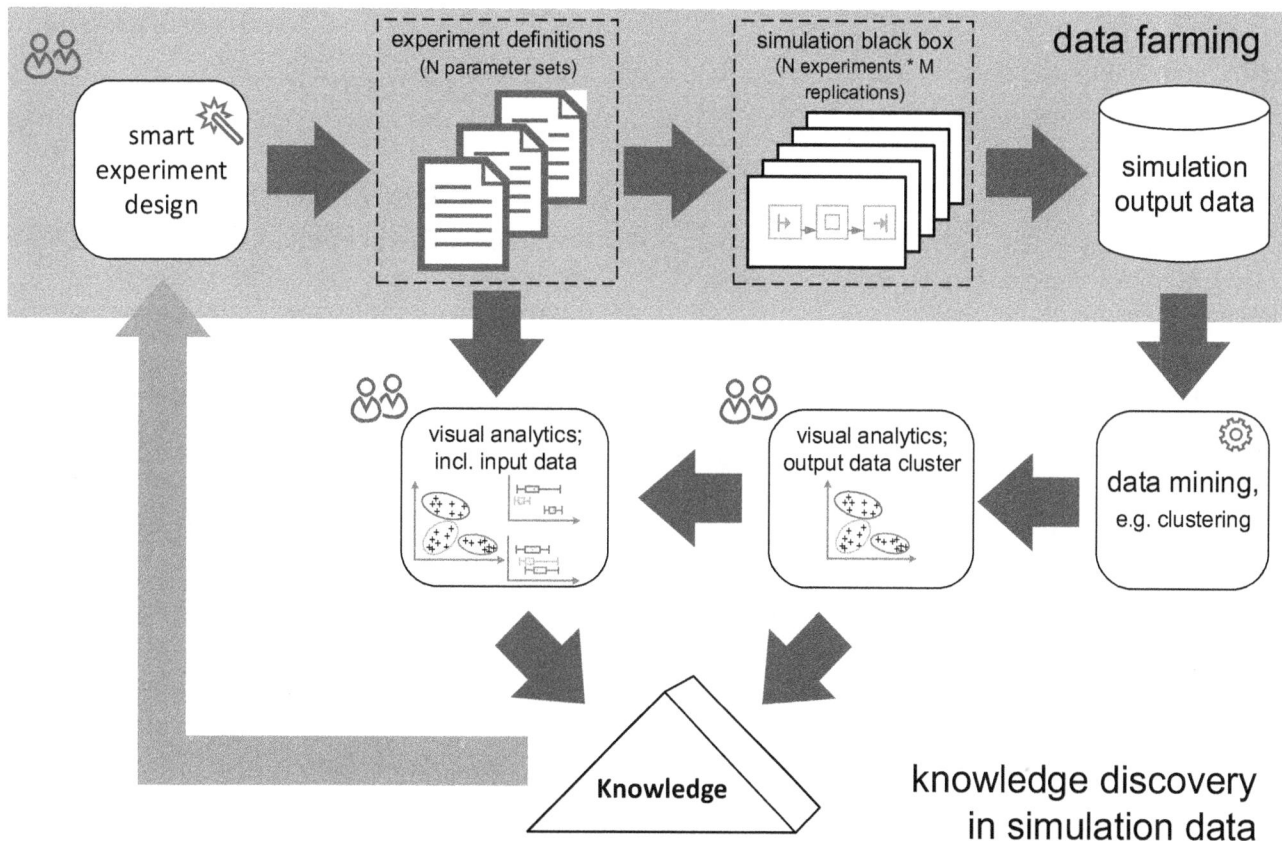

Figure 2. Knowledge discovery process in a discrete event manufacturing simulation.

In a simulation environment, the simulation analyst is always in total control of volume and velocity. The amount of generated output data depends on the experimental setup and furthermore the simulation analyst determines which of the performance measures he wants to observe. At most one may argue that the output data may have a variety of types, so there are at least two v's the analyst is in control of [12].

Figure 2 shows our approach on knowledge discovery in manufacturing simulations. First we have to identify adjustable system input parameters. Next step is estimating bottom and top factor level limits and defining experiments accordingly. Moreover, measurable output parameters have to be defined. This includes possible data types and measurements scales.

After simulation experiments have been conducted, output data can be processed through data mining methods and represented with suitable visualizations. An initial investigation should explore shape and distribution of output parameters and linkage between those. Yet before looking at related input parameters, possible interesting patterns might even be discovered by only looking at output data.

Afterwards, visualizations should establish links between corresponding input and output parameter sets. This eventually yields interesting relationships between corresponding input/output parameter values. Findings should be interpreted and transformed into knowledge by verifying them through the design and conducting of additional experiments in such a way that an iterative process emerges.

As said before, we used a clustering algorithm for the exploration of output data. Since we grow our data as we need, the only thing to do before we can apply a clustering algorithm is to transform the data into a format that fits the algorithms requirements.

Our approach on clustering simulation data means each object in a cluster is one single simulation run. To which cluster a simulation run is allocated is based on selected result parameters of this distinct run. So as a result, experiment runs within the same cluster are similar regarding the selected system performance measures. Figure 3 left side shows a small notional demonstration. Note that this example includes a very small number of simulation runs, respectively cluster points. In a large scale experiment design, the number of cluster points is too big to identify single points, but rather a trend and tendency of point distribution is the focus of visual representation.

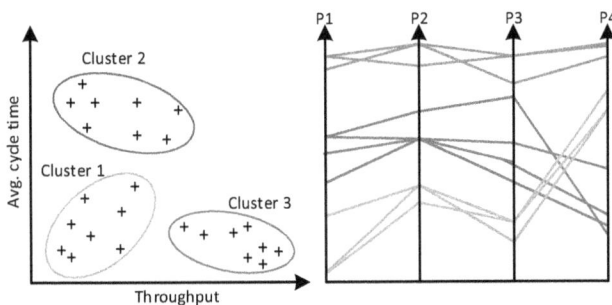

Figure 3. Left side: Two-dimensional representation of simulation output clustering. Each point represents a single experiment and each cluster represents a group of experiments that are similar regarding the two performance measures throughput and average cycle time. Right side: Notional parallel coordinates visualization with four parameters P1-P4.

Furthermore, a two-dimensional representation is feasible only if two variables per simulation run are examined. If the clustering algorithm should process more than two variables, a multidimensional data representation is necessary, like for example the parallel coordinates method as seen in Figure 3 right side.

So what are the actual benefits we can utilize after clustering the simulation outputs?

First of all, we get a visual impression and a quick overview of the performance measures from a large numbers of experiments at once. We also get a first impression on how those experiments are distributed regarding the observed performance measures.

The next step would be investigating the clusters and the experiments they are composed of. An experiment is equivalent to a simulation run which is a dataset composed of a set of output data with corresponding input variables settings. So if we look at a distinct cluster, we also know which input parameter settings are linked to this clusters experiments. Following the iterative process of knowledge discovery, we may apply further statistical methods to gain additional insights on how input parameters values are distributed among the different clusters.

Taking a look at cluster 2 in Figure 3, the system's performance of corresponding experiments is rather poor, whereas system performance of cluster 3 experiments are quite good, with rather high throughputs and low cycle times. From here we can investigate which input settings led to the corresponding systems performance measures that define this cluster.

If we are able to outline a significance of distinct input parameters values that lead to a specific cluster allocation that is yet even unexpected, we actually created new knowledge. At best this knowledge is utilized to support factory planning decisions.

For a better understanding, we clarify the knowledge discovery process with a simple use case example in the following chapter.

4. USE CASE SCENARIO

4.1 Design of Experiments and Prototypical Setup

For a demonstration of this approach, we used an enhanced single server model. In this example, seven different types of products enter the manufacturing system at one single source. Each product type has a distinct processing and setup time. Additionally, each production job gets a unique due date when entering the system. Production jobs are being sorted before entering the processing station and the station has eventually to be set up according to the product type. The time exposure needed to set up the station varies as well depending on the product type. Figure 4 shows a screenshot of Simulation Model.

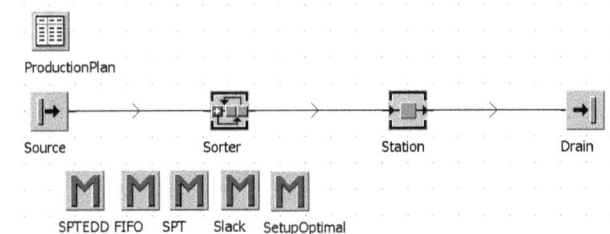

Figure 4. Screenshot of the Plant Simulation Model.

Hence adjustable input variables are: the interval within which jobs are entering the system, the sorter's maximum capacity, the sorting strategy, and the mixture of product types. Measureable output variables are e.g. throughput, mean cycle times, setup times, due date delay and station utilization.

Table 1 shows the design of experiments. For inter arrival times we chose fixed values from 60 seconds up to 240 seconds, which are also the minimum and maximum processing times per job. For sorter capacity we enumerated from 100 to 1000 slots, because preliminary experiments showed that a sorter allocation over 1000 is not expectable, even with a high arrival frequency. Further, we used 5 different sorting strategies: First in first out (FIFO), shortest processing time (SPT), minimum slack time (SLACK), a weighted combination of SPT and earliest due date (SPTEDD) and sorting according to current station setup state.

Table 1. Experimental design

Input Factor	Margins	Levels
Inter arrival time	60s-240s	18
Sorter capacity	10-1000	10
Sorter strategy	5 strategies	5
Product mixture (Seven product types)	0-100% per product	47 Experiments (NOLH-Sampling)
Random number stream	*1-10*	*10*

Due to the stochastic nature of simulation we also conduct replications by varying random number streams. Each replication represents one additional dataset for the knowledge discovery process.

Designing the product mixture experiments is more complicated, because a simple full factorial design from 0%-100% per product type is not feasible, since it would result in at least 7^{101} possible product mixes, and this calculation does not even consider mutual dependencies between the product type proportions. Therefore, a sampling method is necessary. As described above, experiment design through a suitable sampling method manages to reduce the number of experiments dramatically while maintaining the coverage of large parameter spaces.

We created our experiments based on the *nearly orthogonal latin hypercube (NOLH)*, which is a sampling method that offers a realistic distribution of parameter variability. Orthogonal means that these designs try to minimize correlation between input variables and factor-level combinations are evenly sampled [4, 11, 16]. With the sampling design we ended up with 47 manifestations regarding to the product mixture and all input variables combined resulted in a total number of 491.160 experiments. Note that we used the sampling method for the product mixture and full factorial design for the other variables. This is possible because our test scenario is simple. When models become more complex and the number of input variables increases, sampling over all input variables is necessary.

We portioned the simulation runs onto multiple machines and conducted them with Tecnomatix Plant Simulation. For storing input/output datasets we used a MongoDB noSQL database [10]. We choose the noSQL approach, because the schemaless and highly scalable database implementation allows to quickly adapt to dataset modifications while neglecting revision of data schema. Flexible data stores are crucial when adding or removing model

parameters or changing parameter data types after experiments have already been conducted. Another advantage is that a traditional SQL database would slow down the speed of adding new entries due to its data integrity validation mechanisms. Since we are in total control of data creation on the application side, integrity validation can be neglected.

4.2 Clustering Simulation Output Data

As said before, our goal is to group simulation runs into clusters of similar output performance values, so the first question would be which output parameters should be taken into account for the clustering algorithm. Our goal is to group simulation runs into meaningful clusters that are assignable into a hierarchical order from high performance to poor performance runs. Conducting multiple clustering executions with varying parameters is therefore necessary.

Because we observe a large number of output parameters, datasets are multi-dimensional. In multi-dimensional data, similar datasets are composed of subsets that often correlate among each other. Furthermore, correlation among subsets indicates valuable relationships between attributes and eventually hidden casualization [1]. Taking this into account, we can preselect possible parameter combinations by looking at spatial shapes of subsets and searching for interesting patterns.

Figure 5 shows selected output parameters as a scatterplot matrix, which draws a two-dimensional scatterplot for each variable pair of the multi-dimensional data set. This allows us to determine if there are any noticeable, interesting structures among subsets. For example, a rather structure less point cloud with a high proportion of outliers would result in a decrease of the clusters entropy, so pairwise visual investigation of subsets eventually leads to additional insights [14] and therefore meaningful clusters.

In fact there are correlated structures between *throughput, station utilization* and *station setup proportion*. What we see are strongly correlated structures among those parameters, which can be expected in a single server model and also hidden coherences and unexpected distributions between those performance indicators should be very limited in this environment. Still we use those parameters for demonstration of the concept and as a result we get a very clean clustering with good separation between clusters that allows us to build a group hierarchy from good to poor performance runs which is shown in Figure 6. As a counter example, Figure 7 shows a clustering execution with low informational entropy, because the underlying variables have a very high proportion of outliers and are less structured.

This is because the delay value has low influence to the cluster experiment's cluster allocation. Taking a look at the histogram of delay in Figure 5, it shows a high amount of values in the 0-delay class and therefore other variables are nearly uniformly distributed to the 0-delay class.

The final clustering can be seen in Figure 6. The three dimensional data points are represented in a one dimensional parallel coordinates plot as described in section 3. For a better visual representation, each column has been standardized to a 0 mean and a standard deviation of 1, so this visualization is used to evaluate the comparison between experiments, not to look at the actual parameter values. Regardless of cluster allocation, this visual representation gives a quick overview (regarding the three selected performance measures) of almost half a million simulation experiments.

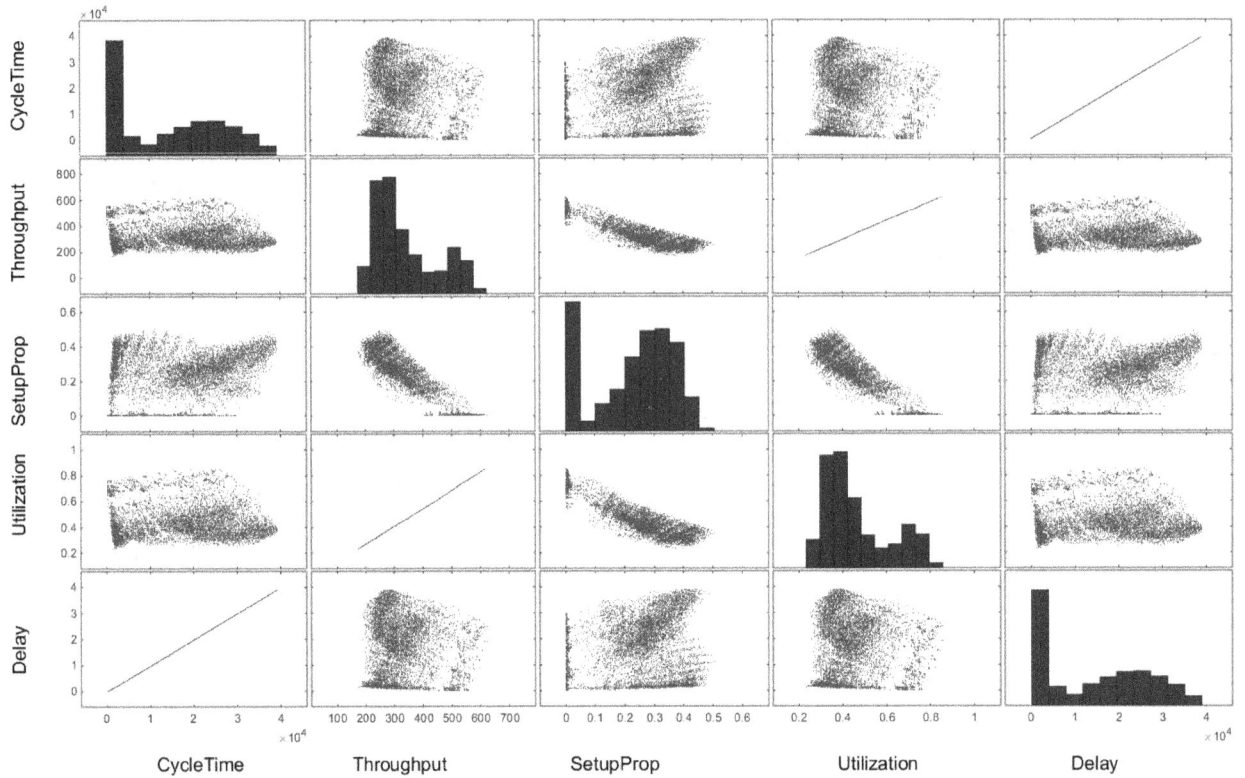

Figure 5. Scatterplot matrix of selected output parameters. This visualization helps to determine parameters which potentially produce well separated clusters.

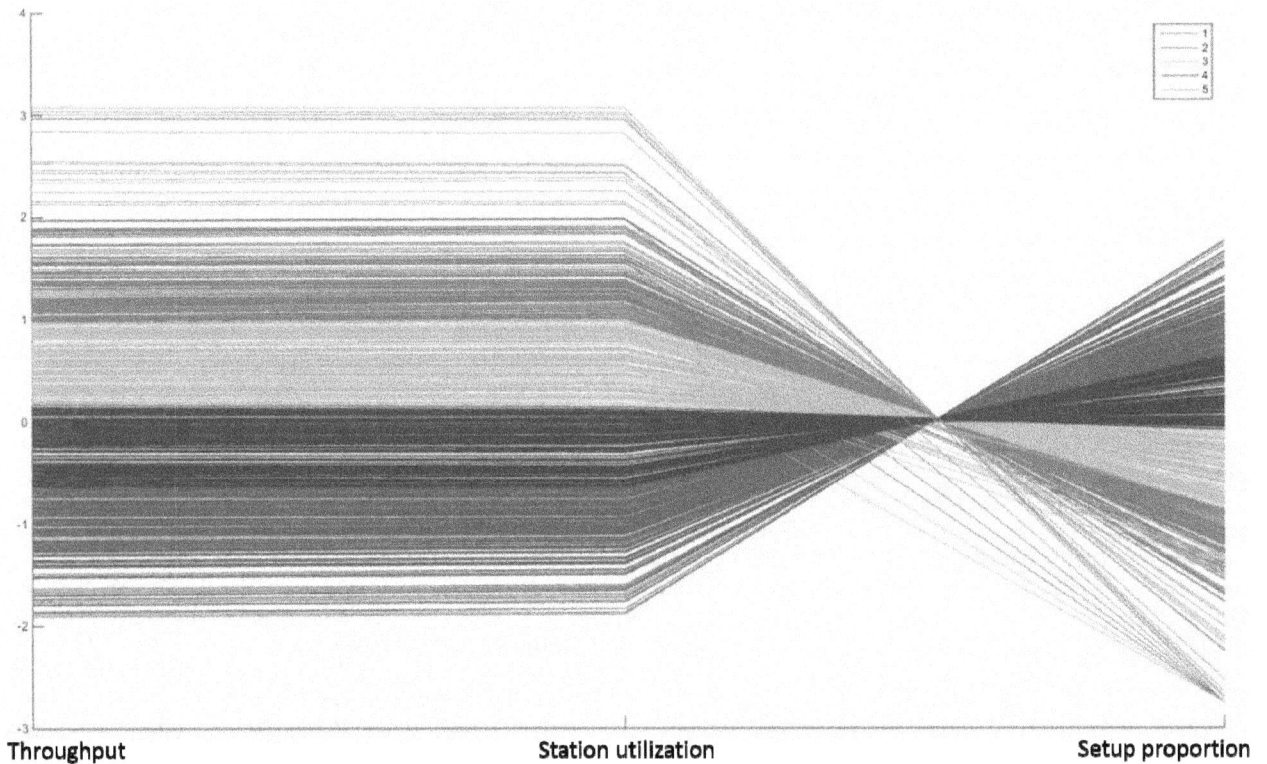

Figure 6. Parallel coordinates visualization of the clustering based on three parameters. Each vertical axis represents one parameter. Parameter values are shown as standardized relative values.

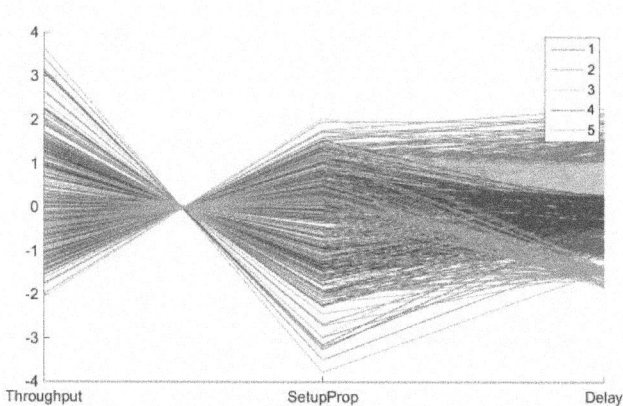

Figure 7. Poorly separated clusters as a result of parameters that don't have a distribution with distinct spatial shape. Clusters are less meaningful so information entropy is low.

Looking at Figure 6, the experiments that compose cluster 1 (blue color) have the lowest performance, with a low throughput, high proportion of machine setups but still low overall station utilization. This performance is worse because e.g. experiments in cluster 4 (purple color) perform much better among throughput and station utilization to the proportion of station setup times. Experiments in cluster 5 (green) and cluster 2 (orange) perform best, even though cluster 2 has a few outlier experiments that have very low setup proportion but don't fulfil the expected linear relation to throughput and station utilization. Further investigation should – among other things - find out why those experiments have lower throughput than cluster 5 experiments despite low setup time proportion.

4.3 Investigation of Relationships to Input Data Parameters

After we grouped the experiments in clusters regarding system performance (of selected parameters), the next step is finding relations to experiment input parameters and investigating on which input parameter values the clusters are composed of.

For example, a certain input parameter value that appears frequently in a distinct cluster indicates that this parameter is influential to the cluster allocation. For that purpose, we used modified boxplots that show the position of an input variable's quartiles per cluster, as shown in Figure 8. The left side of the box marks the location of the 25% quantile and the right side marks the location of the 75% quantile. This means that 50% of all observations are located in the range of the box. Smaller boxes therefore indicate a more specific and less distributed value, because 50% of all observations are located in that range. Additionally, if boxes are not or at least hardly overlapping, the distinct range of value exclusively appears in that cluster, which indicates a strong influence of that value to the cluster allocation.

We also set the height of the box relative to the number of objects in the cluster. That way, a cluster that consists of only a small number of outliers does not lead to wrong interpretations.

Relationships to job inter arrival time

Figure 8 shows that for the input parameter *ArrivalTime*, the high performance cluster number 5 has most of its observations within a value range from 60 to 120 seconds, which shows that low inter arrival time of jobs leads to better system performance. Still this box is partly overlapped by the value range of boxes from other

clusters, which indicates that *ArrivalTime* is not the only input variable that is influential to cluster allocation.

Relationships to product mixture

As said before, the mixture of the seven products was also part of the input parameter setup. Because the proportion values depend on one another they cannot be investigated separately and have to be reviewed together in order to yield meaningful insights.

The common visual representation would be a histogram with seven classes - one class per product type - that shows the proportions of the mixture. Because each simulation run has a different mixture, this would result in half a million different histograms, and plotting those among their cluster allocation would not be a feasible visualization.

As a simplification, we initially limit our investigation to the shape of the mixture that can be represented by one single ratio parameter. This parameter evaluates the balance of the mixture and the number of components in the mix. Based on the Euclidian norm in a two component setting a 100%-0% mix marks the upper end and a 50%-50% mix the lower end of the scale. Because this ratio reduces the product mixture to one single value per observation, we are then able to depict this in a box plot again.

This plot (Figure 8, bottom diagram) shows that the high performance cluster is significantly linked to product mixtures with unbalanced proportions, the best cases being a single product production or mixtures with high proportions of one single product. This is owed to the effect that high proportions of one single product in the mixture lead to less setup processes on the machine, which ultimately reduces the amount of time where the machine is blocked.

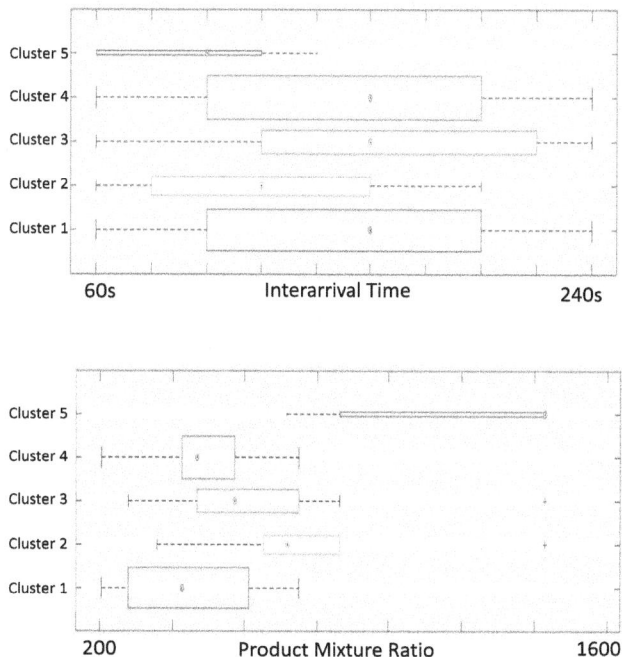

Figure 8. Boxplot that shows distributions of input parameter values per cluster. The top diagram shows the quantile plots for the input parameter *ArrivalTime*, the bottom diagram shows the quantile plots for the product mixture ratio.

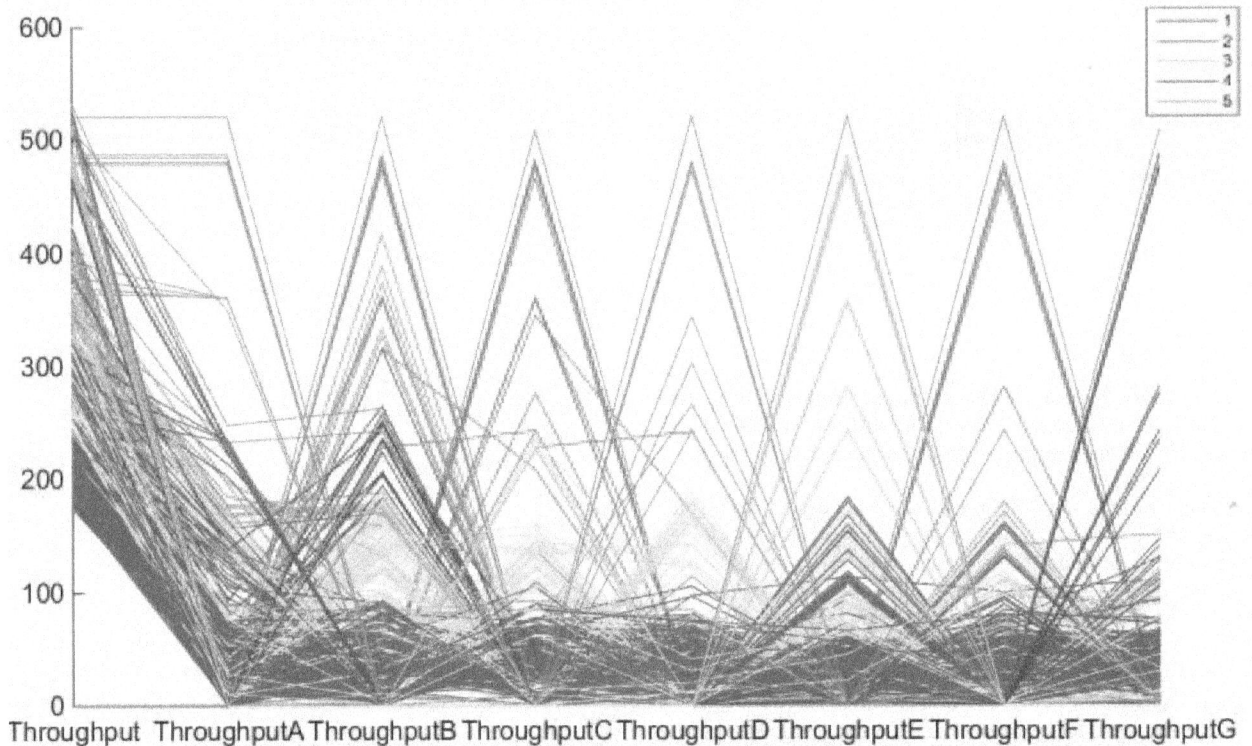

Figure 9. Parallel plot of measured cumulative throughput (parameter on the farthest left) alongside with throughputs per product type (from A to G), color-coded with corresponding cluster membership. Y-axis represents produced parts (absolute values).

Figure 9 supports this assumption by showing that the highest cumulative throughputs (parameter to the farthest left on x-axis) are correlated with very unbalanced proportions of throughput regarding the product type. This can be concluded from the spikes in the parameters showing throughput per product type. The simulation runs in the good (green) cluster have a tendency to prefer product mixes with a single product type leading to the spikes in throughput of this product type (green spikes in product type throughput).

Also from Figure 9 we see that the flatter the lines become, the more balanced is the throughput over the product types, leading to a decreased overall throughput. Moreover, the plot also reflects the hierarchy of clusters from good to poor system performance.

Relationships to job sorting strategy

Another input variable we wanted to investigate is the applied sorting strategy. Since this variable is on a nominal scale and has no numeric ratio, plotting quantiles would be meaningless. An informative visualization should rather show the proportion of the 5 strategies per cluster, so e.g. a possible visualization would be pie charts or a mosaic plot, as shown in Figure 10 and Figure 11.

We see that Cluster 1 does not include experiments conducted with the setup optimal strategy, and therefore this strategy at least does not lead to bad performance. Yet high proportions of experiments in Cluster 2, 3 and 5 indicate that this scheduling strategy leads to good system performance. This is obviously an accurate conclusion since this strategy leads to less machine utilization through setup processes. In summary, regarding to our simple single server model, we found out that short inter arrival times of jobs is the key to a good system performance, at least up

to a break-even point where machine blockings due to setup processes decrease the systems performance.

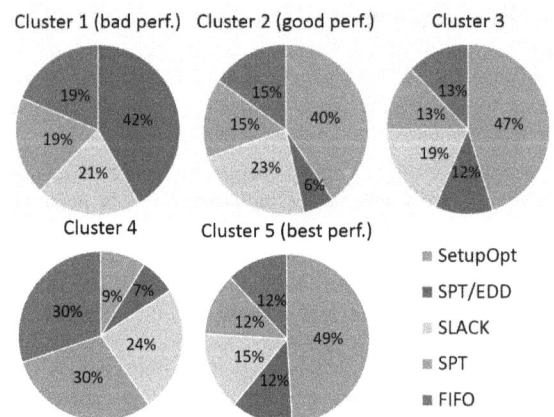

Figure 10. Pie charts of sorting strategy proportion per cluster.

In that situation a setup optimal scheduling strategy lessens this effect. Furthermore, focusing on reducing the product mixture variety is always superior to any sophisticated product mixture, regardless of the applied scheduling strategy.

In line with our proposed iterative process for knowledge discovery, new sets of experiments should be designed to either confirm or dismiss these findings, in order to create knowledge. So the next step would be the design of additional experiments that focus on exploring the limits of those input values that lead to good system performance.

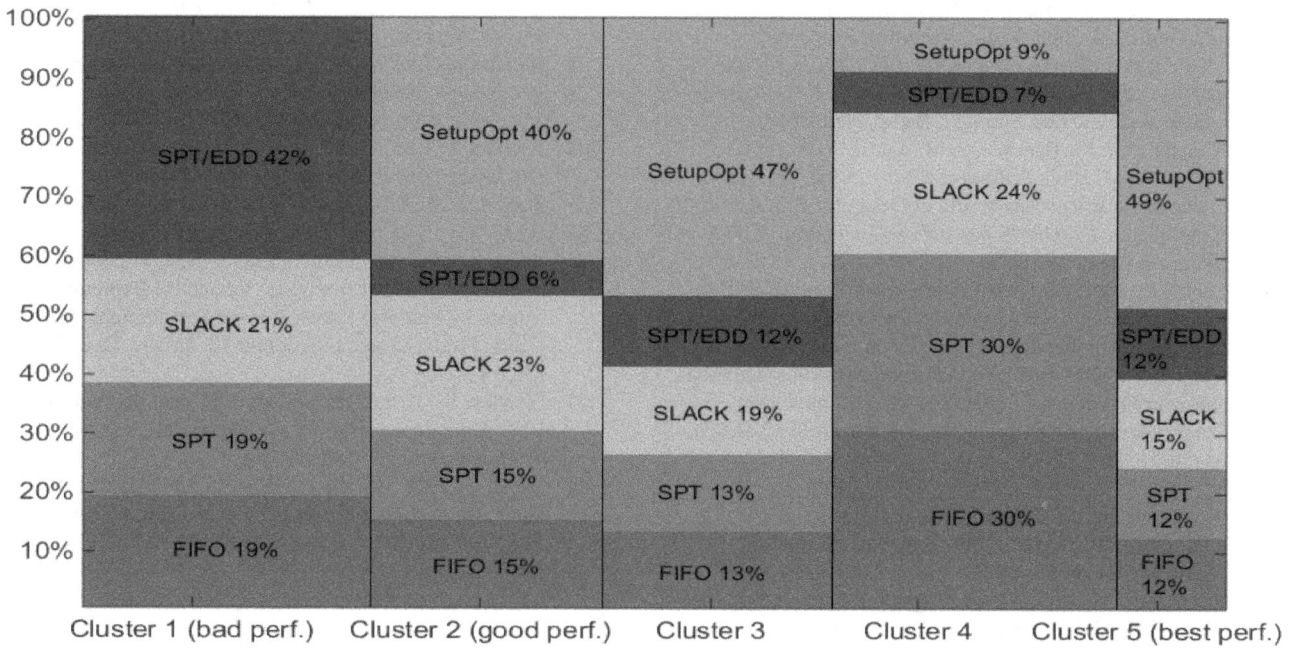

Figure 11. Mosaic plot of sorting strategy proportion per cluster. Note that the width reflects the overall amount of objects in the cluster.

5. DISCUSSION AND SUMMARY

Although options for finding hidden knowledge in a simple single server model are quite limited, we demonstrated how a knowledge discovery process for manufacturing simulation data can be performed. Our approach is based on the knowledge discovery process known from data database sector. We have shown how this process can be adopted for simulation output analysis and how visual analytics combined with elements from big data analytics can be usefully applied in simulation studies.

Our approach brings in an additional viewpoint to discrete event manufacturing simulations analysis, which can be considered alongside traditional experimentation techniques conducted in simulation studies.

Moreover, our approach might be more appealing to people who are not "simulation experts", because in contrast to working through lines of numbers, visualization is a more striking way of handling simulation data. On the other hand it may be less precise since it is more open to interpretation. Planning decisions should always be assisted with traditional simulation studies, but our approach on covering a broadband of system behaviors can help to guideline a certain path.

The above described problem of plotting the scheduling strategy and product mixture made clear that visual linkage between input/output parameters of different scale measurement levels (e.g. nominal and numerical) leads to new challenges in visualization methods in due consideration that visualization should be easily understandable and interpretable. In a best case scenario, the visualization promotes intuitive investigation and knowledge discovery by leveling the tradeoff between correctness, complexity and simplicity. Future research is certainly needed for new visualization methods for these purposes. Taking for example the problem of product mixture, we still face the challenge on how to feasibly plot one single depiction of thousands of experiments with each experiment

having different mixture proportions. Furthermore, visual analytics demands interaction with data, so user interaction should also be incorporated.

Because our proposed method of clustering is just one of many possible investigation methods, future research may also investigate on other data mining and machine learning techniques for simulation data analysis. Promising methods are for example classification methods like decision trees or support vector machines and association rule learning like pattern and sequence mining. Furthermore, online machine learning methods could enable the combination of real world factory data logging and simulation data for a real time data or near-real time data analysis.

6. REFERENCES

[1] Böhm, C., Kailing, K., Kröger, P., and Zimek, A. 2004. Computing Clusters of Correlation Connected Objects. In *Proceeding of the 2004 ACM SIGMOD international conference* (Paris, France, June 13 - 18, 2004). SIGMOD/PODS '04. ACM, New York, NY, 455-466. DOI = http://doi.acm.org/10.1145/1007568.1007620.

[2] Fayyad, U. M., Piatetsky-Shapiro, G., and Smyth, P. 1996. From Data Mining to Knowledge Discovery in Databases. *AI Magazine* 17, 3 (Fall 1996), 37–54.

[3] Han, J. and Kamber, M. 2006. *Data mining. Concepts and techniques*. The Morgan Kaufmann series in data management systems. Elsevier; Morgan Kaufmann, Amsterdam, Boston, San Francisco, CA.

[4] Hernandez, A. S., Lucas, T. W., and Carlyle, M. 2012. Constructing nearly orthogonal latin hypercubes for any nonsaturated run-variable combination. *ACM Trans. Model. Comput. Simul.* 22, 4 (Nov. 2012), 1–17.

[5] Horne, G. E. and Meyer, T. E. 2005. Data Farming: Discovering Surprise. In *Proceedings of the 2005 Winter Simulation Conference* (Orlando, USA, December 04 - 07, 2005), 1082–1087. DOI = http://dx.doi.org/10.1109/WSC.2005.1574362.

[6] Keim, D. A., Mansmann, F., Schneidewind, J., Thomas, J., and Ziegler, H. 2008. Visual Analytics: Scope and Challenges. In *Visual Data Mining: Theory, Techniques and Tools for Visual Analytics*, S. Simoff, M. H. Boehlen and A. Mazeika, Eds. Springer, Berlin, Heidelberg.

[7] Kleijnen, J. P. C., Sanchez, S. M., Lucas, T. W., and Cioppa, T. M. 2005. State-of-the-Art Review: A User's Guide to the Brave New World of Designing Simulation Experiments. *INFORMS Journal on Computing* 17, 3 (Summer 2005), 263–289.

[8] Laney, D. 2001. *3D Data Management: Controlling Data Volume, Velocity, and Variety*. In *Application Delivery Strategies*, Number 949, META Group Inc, Stamford.

[9] Law, A. M. 2003. How to conduct a successful simulation study. In *Proceedings of the 2003 Winter Simulation Conference* (New Orleans, USA, December 07-10, 2003), 66–70. DOI= http://dx.doi.org/10.1109/WSC.2003.1261409.

[10] MongoDB Inc. 2010. *Why Schemaless?* http://blog.mongodb.org/post/119945109/why-schemaless. Accessed 10 February 2015.

[11] Sanchez, S. M. 2011. *NOLHdesigns spreadsheet*. http://harvest.nps.edu/. Accessed 1 February 2015.

[12] Sanchez, S. M. 2014. Simulation Experiments: Better Data, not just Big Data. In *Proceedings of the 2014 Winter Simulation Conference*, (Savannah, USA, December 07-10, 2014), 805–816. DOI = http://dx.doi.org/10.1109/WSC.2014.7019942.

[13] Thomas, J. J. and Cook, K. A. 2005. *Illuminating the Path: The Research and Development Agenda for Visual Analytics*. IEEE Computer Society, Los Alamitos, CA, USA.

[14] Wilkinson, L., Anand, A., and Grossman, R. 2006. High-Dimensional Visual Analytics: Interactive Exploration Guided by Pairwise Views of Point Distributions. *IEEE Trans. Visual. Comput. Graphics* 12, 6 (Nov./Dec. 2006), 1363–1372.

[15] Frawley, W. J., Piatetsky-Shapiro, G., and Matheus, C. J. 1992. Knowledge Discovery in Databases: An Overview. *AI Magazine* 13, 3 (Fall 1992), 57-70.

[16] Ye, K. Q. 1998. Orthogonal Column Latin Hypercubes and Their Application in Computer Experiments. *Journal of the American Statistical Association* 93, 444 (Dec 1998), 1430-1439.

Cost Efficient Short Term Capacity Planning for MTO Enterprises

Ketki Kulkarni
Industrial Engineering and Operations Research
Indian Institute of Technology Bombay
Powai, Mumbai, India 400076
ketki.k@iitb.ac.in

Pallavi Manohar
Xerox Research Center India
Prestige Technology Park-II
Bangalore, India 560103
pallavi.manohar@xerox.com

ABSTRACT

A Make-to-Order (MTO) set-up is one in which production starts only on receiving confirmed orders, and there is no inventory. An enterprise is a group of production sites that may be geographically separated. This paper considers enterprises that operate on the MTO principles. Upon receiving orders for products, the orders are assigned to the different production sites that are geographically distributed. In order to have an efficient production plan, the decision support system must address challenges at the enterprise level, as well as at the individual production site level. In this paper our interest is in an optimal distribution of orders across sites while exploiting individual capacities at those sites. The enterprise level decisions are referred to as routing decisions, while the site level decisions are called scheduling decisions. The planning horizon for these decisions is typically short, that is, a day or a week and hence the proposed solution approach falls under short term capacity planning. A central router is assumed to receive orders on behalf of the enterprise, and is then expected to divide the order workload amongst the sites, in order to minimize the overall costs (production as well as transportation). At each site, an optimal schedule is determined to minimize the maximal completion time, as well as maximize remaining capacity on each machine, after satisfying the workload assigned to it. A framework for cost efficient routing and scheduling while ensuring job deadlines is proposed which allows *iterative interaction* of routing and scheduling modules. The feedback on capacity based on deadline violations at each site is used to iteratively optimize routing of jobs while ensuring job deadlines, along with the objective of cost efficient capacity planning. We present two iterative frameworks one using Mixed Integer Program (MIP) and the second using MIP and discrete event simulation model. The proposed frameworks have been implemented and computational results are presented to compare their performances.

Categories and Subject Descriptors

G.1.6 [**Mathematics of Computing**]: Optimization

General Terms

Algorithms, Performance

Keywords

Capacity Planning; Hybrid Simulation-optimization; Routing; Scheduling

1. INTRODUCTION

Manufacturing set-ups can be classified into two types, Make-to-Order (MTO) and Make-to-Stock (MTS), based on whether the system follows a 'push' or 'pull' strategy. In MTS systems, products are planned in order to stock them as inventory, for future demand. This is a push strategy, where production is based on the demand forecast. As opposed to this, in MTO systems, manufacturing takes place only when an order is received. Such a strategy is called pull strategy, where production is based on the actual or consumed demand.

This paper considers an enterprise group that operates on MTO principles. An enterprise group is a conglomeration of smaller manufacturing units that share the workload of orders received centrally. The smaller units may be owned by a central authority that negotiates the orders on behalf of the group. Alternatively, multiple small units may form an enterprise group through contract, wherein they agree to collectively satisfy orders that would be too large for them to handle individually. Such an arrangement is called as *Horizontal Manufacturing Collaborative Alliance* (HMCA) [4]. A hybrid case is also possible, wherein an enterprise owns a few small manufacturing units and has entered into contract with few other units that it does not own, but which can be a part of the enterprise group, as an outsourcing option.

This paper addresses different decision making challenges in an MTO enterprise environment. The problem description and proposed solution approaches discussed in this paper are valid for HMCA type of groups as well for the hybrid case discussed above. Although the motivation for this research arises from the planning of an enterprise of print shops, the proposed solution approach applies to any MTO enterprise dealing with highly customized end products. From an Operations Research (OR) perspective, the print shop operations resemble an MTO set up, where an order has to be received before a product is processed. In other words, finished product inventory is absent. Products are made only to satisfy existing orders and not in anticipation of future orders.

For each shop, the problem at hand is of scheduling different tasks of jobs across various machines on the shop floor. However, at an enterprise level, before the scheduling issues can be addressed, other decisions such as routing of jobs need to be considered. This paper presents a unified modelling approach, that allows optimization for decisions at various levels of an organization. The short term capacity planning involves scheduling and/or routing decisions over a smaller time horizon, typically a day.

In this paper, we present two iterative modelling schemes for hierarchical decision making in MTO-based enterprises, with geographically distributed production sites. Both these solution methods provide cost efficient routing and scheduling plans for a short planning horizon, while interacting iteratively on a capacity based feedback mechanism.

The rest of the paper description is organized as follows. Section 2 discusses some of the previous work in similar fields and highlights key departures from these. The problem addressed in this paper is formally defined in Section 3. Section 4 describes the MIP-based iterative scheme, along with the mathematical formulations of each model. Section 5 explains the proposed simulation-based iterative scheme. The computational experiments are described in Section 6, along with the results for different scenarios. Section 7 concludes this paper by summarizing the main contributions and highlighting the future extensions of this work.

2. RELATED WORK

We studied several papers dealing with short term capacity planning, different kinds of enterprises and decision making in MTO-based setups. This section summarises the related work. Table 1 presents the various aspects addressed by different papers that were studied. The first column of the table gives the name(s) of the author(s) and the year of the work. The second column indicates the applicability of their research to short term capacity planning. The third column indicates whether systems under consideration in each of these papers follow the MTO principles. The fourth column shows whether or not an iterative scheme was used in the solution approach. The fifth and sixth columns check the relevance of the works for distributed enterprises and shop-level decisions, respectively. The last two columns indicate the choice of models and the industrial application areas. Their relevance to the proposed work in this paper is indicated by the check-mark ($\checkmark$).

It is seen from the last row in the table that none of the related work addresses all of the criteria that are considered by this paper. Each of these papers is briefly described in the remainder of this section.

Chen et al.[3] present a mathematical model that is intended to aid an operations manager in an MTO environment in selecting a set of potential customer orders to maximize the operational profit while ensuring that all the selected orders are fulfilled by their deadline. The output of their model is an optimal capacity plan for the selected orders over a given (finite and short) planning horizon. Chen et al.[3] demonstrate a tradeoff between maximal capacity utilization and optimal operational profit with an example of a small MTO operation. The main decision addressed here is of either accepting or rejecting a potential order based on capacity constraints at the manufacturing facility. Chen et al.[3] do not consider geographically distributed production sites, that is, enterprise planning is not addressed.

Bo et al.[1] consider various costs associated with a typical MTO set up. The output of the model is a schedule, which explains the assignment of various jobs across different geographical locations. The mathematical model described in their paper helps with multiple decisions. First, it either accepts or rejects an order, depending on the technological/functional requirements of the order and the remaining available capacity of the enterprise as a whole. Next, the order is assigned to one of the many production lines, where each sequence of operations is a separate production line. The objective of the model is to minimize total costs, which include production and transportation costs, while ensuring material balance, capacity constraint satisfaction and satisfaction of technological requirements. The approach proposed by Bo et al.[1] is non-iterative, and does not address decisions at the shop-level.

The work by Rai and Lin[10] focusses on distributing the load across the various facilities in an enterprise, in order to minimize the maximum Turn-Around-Time (TAT). Rai and Lin[10] do not consider costs and the mathematical model, although applicable to general scenarios, is tailored for print shops. In the problem under consideration, an enterprise group receives a set of orders, called print jobs. Each print job can be further divided into tasks. Each print shop is assigned one or more of the tasks associated with a job, expressed as a fraction of the total jobs. Not all print shops may be capable of processing the job. For all the print shops that are capable of processing a given job, TAT for that job on that shop is estimated. Using these values for per job TAT, the per shop TAT is estimated. Finally, an optimization algorithm or heuristic is used to solve the min-max problem (minimize the maximum per shop TAT). While this paper is relevant because it considers the application to print shops, it does not address the scheduling decisions at shop-level. Also, Rai and Lin[10] allow splitting of jobs, that is certain tasks of a job may be performed at one site and the remainder of the tasks may be performed at some other site.

Rai and Lin[11] present a different flavour, wherein the mathematical model tries to evaluate options of reducing the number of geographically separated locations. They present a method for evaluating different consolidation options for print shops belonging to the same enterprise, in order to minimize the number of shops with similar capabilities. While consolidating, different factors such as maximum takt rate and capacity requirements are considered. This work is again tailored for print shops, although in principle, it is applicable to a large number of scenarios.

The problem of job routing at the centralised router for a print enterprise has been studied before and the patents are under process. One approach presents a job routing algorithm in real time where there is no buffering of jobs. The shop model considered is very simplistic (assuming single machine) and greedy heuristic to route the jobs is presented to optimize weighted sum of cost and TAT. Another approach proposed allows buffering of jobs as typically due dates for print jobs are in hours or days. The authors present a cost efficient routing algorithm using greedy set cover heuristics. Note that both these patents do not consider optimization at individual shop and do not handle efficient capacity utilization aspect. The solution methods discussed in these papers are not iterative as well. Further, the approaches presented are specific to the print enterprise

Table 1: Classification of literature survey

Authors	Short-term capacity planning	MTO	Iterative models	Distributed enterprise	Shop-level decisions	Mathematical model	Industrial application
Chen et al.[3]	✓	✓	×	×	×	single MIP	-
Bo et al.[1]	✓	✓	×	✓	×	single MIP	Iron and steel
Rai and Lin[10]	×	✓	×	✓	×	single MIP	Print shops
Rai and Lin[11]	×	✓	×	✓	×	single MIP	Print shops
Manohar and Gross (patent in process)	×	✓	×	✓	×	Heuristic	Print shops
Plumettaz et al.(patent in process)	×	✓	×	✓	×	Heuristic	Print shops
Cheng[4]	×	✓	×	✓	×	multi-objective MIP	-
Huang et al.[5]	✓	✓	×	×	×	modular MIPs	Belt pulley
Byrne and Bakir[2]	✓	×	✓	×	×	DES-MIP	-
Kulkarni and Venkateswaran[8]	×	×	✓	×	✓	DES-MIP	-
Proposed paper	✓	✓	✓	✓	✓	modular MIPs	Print shops

where all shops are owned (and hence has complete information) by the enterprise.

In the work of Cheng[4], a bi-objective problem is solved. The first objective is cost minimization, while the second objective is load balancing. This model considers an ad-hoc enterprise formation, called as HMCA, wherein individual manufacturers work in collaboration through contracts for fulfilling an order received by one of the members of the alliance. The different entities of this alliance are similar to geographically distributed production units of an enterprise group.

Huang et al.[5] present an integrated mathematical approach to address the order and product scheduling problems. An order consists of different products; a type of product can be a mart of multiple orders and multiple products of different types can make up an order. The authors factor in resource and machine capacity constraints, order priority and lead time factors in decision making. Huang et al.[5] also presents a unified decision support model. While Huang et al.[5] solve for decisions at a higher management level, our paper solves the routing problem at the central authority level, as well as the scheduling problem at the shop floor level. Also, Huang et al.[5] do not address the geographical distribution of production sites.

After reviewing selected relevant literature, it is observed that although the three fields of MTO, capacity and enterprise planning have been extensively researched separately (or in combination with other OR techniques), their combination remains largely unaddressed, particularly for industries with highly customized individual products.

Our paper presents two iterative schemes; one involving two MIP models and the other involving an MIP and a Discrete-Event Simulation (DES) model. Previous work by Byrne and Bakir[2] demonstrates the use of simulation based iterative techniques for production planning. Kulkarni and Venkateswaran[8] have demonstrated the use of similar techniques for scheduling problems. Our work extends these works to present a solution approach for an integrated planning and scheduling problem.

The next section formally defines this problem, explaining the different aspects in detail.

3. PROBLEM FORMULATION

This paper addresses the short term capacity planning problem faced by an enterprise operating on MTO principles. The enterprise has a central decision making authority and multiple production sites that are geographically distributed. The problem is a hierarchical decision making problem. The first step is a routing problem at the center, where the center assigns a production site to each job received, based on the technological requirements and available capacity in order to minimize cost. Without loss of generality, it is assumed that jobs are a batch of jobs from buffered jobs at the central authority, that needs to be processed. The jobs also need to be routed in such a way that the overall capacity of the enterprise is efficiently utilized, while keeping costs at a minimum. The second step is the scheduling problem at each location, where the production site authority decides the order in which the jobs assigned to it are processed, to achieve objectives such as makespan minimization or maximizing capacity utilization, while ensuring delivery deadlines.

Jobs arrive at the centralized enterprise router and are buffered. Let $J_1, \ldots, J_P$ be the set of jobs that were pulled out from the buffer to be routed to multiple production sites in the enterprise. The iterative routing and scheduling algorithm will be invoked to make routing decisions for these jobs, periodically. The frequency at which the algorithm is invoked depends on the arrival rate and characteristics of the jobs, such as deadline and work-flow of the job. We propose to select a batch of P jobs and make routing decisions for them when 1) There are at least K jobs in the buffer pending to be processed 2) One or more jobs has waited in the buffer for at least T units of time. However, determination of batch sizes and time of batch formation is beyond the scope of this paper, since it involves specifications relating to the application area.

The proposed hierarchical model in this paper is based on certain assumptions. These assumptions are due to business rules and common operational practices.

- Entire job is processed in one location, that is job splitting across locations is not allowed.

- All jobs need to be assigned to some location. Once a job is accepted, then it has to be processed at some location.

- For any given location, each machine is capable of a unique task and each task requires a separate machine. Multiple machines cannot perform the same tasks and multiple tasks of one job cannot be completed on a single machine.

Figure 1 shows the hierarchical decision making for an enterprise. The router has access to a pool of buffered jobs. As mentioned earlier, each location consists of a shop floor with various workstations, performing different tasks. Each workstation consists of a machine preceded by a queue. The machines are represented by circles, with a machine number inside it and the queues are denoted by two horizontal parallel lines before each machine. If a job enters a workstation and finds the machine busy, it joins the queue before the machine, indicated by vertical lines within the queue symbol. The models at the two levels, routing and scheduling, interact iteratively, till a stopping criteria (discussed in later sections) is satisfied.

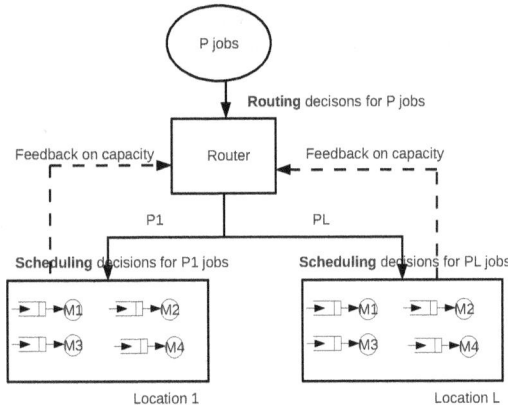

Figure 1: Hierarchical decision making

4. PROPOSED MIP-BASED ITERATIVE FRAMEWORK

The hierarchical decisions discussed so far involve consideration of different constraints and different objectives. This section describes objectives and constraints involved in the routing and scheduling decisions. The modules for routing and scheduling interact with each other, providing necessary information for decision making at each level.

The proposed scheme is intended to address the scheduling needs of multiple shop floors. The number of jobs to be scheduled at any shop floor is a dynamic value, that is not pre-determined, but is rather an output of the routing model. Therefore, it is possible that schedule generation

at one or more of the shop floors may require significantly longer time than others. A single unified model might prove inefficient in such cases. Also, with multiple modules, the model becomes more tractable, wherein it is easier to obtain intermediate solutions while the later stages are still under evaluation. For example, consider the case where the hierarchical model is solved as a single model. Now, it is possible that at one of the sites, the scheduling problem might be a complex one and would take a long time to converge to optimality. In such a situation, the entire solution is delayed, while one segment of the problem is solved. In case of multiple models, the routing results and the schedules at other sites would be reported, while the bottleneck site is still solving its scheduling problem. Considering all these factors, each decision is addressed using separate modules, that are integrated through a common interface.

Figure 2 shows the schematic of the iterative scheme using the various MIP modules. The routing module is executed first for the primary jobs. The scheduling module is then called multiple times, to generate schedules at each of the production sites. The schedules at each site are tested for their adherence to job deadlines. Any violation of these deadlines at a site is reported to the central router. The router then reroutes the jobs by lowering the advertised capacity at that production site and feeding this into the routing module. The scheduling module generates new schedules based on the current routing of jobs. This process continues iteratively, until either all jobs are scheduled within deadlines, or a fixed number of iterations is completed. The number of iterations are chosen based on the computational budget (for example, time allowed for model run).

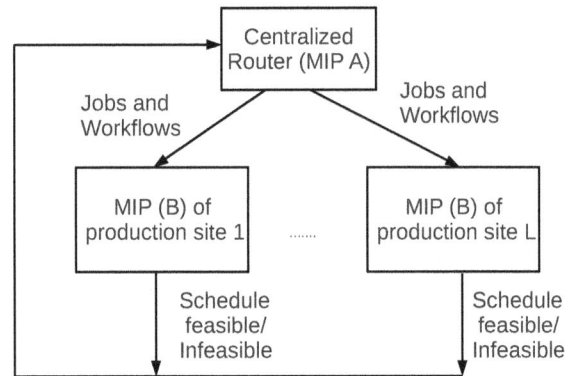

Figure 2: Schematic view of MIP-based iterative framework

Note that the proposed hierarchical model is intended for a short term capacity planning over a finite and small planning horizon. The capacity values used in the model represent the capacity available in the given time horizon. Each decision in the hierarchical model is addressed using a separate module. A Mixed Integer Programming (MIP) formulation is used for each of these. The MIPs are called as A and B and their interaction in the hierarchical model can be observed in Figure 2. Every MIP has a different set of decision variables and objective function(s). The parameters, variables and objectives of these MIPs are described in detail next, along with the constraints.

4.1 MIP for routing: A

The first part of the iterative approach involves decision making at routing level. The central router receives a set of jobs and has to divide these amongst available production sites. While routing, the router has to ensure that the assignments adhere to capacity constraints at each site, while minimizing distance costs and processing costs. The routing model is presented next.

Parameters for routing

d_{jl} geographical distance between job j and site l
c_{ijl} per unit cost of processing job j in machine i at location l
$\hat{c}_{jl}$ per unit cost of transporting job j to site l
f fraction of total capacity, i.e., advertised capacity (input from shops, feedback variable)
R_{il} capacity of machine (in time units) i at site l
p_{ijl} processing time of job j in machine i at site l

Decision Variables

x_{jl} 1 when job j is assigned to site l and 0 otherwise

The processing times can be assumed to be given as fixed values or we can introduce a processing time model to calculate the processing times. We consider the following model which uses job size and processing rates for machines.

Parameters for processing time model

JS_j job size of job j
p_{ijl} processing time of job j in machine i at site l
PR_{il} processing rate of machine i at site l

Processing time model

$$p_{ijl} = \frac{JS_j}{PR_{il}}, \quad j = 1, ..., J, i = 1, ..., I; l = 1, ..., L \quad (1)$$

This model is for illustrative purposes and can be enhanced based on the application area. A linear cost model is assumed for the processing times at each machine, where each unit time of processing at a machine is assigned a cost. However, the unit processing cost is different for different machines and for different sites. It is also possible to use a more advanced cost model, built on industry specific information. Similarly, we consider transportation cost as a linear function of the distance for illustration however more advanced cost models for shipping can be used.

Routing MIP model

$$\min \sum_l \sum_j \sum_i x_{jl} * p_{ijl} * c_{ijl} + \sum_l x_{jl} * d_{jl} * \hat{c}_{jl} \quad (2)$$

$$\text{subject to} \quad \sum_{l=0}^{L} x_{jl} = 1, \quad j = 1, ..., J \quad (3)$$

$$\sum_j x_{jl} * p_{ijl} \leq f * R_{il}, \quad i = 1, ..., I; l = 1, ..., L \quad (4)$$

Expression (2) gives the objective function of the routing model, which is to minimize the total costs. The total cost is a sum of the processing and transportation costs for all the jobs over all the machines at all production sites. Constraint (3) ensures that each job is assigned a site and at most one site. Finally, constraint (4) gives the capacity restrictions for each machine at each site and ensures that the total assigned production time to the machine does not exceed its available capacity. The parameter f is the feedback parameter which is the fraction of the total advertised capacity, that is updated in each iteration, based on the information from the scheduling model. The scheduling model that is used to generate schedules at each site is described next, along with the mathematical formulation.

4.2 MIP for scheduling: B

The Mixed Integer Programming (MIP) formulation by [9] shown below is often used to model the classical deterministic job shop scheduling problem. This formulation guarantees optimality for all small and medium sized problems. The variables and parameters of this formulation are described next, followed by the constraints and objective functions.

Parameters

r_{ilk} 1 if job i requires machine k for task l and 0 otherwise
z_i Due date (in time units) of job i
δ Control parameter with very small value (0.001)
q_i Capacity (in time units) of machine i
p_{ik} processing time of job i in machine k

Decision Variables

s_{ik} start time of job i in machine k
x_{ijk} 1 when job j precedes job i on machine k, and 0 otherwise
$Cmax$ makespan or the completion time of the last job in the shop

Scheduling MIP model

$$\min \left\{ Cmax || \min Cmax + \delta * \sum_{i,j} s_{ij} \right\} \quad (5)$$

$$\text{subject to} \quad \sum_{k=1}^{m} r_{imk}(s_{ik} + p_{ik}) \leq Cmax, \quad i = 1, ..., n \quad (6)$$

$$\sum_{k=1}^{m} r_{imk}(s_{ik} + p_{ik}) \leq z_i \quad i = 1, ..., n \quad (7)$$

$$\sum_{k=1}^{m} r_{imk}(s_{ik} + p_{ik}) \leq \sum_{k=1}^{m} q_k * r_{imk} \quad i = 1, ..., n \quad (8)$$

$$\sum_{k=1}^{m} r_{ilk}(s_{ik} + p_{ik}) - \sum_{k=1}^{m} r_{i,l+1,k} s_{ik} \leq 0, i = 1, .., m; l = 1, .., m-1 \quad (9)$$

$$K(1 - x_{ijk}) + s_{jk} - s_{ik} \geq p_{ik}, \quad k = 1, .., m; 1 \leq i < j \leq n \quad (10)$$

$$K x_{ijk} + s_{ik} - s_{jk} \geq p_{jk}, \quad k = 1, .., m; 1 \leq i < j \leq n \quad (11)$$

Expression (5) presents the two possible choices for the objective of the scheduling problem. The first term stands for minimizing makespan and the second part of the expression tries to start each job as early as possible, while still trying to minimize the makespan. The term δ is a controlling parameter, that decides the weight assigned to the capacity function. If δ is chosen large enough, the model gives priority to reducing idle times and starting jobs as early as possible over minimizing the makespan. This could be desirable if one or more machines need to be freed sooner than others, even at the cost of overall increase in makespan. Constraint (6) gives the lower bound for the objective function $Cmax$. Constraint (7) ensures that the jobs adhere to deadlines. Constraint (8) restricts the last task of each job to finish within the capacity of the machine on which it is scheduled. Constraint (9) ensures that the starting time of job i in operation $l+1$ is not earlier than its finish time in the predecessor operation l. Constraints (10) and (11) ensure that only one job is processed on a machine at any given time. The parameter K is a large number, sometimes taken as sum of all processing times.

Flow shops can be modelled as special cases of job shops. For example, in a job shop, a job can visit machine 1 after machine 2. In a flow shop, however, the jobs may visit machine 2 only after they have finished processing on machine 1 and after reaching machine 2, they are not allowed to revisit machine 1 in future. The flow shop is a special case of the job shop and hence any formulation that is applicable for job shops can be extended to flow shops by making the necessary changes to the work-flow sequence inputs. In the formulation described in this section, the input parameters r_{ilk} contain the work-flow information for every job. The values of these parameters change depending on work-flows. Note that this change in values does not affect the formulation and hence the MIP is applicable for job shops as well as flow shops.

4.3 Iterative feedback based interaction of MIPs

Initially, the router distributes jobs based on the advertised capacities at each site and the processing time requirements of the jobs. At each site, the MIP (B) schedules the jobs for the objectives described above. If a job is seen to violate its deadline, the MIP at that site would terminate as 'infeasible'. Once this infeasibility is detected, this information is passed on to the router. The router notes all the sites where infeasibility has occurred. The available capacity of the 'infeasible' sites is lowered using the parameter α, which could be considered to be a step-size. In the subsequent iteration, the routing MIP (A) uses the capacity $\alpha * f * R_{il}$ for each infeasible site. The choice of α would determine the number of iterations required to obtain feasible schedules at all sites (if at all possible). However, if α is chosen to be too large, it would result in excess idle capacity at sites, leading to reduction in profits.

4.4 Limitations of MIP-based approach

Although, MIP-based approach is an exact framework, it is observed from previous works by [6] and others that the computational efficiency of MIP-based approaches reduces drastically with increase in problem size. This is primarily because, even for a linear increase in the size of the underlying system, the number of decision variables required to model the system often increases exponentially. Scalability is an issue with MIP-based scheduling approaches.

To alleviate this issue of scalability, we can model each site using a discrete-event simulation model, that would also capture operational policies and other non-linearities of the enterprise along with uncertainties and hence would be more realistic. Such a simulation-based iterative framework for cost efficient short term capacity planning can provide a 'good' feasible solution unlike the no solution or no feasible solution resulting from the MIP model. However, this will not provide any guarantee on optimality. Using this framework, however, it would be possible to estimate certain shop level performance measures that can improve the decision making at aggregate level. In particular, using estimates of individual job completion times and idle times, the routing module can ensure meeting of deadlines at the routing level.

In the next section, we present the simulation-based iterative framework for the hierarchical problem discussed so far. The routing model is identical for both the schemes. The difference lies in the models representing the production sites and the nature of feedback between the two levels.

5. PROPOSED SIMULATION-BASED ITERATIVE FRAMEWORK

The output of the routing model is the number of jobs assigned to each site and the work-flow of each job. This data is used to model the shop floors at each site. Each site is modelled using discrete event simulation (DES). The number of machines at a site is fixed and known. The number of jobs assigned, however, changes with the output of the routing model. The DES model reads the output of the routing model and correspondingly configures the shop floor for each site. Each site is represented by a different configuration of the DES model.

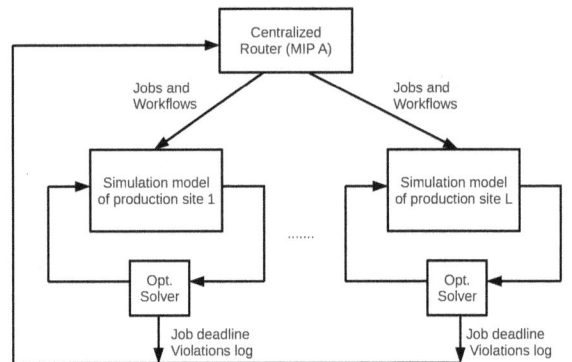

Figure 3: Schematic view of simulation-based iterative framework

Figure 3 shows the schematic of the proposed DES-based iterative framework. As shown in the figure, this scheme involves iterations at both the levels. The outer iterative loop involves interactions between the routing MIP and the various scheduling units. In outer loop, the router generates jobs and work-flow information for each site and a corresponding shop floor is configured in the DES environment. Each simulation model is then run to determine the actual makespan obtained by the shop floor and the completion times for individual jobs. These completion times are compared with the deadlines for the jobs. The jobs for which deadlines are violated are reported in a separate log. This log is used to generate feedback for the routing model. As with the previous iterative scheme, the router MIP distributes the jobs differently across production sites. The new output of the routing model is again tested using DES models for different sites and the process continues iteratively till a termination criterion is satisfied. The termination criterion could either be a fixed number of iterations or the satisfaction of deadlines for all the jobs.

Note that standalone DES models have limited problem solving capabilities. Hence they are often integrated with optimum-seeking packages to enhance their problem solving abilities [8]. The inner loop in this scheme represents the integrated simulation-based optimization solver. Different types of solvers are possible. Kulkarni and Venkateswaran[8] show how a packaged meta-heuristic software such as Anylogic and OptQuest can be used for such problems. [7] demonstrate the use of Linear Programming (LP) methods for solving scheduling problems. Various other heuristics such as Genetic Algorithm (GA) or Particle Swarm Optimization (PSO) can also be used along with the DES model. This paper uses the technique illustrated by Kulkarni and Venkateswaran[8], which uses a meta-heuristic based optimum seeking package called OptQuest (a combination of Tabu search, Scatter search, Integer Programming etc.). The choice of solver is left to the user, since these solvers are typically tailored to suit the application (nature of underlying system).

In this iterative framework, DES provides richer feedback with details about the job violation, thus allows for precise corrective measures within the same iteration. For example, the DES model not only identifies the site at which the deadlines were violated, but also identifies the job, the machine and the amount of time by which the deadline was violated. This helps gauge the extent of corrective measures required as illustrated in the next section.

5.1 Iterative feedback based interaction of MIP-A and DES

Similar to the MIP-based iterative scheme, the DES-based scheme also employs a feedback mechanism to lower the available capacity to the router. However, since DES is able to provide more precise information, the feedback parameters are modified to incorporate the additional information. The feedback parameter is defined as α_{ijk} for job j on machine i at site k.

Using the α_{ijk}, the capacity of a particular machine at a particular site is modified. For illustration purposes, in this paper, we compute α_{ijk} using the duration of violation, that is, the amount of time by which the job deadline was exceeded. Greater the duration, greater the value of α_{ijk}. However, it is possible to design complex feedback mechanisms, where α_{ijk} can be a function of the number of job violations, duration of violations and the priority or importance of the violated job (if any).

6. NUMERICAL RESULTS

The MIP models discussed in the previous sections are implemented in Java using Eclipse IDE. The CPLEX solver has been used to solve the MIP. The models read inputs from different text files. The parameters to the models are set in a wrapper class that is common for all the models. The outputs of each model are written in different text files. A Gantt chart class is called after all models are executed, to visualize the schedule at each site. The DES model is implemented using Anylogic with OptQuest package. The routing model requires various inputs. These are described next.

1. Number of jobs (orders), number of machines in work-flow and number of sites

2. Job size: the number of units that make up a job
3. Work-flow requirements of each job (sequence of machines)
4. Capacity at each site (work-hours on each machine)
5. Percentage of capacity available (initial advertised capacity) at each site
6. Shipping distance requirements of each job from each site
7. Transportation cost per unit distance and per unit job of each job from each site
8. Processing rate of each machine at each site
9. Unit processing cost of each machine

Although the problem definition and mathematical formulations apply to many variants of the MTO and job shop problems, the testing and implementation required that assumptions be made, in order to verify and validate the model. These assumptions are mentioned next.

- The work-flow of every job requires the job to visit every machine in the shop floor.
- Every site has same number of machines.
- While the formulation is valid for both job shops and flow shops, numerical examples will demonstrate flow shops.

The unified model is tested for scenarios involving two types of objectives at scheduling level. In the first case, the model runs to minimize the maximal completion time or makespan. Recall that makespan is the time at which the last job finishes processing at the last machine. The second objective is a combination of two objectives, combining makespan minimization with maximization of residual capacity. When residual capacity is considered, the model not only tries to ensure that the last job leaves the system as soon as possible, but also tries to reduce time wastage on all machines. In this way, additional capacity may be made available on one or more machines at a site.

A task for a job can be performed by similar machines at different sites. These machines may or may not have identical processing rates across sites. The processing time of a task is determined as a function of the size of the job and the processing rate of the machine at which it is processed.

Different input datasets are required for each scenario. Some of the common inputs for all the scenarios are presented in Table 2.

Table 2: Input parameter settings

Parameter	Notation	Value
Total jobs	P	13
Machines	m	4
Production sites	L	5
Fraction of capacity	f	0.8
Feedback parameter	α	0.9

6.1 Choice of objective function for MIP-B

The total capacity of each machine at each production site used for the scenarios in this section is presented in Table 3. The advertised capacity (to the routing MIP-A) by each site is taken to be 80% of the actual capacity.

The scenario discussed next considers scheduling of jobs with a scheduling objective of makespan minimization.

Table 3: Machine capacities at production sites

site	Machine 1	Machine 2	Machine 3	Machine 4
site 0	200	200	200	200
site 1	200	200	200	200
site 2	200	200	200	200
site 3	150	150	150	150
site 4	200	200	200	200

Scheduling jobs with objective of minimizing makespan: Scenario 1

For this scenario, the MIP model provides a decision which distributes the P jobs across just three sites. The remaining two sites are chosen to be idle. Table 4 shows the result summary for this scenario.

Figures 4 to 6 show the Gantt charts for the schedules at each of the three non-idle sites. Each colour indicates a different job.

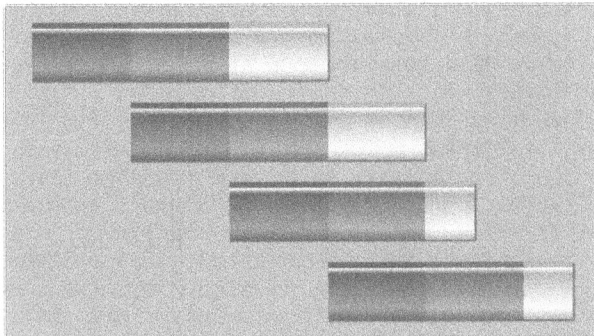

Figure 4: Schedule at site 0

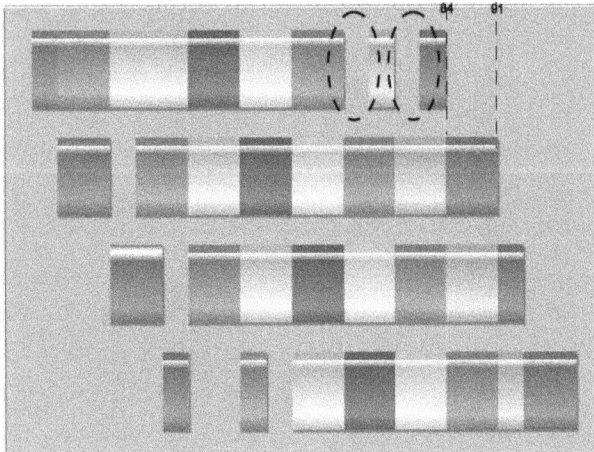

Figure 5: Schedule at site 3

As is seen from Figure 5, there is a possibility of reducing the idle times on machine 1, indicated by the circles, without adversely affecting the overall makespan. The next scenario describes the use of multiple objectives at the scheduling level.

Scheduling objective: minimize makespan and maximize residual capacity: Scenario 2

In a flow shop environment, it is possible to utilize additional capacity on a machine at a site, even if other machines at that site are fully utilized. This is because, a job

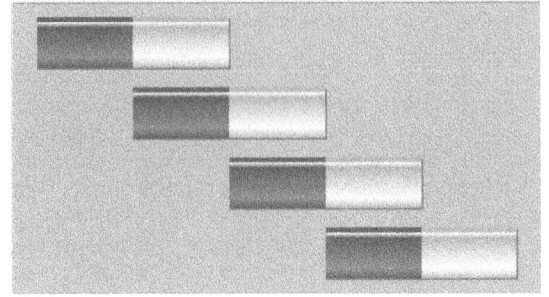

Figure 6: Schedule at site 4

might not require all of the machines at a site. This scenario demonstrates the use of a modified objective, that allows for maximization of remaining capacity, without worsening the makespan of the shop floor. For the scenarios considered in this paper, $\delta = 0.001$ is chosen. This does not impact the overall makespan, since the value of the additional term to the objective is much smaller. However, it allows the generation of alternate schedules for the same makespan, that schedule each task of each job as early as possible, that is, reducing idle times and hence making one or more machines available for additional jobs. Table 5 summarizes the results for this scenario.

Figure 7 shows the Gantt chart corresponding to the schedule at site 3.

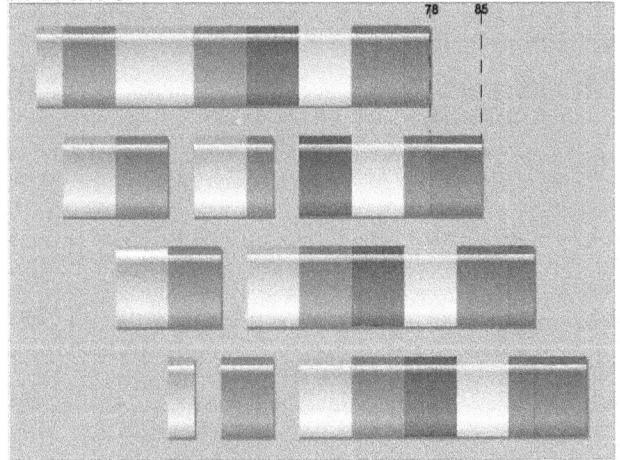

Figure 7: Schedule at site 3

On comparing scenarios one and two, it is observed that in scenario 2, the model is able to obtain the same makespans, but with greater remaining capacity. This is a desirable output, since this capacity can be used to generate additional revenue, either by accepting more jobs from the central router (singly owned enterprises) or by accepting newer orders (for HMCA enterprises).

From tables 4 and 5, it is evident that scheduling more jobs at site 3 is profitable for the enterprise, with two other sites being idle. Therefore, any additional capacity at site 3 can be important. Upon frequent recurrence of such schedules, the consolidation of the unused capacities at the two idle sites can also be considered.

6.2 Iterative MIP vs Iterative simulation based framework

The proposed iterative frameworks based on MIP-based and simulation based scheduling are implemented. Schedul-

Table 4: Result summary for Scenario 1

site	jobs assigned	Makespan	Machine end times	Remaining capacity
site 0	3	59	[31,40,49,59]	[169,160,151,141]
site 1	0	0	-	[200,200,200,200]
site 2	0	0	-	[200,200,200,200]
site 3	8	106	[84,91,99,106]	[66,59,51,44]
site 4	2	50	[21,30,40,50]	[179,170,160,150]

Table 5: Result summary for Scenario 2

site	jobs assigned	Makespan	Machine end times	Remaining capacity
site 0	3	59	[31,40,49,59]	[169,160,151,141]
site 1	0	0	-	[200,200,200,200]
site 2	0	0	-	[200,200,200,200]
site 3	8	106	[**78,85**,99,106]	[**72,65**,51,44]
site 4	2	50	[21,30,40,50]	[179,170,160,150]

ing objective used is to minimize makespan and maximize residual capacity. The scheduling model checks for deadline violations at each site and reports these to the router. If any of the deadlines is not met, the router reroutes the orders across all the sites, by manipulating capacity at the sites where the violation occurred. This process goes on iteratively till either all deadlines are satisfied or a fixed number of iterations are completed.

The MIP-based approach provides limited information, in case of a deadline violation. The solver terminates, declaring the solution as 'infeasible'. However, in the simulation based approach, the simulation model provides detailed information such as the amount of time by which deadline was violated. Using this specific feedback, the simulation based iterative scheme is able to achieve a feasible routing-scheduling plan in much lesser iterations and with reduced costs as well, as shown in Table 6.

As seen in Table 6, the simulation-based method is able to

Table 6: Comparison of iterative schemes

	MIP-based		Simulation-based	
	Routing	Scheduling	Routing	Scheduling
Objective	596	infeasible at site 3	596	job 3 late on machine 4 at site 3 by 7 min
Iterations	30	-	5	-
Objective	636.75	all feasible	598.0	all feasible
Number of sites	4	-	3	-

achieve an 'all feasible' schedule with an overall objective of 598, while the MIP-based scheme achieves an 'all-feasible' schedule for a higher objective of 636.75. The table also shows that the simulation-based method achieves this while still using only 3 of the 5 available sites, while the MIP-based method suggests operations at an additional 4th site. These results were also obtained by the simulation-based method in much lesser iterations (5, as compared with the 30 required by the MIP). Hence, it is observed that the simulation-based method outperforms the MIP-based method for the given example.

7. CONCLUSIONS AND FUTURE EXTENSIONS

In this paper, we have presented an optimization based solution approach for decision making at various levels of an MTO based enterprise (dealing with highly customized end products), with geographically separated manufacturing units, for a short planning horizon. The proposed framework provides the feedback on capacity based on deadline violations at individual sites, to the centralized enterprise router which uses it to iteratively optimize the distribution of jobs (routing) across sites along with the objective of cost efficient capacity utilization.

We first presented a Mixed Integer Programming (MIP) based approach for the enterprise level routing decisions and for the site level scheduling decisions. We then showed that such a MIP-based implementation for scheduling decisions can be further scaled and also richer feedback can be obtained by using a simulation model for each individual production site. We illustrated comparative performance of both the MIP-based and simulation based approaches through numerical evaluations.

The simulation model for individual sites could also capture operational policies and other non-linearities of the enterprise along with uncertainties and hence can be more realistic. As a future extension of this work, our interest is to incorporate uncertainties at the production site which essentially result in stochastic processing times.

8. REFERENCES

[1] H.-g. Bo, S.-r. Zhang, and X.-b. Liu. Research on capacity planning problem in mto enterprises group. In *Proceeding of 2nd International Conference on Information Science and Engineering (ICISE)*, pages 473–477, Hangzhou, China, 4-6 Dec 2010. IEEE Press.

[2] M. D. Byrne and M. A. Bakir. Production planning using a hybrid simulation - analytical approach. *International Journal of Production Economics*, 59(1-3):305 – 311, 1999.

[3] C.-S. Chen, S. Mestry, P. Damodaran, and C. Wang. The capacity planning problem in make-to-order enterprises. *Mathematical and Computer Modelling*, 50(9-10):1461–1473, Nov. 2009.

[4] F. Q. Cheng. A bi-objective order allocation optimization model for horizontal manufacturing

collaborative alliance. *Advanced Materials Research*, 102-104(9-10):836–840, 2010.

[5] P. Huang, H. Li, and L. Han. Order scheduling problems in make-to-order manufacturing systems. In *Proceedings of IEEE International Conference on Mechatronics and Automation*, volume 4, pages 2179–2184, Niagra Falls, Canada, 29 July-1 Aug 2005. IEEE Press.

[6] A. Klemmt, S. Horn, G. Weigert, and K.-J. Wolter. Simulation-based optimization vs. mathematical programming: A hybrid approach for optimizing scheduling problems. *Robotics and Computer-Integrated Manufacturing*, 25-6:917–925, December 2009.

[7] K. Kulkarni and J. Venkateswaran. Iterative simulation and optimization approach for job shop scheduling. In *Proceedings of the 2014 Winter Simulation Conference*, WSC '14, pages 1620–1631, Savannah, Georgia, Dec 7-10 2014. IEEE Press.

[8] K. Kulkarni and J. Venkateswaran. Hybrid approach using simulation-based optimisation. *Journal of Simulation*, 2015. Advance online publication: http://dx.doi.org/10.1057/jos.2014.40.

[9] A. S. Manne. On the job shop scheduling problem. Cowles Foundation Discussion Papers 73, Cowles Foundation for Research in Economics, Yale University, 1959.

[10] S. Rai and J. Lin. Print job allocation system and method, Jan. 25 2007. US Patent App. 11/185,384.

[11] S. Rai and J. Lin. System and method of evaluating print shop consolidation options in an enterprise, Nov. 13 2012. US Patent 8,310,700.

A Media-Rich Curriculum for Modeling and Simulation

Karen Doore, David Vega, Paul Fishwick
Creative Automata Laboratory
University of Texas at Dallas
800 W. Campbell Rd., AT10
Richardson, TX 75080
{kdoore, dxv130830, paul.fishwick}@utdallas.edu

ABSTRACT

We discuss a novel approach for teaching Modeling and Simulation (M&S) using a rich, multi-media focus with an emphasis on student construction and creative representation of simulations for dynamic systems. The increased use of M&S to enhance understanding and analyze problems across an ever-widening range of disciplines means that the diversity and number of professionals who will work with simulations is also increasing. Therefore, it is important that expanded opportunities exist for a wide range of students to take M&S courses as part of their secondary or post-secondary education. In addition to introducing M&S to new audiences, it is important to consider how professionals from these diverse disciplines can enhance and improve the quality and effectiveness of simulations. Courses, which target non-traditional simulation students, can broaden the diversity of expertise within the M&S community. We introduce an M&S course that uses Max/MSP software, which is familiar for many multimedia students and faculty. The course targets a mixed class of graduate students from Art and Technology, Computer Science, and Engineering programs.

Categories and Subject Descriptors

K.3.2 [**Computers and Education**]: Computer and Information Science Education

General Terms
Human Factors

Keywords
Max/MSP, Modeling and Simulation, Education, Data flow, Petri nets, Creativity, IoT, Microcontrollers.

1. INTRODUCTION

With increased use of modeling and simulation across diverse domains, there is a growing need to expand the offering of university courses in modeling and simulation concepts to a wide range of students. Modeling and Simulation (M&S) can be considered a relatively young discipline, and one that is highly multi-disciplinary; this complicates the determination of what should be taught in a graduate-level M&S course [31]. Padilla et al. [36] discuss the diversity of subject areas and fields within the

SIGSIM-PADS'15, June 10–12, 2015, London, UK.
Copyright © 2015 ACM 978-1-4503-3583-6/15/06...$15.00.
DOI http://dx.doi.org/10.1145/2769458.2769471

discipline of Modeling and Simulation, while arguing that it does have enough coherence as a discipline to justify establishing M&S as a science in it's own right. The authors provide a broad overview of M&S as a formal academic discipline with three main components: problem situations, ontological, teleological and epistemological constraints of problem situations, and computational constraints [36].

Fishwick [10] defines computer simulation as 'the discipline of designing a model of a system, executing the model, and analyzing the execution output.' He argues that learning simulation should embody the principle of "learning by doing"; he further emphasizes that "in order to learn about a system, we must first build a model and then make it run." This raises the question of what pedagogical content should be taught to students interested in learning M&S. While there are many factors that should be considered when designing new curricula, there is a growing consensus within the Computing Education Research community that curricula, which engage learners through contextually relevant materials and practices, can often improve learning outcomes [17, 28, 43].

Our course has some unique curriculum-design constraints: *how can we teach Modeling and Simulation to graduate students who have an extreme disparity in their prior knowledge and experience with regards to mathematics, computing, technical and artistic fluency?* Our goal is to challenge all students to approach modeling and simulation from new perspectives with an explicit focus on fostering what Cropley [5] has termed 'functional creativity.' For computer science graduate students, developing simulation programs using a visual data-flow programming paradigm, in addition to a focus on creating sensory-rich simulations requires a different mindset compared to traditional computing courses. For Art and Technology students, the multi-sensory creative approach is well within their comfort zone, as well as using visual data-flow languages, however, our goal was to challenge them to approach the creative process from the perspective of modeling & simulation foundational concepts. Concepts such as message passing, discrete events, state-transitions, feedback, concurrency, parallelism, with an explicit focus on process dynamics are typically not taught in most media art courses, with the possible exception of audio-focused media courses. The software used in our course, Max/MSP, is designed for artists, educators, researchers, working with audio, visual media, and physical computing [29].

We provide an overview of traditional M&S education approaches, which range from teaching applied simulation to curricula with a more theoretical focus. This is followed by a review of some alternative curriculum approaches. Then we examine functional creativity and educational approaches to foster creativity in technical disciplines. We include an overview of data flow programming, data-flow visual languages, and then give a brief overview of Max/MSP software, which was utilized for the course. A survey and discussion of several student projects will provide examples of the benefits of this media-rich approach for teaching modeling and simulation. Finally, we discuss possible extensions to this curriculum, which includes integration between Max/MSP and the Arduino IDE to control microcontrollers like the Arduino Uno.

2. M&S EDUCATION

The rapid expansion and use of simulation across domains, coupled with improvements in ease of use of simulation software systems creates opportunities for teaching M&S to a more diverse target audience [34, 46]. A review of the M&S education literature reveals that there are significant changes in target audiences for simulation courses due to the growing use of simulation in industry [14, 46]. Ideally, curriculum design should be tailored to support the unique learning objectives for each of these diverse groups. Much of the M&S education literature about curriculum and pedagogy seems to be focused on courses taught in engineering, computing, and business schools [14, 18, 25 Kincaid et al. [23] did a review of M&S education literature of graduate-level courses and found that 'these programs are usually focused on the mathematical, hardware, or management aspects of M&S.' We argue that many students from diverse disciplines across the university campus will benefit from courses in M&S; however, these courses should be tailored to support this more diverse set of student interests and background knowledge. In addition, the M&S community can benefit from this type of course, as it may drive interest in M&S careers, where these future artists, educators, designers, and user-experience professionals can use their expertise to enhance M&S products.

2.1 M&S Curriculum Design Factors

We have embraced a learner-centered approach to curriculum design; a similar approach has helped influence how introductory computing courses are being designed to target a wider range of student interests and majors [16, 17, 43]. Szczerbicka et al. define a 'simulationist' as someone who fits within an extremely diverse range of roles, who works with simulations; then the authors discuss the diversity of educational needs for 'simulationists' [46]. Greenwood and Beverstock [14] cite seven reasons which why changes should be implemented to improve M&S curriculum at the university level. Loper et al [27], discuss the wide range of difficulties associated with designing curriculum to support growing need for an M&S educated workforce. Complicating the curriculum design process is the diversity in M&S approaches, such as discrete event simulation (DES), agent based simulation, aggregate approaches to simulation, and hybrid approaches [34]. For each of the simulation categories just mentioned, there are a broad range of software simulation systems, some of which are designed to support teaching / learning while others designed for applied simulation analysis including enterprise-type applications [45].

2.1.1 Education for Applied Simulation

Greenwood and Beverstock [14] suggest curriculum changes that focus on the importance of teaching applied simulation in contrast to more theoretical approaches. They highlight the fact that the role of simulation in the workplace has expanded and that simulation is now an integral part of decision support systems, where most users of simulation systems won't be simulation experts. These 'intermediate' [14] users will more likely be domain experts, using simulation as an applied tool to support

analysis and decision-making. In contrast, Jain [18] expresses concern that simulation courses in many business schools primarily focuses on teaching the use of simulation software rather than teaching students how to build simulations.

2.1.2 Conceptual Modeling Focus

Jové et al. [20] discuss the importance of conceptual models when teaching Discrete Event Simulation (DES) to engineering and computer science students. They recommend a curriculum based on the use of Petri nets as a modeling language to allow students to develop a conceptual model of a system and then to map that to a simulation model implementation, using Arena software. They further note that for these highly technical CS and engineering students, it is critical that they understand fundamental modeling constructs rather than "just teaching the use of certain software" [20]. Jové et al. have identified an important learning objective: 'students must understand the difference between a conceptual model and the implementation of the model.' The Petri net model structure provides a visual language to represent a DES system, where each visual element in a Petri net model corresponds directly to a distinct discrete event simulation concept [52]. In our course we also focused on theoretical and foundational aspects of M&S, this included a unit that focused on the use of Petri nets to model a range of systems.

2.1.3 Blended Approaches

The above approaches represent endpoints within a range curriculum approaches; either a purely applied simulation focus, contrasted with a purely theoretical approach. Kress et al. [25] present a blended approach for a course that targets non-engineering graduate students. They note that these graduate students are primarily from mathematics or science disciplines, and these students typically have extensive experience working with mathematical modeling, numerical simulations, partial differential equations, etc., however they often lack experience with discrete event approaches to simulation. Their goal for the course is 'to prepare these students to work effectively in a typical industry or government-supported simulation modeling group [25].' Accordingly, their curriculum begins with discrete event fundamentals, including a comparison between discrete-event and continuous models, then progresses to cover modeling theory, techniques and applications which were implemented with ExtendSim software. While their target audience has diversity of prior knowledge based on discipline, it appears that they would have similar depth of knowledge of fundamentals of mathematical modeling, to enable the course to cover such a broad range of content in a technically rigorous manner. The target audience for our course lacks the shared depth of knowledge of mathematical modeling concepts, this the primary constraint impacting our curriculum design.

2.1.4 Simulation and Instructional Design

One important aspect of the changing face of Modeling and Simulation is the increased use of simulation for training and instruction. Szczerbicka et al. identify training and education simulation as a major component of the M&S domain, both for training in other disciplines as well as for educating 'simulationists' [46]. Kincaid and Westerlund [23] provide a discipline-oriented taxonomy of M&S knowledge for the purpose of showing the 'breadth of knowledge and skills' of various M&S professionals. The authors specifically discuss the need for professionals in M&S to develop skills in human factors and instructional technology; these skills include UI design, usability, media selection, task analysis, learning theory, to name a few [23]. The design and development of simulations for training for use in areas like medical training, emergency response training, cultural training, or workplace training, requires collaborative teams of professionals with a diverse range of skills.

2.1.5 Multi-Modal Interactive Design

Improvements in technology provide opportunities to create enhanced, media-rich simulations. In order to integrate these multi-sensory components, designers with multi-media expertise will need to collaborate with simulation developers. For example, Taylor et al. [47] are incorporating sonification capabilities in a fluid dynamics simulator, which they've named the 'Virtual Wind Tunnel'. They used Max/MSP software to design and implement their sonification strategy with the goal that integration of multi-modal interaction might enhance user's understanding of complex simulation data [47]. Future iterations of their project will include haptic user-interaction. In a separate project, Taylor and colleagues [48] have used Max/MSP to create an artistic participatory performance as a means to understand collaborative creative behavior, which could be integrated into the design of interactive systems. They also used Max/MSP to integrate remote tangible interfaces that participants used for interaction with the system.

As the art of simulation design evolves to include more diverse media types, it will be important that the design process includes creative artists and designers who can provide enhanced aesthetics for multi-sensory interfaces. For example, Bak et al [2] use Max /MSP software in a course designed to 'provide Interaction Design students with tools and skills to develop complex multimodal, embodied experiences.' We contend that it's not enough to have simulations that present accurate measures of a dynamic system; these systems should be designed to provide an engaging, realistic, multi-sensory, immersive experience. Dance et al. notes that it is important for training to accurately reflect the real-world scenario to support deep learning from the training session [8]. Shams et al. have conducted research that indicates that 'multi-sensory training protocols can better approximate natural settings and are more effective for learning [41]. Our course used a multi-sensory and user-interactivity focus for project assignments. This emphasis was designed to highlight the importance of these factors on end-user understanding of the modeled system, and to encourage students to design system representations from an aesthetic, integrative, and reflective perspective. We argue that an important component of M&S education is for students to develop an understanding of simulation user-experiences in order that they might embrace these aesthetics when they are simulation professionals.

2.2 Insights from Computing Education

While teaching Modeling and Simulation is not the same as teaching introductory programming courses, research in field of Computing Education Research (CER) can inform curriculum design for modeling and simulation courses since there is broad overlap in the nature of concepts. For example, programming and M&S courses have the common goal of teaching students how to design and implement some form of a system based on abstract modeling concepts [40, 9]. The abstract nature of the concepts in these courses means that the software and context of what is taught or modeled can vary greatly across a wide continuum [26, 45]. Curriculum design for these courses is often, at least partially, based on use of a specific software system or language, where trade-offs between factors such as: ease-of use, complexity, cost, and representational expressiveness, have an impact on the how the course is taught [28, 45]. Factors such as problem context, software, and language, can have a large influence on student interest, engagement, and learning outcomes, particularly based on the level of background knowledge and technical fluency of the learner [24,4].

2.2.1 Computing Education for Diverse Audiences

In addition, there has been a recent increase in CS Education research (CER) that has focused on teaching computing concepts to non-majors, where motivation, relevance, context, and representational format are common research themes [16, 17, 28]. The goal of teaching computing concepts to non-experts, with a goal of increased general computing literacy can also provide a lens to improved methods for teaching modeling and simulation to students who will use modeling and simulation in profession as a tool for problem solving, rather than with a goal of becoming a simulation expert. In addition, after graduation, these students may become designers of simulations, where their role is to enhance user experience.

2.2.2 M&S in Computing Education

Another area of research within the CER research community is the use of modeling and simulations to teach computing concepts for the purpose of introducing students to computing. Researchers, including Stroup and Wilensky [44, 53] often use contextualized simulations to teach abstract concepts like cause and effect, distributed or decentralized systems, feedback, rule-based systems, emergent behavior and complex systems. Lin and Tater [26] have studied the difficulties that even advanced CS students have with understanding parallelism, concurrency and coordination concepts. They recommend teaching students to explicitly model coordination, yet also note that for students without strong programming skills, teaching these concepts using traditional programming language constructs such as Java threads can be difficult [26]. We have taken inspiration from computing education research, with a focus on teaching foundational aspects of modeling and simulation, with a necessary focus on connecting these fundamental abstract concepts in a context that is relevant to both media artists and computing graduate students.

2.2.3 Multi-sensory Teaching and Learning

Katai and Toth [21] have conducted research to explore the benefits of teaching abstract computing concepts to undergraduate students using a multi-sensory approach with a well-designed integration of technology and arts. Their study integrated music, video, graphical representations and choreographed dances to provide students with a multi-faceted, sensory experience for a variety of sorting algorithms. Their results indicate that using a multi-sensory, art-integrated method improves students' skill to analyze and design algorithms. They also referred to their prior research study using similar teaching methodology. They found similar improvement in another difficult-to-teach computing concept, resulting in students' improved skill to analyze, design and implement recursive procedures and functions [21]. This improved understanding of abstract concepts through integration of sensory-rich media provides motivation for our use of Max/MSP as the software component for our course.

3. CREATIVITY IN M&S EDUCATION

Cropley suggests that fostering creativity within the domain of Modeling and Simulation can result in improved innovation in both the M&S domain as well as in engineering domains since 'the engineering process is supported and enabled by modeling and simulation' [7]. According to the author, creativity has become a valued and 'vital component of engineering practice' and is seen as a key to innovation, where engineering creativity is articulated as engineering which 'results in the output of novel useful products.' Kaufman [22] notes, 'creativity has been described as the most important economic resource of the 21st century.' Dance and Fishwick [8] note that the ultimate goal in the design of a model is to achieve effective communication of system behaviors to improve understanding of relationships within the model. The authors further argue: 'A model that is aesthetically pleasing will result in enjoyment and improved utilization' [8]. Fishwick urges deeper integration of aesthetic considerations within computing cultures to enrich computing experiences [12]. The notion that a primary role of models and simulations is to function as artifacts for supporting communication means the creative aspects of M&S should be an important part of curriculum design decisions. For these reasons, we argue that it is important to include creativity and aesthetic design as components in an M&S course.

3.1 Creativity and Innovation in Engineering

Cropley et al. [5, 6, 7] provide an overview of the increase in perceived value of creativity within engineering disciplines. He points to the 1957 Sputnik satellite launch as a turning point, where creativity suddenly became an important consideration in evaluating the failure of American engineering innovation in the context of the global 'Space Race'. Cropley notes that Gilford, a preeminent psychologist in the 1950's, identified 'convergent thinking' as a main cause of this lack of creativity and innovation of American engineers [7]. 'Convergent thinking' [15], a term introduced by Gilford, was thought to be the result of teaching approaches that emphasized rapid acquisition of factual knowledge, rapid recall, having clearly defined goals, logical thinking, student compliance, and other similar processes [7]. This is in contrast to Gilford's notion of 'divergent thinking', which involves 'branching out from the given' to explore novel solutions.

3.2 Functional Creativity

Cropley [7] makes a distinction between creativity in the fine arts as compared to engineering creativity. He defines engineering creativity as 'functional creativity', where the focus is on creating *products* to solve problems. Cropley [5] notes that *process* is central component of functional creativity, and he identifies four dimensions of creativity of engineering products and explains how they form a hierarchy that can be used as a lens to view the likely benefits of enhanced creativity in the M&S domain. Cropley's [7] four-dimensional model for defining the creativity of engineering products is: relevance and effectiveness, novelty, elegance, and generalizability. These four dimensions can be used as criteria to evaluate the value of creative products, and can provide guidelines as to inspire creativity when designing products that would range from routine to original, and elegant to innovative solutions.

3.2.1 Fostering Functional Creativity

While Cropley provides strong arguments indicating there is a consensus regarding the importance and value of creativity in engineering domains, he also acknowledges that there is a problematic disconnect because few engineering programs recognize the 'importance of creative thinking as an essential teachable skill' [5]. The author suggests that many engineering curricula are overly focused on 'driving toward ever greater breadth and surface learning in technical topics only', and as a consequence, creativity is not taught or fostered as an integral component of most engineering curricula. As discussed earlier, M&S curriculum designers must also determine how to strike a good balance between covering the breadth or depth of a rapidly expanding discipline.

3.2.2 Simulation-Thinking and Functional Creativity

Cropley and Cropley [6] highlight the notion that links between creativity and engineering are often viewed with an explicit focus on pedagogical changes that could foster creative thinking as an integral part of engineering curricula. Thompson [50] discusses the importance of integrating creative design and analysis in a cohesive manner for engineering curricula. She suggests that simulation courses might provide a good opportunity to have students learn more integrated design-analysis thinking. Thompson coined a new term 'simulation-thinking' to capture a more integrated design-analysis thinking process [50]. Kauffman and Beghetto [22] have developed a model of creativity that can provide insight for fostering creativity as part of the learning process. The authors identify 'mini-c' as a category of creativity, which recognizes the 'creativity inherent in students' unique and personally meaningful insights and interpretations as they learn new subject matter' [22]. It is this type of creativity that we aim to foster in our course; students in our course are expected to explore creative representation in learning modeling and simulation.

3.3 Education and the Art of M & S

Paul et al. raise the question of whether M&S should be taught as a 'science', or whether it's possible to teach so as to provide students with an appreciation that 'simulation is more of an art than science [37].' The authors argue that simulation education should help students recognize that many simulation problems are by their very nature 'not well understood', and recommend that creative problem solving should be a critical component of an M&S course. Paul et al. [37] advocate that M&S education should have four general objectives: teach students how to *learn*, how to *think creatively*, how to *problem solve*, and how to *be professionals*. The authors encourage a course design where students learn that the iterative process of modeling helps clarify problem features, and that 'simulation models are not about being correct or incorrect;' they are a vehicle to elicit discussion and debate in order to allow problem owners to develop an enhanced understanding of their problems [37]. This works best when models are perceived as a representation of the modeled system, and that 'models may be purposefully distorted' in order to enable discovery of enhanced insights about a system [37]. Our course design reflects a similar perspective of M&S, which emphasizes the importance of models as creative products, which are designed through an iterative constructive process, where creative abstraction used to emphasize particular model features in order to create interest or enhance understanding.

4. COURSE: CREATIVE MODELING AND SIMULATION

An important aspect of our course is the process of designing creative system models. This encourages students to engage in creative reflection about how the features of their project can be represented so as to provide an interactive experience so that a user will develop an improved understanding of the system and process being modeled. We want students to embrace the idea of models as creative artifacts, which should be designed to provide insight and to communicate details of a system. In addition, we encourage students to create multi-sensory models and simulations that will be interesting and engaging for users exploring their model. Another important aspect of the course is that it was highly interactive, the course was held in a computer lab with a participatory class environment; where students frequently presented their projects in order to share learning, to generate feedback and to encourage discussion on a regular basis.

Our class size it is generally less than 25 students. Duration of the projects varies, we conduct most projects in a 2-phased approach, the initial phase requires students to submit a project proposal. This gives us an opportunity to provide guidance, which is often needed for such open-ended creative projects. Project duration is approximately three weeks, one week for proposal and one-two weeks for the final implementation. We try to interleave projects so as students are completing implementation of one project they are in the ideation stage for their next project proposal.

4.1 Visual Data Flow for Teaching M&S

We have used Max/MSP software for our course, which is a visual data flow programming language. There are numerous reasons why we feel it is a good fit for use in an M&S course. In the sections below we provide a brief overview of some of the benefits for using visual data flow language like Max for an M&S course.

4.1.1 Data Flow Programming Paradigm

While there are numerous variations of flow based programming approaches, in general, they emphasize the movement of data, where the structure of the program is represented as collections of communicating, asynchronous processes [19, 32]. A primary benefit of the data flow paradigm is that the program structure aligns well with implementation requirements for parallel and distributed processing [32]. In addition, the graphical structure of flow-based programs closely resembles the physical processes that it is modeling [19]. Morrison [31] notes that the technology provides a consistent application view from high-level design all the way down to the implementation. Research has shown that having a mental-model with consistent and explicit mappings from the conceptual level to the program implementation level is critical for program comprehension and understanding [13]. In fact, Johnson et al. cite research showing that most software developers 'naturally think in terms of data flow in the design phase.' [19]

4.1.2 Data Flow for the Internet of Things

Namiot et al. [33] discuss the similarity between data-flow software models and the physical constraints that impact designs for communication between embedded hardware in both Internet of Things (IoT) and Machine-to-Machine (M2M) systems. They have suggest that the flow-based programming paradigm can provide a simple model for M2M communication, where devices would expose interfaces to expose or consume data rather than a more complex API. They argue that a simple protocol would work well for devices like sensors, which don't have support for processing program commands. Max/MSP provides a prototyping environment for IoT and M2M systems [47], since it uses a data-flow paradigm and since it also provides firmware for serial communication with microcontrollers. In our current course, we are using Max to create dynamic prototypes for physical IoT systems, and to provide interactive controls for IoT and M2M systems. The ability to create functioning, virtual-dynamic, rapid-prototypes of physical computing systems provides a powerful teaching environment for M&S. This type of project is discussed in detail in section 5.2.2. Figures 7-9 show examples of this type of mapping from conceptual model to max prototype dynamic-model to physical computing representation model.

4.1.3 Data Flow Visual Programming Languages

Researchers in the field of software engineering have recognized many possible benefits for using data flow visual programming languages (DFWPL) [19, 35]. Johnson et al. have noted that the distinction between requirements, program design and coding phases becomes less obvious when using DFWPL, however, the aesthetics and design of the DFWPL environment have a large impact on the ease of use [19]. The authors also note that visualization and animation are essential components of visual programming environments. Nierstrasz et al. made an early (1992) distinction between application engineering and application development, where they envisioned that application developers would be domain experts who would utilize visual scripting to connect compatible software components in order to create applications [35]. They used the term 'script' to suggest an analogy between the data-flow visual script application and a theatrical performance.

4.1.4 Multi-Media Data Flow Visual Languages

Nierstrasz et al. [35] developed a multimedia platform, which utilized a data-flow paradigm. They chose a multimedia application domain specifically because they envisioned that their 'new ideas might fare better in an area' where inertia and cultural bias against visual scripting wouldn't negatively impact their project. They utilized a 'radically different' approach to OOP application design, as they viewed objects as 'patterns of communicating agents', with the goal of developing better software design methodologies, which emphasized component modularity and reuse [35]. Another benefit of application design in the domain of multimedia is that it provides natural parallels because application components actually resemble 'digital production studio' physical hardware or software processes, which generate audio events [35]. This strong natural connection between data-flow software engineering, media arts, and physical computing can provide a strong bridge for introducing simulation concepts to media artists and designers. It can also provide a fertile test area for the design of immersive, multi-sensory enhanced, interactive simulation systems.

4.2 Max/MSP Features and Architecture

Max/MSP is a visual-language based software system, which employs a data-flow/control-flow visual syntax. Max uses the visual metaphor of analog electronic music components such as amplifiers, synthesizers, etc., where discrete components are connected via patch cords. Data passes through the patch cords encoding a variety of signal-types such as MIDI, audio, text, and JSON formatted data. Max is designed for creating interactive music compositions, and therefore supports both regular and variable time signals; the metronome object represents discrete time, and this object works well for triggering events. In addition, *MSP* (signal processing) components provide oscillating audio signals based on digital signal processing components, which can be used to model dynamic systems. Digital music and media artists use Max/MSP extensively, to create interactive and dynamic compositions including performance art [29].

4.3 Max for Teaching Computing Concepts

Several researchers have discussed the use of Max/MSP software for teaching computing concepts. [2, 9, 28] Manzo [28] notes that the Max data-flow paradigm is intuitive, and the fact that all Max components are objects supports students in learning object-oriented thinking. In addition, Max also provides an API to connect with microcontrollers, and it provides many user-interface components that can be used to control hardware for rapid prototyping of embedded systems. [2, 47] In our M&S course, students were tasked with creating a variety of discrete event models and dynamic simulations. Students were required to incorporate creative visual representation, user interaction, as well as meaningful audio output, using Max objects as construction primitives. Our current iteration of the course has students integrating Max programs with creative physical prototypes of dynamic systems.

4.3.1 Creativity and Aesthetics for M&S Education

As Cropley et al. [5] and others have noted, it's important to nurture creativity, particularly when designing courses situated in technical domains or cultures. Nierstrasz et al. [35] chose a multi-media domain for their software engineering research particularly because they wanted a more creative culture as a test-bed for their application design. We concur with Paul et al. [37] that M&S curricula should encourage creative problem solving in conjunction with traditional M&S concepts. We believe that Max/MSP software provides a solid framework for teaching creative M&S since it uses a visual data-flow format and supports student creation of multi-sensory artistic modeling products. Fishwick suggests that we should endeavor to externalize our mental models as 'real and virtual models, which have sensory and aesthetic qualities [11].' He argues that aesthetics should play an important role in modeling and provides a methodology for incorporating aesthetics into the model design process [11].

- Choose a system to be modeled
- Select model types
- Choose an aesthetic
- Define Mapping
- Create Model

Max allows us to extend this model in two important ways. First, Max allows for rich integration of multiple sensory modalities, along with providing a framework that supports hierarchy and dynamic-encapsulation of model layers, where embedded layers can be designed to reveal visual dynamic features. Second, Max supports integration with microcontrollers, which extends opportunities for creating physical model representations. This support for a creative design progression from conceptual to programmatic to physical models creates a fabulous learning opportunity for students. The process of mapping model concepts, components, coordination structure and aesthetics between these model layers provides students with a rich modeling experience to enhance deep learning.

4.3.2 Brief History of Max/MSP

Max was first developed at IRCAM, by Miller Puckette in the late 1980s; it was initially developed for use with the Macintosh computer [29]. Max was commercially available in 1990 and was chosen as 'Software Innovation of the Year' by readers of Keyboard Magazine in 1991 [29]. In 1996, Puckett started development of Pure Data, (Pd), which is an open-source version of Max/MSP. 'Pd was created to further the Max paradigm by extending data processing to applications other than audio and MIDI, such as real-time video and web interaction [39].' An important distinction between Max and other audio software is that Max is not audio editing software, and it is not a simple audio synthesizer. Max can be considered an 'audio-rendering environment', where all processing is done in real time and the creative process is more analogous to creating a dynamic instrument. [29] Max provides a visual language interface to specify audio and media synthesis and signal processing algorithms in a real-time, live-code environment [29].' This environment provides immediate feedback and the visual format may make it easier to conceptualize signal processing algorithms [29].

4.3.3 Max Data Flow Objects

Max programs are called *patcher* files, and a patcher consists of a number of max objects connected together with patch cords. Max has an extremely large library of built-in objects that can be used to build programs. It also provides several ways to create custom objects, including JavaScript, Java and C++ components. Most Max objects have a number of inlets, which can be connected to the outlet from a different patch. The left-most inlet is a usually a 'hot' inlet, and it is designed to receive control signals indicating that the object should begin executing its behavior. A max object inlet can accept many messages and message-types, depending on arguments defined for that object; in addition, each object also has a large number of attributes, which can be used for initialization and UI-customization. The physical layout of objects on a workspace layer impacts the order of execution, or the ordering of messages sent between objects. Other objects, like *route* and *select*, can be used to explicitly control the order of execution.

4.3.4 Encapsulation and Object Hierarchy

Max is designed to support dynamic viewing and interaction with an executing program across any number of object layers. A patcher file can contain several different levels, which represent object hierarchical relationships. So, a patcher file can be embedded as an object within a parent patcher file; it becomes a sub-patcher with it's own inlets and outlets. Any selection of connected max objects on a workspace can be converted to represent a child sub-patcher object. The basic sub-patcher is represented as a simple rectangular object with the appropriate inlets and outlets as required within the sub-patch for connectivity with the parent patch.

In addition, Max provides the *bPatcher* object, which allows for creation of customized dynamic graphical components. In student example projects below, we will provide a detailed description of bPatcher objects to show how they enable encapsulation of Max sub-patcher objects to create custom visual-dynamic objects. In essence, each layer within Max represents an object that has a hierarchical relationship with other layers in a patcher program. For each object layer, specific objects can be selected to be visible in a presentation-mode view of the program. In addition, Max patches can be edited while they are in dynamic execution mode. The object-oriented, hierarchical design of Max patchers and sub-patchers, combined with powerful flexibility for controlling and customizing the dynamic user-interface components makes Max an extremely interesting option for teaching M&S concepts.

5. CASE STUDIES

We will present a few course project assignments with detailed overview of student project submissions, to explore the creative diversity of student projects as well as to highlight the capabilities of the Max/MSP software for creating interactive representations and implementations of Discrete Event Simulations. For one project, students created a Max implementation of a Petri net system, which could be used as a toolkit for creating dynamic Petri net (PN) models. In addition, students were required to explore the creative representation and implementation of a non-trivial process that could be simulated using their Petri net system.

5.1 Petri Net Project

Fishwick defines Petri nets as a modeling framework, which is primarily used for 'studying dynamic concurrent behavior of systems where there is discrete flow [10].' Peterson notes that a Petri net has static properties that are represented by a directed graph with two distinct node types: circles called places and bars called transitions. The dynamic properties are represented by a token that moves around the graph along directional arcs. [38] Peterson notes that 'the simplicity and power of Petri nets makes them an excellent tool for working with asynchronous, concurrent systems' [38].

Baros [3] and also Jové et al. [20] recommend the use of Petri net models to teach fundamental modeling and computing concepts. Baros notes that students often have difficulty when trying to understand concurrent systems behavior. He argues that, when students construct Petri net models, they develop 'a much more intuitive perception of dependencies (synchronizations) among processes [3].' Jové et al. conclude that having students construct Petri net models, with a focus on conceptual modeling, helps students understand the distinction between a system, a conceptual model, and the implementation of the model [20].

The figures below are examples of one student's Petri net project. This student created an implementation of the Dining Philosophers problem (DP) with his Petri net system. The DP problem can be considered a proxy for studying characteristics of human task coordination, where often a high-level task cannot be decomposed into disjoint parts, so several people must coordinate their activities to complete a task [10]. The first image shows a dynamic, creative representation of five philosophers seated at a dinner table. This figure shows the high level, presentation-view of this Max project. The student created user interface controls to allow a user to start/reset the simulation. He also created several dynamic data-widget elements that provide statistics about the simulation as it progresses in real-time. This dynamic interface indicates which philosophers are currently eating, and shows the location of the unused chopstick. In addition, the student integrated an audio track to provide ambient restaurant sounds, in order to create a multi-sensory presentation.

In Figure 2, the inner-workings of the highest-level Max patcher hierarchy for the DP project is shown. The student has used colored *panel* objects to organize logical sections of patcher code. He has used Max *send* and *receive* objects to provide communication between panels; this hides the patch cords from view and creates an aesthetic design to provide improved visual organization of his project. The figure shows three high-level code sections, the yellow panel represents the clock-signal control, the purple panel contains PN-*Places*, which represent the chopstick resources, and the teal panel contains PN-*Transitions*, which represent the philosophers. This snapshot image shows that

the program is in execution-mode, and Place3 has an active token; this indicates that a chopstick is available. The teal panel, shows that Transition4 is active and highlighted green. This indicates that philosopher4 is currently eating.

This student implemented logic so the PN-transitions have an associated time delay, which corresponds to the time-period when philosophers are eating. Inputs to the philosopher-eating transition are three incoming arcs, which are shown as part of the PN-transition icon, these represent two chopsticks and one food PN-places. There are two outgoing arcs emanating from each PN-transition; these correspond to the chopstick PN-places, so once a transition has completed firing, the two chopstick tokens are returned to their PN-places to enable a different philosopher to have an opportunity to eat.

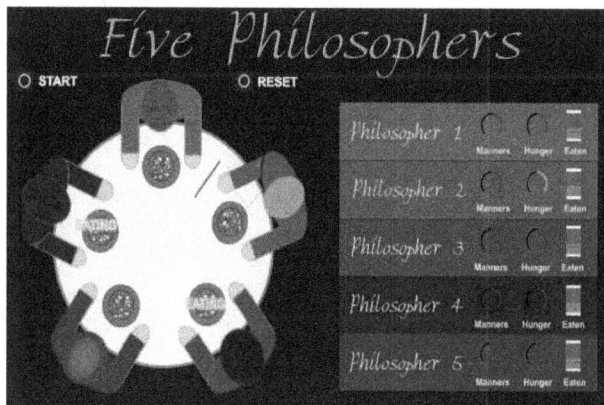

Figure 1. Dining Philosophers in Presentation-View Mode

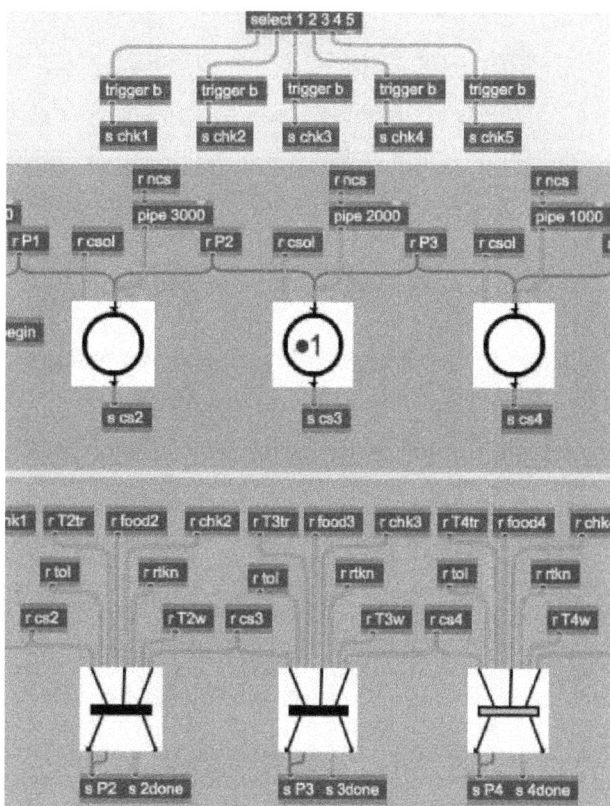

Figure 2. Dynamic Petri-Net Logic Panels

5.1.1 Petri Nets

The process of creating a PN system may provide students insight into subtleties of this modeling paradigm that might otherwise go unnoticed. Some students used the *metro* object as a global clock to send a synchronizing control signal to all transitions in order to have them all fire in parallel. Other students designed their PN transition components to insure fairness in transition ordering; to implement this behavior, students used the Max *urn* object, which generates random numbers without replacement. In Figure 3, which is an embedded sub-patcher designed to control the transition activations, the metro object is connected to an urn object, which controls activation of the transitions. In the image, the output value from the urn object is input to the route object, which provides control-flow capabilities, to activate the selected transition. The bottom of the figure shows that there are six outlets for this sub-patcher, the first outlet is used for testing purposes, while the outer outlets are connected directly to custom designed PN transition objects in the parent patcher. The pink highlighted boxes show that this student has created user-interface elements for the presentation-view of this custom max object. This will show an LED indicator light as each transition is activated via the urn object; currently outlet1 is shown as active.

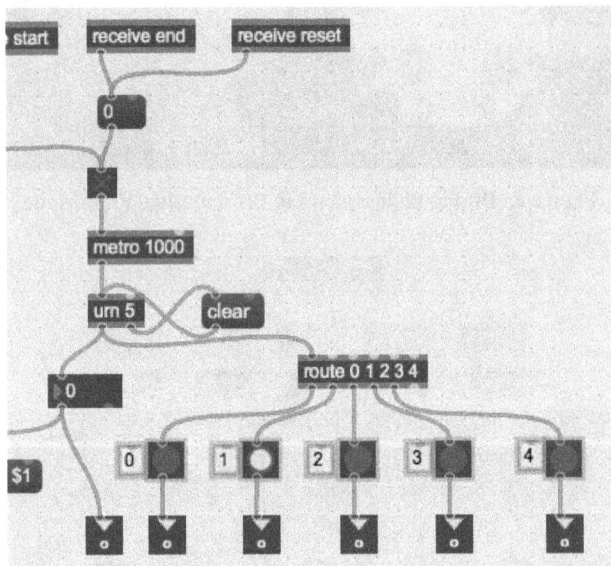

Figure 3. Random Transition Activation Using Urn Object

5.1.2 Event and Object Coordination Messages

Another subtle concept that students discovered when building Petri net components, was that additional messages are required in order to coordinate verification of the state that corresponds to the presence of tokens for PN places associated with incoming arcs, to determine whether a PN transition can fire. Then, once a transition does fire, additional messaging is required to adjust the token state of each associated PN place. Figure 4 shows that four different types of patch cord messages are input into the PN Place object: Place1. The Max objects 's' and 'r' correspond to hidden patch chords, where each send and receive object is connected with some other Max object inlet or outlet, in order to receive or send messages. This layer of message-passing for coordination is often hidden from users when using higher-level simulation software, however these implementation-level details provide concrete demonstration of the importance event orchestration and

system architecture in M&S, which non-major students may not have been exposed to prior to this course.

5.1.3 BPatcher: Custom Visual Dynamic Objects

The PN-place object, which appears as a black circle on a white square in Figures 2, 4 and 5, was created using the Max *bpatcher* object; the PN-place object icon is a visual interface for an embedded sub-patcher of lower-level logic. Figure 5 shows a partial view of the internal logic for a bpatcher PN-place object, which includes three inlets, and three outlets that correspond to the place UI component from Figure 4. While it is difficult to see object details in this figure, it should be clear that the object-oriented architecture of Max, combined with an extensive library of customizable user-interface elements, provides a powerful and creative environment for designing interactive models and simulations. Students in this course created custom bpatcher objects as the primary means to construct interactive representations for their simulation models.

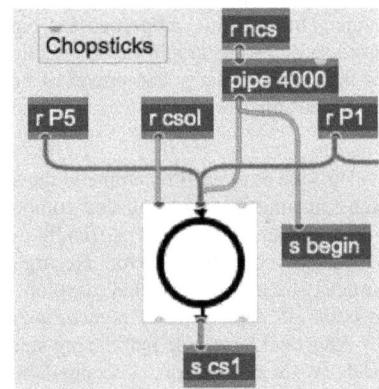

Figure 4. Inlet Messages of Place1 Bpatcher Object

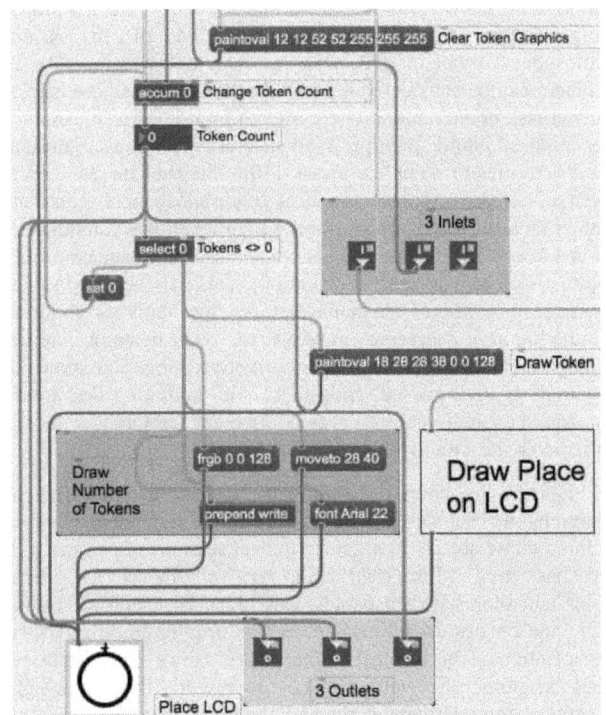

Figure 5. Implementation Details of *Place* Object Sub-Patcher

30

5.1.4 Creative Audio Representation

Max provides many audio objects, and we encouraged students to integrate creative audio for all of their projects. So while it is difficult to share the creative aspect of student designed audio components, this was a very important part of the course. We had several students with strong music performance and audio design backgrounds, and the audio components of their simulations were quite beautiful. We suggested that students integrate audio in a meaningful way with their simulations; often that corresponded to having students analyze their model to find event triggers for audio events. Figure 6 below shows implementation of a Karplus Strong audio generator, which was triggered in conjunction with a Petri net transition firing. The integration of creative audio for these projects helped students view simulations from a more holistic and multi-sensory perspective, it encouraged reflection on their model to determine how audio could be meaningfully integrated.

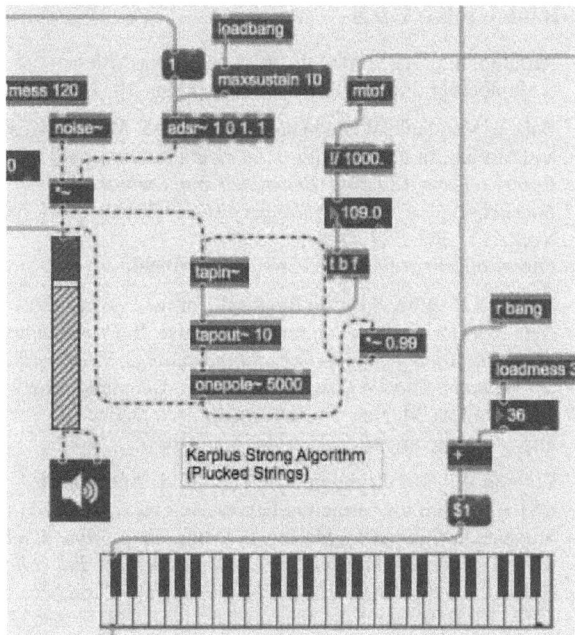

Figure 6. Karplus Strong Integrated Audio Event

5.2 Max: Limitations, Integration with IoT

5.2.1 Limitation: Web Sharing of Programs

Unfortunately, Max patcher programs cannot currently be embedded as interactive components on web pages. This somewhat limits the impact that our student-designed creative simulations can have, because we cannot easily share student projects as interactive online applications. In order to execute a Max program, users must have Max software installed on their system and they must download a patcher file in order to experience and interact with it. However, Max does provide an easy method to share patcher files using a serialized data format that can be copy / pasted in a text editor. In addition, Max has a very robust user community, so there are many resources available online such as videos, tutorials, and an active forum to support users [29]. In addition, within the Max software environment, there is an extensive, well-organized repository of documentation, tutorials, and live-editable code examples for every Max object [29].

5.2.2 Integration with the Internet of Things

Max has an extensive set of objects that provide web integration within a Max patcher. Max components can be used to create user-interfaces to interact and control physical hardware using web protocols. In addition, Max includes firmware to support integration between patcher files and microcontrollers like the Arduino. It is interesting to note that the Arduino microcontroller started as a project for students at the Interaction Design Institute IVREA. One goal of the Arduino project was to create an inexpensive open source microcontroller for student design projects [1]. In our current course, we are using Max to prototype physical simulation models and we are also using Max for designing user-interface controls for these physical, tangible simulation components. Figure 7, below, shows an implementation of the Fibonacci sequence equations, which was created using Max/MSP.

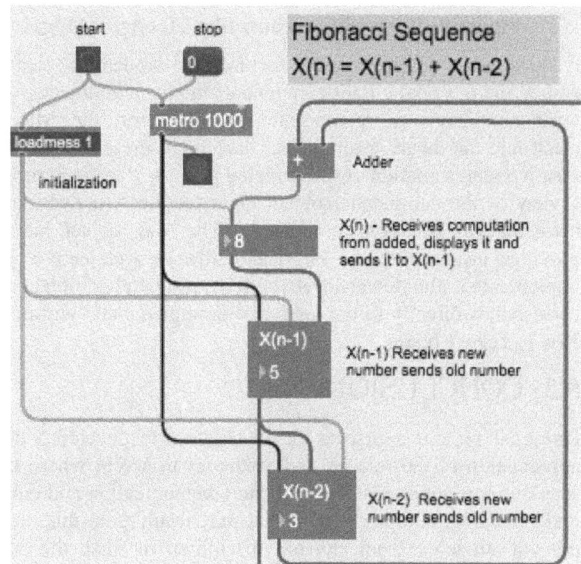

Figure 7. Max Patcher Fibonacci Model

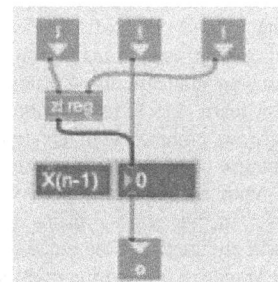

Figure 8. BPatcher Logic for X(n-1) Object

Figure 9 shows the physical prototype of a hardware circuit, which was created using five individual Teensy 3.1 microcontrollers [49]. The physical implementation of the circuit design is isomorphic to the Max patcher. Both models implement synchronous architecture, and utilize serial protocol for communication. The *metro* object in Max, functions as a software clock; it generates a control signal that has a constant (configurable) interval. This architecture is mirrored in the physical circuit where a single Teensy is programmed to behave like the metro object; it sends a control clock signal to each of the other Teensy boards in order to synchronize the data-flow between autonomous components.

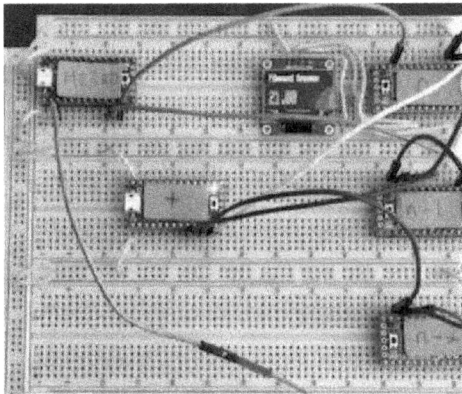

Figure 9. Teensy Microcontroller Fibonacci Model

A third phase of this project requires the student to creatively embed the physical circuit components in physical objects, which must also have an isomorphic mapping with the Max and electronic hardware prototypes; this final project must be a creative representation of the modeled process. Figure 8, provides a view of the sub-patcher object logic for the X(n-1) Fibonacci mathematical equation component. The Max object hierarchy provides insight into the physical hardware architecture we've implemented, the lower-level, custom sub-patcher object logic corresponds directly to the logic that is implemented within a the X(n-1) Teensy board.

5.3 CONCLUSION

One goal for our course is for all students to develop a deeper appreciation of the role art and aesthetics in M&S, where multi-sensory representations can facilitate communication and enhance understanding. Another benefit that may result from this blended mix of students from diverse disciplines is that the shared experience and discourse may inspire students in their professional careers to be more effective communicators and collaborators when working on interdisciplinary team projects. We are utilizing Max/MSP software, which is used by professional media artists, as a means to introduce M&S concepts to Art and Technology students, this creates the opportunity for these students to learn M&S using familiar medium in an environment where we embrace their creative exploration. On the other hand, the use of Max/MSP software provides Computer Science students with a unique perspective; they are working alongside creative media artists, using a visual data flow language. This is likely the first experience for CS students using a visual data flow language for creating multi-sensory projects, we anticipate the experience will encourage them to appreciate and integrate aesthetics of computing in their professional careers. We can also note that the goal of enhancing the creativity of CS students may be more of a challenge than the goal of teaching M&S concepts to Arts and Technology students. We enjoy the challenges and opportunity to cultivate and nurture this creative and technical intermixing of academic cultures.

As this is a new approach for teaching this M&S course, it is difficult to measure the success or impact on student career choices. A key question is whether a topic, like modeling and simulation, is being offered for professional development, vocational training, or as a fundamental area of knowledge required by all students, even those outside of engineering. We take the latter view where our aim the introduction to M&S as a disciplinary area. Thus, validation of the approach lay less with professional follow-through and more with an ability to convey modeling and simulation concepts to non-engineers and non-scientists who nevertheless need an understanding of M&S knowledge to be successful in areas that are already known to rely on this knowledge: such as computer music, animation, virtual reality, and game design and implementation.

6. ACKNOWLEDGMENTS

We thank the Arts and Technology Department and the Computer Science Department at the University of Texas at Dallas. We also thank the office of the Dean of Engineering and Computer Science for the EEF Fellowship sponsorship of the first author. We also would like to thank Joseph Rowe for permitting the use of his Petri net project to be included in this paper.

7. REFERENCES

[1] Arduino, http://en.wikipedia.org/w/index.php?title= Arduino&oldid=646633136. Retrieved Mar. 10, 2015.

[2] Bak, J., Verplank, W. and Gauthier, D. 2015. Motors, Music and Motion. In *Proceedings of the Ninth International Conference on Tangible, Embedded, and Embodied Interaction* (Stanford, CA, January 16-19, 2015). ACM, New York, NY, 367–374. DOI= http://doi.acm.org/10.1145/2677199.2680590.

[3] Barros, J.P. 2002. Specific Proposals for the Use of Petri Nets in a Concurrent Programming Course. In *Proceedings of the 7th Annual Conference on Innovation and Technology in Computer Science Education* (Aarhus, Denmark, June 24-26, 2002). ACM, New York, NY 165–167. DOI= http://doi.acm.org/10.1145/544414.544463

[4] Cohoon, J.P. and Tychonievich, L.A. 2011. Analysis of a CS1 Approach for Attracting Diverse and Inexperienced Students to Computing Majors. In *Proceedings of the 42nd ACM Technical Symposium on Computer Science Education* (Dallas, TX, March 09-12, 2011). ACM, New York, NY, 165–170. DOI=http://doi.acm.org/10.1145/1953163.1953217

[5] Cropley, A.J. and Cropley, D. 2009. *Fostering creativity: A diagnostic approach for higher education and organizations.* Hampton Press Cresskill, NJ.

[6] Cropley, D. H. and Cropley, A. J. 2005. Engineering creativity: A systems concept of functional creativity. In J. C. Kaufman and J. Baer (Eds.), *Creativity Across Domains: Faces of the Muse,* New Jersey: Lawrence Erlbaum Associates Inc., 169-185.

[7] Cropley, D.H. 2007. Applying Creativity in Modeling and Simulation. In *Proceedings of 17th International Council on Systems Engineering (INCOSE 2007): Systems Engineering: Key to Intelligent Enterprises.* (San Diego, CA, June 24-28, 2007) Curan Associates, Inc., 733–741.

[8] Dance, L.K. and Fishwick, P.A. 2001. Methodology for the 3D modeling and visualization of concurrency networks. In *Proceedings of Society of Photo-Optical Instrumentation Engineers (SPIE) 4367, Enabling Technology for Simulation Science* (Orlando, FL, April 16, 2001), 152–163.

[9] Dierbach, C., Hochheiser, H., Collins, S., Jerome, G., Ariza, C., Kelleher, T., Kleinsasser, W., Dehlinger, J. and Kaza, S. 2011. A model for piloting pathways for computational

thinking in a general education curriculum. In *Proceedings of the 42nd ACM Technical Symposium on Computer Science Education* (Dallas, TX, March 09-12, 2011). ACM, New York, NY, 257–262. DOI=http://doi.acm.org/10.1145/1953163.1953243

[10] Fishwick, P. A. 1995. *Simulation Model Design and Execution: Building Digital Worlds.* Englewood Cliffs, New Jersey, Prentice Hall, Inc.

[11] Fishwick, P.A. 2002. Aesthetic programming: Crafting personalized software. *Leonardo.* 35, 4 (2002), 383–390.

[12] Fishwick, P. A. (Ed.) 2006. *Aesthetic computing.* MIT Press, Cambridge, MA, 1-23.

[13] Fix, V., Wiedenbeck, S. and Scholtz, J. 1993. Mental representations of programs by novices and experts. In *Proceedings of the INTERCHI'93 Conference on Human Factors in Computing Systems* (Amsterdam, The Netherlands, April 24-29, 1993). IOS Press, Amsterdam, The Netherlands, 74–79.

[14] Greenwood, A. and Beaverstock, M. 2011. Simulation education-seven reasons for change. In *Proceedings of the 2011 Winter Simulation Conference* (Phoenix, AZ, December 11-14, 2011). Winter Simulation Conference, 20–28.

[15] Guilford, J. P. (1950). Creativity. American Psychologist. 5, 9 (September 1950), 444-454.

[16] Guzdial, M. and Forte, A. 2005. Design process for a non-majors computing course. In *Proceedings of the 36th SIGCSE Technical Symposium on Computer Science Education* (St. Louis, MO, February 23-27, 2005). ACM, New York, NY, 361–365. DOI=http://doi.acm.org/10.1145/1047344.1047468

[17] Haungs, M., Clark, C., Clements, J. and Janzen, D. 2012. Improving first-year success and retention through interest-based CS0 courses. In *Proceedings of the 43rd ACM Technical Symposium on Computer Science Education* (Raleigh, NC, February 27-March 03, 2012). ACM, New York, NY, 589–594. DOI=http://doi.acm.org/10.1145/2157136.2157307

[18] Jain, S. 2014. Teaching of Simulation at Business Schools. In *Proceedings of the 2014 Winter Simulation Conference,* (Savannah, GA, December 07-10, 2014). IEEE Press, Piscataway, NJ, 3684–3695.

[19] Johnston, W.M., Hanna, J.R. and Millar, R.J. 2004. Advances in dataflow programming languages. *ACM Computing Surveys (CSUR).* 36, 1 (2004), 1–34.

[20] Jové, J.F., Petit, A.G., Casas, P.F. and Casanovas-Garcia, J. 2014. Teaching System Modelling and Simulation Through Petri Nets and Arena. In *Proceedings of the 2014 Winter Simulation Conference,* (Savannah, GA, December 07-10, 2014). IEEE Press, Piscataway, NJ, 3662–3673.

[21] Katai, Z. and Toth, L. 2010. Technologically and artistically enhanced multi-sensory computer-programming education. *Teaching and Teacher Education.* 26, 2 (2010), 244–251.

[22] Kaufman, J.C. and Beghetto, R.A. 2009. Beyond big and little: The four c model of creativity. *Review of General Psychology.* 13, 1 (2009), 1–12.

[23] Kincaid, J.P. and Westerlund, K.K. 2009. Simulation in Education and Training. In *Proceedings of the 2009 Winter Simulation Conference* (Austin, TX, December 13-16, 2009). Winter Simulation Conference, 273–280.

[24] Kinnunen, P., Meisalo, V. and Malmi, L. 2010. Have we missed something?: identifying missing types of research in computing education. In *Proceedings of the Sixth International Workshop on Computing Education Research* (Aarhus, Denmark, August 09-10, 2010). ACM New York, NY, 13–22.

[25] Kress, R., Cemerlic, A., Kress, J. and Varghese, J. 2010. Discrete event simulation class for engineering graduate students. In *Proceedings of the 2010 Winter Simulation Conference* (Baltimore, MD, December 05-08, 2010). Winter Simulation Conference, 344–352.

[26] Lin, S. and Tatar, D. 2011. Encouraging parallel thinking through explicit coordination modeling. In *Proceedings of the 42nd ACM Technical Symposium on Computer science education* (Dallas, TX, March 09-12, 2011). ACM, New York, NY, 441–446. DOI=http://doi.acm.org/10.1145/1953163.1953292

[27] Loper, M.L., Henninger, A., Diem, J.W., Petty, M.D. and Tolk, A. 2011. Educating the workforce: M&S professional education. In *Proceedings of the 2011 Winter Simulation Conference* (Phoenix, AZ, December 11-14, 2011). Winter Simulation Conference, 3968–3978.

[28] Manzo, V.J., Halper, M. and Halper, M. 2011. Multimedia-based visual programming promoting core competencies in IT education. In *Proceedings of the 2011 Conference on Information Technology Education* (West Point, New York, October 20-22, 2011). SIGITE '11. ACM, New York, NY, 203–208. DOI=http://doi.acm.org/10.1145/2047594.2047649

[29] Max/MSP Software. https://cycling74.com/company/. Retrieved March 10, 2015.

[30] Cycling74. *Max/MSP History - Where did Max/MSP come from? 2015.* Cycling74. Archived on 2009-06-09. http://web.archive.org/web/20090609205550/http://www.cycling74.com/twiki/bin/view/FAQs/MaxMSPHistory. Retrieved March 10, 2015.

[31] Morrison, J.P. 1994. Flow-based programming. In *Proceedings of the 1st International Workshop on Software Engineering for Parallel and Distributed Systems* (1994). 25–29.

[32] Morrison, J.P. 2010. *Flow-Based Programming, 2nd Edition: A New Approach to Application Development.* CreateSpace Independent Publishing Platform: 2nd Edition, 2010, 1-11.

[33] Namiot, D. and Sneps-Sneppe, M. 2014. On IoT Programming. *International Journal of Open Information Technologies.* 2, 10 (2014), 25–28.

[34] Nance, R.E. and Balci, O. 2001. Plenary session: thoughts and musings on simulation education. In *Proceedings of the 33nd Conference on Winter Simulation* (Arlington, VA, December 09-12, 2001). IEEE Computer Society, Washington, DC, 1567–1570.

[35] Nierstrasz, O., Gibbs, S. and Tsichritzis, D. 1992. Component-oriented Software Development. *Communications of the ACM.* 35, 9 (September 1992), 160–165.

[36] Padilla, J.J., Diallo, S.Y. and Tolk, A. 2011. Do We Need M & S Science ? *SCS M&S Magazine.* 8, (2011). 161–166.

http://www.scs.org/magazines/2011-10/index_file/Files/ Padilla-Diallo-Tolk.pdf. Retrieved March 10, 2015.

[37] Paul, R.J., Eldabi, T. and Kuljis, J. 2003. Perspectives on simulation in education and training: simulation education is no substitute for intelligent thinking. In *Proceedings of the 35th Conference on Winter Simulation: Driving Innovation* (New Orleans, LA, December 07-10, 2003). Winter Simulation Conference, 1989–1993.

[38] Peterson, J.L. 1977. Petri nets. *ACM Computing Surveys (CSUR)*. 9, 3 (1977), 223–252.

[39] Pure Data, 2015 http://puredata.info/. Retrieved Mar. 10, 2015.

[40] Robinson, S. 2011. Choosing the right model: conceptual modeling for simulation. In *Proceedings of the 2011 Winter Simulation Conference (Phoenix, AZ, December 11-14, 2011)*. Winter Simulation Conference, 1423–1435.

[41] Shams, L. and Seitz, A.R. 2008. Benefits of multisensory learning. *Trends in Cognitive Sciences*. 12, 11 (Nov. 2008), 411–417.

[42] Siiman, L.A., Pedaste, M., Tõnisson, E., Sell, R., Jaakkola, T. and Alimisis, D. 2014. A Review of Interventions to Recruit and Retain ICT Students. *International Journal of Modern Education and Computer Science*. 6, 3 (Mar. 2014), 45–54.

[43] Simon, B., Kinnunen, P., Porter, L. and Zazkis, D. 2010. Experience report: CS1 for majors with media computation. In *Proceedings of the fifteenth Annual Conference on Innovation and Technology in Computer Science Education* (Ankara, Turkey, June 28-30, 2010). ACM, New York, NY, 214–218. DOI=http://doi.acm.org/10.1145/1822090.1822151

[44] Stroup, W.M. and Wilensky, U. 2014. On the Embedded Complementarity of Agent-Based and Aggregate Reasoning in Students' Developing Understanding of Dynamic Systems. *Technology, Knowledge and Learning*. 19, 1-2 (July 2014), 19–52.

[45] Stahl, I. 2000. Teaching methods: how should we teach simulation? In *Proceedings of the 32nd Conference on Winter Simulation* (Orlando, FL, December 10-13, 2000).

Society for Computer Simulation International, San Diego, CA. 1602–1612.

[46] Szczerbicka, H., Banks, J., Rogers, R.V., Ören, T.I., Sarjoughian, H.S. and Zeigler, B.P. 2000. Conceptions of curriculum for simulation education: panel. In *Proceedings of the 32nd Conference on Winter Simulation* (Orlando, FL, December 10-13, 2000). Society for Computer Simulation International, San Diego, CA. 1635–1644.

[47] Taylor, R., Kazakevich, M., Boulanger, P., Garcia, M. and Bischof, W.F. 2007. Multi-modal Interface for Fluid Dynamics Simulations Using 3–D Localized Sound. In *Proceedings of the 8th International Symposium on Smart Graphics* (Kyoto, Japan, 2007). Springer-Verlag, Berlin, Heidelberg 182–187.

[48] Taylor, R., Boulanger, P. and Olivier, P. 2008. dream. Medusa: A participatory performance. In *Proceedings of the 9th International Symposium on Smart Graphics* (Rennes, France, 2008). Springer-Verlag, Berlin, Heidelberg, 200–206.

[49] Teensy, 2015 https://www.pjrc.com/teensy/teensyduino.html. Retrieved March 10, 2015.

[50] Thompson, M.K. 2009. Simulation thinking: Where design and analysis meet. *In Proceedings of the 2009 Winter Simulation Conference* (Austin, TX, December 13-16, 2009). Winter Simulation Conference, 3099–3108.

[51] Trifonova, A., Brandtsegg, Ø. and Jaccheri, L. 2008. Software engineering for and with artists: a case study. In *Proceedings of the 3rd international conference on Digital Interactive Media in Entertainment and Arts* (Athens, Grece, September 10-12, 2008). ACM, New York, NY, 190–197. DOI=http://doi.acm.org/10.1145/1413634.1413671

[52] Wang, J. 2007. Petri nets for dynamic event-driven system modeling, in: *Handbook of Dynamic System Modeling*, Ed: Paul Fishwick, CRC Press, 2007.

[53] Wilensky, U. and Reisman, K. 2006. Thinking like a wolf, a sheep, or a firefly: Learning biology through constructing and testing computational theories—an embodied modeling approach. *Cognition and instruction*. 24, 2 (2006), 171–209.

Microcontroller Based Water Computer: An Experiment with Tangible System Dynamics Modeling

David Vega, Michael Howell, Karen Doore, Paul Fishwick
University of Texas at Dallas
800 West Campbell Road, AT10
Richardson, TX 75080-3021 USA
{dxv130830, howell, kdoore, paul.fishwick}@utdallas.edu

ABSTRACT

The goal of designing effective methods to teach systems-thinking concepts has been an important focus within the education community. We propose a novel approach to introduce systems-thinking concepts in informal education environments by the use of a tangible user interface. We have designed an analog water computer based on the System Dynamics modeling framework in order to create a physical machine that exhibits complex system behaviors. Our model specifically facilitates enhanced understanding of differential equations and provides visual feedback of the system in real -time. Our tangible and interactive water computer simulates the behavior of the Lotka-Volterra differential equations model and provides an intuitive visual interface that maps symbolism in mathematical equations to discrete physical components of our machine. In addition, our machine has been designed to provide tangible interaction capabilities so that changes to the physical system will provide learners with a deeper understanding of mathematical relationships that are represented by the machine components. The objective is to narrow the gap which exists between the mathematically abstract and the real physical world, and to encourage exploration and stimulate curiosity as these intangible factors are important to foster learner engagement particularly in informal learning environments.

Categories and Subject Descriptors

I.6.3 [**Simulation and Modeling**]: Applications; C.1.3 [**Other Architectural Styles**]: Analog computers.

General Terms

Experimentation, Design, Theory

Keywords

Simulation, Modeling, System Dynamics, Tangible, Analog Computing

SIGSIM-PADS '15, June 10 - 12, 2015, London, United Kingdom
© 2015 ACM. ISBN 978-1-4503-3583-6/15/06...$15.00
DOI: http://dx.doi.org/10.1145/2769458.2769469

1. INTRODUCTION

Forrester [14] notes "The fragmentary nature of traditional education becomes less relevant as society becomes more complex, crowded and tightly interconnected". While novel approaches like Massively Open Online Courses, (MOOCs) are emerging to provide alternative pedagogical models, their focus group is primarily higher education and adult learners [1]. We contend it is essential to develop novel, effective, and engaging approaches to introduce these important skills to a more diverse range of students. A pilot study conducted by Roberts [36] showed that "dynamic feedback, systems thinking concepts can be taught to children as young as ten and eleven years old". Roberts's study determined that it is possible for fifth and sixth graders to learn skills previously taught to graduate MIT students. However, introducing System Dynamics to pre-college students should be addressed using a different strategy than the one applied to higher education. Forrester notes that SD is not a tool that fits well with the lecture-based educational model, he argues that SD knowledge cannot be acquired by acting as a spectator watching from the stands. Sterman suggests that learning to understand causal dynamic systems is a complex process in itself [42].

diSessa's [8] research suggests that understanding results from conceptual changes to a learner's existing mental model. His research emphasizes the view that learning in children can occur through an emergent process of constructing 'different models out of their intuitive resources [8]'. To support this type of learning process, our water computer can serve as a learning-artifact; it can inspire student curiosity to promote inquiry. diSessa's theory of emergence as an important learning mechanism, requires that students have an 'explanatory goal' to inspire them to develop, test, and modify explanations to explain the observed focal phenomena [8]. We hypothesize that building on a learner's existing understanding of water-flow through containers may allow users to develop enhanced understanding of dynamic system concepts in order to integrate those concepts with their existing mental models [3, 18]. We have developed a physical prototype of an interactive SD model in order to provide students with an immersive learning experience to enhance their understanding of SD concepts. Our Lotka-Volterra (LV) microcontroller based water-computer is a hybrid analog/digital computer [26, 49] that dynamically solves a pair of differential equations, using flowing water, as the computation medium. The water machine's operation visually represents the dynamic system composed of a predator species and a prey species, and simulates the behavior of their populations changing over time. This model can be used in informal education environments [39] as a learning artifact that demonstrates how coupled differential equations operate.

The Internet of Things (IoT) refers to an evolving trend in electronics and software, where computing is ubiquitous [20, 48]. This ubiquity began in the 1990s with computing elements forming the basis of ever-smaller products, from badges and cards to wearables. Our use of IoT in the Creative Automata Laboratory is focused on making "modular systems" that are tangible representations of abstract artifacts from mathematics and computing. The water computer described in this paper is an example of such a tangible representation of a System Dynamics model for ecology. A modular system is one where components are connected together to achieve an IoT collective presence. We begin with modular networks represented in Max/MSP, a visual programming language that employs a data-flow and block diagram representation of objects. From the patches developed with Max/MSP, we proceed in one of two paths: (1) to connect a patch directly to hardware for both input (i.e., sensing) and output (i.e. actuation), or (2) to treat the patch as an interactive virtual prototype for a physical system. The water computer described in this paper stems from exploration using the 2nd path.

2. WATER COMPUTING

 The term "Computer" refers to an object or device that performs a computation or calculation. The earliest analog computation tool known is the abacus, invented in Babylon around 2400 BC. Water computing is a term that originated in the Soviet Union around 1928 where analog computers were being researched. The "Water Integrator" was a machine capable of solving differential equations with fine precision (fractions of a millimeter) by manipulating water through various chambers. The water represented data and the flow represented mathematical operations. These computers were used in the Soviet Union until the late 80's for the modeling of dynamical systems [45].

The Monetary National Income Analogue Computer (MONIAC) is another example of analog computers that uses water for data representation [4]. Unlike the water integrator, the MONIAC was designed for educational purposes. It was created in 1949 by the economist William "Bill" Phillips in New Zealand to model the economic processes of the United Kingdom. This model is currently being used as a learning tool in the University of Leeds's Business School to aid in the "understanding of complex ideas of economics, particularly dynamics" [4]. We can appreciate by this example the potential of these water analog computers in the educational environment not only because their computing power (which is limited compared to digital computers) but for its ability to engage the student due to its tangibility [25].

Analog water computers provide learners with a physically observable process where water flow creates a dynamic, visual representation of data being transferred or translated from one place to another. Students using the MONIAC can understand how the data is being manipulated to get the expected or desired results in real time [4]. These computational models introduce the concept of integration in an intuitive form consisting of water flow and water accumulation. Forrester [16] notes that "a child that can fill a glass of water understands the concept of accumulation". These analogous properties can be harnessed and integrated in the design of learning environments to teach complex system concepts like causality, material flows, accumulation, and feedback. These concepts are found to be the building blocks of the System Dynamics language. In subsequent sections, we describe modeling and simulation of dynamic systems and further discuss the design and educational goals of our interactive water computer and how it can be used in System Dynamics education.

3. DYNAMIC SYSTEMS

To provide a foundation for understanding System Dynamics modeling concepts, we review some of the fundamental principles of complex dynamic systems. Dynamic Systems Theory emerged from physics and mathematics, driven by the human necessity to explain the world around us. It was conceived based on the simple idea that everything changes over time, or in mathematical form:

$$x(t + 1) = f\big(x(t)\big) \qquad (1)$$

This denotes that a state or variable x at time $t+1$ was conceived by a function at time t. With this in mind if we declare x to be a system, it can be clearly observed that a change on a variable inside $f(x(t))$ will affect the overall outcome of the entire system [7]. It is important to notice that dynamic systems require an initial state, a set of values that specify the current state of the system at time $t0$, and that depending on this initial state different behaviors, can be observed at the output during a particular instance of time.

3.1 Differential Equations of Dynamic Systems

Newton stated in his Method of Fluxions book [31] that the world communicates through "Fluxions", more commonly known as differential equations (DE). Applications of DE are common in engineering, physics and biology, but can be extended as far as management and the humanities. Differential equations are a tool that supports and enables analysis, understanding, and prediction of the complex behaviors exhibited by dynamic systems.. Differential equations are also referred to as mathematical models, since they accurately represent the way physical phenomenon reacts to a particular stimulus.

College students, and others, often struggle to understand DEs and the complexity that these systems represent because they fail to connect all of the interlinked pieces necessary to understand the main problem [24, 52]. Sometimes the lack of unique solutions, which is common for these systems, makes the task even more laborious [17]. Nevertheless, even if differential equations are what gave birth to dynamic systems theory one can argue that they are not needed to comprehend the overall behavior and principles that drive them [46]. With the introduction of our analog water computer model for informal education, our goal is to minimize these difficulties by building on student's existing physical intuitions and their embodied experience with water-flow to enhance their systems thinking abilities.

3.2 Lotka-Volterra Model

Alfred J. Lotka first introduced the Lotka-Volterra (LV) predator-prey model in the beginning of the 19th century but it was not until 1925 when he used it to analyze predator-prey interactions in a book he published in biomathematics. Vito Volterra made a deep statistical analysis in 1926 independently. With over 50 published papers this is one of the best studied models of predator-prey behavior [27, 34].

A pair of first-order, non-linear, differential equations mathematically describes the LV model. This model is not only used to describe the interaction dynamics of predator-prey biological systems, it is applicable to systems in economics and can be useful whenever describing competition among agents [34]. Although the system proves to be a target of numerous studies and research, the mathematical model describing the system over time can hide the role of each component behind symbols and operands.

The LV equations are:

$$\frac{dH}{dt} = Hr - aHP \qquad (2)$$

$$\frac{dP}{dt} = -Pm + bPH \qquad (3)$$

Where

$P = P(t) = Population\ of\ predators$

$H = H(t) = Population\ of\ prey$

$r > 0\ Birth\ rate\ of\ Prey$

$a > 0\ Death\ rate\ of\ Prey\ by\ Predator$

$m > 0\ Death\ rate\ of\ Predators$

$b > 0\ Birth\ rate\ of\ Predators\ by\ eating\ Prey$

4. MODELS IN EDUCATION

Modeling and simulation (M&S) is applied extensively throughout a variety of fields: engineering, biology, economics, management, computer science, telecommunications, and defense just to name a few [10]. A model can be described as "something used in place of something else" [37]. Models often used to study and gather information about systems or any process of change that sometimes is difficult and/or expensive to test in physical form.

Forrester notes that people's daily decisions are based on our perceptions of the world [16]. These assumptions can be referred to as mental models. However, the human mind can be unreliable; our mental model is shaped by, and therefore biased by our experiences. Sterman [42] highlights the need for tools to shape our understanding so that we can improve our mental models: 'where the world is dynamic, evolving, and interconnected, we tend to make decisions using mental models that are static, narrow, and reductionist'. Forrester asserts that "students should learn that all decisions are made on the basis of models" and that "they should appreciate how computer simulation models can compensate for weaknesses in mental models" [16]. Senge reasons that 'The problems with mental models lie not in whether they are right or wrong - by definition, all models are simplifications. The problems with mental models arise when they become implicit - when they exist below the level of our awareness [41]. Bruner states: "the most basic thing that can be said about human memory... is that unless detail is placed into a structured pattern, it is rapidly forgotten" [5]. Forrester adds that the structure Bruner defines "should show the dynamic significance of the detail" [14, 15]. However, current educational models uncover just a fragment of the real world in a static framework. A different approach is required to obtain a reliable mapping of the real dynamic world to the student's mental model.

4.1 System Dynamics

System Dynamics was developed by Jay Forrester in the late 1950s [14]. SD emerges out of Forrester's experience in servomechanisms engineering, not from a general systems theory or cybernetics perspective [35]. Richardson notes that Forrester first published his SD theory based on his experience applying an engineering approach to understand complex business management problems. Forrester later applied this same modeling methodology to improve understanding and of the dynamics of urban demographics [35]. Since then, SD methodologies have been extensively applied in the modeling and simulation of complex systems across a broad range of diverse disciplines [6, 40, 47].

Forrester argues that current pre-college educational approaches do not adequately prepare students to deal with real world situations, because they do not guide students to think about the causal roots of issues [14]. SD utilizes an iconographic language to represent elements of complex dynamic systems using feedbacks, stock, flows, and time delays (see Figure 1) as the building blocks of this modeling method. However, researchers have discovered that many students encounter difficulties when trying to understand the fundamental SD concepts, such as how flow and flow rates impact the dynamic level of a material within a system [44]. Dynamic complexity and information availability are some of the time consuming barriers blocking the students conceptual reasoning [33]. One limitation of using a diagrammatic modeling approach like SD in addressing these complicated concepts is the fact that the notation itself creates a static representation of a dynamic phenomenon., To overcome this limitation, SD modeling requires interactivity. A more dynamic representation of the concepts will enable students to form a more reliable mental model of the system [19, 53].

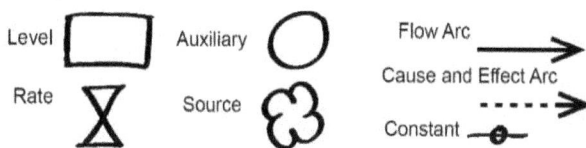

Figure 1 SD Language Symbols

4.2 System Dynamics Modeling

System Dynamics modeling is a formalism used to describe complex systems that alter their state during any given instance of time due to different external or internal factors [43]. Furthermore, SD modeling is used across a wide variety of disciplines including business, management, and the sciences [2, 11, 32]. Different languages or approaches can also be used to model structure and behavior of dynamic systems, including Petri nets, Bode Plots, and Finite State Machines. We will describe and compare isomorphic models of the LV system using a functional block model (see Figure 2) as compared to a SD model [12].

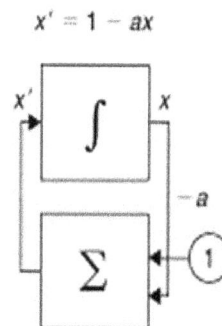

Figure 2 Block Diagram of a Differential Equation [9]

The system described by Figure 2 is a simple first order differential equation. Although the equation is described in mathematical notation as a differential, using the derivative operator (x') symbolism, one should note that none of the blocks in the diagram actually contain this derivative symbol. Forrester [14, 16] states that "nature only integrates or accumulates, it doesn't derivate", he claims that the idea of accumulation is compatible with the mental models people use every day. As a motivating example, we can observe in Figure 3 the implementation of the LV equations in block diagram.

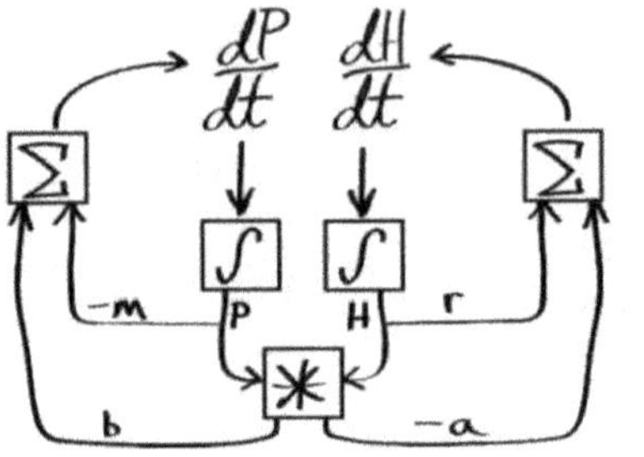

Figure 3 LV Block Diagram Representation [23]

Using block diagrams provides an accurate, and slightly more intuitive way of representing a differential equation model, when compared to the mathematical equations [17]. However, it is also a static representational format, which fails to capture the dynamic behavior of the LV system of equations. We can compare this block-model format to our slightly stylized version of an SD model shown in Figure 4. One can see that this model uses a water-flow analogy, where flow and accumulation correspond to basic intuition that most people can relate to: water flowing through plumbing and into a bathtub [14, 36]. The intuitive nature of SD inspires us to extend this model into the physical world; where the dynamic behavior of the flow of data can be represented by actual water flowing on a continuous basis.

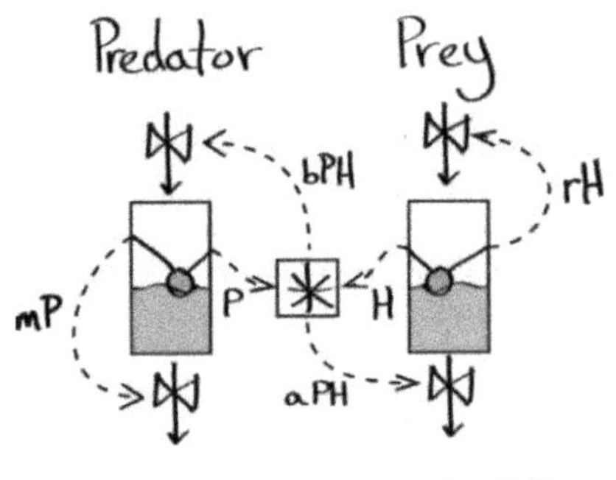

Figure 4 LV SD Representation [23]

5. MODEL IMPLEMENTATION

5.1 LV Water Computer Model

A translation from the abstract equations model to the block diagram form was implemented in Max/MSP software. Using Max/MSP objects and its data-flow computation capabilities we constructed a program based on the SD model shown in Figure 3. It consists of addition, subtraction and multiplication blocks that perform mathematical operations. To compute integration we use the "history" object, which allows feedback though the insertion of a single-sample delay. To exploit Max/MSP processing proficiency, we used the gen~ object, which is a lower-level visual programming environment, shown in the middle of Figure 5. It allows regular objects to be computed using MSP's signal processing capabilities.

Four interactive input-controllers represent each of the four parameters that change the behavior of the differential equations, which can be manipulated in real time by the user. Figure 6 shows the object structure inside the gen object.

An analysis of the limitations and boundaries encountered through experimentation within the virtual Max/MSP prototype served as a basis for the design and development of the tangible microcontroller based water computer shown in Figure 7.

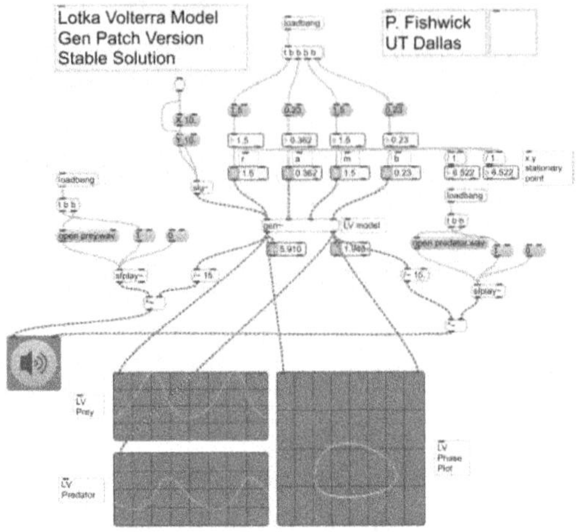

Figure 5 Max/MSP LV Simulation

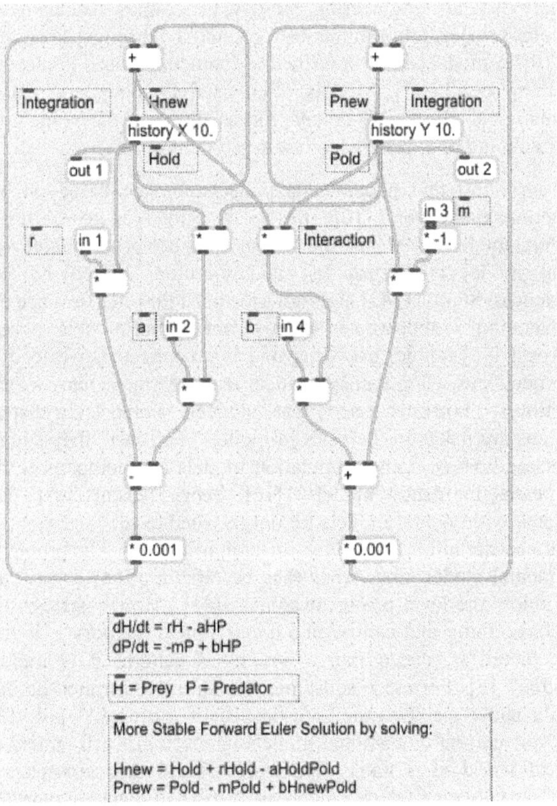

$$dH/dt = rH - aHP$$
$$dP/dt = -mP + bHP$$

H = Prey   P = Predator

More Stable Forward Euler Solution by solving:

Hnew = Hold + rHold - aHoldPold
Pnew = Pold - mPold + bHnewPold

Figure 6 Max/MSP LV Model

The model operates as follows:

Two water pumps drive water from a 22" x 16" reservoir water container located on the bottom of the device through clear plastic tubes, which are independent of each other.

Each of these water tubes connect to a proportional valve that is controlled by a servo-motor and is located at the top of one of the two 4" x 12" cylindrical water containers on the device. These valves are controlled by the positive terms for each of the LV differential equations. They represent the births, or increase of population of the predators and the prey. At the bottom of the cylindrical water containers, another two proportional valves are located. These valves are controlled by the negative terms of the differential equations, and represent the deaths for each of the two populations. These valves are a physical translation from the rates utilized in SD language. The movement of these valves throughout the simulation provides a physical feedback to the user about what is occurring in the model and how this affects directly the solution of the system of equations.

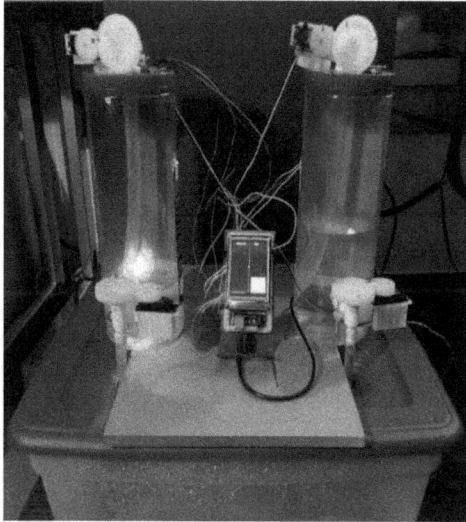

Figure 7 LV Microcontroller Based Water Computer – Prototype I

An ultrasonic distance sensor located at the top lid of each of the cylindrical water containers, measures the water (population) level inside the container, at a 5Hz rate and feeds that data back to the microcontroller unit.

The microcontroller functions as the digital brain of the system, it solves the differential equations using the analog ultrasonic sensor's input and the rates introduced by the student. Using the equation-based approach in constraint modeling [9], converting the differential equation system to a discrete-time difference equation and applying Euler's method to solve them, we approximate the solutions to the differential equations. The computed values for the populations' increasing and decreasing rates are then quantized, normalized and then sent to the proportional valves, which modify their position and therefore increase or decrease the water (population) level accordingly. The water level translates directly from SD to the physical water container and represents the solved equation as time passes.

Using proper labeling, visual indicators, (see Figure 8) and the interactivity of the model, we aim to inspire student curiosity and encourage them to explore the model in further detail; interconnecting the variables and constants to form an accurate mental model from the dynamic simulation model that is reliable and remains true to the real system.

5.2 Future Directions

Cyberlearning examines how the advances in technology can be integrated with the advances in the sciences of learning [30]. The iLab project developed by MIT, represents an implementation of this field. It evolved from the idea that students could use the same piece of equipment that a professional scientist uses. This allows the student to experience how classroom-learning concepts are applied in a real world laboratory [21]. Today's students have

grown up with 21st century tools that are second nature to them [29]. Cyberlearning seeks to exploit this quality to help the student understand the skill they are learning and how to apply it.

Furthermore, current research about incorporation of IoT technologies for educational purposes suggests promising advances for education methodologies [51]. Using a web interface, that is currently being developed, students will be able to continue their interaction with our physical model beyond the confines of formal or informal learning facilities.

To make remote interaction possible, we are implementing a configuration, which will use an IP enabled webcam to provide real-time visual feedback to students of the physical model in our lab. To enhance this experience, students are able to interact with the rate parameters that correspond to the LV equation and observe in real time how this affects the behavior of the water and the valves in our system. We anticipate that some user-interactions may produce unstable conditions in the physical model depending on the volume of feedback sent at any given time, some restrictive constrains will need to be implemented. We are currently evaluating several different implementation options to minimize the impact of de-stabilizing actions.

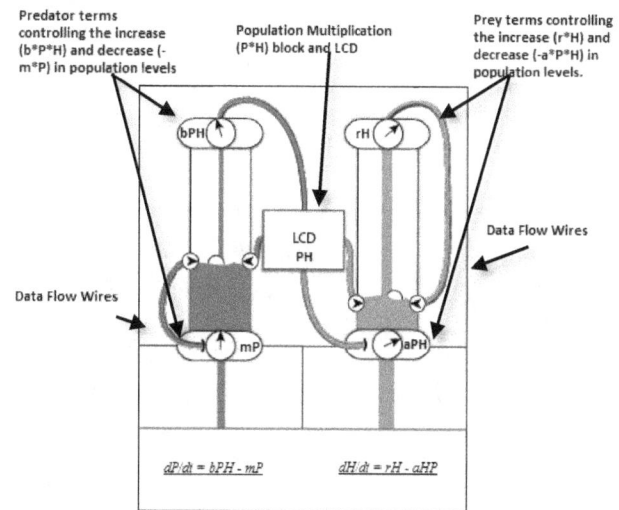

Figure 8 LV Labeling Map

6. CONCLUSIONS

Integration of Forrester's SD representations with tangible user interfaces with engaging interactivity is a rich area for further research opportunities. We envision educational benefits from using our models that should encourage continuing exploration on how these tangible interfaces can be used to improve the learning experience [22, 28, 38]. Ishii asserts that "an SD model is abstract" and continues "children engage with concrete activities that are meaningful to them" [27]. As Ishii states our challenge in the Creative Automata Laboratory is to "make the abstract, concrete". We intend to create immersive SD learning-artifacts, creating interactive models to broaden students' learning experiences.

While we have not yet conducted formal human-subject evaluations of our water-computer, we have displayed it publically during both an Engineering Week event and as part of an Arts & Technology Art exhibit at our university. The water-computer has succeeded in driving interest and engagement, as it has been an extremely popular exhibit. In addition, we are using these events to observe user-interaction, in order to inform HCI design decisions for our iterative prototypes. One important design issue resulting from observation of users interacting with our tangible SD model concerns the affordances of our model, which mirror the affordances of SD stock-flow diagram notation. It seems that users assume that the flow-control indicator dials also provide the ability to control material flows; users try to turn knobs in order to change instantaneous flows. They are exploring ways to interact and manipulate the system. In other words, our tangible SD system has surfaced some interface-affordance issues, which are mirrored in typical SD notation. These representational affordances may lead users to misunderstand of the nature of SD systems.

Specifically, if users of SD software or our tangible system believe that they can directly control the inflow and outflow of instantaneous material flow, this indicates they may not understand the nature of feedback within the system. In the LV system, feedback corresponds to the current population level, where this is multiplied by an auxiliary variable to determine the instantaneous material flow. While the auxiliary variables can be considered as modifiable leverage points for the system, the population levels are features of the system that can't be directly modified. Therefore, if the representational format of instantaneous flow provides an affordance that indicates it is directly modifiable, this may cause difficulties for understanding the nature of complex dynamic systems. We plan to explore this issue more deeply in future iterations of our SD learning artifacts. This discovery might suggest that SD stock-flow-diagram notation should also be re-examined to determine if there are representational affordances that may incorrectly cue users trying to understand complex dynamic systems.

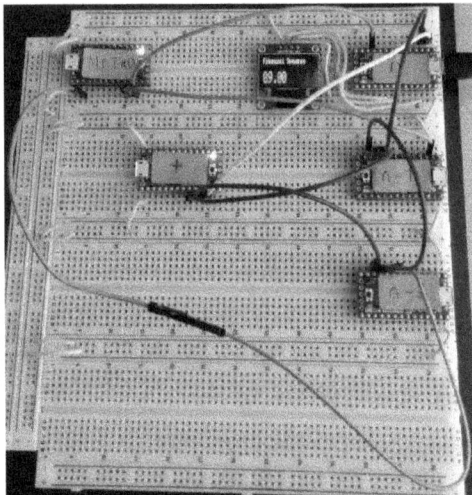

Figure 9 Fibonacci SD Representation

As a future work, in conjunction with our microcontroller based water computer we are also exploring how SD could be implemented using tangible Montessori-inspired manipulatives [50, 54, 55]. This mapping from our Max/MSP prototyping tool to a set of tangible objects can provide students with deeper understanding of what the algorithms built inside Max/MSP are actually doing. As an example we created a representation of the Fibonacci sequence algorithm using microcontrollers (see Figure 9). Although further experimentation is needed to provide metrics and feedback, based on previous research we anticipate that our models could expand current SD methodologies and broaden the path to a different way of education that has the potential of advancing the 21st century learning experience.

7. ACKNOWLEDGMENTS

This research was supported through a startup fund provided for the Creative Automata Laboratory.

REFERENCES

[1] Ahn, J., Weng, C. and Butler, B.S. 2013. The Dynamics of Open, Peer-to-Peer Learning: What Factors Influence Participation in the P2P University? In *Proceedings of the 2013 46th Hawaii International Conference on System Sciences,* (Washington, DC, USA, Jan 7-10, 2013). IEEE, New York, NY, 3098–3107.

[2] Angerhofer, B.J. and Angelides, M.C. 2000. System dynamics modelling in supply chain management: research review. In *Proceedings of the Winter Simulation Conference,* (Orlando, FL, USA, Dec 10-13, 2000). IEEE, New York, NY, 342–351.

[3] Arnold, M. and Millar, R. (1996). Exploring the use of analogy in the teaching of heat, temperature and thermal equilibrium. *Research in science education in Europe,* Routledge, (London, UK, 2005), *22-35.*

[4] Bissell, C. 2007. Historical perspectives - The Moniac A Hydromechanical Analog Computer of the 1950s. *IEEE Control Systems,* 27, 1 (Feb. 2007), 69–74.

[5] Bruner, Jerome S., 1963. *The Process of Education,* New York: Vintage Books, (1963).

[6] Checkland, P. 1999. *Systems Thinking, Systems Practice: Includes a 30-Year Retrospective.* Journal-Operational Research Society, 51, 5, (16 September 1999), 647-647.

[7] De Bot, K., Lowie, W. and Verspoor, M. 2007. A Dynamic Systems Theory approach to second language acquisition. *Bilingualism: Language and Cognition,* 10, 01 (Apr. 2007), 7-7.

[8] diSessa, A.A. 2014. The Construction of Causal Schemes: Learning Mechanisms at the Knowledge Level. *Cognitive Science,* 38, 5 (2014), 795–850.

[9] Fishwick, P. A. 1995. *Simulation model design and execution: building digital worlds.* Prentice Hall PTR, 206-209.

[10] Fishwick, P. A. (Ed.). 2007. *Handbook of Dynamic System Modeling,* Boca Raton: Chapman & Hall/CRC, 17-37.

[11] Fogel, A. 2011. Theoretical and Applied Dynamic Systems Research in Developmental Science: Dynamic Systems Research. *Child Development Perspectives,* 5, 4 (Dec. 2011), 267–272.

[12] Forrester, J. W. 1961. *Industrial Dynamics.* MIT Press: Cambridge, MA. Productivity Press, 464-465.

[13] Forrester, J. W. 1996. *Road Map 1: System Dynamics and K-12 Teachers.* MIT System Dynamics in Education Project, http://web.mit.edu/sysdyn/sdep.html, (April 1 2015).

[14] Forrester, J.W. 1992. System Dynamics and Learner-Centered-Learning in Kindergarten through 12th Grade Education. Technical Report D-4337, MIT. *http://www.mitocw.espol.edu.ec/courses/sloan-school-of-management/15-988-system-dynamics-self-study-fall-1998-spring-1999/readings/learning.pdf,* (May 9, 2015).

[15] Forrester, J.W. 1994. Learning through system dynamics as preparation for the 21st century. *Keynote Address for Systems Thinking and Dynamic Modeling Conference for K-12 Education,* (Concord, MA, USA, June 27-29, 1994).

[16] Forrester, J.W. 2009. Some basic concepts in system dynamics. Sloan School of Management, Massachusetts Institute of Technology, (2009). *Retrieved from http://clexchange.org/ftp/documents/system-dynamics/SD2009- 02SomeBasicConcepts.pdf*, (Jan 23 2015).

[17] Franklin, G.F., Powell, D.J. and Emami-Naeini, A. 2001. Feedback Control of Dynamic Systems, *Prentice Hall PTR, Upper Saddle River, NJ,* (2001), 22-57.

[18] Gentner, D. (1983). Structure-Mapping: A Theoretical Framework for Analogy. *Cognitive science, 7, 2, (1983), 155-170.*

[19] Größler, A. and Strohhecker, J. (2012). Tangible Stock/Flow Experiments-Addressing Issues of Naturalistic Decision Making. In *Proceedings of the 30th International Conference of the System Dynamics Society (St. Gallen, Switzerland, July 22-26, 2012).*

[20] Gubbi, J., Buyya, R., Marusic, S. and Palaniswami, M. 2013. Internet of Things (IoT): A vision, architectural elements, and future directions. *Future Generation Computer Systems,* 29, 7, (Sep. 2013), 1645–1660.

[21] Harward, V.J., del Alamo, J.A., Lerman, S.A., Bailey, P.H., Carpenter, J., DeLong, K., Felknor, C., Hardison, J., Harrison, B., Jabbour, I., Long, P.D., Mao, T., Naamani, L., Northridge, J., Schulz, M., Talavera, D., Varadharajan, C., Wang, S., Yehia, K., Zbib, R. and Zych D. 2008. The iLab Shared Architecture: A Web Services Infrastructure to Build Communities of Internet Accessible Laboratories. In *Proceedings of the IEEE,* 96, 6 (Beijing, China, May 19-23, 2008). IEEE, New York, NY, 931–950.

[22] Horn, M.S., Crouser, R.J. and Bers, M.U. 2012. Tangible interaction and learning: the case for a hybrid approach. *Personal and Ubiquitous Computing,* 16, 4, (Apr. 2012), 379–389.

[23] Howell, M., Vega, D., Doore, K., and Fishwick, P. (2014, December). Enhancing model interaction with immersive and tangible representations: a case study using the Lotka-Volterra model. *In Proceedings of the 2014 Winter Simulation Conference,* (Savannah, GA, Dec 7-10, 2014). IEEE, New York, NY, 3572-3583

[24] Hubbard, J. H., and West, B. H. (Eds.). 1995. Differential Equations: A Dynamical Systems Approach: A Dynamical Systems Approach. Part II: Higher Dimensional Systems (Vol. 5). *Springer Science & Business Media,* New York: Springer-Verlag, (1995).

[25] Ishii, H. 2008. The tangible user interface and its evolution. *Communications of the ACM,* 51, 6 (2008), 32–36.

[26] Korn, G. A. 1962. The impact of hybrid analog-digital techniques on the analog-computer art. In *Proceedings of the IRE, 50, 5, (New York, NY, March 26-29, 1962).* IRE, New York, NY, *1077-1086.*

[27] Malcai, O., Biham, O., Richmond, P. and Solomon, S. 2002. Theoretical analysis and simulations of the generalized Lotka-Volterra model. *Physical Review Letters, 66, 3,* 031102.1-031102.6

[28] Marshall, P. 2007. Do tangible interfaces enhance learning? In *Proceedings of the 1st international conference on Tangible and embedded interaction,* (Baton Rouge, LA, Feb 15-17, 2007). ACM, New York, NY, 163-170.

[29] National Education Association. Preparing 21st Century Students for a Global Society: An Educators Guide to the "Four Cs". *Retrieved February 21, 2015, from the National Education Association.* https://www.nea.org/assets/docs/A-Guide-to-Four-Cs.pdf, *(May 5, 2015).*

[30] Navarro, P., and Shoemaker, J. (1999). The power of cyberlearning: An empirical test. *Journal of computing in Higher Education, 11, 1, 29-54.*

[31] Newton, I., and Colson, J. 1736. The Method of Fluxions and Infinite Series; with Its Application to the Geometry of Curve-lines... Translated from the Author's Latin Original Not Yet Made Publick. To which is Subjoin'd a Perpetual Comment upon the Whole Work, by J. Colson. http://books.google.com/books?id=WyQOAAAAQAAJ&printsec=frontcover&source=gbs_ge_summary_r&cad=0#v=onepage&q&f=false, (May 9, 2015).

[32] Olfati-Saber, R. 2006. Flocking for Multi-Agent Dynamic Systems: Algorithms and Theory. *IEEE Transactions on Automatic Control,* 51, 3 (Mar. 2006), 401–420.

[33] Qudrat-Ullah, H. (2010). Perceptions of the effectiveness of system dynamics-based interactive learning environments: an empirical study. *Computers & Education,* 55(3), 1277-1286.

[34] Reichenbach, T., Mobilia, M. and Frey, E. 2006. Coexistence versus extinction in the stochastic cyclic Lotka-Volterra model. *Physical Review Letters,* 74, 051907. http://dx.doi.org/10.1103/PhysRevE.74.051907 (May 9 15).

[35] Richardson, G.P. 2011. Reflections on the foundations of system dynamics: Foundations of System Dynamics. *System Dynamics Review,* 27, 3 (Jul. 2011), 219–243.

[36] Roberts, N. 1978. Teaching Dynamic Feedback Systems Thinking: An Elementary View. *Management Science,* 24, 8 (Apr. 1978), 836–843.

[37] Rogers, R.V. 1997. What makes a modeling and simulation professional?: The consensus view from one workshop. In *Proceedings of the 29th Winter Simulation Conference,* (1997). IEEE, New York, NY, 1375–1382.

[38] Schneider, B., Jermann, P., Zufferey, G. and Dillenbourg, P. 2011. Benefits of a Tangible Interface for Collaborative Learning and Interaction. *IEEE Transactions on Learning Technologies,* 4, 3 (July 2011), 222–232.

[39] Scribner, S., and Cole, M. (1973). Cognitive consequences of formal and informal education. *Science, 182(4112), 553-559*

[40] Senge, P.M. and Stesman, J.D. 1992. Systems thinking and organizational learning: acting locally and thinking globally in the organization of the future. *European journal of operational research, 59, 1* (May 26, 1992), 137-150.

[41] Senge, P. M. 2010. The Fifth Discipline: The Art & Practice of the Learning Organization. *Crown Publishing Group,* 166.

[42] Sterman, J. D. 2006. Learning from Evidence in a Complex World. *American Journal of Public Health, 96, 3, 505-514.*

[43] Sterman, J.D. 2001. System dynamics modeling. *California management review*, 43, 4 (2001), 8–25.

[44] Sweeney, L. B., Sterman, J. D. 2000. Bathtub Dynamics: Initial Results of a Systems Thinking Inventory. *System Dynamics Review, 16, 4,* 249–86.

[45] Szücs, E. 1980. *Similitude and modelling.* Fundamental Studies in Engineering, 2, *Elsevier Scientific Publishing Company*, (Amsterdam, Netherlands, 1980).

[46] Thelen, E. and Smith, L.B. 1998. *Dynamic systems theories.* Handbook of child psychology, Wiley Publishing, (Hoboken, NJ, 1998), 563-635.

[47] Van Ackere, A. 1993. Systems Thinking and Business Process Redesign: An Application to the Beer Game. *European Management Journal,* 11, 4, (1993), 412-423.

[48] Weiser, M. 1991. The Computer in the 21st Century. *Scientific American*, (September 1991), 78-89.

[49] Wolfe, P. T. 1990. U.S. Patent No. 4,953,089. U.S. *Patent and Trademark Office,* Washington, DC, (1990).

[50] Xie, L., Antle, A.N. and Motamedi, N. 2008. Are tangibles more fun?: comparing children's enjoyment and engagement using physical, graphical and tangible user interfaces. In *Proceedings of the 2nd international conference on Tangible and embedded interaction,* (Bonn, Germany, Feb. 18-21, 2008). ACM, New York, NY, 191–198.

[51] Yan-lin, L. L. Y. Z. 2010. The Application of the Internet of Things in Education. *Modern Educational Technology,* 2, (Ontario, Canada, 2010), 8-10.

[52] Zill, D. 2012. A first course in differential equations with modeling applications. *Cengage Learning*, Boston, MA, (2012).

[53] Zuckerman, O. and Resnick, M. 2003. A physical interface for system dynamics simulation. *CHI'03 extended abstracts on Human factors in computing systems,* (Fort Lauderdale, FL, April 5-10, 2003). ACM, New York, NY, 810–811.

[54] Zuckerman, O. and Resnick, M. 2004. Hands-on modeling and simulation of systems. In *Proceedings of the 2004 conference on Interaction design and children: building a community,* (Baltimore, MD, June 1-3, 2004). ACM, New York, NY, 157–158.

[55] Zuckerman, O., Arida, S. and Resnick, M. 2005. Extending tangible interfaces for education: digital montessori-inspired manipulatives. In *Proceedings of the SIGCHI conference on Human factors in computing systems,* (Portland, OR, April 2-7, 2005). ACM, New York, NY, 859–868.

Layered Simulations for Teaching Methodologies

Michael Howell, Brian Merlo, Paul Fishwick

University of Texas at Dallas

800 W. Campbell Rd., AT10

Richardson, TX 75080

{howell, brian.merlo, paul.fishwick}@utdallas.edu

ABSTRACT

Modeling & Simulation are invaluable at helping us understand and predict systems at every scale. We strive to enrich learning by implementing a layered framework which is engaging and straightforward to the student. Additionally, we can communicate system dynamics by integrating well-known concepts to function as stepping stones towards complex subjects. This is primarily achieved by leveraging the data-flow language, which can accommodate a diverse range of students. We show how to develop a framework for implementing our teaching methodology using Max/MSP, and an instance of the implementation using auditory and visual presentations.

Categories and Subject Descriptors

K.3.2 [**Computers and Education**]: Computer and Information Science Education – *Computer science education, Curriculum, Literacy.*

General Terms

Design, Experimentation, Human Factors.

Keywords

Interdisciplinary Approaches.

1. INTRODUCTION

In the School of Arts Technology and Emerging Communication at The University of Texas at Dallas there exists an interdisciplinary learning environment between engineering, computer science, design and visual arts. The diversity of this population of students requires a broader approach for teaching Modeling & Simulation for a variety of applications, e.g. agent-based interactions within complex networks. To teach these concepts, we choose a layered approach, facilitated by the visual, dataflow language of Max/MSP. We find that the Max/MSP is a language that can serve as a functional analogue to Forrester's language in system dynamics Modeling & Simulation. Forrester proposed that the use of active-learning experiences draws students into a deeper understanding of the subject matter [2]. This type of learning leverages the student's reasoning skills by observing causality in a system. The students develop their own

SIGSIM-PADS '15, June 10-12, 2015, London, United Kingdom

ACM 978-1-4503-3583-6/15/06.

http://dx.doi.org/10.1145/2769458.2769488

method, and with the aid of computer processing, employ the corresponding learning approach within their personalized, layered simulation.

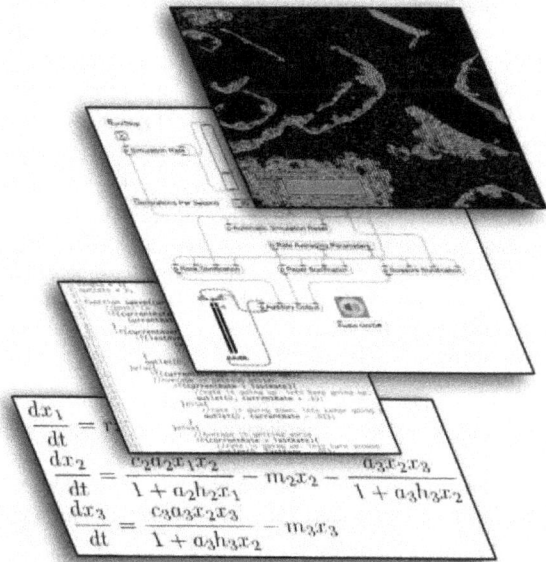

Figure 1. The four layers of an implemented design.

2. LAYERED SIMULATION

Our paradigm for authoring a simulation uses encapsulated layers to form an integrated architecture. We split the implementation of the model into four layers of abstraction (Figure 1). The sublayers are coupled together in terms of function, but are themselves self-contained sub models. While interior layers are functionally tied to the adjoining layers, the intent for the student is that each layer can be experienced and studied independently. We keep the layers independent so that smaller systems can be taught without crossover between abstractions [1].

The first layer is the presentation. The presentation provides a visual aesthetic meant to be experienced, enjoyed, and extended by the student. The aesthetic result is not limited to the visual spaces, but also includes audio and touch wherever possible.

The second layer consists of the emulation of both the system's inherent structures and the intermediary results between functions. It serves as a conceptual model of the system which supports a high degree of traceability. Normally, intermediary results and visuals are extraneous to the presentation, but for the novice, they serve as subsystems of the simulation which explains how the presentation is formed.

The third layer is the implementation of languages and structures defined by the user. The structures are used to create simulation visualizations, which in turn aid in understanding the flow of the Max/MSP model in the preceding layer. Additionally, the results of the simulation visualizations are coupled together to form the presentation.

The fourth layer is the core framework of the simulation. It is the mathematical foundation and fundamental theory that describes the system's behaviors. A firm understanding of this layer allows the students to create new derivative works.

3. IMPLEMENTATION

Our implementation of a layered simulation presents the student with aural and visual feedback that represents a dynamic system. We add parametric control and interactive elements to facilitate personalization of the model. The abstract model driving the simulation is an ordinary differential equation of three dimensions [6]. Differential equations with greater than two dimensions can be reduced into lower-ordered systems. This reduction of the problem provides a pathway to teach about those simpler relationships.

The visual presentation began as a static display, but became more dynamic through a hybrid of trace-driven and self-driven input. We utilized participant interaction via webcam to add data into the active simulation. The interactions gave users the ability to test and experiment with the results. This tangible interaction provided a sense of connection to the model, which could not be observed in previous versions [5].

To illustrate the paths of logic, intermediate simulation visualizations were spread throughout the work, allowing for smaller and more manageable simulations. We showed visualizations of the significant steps in the simulation, which includes initialization, random variation, and partial solutions.

Details of the described methods for visualizations and sonification were further encapsulated into subsystems, such that the student was able to draw a clear path between logical steps without obfuscating the structures. We implement an auditory presentation in parallel to reinforce the concepts and include an extra mode of sensory perception.

Sensory perception is how we perceive the world and interface with our environment [4]. We operate under the premise that including extra modes of perception to Modeling & Simulation enhances the qualitative understanding of system behaviors. For example, assume there is a multi-variable system in which we are able to analyze a discrete event for a period of 1 second. The visual interface -- confined to the x-y plane, with the possibility of a superimposed z-axis (3rd dimension) -- would be underutilized without the addition of time domain information. This interface yields a maximum of six discernable relations i.e., each plane with respect to its adjacent plane. The same system that incorporates a sonic component could define an additional 16 permutations to which system data is functionally mapped to sonic outputs, e.g. amplitude, frequency, timbre, and envelope of a sound wave with respect to the three spatial dimensions. We refer to this as the "auditory display," or sonification of a system.

Sonification can generally be divided into two different orders. First order sonification can create discernible changes in the sonic output and ultimately convey the behaviors of a modeled system. Second order sonification applies time-based algorithms, giving the designer a larger range of freedom to develop the auditory

display. This is facilitated by leveraging musical structures, such as rhythm, harmony, and melody, so that we can make creative choices for representing system dynamics that are more palatable to the listener [3].

4. CONCLUSIONS AND FUTURE WORK

We promote the use of Modeling & Simulation as a means of learning abstract models. We provide a framework for creating simulations which are purposed for hands-on and personal teaching methods. To test our framework we show a simulation model of cellular automata. We extend the model to include sonification and user interaction. We find that the art aesthetic elicits questions in the observer and allows for a more memorable interaction. This provides feedback in which the user is able to test their assumptions.

There is evidence that we are moving towards a new and effective avenue for Modeling & Simulation education, but want to see further work on applying the model to a variety of topics and formally study the effectiveness of this strategy. This work would benefit from developing several more designs based on the architecture that extends the breadth of its application. An informal study would greatly enhance the confidence in further development of this methodology. We believe a user study could provide us with a stronger understanding of the effectiveness of the layered approach. We want to understand how simulation traversability affects the student's ability to learn abstract models, and if a personalized approach to learning is equally as effective as traditional methods.

5. ACKNOWLEDGMENTS

Our thanks to our colleagues in the Creative Automata Lab at The University of Texas at Dallas for the discussions and feedback while developing this work, and we thank Scot Gresham-Lancaster for his valuable critiques on our sonification. The authors also thank the anonymous reviewers for their valuable suggestions and comments which improved upon the quality of this work.

6. REFERENCES

[1] Fishwick, P. A. 1995. *Simulation Model Design and Execution: Building Digital Worlds*. Prentice-Hall, Upper Saddle River.

[2] Forrester, Jay W. 1994. Learning through System Dynamics as Preparation for the 21st Century. *In Keynote Address for Systems Thinking and Dynamic Modeling Conference for K-12 Education, (Concord Academy, Concord, MA, USA, 1994)*. Waltham, MA. Pegasus Communications.

[3] Gresham-Lancaster, S. 2012. Relationships of Sonification to Music and Sound Art. AI Soc. 27, 2, 207-212. http://dx.doi.org/10.1007/s00146-011-0337-3

[4] Jung, C. G. 1971. *Psychological Types*. Princeton University Press, Princeton, N.J.

[5] Ishii, H. 2008. Tangible bits: beyond pixels. *In Proceedings of the 2nd International Conference on Tangible and Embedded Interaction, (Bonn, Germany, February 18-20, 2008)*. ACM, New York, NY, xv-xxv.

[6] Hastings, A. 2011. Gross, L. ed. *Sourcebook in Theoretical Ecology*. Berkeley, California University of California Press.

A Prototype HLA Development Kit: Results from the 2015 Simulation Exploration Experience

Alfredo Garro
Alberto Falcone
DIMES
University of Calabria, Rende (CS), Italy
firstname.lastname@dimes.unical.it

Nauman R. Chaudhry, Omar-Alfred Salah,
Anastasia Anagnostou, Simon J.E. Taylor
Department of Computer Science
Brunel University, Uxbridge, UK
firstname.lastname@brunel.ac.uk

ABSTRACT

The IEEE 1516-2010 High Level Architecture for distributed simulation is used to facilitate the development of large-scale simulations. However, there is a steep learning curve. The annual Simulation Exploration Experience (SEE) presents the opportunity for multiple international student-led teams to gain experience in developing distributed simulations in an interesting lunar-based scenario. To support the student learning process, a prototype HLA Development Kit has been created that has the goal of reducing the complexity of distributed simulation design and implementation. A student-led team used the Kit to create a lunar excavator federate using agent-based simulation implemented in REPAST. The excavator federate successfully interoperated with the University of Liverpool UAV during SEE 2015. This paper presents a short overview of the Kit and experiences in developing the lunar excavator federate.

Categories and Subject Descriptors

I.6.3 [**Simulation and Modeling**]: Applications; I.6.5 [**Simulation and Modeling**]: Model Development - *modeling methodologies*; I.6.8 [**Simulation and Modeling**]: Types of Simulation - *agent, distributed.*

General Terms

Management, Design, Experimentation

Keywords

Distributed Simulation; High Level Architecture; Agent-based Simulation.

1. INTRODUCTION

Despite the IEEE 1516-2010 High Level Architecture (HLA) standard, building complex and large distributed simulations systems remains a challenging task and requires considerable expert knowledge. Development and testing of *HLA Federates* is generally difficult and requires significant expertise. These challenges make it difficult to develop educational programs to give students key skills in distributed simulation development. In response to this, the annual Simulation Exploration Experience (SEE) was created to give international student-led teams experience in developing distributed simulations in an interesting lunar-based scenario [1, 2]. The event is organized by the Simulation Interoperability Standards Organization (SISO) in collaboration with NASA and other research and industrial partners. Building on experience from participation in this event, a prototype general-purpose, domain-independent framework that attempts to ease the development of HLA Federates has been created. This paper presents a short overview of the framework and brief experiences in developing the lunar excavator federate.

2. HLA DEVELOPMENT FRAMEWORK

The HLA Development Kit software Framework (DKF) is a general-purpose, domain-independent framework, released under the open source policy Lesser GNU Public License (LGPL), which facilitates the development of HLA Federates. The DKF allows developers to focus on the specific aspects of their own Federates rather than dealing with the common HLA issues such as the management of the simulation time; the connection/disconnection on/from the HLA RTI; the publish, subscribe and updating of *ObjectClass* and *InteractionClass* elements. The DKF is designed and developed by the SMASH-Lab (System Modeling And Simulation Hub - Laboratory) of the University of Calabria (Italy) working in cooperation with the NASA JSC (Johnson Space Center), Houston (TX, USA). The DKF is fully implemented in the Java language. The architecture of a DKF-based Federation is composed of three main layers (see Figure 1): (i) *Application Layer*, which contains the Federates that can interact with both the DKF and the HLA RTI by using their APIs; (ii) *DKF Layer*, which represents the core of the architecture and provides a set of domain-independent APIs that are used to access the DKF capabilities; and (iii) *HLA RTI Infrastructure*, which represents the RTI that host the federation.

The *DKF* is organized into a hierarchy of packages and sub-packages; each of which contains a set of Java classes and interfaces that implement specific functionalities. For example, the *core* package implements the kernel of the DKF. It includes the fundamental *DKFAbstractFederate* and *DKFAbstractFederateAmbassador* classes that provide the basic functionalities to manage a Federate. The *config* package contains the collection of classes that manage the Federation Execution and RTI connection configuration parameters provided by a ".json" file. The *model* package contains some classes to facilitate publishing, subscribing and the data updating of both an *ObjectClass* and an *InteractionClass* through Java annotations. A *coder* package contains the classes used to coding and decoding both *ObjectClass* and *InteractionClass* instances. Finally, the

SIGSIM-PADS '15, June 10-12, 2015, London, United Kingdom
ACM 978-1-4503-3583-6/15/06.
http://dx.doi.org/10.1145/2769458.2769489

application domain extension *see.smackdown* package, contains some SEE domain-specific classes, which are used by the *core* components of the *DKF* to handle some specific aspects related to the SEE Federation such as transformations among *SEE Coordinate Reference Frames*, the publish and subscribe of *PhysicalEntities*, and the management of the *SISO Space Federation Object Models*.

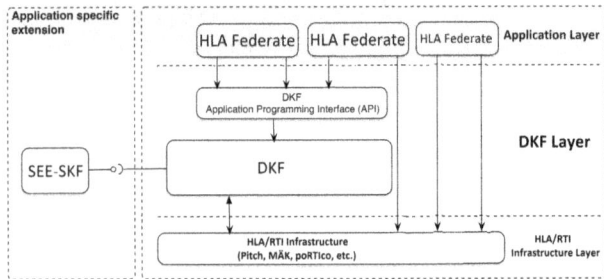

Figure 1: The architecture of a DKF-based Federation.

Figure 2 shows an example architecture of a Federate created by using the capabilities of both the DKF and its SEE-specific extensions, the SEE Starter Kit Framework-SKF. The classes *SEEAbstractFederate* and *SEEAbstractAmbassador*, which are in grey, define the behavior of a SEE Federate, while the classes in yellow belong to the DKF application independent part. The *SEEAbstractFederate* class implements the methods of the *DKFAbstractFederate* class. This latter class provides functionalities to configure and connect/disconnect a Federate to/from a Federation Execution. In particular, the *DKFAbstractFederate* class provides a concrete SEE Federate with the management of its life cycle (FLCM), as a consequence, a SEE working team has only to define the specific behavior of its SEE Federate without worrying about low-level implementation details since the DKF manages them. Specifically, the pro-active part of the behavior of a Federate is specified in the "processing and update data" composite state, which is accessed between a TAG and TAR request; whereas, the re-active part of the behavior of a Federate is specified in the "processing interaction" composite state so as to indicate how to handle the RTI callbacks about the interactions/objects that the Federate has subscribed. The *SEEAbstractAmbassador* class implements the *DKFAbstractFederateAmbassador* class in order to interact with the RTI services. Finally, the *ExecutionThread* class handles the execution of a HLA Federate in the simulation environment.

3. DEVELOPING THE EXCAVATOR FEDERATE

As part of SEE 2015, Brunel hosted a student-led team consisting of postgraduate and undergraduate students. The ultimate goal of the excavator agent-based simulation was to explore how excavator "robots" could self-organize in the coordination of the extraction of lunar regolith materials. The excavator simulation was first created using the REPAST agent-based simulation language. This was then implemented using the DKF and SEE-specific extensions (SEE SKF). The federate interoperates with a UAV federate produced by the University of Liverpool that flies over the area taking magnetometer readings to guide the excavator search for material. The agent-based simulation consists of the *JExcavatorsBuilder*, *Excavator* and *Mineral* classes. *JExcavatorsBuilder* implements the REPAST *ContextBuilder* interface to create the simulation environment for the excavators.

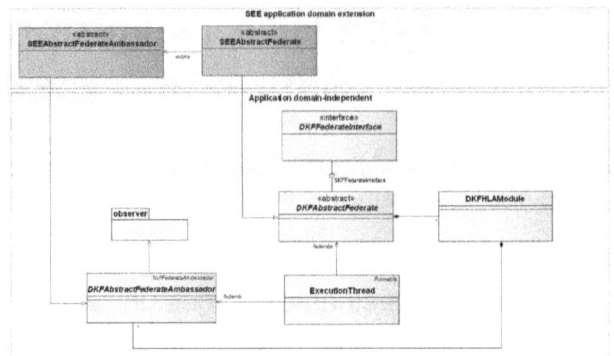

Figure 2: Example architecture of the DKF-based Federate developed for the SEE 2015.

Using the DKF approach, the students follow four steps to create a federate: (1) create a FOM to reflect the interaction between the two federates. Within the *Excavator* class Java annotations were used to identify key items used by the DKF (object class, attributes, etc.). DKF *coders* were then added to support the communication of attributes to/from the federate. The *SEEAbstractFederate* class was then extended to create the *ExcavatorFederate* classes; (2) within the *ExcavatorFederate* class the *configureAndStart()* method of the DKF remained unchanged. The DKF *doAction()* method was modified to advance the agent-based simulation by first obtaining the current state (context) of the simulation, finding all agents (objects) and then running the REPAST *step()* method in the agents, and finally calling *updateElement()* to output the new state of the excavator Federate's attributes; (3) involved the simple extension of the *SEEAbstractFederateAmbassador* class with as the *ExcavatorFederateAmbassador*; (4) identify the main() method to execute the simulation.

4. FUTURE WORK

SEE 2015 finished successfully in April 2015. Experiences from the event will feed into a new version of both the DKF and SEE SKF. The goal for the next year is to use the DKF with more student-led teams and to further develop educational materials for tutors to use the framework in degree-level courses.

5. REFERENCES

[1] Falcone, A., Garro, A., Longo, F. and Spadafora, F. 2014. Simulation Exploration Experience: A Communication System and a 3D Real Time Visualization for a Moon base simulated scenario. In *Proceedings of the 18th IEEE/ACM International Symposium on Distributed Simulation and Real Time Applications* (ACM/IEEE DS-RT), Toulouse (France), October 1-3, 2014, Published by the IEEE Computer Society, Los Alamitos, CA.

[2] Taylor, S.J.E., Revagar, N., Chambers, J., Yero, M., Anagnostou, A., Nouman, A. and Chaudhry, N.R. 2014. Simulation Exploration Experience: A Distributed Hybrid Simulation of a Lunar Mining Operation. In *Proceedings of the 18th IEEE/ACM International Symposium on Distributed Simulation and Real Time Applications* (ACM/IEEE DS-RT), Toulouse (France), October 1-3, 2014. Published by the IEEE Computer Society, Los Alamitos, CA.

Time-Sharing Time Warp
via Lightweight Operating System Support

Alessandro Pellegrini and Francesco Quaglia
DIAG – Sapienza, University of Rome
Via Ariosto 25, 00185 Rome, Italy
{pellegrini, quaglia}@dis.uniroma1.it

ABSTRACT

The order according to which the different tasks are carried out within a Time Warp platform has a direct impact on performance, given that event processing is speculative, thus being subject to the possibility of being rolled-back. It is typically recognized that not-yet-executed events having lower timestamps should be given higher CPU-schedule priority, since this contributes to keep low the amount of rollbacks. However, common Time Warp platforms usually execute events as atomic actions. Hence control is bounced back to the underlying simulation platform only at the end of the current event processing routine. In other words, CPU-scheduling of events resembles classical batch-multitasking scheduling, which is recognized not to promptly react to variations of the priority of pending tasks (e.g. associated with the injection of new events in the system). In this article we present the design and implementation of a time-sharing Time Warp platform, to be run on multi-core machines, where the platform-level software is allowed to take back control on a periodical basis (with fine grain period), and to possibly preempt any ongoing event processing activity in favor of dispatching (along the same thread) any other event that is revealed to have higher priority. Our proposal is based on an ad-hoc kernel module for Linux, which implements a fine grain timer-interrupt mechanism with lightweight management, which is fully integrated with the modern top/bottom-half timer-interrupt Linux architecture, and which does not induce any bias in terms of relative CPU-usage planning across Time Warp vs non-Time Warp threads running on the machine. Our time-sharing architecture has been integrated within the open source ROOT-Sim optimistic simulation package, and we also report some experimental data for an assessment of our proposal.

Categories and Subject Descriptors

D.4.1 [**Operating Systems**]: Process Management—*Threads*;
I.6.8 [**Simulation and Modeling**]: Types of Simulation—*Discrete Event, Parallel*

General Terms

Algorithms, Performance

Keywords

PDES; Speculative Processing; Preemptive Scheduling

1. INTRODUCTION

Time Warp [10] is the reference synchronization protocol for optimistic parallel processing of discrete event simulation models. It allows the worker threads operating within the simulation platform to process simulation events speculatively, with no preliminary assessment of their safety. On the other hand, in case processed events are eventually revealed as non-causally consistent, their effects on the simulation model execution trajectory are undone via rollback schemes based on state recovery techniques exploiting either checkpointing [19, 21, 18] or reverse computing [5, 24]. The relevance of Time Warp (and of simulation platforms based on this synchronization paradigm) lies in that it allows for extremely high scalability. In fact, as recently shown by the results provided in [12], Time Warp systems exhibit the potential for scaling up to millions of processing units.

As for software development, beside some historical proposal along the path of developing Time Warp as a special-purpose operating system oriented at supporting discrete event applications [11], the common trend is the one according to which Time Warp systems are built as user-space platforms, to be hosted on top of general-purpose operating systems (see, e.g., [4, 17, 14, 6]). As a consequence, the platform-level software within the whole Time Warp architecture is seen by the application-level code (namely, the simulation model) as a library offering a specific API (e.g., for injection and CPU-dispatching of simulation events) and, in the most advanced cases (see [18]), providing application transparent support for recoverability[1].

The major consequence by the library-based approach is that control is bounced back to the platform-level software (along any worker thread) only upon the occurrence of specific run-time events, such as the end of the execution of the last CPU-dispatched simulation event or the interception of, e.g., memory update operations that trigger platform-level recoverability capabilities ultimately allowing to restore a

---

[1]As an example, in some proposals compile/link time (instrumentation) directives are used to allow the platform-level library to intercept memory updates issued by the application code so as to transparently support log/recovery of the application-level data structures.

previous simulation model's state. In other words, all the simulation events processed within conventional Time Warp systems are actually CPU-dispatched according to a classical batch-multitasking scheme, where the platform-level software is not allowed to take back control independently of the activities that are carried out by the application code. As a consequence, the platform-level software is not allowed to re-evaluate CPU assignment until the completion of the last-dispatched simulation event. Therefore, it is not able to CPU-dispatch any other simulation event that may have been produced in the system, which may have a higher priority (e.g., a lower timestamp) compared to the one currently being processed by the CPU [22].

Regaining control frequently, with re-evaluation of the assignment of the CPU, can be a relevant means for improving performance (thanks to the reduction of the incidence of rollback) given that the CPU capacity can be dynamically assigned to simulation events that currently require more prompt execution, e.g. due to their lower timestamps, and thus can more likely give rise to dependencies affecting the virtual time window that is currently covered by the worker threads processing activities. We note that this aspect is also related to improving the energy efficiency of Time Warp platforms, given that reducing the amount of rollbacks in the parallel run means reducing the overall energy used for any individual productive unit of work done (namely, eventually committed events) [20].

Clearly, the period according to which the platform-level software re-gains control needs to be fine grain, especially in contexts where CPU-requirements for processing simulation events are on the order of (tens of) microseconds. Hence classical timer-interrupt settings supported by conventional operating systems do not suffice for this purpose. As an example, common Linux configurations lead the timer to interrupt the current thread running on any CPU-core with period on the order of 1 to 4 milliseconds (higher values are typically used on machines with larger amounts of CPU-cores given that CPU preemption and reassignment is less critical on these systems compared to those with reduced number of cores). Also, bouncing control back to the platform-level software via standard temporized signals, such as the POSIX `SIGALRM` signal, would be unfeasible because of the overhead, given that this approach would require the whole chain of signal management mechanisms to be passed through at kernel level.

In this article we present the design and implementation of a time-sharing Time Warp system, to be hosted on top of multi-core machines running Linux, where the platform-level software is allowed to take back control on a periodical basis, with very fine grain period (e.g. on the order of tens of microseconds) and is allowed to re-evaluate CPU assignment, and to dynamically schedule higher priority simulation events. This is achieved with minimal overhead thanks to the capabilities of an ad-hoc Linux module for timer management that we have developed, which allows for (periodical) control flow variations along any running thread with no intervention by the chain of kernel mechanisms used for supporting POSIX signals. Our proposal is fully compliant with the conventional and scalability oriented top/bottom-half timer-interrupt management offered by Linux, and does not create any bias in terms of actual CPU-assignment across the threads (including kernel-level threads) operating in the system. In other words, Time Warp threads are allowed to see

their original CPU ticks (those natively assigned by the operating system) as partitioned into sub-intervals (with proper control flow management at the end of each sub-interval), while any other active thread in the system (which is not a Time Warp worker thread) is not subject to any partitioning of its assigned ticks. This prevents to impair fairness, which is an essential pre-requisite given that the time-sharing Time Warp platform might run on a multi-user conventional platform. This aspect is clearly relevant also when considering fairness across Time Warp worker threads and kernel-level threads used by the operating system for housekeeping.

Besides the ability to optimize CPU assignment depending on the (dynamic) priority of the tasks to be performed within the Time Warp system, our proposal has also the capability to address some specific liveness problems related to the speculative nature of Time Warp, such as application-level infinite loops that may arise when reaching an application non-admissible state due to out of order events' executions [15]. These loops can be (timely) broken thanks to our time-sharing approach which can be exploited for supporting preemptive rollback operations leading to the squash of the non-admissible state trajectory.

The fully featured time-sharing architecture we have developed has been integrated within the open source ROOT-Sim package[2] [17, 9], and operates in a fully transparent way to the overlying application code. Hence, the benefits from it come with no explicit intervention by the application programmer. We also report experimental data for an assessment of the time-sharing Time Warp proposal in terms of both overhead by the extra-ticks and final delivered performance with a real-world case study application in the area of simulation of wireless systems.

The remainder of the article is structured as follows. In Section 2 we discuss related work. The whole time-sharing architecture is presented in Section 3. Experimental data are provided in Section 4.

2. RELATED WORK

In the wide area of High-Performance-Computing (HPC) systems, some literature studies exist on the relation between performance and timer-interrupt frequency. The common idea underlying most of the outcoming performance optimization proposals is that the lower the timer-interrupt frequency, the better the final delivered performance [7, 8, 25]. The exacerbation of this approach led to defining *tickless* operating systems (namely, with extremely reduced frequency of the timer-interrupt) as the best configuration for hosting HPC applications. However, these studies have been tailored to the case of non-speculative processing, where any work carried out by the thread running on whichever CPU-core is actually useful, hence there is no actual need to change the software execution flow (e.g. periodically) in order to optimize synchronization dynamics in terms of reduction of wasted computation, which is instead the case optimistic Time Warp systems. Also, the above studies have been tailored to evaluate the effects of the variation of the timer-interrupt frequency in contexts where the actual management of the timer-interrupt is still based on the native rules applied by the operating system kernel. In other words, the above proposals have been aimed at simply configuring the timer-interrupt behavior (limited to its frequency)

---

[2] Available at `http://github.com/HPDCS/ROOT-Sim`.

in HPC contexts, not at introducing ad-hoc software modules for exploiting timer events, which is instead the path we followed. In fact, our proposal puts in place a special (and lightweight) mechanism for handling timer-interrupts. Overall, we follow an approach which is completely different from the one dealt with by those literature studies in terms of both reference scenario (speculative vs non-speculative processing) and architectural impact on the system organization.

In the context of optimistic PDES systems, the only work we are aware of which deals with the relation between performance and timer-interrupt configuration is the one in [3]. Here the author proposes an approach which is opposite to ours, where the Time Warp threads are allowed to take CPU control for longer periods (thus being not interrupted for a while) in order to be able to fully execute a simulation model with no interference by other workload on the system, and to deliver the output in real-time. This solution is still along the path of tick-less operating systems, with the difference that the tick-less behavior is triggered on-demand (namely whenever a time-critical parallel simulation needs to be executed), hence it is not a static configuration of the underlying operating system. Our approach is fully orthogonal to this one because our target is the reduction of wasted time, thanks to an appropriate periodic variation of the control flow along Time Warp threads. Also, while the proposal in [3] is based on reserving the computing capacity for Time Warp programs—thus excluding the possibility for other tasks to be run on the system for a while—in our approach we do not create any bias in the usage of the computing system across Time Warp threads and other kinds of threads. We only allow the Time Warp threads to see their own ticks as partitioned into sub-intervals (as hinted, with proper control flow management at the end of each sub-interval). This leads our proposal to be suited also for context where the computing platform is shared across different users and applications.

As pointed out, our time-sharing Time Warp proposal also entails the capability of supporting preemptive rollback of the currently (incorrectly) executed simulation event. The topic of preemptive rollback in optimistic discrete event simulation has been studied in literature, mainly in [6, 23]. The Time Warp platform presented in [6] supports event preemptive rollback for optimistic parallel simulation on shared memory machines, and is based on direct manipulation of the event list of the recipient simulation object by the thread along which the generation of a new event is handled. With this solution, the sender thread is able to determine the current simulation time of the recipient simulation object and whether any message/anti-message being sent to that object violates causality. If this is the case, the sender thread notifies the violation to the thread handling the recipient object, which is done to timely interrupt any in-progress activity in order to execute rollback operations. Our solution is different since it does not rely on cross-thread signaling. Also, in our approach, any Time Warp thread is allowed to change its current flow (and dynamically dispatch a different simulation event after preemption of the last dispatched one) independently of the actual materialization of a causality violation, rather when we also must give higher priority to a different simulation event, possibly to be executed at a simulation object different from the currently running one, anyhow currently bound to the worker thread (e.g., in or-

der to reduce the likelihood of future rollback generation). This is basically due to the fact that our time-sharing Time Warp system is not limited to the support for preemptive rollback. As for the preemptive rollback approach in [23], it is suited for distributed memory systems (based on Myrinet interconnection) while we deal with shared memory multi-core machines. Also, the solution in [23] is based on polling, and the polling code to periodically verify the causal consistency of the current event needs to be nested by the application programmer in proper points of the application native code. Instead, our proposal is based on interrupts, and is fully transparent to the application code (and thus to the developer). Finally, similarly to [6], the solution in [23] does not cope with control flow variations associated with the dynamic generation of higher-priority events (namely with timestamps lower than that of the event currently executed along the thread) that are not currently giving rise to a rollback operation.

As a matter of fact, our time-sharing Time Warp approach is based on a kind of dual-mode execution, where control is periodically pushed back to platform mode via the kernel-level extra ticks' management system. Dual-mode execution in Time Warp systems has been already studied in [16], however this work is focused on the management of different memory views (via operating system-level ad-hoc facilities) so that when running in application mode, only a sub-portion of the whole address space is accessible by the Time Warp worker thread, namely the sub-portion keeping the memory layout of the dispatched simulation object. Any access to the state of another object generates a trap that gives control back to the platform code, which actuates proper thread synchronization mechanisms so as to allow the access to any valid memory location by any event processing routine (as for classical sequential style coding of DES models). Rather, the present proposal is tailored to variations of the control flow in order to react to the generation of higher priority simulation events or tasks (such as rollbacks to be processed) and to the dynamical assignment of CPU to these events. Still, like the proposal in [16], we retain application transparency.

Finally, the present proposal is clearly related to the seminal work in [11], where Time Warp is instantiated as a special-purpose operating system (although operating in user space), destined to host discrete event applications according to a speculative processing paradigm. The core difference between what we are presenting and the proposal in [11] lies in that such an approach is still based on batch-processing of the events, with preemption only used in case of causality errors affecting the currently-dispatched simulation event. Rather, our approach is a truly time-sharing one, which is achieved thanks to the employment of kernel-level ad-hoc (and lightweight) modules specifically oriented to the management of control flow variations (hence preemption in its wide usage) on a fine-grain periodical basis.

3. THE TIME-SHARING ARCHITECTURE

3.1 Basics on Linux Timer-Interrupts

As for our target machines, namely x86 ones, modern processors are equipped with various timer facilities, among which one is ultimately exploited to drive the passage of time on each individual CPU-core. This is the LAPIC-timer component supported by APIC (Advanced Programmable

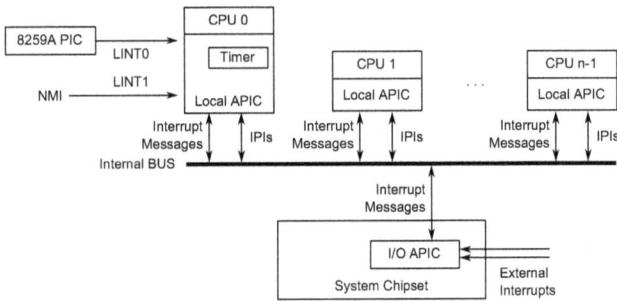

Figure 1: x86 interrupt system.

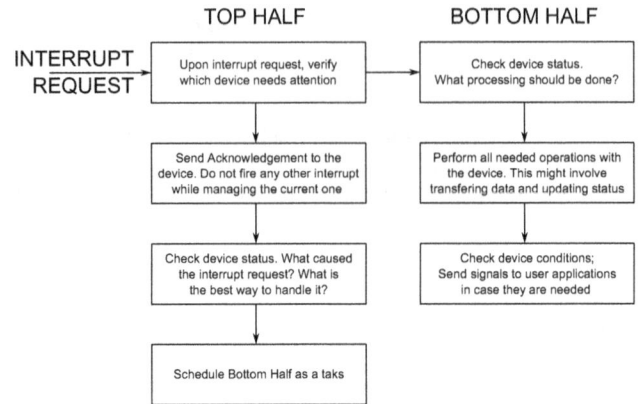

Figure 2: Top/bottom-half general scheme.

Interrupt Controller), which is a timer-component local to any CPU-core in the system. The general hardware organization on x86 architectures regarding interrupt management is depicted in Figure 1.

The LAPIC-timer can be configured to operate in different modes, among which the one used by the Linux kernel is the periodic-interrupt mode. More specifically, at kernel startup, a so called calibration procedure is executed such that the LAPIC-timer is setup (in terms of its internal hardware counter, upon the expiration of which the interrupt is issued towards the associated CPU-core) so as to periodically generate interrupts according to the frequency established by the CONFIG_HZ parameter defined at kernel compile time. As hinted, classical interrupt periods for entry level to medium-end machines range from 1 to 4 milliseconds, which is reflected to values of CONFIG_HZ ranging from 1000 to 250. Once setup at startup, the configuration of the LAPIC-timer is never changed, thus the same interrupt period is always used at system steady state.

As for software-side management of the interrupt, we have that the actual management scheme supported by Linux is based on the top/bottom-half paradigm. More specifically, upon the receipt of the LAPIC-timer interrupt, a very minimal piece of code is executed by the CPU-core, which is only used to update timing information and to possibly flag the current thread in such a way that eventually the scheduler is called and a context switch (that switches this thread off the CPU) can take place. Actually, a thread that has been dispatched on CPU is typically allowed to run for various timer-ticks before being flagged for re-schedule. The general scheme for top/bottom-half management, for the sake of clarity, is reported in Figure 2.

All the above (fine grain) actions are representative of the top-half portion of the timer-interrupt handler. On the the other hand, the call to the kernel schedule() function for performing actual context switches (if requested) is actuated right prior to leaving kernel mode[3]. Therefore, the schedule() function, which represents the core part of the bottom-half of the timer-interrupt manager, is executed only in case no kernel-level critical task is being executed by the thread. This allows for scalability on multi-core processors, given that de-scheduling a thread during the execution of any kernel-level critical task, such as a spinlock-protected kernel-level critical section, would lead the critical section to be locked up to the point in time where this same thread will be CPU-rescheduled, an operation that may occur after

an unpredictable amount of time (also depending on system workload and relative thread priorities).

3.2 The Extra-Tick Logic

As hinted, our time-sharing architecture is based on a kernel-level differentiation between Time Warp threads and other kinds of threads (running generic applications), since only the former ones need to be managed according to the lightweight extra-tick scheme. To this end, we have developed a Linux module offering support for a special device file called dev_extra_tick such that:

- this special device file is single instance, hence no two different concurrently-opened I/O sessions on it are allowed. This is compliant with the idea that a single process (namely the multi-thread Time Warp platform running on the multi-core machine) needs to use the facilities offered by the special device file for supporting the execution of all of its worker threads;

- a thread can register itself as a Time Warp worker-thread by issuing as simple ioctl call towards the device file.

Registering a thread on the special device file allows the kernel to know that the thread needs to undergo the extra-tick policy. Actually, registration means that the thread identifier (as seen by the kernel, not by the pthread library, since the two are typically different), is registered into a fast access hash table, which is installed as part of the kernel module data structures implementing the special device file driver.

At this point, the portions of the whole kernel architecture that need to know whether some thread is registered and needs ad-hoc tick management are two: the kernel scheduler, and the top-half of the timer-interrupt. The external module implementing the management logic for the dev_extra_tick device file is also in charge of redefining the actual behavior of the kernel scheduler and of the top-half of the timer-interrupt so that their logic is modified so as to become compliant with extra-tick management requirements.

Rather than providing a recompiled version of the kernel with the aforementioned changes already implemented, our module adopts a *dynamic patching* approach where parts of the executable image of the kernel are rewritten at startup of the external module implementing the device file.

---

[3] A minor variation is in place for the case of kernel threads, which never leave kernel mode operations.

To patch the kernel `schedule()` function, we retrieve the memory position of the corresponding machine instructions block from the system-map (typically available in Linux installations from the `/boot` directory of the root file system), and we inject into this routine an execution flow variation such that control goes to a `schedule_hook()` routine offered by the external module right before the `scheduler()` would execute its finalization part (e.g. stack realignment and return). A scheme of this patching approach is shown in Figure 3, which has been tested on Linux kernels from 2.6 to 3.2. The red block of code implementing the finalization part of original `schedule()` function is initially sampled and copied at the end of the `schedule_hook()` function by also adjusting relative memory references (if present) in the copy. Then we replace the red block of code in the original version of `schedule()` with a block of machine code (the yellow part) which allows passing control to `schedule_hook()` so that the actual final part of the scheduling process is under the control of our external module. In the end, the `schedule_hook()` function will simply execute the same return actions originally planned by the kernel's `schedule()` function. However, patching the original scheduler in this way allows the hook to take control when the decision about what thread needs to take control of the CPU-core[4] is already finalized. Hence, we know what thread will have control of the CPU-core for the current set of ticks.

As a consequence, the hook is able to check whether the thread is a registered one (so that it needs to be extra-ticked) by consulting the aforementioned fast access hash table implementing the registration record, and in the positive case it executes the following additional steps:

(A) It changes the LAPIC-timer period by scaling it on the basis of a configuration parameter supported by our kernel module. The scaling factor is what determines the length of the extra-tick interval.

(B) It records in a per CPU-core entry of a proper control table (still managed by the module) that the current CPU-core is working in extra-tick mode.

(C) It records in a proper per registered-thread entry of a control table (again managed by the module) a counter of extra-ticks not yet consumed by such a thread within the current tick period.

Clearly, the information recorded in point B is also used in order to revert the LAPIC-timer configuration to the original one. More in detail, if the scheduler passes control to a non-registered thread, and the current CPU-core is registered as operating in extra-tick mode, then the LAPIC-timer is restored to its initially configured counter value, thus the scheduled thread will run with a classical tick length, and the control record associated with the CPU-core is reset in order to reflect that the CPU-core is no longer operating in extra-tick mode. Note that this approach works also in scenarios where the thread registered within the `dev_extra_tick` device file looses control of the CPU-core because of a passage into a sleep state (e.g. for an I/O interaction). Overall the above scheme allows restoring the LAPIC-timer configuration to the original one each time a non-registered thread is

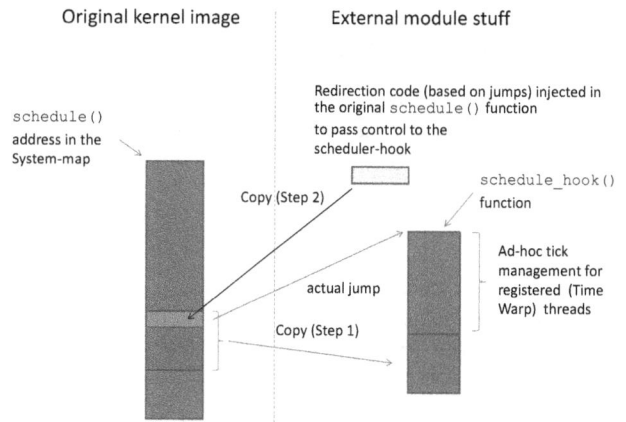

Figure 3: Dynamic patching of the kernel scheduler.

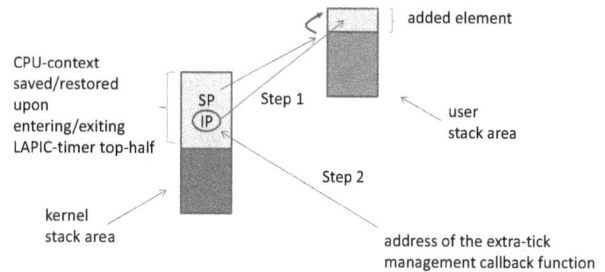

Figure 4: Stack and CPU context management by the LAPIC-timer top-half hook.

(re)scheduled independently of any state-transition of registered (hence extra-ticked) threads in the operating system state diagram.

Let us now analyze how the original top-half of the LAPIC-timer interrupt has been patched in our architecture, so that the extra-ticks can be actually exploited for control flow variations of the `dev_extra_tick` registered threads, namely the ones that in our overall architectural organization run within the Time Warp platform. The patch has been developed by targeting kernel version 3.16.7, but it is of general use (except for a few minor modifications that might be required for other kernel versions depending on the exact path of execution of, e.g., very basic actions in the preamble of the actual timer-interrupt management logic—details on this aspect will come shortly).

Top-half modules in conventional Linux configurations are made up by two different code blocks, a launcher and an actual top-half procedure. The launcher takes control when the CPU-core firmware accepts the interrupt. It is in charge of aligning the kernel-level stack of the interrupted thread to a proper snapshot and then of calling the actual top-half module. Such a snapshot also includes the CPU-context to be restored once the interrupt top-half procedure ends. This includes the stack pointer (SP) and the instruction pointer (IP) associated with the interrupted execution flow, which will play a major role in our time-sharing architecture.

In our patching approach of the LAPIC-timer interrupt management logic, we have still exploited the system-map to locate the launcher code block in the kernel memory image, and then we patched it by replacing the call to the original top-half with one to a top-half hook function offered by the

---

[4]It has actually already taken control of the CPU-core, since we are returning from the scheduling process.

external module that we have developed, which therefore fully replaces the original top-half procedure. This top-half hook is in charge of executing the same identical basic actions as those executed by the original top-half procedure (such as acknowledging the accepted interrupt). However, it discriminates if the interrupted thread is a `dev_extra_tick` registered one (namely, one subject to extra-tick management), and in the positive case it executes the following actions:

(i) It decreases the extra-tick counter associated with the thread (as pointed out, this is the counter that is set upon the reschedule of any thread registered on the `dev_extra_tick` device file).

(ii) If the counter reaches the value zero, then it means that a whole originally-sized tick-period has expired (hence the thread consumed all the extra-ticks granted to it in its current tick period). In this case, the top-half hook calls the actual kernel function used to update kernel-level timing information (in most of the recent kernel versions this work is carried out via the `lo-cal_apic_timer_interrupt()` kernel function). This mimics the behavior of the original top-half manager execution path, given that it would trigger the timing information update function exactly at the end of each originally-sized tick-period, hence upon any LAPIC-timer interrupt when using the classical timer calibration.

(iii) The top-half hook changes the IP kept by the processor image registered into the system stack upon interrupt acceptance, so that the interrupted thread will gain control in a proper machine code block upon the restore of that image onto the CPU-core (namely, when returning from LAPIC-timer interrupt). Consequently, the top-half hook also changes the application-level stack layout of the thread by adding a program-counter return value that will allow that code block to exactly return control to the instruction interrupted by the extra-tick (namely, the original IP value logged into the CPU-context snapshot on the system stack). This is done by exploiting the SP value from the logged CPU-context, which then is also modified in order to reflect the insertion of a new element at the top of the user level stack. A schematization of the performed operations is provided in Figure 4.

(iv) Finally, in case the extra-tick counter of the thread registered within the `dev_extra_tick` device file reached the value zero—see point (ii)—the thread is again filled with the number of extra-ticks (say N) it is allowed to receive in the next tick period.

In our time-sharing Time Warp architecture, the address of the code block that will take control thanks to the instruction pointer variation in point (iii) represents an ad-hoc callback function of the Time Warp platform, which will periodically (namely, at each extra-tick expiration) bring control to the platform-level software along any Time Warp worker thread. This address is posted to the kernel when calling the same `ioctl` system call that is used for registering the thread in the `dev_extra_tick` device file as one to be extra-ticked. Overall, a Time Warp thread can atomically register itself for being subject to extra-ticks and post the address of the

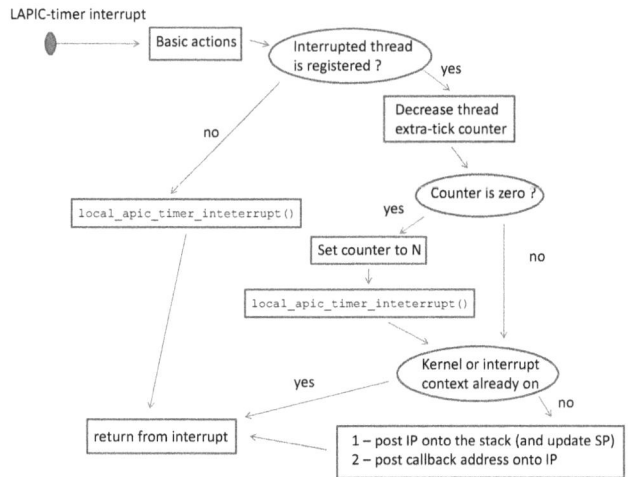

Figure 5: Behavior of the top-half hook for the LAPIC-timer interrupt.

callback function whose execution is activated thanks to the actions by the top-half hook of the LAPIC-timer interrupt we provide within our module.

The actual scheme according to which our top-half hook for the LAPIC-timer interrupt works is depicted in Figure 5. As one may observe, the hook version of the LAPIC-timer interrupt manager is still lightweight given that the additional actions it performs (compared to the original version of the top-half procedure) have constant time and are mostly related to decrementing and (possibly) setting a counter (the per-registered-thread extra-tick counter) and setting a few memory locations, one in the application-level thread stack (see point 1 in the bottom-right box of Figure 5, where the IP present in the snapshot of the user level CPU-context, which is already logged in the system level stack upon entering the top-half hook, is saved onto the user level stack), and the other ones in the user level CPU-context logged in the stack (namely IP and SP values, that will be then restored upon exiting the interrupt procedure).

As an additional note, care must be taken when receiving an extra-tick along a thread which is already working at kernel level. This may happen in case the extra-ticked thread called a system call, or if it entered kernel mode because of the receipt of a generic interrupt by some device (see Figure 1) or even because of a generic trap (e.g. an empty-zero memory access requiring the physical allocation of the requested page). In this case, variation of the flow control must not be actuated given that it would violate any, e.g., atomicity rule for the execution of already activated kernel-level code. This is reflected in our scheme by having that the control flow variation is actuated only if the interrupted thread was not already working in kernel mode or was not already subject to an interrupt. Such a check has been implemented in our top-half hook by simply checking whether the IP to be restored contains a kernel-level address, and by also checking whether an interrupt context was already active on the current CPU-core (a check that is anyhow already assessed by the basic actions that are carried out also by the original top-half procedure).

The periodic execution flow variation induced via extra-tick management, although being similar in spirit to the one adopted for handling POSIX signals, is still much more lightweight, given that on demand usage of temporized signals would require passing through the whole scheduling process (and also trough system calls for requesting the activation of each individual alarm). Also, conventional signal handlers for temporized signals cannot operate with the same time granularity we can impose in our architecture (namely the extra-tick period) just because, in the worst case, a whole tick period might be requested in order for the kernel to take control back and determine that some alarm has expired for the thread.

As a final note, we ensure execution safety while mounting the kernel module[5] by synchronizing all the CPU-cores during the mounting operation via the `smp_call_function()` kernel function. This can be used to trigger the execution of a same code block on all the cores. We have used it to implement a master/slave protocol, similar in spirit to the one used while booting the Linux kernel, where a single CPU-core executes the actual patching of the kernel code (by also temporarily disabling write protection on the kernel image) during module startup, while the other CPU-cores wait for the master to finish. In this way, no critical race will take place, preventing any CPU-core from accessing the not yet finalized image of the kernel.

3.3 Detection and Management of Event and Task Priority Variations

The extra-tick architecture presented in the previous section is of general applicability, in terms of its ability to periodically bring control back to a specific portion of the platform-level software, and to dynamically (re)schedule on CPU higher-priority tasks. On the other hand, how to exploit it within an optimistic PDES platform depends on proper platform internals.

In this section we discuss the integration we performed between the extra-tick manager and the ROOT-Sim open source optimistic simulation platform. However, given that this platform implements some relevant reference architectural solutions specifically tailored for multi-core environments (see [27]), the presented integration, beyond giving rise to a specific time-sharing Time Warp solution, can also be seen as one providing reference guidelines for time-sharing organizations of optimistic PDES.

The core ROOT-Sim aspect that is of interest in this discussion is the management of the message (or anti-message) exchange across different worker threads operating within the platform. More in detail, given that ROOT-Sim manages any subset of simulation objects, say S, by (temporarily) binding them to a specific worker thread, say t, and the adopted CPU-dispatching rule is the classical Lowest-Timestamp-First (LTF), the CPU-dispatched event associated with the objects in S is always the one with highest priority.

The only exception is when messages, or anti-messages, produced while concurrently running other simulation objects along other worker threads, and destined to some object belonging to the set S handled by t, will carry a timestamp which is lower than the one associated with the last-dispatched lowest-timestamp event. Clearly, this cannot be known before the CPU-schedule operation along thread t.

In ROOT-Sim, the exchange of messages/anti-messages across different worker threads does not take place by directly incorporating the corresponding information into the destination object event queue. Rather, messages are exchanged according to a top/bottom-half approach, still oriented to scalability. Particularly, each worker thread manages a set of bottom-half queues (one for each simulation object it is currently handling) such that any other worker thread in the system can notify the presence of new data to be ultimately incorporated into the destination object's event queue via the corresponding bottom-half queue. Checking whether some new data is present into a bottom-half queue, and actual processing of the data with incorporation into the destination event queue, is carried out exclusively by the worker thread in charge of (currently) handling the destination object. This scheme is complemented by a constant-time management of the critical section for inserting/deleting elements into/from any bottom-half queue, which leads actual thread synchronization to scale.

The above scheme has been extended in order to perform the integration with the extra-tick management architecture along the following lines. First, each worker thread t operating in the Time Warp platform has been associated with a BH_min_t record, which represents at any time instant the minimum timestamp of any message/anti-message that has been recorded in any of the bottom-half queues associated with the simulation objects that t is currently managing, since the last flush operation of these queues. In other words, BH_min_t represents the minimum value among the timestamps of information in transit (if any), which is destined to some simulation object handled by t.

This record is initialized to the special macro INFTY (via a single atomic assignment operation) when the worker thread t accesses its bound bottom-half queues an flushes the data into the corresponding event queues. Whenever a different worker thread inserts a bottom-half record into any of the bottom-half queues associated with the simulation objects managed by t, the reduction $BH\_min_t = Min(BH\_min_t, T)$ is performed, where T represents the timestamp of the message/anti-message that is being placed into the destination bottom-half queue. In our implementation, this reduction is performed via an atomic Compare-And-Swap (CAS) instruction. This allows manipulating BH_min_t while not requiring worker threads that concurrently access two distinct bottom-half queues bound to t to execute a conflicting critical section[6].

Another record, called $current\_time_t$, is associated with each worker thread t. It is used to keep track of the timestamp of the current simulation event, if any, that has been CPU-dispatched along t (this is the lowest-timestamp event according to LTF). The value of $current\_time_t$ is set to the special value -1 in case thread t is not currently processing any event (e.g. it is running housekeeping operations within the Time Warp platform).

The values of $current\_time_t$ and BH_min_t are used by the callback function that takes control via the extra-tick mechanism in order to determine whether some higher priority task (compared to the one currently processed by the CPU along thread t) needs to be CPU-dispatched. Particu-

---

[5]We recall that during the mount operation, the module initialization function rewrites some parts of the kernel code at run-time, which is a critical procedure.

[6]In fact, each of them needs to temporarily lock a different bottom-half queue for data insertion, which helps not hampering concurrency [27].

larly, the callback function executing along t has the following simple structure:

---

void **tick-manager()**
1. **if** ($current\_time_t \leq BH\_min_t$)
2.   **return**;
3. **else**
4.   `switch_to_platform_context()`;

The above structure allows changing the current execution flow along thread t in case:

1) The simulation object currently dispatched for event execution along t needs to rollback, since it is the recipient of a message or anti-message in its past (namely BH_min_t corresponds to the timestamp of a message/ anti-message destined to the currently running simulation object). In this case the rollback operation will take place according to a preemptive mode just based on the time-sharing organization and on the (periodic) regain of control at the Time Warp platform level.

2) Some generic simulation object managed by t dynamically gains a priority higher than that of the currently running one, since it becomes the recipient of some message or anti-message with a timestamp lower than that of the last lowest-timestamp CPU-scheduled event. The case of an incoming anti-message is again representative of a causal inconsistent execution at the destination simulation object, given the adopted LTF rule for the CPU-dispatching of the events by any worker thread t.

Overall, in either case, control must return to the Time Warp platform layer, so that the higher priority task (either a rollback operation or not) is promptly executed. In the pseudo-code this is achieved via the invocation of the `switch_to_platform_context()` function, whose actual support, as well as the support for correct management of individual (and separate) simulation object contexts, is described in the next section.

On the other hand, in case no higher priority task needs to be executed, the forward execution of the last CPU-dispatched event is immediately resumed given that the tick-manager callback function simply returns, thus taking control back to the point where the original execution flow was interrupted by the extra-tick at the heart of the time-sharing architecture.

3.4 Support for Context Switches

The management of different per-simulation-object contexts (as well as the platform context) is based on the ROOT-Sim support that has been introduced in [16] to create stack separation across the different simulation objects. This is achieved by locating the stack of each object in a portion of memory destined for object usage (e.g. when memory chunks are dynamically requested while executing events at that object) via proper (and application transparent) allocation layers [16, 26]. On the other hand, each worker thread t also has a platform context associated with it, which is in turn associated with a proper stack area located in a different, and disjoint, memory region.

Execution resume in the different stacks, such as when `switch_to_platform_context()` is executed, has been supported via `setjump` and `longjump` POSIX APIs. They have also been used as the support for, e.g. squashing the stack image of the currently-executing simulation object in case a preemptive rollback occurs within the time-sharing Time Warp system (which eventually leads the object to resume execution with a different context, namely a logged one that is then put back in place).

3.5 Support for Safe Platform Mode Execution

A final core aspect deals with the fact that in an advanced Time Warp platform applications are supported by allowing the actual application code to live in a piece-wise-deterministic environment which is able, transparently to the application code, to support recovery of any incorrect trajectory of the application state possibly caused by causality errors in the speculative execution path.

A classical way to achieve this is the one where any interaction between the application code and external services, such as those offered by standard third-party programming libraries, is intercepted by the Time Warp environment and is handled according to proper rules. Classical examples are the ones where recoverable dynamic memory services and/or recoverable I/O services are exposed to the application via standard interfaces (e.g. `malloc` or `printf`) but are handled (to make them actually recoverable) via proper logic at the level of the Time Warp platform. Such a kind of application-transparent intervention by the platform-level software may reach a granularity so fine that even a single machine instruction can be intercepted and made recoverable, as when relying on binary code instrumentation to run-time track memory writes, and to dynamically log recoverability data so as to retain the possibility to undo the update [18].

According to this view, independently of the presence of any time-sharing support like the one we provide, an advanced Time Warp platform can be already seen as a system working according to a dual-mode execution model, where the application can trap into platform mode just because of some (seamless) access to one of the above mentioned services. On the other hand, the actual implementation of such platform-level services, for being correct, may require atomicity. Just to mention an example, locks on specific data structures or memory regions might be acquired by some worker thread once the application has trapped into platform mode along that thread in order to correctly manage the triggered service [1].

This atomicity must be guaranteed also in case of the time-sharing architecture we provide. Hence, if the tick-management callback is triggered while the running thread has already trapped into platform mode in a seamless manner on behalf of the application code processing the current simulation event, our choice is to avoid any variation of the control flow (independently of the actual presence of higher priority tasks), so as not to interfere with the already entered platform-level code block. In order to achieve this target in ROOT-Sim, we have reorganized the platform-level software such in a way that any entry point for actual platform operations has been augmented by a wrapper that atomically sets a flag indicating that the thread is running in platform mode. The reverse action, which resets the flag to application mode, is actuated via wrappers intercepting the return

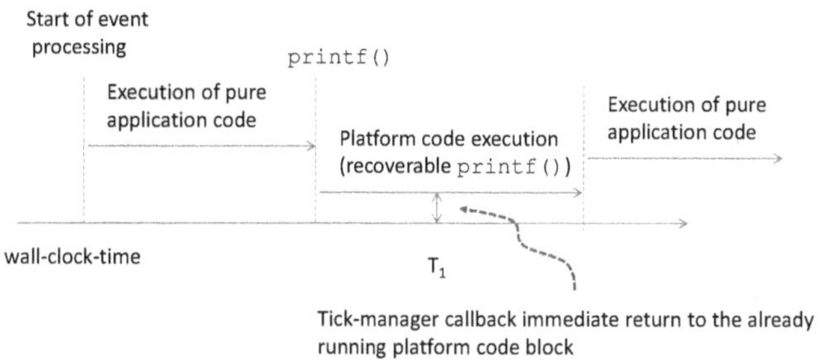

Figure 6: Management of extra-ticks in the interleave between application and platform code blocks within an event processing wall-clock-time window.

of any platform-level service possibly activated while processing some event via the aforementioned trap/interception mechanism. In case a callback for managing some extra-tick is received while running a platform-mode phase during the processing of an event in the application software, then the callback simply returns control to the interrupted execution point.

A schematization of this behavior is provided in Figure 6, where we show the arrival of an extra-tick at wall-clock-time T_1, with consequent activation of the extra-tick management callback function, and where the callback simply returns given that at the same time instant the platform-level software was already handling, possibly via proper recoverability rules, some I/O operation invoked by the event processing code implemented at the application level.

We also note that the approach where no control flow variation is actuated in case the platform mode has been already entered, e.g., because of an interception of some third-party library call while processing the current event by some worker thread, also allows safety of the execution of any platform-level facility ultimately relying on external user space libraries, such as libc-xx.so, given that the flow control in these libraries is never changed by any extra-tick arrival.

4. EXPERIMENTAL RESULTS

We have executed experiments with the time-sharing version of ROOT-Sim by running this platform of top of a 32-core 64-bit NUMA machine, namely an HP ProLiant server, equipped with four 2GHz AMD Opteron 6128 processors (each one equipped with 8 CPU-cores) and 64 GB of RAM. The operating system is Linux SUSE, kernel version 3.16.7 augmented with our extra-tick management architecture. In the original configuration of the kernel, the LAPIC-timer was set to issue an interrupt each 1 millisecond. When running in extra-tick mode we configured the LAPIC-timer to send an interrupt 10 times more frequently, thus each 100 microseconds.

As the benchmark for assessing the effectiveness of our time-sharing proposal, we used a real-world cellular system simulator, which has already been used as a reference benchmark application in a number of other studies oriented to optimistic PDES (see, e.g., [18]). In this application, each simulation object models a wireless cell, and we selected a total number of 1024 cells (represented as hexagons), each one managing 1000 wireless channels, which provide coverage to mobile devices in a squared region. The model is high fidelity in terms of how interference across different chan-

nels within a same cell, and power management upon call setup/handoff is captured/actuated. Particularly, the application handles power management simulation according to the results in [13]. The application is also highly parameterizable by allowing the recalculation of fading coefficients and actual Signal-to-Interference Ratio (SIR) both on the occurrence of specific events (e.g. the startup of a call) and periodically (so as to account for, e.g., changes of conditions in the coverage area). Also, the inter-arrival of calls to mobile devices residing in the coverage area can be configured, thus leading to different values for the wireless channels' utilization factor. This, in its turn, affects both memory and CPU demand by the simulation given that higher utilization factors lead to the need for keeping more records for simulating the concurrently active calls in any cells, and also to more costly operations for scanning and (possibly) updating these records. As a final preliminary note, the interaction across the different simulation objects takes place upon the occurrence of a handoff of a mobile device involved in an ongoing communication, in which case the wireless channel at the source cell is released, and a new one in the destination cell is attempted to be reserved.

On our experimentation we set the average residual residence time in the current cell for a mobile device involved in an on-going call to the value 5 min, while the average call duration was set to 2 min. Both these values have been set to follow exponential distributions. Also, we have run this model with three different settings for the channel utilization factor, namely 25%, 50% and 75%, determined by different call inter-arrival rates, with balanced workload on all the simulation objects (fairly distributed on 32 worker threads operating within the ROOT-Sim platform on top of the 32 CPU-core machine), and with periodic recalculations of the fading coefficients of active channels. This settings gives rise to variations of the simulation event's average CPU requirement from about 70/80 microseconds, to about 150 microseconds. This way we achieved differentiated configurations in terms of the relation between the event execution granularity, and the granularity of the extra-ticks' interval (recall this has been set to 100 microseconds). In other words, the adopted settings allowed us to determine different actual likelihoods for an extra-tick to interrupt an on going event (in fact such a likelihood is higher when the event granularity is greater), which gave us the possibility to assess our time-sharing architecture when changing the likelihood that a higher priority task can be detected as standing while the execution of an event is in progress. Further, the configuration with finer granularity of the events (namely the one with 25% channel utilization factor) looks also good for assessing the overhead by our proposal, just given the reduced likelihood for the extra-tick to occur while an event is in progress, rather while we are running any platform-level housekeeping operations, which leads to a case where the extra-tick simply returns control to the original point (but cost has anyhow been spent for delivering it, hence for delivering control to the callback offered by the Time Warp system).

In this experimentation we compare the original execution dynamics of ROOT-Sim, namely those based on the classical batch-multitask paradigm for processing the events (where control is returned to the underlying platform for dispatching other events/tasks only at the end of the event-handler processing routine) with those achieved via the integration

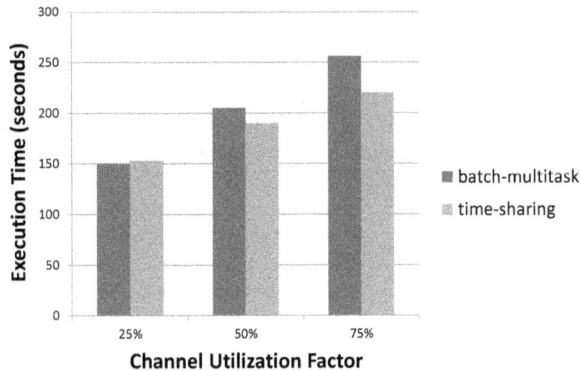

Figure 7: Execution time results.

	Channel Utilization Factor		
	25%	50%	75%
execution time (sec)	3500	5145	7610

Table 1: Performance of the serial simulator.

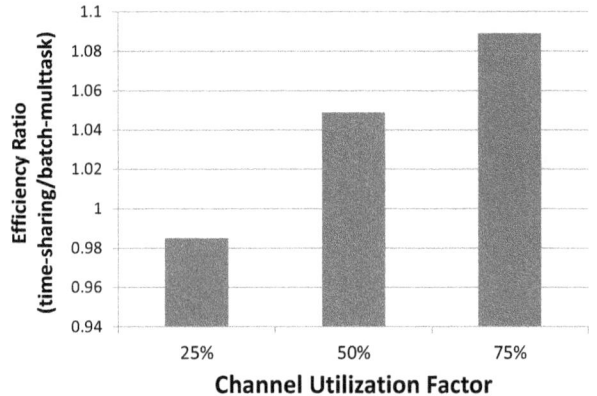

Figure 8: Time-sharing efficiency over batch-multitask efficiency.

of the time-sharing support (which allows for passing control to events/tasks that dynamically reveal as higher priority ones). Particularly, in Figure 7 we report the execution time (computed as the average over 5 different samples, each referring to a different settings of the pseudo-random seeds used for stochastically driving model execution) for simulating a specific virtual time interval in the different configurations of the benchmark application and with either batch-multitask or time-sharing support. Also, we decided to run with checkpoint interval fixed to the value 10 for all the simulation objects in order not to introduce fluctuations and/or variations in performance possibly caused by some adaptive mechanism to select the checkpoint frequency, which might interfere with the actual performance variations natively imputable to the two different execution schemes we are comparatively studying, namely time-sharing vs batch-multitask. By the data we can draw the following main observations. First, the results related to the configuration with 25% channel utilization factor, which as hinted before is essentially useful for overhead assessment, actually show a minimal overhead by the time-sharing support, given that the execution times for the two different supports is essentially the same. On the other hand, as soon as the event granularity is increased (namely for higher values of the channel utilization factor) we get an actual reduction of the execution time achieved with the time-sharing support (as compared to the traditional batch-multitask support). Specifically, the gain in performance is of the order of 8% for the case of utilization factor set to 50%, and of the order of 15% when the utilization factor is further increased up to 75%. For completeness, we also report in Table 1 the corresponding execution times for the case of a serial execution of the same identical application code on top of a sequential scheduler based on the Calendar-Queue data structure [2], which allows determining the speedup of the parallel runs, and hence whether this study refers to competitive parallel performance.

By the data in Figure 8, we get the explanation of the actual source of the performance gain by the time-sharing support compared to the batch-multitask one. Specifically,

we report in this figure the variation of the ratio between the optimistic run efficiency observed with the time-sharing support and the one observed with the batch-multitask support. We recall that the efficiency of an optimistic PDES run represents the percentage of productive work executed (processed simulation events that are not eventually rolled back). Hence it is an expression (and a derivation) of the actual rollback pattern (and amount). By the data we see that, for the configuration with 25% channel utilization factor, the two different supports provide in practice the same efficiency values. This is aligned with our previous observations in relation to the application configuration with finer-event granularity, which exhibits a reduced likelihood of actual interruption of an event processing phase by the extra-ticks, with consequent reduction of the possibility to change the rollback pattern in the time-sharing support by passing control to some higher priority task (e.g. a simulation event with smaller timestamp) dynamically injected in the system. On the other hand, increasing the event granularity leads to scenarios with increased ability by the time-sharing support to actually track (while an event is already being processed in CPU) whether higher priority activities need to be carried out along the same worker thread and dynamically reschedule them in CPU, which leads to limit the negative impact of, e.g. out-of timestamp order processing. This, in its turn, leads the relative efficiency by the time-sharing support to increase, compared to the batch-multitask one, up to 9%. Overall, the time-sharing configuration shows higher likelihood to perform useful (not eventually rolled back) work, especially for the case of larger granularity events, and this is achieved with negligible overhead (by the time-sharing support), with positive effects on performance.

In Figure 9 we provide an additional plot where we show the variation of the amount of actual event preemptions (hence execution flow variations) per execution time unit achieved while running in time-sharing mode for the three different configurations of the channel utilization factor we have considered in this study. Aligned with the previous results, the data reported in this plot show how the configurations with larger event granularity (namely, higher channel utilization factor) manifest a larger percentage of actual preemptions per wall-clock-time unit. On the other hand, the interesting point in this plot is that it does not scale linearly, which is a reflection of the fact that greater event

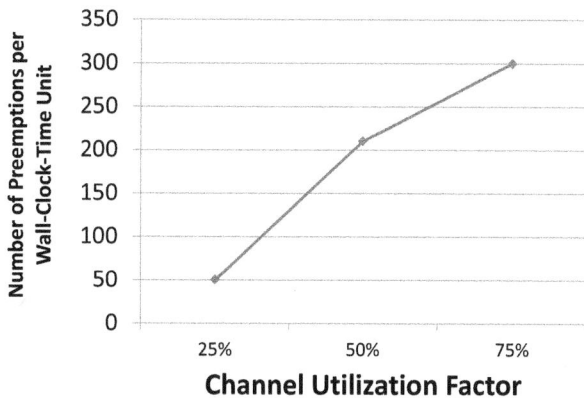

Figure 9: Number of preemptions per wall-clock-time unit when running in time-sharing mode.

granularity on the one hand allows for more opportunities of preemption (since extra-ticks more likely will be delivered while simulation-event processing is in progress), but on the other hand, parallel runs with larger grain events are typically (at least for balanced models like the ones we are considering) less subject to divergence of the simulation clocks of the different concurrent simulation objects, which leads to reduced likelihood that the extra-tick callback function actually finds some higher priority task (e.g. the rollback of the currently running simulation object) to be carried out. However, this somehow no linear shape of the curve in Figure 9 looks intrinsic to the nature of Time Warp dynamics, hence not being a specific limitation of the time-sharing Time Warp approach we have presented.

5. CONCLUSIONS

In this article we have presented a lightweight support for allowing time-shared execution of Time Warp platforms on top of conventional operating systems, such as Linux, and multi-core machines.

In our proposal, any individual worker thread operating within the Time Warp system can be interrupted with high frequency (a frequency much higher than conventional timer interrupts in classical operating systems' configurations) and with low interrupt-management overhead, in order to determine whether any higher priority task (e.g. a rollback to be promptly processed) or event (e.g. with lower timestamp compared to the currently executed one) needs to be CPU-dispatched. This allows for reacting to actual changes of the priorities of the activities to be carried out within the Time Warp run, with consequent (possible) advantages in terms of reduction of the amount of wasted work.

Our operating system based support for time-sharing has been integrated into an open source Time Warp platform, and we also report experimental data for an assessment of both the overhead by our proposal and its final effectiveness in terms of improvements of the execution speed of Time Warp simulations on multi-core machines.

6. REFERENCES

[1] F. Antonacci, A. Pellegrini, and F. Quaglia. Consistent and efficient output-streams management in optimistic simulation platforms. In *Proceedings of the ACM SIGSIM Conference on Principles of Advanced Discrete Simulation, (SIGSIM-PADS), Montreal, QC, Canada, May 19-22, 2013*, pages 315–326, ACM Press, 2013.

[2] R. Brown. Calendar queues: a fast O(1) priority queue implementation for the simulation event set problem. *Communications of the ACM*, 31(10):1220–1227, 1988.

[3] C. D. Carothers. Xsim: real-time analytic parallel simulations. In *Proceedings of the Workshop on Parallel and Distributed Simulation (PADS), Washington, D.C., USA, May 12-15, 2002*, pages 27–34, IEEE Computer Society, 2002.

[4] C. D. Carothers, D. W. Bauer, and S. Pearce. ROSS: A high-performance, low-memory, modular time warp system. *Journal of Parallel and Distributed Computing*, 62(11):1648–1669, 2002.

[5] C. D. Carothers, K. S. Perumalla, and R. M. Fujimoto. Efficient optimistic parallel simulations using reverse computation. *ACM Transactions on Modeling and Computer Simulation*, 9(3):224–253, 1999.

[6] S. R. Das, R. M. Fujimoto, K. Panesar, D. Allison, and M. Hybinette. GTW: a time warp system for shared memory multiprocessors. In *Proceedings of the 26th Winter Simulation Conference*, pages 1332–1339. Society for Computer Simulation International, 1994.

[7] P. De, R. Kothari, and V. Mann. Identifying sources of operating system jitter through fine-grained kernel instrumentation. In *Proceedings of the IEEE International Conference on Cluster Computing, 17-20 September 2007, Austin, Texas, USA*, pages 331–340, IEEE Computer Society, 2007.

[8] K. B. Ferreira, P. Bridges, and R. Brightwell. Characterizing application sensitivity to OS interference using kernel-level noise injection. In *Proceedings of the 2008 ACM/IEEE Conference on Supercomputing (SC), November 15-21, 2008, Austin, Texas, USA*, pages 19:1–19:12, ACM Pess, 2008.

[9] HPDCS Research Group. ROOT-Sim: The ROme OpTimistic Simulator - v 1.0. *http://www.dis.uniroma1.it/~hpdcs/ROOT-Sim/* (last accessed: May 2015).

[10] D. R. Jefferson. Virtual Time. *ACM Transactions on Programming Languages and System*, 7(3):404–425, 1985.

[11] D. R. Jefferson, B. Beckman, F. Wieland, L. Blume, M. D. Loreto, P. Hontalas, P. Laroche, K. Sturdevant, J. Tupman, L. V. Warren, J. J. Wedel, H. Younger, and S. Bellenot. Distributed simulation and the Time Warp operating system. In *Proceedings of the Eleventh ACM Symposium on Operating System Principles (SOSP), Austin, Texas, November 8-11*, pages 77–93, ACM Press, 1987.

[12] P. D. B. Jr., C. D. Carothers, D. R. Jefferson, and J. M. LaPre. Warp speed: executing Time Warp on 1,966,080 cores. In *Proceedings of the ACM SIGSIM Conference on Principles of Advanced Discrete Simulation, (SIGSIM-PADS), Montreal, QC, Canada, May 19-22, 2013*, pages 327–336, ACM Press, 2013.

[13] S. Kandukuri and S. Boyd. Optimal power control in interference-limited fading wireless channels with outage-probability specifications. *IEEE Transactions on Wireless Communications*, 1(1):46–55, 2002.

[14] D. E. Martin, T. J. McBrayer, and P. A. Wilsey. WARPED: A Time Warp simulation kernel for analysis and application development. In *Proceedings of the 29th Hawaii International Conference on System Sciences (HICSS), Volume 1: Software Technology and Architecture, January 3-6, 1996, Maui, Hawaii, USA*, pages 383–386. IEEE Computer Society, 1996.

[15] D. M. Nicol and X. Liu. The dark side of risk (what your mother never told you about Time Warp). In *Proceedings of the Eleventh Workshop on Parallel and Distributed Simulation (PADS), Lockenhaus, Austria, June 10-13, 1997*, pages 188–195, IEEE Computer Society, 1997.

[16] A. Pellegrini and F. Quaglia. Transparent multi-core speculative parallelization of DES models with event and cross-state dependencies. In *Proceedings of the ACM SIGSIM Conference on Principles of Advanced Discrete Simulation, (SIGSIM-PADS), Denver, CO, USA, May 18-21, 2014*, pages 105–116, ACM Press, 2014.

[17] A. Pellegrini, R. Vitali, and F. Quaglia. The ROme OpTimistic Simulator: Core internals and programming model. In *Proceedings of the 4th International ICST Conference on Simulation Tools and Techniques (SIMUTools), Barcelona, Spain, March 22 - 24*, pages 96-98, ICST, 2011.

[18] A. Pellegrini, R. Vitali, and F. Quaglia. Autonomic state management for optimistic simulation platforms. *IEEE Transactions on Parallel and Distributed Systems (preprint)*, May 2014, doi:10.1109/TPDS.2014.2323967.

[19] B. R. Preiss, W. M. Loucks, and D. MacIntyre. Effects of the checkpoint interval on time and space in Time Warp. *ACM Transactions on Modeling and Computer Simulation*, 4(3):223–253, 1994.

[20] P. Putnam, P. A. Wilsey, and K. V. Manian. Core frequency adjustment to optimize Time Warp on many-core processors. *Simulation Modelling Practice and Theory*, 28:55–64, November 2012.

[21] F. Quaglia. A cost model for selecting checkpoint positions in Time Warp parallel simulation. *IEEE Transactions on Parallel and Distributed Systems*, 12(4):346–362, 2001.

[22] F. Quaglia and V. Cortellessa. On the processor scheduling problem in Time Warp synchronization. *ACM Transactions on Modeling and Computer Simulation*, 12(3): 143-175, 2002.

[23] A. Santoro and F. Quaglia. Software supports for event preemptive rollback in optimistic parallel simulation on myrinet clusters. *Journal of Interconnection Networks*, 6(4):435–457, 2005.

[24] S. K. Seal and K. S. Perumalla. Reversible parallel discrete event formulation of a tlm-based radio signal propagation model. *ACM Transactions on Modeling and Computer Simulation*, 22(1):4:1–4:23, 2011.

[25] S. Seelam, L. L. Fong, A. N. Tantawi, J. Lewars, J. Divirgilio, and K. Gildea. Extreme scale computing: Modeling the impact of system noise in multicore clustered systems. In *Proceednngs of 24th IEEE International Symposium on Parallel and Distributed Processing (IPDPS), Atlanta, Georgia, USA, 19-23 April 2010*, IEEE Computer Society, pages 1–12, 2010.

[26] R. Toccaceli and F. Quaglia. DyMeLoR: Dynamic Memory Logger and Restorer library for optimistic simulation objects with generic memory layout. In *Proceedings of the Workshop on Principles of Advanced and Distributed Simulation (PADS), Roma, Italy, June 3-6*, pages 163–172. IEEE Computer Society, 2008.

[27] R. Vitali, A. Pellegrini, and F. Quaglia. Towards symmetric multi-threaded optimistic simulation kernels. In *Proceedings of the Workshop on Principles of Advanced and Distributed Simulation (PADS), Zhangjiajie, China, July 15-19*, pages 211–220. IEEE Computer Society, Aug. 2012.

NUMA Time Warp

Alessandro Pellegrini and Francesco Quaglia
DIAG – Sapienza, University of Rome
Via Ariosto 25, 00185 Rome, Italy
{pellegrini, quaglia}@dis.uniroma1.it

ABSTRACT

It is well known that Time Warp may suffer from large usage of memory, which may hamper the efficiency of the memory hierarchy. To cope with this issue, several approaches have been devised, mostly based on the reduction of the amount of used virtual memory, e.g., by the avoidance of checkpointing and the exploitation of reverse computing. In this article we present an orthogonal solution aimed at optimizing the latency for memory access operations when running Time Warp systems on Non-Uniform Memory Access (NUMA) multi-processor/multi-core computing systems. More in detail, we provide an innovative Linux-based architecture allowing per-simulation-object management of memory segments made up by disjoint sets of pages, and supporting both static and dynamic binding of the memory pages reserved for an individual object to the different NUMA nodes, depending on what worker thread is in charge of running that simulation object along a given wall-clock-time window. Our proposal not only manages the virtual pages used for the live state image of the simulation object, rather, it also copes with memory pages destined to keep the simulation object's event buffers and any recoverability data. Further, the architecture allows memory access optimization for data (messages) exchanged across the different simulation objects running on the NUMA machine. Our proposal is fully transparent to the application code, thus operating in a seamless manner. Also, a free software release of our NUMA memory manager for Time Warp has been made available within the open source ROOT-Sim simulation platform. Experimental data for an assessment of our innovative proposal are also provided in this article.

Categories and Subject Descriptors

D.4.2 [**Operating Systems**]: Storage Management—*Virtual Memory*; I.6.8 [**Simulation and Modeling**]: Types of Simulation—*Discrete Event, Parallel*

General Terms

Algorithms, Performance

Keywords

PDES; Non-uniform Memory Access; Speculative Processing

1. INTRODUCTION

Speculative computing techniques are widely recognized as a means to achieve scalability of parallel/distributed applications thanks to the (partial) removal of the cost for coordinating concurrent processes and/or threads from the critical path of task processing [16, 30]. In the context of Parallel Discrete Event Simulation (PDES), the speculative paradigm is incarnated by the well-known Time Warp synchronization protocol [18], which has been recently shown to provide scalability up to thousands or millions of CPU-cores [20].

On the other hand, it is also known that a core pitfall of speculative processing schemes lies in their large usage of memory, given that they typically require maintaining (and accessing) histories of speculatively-produced data records and/or recoverability data to cope with misspeculation scenarios. This leads to reduced application locality and consequent suboptimal behavior of the memory hierarchy, given that the working set of the application will more likely exceed cache-storage.

As for Time Warp, its large usage of virtual memory has been shown to represent a potentially insurmountable obstacle to the delivery of adequate performance, as for cases where uncommitted data records saturate RAM (or even virtual memory) thus requiring secondary storage support for the parallel run. On the one hand, such extreme scenarios have been shown to be faceable by proper memory management protocols explicitly aimed at limiting the level of speculation within the Time Warp run (see, e.g., [11]). On the other hand, the classical approach that is employed for reducing the memory footprint of Time Warp applications, and hence for improving their locality, consists in reducing the amount of memory that is kept for allowing recoverability of the state of the concurrent simulation objects (also known as Logical Processes—LPs). Along this path we can find solutions based on infrequent and/or incremental checkpointing of the snapshot of the simulation object's state (or a combination of the two approaches) [25, 27, 28] or on the usage of reverse computing techniques [9]. The latter may (at least in principle) fully avoid keeping state recoverability data, at the expense of an increase in CPU requirements for rebuilding a past state snapshot.

However, despite the wide literature in the area of reducing the memory usage for state recoverability data, the large usage of virtual memory and the reduced locality in Time Warp still stand as intrinsic to this synchronization approach. As an example, event records keeping information about events that have already been processed, but which cannot yet be discarded because their commitment is still undetermined, contribute to enlarging the amount of virtual memory to be managed. Also, this memory is requested to be scanned upon *fossil collection* for buffer release to the underlying allocator, which gives rise to a change of the locality from the live event buffers' portion to the obsolete one. Hence, the efficiency according to which the cache/RAM hierarchy is exploited still stands as a core issue to be addressed while building high performance Time Warp systems.

In this article we tackle the above issue by presenting a memory management architecture that is aimed at reducing the actual latency for the access to memory locations when running Time Warp systems on top of multi-core Non-Uniform-Memory-Access (NUMA) platforms. The relevance of the NUMA architectural paradigm lies in that systems continuously increase their number of processors and the overall size of RAM storage. Hence it is increasingly difficult to build large platforms with uniform memory access latency. Nowadays, medium-end parallel machines equipped with non-minimal amounts of CPU-cores and/or RAM are de-facto configured to have different RAM zones *close* to specific CPU-cores, hence providing low latency and high throughput of memory access, while other zones are *far* from these same CPU-cores and induce higher latency and a reduced memory access throughput. This de-facto standard configuration has led system-software developers to recently include facilities for optimizing memory management in NUMA contexts, such as for the case of Linux, which starting from version 2.6.18 supports NUMA specific services that are exposed to the application-level software via system calls.

We exploit such services offered by Linux, and reflect them into a NUMA-aware memory management architecture operating at the level of the Time Warp platform, particularly in the context of multi-threaded Time Warp systems. Specifically, we provide an architectural organization where any information record logically bound to a specific simulation object (such as its event records, keeping either already processed or unprocessed events, and its state recoverability data, as well as its live state) is guaranteed to be kept on private memory pages. Hence, the simulation objects (including their event buffers) are actually allocated on disjoint sets of memory pages. Also, the memory pages associated with data for an individual simulation object are guaranteed to be located on the NUMA node where the worker thread currently in charge of running the simulation object resides. This leads the worker thread to benefit from minimum RAM-access latency and maximal throughput when performing read operations (e.g. while scanning data associated with the simulation object).

The association of the simulation object's private pages with the correct NUMA node is operated in our architecture according to both static and dynamic policies. The latter approach is actuated according to an non-intrusive daemon-based solution, where a thread (similar in spirit to the Linux `kswapd`) is in charge of periodically checking whether a migration from a source to a destination NUMA node is requested for the memory pages of any simulation object, and in the positive case executes the migration non-intrusively. Hence, our proposal guarantees NUMA-efficient memory access even in contexts where a specific simulation object is migrated from one worker thread to another one (possibly operating on a CPU-core close to a different NUMA node), such as for the case of load-sharing with dynamic migration of the objects within a multi-thread Time Warp platform [36] or when the number of worker threads is dynamically changed with consequent re-distribution of the simulation objects across the still active worker threads [38]. Further, our proposal entails optimized NUMA management also in relation to the memory buffers used for exchanging events across the concurrent simulation objects.

We finally stress that our proposal is fully application-transparent, hence allowing the application-level programmer to still rely on classical (dynamic) memory management services, such as the `malloc` library, for memory allocation/deallocation within the simulation model. Also, the presented NUMA-oriented architecture has been made freely available by having it been integrated within the open source ROOT-Sim (ROme OpTimistic Simulator) package [24][1]. Experimental data for an assessment of our proposal are also presented in this article.

The remainder of the article is structured as follows. In Section 2 we discuss related work. The NUMA-oriented memory management architecture is presented in Section 3, together with the support for dynamic migration of the memory pages destined to an individual simulation object across different NUMA nodes. Experimental data are provided in Section 4.

2. RELATED WORK

Optimized approaches and architectures supporting state recoverability in optimistic PDES systems [25, 27, 28, 29, 31, 40] can be also considered as general solutions aimed at reducing the memory demand by the optimistic simulation environment, thanks to the infrequent and/or incremental nature of the employed checkpointing techniques. Such a reduction, which can lead to improving the memory locality and the cache/RAM hierarchy efficiency, can be considered as a reflection of the whole optimization process leading to well-suited tradeoffs between log and restore overheads. However, these literature solutions do not directly tackle the issue of memory-access efficiency in NUMA platforms. In fact, they do not integrate policies for controlling the delivering of memory buffers for logging state recoverability data so as to make memory accesses NUMA optimized, which is instead the target of this article. Overall, our proposal is fully complementary to (and can be integrated with) any of the above mentioned solutions. The same is true when considering the alternative recoverability method based on reverse computation (rather than checkpointing) [9].

As hinted, the memory demand by optimistic platforms does not only involve log operations, but the need for temporary maintaining event buffers that are not yet detected as already committed (since Global Virtual Time—GVT—is

---

[1]Please refer to `https://github.com/HPDCS/ROOT-Sim` for the actual free software package.

typically re-evaluated periodically), and the need for supporting speculative scheduling of future events. The latter aspect may entail high frequency of buffer allocation requests just due to the fact that purely optimistic approaches can allow the simulation objects to run far ahead of the currently committed horizon in case of the absence of blocking or throttling strategies. As for memory requirements related to the already committed portion of the computation, some advanced fossil collection mechanisms have been proposed [10] that, by means of dissemination of information about causality relations among events, are aimed at the identification of the fossils (hence of memory to be recovered) in a complementary manner compared to the classical ones based on GVT computation. Still, these approaches do not provide NUMA optimized memory management approaches, rather general solutions for prompt release (thus re-usage) of memory buffers as a general approach for reducing memory demand and increasing locality.

The effects of the cache/RAM hierarchy and of the underlying virtual memory system on the performance of specific tasks (such as state saving) and/or of the overall simulation run have also been (empirically) studied by several works [2, 3, 8, 14], some of which deal with the context of NUMA platforms. Outcomes by these studies show how both caching and virtual memory may have a relevant impact on performance, thus posing the need for optimizing platform level configuration and/or design in order to limit the performance degradation phenomenon. This is exactly what we do with our memory management proposal oriented to NUMA platforms.

Interesting proposals aimed at the integration of advanced memory management schemes specifically tailored to optimistic PDES platforms can be found in [13, 19, 21, 26]. Here the authors propose techniques, such as cancelback, pruneback or artificial rollback, which are aimed at achieving efficient executions of the optimistic paradigm when considering limited available memory. This is achieved by, e.g., artificially squashing portions of speculated computation in order to avoid maintaining the related information (such as the buffers for speculatively scheduled events) when memory demand becomes critical (e.g. when page-swapping phenomena in the virtual memory system would tent to appear). With this type of integrations, the optimistic approach has been shown to be able to complete the run at reasonable performance by using an amount of memory similar (or slightly larger than) the one requested by a sequential, non-speculative run of the same simulation application. Further, the performance tradeoffs associated with these schemes have been thoroughly investigated both analytically and empirically (see, e.g., [12]). Again, these solutions are complementary to the one we provide since none of them is specifically oriented to optimizing the efficiency of the cache/RAM hierarchy in NUMA systems.

Different approaches, still tailored to the tradeoff between memory management and performance, relate to the reduction of the number of memory copies for supporting event exchanges within the optimistic platform. Particularly, the proposal in [32] provides a so called zero-copy message passing approach, suited for both conservative and optimistic simulation, which allows reducing the whole memory demand due to message buffering on shared memory architectures, thanks to the reduction of the amount of virtual memory buffers used for keeping the messages. However, this approach is not directly oriented to improving the efficiency of memory accesses in NUMA platforms.

The work in [15] faces the cache hierarchy misuse in optimistic simulators by pointing out the relevance of buffer delivery mechanisms that are cache-friendly in shared memory contexts. The work exclusively accounts for buffers reserved for exchanged messages. It presents a new approach that partitions the memory destined to messages so that the pages are accessed only by the two processes that participate in the communication, providing a reduction of the cache-coherence overhead and the cache invalidation. Our proposal intrinsically offers the same advantage, but additionally copes with memory access efficiency to live states of the simulation objects and recoverability data, also in contexts where the simulation objects can be dynamically migrated across worker threads operating in different NUMA nodes.

The work in [34] presents a partitioning of the data structures typically employed in optimistic PDES systems in order to determine the so called access-intensive vs access-mild portions, the latter being the portions of data that unlikely will be accessed in the future. Access-mild data are mapped onto virtual addresses that collide on the same cache portion, so as to avoid that write operations when generating these data will erase access-intensive data from the cache. This approach does not aim at improving data movement in the cache/RAM hierarchy, e.g., in NUMA machines, rather it is aimed at increasing cache hits.

Finally, the work in [39] presents a performance study of multi-thread optimistic PDES systems (particularly a multi-thread variant of ROSS [7]) where various optimizations are considered, one of which is related to memory management in NUMA machines. Specifically, this work studies the effects of (re-)using memory buffers belonging to the destination memory pool when exchanging events across the simulation objects, so as to increase the likelihood that the buffer is actually located on the NUMA node where the thread running the destination simulation object resides. This solution does not directly cope with empty-zero memory, thus the buffer is guaranteed to be hosted on the correct NUMA node only in case it resides on non-empty-zero memory previously touched by the destination thread. This is due to the fact that the actual memory allocation policy is intrinsically based on default local-policies adopted by NUMA-oriented operating system kernels. We overcome this problem in our approach; further, we optimize NUMA access by explicitly considering the mapping of both the live state of the simulation object and its recoverability data, and by also offering support for dynamic migration of the object (and of all its associated data) across threads running on different NUMA nodes, aspects that are not considered by the proposal in [39].

3. THE MEMORY MANAGEMENT ARCHITECTURE

3.1 Architectural Context

We target optimistic PDES systems based on the multi-thread paradigm (rather than multi-process ones), which have been recently shown to be highly suited for shared memory platforms thanks to the possibility of optimizing aspects such as data exchange and balanced usage of the

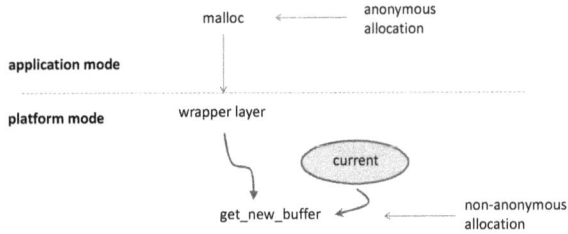

Figure 1: The dual-mode execution model.

computing power [36, 37] in application transparent manner. Also, we consider a convenient execution model where a simulation object, which we denote as $SOBJ_i$, is temporarily bound to a specific worker thread WT_j along a given wall-clock-time window. Hence the simulation objects can be periodically migrated across the worker threads, e.g., for load-sharing purposes.

On the basis of recent results in the design and development of optimistic PDES platforms, such as [23], we assume that the PDES system runs according to a dual-mode scheme where we distinguish between *application* vs *platform* modes. When a worker thread dispatches some simulation object for execution, then the application mode is entered. When the dispatched application callback function returns control to the underlying PDES environment along the running thread we (re)enter platform mode. With no loss of generality we assume that any worker thread WT_j has a notion of *current* simulation object, indicating the identity of the simulation object that has been dispatched for application execution along the thread.

Still in compliance with recent results in the area of multi-thread optimistic PDES platforms, we consider the scenario where the live state of a simulation object, its recoverability data, and its input and output queues are manipulated by a single worker thread at a time, namely the worker thread to which the object is currently bound. As a result, any event record (or anti-event record) exchanged across different simulation objects is never directly inserted into the destination queue. Rather, it is posted on a bottom-half queue, and later extracted and manipulated by the correct thread, namely the one in charge of running the destination simulation object. Also, we consider a software architecture where memory allocation/deallocation services by the application code are not directly issued towards the standard malloc library. Instead, they are transparently intercepted by the underlying PDES environment and redirected to proper allocators. As shown in [25], this can be achieved by simple compile/link time directives, where dynamic memory APIs, as well as third party libraries linked to the application code, can be wrapped so as to bounce control back to the underlying environment upon any call to these API functions.

According to the above premise, we target the scenario depicted in Figure 1 where:

- whenever the application code calls a standard-library memory management API (such the malloc service), the underlying environment can detect which is the invoking simulation object;

- the platform layer can perform non-anonymous memory allocation/deallocation operations where the platform internal API for these operations is aware of which

simulation object is associated with the operation. Particularly, the function get_new_buffer(int sobj_id, size_t size) can be invoked so that buffer allocation will be executed selectively, on the basis of the identity of the simulation object for which data need to be stored. A malloc call by the application, ultimately intercepted by the platform layer, is served via a non-anonymous allocation operation in a transparent way to the application. Also, a platform level allocation, e.g. of some event buffer destined to keep data for a specific simulation object, is also executed non-anonymously.

3.2 Memory Allocator

As pointed out before, we operate in a context where the platform layer allocates memory (either for platform usage or for application usage) by relying on some allocation service get_new_buffer that is non-anonymous. The actual implementation of this service can be disparate. For convenience we resort on the open-source DyMeLoR allocator [33] for actual allocation of memory destined to the application, which is based on pre-allocation of large memory segments (originally via the actual malloc library), which are then logically partitioned into chunks. This allocator, besides delivering memory for usage by the caller, has also facilities for keeping the memory map of non-anonymously allocated chunks for a specific simulation object (via compact bitmaps) and making it recoverable. Hence it is well suited for serving memory requests originally issued by the application code, which give rise to memory layouts of the simulation objects that need to be made recoverable at past logical time values. We also developed a variant of DyMeLoR where recoverability data structures are fully removed. This variant is used in our final architecture to serve memory allocations/deallocations for platform level usage (which do not need to be made recoverable). However, we note that the actual NUMA memory management architecture we are presenting can be integrated with other kinds of user-level allocators. In fact the NUMA manager acts as the final (back-end) memory allocation service for the adopted user-level allocator.

Essentially, our NUMA manager can pre-reserve memory segments to be delivered to the overlying (user-level) chunk allocator. This is done non-anonymously, in fact the NUMA manager exposes a segment allocation function void* allocate_segment(int sobj, size_t size), to be used for pre-reserving memory that will ultimately be used for managing chunks (hence data) associated with a specific simulation object. The overlying user-level allocator can install whatever information onto the segments, such as meta-data for managing the free room within the same segment (just like the malloc library does after pre-reserving memory from the operating system).

Pre-reserving is supported via the POSIX mmap system-call, which allows for validating in the process memory map a set of contiguous virtual pages, whose global size complies with the size of the segment allocation request. The NUMA allocator keeps, for each simulation object, a meta-data record mem_map which records the following fields:

```
void*   base;
size_t size;
int     active;
```

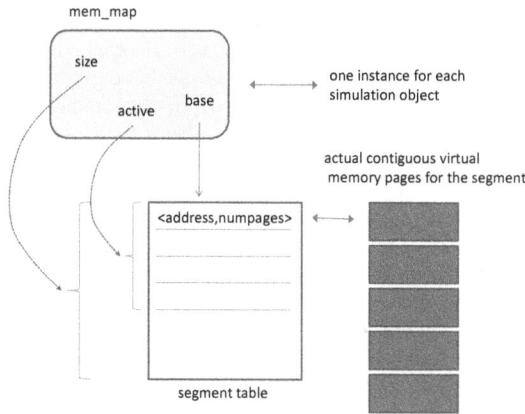

Figure 2: `mem_map` data structures.

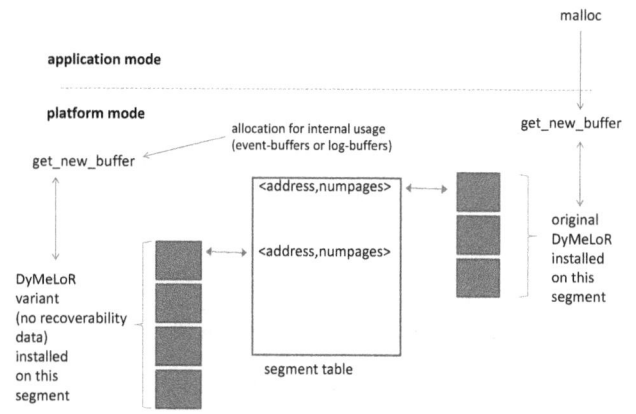

Figure 3: Memory allocation for platform and application usage.

where **base** is a pointer to a non-anonymous segment table, **size** indicates how many entries are currently present in the table, and **active** indicates how many of these entries are currently valid. The scheme is shown in Figure 2. Each time a new segment allocation is requested, the first free entry in the segment table associated with a specific simulation object is reserved, and after the **mmap** service is called the entry is used to keep the tuple $\langle address, numpages \rangle$ indicating the actual address of the sequence of pages that have been validated by the underlying operating system, and the total number of these pages. In case the segment table gets exhausted it is simply reallocated (again via **mmap**) with doubled size. On the other hand, in case a segment previously allocated is released, then the busy entries in the segment table are re-compacted at the top of the table by copying the last valid entry into the one of the released segment. This allows for $O(1)$ time complexity for segment allocation/deallocation (except for the cases where the table needs to be resized).

Overall, as shown in Figure 3, anytime some worker thread needs to allocate a buffer for platform level usage, which is destined to keep input or output events of a specific simulation object, or which is needed to record recoverability data for the simulation object state (namely a checkpoint), the **get_new_buffer** interface of the DyMeLoR user-level allocator (particularly the variant not keeping allocation/deallocation recoverability data) is called, and an actual buffer is delivered by this allocator which will necessarily reside on a non-anonymous segment pre-reserved by DyMeLoR. The same happens when the platform level software issues a call to the **get_new_buffer** service after having intercepted a **malloc** call issued from the application, particularly from the current simulation object dispatched along the worker thread (with the only difference that the instance of DyMeLoR is this time the one keeping allocation/deallocation recoverability data). Hence also the chunks belonging to the live state of the simulation object will be actually located on a non-anonymous memory segment.

By the above architectural organization, the NUMA memory manager guarantees that the set of virtual memory pages destined to keep event buffers, live state and recoverability data for any individual simulation object is actually disjoint from the set of virtual memory pages used for storing data associated with other simulation objects hosted by the multi-thread PDES system.

Let us now discuss the aspect of how these virtual memory pages are allocated on the different NUMA nodes. As well known, once a memory segment is allocated by the NUMA manager via the **mmap** system-call, its pages do not actually exist in physical memory (they are referred to as empty-zero) and will be allocated only upon a real access by the software (these are the so called minor-faults in operating system terminology). Modern operating system kernels, such as Linux 2.6.18 (or later versions) expose system-calls driving the actual allocation of pages onto NUMA nodes, e.g., upon the occurrence of minor faults. Particularly, the **set_mempolicy** system-call allows to specify the rules according to which the allocation of virtual to physical memory needs to be carried out. In our design, this system-call is employed upon starting up the NUMA manager in order to post a strict binding policy so that empty-zero memory is materialized on the NUMA node associated with the CPU-core where the memory access is performed. This policy, together with the memory access rules we consider, such that the memory pages destined for keeping data (chunks) associated with a specific simulation object are only accessed by the worker thread to which the object is bound, leads the physical memory allocation to occur on the NUMA node associated with the CPU-core where the thread is running.

The above management rules well fit scenarios where the worker thread is statically bound to a specific CPU-core (such as when running with the **sched_setaffinity** service posted) and the simulation objects are statically bound to a specific worker thread. How to cope with dynamic scenarios where these constraints are not met will be discussed in Section 3.4.

3.3 Management of Data Exchange

Clearly, page-disjoint access by the worker threads to the chunks hosting data for the different simulation objects can be guaranteed for input/output event queues, for the live state of the object and for state recoverability data. However it cannot be guaranteed when we need to exchange events (or anti-events) across the different simulation object. In order to provide effective NUMA-oriented support for the exchange operation of events across different simulation objects, we provide a NUMA-oriented implementation of the scheme originally described in [37], based on the bottom-half paradigm.

In particular, when a worker thread needs to post a new event/antievent having with destination $SOBJ_k$, no direct access to the event queue of the target object is performed. In fact, in case the memory pages keeping the records of the event queue of $SOBJ_k$ were located on a different NUMA node, the access (for scanning records and correctly installing the new one) might be costly. Rather, the event is posted on an intermediate queue (the bottom-half queue of $SOBJ_k$) and the actual incorporation into the recipient event queue will be carried out by the worker thread in charge of running $SOBJ_k$ (which will access close memory while manipulating the queue). The NUMA-oriented optimization lies in that the bottom-half queue is guaranteed to be hosted by the NUMA node where the destination object (hence thread) operates.

More in detail, the `mem_map` data structure (recall that an individual instance of this data structure is associated with any simulation object) previously presented has been augmented with the additional fields:

```
void*  live_bh;
int    live_msgs;
int    live_boundary;
```

where `live_bh` points to a page aligned buffer that is used as the buffer for hosting the exchanged events, `live_msgs` is the counter of currently available messages into the bottom-half buffer, and `live_boundary` is the offset (into the buffer) where free room is available for additional events to be sent towards the destination ([2]). The pages forming the bottom-half buffer are allocated again via the `mmap` system-call, hence we guarantee that the different bottom-half queues are located on disjoint sets of memory pages for the different simulation objects. Overall, all the worker threads sending an event (or anti-event) towards a specific simulation object will deliver the information on specific memory pages reserved for the bottom-half queue of the destination. On the other hand, the bottom-half pages are materialized (namely they switch off the empty-zero state) upon their first access, which can take place by whichever worker thread (running on whichever NUMA node). Hence on the basis of the employed operating system memory policies, depicted in the previous section, the bottom-half queue pages will not necessarily reside on the NUMA node where the thread hosting the destination simulation object is running. The realignment (if requested) of these pages on the correct NUMA nodes will be dealt with in Section 3.4, where we cope with the mechanisms for (dynamically) migrating pages across the different NUMA nodes.

Overall, with our architecture we guarantee that the pages forming the bottom-half buffer associated with a specific simulation object will reside (or will be migrated to) the NUMA node where the worker thread, say WT_j, managing this object is running. Hence the read operations by WT_j for reading the messages and incorporating the content into the destination object event queues will occur from close memory. This will not penalize the event-send operations by the other threads (possibly operating in different NUMA nodes) given that the NUMA architecture is not adverse to

memory writes on remote NUMA nodes (thanks to the fact that writes occur into the cache) rather, they are adverse to reads (in case these are not served via cached data).

An additional optimization has been introduced in order not to hamper concurrency in the management of the bottom-half queue. In fact, given that multiple worker threads can concurrently send data towards the same destination simulation object, any insertion of an element in the bottom-half queue must occur in a critical section (protected by spin-locks in our implementation). The same would be true for the reads from the bottom half, in case the bottom-half buffer would be handled as a circular buffer. To avoid explicitly synchronizing read and write operations onto the bottom-half queue, we extended the bottom-half queue support by having two different bottom-half buffers. One is the live buffer (as illustrated above) which is managed via the aforementioned fields kept by the `mem_map` record. A second one is the *expired* buffer, which is a clone of the live one, in terms of implementation and data structures. The read operations occur from the expired buffer (and given that they are carried out by a single worker thread, namely the one managing the destination simulation object, they are not subject to concurrency problems), while the write operations occur into the live one. Each time a read operation is issued on an empty expired buffer, live and expired buffers are exchanged (so as to give rise to a new era of their usage), which occurs in a fast critical section, e.g., by switching the respective pointers to the actual buffers. In this way, we do not need to synchronize reads with writes (except for the start of a new era), rather only write operations need to occur in critical sections. Also, a dynamic resize mechanism is employed so that when a new era is started, and the occupancy in the bottom-half buffers exceeds a threshold percentage, then these buffers enlarged by reallocating them (still via `mmap`), which allows resizing the memory used for in transit messages across different worker threads depending on the frequency of messages arrival towards specific destinations.

3.4   The Page Migration Daemon

A core additional component complementing the above presented memory management architecture is the page migration daemon, which we refer to as `pagemigd`. This daemon, which runs as a set of CPU non-intrusive threads, is in charge of periodically moving the memory pages associated with the memory map of a specific simulation object to a target NUMA node. The work by this daemon is based on an additional data structure, which we name `map_move`, instantiated on a per-simulation object basis. This data structure has the following fields:

```
pthread_spinlock_t spinlock;
unsigned           target_node;
int                need_move;
```

where `need_move` indicates whether a request to migrate the whole memory map associated with a given simulation object has been posted, and (if posted) `target_node` indicates the target NUMA node for the move operation. The `spinlock` field is used to make the access to this data structure atomic, and to make atomic also the actual move of the memory map towards the target node (in case a move has been requested). The move request can be posted to the daemon via the function `void move_sobj(int sobj_id, unsigned target_node)`, which can be called by the worker

---

[2]The reason why we use the term *live* in the names of the data structures will be clarified later in this same section.

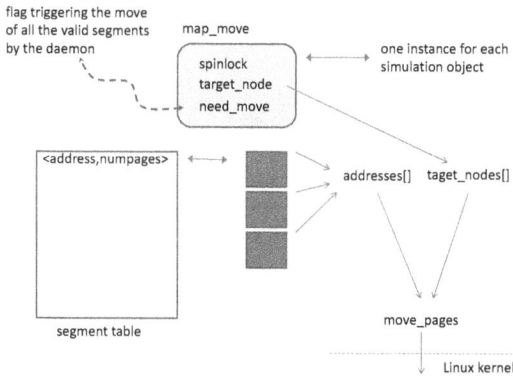

Figure 4: Segment migration operation.

threads operating with the PDES platform. In case a move request is found to be posted (i.e. the flag `need_move` is found to be raised), `pagemigd` accesses the `mem_map` data structure associated with the object to move, and migrates (one after another) all the currently active segments, namely the ones registered within the segment table of that simulation object. As already pointed out, a valid entry provides the initial address of the segment of contiguous pages to be moved, and the number of these pages. Hence, being the page size fixed on the target architecture and operating system (say 4KB), the address of any page belonging to a given segment is also known (in fact it is determined on the basis of a simple offset rule from the segment start address).

The actual move of the pages belonging to an individual segment is carried out by invoking the `move_pages` system call which is supported in Linux starting from kernel 2.6.18. Among other parameters, this system call takes as input two arrays, one is the array of virtual addresses of pages to be moved, the second one is the array telling to which NUMA nodes the pages need to be moved. Hence, the actual activities for moving the segment towards the target NUMA node are the ones schematized in Figure 4.

We underline that the support for the `move_pages` system-call in the Linux kernel logically treats the move of an individual page from a NUMA node to another one as a couple of swap-out/swap-in operations (but with no mandatory inter-action with stable storage). Particularly, the page logically disappears from memory (namely from the origin node) and is then faulted-in towards the target node. In case some worker thread issues a memory access to a page that is currently being moved, then the access is treated similarly to a minor fault, hence at low cost. On the other hand, in case the access occurs after the page move has already been finalized, then no fault occurs along the execution of the worker thread. Also, empty-zero pages are ignored by the kernel, hence using the above approach leads to pay no cost for virtual memory that is actually not yet allocated in RAM.

Other aspects deserving attention in the above organization is related to migrating the pages reserved for the bottom-half queues. Recall that these pages are not registered within the segment table associated with the simulation object, rather they are directly accessible via the meta data kept by the `mem_map` record. In particular, `pagemigd` always attempts to move these pages towards the last value registered in `target_node` for a specific simulation object, independently of whether the `need_move` flag is raised. This

is because, as pointed out before, these pages can be materialized as non-empty-zero on generic NUMA nodes, depending on which worker thread issued the first access to the bottom-half buffer (i.e. to any generic page of that buffer) while sending events/anti-events to the destination simulation object. Issuing the move request periodically via `pagemigd` allows the pages hosting the bottom-half queue to be promptly migrated towards the correct NUMA node (even if originally allocated on a different node). On the other hand, in case these pages are already located on the correct node, the `move_pages` system-call will simply return by ignoring the move operation, thus inducing minimal overhead for useless calls.

In our design, the operation of moving the pages hosting the bottom-half queues does not lock the `spinlock` in the `map_move` data structure, and is executed in full concurrency with the actual access to the bottom-half buffers by the worker threads. To allow safe access to the addresses of the pages forming these buffers, the `pagemigd` daemon does not use the `live_bh` and the `expired_bh` pointers in the `mem_map` data structure. In fact, these are switched (although infrequently, namely at the start of a new era for the bottom-half buffers usage) and would need to be accessed atomically for correct determination of the page address. To overcome this issue, as shown in Figure 5 these addresses are duplicated at startup and recorded in two stable pointers in the array `bh_addresses[]`. The only situations in which these pointers are changed is when dynamic resize of the bottom-half buffers is carried out (as hinted, this occurs when a threshold occupancy is reached). The resize implies that the buffers are reallocated via `mmap` so that the `bh_addresses[]` are updated. Given that the `pagemigd` daemon uses the pointers stored in `bh_addresses[]` to issue the page move request to the kernel for migrating the pages forming the bottom-half buffers towards the target NUMA node, a fast critical section (implemented via CAS instructions) is used in order to lock the content of `bh_addresses[]` so that any resize operation leads to temporary block the page move action up to the finalization of the `bh_addresses[]` content.

Overall, the `spinlock` in the `map_move` data structure is only used for (i) avoiding races when posting new move requests towards `pagemigd`, (ii) avoiding that the segment table is changed while a move is in progress. In fact, each time the upper level allocator, say DyMeLoR, pre-allocates memory (or releases) memory segments, this operation blocks the `spinlock` associated with the memory map so as to prevent the `pagemigd` daemon to scan the segment table while it is being modified.

Summarizing, the presence of `pagemigd` allows the whole NUMA-oriented architecture to:

- dynamically rebind the pages keeping the data (event buffers, live state, and recoverability information) of any simulation object to the NUMA node that is closest to the CPU-core where the worker thread managing the simulation object runs, which is useful both when the migration of an object from a worker thread to another one is performed (e.g. for load-sharing purposes [36]) and when the worker threads are switched across CPU-cores operating in different NUMA nodes;

- dynamically move the pages used for data exchange towards the NUMA node where the destination simulation object of the data is hosted (given that the

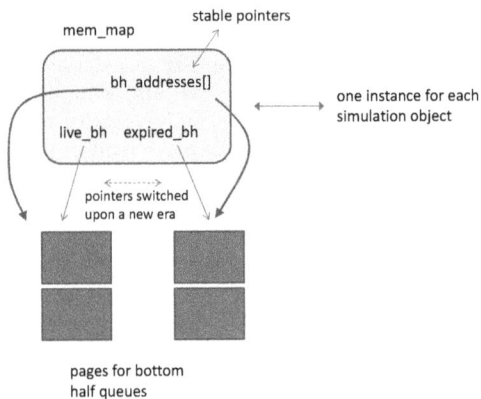

Figure 5: Data structures for bottom-half queues maintenance and migration.

worker thread managing it runs on a CPU-core close to that NUMA node).

As a final aspect, our `pagemoved` is not forced to be executed as a single non-CPU intrusive thread. Rather the number of threads `Num_pagemoved` forming the daemon (as well as their wake-up period) can be selected at startup of the NUMA memory management architecture. Each of these threads is in charge of checking the request for migration, and of actually migrating, a subset of the simulation objects (selected according to a balanced hashing scheme based on thread identifiers). The reason for this kind of load-sharing across multiple page-migration threads is twofold. First, if a move request is standing, it will more likely be observed promptly after the thread wake-up from the sleep period. Second, avoiding to perform the whole migration work along a single thread leads to avoiding the `pagemigd` daemon (although being CPU non-intensive) to interfere in a highly unbalanced manner with the worker threads operating in the PDES environment, rather, upon their periodic wake-up, all the `pagemigd` threads will lead to (more) proportionally slow down the worker threads, which allows not to increase the skew in the advancement of the simulation objects along the logical time axis [39]. Consequently, this approach likely not favors the generation of additional rollbacks due to the `pagemigd` daemon interfering work-load.

4. EXPERIMENTAL STUDY

As hinted, we have integrated all our solutions into the ROme OpTimistic Simulator (ROOT-Sim) [24, 22, 17], an optimistic simulation platform based on the Time Warp protocol [18] and tailored for UNIX-like systems. ROOT-Sim is designed to be a general-purpose platform, that can support any kind of discrete event model developed by adhering to a very simple and intuitive programming model (in fact, the platform transparently handles all the mechanisms associated with parallelization and synchronization). Particularly, the programmer is only requested to code the logic implementing the callback entry points to the application code, whose execution is triggered by the underlying ROOT-Sim platform along any worker thread right upon CPU-dispatching the execution of some event targeting a specific object, or when inspecting some newly committed state of the simulation object. Also the programmer can use a very simple API offered by ROOT-Sim for injecting new events in the system, destined to whichever simulation object.

The hardware architecture used for running the experiments is a 64-bit NUMA machine, namely an HP ProLiant server, equipped with four 2GHz AMD Opteron 6128 processors and 64 GB of RAM. Each processor has 8 cores (for a total of 32 cores) that share a 12MB L3 cache (6 MB per each 4-cores set), and each core has a 512KB private L2 cache. The operating system is 64-bit Debian 6, with Linux Kernel version 2.6.32.5. The compiling and linking tools used are `gcc` 4.3.4 and binutils (`as` and `ld`) 2.20.0. Also, the architecture entails 8 different NUMA nodes, each one close (distance 10) to 4 CPU-cores and far (distance 20) from all the others.

As a test-bed application, we have used *traffic*. This application simulates a complex highway system (at a single car granularity), where the topology is a generic graph, in which nodes represent cities or junctions and edges represent the actual highways. Every node is described in terms of car inter-arrival time and car leaving probability, while edges are described in terms of their length. At startup phase, the simulation model is asked to distribute the highway's topology on a given number of simulation objects. Every object therefore handles the simulation of a node or a portion of a segment, the length of which depends on the total highway's length and the number of available simulation objects.

Cars enter the system according to an Erlang probability distribution, with a mean inter-arrival time specified (for each node) in the topology configuration file. They can join the highway starting from cities/junctions only, and are later directed towards highway segments with a uniform probability. In case a car, after having traversed part of the highway, enters a new junction, according to a certain probability (again specified in the configuration file) it decides whether to leave the highway. Whenever a car is received from any simulation object, it is enqueued into a list of traversing cars, and its speed (for the particular object it is entering in) is determined according to a Gaussian probability distribution, the mean and the variance of which are specified at startup time. Then, the model computes the time the car will need to traverse the node, adding traffic slowdowns which are again computed according to a Gaussian distribution. In particular, the probability of finding a traffic jam is a function of the number of cars which are currently passing through the node. A `LEAVE` event is scheduled towards the same simulation object at the computed time. Additionally, when a car is enqueued, the whole list of records associated with cars is scanned, in order to update their position in the queue, which reflects updates on the relative positions of the cars along the path they are traversing. Note that this does not involve time stepped execution of the simulation model.

Accidents are derived according to a probability function as well. In particular, they are more likely to occur when the amount of cars traversing the highway portion modeled by a simulation object is about half of the cars which can be hosted altogether. In fact, if few cars are in, accidents are less frequent. Similarly, if there are many, the traffic factor produces a speed slowdown, thus reducing the likelihood of an accident to occur. Therefore, the model discretizes a Normal distribution, computing the Cumulative Density Function in a contour defined as *cars in the node* $\pm \frac{1}{2}$, having as the mean half of the total number of cars which are at the current moment in the system, and as the variance a factor which can be specified at startup. The total number of cars which can be hosted by a simulation object is computed according to the actual length of the simulated road, which is determined when the model is initialized. When an accident occurs, the cars are not allowed to leave the path portion modeled by the corresponding simulation object, until the road is freed. In fact, if a LEAVE event is received, but its execution is associated with a car involved in an accident, the record associated with the car is not removed from the queue. Rather, its leave time is updated according to the accident's durations, and a new LEAVE event is scheduled. The duration of an accident phase is determined according to a Gaussian distribution, the mean and the variance of which are again specified at startup.

During the scan of the queue entries, with a certain small probability (specified at startup), a car decides to stop for a certain amount of time (e.g. for fuel recharge). This is reflected by setting a special flag in the record, and a duration for the stop is drawn from a Gaussian distribution. In this case, if a LEAVE event is received associated with a stopped car, the behavior of the model is the same as in the case of an accident. During a queue scan, if a stopped car expires its stop time, the relevant flag is reset, so that the next LEAVE event will allow it to exit from the path portion modeled by the current simulation object.

In our execution, we have simulated the whole Italian highway network. We have discarded the highways segments in the islands in order to simulate an undirected connected graph, which allows to have the actual workload migrating overall the highway. The topology has been derived from [4], and the traffic parameters have been tuned according to the measurements provided in [5]. The average speed has been set to 110 Km/h, with a variance of 20 Km/h, and accident durations have been set to 1 hour, with 30 minutes variance. This model has provided results which are statistically close to the real measurements provided in [1]. Overall, the used application is a real world one, that we have produced in cooperation with colleagues from Logistic Engineering such in a way to provide support to decision making processes (such as scheduling of delivery services across the country). We consider this application benchmark to be significant for showing how our proposed NUMA memory management architecture is able to capture the differentiated memory access patterns, and react via proper migration of memory pages towards the most access-intensive NUMA nodes.

For this benchmark application, we report performance data when running according to differentiated modes. In one mode, the Italian highway has been modeled via 137 simulation objects (individually handling up to 130 Km) in a configuration fairly balanced and stable in terms of workload by the different simulation objects, which is achieved by having the traffic parameters set to simulate scenarios where jams due to, e.g., accidents are very infrequent. This configuration does not require dynamic re-mapping of the simulation objects across the 32 worker threads operating within the ROOT-Sim platform in order to achieve competitive parallel executions[3]. For this balanced case, we compare

[3]In all the experiments, the worker threads are run with CPU-affinity setup, which is the classical approach for avoiding cross CPU-core migration of highly CPU intensive applications, which may induce overhead. As a reflection, any worker thread constantly operates on a specific NUMA node.

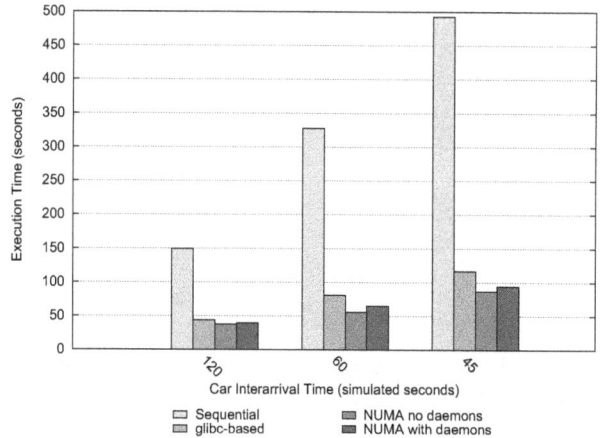

Figure 6: Balanced configuration: total execution time.

the execution time achieved with (i) a traditional sequential execution (carried out on top of a properly-optimized scheduler based on a Calendar-Queue [6]), (ii) a parallel execution relying on memory management based on the standard glibc library, and (iii) a parallel execution relying on our NUMA memory management architecture. The sequential execution is a baseline one, which allows us to verify the level of speedup achievable via parallel runs. On the other hand, the glibc-based parallel run is a reference one allowing us to assess the effectiveness of the ad-hoc NUMA-oriented memory management support for Time Warp (when compared with standard memory allocation and management facilities).

In Figure 6, we provide the execution times for such balanced configuration of the *traffic* application, while varying the car inter-arrival time. Specifically, we have set all the source nodes (namely, all the junctions) in the highway topology to have a inter-arrival time set to 120 (less loaded), to 60, and to 45 (more loaded), respectively. Also, for the NUMA-oriented memory management architecture, we have considered two different settings. In one we do not activate pagemoved daemons. In the other one we set the number of pagemoved daemons to 32 (one per each CPU-core), and we set an aggressive activation period for them of one second. This produces a high interference with the actual simulation work carried out by the worker threads, and furthermore it provides no actual benefit, as the number of page migrations required is extremely low, due to the balanced nature of the workload. Overall, we consider a kind of worst case configuration for the parallel runs given the relatively reduced workload (in terms of cars to be managed per virtual time unit), which tends not to favor speedup by parallel executions, and also leads to reduced efficiency in optimistic synchronization, given the fine granularity of the events. The worst case profile for NUMA is further related to interference by the pagemigd daemons (in case they are activated).

By the results, we see that the parallel runs provide anyhow speedup vs the sequential execution, which increases while increasing the workload. On the other hand, the performance achieved by our NUMA-oriented memory manager is up to 27% better than the one of the glibc configuration in case no pagemigd daemons are activated, and up to 20% better in case these daemons are activated. This is a rele-

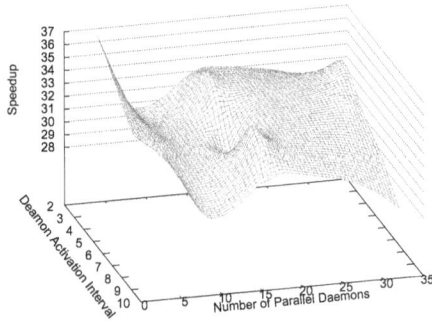

Figure 7: Unbalanced configuration: speedup of the NUMA memory manager vs sequential execution.

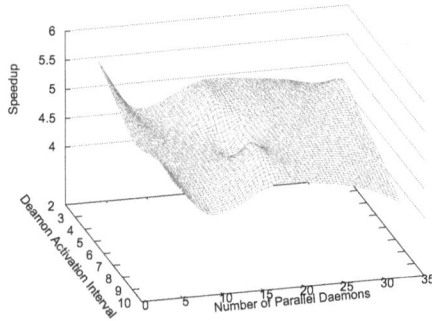

Figure 8: Unbalanced configuration: speedup of the NUMA memory manager with daemons vs with no-daemon.

vant achievement when considering that the maximum efficiency (namely, the percentage of work that is not eventually rolled back) which has been observed in the optimistic parallel runs is on the order of 65% (this is achieved when the car inter-arrival time is set to 45 simulated seconds, which gives rise to an increased simulation workload compared to the other configurations, with consequent increase of the average event granularity), which means that the ROOT-Sim Time Warp system is actually executing significant volumes of memory operations (allocation/deallocation and accesses) for either forward and rollback modes, which allows assessing the dynamics of our NUMA-oriented memory manager (vs glibc) according to a relatively wide spectrum of memory related activities. Also, the actual rollback pattern seems not to be significantly influenced by the interference caused by the pagemigd daemons, given that they lead to a reduction in performance (compared to the NUMA-oriented memory manager with no daemons) which is upper bounded by 10%.

In Figures 7-9 we report results related to a different configuration of the *traffic* application, where the volume of cars managed is greater (particularly, the car inter-arrival frequency is derived from [5]), and where we consequently get the possibility of accidents to occur according to the aforementioned statistical distribution. This gives rise to dynamic unbalance of the workload across the simulation objects, such that the dynamic re-balance of the actual workload on the computing platform is actuated by ROOT-Sim according to the simulation-object-to-worker-thread migration policy presented in [35]. Also, for this scenario we improve the level of granularity of the representation of the Italian highway by increasing the total number of simula-

tion objects to 1024 (hence each object simulates a shorter potion of the highway, which allows for a finer grain representation of the –relative– movement of vehicles). Therefore, this configuration allows us to assess whether the page migration facility embedded in our NUMA memory manager is able to promptly respond to variations of the workload and to the rebinding of the simulation objects towards the worker threads (hence to the variations of the memory access pattern by these threads). Additionally, in order to study how the pagemigd daemons' activation frequency and interference affects the overall execution, we have varied the number of parallel daemons in the interval [4, 32], and the activation frequency in the interval [2, 10] seconds.

By the results we see that the speedup achieved by the parallel run based our NUMA memory management architecture vs the sequential run (see Figure 7) is up to the order of 37 (this is achieved with a few pagemoved daemons, activated relatively frequently), and is at least on the order of 28/30 (for any other suboptimal configuration of the daemons, in terms of their number of instances and activation frequency). These higher speedup values, as compared to the balanced configuration of *traffic* are clearly due to the higher granularity of simulation events, which comes from the higher workload of cars that are simulated. As for the peak speedup configuration, we might expect it to appear in the actual observed point given that, as hinted before, accidents duration is set to the average value of 1 simulated hour, which leads to the scenario where each new imbalance persists for a limited amount of wall-clock-time. Hence frequent activation of even a few page move daemons represents a configuration that is able to promptly react to the re-balance phase and to promptly put in place a new RAM optimized placement of virtual memory pages. Also, running with pagemigd daemons allows the NUMA architecture to achieve up to 5.5 speedup compared to the case where the daemons are not activated (see Figure 8), which is clearly due to the fact that the migration of simulation objects for re-balance purposes is not fully complemented by the migration of the associated virtual pages towards the correct NUMA node in case of daemons' exclusion. Finally, the NUMA management architecture achieves up to 7x performance improvements compared to the case where the glibc library is used in combination with simulation object migrations across the worker threads as supported by ROOT-Sim (see Figure 9). In fact, the glibc memory manager exhibits a twofold performance loss vs the NUMA-oriented memory manager we have presented: (1) is does not ensure optimized NUMA access (even for balanced workload, as we already observed from data in Figure 6) – (2) it does not allow to move pages across NUMA nodes in order to follow the migration of simulation objects across the different worker threads (in their turn operating in the different NUMA zones). Both the aspects are dealt with by our NUMA memory management architecture, with relevant impact on performance improvements.

5. CONCLUSIONS

In this article we have presented a fully featured NUMA-oriented memory management architecture to be employed in Time Warp platforms running on top of multi-core machines. The architecture is based on NUMA specific allocation facilities that allow all the virtual pages destined to store application or platform level data bound to different

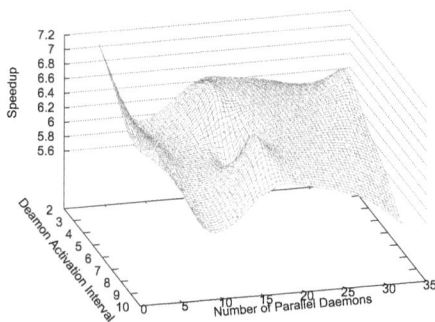

Figure 9: Unbalanced configuration: speedup of the NUMA memory manager with daemons vs glibc.

simulation objects (such as the object live state, its recoverability data and its events) to belong to disjoint sets of pages. Also, the pages associated with each simulation object are recorded onto proper memory maps that are also managed by daemons that support dynamic page migration towards the correct NUMA zone any time this might be requested for performance optimization purposes (such has when migrating the simulation objects across different worker threads for load balancing purposes). The NUMA memory management architecture has been released as free software and integrated in a reference open source Time Warp platform. Further, experimental data are reported in this article demonstrating its effectiveness for the case of a real word simulation application (particularly, a vehicular network simulation application) run in top of an off-the-shelf 32 CPU-core Linux machine equipped with 64 GB of RAM.

6. REFERENCES

[1] ACI. Dati e statistiche. *http://www.aci.it/?id=54* (last accessed: May 12, 2015).

[2] I. F. Akyildiz, L. Chen, S. R. Das, R. Fujimoto, and R. F. Serfozo. Performance analysis of "Time Warp" with limited memory. In *Proceedings of the International Conference on Measurement and Modeling of Computer Systems (SIGMETRICS), Newport, Rhode Island, USA, June 1-5, 1992*, pages 213–224, ACM Press, 1992.

[3] I. F. Akyildiz, L. Chen, S. R. Das, R. Fujimoto, and R. F. Serfozo. The effect of memory capacity on Time Warp performance. *Journal of Parallel and Distributed Computing*, 18(4):411–422, 1993.

[4] AUTOMAP. Atlante stradale italia. *http://www.automap.it/* (last accessed: May 12, 2015).

[5] Autostrade per L'Italia S.p.A. Reportistica sul traffico. *http://www.autostrade.it/it/la-nostra-rete/dati-traffico/reportistica-sul-traffico* (last accessed: May 12, 2015).

[6] R. Brown. Calendar queues: a fast O(1) priority queue implementation for the simulation event set problem. *Communications of the ACM*, 31(10):1220–1227, 1988.

[7] C. D. Carothers, D. W. Bauer, and S. Pearce. ROSS: A high-performance, low-memory, modular Time Warp system. *Journal of Parallel and Distributed Computing*, 62(11):1648–1669, 2002.

[8] C. D. Carothers, K. S. Perumalla, and R. Fujimoto. The effect of state-saving in optimistic simulation on a cache-coherent non-uniform memory access

architecture. In *Proceedings of the Winter Simulation Conference (WSC), Phoenix, AZ, USA, December 5-8, 1999*, pages 1624–1633, SCS, 1999.

[9] C. D. Carothers, K. S. Perumalla, and R. M. Fujimoto. Efficient optimistic parallel simulations using reverse computation. *ACM Transactions on Modeling and Computer Simulation*, 9(3):224–253, july 1999.

[10] M. Chetlur and P. A. Wilsey. Causality information and fossil collection in Time Warp simulations. In *Proceedings of the Winter Simulation Conference (WSC), Monterey, California, USA, December 3-6, 2006*, pages 987–994, SCS, 2006.

[11] S. R. Das and R. Fujimoto. An adaptive memory management protocol for Time Warp simulation. In *Proceesings of the Conference on Measurement and Modeling of Computer Systems (SIGMETRICS), Vanderbilt University, Nashville, Tennessee, USA, May 16-20*, pages 201–210, ACM Press, 1994.

[12] S. R. Das and R. M. Fujimoto. A performance study of the cancelback protocol for Time Warp. *ACM SIGSIM Simulation Digest*, 23(1):135–142, ACM Press, 1993.

[13] S. R. Das and R. M. Fujimoto. Adaptive memory management and optimism control in Time Warp. *ACM Transactions on Modeling and Computer Simulation*, 7(2):239–271, 1997.

[14] S. R. Das and R. M. Fujimoto. An empirical evaluation of performance-memory trade-offs in Time Warp. *IEEE Transactions on Parallel and Distributed Systems*, 8(2):210–224, 1997.

[15] R. M. Fujimoto and K. S. Panesar. Buffer management in shared-memory time warp systems. In *Proceedings of the Ninth Workshop on Parallel and Distributed Simulation (PADS), Lake Placid, New York, USA, June 14-16, 1995*, pages 149–156, IEEE Computer Society, 1995.

[16] S. Hirve, R. Palmieri, and B. Ravindran. Archie: a speculative replicated transactional system. In *Proceedings of the 15th International Middleware Conference, Bordeaux, France, December 8-12, 2014*, pages 265–276, ACM Press, 2014.

[17] HPDCS Research Group. ROOT-Sim: The ROme OpTimistic Simulator - v 1.0. *http://www.dis.uniroma1.it/~hpdcs/ROOT-Sim/* (last accessed: May 12, 2015).

[18] D. R. Jefferson. Virtual Time. *ACM Transactions on Programming Languages and System*, 7(3):404–425, July 1985.

[19] D. R. Jefferson. Virtual Time II: storage management in conservative and optimistic systems. In *Proceedings of the Ninth Annual ACM Symposium on Principles of Distributed Computing (PODC), Quebec City, Quebec, Canada, August 22-24*, pages 75–89. ACM Press, 1990.

[20] P. D. B. Jr., C. D. Carothers, D. R. Jefferson, and J. M. LaPre. Warp speed: executing Time Warp on 1,966,080 cores. In *Procesing of the ACM SIGSIM Conference on Principles of Advanced Discrete Simulation, (SIGSIM-PADS), Montreal, QC, Canada, May 19-22, 2013*, pages 327–336, ACM Press, 2013.

[21] Y.-B. Lin and B. R. Preiss. Optimal memory management for Time Warp parallel simulation. *ACM Transactions on Modeling and Computer Simulation*, 1(4):283–307, 1991.

[22] A. Pellegrini and F. Quaglia. The ROme OpTimistic Simulator: A tutorial (invited tutorial). In *Proceedings of the 1st Workshop on Parallel and Distributed Agent-Based Simulations (PADABS), Aachen, Germany, August 26-27*, LNCS, Springer-Verlag, pages 501–512, 2013.

[23] A. Pellegrini and F. Quaglia. Transparent multi-core speculative parallelization of DES models with event and cross-state dependencies. In *Proceedings of the ACM SIGSIM Conference on Principles of Advanced Discrete Simulation (SIGSIM-PADS), Denver, CO, USA, May 18-21*, pages 105–116. ACM Press, May 2014.

[24] A. Pellegrini, R. Vitali, and F. Quaglia. The ROme OpTimistic Simulator: Core internals and programming model. In *Proceedings of the 4th International ICST Conference on Simulation Tools and Techniques (SIMUTools), Barcelona, Spain, March 22-24*, pages 96–98, ICST, 2011.

[25] A. Pellegrini, R. Vitali, and F. Quaglia. Autonomic state management for optimistic simulation platforms. *IEEE Transactions on Parallel and Distributed Systems (preprint)*, May 2014, doi:10.1109/TPDS.2014.2323967.

[26] B. R. Preiss and W. M. Loucks. Memory management techniques for Time Warp on a distributed memory machine. In *Proceedings of the Ninth Workshop on Parallel and Distributed Simulation (PADS), Lake Placid, New York, USA, June 14-16*, pages 30–39, IEEE Computer Society, 1995.

[27] B. R. Preiss, W. M. Loucks, and D. MacIntyre. Effects of the checkpoint interval on time and space in Time Warp. *ACM Transactions on Modeling and Computer Simulation*, 4(3):223–253, July 1994.

[28] F. Quaglia. A cost model for selecting checkpoint positions in Time Warp parallel simulation. *IEEE Transactions on Parallel and Distributed Systems*, 12(4):346–362, 2001.

[29] F. Quaglia and A. Santoro. Non-blocking checkpointing for optimistic parallel simulation: Description and an implementation. *IEEE Transactions on Parallel and Distributed Systems*, 14(6):593–610, 2003.

[30] P. Romano, R. Palmieri, F. Quaglia, N. Carvalho, and L. Rodrigues. On speculative replication of transactional systems. *Journal of Computer and System Sciences*, 80(1):257–276, 2014.

[31] R. Rönngren, M. Liljenstam, R. Ayani, and J. Montagnat. Transparent incremental state saving in Time Warp parallel discrete event simulation. In *Proceedings of the 10th Workshop on Parallel and Distributed Simulation (PADS), Philadelphia, PA, USA, May 22-24*, pages 70–77. IEEE Computer Society, 1996.

[32] B. P. Swenson and G. F. Riley. A new approach to zero-copy message passing with reversible memory allocation in multi-core architectures. In *Proceedings of the 26th Workshop on Principles of Advanced and Distributed Simulation (PADS), Zhangjiajie, China, July 15-19, 2012*, IEEE Computer Society, pages 44–52, 2012.

[33] R. Toccaceli and F. Quaglia. DyMeLoR: Dynamic Memory Logger and Restorer library for optimistic simulation objects with generic memory layout. In *Proceedings of the Workshop on Principles of Advanced and Distributed Simulation (PADS), Roma, Italy, June 3-6, 2008*, pages 163–172. IEEE Computer Society, 2008.

[34] R. Vitali, A. Pellegrini, and G. Cerasuolo. Cache-aware memory manager for optimistic simulations. In *Proceedings of the International Conference on Simulation Tools and Techniques (SIMUTOOLS) Sirmione-Desenzano, Italy, March 19-23, 2012*, pages 129–138, ICST, 2012.

[35] R. Vitali, A. Pellegrini, and F. Quaglia. A load sharing architecture for optimistic simulations on multi-core machines. In *Proceedings of the 19th International Conference on High Performance Computing (HiPC), Pune, India, December 18-22, 2012*, pages 1–10. IEEE Computer Society, 2012.

[36] R. Vitali, A. Pellegrini, and F. Quaglia. Load sharing for optimistic parallel simulations on multi core machines. *SIGMETRICS Performance Evaluation Review*, 40(3):2–11, 2012.

[37] R. Vitali, A. Pellegrini, and F. Quaglia. Towards symmetric multi-threaded optimistic simulation kernels. In *Proceedings of the Workshop on Principles of Advanced and Distributed Simulation (PADS), Zhangjiajie, China, July 15-19, 2012*, pages 211–220, IEEE Computer Society, 2012.

[38] J. Wang, N. B. Abu-Ghazaleh, and D. Ponomarev. Interference resilient PDES on multi-core systems: towards proportional slowdown. In *Proceedings of the ACM SIGSIM Conference on Principles of Advanced Discrete Simulation, (SIGSIM-PADS), Montreal, QC, Canada, May 19-22, 2013*, pages 115–126, ACM Press, 2013.

[39] J. Wang, D. Jagtap, N. B. Abu-Ghazaleh, and D. Ponomarev. Parallel discrete event simulation for multi-core systems: Analysis and optimization. *IEEE Transactions on Parallel and Distributed Systems*, 25(6):1574–1584, 2014.

[40] D. West and K. Panesar. Automatic incremental state saving. In *Proceedings of the Workshop on Parallel and Distributed (PADS), Philadelphia, PA, USA, May 22-24, 1996*, pages 78–85, IEEE Computer Society, 1996.

Fidelity Evaluation based Time Dilation in Hybrid Network Emulation

Siming Lin, Zhouyi Zhou, Wenyang Deng, Liang Chang, Chao Wang, Liang Liang
Institute of Computing Technology
Chinese Academy of Sciences
Bejing, China 100080
{linsiming, yizhouzhou, dengwenyang, liangliang}@ict.ac.cn
{changliang, wangchao}@software.ict.ac.cn

ABSTRACT

Hybrid network emulation has emerged as a new way to exploit advantages of both network simulation and emulation. Hybrid network emulation often uses a technology called time dilation to combat performance limitation. In order to implement accurate time dilation, we define the concept of Emulation Fidelity. We calculate the time dilation factor by evaluating Emulation Fidelity. Fidelity evaluation based time dilation improves correctness of large-scale high-throughput network emulation with maximum efficiency.

Categories and Subject Descriptors

C.4 [**Computer Systems Organization**]: Performance of Systems – *modeling techniques*;

General Terms

Measurement, Performance, Experimentation

Keywords

Simulation; Emulation; Emulation Fidelity; Time Dilation; Virtualization

1. INTRODUCTION

Network researches should be evaluated during the stages of protocol design, system development and after-implementation maintenance. Discrete event simulator is an import tool to analyze network performance. Parallel distributed discrete event simulator is suitable for large-scale, heterogeneous network simulation. On the other hand, behavior realism of simulation is a difficult problem. Emulation testbeds using virtualization technologies can directly run actual implementation code. But they do not scale as well as simulators. Hybrid approach has emerged as a new way to exploit advantages of both simulation and emulation. Hybrid network emulation will encounter performance limitation in large-scale high-throughput scenery. We use a technology called time dilation to allow large-scale high-throughput emulation. Time dilation in the field of network emulation is defined as the real time scheduler schedule the network events at a slower rate than virtual time by a specific factor named time dilation factor (TDF). Lee [2] uses adaptive time dilation to combat hybrid network emulation overload.

SIGSIM-PADS'15, June 10–12, 2015, London, United Kingdom
ACM 978-1-4503-3583-6/15/06.
http://dx.doi.org/10.1145/2769458.2769486

The work in progress hybrid network emulation system consists of simulator NSMEE, revised qemu-kvm hypervisor and a TDF synchronizer as shown in Figure 1.

NSMEE is extended from NSME [3] with adaptive time control, We also adjust the virtual clock of revised qemu-kvm hypervisor according to current TDF.

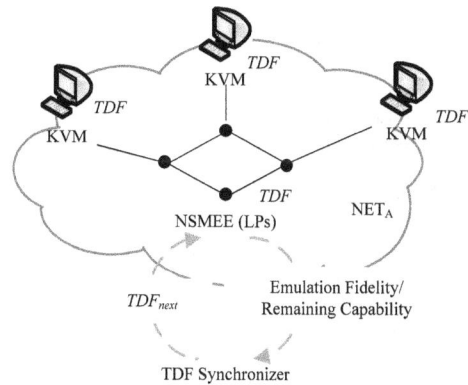

Figure 1: System architecture

In previous works on network emulation time control, external factors are used to calculate TDF. Grau [1] computes TDF by counting CPU cycles; Lee [2] computes TDF by retrieving CPU load. We think deducing TDF from external factors are inadequate: we can't enumerate all external affecting factors, and influence of each TDF affecting factor (CPU pressure, memory shortage, *etc.*) is hard to define.

Our work evaluates TDF in a more accurate way by introducing concept of Emulation Fidelity which directly reflects emulation pressure.

$$F(t_i, t_i + \tau) = \frac{V(E_{last(t_i, t_i + \tau)}) * TDF - V(E_{first(t_i, t_i + \tau)}) * TDF}{W(E_{last(t_i, t_i + \tau)}) - W(E_{first(t_i, t_i + \tau)})} \quad (1)$$

In equation 1, $F(t_i, t_i + \tau)$ is defined as Emulation Fidelity for sampling interval $(t_i, t_i + \tau)$. $E_{last}(t_i, t_i + \tau)$ is defined as last event being scheduled during $(t_i, t_i + \tau)$. $E_{first}(t_i, t_i + \tau)$ is defined as first event being scheduled during $(t_i, t_i + \tau)$. Function V is defined as event's virtual start time. Function W is defined as event's wall-clock start time. The ideal behind Emulation Fidelity is that, when network emulator encounters performance limitation, events' actual start time lagging will become more serious. Note Emulation Fidelity falls between 0 and 1 because event's projected start time never overruns event's actual start time.

When NSMEE has abundant processing capability, maintaining higher than enough TDF value losses processing efficiency. Thus we introduce concept of Remaining Capability.

$$R(t_l, t_l + \tau) = 1 - \frac{\sum\limits_{W(E) \in (t_l, t_l + \tau)} P(E)}{\tau} \quad (2)$$

In equation 2, Function P is defined as processing time of event. Remaining Capability is logical processes' idle percentage.

The TDF for next adjusting period: TDF_{next} is calculated by algorithm 1.

Algorithm 1 TDF estimation for next adjust period

$R_{min} = \min\limits_{l \in \text{logical processes}} \{R_l\} \quad F_{min} = \min\limits_{l \in \text{logical processes}} \{F_l\}$

if $R_{min} > 0$ **then**

$\quad TDF_{next} = \min(1, TDF \times (1 - R_{min}))$

else

$\quad TDF_{next} = TDF / F_{min}$

end if

We take minimal values of Emulation Fidelities and Remaining Capabilities to ensure all logic processes are not overloaded.

2. EVALUATION

To evaluate performance of our proposed system, we setup a experimental environment which consists of 6 Intel Xeon E5410 servers with 16GB main memory. One of the servers runs TDF synchronizer, while other 5 servers have NSMEE and revised qemu-kvm hypervisor run on them. We choose P2P live streaming system as our evaluation target. Our evaluation topology consists of 5 subnets where Peers register themselves to the Tracker and get the peer list and report their videos' information to Program Server. Program Server records the peers' information to database. Media Server holds the full content of all the videos and provides them to the Peers.

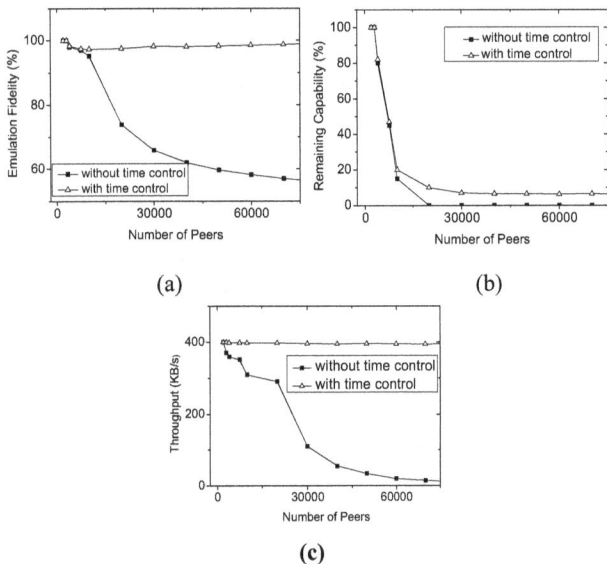

(a)　　　　　　(b)

(c)

Figure 2: Emulation with increasing number of Peers

Accompanying the growth of Peer number, the emulation system will suffer from performance overload. In Figure 2 (a) and Figure 2 (b), lines with rectangular points show the average Emulation Fidelity and average Remaining Capability of logical processes without time control. Both Emulation Fidelity and Remaining Capability drop as Peer number increases. When there are time control, the average Emulation Fidelity is stable as shown from lines with triangle in Figure 2 (a). Figure 2 (c) shows the maximum emulated Peer throughput with and without time control. Maximum emulated Peer throughput maintains its top limit (400KB/s) under our adaptive time control. Figure 3 below shows effects of adaptive time control with different values of sampling interval: τ and TDF adjusting interval: M (To avoid system tremors caused by frequent TDF adjusting, we estimate the TDF M sampling intervals ahead using linear regression and adjust TDF every M sampling intervals).

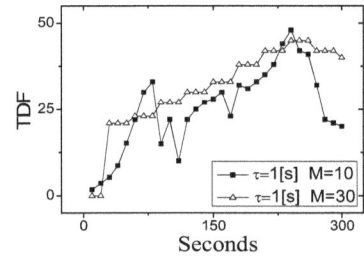

Figure 3: Evaluation of time control with 60000 Peers

We can see from Figure 3 that the TDF is more jittered when $M = 10$. Longer the TDF adjust period, more stable the TDF. But if M is too large, our adaptive time control system will be obtuse towards emulation overload. Similarly the choose of τ should balance between measure accuracy and system efficiency. From experiments, $\tau = 1[s]$ and $M = 30$ are good candidates to serve as system parameters.

3. ACKNOWLEDGMENTS

This work is supported by the National Natural Science Foundation of China (61202058).

4. REFERENCES

[1] Grau, A., Herrmann, K., and Rothermel, K. 2009. Efficient and scalable network emulation using adaptive virtual time. In *Proceedings of the 18th International Conference on Computer Communications and Network* (San Francisco, CA, USA, August 03-06, 2009).ICCCN'09. IEEE, 1-6.

[2] Lee, H. W., Thuente D., and Sichitiu, M. L. Integrated simulation and emulation using adaptive time dilation. In *Proceedings of the 2nd ACM SIGSIM/PADS Conference on Principles of Advanced Discrete Simulation* (Denver, CO, USA, May 18-21, 2014). SIGSIM-PADS'14. ACM, New York, NY, 167-178.

[3] Lin, S. M., Cheng, X. Q., and Lv, J. M. A visualized parallel network simulator for modeling large-scale distributed applications. In *Proceedings of the 8th International Conference on Parallel and Distributed Computing, Applications and Technologies*, (Adelaide, SA, Australia, December 03-06, 2007). PDCAT'07. IEEE, 339-346.

Analyzing Data Dependencies for Increased Parallelism in Discrete Event Simulation

Mirko Stoffers*, Torsten Sehy*, James Gross‡, Klaus Wehrle*
*Communication and Distributed Systems, RWTH Aachen University
‡School of Electrical Engineering, KTH Royal Institute of Technology
stoffers@comsys.rwth-aachen.de, torsten.sehy@rwth-aachen.de,
james.gross@ee.kth.se, wehrle@comsys.rwth-aachen.de

ABSTRACT

To parallelize simulations, independent events have to be identified, which can be executed concurrently. The highest level of parallelism is achieved if the number of events identified as independent is maximized. Traditionally, this identification is based on time and location of events, only allowing parallelization if events on the same simulation entity are executed in timestamp order. To increase the level of parallelism, we propose a novel approach investigating another criterion for independence: If two events on the same simulation entity do not access the same data items in a conflicting manner, they can as well be executed in parallel. To this end, we propose static analysis of the model code for data access. To ease this process we develop the simulation language PSimLa similar to C++ but modified where necessary to increase analyzability without removing essential C++ features. First evaluation results show the potential of this approach and increase the confidence that data-dependency analysis can improve future parallel simulation.

Categories and Subject Descriptors

I.6.2 [**Simulation and Modeling**]: Simulation Languages

General Terms

Languages, Performance, Algorithms

Keywords

Parallel simulation; Static code analysis; Data dependencies

1. INTRODUCTION

The demand for simulation of more complex systems in higher degree of detail drives the need for parallel execution of simulation software. The parallelization gain primarily depends on the number of events identified as independent, commonly evaluated on time and location of events using the local causality constraint, which is fulfilled "if and only if each Logical Process (LP) processes events in nondecreasing

SIGSIM-PADS'15, June 10–12, 2015, London, United Kingdom.
ACM 978-1-4503-3583-6/15/06.
http://dx.doi.org/10.1145/2769458.2769487.

timestamp order" [3, p. 32]. While this guarantees correct results [4], we argue that this is not a necessary condition. Two events can be independent even if their re-ordering violates the causality constraint, if they don't have data-dependencies. Today, there is only a single approach analyzing data-dependencies at compile time to increase parallel simulation performance [2]. However, this approach does not incorporate the challenging part of analyzing data access by pointers or references, hence it is restricted to a very small domain of models built without pointer or reference access. Hence, it is necessary to develop an approach applicable to Discrete Event Simulation (DES) models implemented in a structured language without removing essential features.

However, certain features of common general purpose languages like C++, especially pointers, do render data access tracking difficult to infeasible [1, 5]. Unfortunately, the huge set of Domain-Specific Languages (DSLs) for parallel simulation does not help solving this issue since neither of them is optimized for static analyzability. Instead, we propose a simulation language similar and compatible to C++, but aiming at increasing analyzability though not removing essential features without providing proper alternatives.

In this paper, we introduce the basic design of our language PSimLa, the current state of our proof-of-concept compiler implementation, and a first analysis approach. First evaluation results show that this approach is promising to speed up otherwise hard-to-parallelize simulation models.

2. THE PSimLa LANGUAGE

We design our DSL PSimLa for data-dependency based parallel simulation as a derivative of C++. To allow implementation of any DES model realizable in a general purpose language, PSimLa must be *Turing complete*. By *maximizing analyzability* the language design aids analyzing the code for data-dependencies. Under this constraint we *optimize execution performance* of the translated programs. To ease model development we *use well-established concepts* where possible and *maintain compatibility* to existing C++-code to enable step-by-step translation of preexisting models.

We base our language on C++ and the simulation elements of OMNeT++, and shape the compilation process in a way that PSimLa programs are first code-to-code translated into C++. During this step we also perform static analysis of PSimLa code for data-dependencies, which we then represent by additional C++ code. By compiling the output with a standard C++ compiler and running it with a modified version of OMNeT++, the provided dependency information can be used to gain additional speedup (see Sec. 3).

```
module MyMod {
  parameters:
    int myParam;
  gates:
    input myInputGate;
    output myOutputGate;
  private:
    int myInt;
    int myFn(int p1) { return p1+myParam; }
  protected:
    void initialize() { myInt=0; }
    void handleMessage(Message msg) {
      if(msg.getKind()==1) myInt=0;
      if(msg.getKind()==2) myInt=myFn(myInt);
      sendDelayed(msg,0,"myOutputGate");
    }
}
```

Figure 1: Example PSimLa Module.

For the language syntax, we adopt the building blocks and paradigms from OMNeT++. A *Module* can be defined similar to a class in C++. It is equivalent to a Simple Module in OMNeT++, hence developers need to implement an event handler and may provide an initialization and a teardown function. Additionally, PSimLa provides the standard syntax elements of C++ like primitive data types, classes, branches, and loops. However, the proof-of-concept implementation of our PSimLa compiler does not yet support every syntax element, but enough features are implemented to provide equivalent alternatives. For example, **for** loops can be replaced by **while** loops, changing neither semantics nor complexity. An example Module is depicted in Fig. 1.

The major difference between PSimLa and C++, however, is that PSimLa provides no pointer types, but only references. Under the hood, PSimLa translates references to C++11 smart pointers, enabling reference counting and deletion of objects at the end of their life cycles.

3. ANALYSIS TECHNIQUES

To investigate the analyzability of PSimLa we implemented a first analysis approach that aims at identifying data-dependencies between events. To this end, we assume that each data item can only be accessed by a single Module at a time. This is a common assumption in Parallel Discrete Event Simulation (PDES), e.g., when a simulation is decomposed into LPs where each LP can only access local data. However, while the local causality constraint [3] forces the events at each simulation entity to be executed in-order, our data-dependency information can help relaxing this constraint without changing simulation results. Hence, a Module can already process a future event even if another event with an earlier timestamp is executed later, finally eliminating too restrictive synchronization barriers.

Our static analysis works in five steps. 1. We identify and categorize events into different types. This allows us to store the derived dependencies on an event type basis, as the concrete event instances are not known at compile time. 2. We track, which data items are accessed by events of the different types. Since different events of the same type might access different data items and the Turing-completeness of PSimLa does not allow to reliably detect, for example, which branch the program flow will take at runtime, we chose to conservatively overestimate the data accesses. This means that two independent events might not be executed in par-

allel if we cannot guarantee this independence based on the information gathered. 3. We determine the scheduling relations, i.e., which other events an event handler will schedule at runtime. This is important to avoid conflicts with those events if another event is executed early. 4. We infer the event dependencies and store which event types depend on which other event types. To this end, we generate C++-code that allows determining the type of a given event instance and deriving its dependencies. 5. At runtime, we access this information to yield decisions whether the next event can be safely executed in parallel immediately, even if the local causality constraint could not guarantee correctness.

4. EVALUATION AND CONCLUSION

We performed first evaluations of the analysis approach. Synthetic benchmarks of simple events only performing read operations – which where previously not parallelizable due to causal violations – show almost linear speedup on a 12-core simulation platform, while the same model with write operations cannot be speeded up. This confirms that the approach correctly identifies event dependencies and independencies in these scenarios. A case study of a 57 node Wireless Mesh Network, which is speeded up by traditional parallel simulation only by a factor of 3 to 4, can as well gain close-to-linear speedup by our data-dependency analysis.

We conclude that data-dependency analysis is a promising technique for future improvements on parallel simulation. To this end, it does not suffice to account only for member variables of modules, but data items accessed by pointers or references have to be incorporated into the analysis to include a wide set of simulation models. To circumvent the infeasible problem of pointer analysis [1, 5], a language designed with analyzability in mind, like PSimLa, can aid the analysis without restricting the opportunities necessary for model development. Future efforts in enhancing the PSimLa compiler implementation and the analysis approach allow investigation of the feasibility of data-dependency analysis on a broad range of simulation models.

Acknowledgments

This work has been co-funded by the German Research Foundation (DFG) within the Collaborative Research Center (CRC) 1053 – MAKI.

5. REFERENCES

[1] D. Binkley. Source Code Analysis: A Road Map. In *Proc. of Future of Software Engineering*, (Minneapolis, MN, May 23–25, 2007) IEEE, Los Alamitos, CA, 104–119, 2007.

[2] W. Chen, X. Han, and R. Dömer. Out-of-Order Parallel Simulation for ESL Design. In *Proc. of the 2012 Conf. on Design, Automation & Test in Eur.*, (Dresden, Germany, March 12–16, 2012) IEEE, Los Alamitos, CA, 141–146, 2012.

[3] R. Fujimoto. Parallel Discrete Event Simulation. *Communications of the ACM*, 33(10):30–53, 1990.

[4] R. Fujimoto. Parallel and Distributed Simulation. In *Proc. of the 31st Winter Sim. Conf.*, (Phoenix, AZ, Dec. 5–8, 1999) ACM, New York, NY, 122–131, 1999.

[5] M. Hind. Pointer Analysis: Haven't We Solved This Problem Yet? In *Proc. of the 2001 ACM Workshop on Prog. Analysis for SW Tools and Eng.*, (Snowbird, UT, June 18–19, 2001) ACM, New York, NY, 54–61, 2001.

Experiments with Hardware-based Transactional Memory in Parallel Simulation

Joshua Hay
Intel Corporation
Portland, Oregon
hayjo813@gmail.com

Philip A. Wilsey
University of Cincinnati
Cincinnati, OH 45221-0030
wilseypa@gmail.com

ABSTRACT

Transactional memory is a concurrency control mechanism that dynamically determines when threads may safely execute critical sections of code. It provides the performance of fine-grained locking mechanisms with the simplicity of coarse-grained locking mechanisms. With hardware based transactions, the protection of shared data accesses and updates can be evaluated at runtime so that only true collisions to shared data force serialization. This paper explores the use of transactional memory as an alternative to conventional synchronization mechanisms for managing the pending event set in a Time Warp synchronized parallel simulator. In particular, we explore the application of Intel's hardware-based transactional memory (TSX) to manage shared access to the pending event set by the simulation threads. Comparison between conventional locking mechanisms and transactional memory access is performed to evaluate each within the WARPED Time Warp synchronized parallel simulation kernel. In this testing, evaluation of both forms of transactional memory found in the Intel Haswell processor, Hardware Lock Elision (HLE) and Restricted Transactional Memory (RTM), are evaluated. The results show that RTM generally outperforms conventional locking mechanisms and that HLE provides consistently better performance than conventional locking mechanisms, in some cases as much as 27%.

Categories and Subject Descriptors

D.1.3 [**Programming Techniques**]: Concurrent Programming—*parallel programming, distributed programming*
; I.6.8 [**Simulation and Modeling**]: Types of Simulation—*parallel, distributed, discrete event*

Keywords

Transactional memory, parallel simulation, optimistic synchronization, pending event set

SIGSIM-PADS'15, June 10 - 12, 2015, London, United Kingdom
ACM ISBN 978-1-4503-3536-6/15/06 ...$15.00.
DOI: http://dx.doi.org/10.1145/2769458.2769462 .

1. INTRODUCTION

Multi-core processors introduce an avenue for increased software performance and scalability through multi-threaded programming. However, this avenue comes with a toll: the need for synchronization between multiple threads of execution, especially during the execution of critical sections. By definition, a critical section is a segment of code accessing a shared resource that can only be executed by one thread at any given time [20]. For example, consider a multi-threaded application that is designed to operate on a shared two-dimensional array. For the sake of simplicity, the programmer uses coarse-grained locking mechanisms to control access to the critical section, *e.g.*, a single atomic lock for the entire structure. The critical section reads a single element, performs a calculation, and updates the element of the array. Once a thread enters the critical section, it locks all other threads out of the entire array until it has completed its task, thus forcing the collection of threads to essentially execute sequentially through the critical section even when they are accessing completely independent parts of the array. This results in lock contention, and consequently negatively impacts performance, as threads must now wait for the currently executing thread to relinquish access to the shared resource. Programmers can employ more fine-grained locking mechanisms to expose concurrency, such as locking individual rows or even individual elements in the previous example. However, this approach is vastly more complicated and error prone [18]; this approach requires the programmer to define and maintain a separate lock for each row or each element. Unfortunately, programmers are limited to using static information to decide when threads must execute a critical section regardless of whether coarse-grained or fine-grained locking is used.

Transactional memory (TM) is a concurrency control mechanism that attempts to eliminate the static sequential execution of a critical section by dynamically determining when accesses to shared resources can be executed concurrently [18]. In the above example, instead of using locks, the programmer identifies the critical section as a transactional region (hereafter, the terms *critical region* and *transaction* will be used interchangeably). As the threads enter the transactional region, they attempt to "atomically" execute the critical section. The TM system records memory accesses as the transactions execute and finds that the transactions operate on independent regions of the data structure, *i.e.*, there are no conflicting memory accesses. Instead of being forced to execute sequentially by the conventional locking mechanisms, the threads are allowed to safely execute the critical section concurrently. TM is analogous to traffic roundabouts whereas conventional synchronization mechanisms are analogous to conventional traffic lights [16].

Transactional memory operates on the same principles as database transactions [9]. The processor atomically commits *all* memory operations of a successful transaction or discards *all* memory operations if the transaction should fail (a collision to the updates by the multiple threads occurs). In order for a transaction to execute successfully, it must be executed in isolation, *i.e.,* without conflicting with other transactions/threads memory operations. This is the key principle that allows transactional memory to expose untapped concurrency in multi-threaded applications.

One problem space that could benefit from transactional memory is that of Parallel Discrete Event Simulation (PDES). A key challenge area in PDES is the need for contention-free pending event set management solutions [5]. Transactional memory can help alleviate contention for this shared structure and potentially expose untapped concurrency in the simulation's execution.

This paper explores the use of transactional memory to manage the pending event set schedule queue in the WARPED parallel simulation kernel. In particular, we will integrate the hardware-based transactional memory primitives from the Intel Haswell platform to manage the pending event set data structures of the WARPED parallel discrete event simulation engine. While WARPED has multiple shared data structures in the kernel, the focus of this work is on the pending event set. It is the primary bottleneck in PDES applications, and hence the primary motivation for this study.

The remainder of this paper is organized as follows. Section 2 provides a general overview of transactional memory. It gives some examples of other TM implementations and discusses why they do not work as well as TSX. It provides examples of related studies. Finally, it provides an overview of how TSX works and how it is implemented in software. Section 3 provides some background of the PDES problem space. It introduces WARPED and some of the implementation details relevant to this study. Previous studies with the WARPED pending event set are also briefly discussed. Section 4 discusses how TSX is incorporated into the WARPED pending event set implementation. It also provides a brief overview of the critical sections utilizing TSX and why TSX will be beneficial. Section 5 presents the experimental results of this research for different simulation configurations. Finally, Section 5.2 contains some concluding remarks.

2. BACKGROUND

This section provides a high level explanation of how transactional memory operates. It then introduces other implementations, as well as reasons why they were not explored in this study. Next, it provides some examples of related studies with transactional memory, specifically the implementation used in this study. Finally, it provides an overview of Intel's implementation, Transactional Synchronization Extensions (TSX) and how the programmer can develop TSX enabled multi-threaded applications.

2.1 Transactional Memory Overview

Transactional memory (TM) is a concurrency control mechanism that dynamically determines when two or more threads can safely execute a critical section [18]. The programmer identifies a transactional region, typically a critical sec-

tion, for monitoring. When the transaction executes, the TM system, whether it is implemented in hardware or software, tracks memory operations performed within the transactional region to determine whether or not two or more transactions conflict with one another, *i.e.,* if any memory accesses conflict with one another. If the threads do not conflict with one another, the transactions can be safely and concurrently executed. If they do conflict, the process must abort the transaction and execute the critical section non-transactionally, *i.e.,* by serializing execution of the critical section with conventional synchronization mechanisms.

As a transaction is executed, the memory operations performed within the transaction are buffered, specifically write operations. Write operations will only be fully committed when the transaction is complete and safe access has been determined. Safe access is determined by comparing the set of addresses each transaction reads from (called the *read-set*) and the set of addresses each transaction writes to (called the *write-set*). Each transaction builds its own read-set and write-set as it executes. While a thread is executing transactionally, any memory operation performed by any other thread is checked against the read-set and write-set of the transactionally executing thread to determine if any memory operations conflict. The other threads can be executing either non-transactionally or transactionally. If the transaction completes execution and the TM system has not detected any conflicting memory operations, the transaction atomically commits all of the buffered memory operations, henceforth referred to simply as a *commit*.

Whenever safe access does not occur, the transaction cannot safely continue execution. This is referred to as a *data conflict* and only occurs if: (i) one transaction attempts to read a location that is part of another transaction's write-set, or (ii) a transaction attempts to write a location that is part of another transaction's read-set or write-set [11]. Once a memory location is written to by a transaction, it cannot be accessed in any way by any other transaction; any access by any other transaction results in a race condition. If such a situation arises, all concurrently executing transactions will abort execution, henceforth referred to simply as an *abort*.

By definition, a transaction is a series of actions that appears instantaneous and indivisible possessing four key attributes: (1) atomicity, (2) consistency, (3) isolation, and (4) durability [9]. TM operates on the principles of database transactions. The two key attributes for TM are atomicity and isolation; consistency and durability must hold for all multi-threaded operations in multi-threaded applications. Atomicity is guaranteed if: (1) all memory operations performed within the transaction are completed successfully, or (2) it appears as if the performed memory operations were never attempted [9]. Isolation is guaranteed by tracking memory operations as the transactions execute and aborting if any memory operations conflict. If both atomicity and isolation can be guaranteed for all memory operations performed within a critical section, that "critical section" can be executed concurrently [18].

In the case of a commit, the transaction has ensured that its memory operations are executed in isolation from other threads and that *all* of its memory operations are committed, thus satisfying the isolation and atomicity principles. Note that only at this time will the memory operations performed within the transaction become visible to other threads, thus satisfying the appearance of instantaneousness. In the case of an abort due to a data conflict, it is clear that the isolation principle has been violated. It should be noted that transactions can abort for a variety of reasons depending on the implementation [12, 3], but the primary cause is data conflicts. Upon abort, all memory operations are discarded to maintain atomicity.

2.2 Related Studies

There have been many implementations of TM systems since its conception, mostly in software [25, 2, 4, 3, 22, 7, 1]. As the name suggests, Software Transactional Memory (STM) systems implement the memory tracking, conflict detection, write buffering and so on in software. Most systems are implementation specific, but memory tracking is typically done through some form of logging. While this allows transactional memory enabled applications to be executed on a variety of platforms, performance usually suffers. Gajinov et al performed a study with STM by developing a parallel version of the Quake multi-player game server from the ground up using OpenMP parallelizations pragmas and atomic blocks [7]. Their results showed that the logging overhead required for STM resulted in execution times that were 4 to 6 times longer than the sequential version of the server. In general, STM has been found to result in significant slowdown [1]. Although STM is more widely available than HTM, its use in this this study was dismissed due to the significant performance penalty.

Hardware Transactional Memory (HTM) provides the physical resources necessary to implement transactional memory effectively. Many chip manufacturers have added, or at least sought to add, support for HTM in recent years. IBM released one of the first commercially available HTM systems in their Blue Gene/Q machine [22]. Even though they found that this implementation was an improvement over STM, it still incurred significant overhead. AMD's Advanced Synchronization Facility and Sun's Rock processor included support for HTM [3, 4]. However, AMD has not released any HTM enabled processors as of this study, and Sun's Rock processor was canceled after Sun was acquired by Oracle.

With the release of Intel's Haswell generation processors, Intel's Transactional Synchronization Extensions (TSX) is currently the only widely available commercial HTM-enabled system. Numerous studies have already been performed with TSX, primarily evaluating its performance capabilities. Chitters et al modified Google's write optimized persistent key-value store, LevelDB, to use TSX based synchronization instead of a global mutex. Their implementation shows 20-25% increased throughput for write-only workloads and increased throughput for 50% read / 50% write workloads [2]. Wang et al studied the performance scalability of a concurrent skip-list using TSX Restricted Transactional Memory (RTM). They compared the TSX implementation to a fine-grain locking implementation and a lock-free implementation. They found that the performance was comparable to the lock-free implementation without the added complexity [24]. Yoo et al evaluated the performance of TSX using high-performance computing (HPC) workloads, as well as in a user-level TCP/IP stack. They measured an average speed up of 1.41x and 1.31x respectively [25]. The decision to use Intel's TSX for this research was based on its wide availability and the performance improvements observed in other studies.

2.3 Transactional Synchronization Extensions (TSX)

Intel's Transactional Synchronization Extensions (TSX) is an extension to the x86 instruction set architecture that adds support for HTM. TSX operates in the L1 cache using the cache coherence protocol [12]. It is a best effort implementation, meaning it does not guarantee transactions will commit [11]. TSX has two interfaces: (1) Hardware Lock Elision (HLE), and (2) Restricted Transactional Memory (RTM). While both operate on the same principles of transactional memory, they have subtle differences. This section discusses some of the implementation details of TSX as well as how the programmer utilizes TSX.

The **_Hardware Lock Elision_** (HLE) interface is a legacy-compatible interface introducing two instruction prefixes, namely: `XACQUIRE` and `XRELEASE`.

The `XACQUIRE` prefix is placed before a locking instruction to mark the beginning of a transaction. `XRELEASE` is placed before an unlocking instruction to mark the end of a transaction. These prefixes tell the processor to elide the write operation to the lock variable during lock acquisition/release. When the processor encounters an `XACQUIRE` prefixed lock instruction, it transitions to transactional execution. Specifically, it adds the lock variable to the transaction's read-set instead of issuing any write requests to the lock [11]. To other threads, the lock will appear to be free, thus allowing those threads to enter the critical section and execute concurrently. All transactions can execute concurrently as long as no transactions abort and explicitly write to the lock variable. If that were to happen, a data conflict technically occurs — one transaction writes to a memory location (the lock) that is part of another transaction's read-set.

The `XRELEASE` prefix is placed before the instruction used to release the lock. It also attempts to elide the write associated with the lock release instruction. If the lock release instruction attempts to restore the lock to the value it had prior to the `XACQUIRE` prefixed locking instruction, the write operation on the lock is elided [11]. It is at this time that the processor attempts to commit the transaction.

However, if the transaction aborts for any reason, the region will be re-executed non-transactionally. If the processor encounters an abort condition, it will discard all memory operations performed within the transaction, return to the locking instruction, and resume execution without lock elision, *i.e.,* the write operation will be performed on the lock variable. If another thread is executing the same transactional region, those transactions will also abort. The aborted transaction thread performs an explicit write on the lock, resulting in a data conflict for any other transaction as the lock variable is part of the other transaction's read-set. The re-execution of the critical section using conventional synchronization is necessary to guarantee forward progress [11].

To enable HLE synchronization, the programmer merely adds the HLE memory models to the existing locking intrinsics (Figure 1). The `_ATOMIC_HLE_ACQUIRE` tells the thread to execute an `XACQUIRE` prefixed lock acquire instruction when another thread releases the lock. The combination of memory models, `__ATOMIC_HLE_ACQUIRE|__ATOMIC_ACQUIRE)` allows for the locking instructions to be executed with or without elision. The local thread can be synchronized to a `XRELEASE` prefixed lock release instruction or a standard lock release instruction.

HLE is legacy compatible. Code utilizing the HLE inter-

```
/* Acquire lock with lock elision if possible */
/* Loop until the returned value
   indicates the lock was free */
while(__atomic_exchange_n(&lock, 1,
       __ATOMIC_HLE_ACQUIRE|__ATOMIC_ACQUIRE)):

/* Begin executing critical section/
   transactional region */
...
/* End critical section/transactional region */

/* Free lock with lock elision if possible */
__atomic_store_n(&lock, 0,
         __ATOMIC_HLE_RELEASE|__ATOMIC_RELEASE);
```

Figure 1: Generic HLE Software Implementation

face can be executed on legacy hardware, but the HLE prefixes will be ignored [11] and the processor will perform the write operation on the locking variable and execute the critical section non-transactionally. While this interface does nothing for multi-threaded applications on legacy hardware, it does allow for easier cross-platform code deployment.

The *Restricted Transactional Memory* (RTM) interface for HTM introduces four new instructions, namely: XBEGIN, XEND, XABORT, and XTEST.

The XBEGIN instruction marks the start of a transaction, while the XEND instruction makes the end of a transaction. The XABORT instruction is used by the programmer to manually abort a transaction. Finally, the XTEST instruction can be used to test if the processor is executing transactionally or non-transactionally.

The XBEGIN instruction transitions the processor into transactional execution [11]. Note that the XBEGIN instruction does not elide the locking variable as HLE does. Therefore, the programmer should manually add the locking variable to the transaction's read-set by checking if the lock is free at the start of the transaction. If it is free, the transaction can execute safely. Once execution reaches the XEND instruction, the processor will attempt to commit the transaction.

As previously mentioned, the transaction can abort for many reasons. One case specific to RTM occurs when the lock is not free upon entering the transaction. In this case, the programmer uses the XABORT instruction to abort the transaction. But no matter the reason for the abort, execution jumps to the fallback instruction address [11]. This address is specified as an operand of the XBEGIN instruction.

It is this fallback path that makes RTM a much more flexible interface than HLE because it is entirely at the discretion of the programmer to determine precisely what happens on failure of a transaction. Even so, the programmer must still provide an abort path that guarantees forward progress [11]. Therefore, the abort path should use explicit synchronization, *e.g.*, acquire a lock, to ensure forward progress. However, the programmer can use this abort path to tune the performance of RTM enabled applications. For instance, a retry routine can be used to specify how many times the processor should attempt to enter transactional execution before using explicit synchronization. Furthermore, the EAX register reports information about the condition of an abort [11], such as whether or not the abort was caused by the XABORT instruction, a data conflict, so on. The programmer

```
if (_xbegin() == _XBEGIN_STARTED) {
    /* Add lock to read-set */
    if (lock is not free) {
        /* Abort if lock is already acquired */
        _xabort(_ABORT_LOCK_BUSY);
    }
} else {  /* Abort path */
    acquire lock
}

/* Begin critical section/transactional region */
...
/* End critical section/transactional region */

if (lock is free) {
    /* End transaction and commit results*/
    _xend();
} else {
    release lock
}
```

Figure 2: Generic RTM Software Implementation

can use this information to make more informed decisions regarding reattempting transactional execution.

The RTM implementation is more involved because it uses entirely new instructions. The general algorithm for the RTM software interface is shown in Figure 2. The programmer moves the existing locking mechanism inside an else clause of the XBEGIN if statement, which will determine if the processor transitions to transactional execution or takes the abort path. As previously mentioned, the processor will also return to this point should the transaction abort in the middle of execution. Moving the locking mechanism into the RTM abort path ensures that the abort path ultimately uses explicit synchronization and guarantees forward progress. GCC 4.8 and above includes support for the _xbegin, _xabort, and _xend intrinsics [21].

While RTM is a more flexible interface than HLE, it can only be used on supported Haswell platforms. If a legacy device attempts to execute one of the RTM instructions, it will throw a General Protection Fault. It should be noted that execution of the XEND instruction outside of a transaction will result in a General Protection Fault as well [12].

3. PDES AND WARPED

Discrete Event Simulation (DES) models a system's state changes at discrete points in time. In a DES model, physical processes are represented by Logical Processes (LPs) [14]. For example, in an example epidemic simulation (an example of which is used in this study), LPs can represent geographical locations containing a subset of the total population. The LP's state represents the diffusion of the disease within the location and the status of the occupants at that location. Executed Events in this simulation represent the arrival or departure of individuals to or from that location, the progression of a disease within an individual at that location, the diffusion of a disease throughout that location, etc [17]. To effectively model epidemics, a significant population size and number of locations needs to be simulated.

WARPED is a publicly available Discrete Event Simulation (DES) kernel implementing the Time Warp protocol [13, 6]. It was recently redesigned for parallel execution on

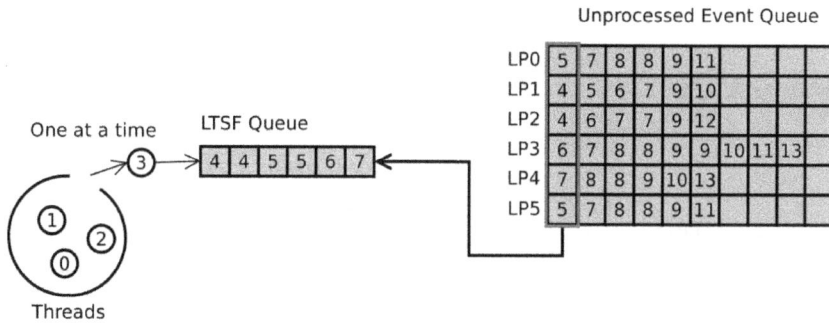

Figure 3: Pending Event Set Scheduling

multi-core processing nodes [15]. It has many configuration options and utilizes many different algorithms of the Time Warp protocol [6].

The pending event set is maintained as a two-level structure in WARPED (Figure3) [5]. Each LP maintains its own event set as a time-stamp ordered queue. As previously mentioned, each LP maintains an unprocessed queue for scheduled events yet to be executed and a processed queue to store previously executed events. A common Least Time-Stamped First (LTSF) queue is populated with the least time stamped event from each LP's unprocessed queue. As the name suggests, the LTSF queue is automatically sorted in increasing time-stamp order so that worker threads can simply retrieve an event from the head of the queue. This guarantees the worker thread retrieves the least time-stamped event without having to search through the queue. The LTSF queue is also referred to as the schedule queue in WARPED; these terms will be used interchangeably.

3.1 Pending Event Set Data Structures

The implementation of the pending event set is a key factor in the performance of the simulation [19]. The WARPED simulation kernel has two functional implementations: (1) the C++ Standard Template Library (STL) multi-set data structure, and (2) the splay tree data structure. The way that these data structures are accessed and, more importantly, self-adjust will be relevant to how effectively TSX can be used to access these structures. Due to space considerations, only performance results with the multi-set data structure are shown. Results with splay trees are consistent with those described in this manuscript. Interested readers can find those details in [10].

The sorted STL multi-set data structure is an abstract data structure implemented as a self-balancing, red-black binary search tree [8]. Look-up, insertion, and deletion operations performed in a red-black tree with n elements are performed in average O(log n) time. When insertion or deletion operations are performed, the tree is rebalanced by a tree rearrangement algorithm and a "painting" algorithm taking average O(1) and O(log n) time respectively.

In the STL multi-set, the lowest value element will always be the left most child node of the tree. To access the least time-stamped event at the head of the LTSF queue, multi-set red-black tree must be traversed to the left most child node. Any insertion or removal of events requires that the red-black tree rebalance itself.

One concern with these data structures in relation to TSX

is self-adjustment. When these data structures have to self-adjust, the read-set and write-set of the transaction can grow significantly; all transactions operating on that data structure may then need to abort. However, the self-adjustment is a necessary evil. Events need to retrieved from the pending event set and executed in least time-stamped order. If a thread had to search for the least time-stamped event every time it retrieved an event, execution of the simulation would be cripplingly slow. Instead, the pending event set is sorted in order of increasing time-stamp, and the thread can simply fetch the top event in the queue [15]. That being said, there are still opportunities where these data structures may try to self-adjust, but not actually need to write any changes to the structure, *i.e.*, the multi-set queue may already be sorted after insertion. In these situations, only the read-set of the transaction in question will grow, and all concurrently executing transactions may proceed.

We conducted some preliminary studies using TSX with simple data structures such as std:list and std:forward_list for the pending event set. However, the performance results were much worse due to sorting overheads. Perhaps there are alternate simple data structures or queue organizations that may uncover improved results with TSX, but as of yet we have not uncovered any. Therefore, the experiments reported in this manuscript are restricted to the more complex multi-set and splay tree data structures.

3.2 Worker Thread Event Execution

Within a WARPED simulation, a manager thread on each processing node initiates n worker threads at the beginning of the simulation. It can also suspend inactive worker threads if they run out of useful work (events in the pending event set). When a worker thread is created, or resumes execution after being suspended by the manager thread, it attempts to lock the LTSF queue and dequeue the least time-stamped event. If the worker thread successfully retrieved an event, it executes that event as specified by the simulation model. It then attempts to lock the unprocessed queue for the LP associated with the executed event, and dequeue the next least time-stamped event. The dequeued event is inserted into the LTSF queue, which resorts itself based on the event time-stamps. An abstract event processing algorithm is shown in Figure 4 [5]. Note that the worker threads perform many other functions as well.

3.3 Contention

Only one worker thread can access the LTSF queue at a

```
worker_thread()

   lock LTSF queue
   dequeue smallest event from LTSF
   unlock LTSF queue

   while !done loop

     process event (assume from LPi)

     lock LPi queue
     dequeue smallest event from LPi
     unlock LPi queue

     lock LTSF queue

     insert event from LPi
     dequeue smallest event from LTSF

     unlock LTSF queue
   end loop
```

Figure 4: Generalized event execution loop for the worker threads. Many details have been omitted for clarity.

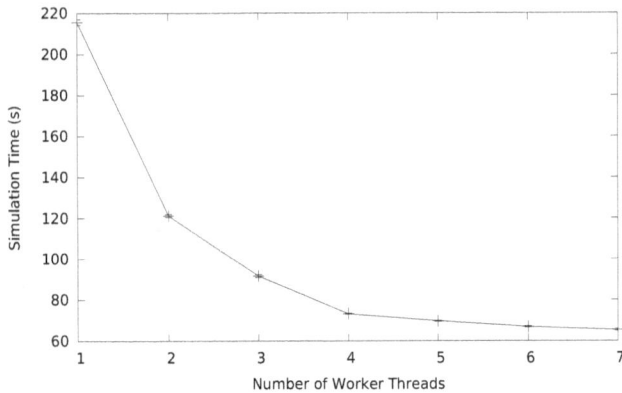

Figure 5: warped Simulation Time versus Worker Thread Count for Epidemic Model

time. This creates a clear point of contention during event scheduling as each thread must first retrieve an event from the LTSF queue. The LTSF queue must also be updated when events are inserted into any of the LP pending event sets. This occurs when new events are generated or the simulation encounters a causality error and must rollback.

The initial WARPED implementation execution time was measured and analyzed using 1 to 7 worker threads on an Intel i7-4770 with 2-way hyperthreading on 4 processing cores. These results can be seen in Figure 5. It is evident that simulation time becomes less and less affected by increasing the worker thread count, especially when the worker thread count surpasses 4. This is attributed to the increased contention for the LTSF queue; with more threads, each thread has to wait longer for access to the LTSF queue. The multicore processor trend will continue to increase the number of simultaneous execution threads available, consequently increasing the contention problem.

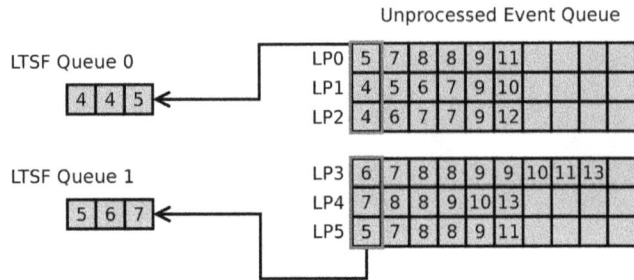

Figure 6: Pending Event Set Scheduling with Multiple LTSF Queues

3.4 Previous Solutions to Contention

Dickman *et al* explored the use of various data structures in the WARPED pending event set implementation, specifically, the STL multi-set, splay tree, and ladder queue data structures [5]. A secondary focus of this study will expand upon the use of splay tree versus STL multi-set data structures; at the time of this work, the ladder queue implementation was being heavily modified and could not be included in this study.

Another focus of the Dickman *et al* study was the utilization of multiple LTSF queues [5]. Multiple LTSF queues are created at the beginning of the simulation. Each LP is assigned to a specific LTSF queue as shown in Figure 6. In a simulation configured with four LPs, two worker threads, and two LTSF queues, two LPs and one thread are assigned to each queue. This significantly reduced contention as each thread could access separate LTSF queues concurrently. The initial implementation statically assigned LPs to LTSF queues. This resulted in an unbalanced load distribution, leading to an increased number of rollbacks and reduced simulation performance. This was corrected using a load balancing algorithm to dynamically reassign LPs to LTSF queues [5]. This study expands upon the previous multiple LTSF queue study to evaluate if contention can be reduced even further with TSX.

3.5 Thread Migration

Another potential solution to contention is to distribute worker threads that migrate events from the LPs to subsequent LTSF queues. That is, in the original scheduling scheme, worker threads are assigned to a specific LTSF queue. The worker thread would insert the next event into the same LTSF it had just scheduled from as seen in Figure 4. In this implementation, the worker thread inserts the next event into a different LTSF queue, based on a circularly incremented counter. This approach dynamically reassigns worker threads LTSF queues by migrating the threads to new LTSF queues. It also implicitly balances the load between the all the LTSF queues. The number of LTSF queues is specified in a configuration file, and has no restrictions as in the static assignment.

In a separate (unpublished) study, UC researchers discovered that this implementation resulted in poor performance on Non-uniform Memory Access (NUMA) architectures. Jingjing Wang *et al* also noticed similar performance degradation, which they attributed to poor memory locality due to the movement of LPs to different threads [23]. To offset these performance hits, a migration count was im-

```
worker_thread()

  i = fetch-and-add LTSF queue index
  lock LTSF[i]
  dequeue smallest event from LTSF[i]
  unlock LTSF[i]

  while !done loop

    process event (assume from LPi)

    lock LPi queue
    dequeue smallest event from LPi
    unlock LPi queue

    i = fetch-and-add LTSF queue index

    lock LTSF[i]

    insert event from LPi into LTSF[i]
    dequeue smallest event from LTSF[i]

    unlock LTSF queue
  end loop
```

Figure 7: Generalized event execution loop for migrating worker threads. Many details have been omitted for clarity.

plemented in this scheme. Instead of continuous migration, threads are reassigned to their original LTSF queue after executing a certain number of events. The threads will continue to schedule events from their original LTSF queue for the remainder of the simulation.

4. WARPED WITH TSX

This section discusses the various critical sections of WARPED that use the TSX mechanism for this study. As previously mentioned, the primary focus of this study is the shared LTSF queue. The LP event queues also modified to use the TSX mechanism. In this study, experiments with both the RTM and HLE mechanisms are explored.

The following functions require synchronization to access the LTSF queue:

- `insert()`: copy the least time-stamped event from a specific LP's unprocessed queue into the LTSF queue.

- `updatedScheduleQueueAfterExecute()`: find the source LP of the previously executed event, and copy the least time-stamped event from that LP's unprocessed queue into the LTSF queue using the `insert()` function above.

- `nextEventToBeScheduledTime()`: return the time of the event at the beginning of the LTSF queue.

- `clearScheduleQueue()`: clear the LTSF queue.

- `setLowestObjectPosition()`: update the lowest object position array.

- `peek()`: dequeues the next event for execution from the head of the LTSF queue.

- `peekEvent()`: if a simulation object is not specified, call `peek()`.

Most of these critical sections involve write operations, typically through queuing and dequeuing events. Queuing and dequeuing requires the multi-set and splay tree data structures to readjust themselves thus adding more memory locations to the transaction's read-set and write-set. `nextEventToBeScheduleTime()` is the only critical section that performs strictly read operations. Furthermore, many of these critical sections overlap with critical sections from the unprocessed and processed queues, which are described below.

The functions described above perform a variety of memory operations and any thread can execute any critical section at any time. Based on static analysis, there's no way of knowing which threads will access what structure in what way, hence the need for synchronization. However with TSX, functions that do not interfere can execute concurrently. TSX tracks read and write memory operations separately in the transaction's read-set and write-set respectively. Transactions only interfere if a data conflict occurs, *i.e.,* a thread attempts to write to a memory location in another transaction's read-set, or a thread attempts to read a memory location in another transaction's write-set.

For example, one worker thread calls `nextEventToBeScheduleTime` to get the time-stamp of the event at the head of the LTSF queue. There is a possibility that a different worker thread is currently updating the LTSF queue or will attempt to update the LTSF queue while the first worker thread is in the middle of executing `nextEventToBeScheduleTime`. This scenario necessitates synchronization. However, in a different scenario, instead of the second worker thread writing to the LTSF queue, it also calls `nextEventToBeScheduleTime`. Both are read operations and do not interfere with each other. TSX recognizes this scenario and allows the worker threads to execute concurrently, whereas locks force one worker thread to wait until the other is done with the LTSF queue.

Several similar scenarios can arise during simulation execution. While there are too many possible scenarios to identify specifically where TSX can be beneficial, the potential to expose concurrency through dynamic synchronization is too great to be dismissed. Note, there is also no guarantee that TSX will work 100% of the time; there are several runtime events that can cause transactions to abort, as well as physical limitations.

4.1 TSX Implementation

This section discusses how both TSX interfaces were implemented in WARPED.

4.1.1 Hardware Lock Elision (HLE)

The generic algorithm presented in Figure 1 only works for locks with a binary value, *i.e.,* the lock is free or it is not free. The WARPED locking mechanism assigns the thread number to the lock value to indicate which thread currently holds the lock. To comply with this implementation, custom HLE lock acquire and lock release functions were implemented. GCC inline assembly functions were developed appending the appropriate HLE prefixes to the CMPXCHG lock instruction.

These functions are shown in Figures 8 and 9. The `_xacquire()` function loads the value 0xFFFF (the value indicating the

```
static inline int _xacquire(int *lockOwner,
    const unsigned int *threadNumber)
{
  unsigned char ret;
  asm volatile("mov $0xFFFF, %%eax\n"
         _XACQUIRE_PREFIX "lock cmpxchg %2, %1\n"
         "sete %0"
         : "=q"(ret), "=m"(*lockOwner)
         : "r"(*threadNumber)
         : "memory", "%eax");
  return (int) ret;
}
```

Figure 8: HLE _xacquire Inline Assembly Function

```
static inline int _xrelease(int *lockOwner,
    const unsigned int *threadNumber)
{
  unsigned char ret;
  asm volatile("mov %2, %%eax\n"
         _XRELEASE_PREFIX "lock cmpxchg %3, %1\n"
         "sete %0"
         : "=q"(ret), "=m"(*lockOwner)
         : "r"(*threadNumber), "r"(0xFFFF)
         : "memory", "%eax");
  return (int) ret;
}
```

Figure 9: HLE _xrelease Inline Assembly Function

lock is free) into a specific register, then compares the lockOwner variable with the the previously loaded value to determine if the lock is free. If the values are the same, the CMPXCHG instruction will write the value of the threadNumber variable into the lockOwner variable and return the result. The _xrelease() function loads the value of the lockOwner variable into a specific register, then compares the threadNumber variable with the previously loaded value. If the lockOwner value is the same as the thread number, the cmpxchg writes the value 0xFFFF into the lockOwner variable to indicate the lock is free. Of course, if the processor successfully transitions into transactional execution with the HLE prefixes, the write operations technically never occur. They only *appear* to occur to the local thread. Any other thread still sees the lock as free.

4.1.2 Restricted Transactional Memory (RTM)

RTM allows the programmer to specify an abort path to be executed upon a transactional abort. This allows better tuning of RTM performance. The RTM algorithm implemented in WARPED includes a retry algorithm described below in Figure 10. Instead of immediately retrying transactional execution, the algorithm decides when and if the transaction should be retried based on the condition of the abort. If the transaction was explicitly aborted for reasons other than another thread owning the lock, do not retry transactional execution. The programmer used the _xabort() function to explicitly abort the transaction. If the lock was not free upon entering the transaction, wait until it is free to retry transactional execution. If a data conflict occurred, wait before retrying by using the _mm_pause busy-wait loop to try and offset the execution of the conflicting threads. This is done in hopes that the conflicting

```
while retry count is less than retry limit
   status = _xbegin()

   if status == XBEGIN
     if lock is free
        execute transactional region
     else
        _xabort

   update abort stats

   if transaction will not succeed on retry or
      _xabort was called due to reasons other
      than the lock not being free

      break

   else if _xabort was used because the lock
      was not free

      wait until the lock becomes free to retry

   else if a data conflict occurred

      wait before retry using _mm_pause busy-wait loop

   increment retry count
end loop

acquire lock

execute critical section
```

Figure 10: RTM Retry Algorithm

memory operations will be performed at different times on the next retry.

The RTM retry limit is specified at compile time. Each data structure maintains its own retry limit initially set to the global limit. A back-off algorithm is used to reduce the retry limit for a specific data structure. If the transactions for this data structure abort more often than not, the retry limit is reduced. This ideally reduces the number of transaction attempts for an extended period of time. If the transaction commit rate increases, the retry limit increases up to the initial limit specified at compile time. The retry limit increases if the commit rate passes the abort to commit rate ratio threshold.

Furthermore, if transactions for the data structure consistently abort for an extended period of time with no successful commits, transactional execution is not attempted for the remainder of the simulation.

5. EXPERIMENTAL ANALYSIS

This study compares the performance of the WARPED simulation kernel using conventional synchronization mechanisms, Hardware Lock Elision (HLE), and Restricted Transactional Memory (RTM). All simulations were performed on a system with an Intel i7-4770 running at 3.4 GHz with 32GB of RAM. The average execution time and standard deviation were calculated from a set of 10 trials for each simulation configuration. When comparing synchronization

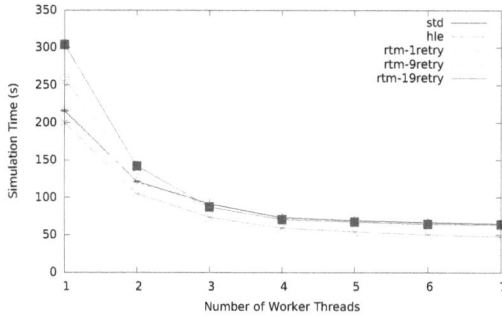

Figure 11: Performance of a Single Multi-set LTSF Queue

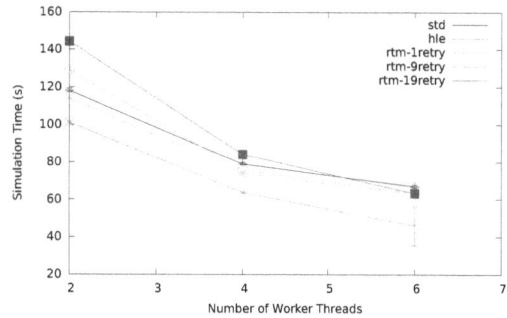

Figure 12: Performance of Multiple Worker Threads, 2 LTSF Queues

mechanisms, the simulation execution times are compared for the same LTSF queue and worker thread configurations. When comparing the LTSF queue configurations, the multiple LTSF queue configuration execution time is compared with the execution time of the same configuration with 1 LTSF queue.

The simulation model used to obtain the following results is an epidemic model. It consists of 110998 geographically distributed people in 119 separate locations requiring a total of 119 LPs. The epidemic is modeled by reaction processes to model progression of the disease within an individual entity, and diffusion processes to model transmission of the disease among individual entities.

5.1 The Default Multi-set Schedule Queue

The default implementation of the LTSF queue is the STL multi-set data structure. It is a self-adjusting binary search tree which keeps the least time-stamped event in the left most leaf node of the tree.

5.1.1 Static Thread Assignment

In the original WARPED thread scheduling scheme, threads are statically assigned to an LTSF queue. Contention will clearly be a problem if the simulation only schedules from one LTSF queue as every worker thread is assigned to that queue.

The first part of this study compares the performance of the WARPED pending event set static thread scheduling implementation using one LTSF queue synchronized with:

1. atomic locks,
2. HLE,
3. RTM with 1 retry,
4. RTM with 9 retries, and
5. RTM with 19 retries.

These results are shown in Figure 11. It is clear that using HLE improves simulation performance, but still suffers from the same rise in contention as the number of worker threads is increased. The performance using RTM for any retry count used is worse than the standard locking mechanism initially. As the number of worker threads is increased, the performance using RTM is slightly better than the standard locking mechanism, but only by about 2 or 3%.

It is evident from Figure 11 that contention is increasing as the number of worker threads increases, regardless of the synchronization mechanism used. This is somewhat expected as contention is still high for the single LTSF queue.

Transactional memory exposes concurrency where it can, but some critical sections simply cannot be executed concurrently. It should be noted that the performance of HLE does not flatten quite as much as the other synchronization mechanisms.

The initial solution to alleviate contention for the LTSF queue is the utilization of multiple LTSF queues. The data for different numbers of schedule queues is limited by the necessity to have a number of LTSF queues evenly divisible by the number of worker threads. This is because of the way threads are assigned to LTSF queues; if the numbers are not evenly divisible, the simulation becomes unbalanced. LPs assigned to a certain LTSF queue can get far ahead or behind of other LPs on different LTSF queues resulting in significant rollbacks and thus performance degradation.

Figure 12 shows the simulation results for varying worker thread configurations using 2 LTSF queues. The load balancing restrictions discussed above restrict the available data for these results. Each synchronization configuration yields roughly the same increasing performance trend. RTM performance seems to be worse with more retries with a lower worker thread count, but eventually converges with the single retry scheme. On the other hand, HLE synchronized simulations consistently outperform simulations using the standard synchronization.

The LTSF queue count configuration per worker thread configuration results are shown Figure 13. Using 2 LTSF queues with 2 statically assigned worker threads appears to alleviate contention. Using HLE, simulation execution time was reduced by 13-14% regardless of the number of LTSF queues used. RTM improved performance using only 1 retry, but only by about 1-3%. Using any more retries resulted in worse performance. Using the standard locking mechanisms, simulation execution time reduced by about 2.5% increasing the LTSF queue count from 1 to 2. With TSX, simulation execution time reduced by about 4% when increasing the LTSF queue count from 1 to 2. While only a small difference, TSX managed to reduce contention a bit more in conjunction with multiple LTSF queues.

While TSX, specifically HLE, substantially improved simulation performance, as much 22%, simulation execution time increased as the number of LTSF queues used was increased in other configurations. It was noted that these simulations resulted in significantly higher rollbacks, the most likely cause of the increased execution time. These poor performance results could be attributed to the lack of a proper

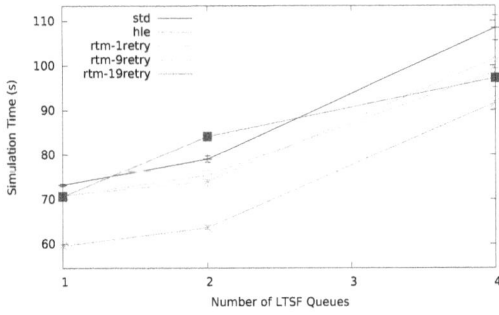

Figure 13: Performance of Multiple Multi-set LTSF Queues, 4 Statically Assigned Worker Threads

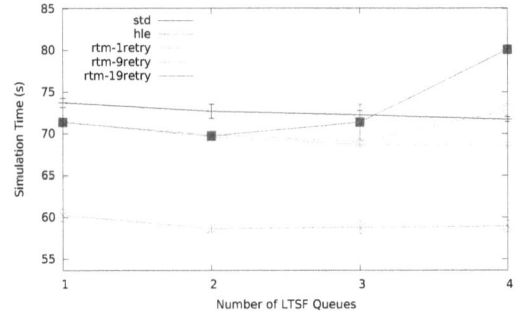

Figure 15: Performance of Multiple Multi-set LTSF Queues, 4 Dynamically Assigned Worker Threads

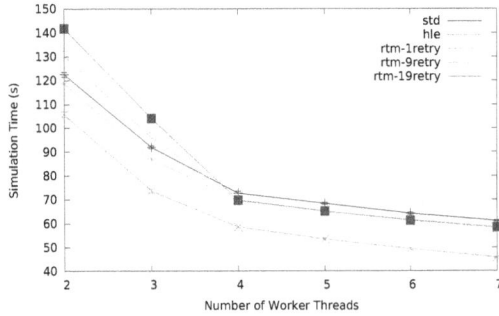

Figure 14: Performance of Multiple Dynamically Assigned Worker Threads, 2 LTSF Queues

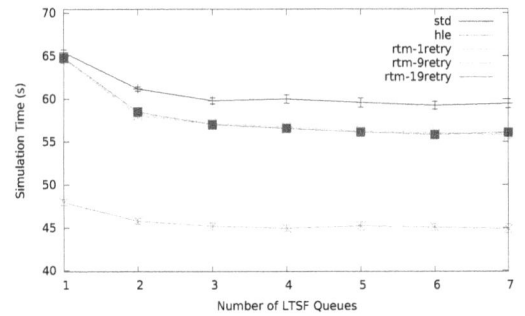

Figure 16: Performance of Multiple Multi-set LTSF Queues, 7 Dynamically Assigned Worker Threads

load balancing procedure, which is addressed with dynamic thread assignment.

5.1.2 Dynamic Thread Assignment

Another solution to contention is to distribute worker threads that try to simultaneously access the same LTSF queue to different LTSF queues. Worker threads are dynamically assigned to LTSF queues rather than statically.

The first solution continuously migrates the worker threads to the next LTSF. That is, the worker thread processes an event from $LTSF_i$ and then $LTSF_{(i+1)modn}$ where n is the number of LTSF queues. As the worker thread moves among the LTSF queues, the worker thread also moves the next event from the just processed LP to the next LTSF queue. This also helps distribute the critical path of events in the LPs around the LTSF queues. This solution implicitly balances the work load between LTSF queues. Therefore, any number of LTSF queues can be used with any number of worker threads.

Figure 14 shows the simulation results for 2 LTSF queues using the continuous migration scheme as the number of worker threads is varied. Similarly to the static scheduling scheme, the simulations for each synchronization mechanism seem to follow almost the same trends. The more retries the RTM algorithm attempted, the worse performance was for 2 and 3 worker threads. However, the number of retries did not affect the RTM performance for 4 or more worker threads.

Simulation execution time decreased slightly by increasing the number of LTSF queue with 4 worker threads (Figure 15). Each multiple LTSF configuration reduced simula-

tion execution time by 2-3% when compared to the single LTSF queue configuration. The only exception to this trend is the 4 LTSF queue configuration with HLE; it reduced simulation execution time slightly less than standard locking mechanisms, but the difference seems trivial. While RTM performed well for lower LTSF queue counts, the increased retry counts resulted in worse performance for greater LTSF queue counts. In any configuration, HLE still reduces execution time by about 18%, while RTM generally generally reduces execution time by about 3-4% when comparing the two to standard locking mechanisms.

The final simulation configuration uses 7 worker threads with 1 to 7 LTSF queues (Figure 16). Using standard locking mechanisms with multiple LTSF queues reduces execution time by 6% to 9% as the number of LTSF queues is increased. Surprisingly, HLE only reduces execution time by 3% to 5%. But again, HLE still well outperforms the standard locking mechanisms by as much as 27%. RTM only outperforms standard locking mechanisms by about 5%. However, it becomes much more effective with more LTSF queues. Execution time improvements increased from 9% to almost 14% when using RTM with increasing LTSF queues counts.

As previously discussed, the continuous thread migration approach does not work well for NUMA architectures due to memory locality issues. The thread migration scheme was modified to migrate threads between LTSF queues for the first 50 events a thread executes. In the first implementation of this scheme, after a thread executes 50 events, it is no longer reassigned to a different LTSF queue. It continues to schedule from the same LTSF queue as it did for the 50th event for the remainder of the simulation.

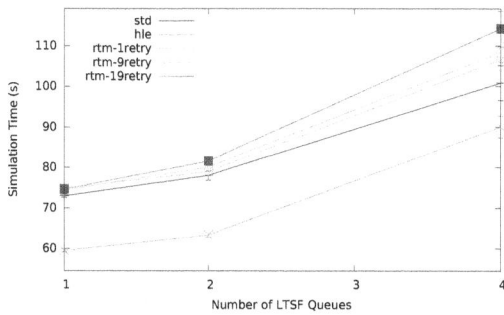

Figure 17: Simulation Time versus Number of STL Multi-set LTSF Queues for 4 Worker Threads

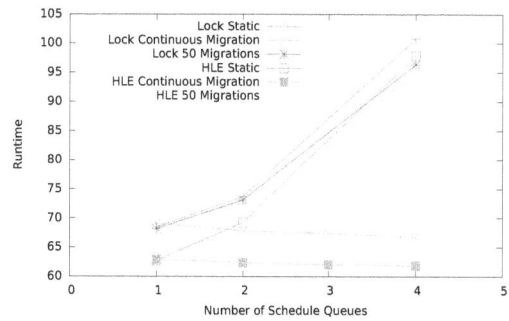

Figure 18: Comparison of Migration Schemes for 4 Worker Threads with X LTSF Queues

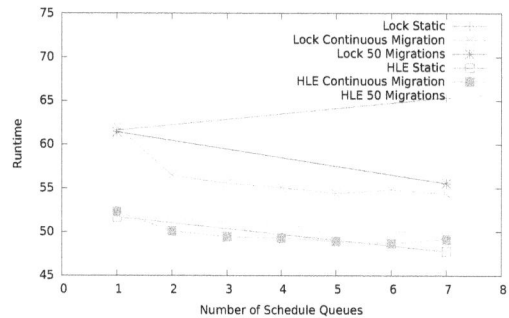

Figure 19: Comparison of Migration Schemes for 7 Worker Threads with X LTSF Queues

While the continuous migration scheme is not problematic for the system under test, the comparison was made to thoroughly evaluate TSX using this scheme as a viable solution to contention. TSX may also one day become available on NUMA architectures. Further testing would need to be performed, but at least it will be known if this solution has any significant impact on contention.

These results are shown in Figure 17. It is evident that any static thread to LTSF queue assignment suffers from the same problems. Except for the 2 worker thread, 2 LTSF queue and 3 worker thread, 3 LTSF queue configurations, performance suffers as the number of LTSF queues is increased. Load balancing becomes an issue with this migration scheme because worker threads can become unevenly divided among the LTSF queues leading.

The second implementation attempts to address the load balancing issue by reassigning worker threads to their original LTSF queues after successfully executing the specified number of events. After a thread is reassigned to its original LTSF queue, it continues to schedule events from that queue for the remainder of the simulation.

Unfortunately, the simulation results were incredibly inconsistent using this scheduling scheme. A significant portion of the simulations did not complete execution in the allotted time. The longer running simulations experienced significantly higher rollbacks. When the simulation does appear to run normally, it executes slightly faster than the strictly static thread assignment scheme. However, the instability of this migration scheme made it infeasible to obtain data.

The migration scheme makes a significant difference in contention and load balancing. Figures 18 and 19 show the comparison of the migration schemes used. The first implementation of the event limited migration scheme is shown below since the second implementation performance could not be adequately measured.

5.2 Conclusions

This paper explored the use of Intel's transactional memory implementation, Transactional Synchronization Extensions (TSX) in the multi-threaded WARPED PDES kernel to alleviate contention for the pending event set. The WARPED pending event set consists of a global Least Time-Stamped First (LTSF) queue and local event set queues for each LP.

Based on the results, it clear that TSX improved the performance of WARPED. HLE consistently shows speedup over conventional synchronization mechanisms. It even slightly reduces execution time when the simulation only uses one LTSF queue. In other configurations, HLE reduces execution time by as much as 27% and consistently reduces execution time by 20%.

While HLE is the superior synchronization mechanism, RTM still showed increases in performance, generally by about 5%. It also works with multiple LTSF queues better than HLE. This is most likely attributed to the retry algorithm. HLE transactions only have one chance to execute a transaction. If contention is high at certain times, the transaction will most likely abort. The RTM retry algorithm uses abort information to decide when to retry transactional execution, rather than immediately aborting the transaction or using conventional synchronization mechanisms. RTM might not perform as well as HLE due to the overhead associated with RTM. The retry algorithm requires abort statistics to be calculated and maintained which adds a bit more overhead to RTM.

TSX is not likely to allow simultaneous access to the same LTSF queue when the structure is being written. TSX synchronization mechanisms also appear to be more expensive. The performance increases seen with TSX are most likely result from the concurrent execution of critical sections involving only read operations. Furthermore, some critical sections bypassed their write operations under certain conditions. For example, a check was performed within a critical section to ensure the LTSF queue was not empty. If the queue was empty, the critical section ended without performing any operations. With standard synchronization, this critical section would still suffer from the locking overhead, even though it wasn't necessary. With TSX synchronization, the check could potentially execute concurrently with another thread. The same scenarios apply to each LP's processed and unprocessed queue. Overall, TSX reduced unnecessary contention.

In conclusion, TSX significantly improves simulation performance for the WARPED PDES kernel. While other solutions to contention showed improvements in performance, they were not nearly as significant as TSX, especially HLE. TSX only showed slight improvements in its own performance when combined with these other solutions. Regardless, TSX is powerful solution to contention.

Acknowledgments

Support for this work was provided in part by the National Science Foundation under grant CNS–0915337.

6. REFERENCES

[1] C. Cascaval, C. Blundell, M. Michael, H. W. Cain, P. Wu, S. Chiras, and S. Chatterjee. Software transactional memory: Why is it only a research toy? *Communications of the ACM*, 51(11):40–46, 2008.

[2] V. Chitters, A. Midvidy, and J. Tsui. Reducing synchronization overhead using hardware transactional memory. Technical report, University of California at Berkeley, Berkeley CA, 2013.

[3] J. Chung, L. Yen, S. Diestelhorst, M. Pohlack, M. Hohmuth, D. Christie, and D. Grossman. ASF: AMD64 extension for lock-free data structures and transactional memory. In *43rd Annual IEEE/ACM International Symposium on Microarchitecture (MICRO)*, pages 39–50, New York, NY, 2010. ACM.

[4] D. Dice, Y. Lev, M. Moir, and D. Nussbaum. Early experience with a commercial hardware transactional memory implementation. In *Proc of the 14th International Conference on Architectural Support for Programming Languages and Operating Systems*, pages 157–168, 2009.

[5] T. Dickman, S. Gupta, and P. A. Wilsey. Event pool structures for pdes on many-core beowulf clusters. In *Proc of the 2013 ACM SIGSIM Conference on Principles of Advanced Discrete Simulation*, pages 103–114, New York, NY, 2013. ACM.

[6] R. Fujimoto. Parallel discrete event simulation. *Communications of the ACM*, 33(10):30–53, Oct. 1990.

[7] V. Gajinov, F. Zyulkyarov, U. Osman S, A. Cristal, E. Ayguade, T. Harris, and M. Valero. Quaketm: Parallelizing a complex sequential application using transactional memory. In *Proc of the 23rd International Conference on Supercomputing (ICS'09)*, pages 126–135, 2009.

[8] S. Hanke. The performance of concurrent red-black tree algorithms. Technical report, Institut fur Informatik, University of Freiburg, 1998.

[9] T. Harris, J. R. Laurus, and R. Rajwar. *Transactional Memory*. Morgan and Claypool, 2nd edition, 2010.

[10] J. Hay. Experiments with hardware-based transactional memory in parallel simulation. Master's thesis, School of Electronic and Computing Systems, University of Cincinnati, Cincinnati, OH, June 2014.

[11] Intel. *Intel Architecture Instruction Set Extensions Programmer Reference. Chapter 8: Intel Transactional Synchronization Extensions*, Feb. 2012.

[12] Intel. *Intel 64 and IA-32 Architectures Optimization Reference Manual. Chapter 12: Intel TSX Recommendations*, July 2013.

[13] D. E. Martin, T. J. McBrayer, and P. A. Wilsey. Warped: A time warp simulation kernel for analysis and application development. In *29th Hawaii International Conference on System Sciences (HICSS-29)*, volume Volume I, pages 383–386, Jan. 1996.

[14] J. Misra. Distributed discrete-event simulation. *ACM Computing Surveys*, 18(1):39–65, Mar. 1986.

[15] K. Muthalagu. Threaded warped: An optimistic parallel discrete event simulator for clusters of multi-core machines. Master's thesis, School of Electronic and Computing Systems, University of Cincinnati, Cincinnati, OH, Nov. 2012.

[16] M. Neuling. What's the deal with hardware transactional memory?, 2014.

[17] K. S. Perumalla and S. K. Seal. Discrete event modeling and massively parallel execution of epidemic outbreak phenomena. *Simulation*, 88(7):768–783, July 2012.

[18] R. Rajwar and J. R. Goodman. Speculative lock elision: Enabling highly concurrent multithreaded execution. In *Proc of the 34th Annual ACM/IEEE International Symposium on Microarchitecture*, pages 294–305, New York, NY, 2001. ACM.

[19] R. Ronngren, R. Ayani, R. M. Fujimoto, and S. R. Das. Efficient implementation of event sets in time warp. In *Proc of the Seventh Workshop on Parallel and Distributed Simulation*, pages 101–108, 1993.

[20] A. Silberschatz, P. B. Galvin, and G. Gagne. *Operating System Concepts*. John Wiley and Sons, Inc., 8th edition, 2008.

[21] R. M. Stallman et al. *Using the GNU Compiler Collection*. Free Software Foundation, Inc., 2013.

[22] A. Wang, M. Gaudet, P. Wu, J. N. Amaral, M. Ohmacht, C. Barton, R. Silvera, and M. Michael. Evaluation of blue gene/q hardware support for transactional memories. In *Proc of the 21st International Conference on Parallel Architectures and Compilation Techniques (PACT-12)*, pages 127–136, 2012.

[23] J. Wang, N. Abu-Ghazaleh, and D. Ponomarev. Interference resilient pdes on multi-core systems: Towards proportional slowdown. In *Proc of the 2013 ACM SIGSIM Conference on Principles of Advanced Discrete Simulation*, pages 115–126, New York, NY, 2013. ACM.

[24] Z. Wang, H. Qian, H. Chen, and J. Li. Opportunities and pitfalls of multi-core scaling using hardware transactional memory. In *Proc of the 4th Asia-Pacific Workshop on Systems*, pages 3:1–3:7, 2013.

[25] R. M. Yoo, C. J. Hughes, K. Lai, and R. Rajwar. Performance evaluation of intel transactional synchronization extensions for high-performance computing. In *Proc of the International Conference on High Performance Computing, Networking, Storage and Analysis*, pages 19:1–19:11, 2013.

Improving Accuracy and Performance Through Automatic Model Generation for Gate-Level Circuit PDES with Reverse Computation

Elsa Gonsiorowski, Justin M. LaPre, Christopher D. Carothers
Rensselaer Polytechnic Institute
Troy, NY 12180
{gonsie,laprej,chrisc}@cs.rpi.edu

ABSTRACT

Gate-level circuit simulation is an important step in the design and validation of complex circuits. This step of the process relies on existing libraries for gate specifications. We start with a generic gate model for Rensselaer's Optimistic Simulation System (ROSS), a parallel discrete-event simulation framework. This generic model encompasses all functionality needed by optimistic simulation using reverse computation. We then describe a parser system which uses a standardized gate library to create a specific model for simulation. The generated model is comprised of several functions including those needed for an accurate model of timing behavior.

To quantify the improvements that an automatically generated model can have over a hand written model we compare two gate library models: an automatically generated LSI-10K library model and a previously investigated, handwritten, simplified GTECH library model [19]. We conclude that the automatically generated model is a more accurate model of actual hardware. The generated model also represents the timing behavior with an approximately 50 times higher degree of fidelity. In comparison to previous results, we find that the automatically generated model is able to achieve better optimistic simulation performance when measured against conservative simulation. We identify peak optimistic performance when using 128 MPI-Ranks on eight nodes of an IBM Blue Gene/Q machine.

Categories and Subject Descriptors

D.1.2 [**Programming Techniques**]: Automatic Programming; D.1.3 [**Programming Techniques**]: Concurrent Programming—*Parallel Programming*

General Terms

Design, Performance

Keywords

Parallel discrete-event simulation; digital logic simulation; automatic logic generation; design automation

1. INTRODUCTION

In the world of simulation, model creation can be a complex act of creativity and ingenuity. Model developers must create a detailed representation of a complex real-world system. In addition, this representation must be built within a specific simulation framework. When working with a discrete-event simulation tool, developers must account for model memory and understand the details of how a model's state may change over time. By creating a generic model for a common simulation use case, we increase model flexibility to allow for any set of specific details. A user can then make use of an existing parser to transform a domain-specific description into code used by the generic model.

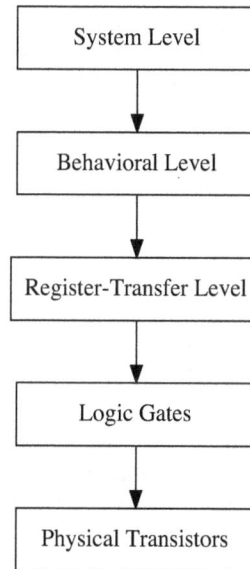

Figure 1: Levels of abstraction within the circuit design process. Automatic tools perform synthesis on a given design to generate the design at the next (lower) level. This design is then validated through one or more tests.

The process for designing large integrated circuits (such as processors) involves simulation at many levels of abstraction (see Figure 1). Gate-level simulation usually begins with circuit designs at the Register-Transfer Level (RTL), written in the Verilog Hardware Description Language [23, 24]. To synthesize the RTL description, one must select a gate library. This library contains descriptions of the logic gates available. While this can be as simple as the set of *and*, *or*, and *not* boolean logic gates, more extensive gate libraries are often used. Commercial gate libraries will describe the electrical properties of a gate, such as its power draw and resistance.

At the logic gate level of circuit abstraction there are many functional validation tests that are performed. Here, simulation is a common tool. Simulation is used to test expected output signals (given a known set of input signals). Simulation can also be used as a virtual oscilloscope to verify electrical signals at various places within the circuit.

Integrated circuits have become so complex that sequential simulation tools are no longer adequate. Many commercial gate-level simulation tools have limited parallel capability, thus limiting simulation to sub-components of the larger circuit. Large circuits have a wealth of inherent parallelism that can be fully exploited with parallel discrete-event simulation.

This paper describes a generic model for logic-level (gate-level) circuit simulation. This generic model provides the core capability upon which any particular logic gate library can be modeled and simulated. Here we demonstrate that by using a generic model with automatically generated library details the overall simulation is more accurate and has better performance for optimistic simulation, when compared to conservative simulation. To our knowledge, our contributions include the first ever results of gate-level circuit simulation on a modern supercomputing platform, namely the IBM Blue Gene/Q.

We begin with a review of simulation and gate-level circuit modeling, including essential terminology, in Section 2. Next, details of the generic model are described in Section 3. We then describe the process of parsing an existing gate description written to domain-specific Liberty language in Section 4. In Section 5, we illustrate improved accuracy and performance by comparing a handwritten model with the generic model with automatically generated gate library details. Section 6 presents related research in the area of automatic model generation and highlights the importance of logic-level simulation. Finally, we present a summary of the value and importance of tools for automatic model generation in Section 7.

2. BACKGROUND

Computer simulations model real world behavior in order to understand a complex system over time. Within discrete-event simulations the state of the modeled system can only be modified through a sequence of time-stamped events [39]. Thus these simulations are from constructed of two entities:

- **Events**
  Each event occurs at a particular instance in time and contains a specific piece of information. An event will directly affect only one logical process, but a series of events can be said to be causally linked.

- **Logical Processes or LPs**
  These entities encapsulate the particular state of a portion of the modeled system. LPs are directly affected by events, and can cause change to other parts of the system by "sending" or "scheduling" events in the future.

When a simulation engine exists within a parallel or distributed environment it falls in the research area of *Parallel Discrete-Event Simulation* (PDES). The primary challenge that a legitimate PDES engine must address is that of unique event serializability [17]. That is, the ordering of events within a simulation must be deterministic across any underlying configuration of execution hardware (whether executed in a single processor environment or on any number of parallel processor configurations). There are two approaches used by parallel simulation engines to achieve the strict

and reproducible order of events: conservative and optimistic synchronization [17].

2.1 Conservative Synchronization

Conservative synchronization within a parallel simulation engine ensures that there is both local and global in-order execution of events. That is, through a conservative synchronization algorithm, no LP is allowed to process an event unless it can be proven that all earlier events which affect the given LP have already been processed.

The YAWNS algorithm is most common conservative synchronization algorithm used in modern simulation engines [35,36]. This conservative algorithm uses global synchronization coupled with a local processing window (called the *global lookahead* window). The global lookahead is used to determine the minimum allowable timestamp increment for events. That is, upon processing an event at time t, the given LP can only schedule events at a time greater than $t + global\ lookahead$.

The relationship between lookahead window size and the average length of event delay within in a system greatly impacts the speedup that can be achieved by a conservative simulation [11]. If the lookahead window is relatively small in comparison the average event delay, there will negative impact on conservative performance. This is due to the fact that global synchronization must happen more frequently as the simulation progresses. If all event delays are of a uniform size, then the lookahead window can be quite large and conservative simulation can perform increasingly well.

2.2 Optimistic Synchronization

Within optimistically synchronized parallel simulations there are no guarantees of global in-order execution of events. This means that an LP may process a sequence of events out of serial order. The most prevalent algorithm in this area is Time Warp [26]. This method keeps track of inter-event causality. As such, when an out-of-order event is detected, the system is able to recover [31].

System recovery occurs at an LP level. One method of LP recovery is called *reverse computation* [12]. This method uses a function to "un-process" a given event. This allows LPs to *rollback* or *reverse* the effects of a series of events and begin forward event processing with a more correct ordering. Usually, the onus of writing the function for reversing the state of an LP lies on the model developer.

When an LP detects out-of-order event, the event is said to cause the LP to *rollback*. This rollback may require that certain messages be canceled. This cancellation process is done through *anti-messages*. Within Time Warp systems there are two categories of rollbacks [17]:

- **Primary Rollback**
  A rollback triggered by receiving a late message. For an LP at time t, a primary rollback occurs when it receives an event at a time less than t. This may cause some anti-messages to be sent.

- **Secondary Rollback**
  A rollback triggered by an anti-message corresponding to a message which has already processed by an LP.

2.3 ROSS

Rensselaer's Optimistic Simulation System, ROSS, is a prominent PDES engine [7, 10, 12, 21]. This ANSI C engine includes a reversible random number generator and is designed for fast and efficient performance. ROSS performs conservative simulation using the YAWNS protocol and optimistic simulation using the Time Warp algorithm with reverse computation. Recently, ROSS has been shown to be remarkable scalable [6].

2.4 Circuit Design Process

Circuit design for modern processors is a complex activity. The design process involves several levels of abstraction and uses simulation for verification. When a circuit design is finally realized at the logic gate level, the size of the problem to be simulated has increased greatly. Traditionally, this digital logic simulation step has been a bottle neck in the design process [9].

Parallel simulation, particularly PDES, has been found to be quite appropriate for this problem [5,9]. Implementations of parallel digital logic simulation exist for many flavors of the viable PDES algorithms, as this was once an engaging area of research [9,34,40,41]. More recently, however, there has been a lack of activity in this field, with some believing that there is little room for improvement on existing techniques [22]. This limited view uses traditional metrics which only evaluate the simulation systems themselves [5, 13, 16], without perspective on the larger circuit design process.

The research presented here involves several concepts from electrical engineering, including the following terms:

- **Gate**
  A small component that performs a logic operation on a set of inputs to produce a set of outputs. A *nand* gate is an example of one boolean logic gate. Some gates may be able to store data and have an internal state (e.g., a *latch*).

- **Pin**
  A point of contact for an electrical component within a circuit. Electrical signals are carried in to and out of a logic gate along its pins. When a gate has an internal state, the data is said to reside on "internal pins."

- **Netlist**
  A list of all components (gates) and their connections for a given circuit. A particular netlist description of a circuit uses components specified in a provided gate library.

3. GENERIC MODEL

The generic gate model is the foundation for any gate instance LP. This generic model encompasses all nonspecific gate behavior, including: state initialization, message passing, event handling, and reverse event handling. The specific functions of a particular gate type are abstracted away with function pointers. By implementing the fundamentals of a gate model in a nonspecific way, any number of gates types can be modeled. In the subsequent section, we review the common functionality that the generic gate model provides.

3.1 Gate State

An LP's *state* in ROSS must be flexible enough to encapsulate the state of any logic gate. By condensing the core characteristics of any logic gate into a defined set, we created a generic gate model. This is relatively straightforward for logic gates and they can be defined by the following characteristics:

- **Type**
  This attribute simply identifies which type of gate (from the provided gate library) this instance represents.

- **Input Pins**
  This vector represents the pins where electrical signals are received. The number of incoming wires to a single input pin of a gate is called *fanin*. Fanin is usually limited as no more than one wire connects to an input pin.

- **Internal Pins**
  This vector represents the internal state of a logic gates and is only used by some more complicated gate types, such as flip-flops and latches.

- **Output Pins**
  This vector represents the outgoing electrical signals a gate can produce. The number of outgoing wires from any output pin is called *fanout*. Fanout is not limited, meaning several wires can connect from one output pin.

3.2 State Initialization

During LP initialization, a particular circuit model is instantiated. The generic gate model works with a description of a particular circuit that has been pre-processed for fast parallel instantiation. Each LP is provided with a predefined-size chunk of string data which it parses into its gate type and pin connections.

One challenge of LP initialization is unconstrained fanout for a particular logic gate instance. A classic example of this is a poorly defined clock tree, where one logic gate defines the clock signal for an entire circuit. In the OpenSPARC T2 example (in Section 5), a single gate experiences a fanout of over 5,000 wires. The issue arises during pre-processing, when a logic gate instance must be defined in a pre-determined amount of space. This ensures fast startup, but cannot include all information about a gate instance's outgoing connections. Instead, we provide a size for the output pins vector, and perform a 2-phase initialization. First, each LP allocates memory based upon the gate instance information read from the initialization file. Second, each LP sends a message to the LPs connected on its input pins notifying them of a link.

3.3 Messages

In any discrete-event simulation, the messages represent small packets of communication between LPs. These messages trigger any and every change within the system. When using ROSS's optimistic mode with reverse computation, the messages gain additional importance. The same message processed during forward event handling is un-processed as an *anti-message* during reverse event handling. We take advantage of this fact by using the message to store pieces of LP state that are destroyed during forward event handling. These values are easily restored from the anti-message during rollback.

Messages store the following:

- **Sender Information**
  This includes the sender ID and which pin the value was sent from.

- **Receiver Information**
  This includes which pin the value is received upon.

- **Signal Information**
  This may be a high or low value (some gate libraries make use of more than two possible signal values).

Additional space in the message is allocated for latch-style gates with internal logic pins. These gates store information in internal state that must be state-saved to the message during forward event handling.

3.4 Forward Event Handling

Event handling during simulation is relatively straightforward for any generic logic gate model. Upon receiving an electrical signal (such as a digital 1 or 0) on an input pin, the gate calculates signals to send through its output pins. The model LPs then send messages with a specific delay. For a code snippet, see Figure 2. It is important to note that any LP state value that is overwritten is saved to the message before destruction. The message processed here becomes the anti-message which is processed during an optimistic simulation rollback.

The flexibility to model any given library of gates is done through type defined function pointers. For each gate type-defined in the Liberty library, several functions are generated. The most essential function is the logic function. Each gate type generates a logic function adhering to the type definition: `typedef void (*logicFunction) (int input[], int internal[], int output[])`. The values of the output pins are then sent through a message simulating an electrical signal. These messages have a delay associated with them, depend on whether the incoming input signal was rising or falling. We use the following delay function type: `typedef float (*delayFunction) (int inputPin, int outputPin, int risingFlag)`.

To make these specific functions easily accessible by the generic model, they are placed in an array. These arrays can be referenced by the integer defining an LP's particular gate type.

3.5 Reverse Event Handling

The ability of an LP to rollback, or revert to its state to a previous point in time, is a key property of any optimistic simulation model. Being able to achieve this in a programmatic manner is not always an easy task, particularly if a model has large state or encapsulates complex logic. This is decidedly not the case when it comes to simple logic gates. The crucial detail of a logic gate is that the output signals can be calculated from the given set of input (and possibly internal) pins. Thus, an event that stores information used by the forward event handler can easily store the same information needed to revert the LP state.

The reverse event handler for the generic gate model is surprising uncomplicated (see Figure 3). The ROSS engine does the hard work of tracking event causality. An individual LP needs to only "un-process" an anti-message. For the generic model, that involves using values stored the anti-message to revert the state. These are the same values that were saved to the message during the forward event handling.

For any given gate library, there is no need to undo any logic which took place within the gate. The output pins will be re-evaluated during the next forward execution of an event. This elementary aspect of logic gates makes the automatic generation of any model straightforward.

4. MODEL GENERATION

To model the specific behavior of gates in a specified library, the library description file must be parsed. The goal for this process is to transform the domain-specific gate descriptions into an equivalent model for ROSS written in C. Currently, our generic model (Section 3) uses only the timing and boolean-logic data for each gate. The simplicity of the generic model makes it easy to extend to other gate properties, such as power usage.

This parsing is straight forward for any library that adheres to the domain-specific Liberty format [30]. To parse the grammar defined by Liberty, we created a Python Lex-Yacc LR-parser [8].

This parsers builds a collection of Gate_Type objects, consisting of pins and "special" internal functions. Each pin is associated with a direction, and output pins are associated with a boolean expression representing a logic function. Once this object hierarchy is created from the input Liberty file, each Gate_Type preforms a local analysis to its rename pins with array references. Finally, the model C code is generated.

Figure 4 shows an example of this transformation from Liberty format to equivalent C code. This automatically generated model not only includes the logic function of each gate, but encompasses the timing information as well. For validation, the generated code can be directly compared to the provided gate library definition. With automatic model generation, an end-user can experiment with many different gate libraries. This allows the simulated model to be consistent with the gates used during fabrication.

By creating an automatic generation tool, we have remove the need for a human to hand write model code. For example, the LSI-10K library (discussed in Section 5) details 163 different logic gates. The model code describing this library is over 9,000 lines-of-code. The flexibility of our approach allows for any standardized library to be used within ROSS by simply running a script. In the remainder of this section we describe the important elements of this model generation process.

4.1 Pin Names

The pins associated with a particular logic gate are guaranteed to have unique names. These names can be easily alphabetized, creating a lexicographical ordering. It is this alphabetically order that maps pin names to array indices. This name mapping takes place when a boolean expression (i.e., the logic function for an output pin) is converted to the equivalent C representation.

For example, take a Liberty defined OR gate with two input pins, A and B, and one output pin Z (see Figure 4). This becomes an instantiation of a generic gate model with an input pin array of size two and an output pin array of size one. Any reference to pin A is transformed to a reference to `input[0]`, pin B becomes `input[1]`, and pin Z becomes `output[0]`. Thus, the logical OR function defined by the Liberty description ("A+B") is rewritten using the boolean operations available in C: (`input[0] || input[1]`).

4.2 Predefined LPs Types

Circuit design netlists are made up of a few components: gates, wires, and input and output connections (external to the current circuit). Each gate or "net" in a netlist becomes an LP during simulation (defined by the generic gate model). Straight wires (wires connecting two pins) do not become LPs and instead the direct connection information is stored within a gate's state. In contrast, wires which represent a fanout (where one output pin connects to two or more input pins) do become LPs. These *fanout* LPs, along with special *input* and *output* LPs are treated as generic gate types that are not defined by the Liberty gate library. Instead, they created by default during automatic model generation.

4.2.1 Input and Output LPs

Input LPs represent signals coming from other circuit components. In the example discussed in Section 5, these LPs randomly feed high and low signals into the circuit during simulation.

Output LPs represent signals exiting the current circuit module. Currently these LPs act as a sink for any incoming signals.

4.2.2 Fanout LPs

In most circuit designs, there is no fanin. That is, a single input pin on any gate is connected to only one wire. This is not the case for fanout as one output pin may connect many wires, each leading to separate input pins. These fanout wires are represented as LPs

```
void gates_event(gate_state *s, message *in_msg){

    if (in_msg->type == LOGIC_MSG) {
        int in_pin = in_msg->id;

        if (s->inputs[in_pin] == in_msg->value) return; // no change for input pins

        int rising = (s->inputs[in_pin] < in_msg->value);

        // save current state of input and internal pins in case of reverse event
        // we store old values in the current message, which is used during reverse
        SWAP(&(s->inputs[in_pin]), &(in_msg->value));
        if (gate_internal_size[s->gate_type] > 0) {
            in_msg->internal_pin0 = s->internals[0];
            in_msg->internal_pin1 = s->internals[1];
        }

        // perform logic operation
        logic_function_array[s->gate_type](s->inputs, s->internals, s->output_val);

        // send messages to my output pins
        for (int i = 0; i < gate_output_size[s->gate_type]; i++){
            // calculate the delay for outgoing signals
            float delay = delay_function_array[s->gate_type](in_pin, i, rising);
            // ...
}
```

Figure 2: Snippet of generic gate forward event handler.

```
void gates_event_rc(gate_state *s, message *in_msg){

    if (in_msg->type == LOGIC_MSG) {

        if (s->inputs[in_msg->id] == in_msg->value) return;

        // restore the state of input and internal pins
        SWAP(&(s->inputs[in_msg->id]), &(in_msg->value));
        if (gate_internal_size[s->gate_type] > 0) {
            s->internals[0] = in_msg->internal_pin0;
            s->internals[1] = in_msg->internal_pin1;
        }

        // No need to undo changes to output pins
        // ROSS handles event causality

    }
}
```

Figure 3: Snippet of generic gate reverse event handler.

which simply forward an incoming signal to all connected outputs. These LPs use an event delay which is smaller than the smallest gate delay in the current library.

5. ILLUSTRATIVE EXAMPLE

To understand the value of using automatic model generation, we compare an automatically generated model to a handwritten one. A comparison of the details of these two models can be seen in Table 1. Both models were used to simulate the crossbar switch (CCX) from the OpenSPARC T2 processor [38]. The simulations of the CCX models lasted for 3,000 simulation time units which is equivalent to 3,000 clock cycles for the handwritten model and 3000 ns for the automatically generated model. Both models use a similar round-robin style partitioning scheme. This scheme makes no attempt to group the LPs by communication patterns and leads to a very high percentage of messages set to an LP within another MPI rank.

Table 1: Detail comparison between a handwritten simplification of a GTECH model and an automatically generated timing-accurate LSI-10K model. These details are from the simulation of the crossbar switch module from an OpenSPARC T2 processor.

	Handwritten GTECH Simplified Model	Auto-Generated LSI-10K Model
Gate Count	211,001	200,981
Net Events	1.4 Billion	0.2 Billion
Time Unit	Clock Cycle	Nanosecond
Lookahead	0.4	0.009

The handwritten model used as the basis for comparison has been previously presented in [19]. This model was a dramatic simplification of the GTECH standard cell library provided by Synopsis [37]. While the GTECH library contains over 100 gates, the

91

```
cell(OR2) {
  pin(A) {
    direction : input;
  }
  pin(B) {
    direction : input;
  }
  pin(Z) {
    direction : output;
    function : "A+B";
    timing() {
      intrinsic_rise : 0.38;
      intrinsic_fall : 0.85;
      related_pin : "A";
    }
    timing() {
      intrinsic_rise : 0.38;
      intrinsic_fall : 0.85;
      related_pin : "B";
    }
  }
}
```

(a) LSI-10k Liberty code

```
void OR2_func
(int input[], int internal[], int output[]) {
  //Z : A+B
  output[0] = (input[0] || input[1]);
}

float OR2_delay_func
(int in_pin, int out_pin, int rising) {
  //['Z']
  if (out_pin == 0) {
    //['B']
    if ( in_pin == 1 ) {
      if (rising) return 0.38;
      if (!rising) return 0.85;
    }
    //['A']
    if ( in_pin == 0 ) {
      if (rising) return 0.38;
      if (!rising) return 0.85;
    }
  }
}
```

(b) The corresponding, automatically generated C code

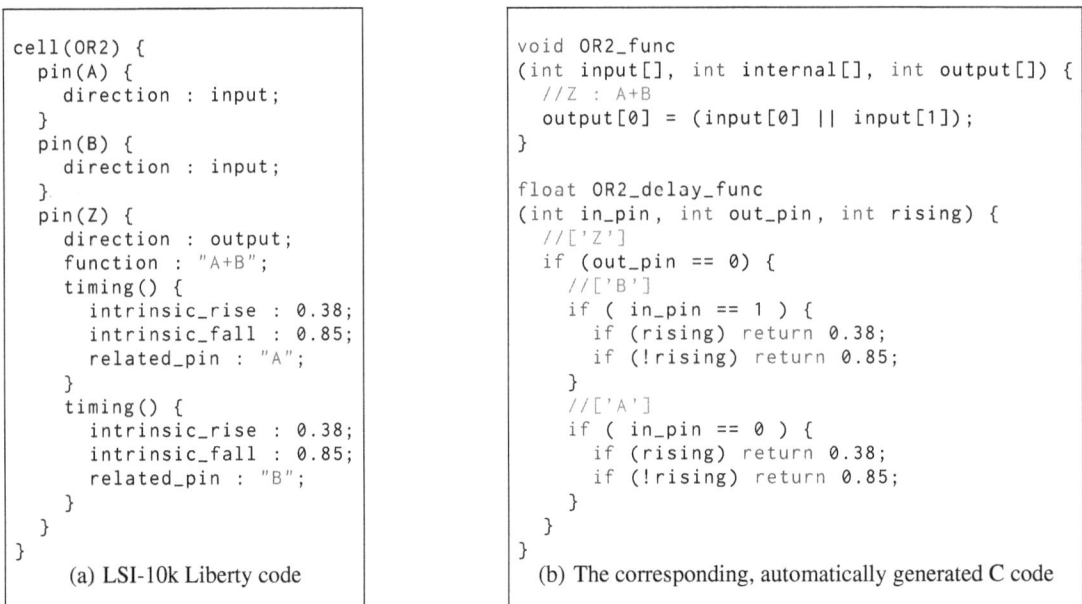

Figure 4: Example of an OR logic gate defined in the LSI-10k Liberty library and the automatically generated functions used by the ROSS generic gate model. Note that one can do a line-by-line comparison to validate both the logic and timing information.

handwritten model consisted of an over decomposition of each logic gate into one of eight basic gates: *repeater*, *not*, *and*, *nand*, *or*, *nor*, *xor*, and *xnor*. This decomposition transformation was accomplished by a parser provided by Li et al. [29] and is written in Lex and Yacc [28].

Due to a lack of timing information for the GTECH library, a very simplistic timing model was used, with each logic gate having a uniform, single clock-cycle delay. This delay was achieved through the use of self-scheduled wakeup messages. These messages carried no logic, but contributed to a large event population for the simulation as a whole. This simplistic timing model also had an effect on the lookahead value that could be used for conservative simulation. With such a regularly timed model, lookaheads of 0.4 time units were used. This is quite large in comparison to the average event "in-flight" time of 0.5 time units.

For our automatically generated model, we use the LSI-10k library written in Liberty format [30]. This generated model is approximately 10,000 lines of code. This code includes the logic function for each gate type, as well as a function to calculate a gate's internal delay (see Figure 4). The generated C code can be compared on a line-by-line basis with the Liberty library description for verification of both the logic and timing information.

For any automatically generated model, the lookahead value used during conservative simulation must be derived from the timing values in the provided gate library. Within the LSI-10k model, the smallest defined timing delay is 0.01 ns. Thus we safely set the lookahead window at 0.009 ns for this model. The smaller lookahead window represents an increase of fidelity of the timing behavior model. In this respect, the automatically generated model is nearly 50 times more accurate than the handwritten model.

We have shown that the automatically generated model leads to an accurate representation of the gates being modeled and simulated. The next task is to determine any effects the automatically generated model on simulation performance. We address this by recreating and comparing results with an experiment described in [19], where a handwritten gate model was used.

5.1 Experimental Setup

The circuit design chosen was the CCX component of the OpenSPARC T2 processor. We start with the open source RTL description. This source was then synthesized into a gate-level netlist using the Synopsys Design Compiler and the selected gate library (either GTECH or LSI-10k).

The experiments with the handwritten model were performed on an IBM Blue Gene/L with cores operating at 700 MHz [19]. This supercomputer debuted in 2004 as the first of its class. It was designed around a relatively slow processor speed, allowing for a lower overall power consumption [18]. It also introduced a system-on-a-chip design, with all node components (including two processor cores) embedded in one chip. These nodes were connected to several global communication networks, including a separate network for global MPI communications (e.g., *all reduce*).

To create a similar experimental setup, the automatically generated model was run on an IBM Blue Gene/Q machine, with cores running at 1.6 GHz. This is the latest edition of the IBM supercomputer line. The Blue Gene/Q features 18 processor cores per chip [20]. 16 of the 18 cores are devoted to application use; one core is dedicated to operating system functionality; the final core is a spare, used when another core within the chip fails. While the Blue Gene/Q is capable of running up to four hardware threads per core, this work only uses one hardware thread per core (i.e., one MPI rank per core).

On both Blue Gene systems, ROSS benefits from the high-speed communication networks [7,21]. For these results and the previous results pertaining to the handwritten model, we use the terms *MPI rank* and *core* interchangeably.

5.2 Results

To understand the impact on overall simulation performance of an automatically generated model, we examine the relationship between the performance of optimistic and conservative simulation. Figure 5 shows the optimistic/conservation comparison during strong scaling for the handwritten model. Here, conservative performance continues to improve as parallelism increases. In contrast, as par-

92

**Handwritten Basic Gate Library
on IBM Blue Gene/L**

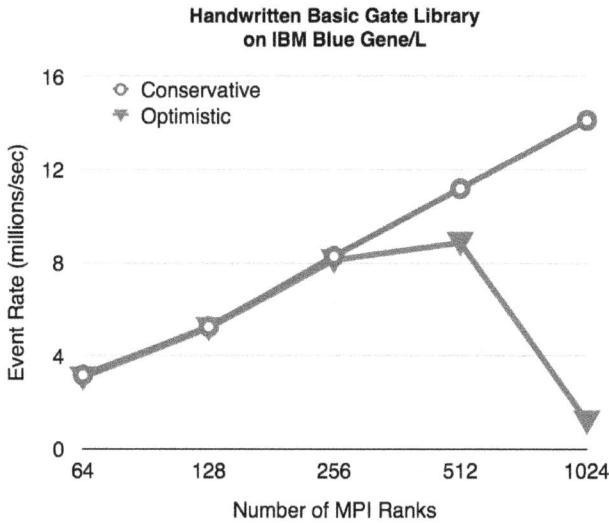

Figure 5: Single crossbar experiments on 700 MHz Blue Gene/L cores. Inputs are generated randomly every two simulation time units. This experiment was originally published in [19].

**Auto-generated LSI-10k Gate Library
on IBM Blue Gene/Q**

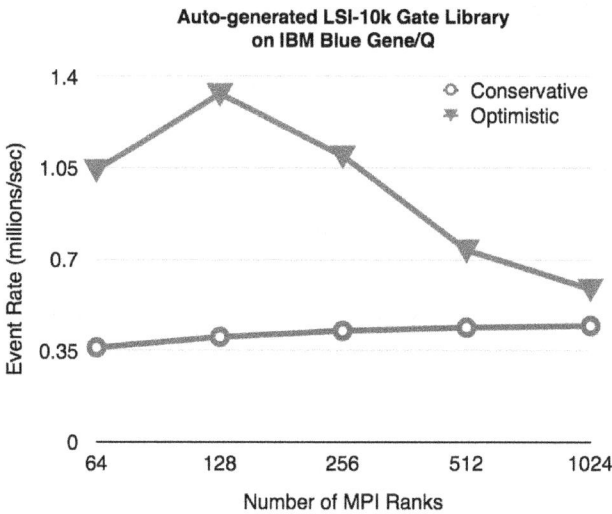

Figure 6: Single crossbar experiments on 1.6 GHz Blue Gene/Q cores. Inputs are generated randomly every two simulation time units. Note that the lower event rate (when compared to Figure 5) is due to a decrease in overall event population as well as an increase in event complexity.

allelism increases optimistic simulation never outperforms conservative and in fact becomes under decomposed and experiences a decrease in performance.

Optimistic simulation is usually expected to outperform conservative. This result was attributed to the over-simplification of the handwritten model. As concluded in [19]:

"The lookahead of 0.4 time units (in relation to the timestamp increment of 0.5 time units) is in the medium to large range, based on the performance study by Carothers and Perumalla [11]. From this study, we note that conservative synchronization outperforms optimistic synchronization for medium and large lookahead up to 8,192 cores. We observe the same phenomena here. Should the

Number of Primary and Secondary Rollbacks

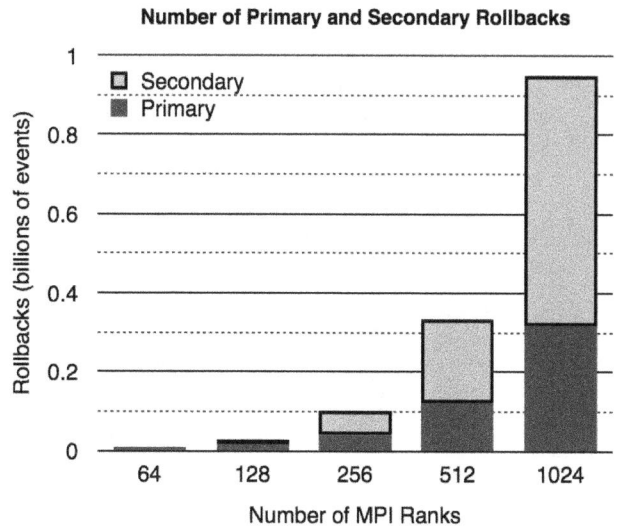

Figure 7: This graph shows the total number rollback events as a sum of the primary and secondary rollbacks. Note that there are total of 200 million net events in the simulation.

lookahead become smaller due to changes in the model or core count increase, we expect optimistic performance to improve and potentially overtake conservative performance."

We can now demonstrate the observation that a smaller lookahead value will positively affect optimistic performance.

Figure 6 compares optimistic and conservative simulation performance for the automatically generated model. Here, optimistic synchronization outperforms conservative performance. Again, there is the same increase, then decrease in optimistic performance as number of MPI ranks grows. We can again contribute this to the fact that the overall model is small, on the order of 200,000 total LPs. With more than 128 MPI ranks, the model is under decomposed and the communication overhead of synchronization outweighs the total work done on any individual core.

A greater understanding of the under decomposition which occurred during the optimistic simulations can be gained through analyzing the rollbacks. Figure 7 shows that the total number of rollbacks as a sum of the primary and secondary rollbacks. It is important to remember that the number of net events in a full run of the simulation is 200 million. At 256 MPI ranks, optimistic simulation experiences approximately 100 million rollback events, on the order of one half the total number events which need to be processed. Put another way, for event two events which are processed, one of them is eventually rolled back. It is at this point (256 MPI ranks) that we begin to see a decrease in overall optimistic simulation performance.

We can further explore the relationship between primary and secondary rollbacks by analyzing them as a percentage of total rollbacks (seen in Figure 8). For the two experiments where optimistic simulation improves with parallelism (64 and 128 MPI ranks), less than half of the total rollbacks are secondary rollbacks. This means that most anti-messages were received before their counterpart forward message was processed by the receiving LP. The large portion of secondary rollbacks for the large experiments indicates that some MPI ranks within simulation are much farther ahead in time than others.

Primary and Secondary Rollbacks as a Percentage of Total Number of Rollbacks

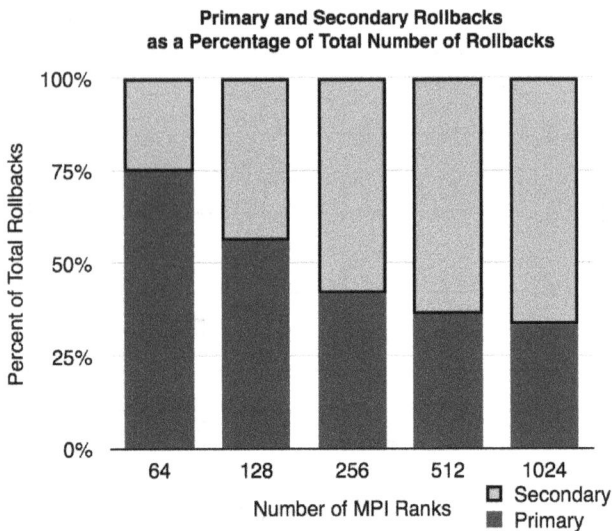

Figure 8: This graph shows the percentage breakdown of the total number of rollback events in terms of primary and secondary rollbacks. The large percentage of secondary rollbacks indicate a large disparity of virtual time across different MPI Ranks.

6. RELATED WORK

Automatic model generation is not a new area of study. The idea of predefining a conceptual (or generic) model shows up in many fields where simulation is an important part of a larger workflow. One such example comes from supply chain management [42]. This work identifies the key elements of the supply chain and how they relate to each other. With the generic definitions in place, it is possible to simulate the specifics of any number of configurations.

For decades, automatic model processing has been a part of the circuit design process (refer to Figure 1). This includes everything from generating behavior models within proprietary systems [25] to generating the schematic diagrams [1] to extracting a gate model from an existing transistor design [27]. Automatically generating gate level models for sequential circuit simulation has not been extensively studied academically, but is a highly patentable area (most recently in [15]).

Parallel digital logic simulation is a highly investigated area of research. This includes several investigations of the merits of both conservative and optimistic synchronization algorithms [3, 4, 14, 32]. The findings are usually mixed as both methods have their merits and either one may be more suitable for a particular circuit model. More recently, research has focused on improving the performance of optimistic simulation through a bottom-up implementation of a digital logic-specific simulation framework [2, 29, 33, 43].

7. CONCLUSIONS

In a typical integrated circuit design workflow, gate-level simulation is done using proprietary, domain-specific simulation software. By creating a generic model and the tools required for parsing domain-specific descriptions, we have enabled substantial increases in modeler efficiency through the use of a high performing PDES implementation. The automatic model generation tool allows for any gate model written in Liberty to be realized in the ROSS framework. This flexibility will allow for an increase in use-

fulness of simulation within the circuit design and verification cycle.

In this paper we have described a generic model for gate-level circuit simulation within a conservative and reverse-computation-based optimistic simulation engine. This generic model is coupled with an automatic system which can generate model details from a Liberty-formated gate library. The accuracy of the automatically generated model can be validated through a side-by-side comparison of the original Liberty description and the resulting C code. This model also allows for greater precision in the model of timing behavior, which is evident in lookahead value used by conservative simulation.

To investigate the performance impact of the automatically generated model we compared the relationship of optimistic and conservative simulation performance to an existing set of results which used a handwritten model. The experiments conducted for this paper were preformed on an IBM Blue Gene/Q and represent some of the first PDES results on this machine. We found that the increased accuracy of model timing (and decrease in lookahead window size) contributed to improved performance of optimistic simulation over conservative simulation. We observed that when the high-fidelity model was executed on 128 MPI ranks, optimistic outperformed conservative simulation by a factor of 3.3. As the number of MPI ranks increased, to a maximum of 1024 ranks, optimistic did not drastically outperform conservative simulation due to a substantial increase in primary and secondary rollbacks.

8. ACKNOWLEDGMENTS

This material is based on research sponsored by Air Force Research Laboratory under agreement number FA8750-11-2-0065. The U.S. Government is authorized to reproduce and distribute reprints for Governmental purposes notwithstanding any copyright notation thereon. The views and conclusions contained herein are those of the authors and should not be interpreted as necessarily representing the official policies or endorsements, either expressed or implied, of Air Force Research Laboratory or the U.S. Government.

9. REFERENCES

[1] A. Arya, V. Swaminathan, A. Misra, and A. Kumar. Automatic Generation Of Digital System Schematic Diagrams. In *Proceedings of the 22nd ACM/IEEE Design Automation Conference*, DAC '85, pages 388–395, Las Vegas, NV, USA, 23–26 June 1985. IEEE Computer Society.

[2] H. Avril and C. Tropper. Clustered time warp and logic simulation. In *Proceedings of the Ninth Workshop on Parallel and Distributed Simulation*, PADS '95, pages 112–119, Lake Placid, New York, USA, 13–16 June 1995. IEEE Computer Society.

[3] R. Bagrodia, Y.-a. Chen, V. Jha, and N. Sonpar. Parallel Gate-level Circuit Simulation on Shared Memory Architectures. *ACM SIGSIM Simulation Digest*, 25(1):170–174, 1995.

[4] R. Bagrodia, Z. Li, V. Jha, Y. Chen, and J. Cong. Parallel Logic Level Simulation of VLSI Circuits. In *Proceedings of the 26th Conference on Winter Simulation*, WSC '94, pages 1354–1361, Orlando, FL, USA, 11–14 Dec. 1994. Society for Computer Simulation International.

[5] M. L. Bailey, J. V. Briner, Jr., and R. D. Chamberlain. Parallel Logic Simulation of VLSI Systems. *ACM Computing Surveys*, 26(3):255–294, Sept. 1994.

[6] P. D. Barnes, Jr., C. D. Carothers, D. R. Jefferson, and J. M. LaPre. Warp Speed: Executing Time Warp on 1,966,080

Cores. In *Proceedings of the 2013 ACM SIGSIM Conference on Principles of Advanced Discrete Simulation*, PADS '13, pages 327–336, Montreal, Canada, 19–22 May 2013. ACM.

[7] D. Bauer, C. Carothers, and A. Holder. Scalable Time Warp on Blue Gene Supercomputers. In *Proceedings of the 23rd ACM/IEEE/SCS Workshop on Principles of Advanced and Distributed Simulation*, PADS '09, pages 35–44, Lake Placid, NY, USA, 22–25 June 2009. IEEE Computer Society.

[8] D. Beazley. PLY: Python Lex-Yacc. *http://www.dabeaz.com/ply/index.html*, 2000–2011. Last access 11 April 2015.

[9] J. V. Briner, Jr., J. L. Ellis, and G. Kedem. Breaking the Barrier of Parallel Simulation of Digital Systems. In *Proceedings of the 28th ACM/IEEE Design Automation Conference*, DAC '91, pages 223–226, San Francisco, California, USA, 17–21 July 1991. ACM.

[10] C. Carothers, D. Bauer, and S. Pearce. ROSS: A High-Performance, Low Memory, Modular Time Warp System. In *Proceedings of the 14th Workshop on Parallel and Distributed Simulation*, PADS '00, pages 53–60, Bologna, Italy, 28–31 May 2000. IEEE Computer Society.

[11] C. Carothers and K. Perumalla. On Deciding Between Conservative and Optimistic Approaches on Massively Parallel Platforms. In *Proceedings of the 42nd Conference on Winter Simulation*, WSC '10, pages 678–687, Baltimore, MD, USA, 5–8 Dec. 2010.

[12] C. Carothers, K. Perumalla, and R. Fujimoto. Efficient Optimistic Parallel Simulations Using Reverse Computation. In *Proceedings of the 13th Workshop on Parallel and Distributed Simulation*, PADS '99, pages 126–135, Atlanta, GA, USA, 1–4 May 1999. IEEE Computer Society.

[13] R. D. Chamberlain. Parallel Logic Simulation of VLSI Systems. In *Proceedings of the 32nd Annual ACM/IEEE Design Automation Conference*, DAC '95, pages 139–143, San Francisco, California, USA, 12–16 June 1995. ACM.

[14] Y.-a. Chen, V. Jha, and R. Bagrodia. A Multidimensional Study on the Feasibility of Parallel Switch-level Circuit Simulation. *ACM SIGSIM Simulation Digest*, 27(1):46–54, June 1997.

[15] S. C. Cismas, K. J. Monsen, and H. K. So. *Automatic Code Generation for Integrated Circuit Design*, Feb. 7 2006. US Patent 6,996,799.

[16] A. Costa, A. de Gloria, P. Faraboschi, and M. Olivieri. An Evaluation System for Distributed-time VHDL Simulation. In *Proceedings of the Eighth Workshop on Parallel and Distributed Simulation*, PADS '94, pages 147–150, Edinburgh, Scotland, United Kingdom, 6–8 July 1994. ACM.

[17] R. M. Fujimoto. *Parallel and Distributed Simulation Systems*. John Wiley & Sons, Inc., New York, NY, USA, 1st edition, 1999.

[18] A. Gara, M. A. Blumrich, D. Chen, G.-T. Chiu, P. Coteus, M. E. Giampapa, R. A. Haring, P. Heidelberger, D. Hoenicke, G. V. Kopcsay, et al. Overview of the Blue Gene/L System Architecture. *IBM Journal of Research and Development*, 49(2.3):195–212, 2005.

[19] E. Gonsiorowski, C. Carothers, and C. Tropper. Modeling Large Scale Circuits Using Massively Parallel Discrete-Event Simulation. In *Proceedings of the 20th IEEE International Symposium on Modeling, Analysis Simulation of Computer and Telecommunication Systems*, MASCOTS '12, pages 127–133, Arlington, VA, USA, 7–9 Aug. 2012.

[20] R. A. Haring, M. Ohmacht, T. W. Fox, M. K. Gschwind, D. L. Satterfield, K. Sugavanam, P. W. Coteus, P. Heidelberger, M. A. Blumrich, R. W. Wisniewski, et al. The IBM Blue Gene/Q Compute Chip. *Micro, IEEE*, 32(2):48–60, 2012.

[21] A. O. Holder and C. D. Carothers. Analysis of Time Warp on a 32,768 Processor IBM Blue Gene/L Supercomputer. In *Proceedings of the 20th European Modeling and Simulation Symposium*, EMSS '08, pages 284–292, Amantea, Italy, 17–19 Sept. 2008. CAL-TEK SRL.

[22] K. hui Chang and C. Browy. Parallel Logic Simulation: Myth or Reality? *Computer*, 45(4):67–73, April 2012.

[23] IEEE Standard for Verilog Hardware Description Language. *IEEE Standard 1364-2005 (Revision of IEEE Standard 1364-2001)*. *http://dx.doi.org/10.1109/IEEESTD.2006.99495*, 2006. Last access 12 May 2015.

[24] IEEE Standard for Verilog Register Transfer Level Synthesis. *IEEE Standard 1364.1-2002*. *http://dx.doi.org/10.1109/IEEESTD.2002.94220*, 2002. Last access 12 May 2015.

[25] R. G. Ingalls. Automatic Model Generation. In *Proceedings of the 18th conference on Winter simulation*, WSC '86, pages 677–685, Washington, DC, USA, 8–10 Dec. 1986. ACM.

[26] D. R. Jefferson. Virtual time. *ACM Transactions on Programming Languages and Systems*, 7(3):404–425, 1985.

[27] S. Kundu. Gatemaker: A Transistor to Gate Level Model Extractor for Simulation, Automatic Test Pattern Generation and Verification. In *Proceedings of the 1998 International Test Conference*, ITC '98, pages 372–381, Washington, DC, USA, 18–23 Oct. 1998. IEEE Computer Society.

[28] J. Levine, T. Mason, and D. Brown. *Lex & Yacc*. A Nutshell Handbook. O'Reilly & Associates, Sebastopol, CA, USA, 1992.

[29] L. Li, H. Huang, and C. Tropper. DVS: An Object-Oriented Framework for Distributed Verilog Simulation. In *Proceedings of the 18th Workshop on Parallel and Distributed Simulation*, PADS '03, pages 173–180, San Diego, CA, USA, 10–13 June 2003. IEEE Computer Society.

[30] Liberty, Version 2009.06. *IEEE-ISTO*. *http://www.opensourceliberty.org*, September 2009. Last access 12 May 2015.

[31] Y.-B. Lin and E. D. Lazowska. A Study of Time Warp Rollback Mechanisms. *ACM Transactions on Modeling and Computer Simulation*, 1(1):51–72, Jan. 1991.

[32] D. Lungeanu and C.-J. R. Shi. Distributed Simulation of VLSI Systems Via Lookahead-Free Self-Adaptive Optimistic and Conservative Synchronization. In *Proceedings of the 1999 IEEE/ACM International Conference on Computer-Aided Design*, ICCAD '99, pages 500–504, San Jose, CA, USA, 7–11 Nov. 1999. IEEE Computer Society.

[33] S. Meraji, W. Zhang, and C. Tropper. On the Scalability of Parallel Verilog Simulation. In *Proceedings of the 38th International Conference on Parallel Processing*, ICPP '09, pages 365–370, Vienna, Austria, 22–25 Sept. 2009. IEEE Computer Society.

[34] R. Mueller-Thuns, D. Saab, R. Damiano, and J. Abraham. VLSI Logic and Fault Simulation on General-Purpose Parallel Computers. *IEEE Transactions on Computer-Aided Design of Integrated Circuits and Systems*, 12(3):446–460, Mar 1993.

[35] D. Nicol. The Cost of Conservative Synchronization in Parallel Discrete Event Simulations. *Journal of the ACM*, 40(2):304–333, 1993.

[36] D. Nicol and P. Heidelberger. Parallel Execution for Serial Simulators. *ACM Transactions on Modeling and Computer Simulation*, 6(3):210–242, July 1996.

[37] S. Palnitkar. *Verilog HDL: A Guide to Digital Design and Synthesis*. Prentice Hall Press, Upper Saddle River, NJ, USA, second edition, 2003.

[38] I. Parulkar, A. Wood, S. Microsystems, and S. Mitra. OpenSPARC : An Open Platform for Hardware Reliability Experimentation. In *Proceedings of the Fourth Workshop on Silicon Errors in Logic System Effects*, SELSE '08, Austin, TX, USA, 26–27 Mar. 2008. IEEE Computer Society.

[39] S. Robinson. *Simulation: The Practice of Model Development and Use*. John Wiley & Sons, Hoboken, NY, USA, 2004.

[40] L. Soulé and A. Gupta. An Evaluation of the Chandy-Misra-Bryant Algorithm for Digital Logic Simulation. *ACM Transactions on Modeling and Computer Simulation*, 1(4):308–347, Oct. 1991.

[41] W.-k. Su and C. L. Seitz. *Variants of the Chandy-Misra-Bryant Distributed Discrete-Event Simulation Algorithm*. Technical report, California Institute of Technology, Pasadena, CA, USA, 1988.

[42] G. E. Vieira and O. C. Júnior. A Conceptual Model for the Creation of Supply Chain Simulation Models. In *Proceedings of the 37th conference on Winter Simulation*, WSC '05, pages 9–pp, Orlando, FL, USA, 4–7 Dec. 2005. IEEE Computer Society.

[43] Q. Xu and C. Tropper. XTW, A Parallel and Distributed Logic Simulator. In *Proceedings of the 19th ACM/IEEE/SCS Workshop on Parallel and Distributed Simulation*, PADS '05, pages 181–188, Kufstein, Austria, 1–3 June 2005. ACM.

Towards HLA-based Optimistic Synchronization with CSPs

Steffen Strassburger
Ilmenau University of Technology
P.O. Box 100 565
98684 Ilmenau
+49-3677-694051
steffen.strassburger@tu-ilmenau.de

ABSTRACT

The High Level Architecture for Modeling and Simulation (HLA) comes with the promise of facilitating interoperability between a wide variety of simulation systems. HLA's time management offers a unique support for heterogeneous time advancement schemes and differentiates HLA from other general interoperability standards. While it has been shown that HLA is applicable for connecting commercial off-the-shelf simulation packages (CSPs), the usage of HLA time management in this specific application area is virtually always limited to conservative synchronization. In this paper, we investigate HLA's capabilities concerning optimistic synchronization and the imposed requirements on CSPs. For the first time, we outline its use in combination with a CSP, namely the Simulation Language with Extensibility (SLX). We report on initial performance results and potential limitations in the current HLA 1516.1-2010 standard and its interpretation by RTI vendors.

Categories and Subject Descriptors

I.6.8 [**Simulation and Modeling**]: Types of Simulation – *distributed.*

General Terms

Algorithms, Performance, Experimentation, Standardization.

Keywords

Optimistic synchronization, HLA, SLX.

1. INTRODUCTION

HLA has been used for facilitating interoperability between CSPs for quite a number of years. First investigations into the subject were based on SLX [5] and were soon followed by several other studies involving CSPs such as Simul8 [3].

The synchronization aspect of the HLA integration of CSPs requires the user to have some influence on the event scheduling mechanism of the CSP. The vast majority of know publications is in that regard limited to the application of conservative synchronization schemes. Often, even time stepped approaches have been applied. While conservative synchronization schemes are rather easy to use and implement, their performance depends

SIGSIM-PADS '15, June 10-12, 2015, London, United Kingdom
ACM 978-1-4503-3583-6/15/06.
http://dx.doi.org/10.1145/2769458.2769483

on the ability to specify (desirably large) Lookahead values for each simulation model. Lookahead is highly dependent on the simulation problem at hand. In the worst case, Lookahead values of zero have to be assumed, leading to a quasi-sequential execution of the CSPs in the distributed simulation.

Optimistic synchronization provides hope for faster model execution, but has not been used in CSPs, as they typically do not provide any state-saving capabilities.

The objective of the research presented here was to practically investigate, whether HLA based optimistic synchronization could actually be integrated into a CSP of our choice. With SLX, a CSP was found which fulfilled the basic requirement of a state saving capability. Our investigation focused on options of integrating optimistic synchronization into an existing HLA interface of this CSP and on ways for transparently offering optimistic synchronization to SLX.

2. REQUIREMENTS

Several requirements are imposed on a CSP when optimistic synchronization shall be applied. The most prominent requirement results from the need for a recovery mechanism. A recovery mechanism must be capable of undoing the potentially damaging results that out-of-order-processing of messages can incur.

As part of a recovery mechanism, a previous state of the simulation must be restored. This can be achieved by applying a state saving and restoration technique. This technique must be capable of storing all relevant state information during a simulation run at arbitrary simulation time stamps. Relevant state information includes the state of the user model (e.g., state variables, object instances) as well as system state (e.g., position of random number generators, event lists, etc.).

Other requirements needed to recover from causality violations are the need to cancel any sent messages that become invalid, because a straggler message has been received. To be able to cancel such messages, a federate must keep a log of all sent messages and their time stamp. To be able to reprocess any received messages after a state rollback, an optimistic federate must also keep a log of all incoming messages including their time stamps. In the HLA, all calls to services of the federate interface specification that carry time stamps should be considered as relevant messages. Such services return message retraction handles needed to identify and retract (i.e. cancel) a message. Relevant HLA services include *updateAttributeValues* (UAV) and *sendInteraction* (SI).

Further requirements imposed by optimistic synchronization protocols include the need to perform "global virtual time" (GVT) calculations [2] as well as the need for a mechanism to correctly determine the simulation end condition.

3. SLX-HLA-INTERFACE EXTENSIONS

SLX offers a state-saving and restoration capability originally intended for purposes such as saving a model state after a warmup-period (e.g. for efficiently performing replications in non-terminating simulations). This capability was investigated and found fit to be the base for a rollback mechanism in optimistic synchronization.

The guiding principle in designing the optimistic extensions for the SLX-HLA-Interface was to make usage of optimistic synchronization as easy as possible for the modeler. With that in mind, as much implementation as possible was put into the SLX-HLA-Interface library, following the idea of an external rollback controller put forward by other authors [7].

It takes care of bookkeeping tasks, such as keeping message logs of received and sent messages, the detection of causality violations, and the processing of incoming and outgoing message retraction requests ("cancellations").

The most important concern which conceptually had to be placed on the side of the SLX model relates to the state saving and restoration approach. It involves issuing the "SLXCheckpoint" and "SLXRestore" command when appropriate. Also, the management of releasing obsolete checkpoints using "SLXReleaseCheckpoint" had to be implemented. Further extensions needed in the SLX-HLA-Interface include the addition of RTI_FlushQueueRequest to the interface, which is needed for requesting out-of-order delivery of messages from the RTI.

4. EXPERIMENTAL VALIDATION

A small case study based on the bounded buffer CSP interoperability reference model IRM A.2 [4] was used to test the validity of the implemented optimistic synchronization approach. This IRM imposes a zero Lookahead requirement.

Two federates were implemented in SLX (Version 2.3, Build EP 264). The commercial pRTI 5.0.0.0 (Build 1887) from Pitch was used as RTI software. The implementation of the SLX-HLA-Interface uses the HLA 1516.1-2010 ("HLA-Evolved") C++ API.

Both federates and the RTI were executed on a single PC with an Intel i5-3470 Multi-Core-Processor with 3.20 GHz and a main memory capacity of 16 GB.

In the experiments, the behavior of federate 1 was kept constant. It produces entities following a uniform distribution, processes the entities in a workstation and tries to transfer them to federate 2. If the queue in federate 2 is full, federate 1 will block processing at its last workstation. To induce different requirements on the synchronization algorithm, the behavior of federate 2 was varied and different sets of experiments were conducted.

Initial performance results show that optimistic synchronization outperforms conservative synchronization in the zero Lookahead case on every occasion. While these findings are very positive, there is obviously more experimentation needed. This will involve both more complex models and fairer conditions for the conservative approach (Lookahead values larger than zero).

5. PROBLEMS WITH GVT AND FQR

An important feature needed for optimistic synchronization is the determination of a value called Global Virtual Time (GVT). GVT imposes a lower bound on how far back a rollback can occur and is essential for fossil collection.

The design of HLA Time Management intended the *flushQueueRequest* (FQR) service in conjunction with the *timeAdvanceGrant* (TAG) service to provide such GVT determination capabilities to optimistic federates [1, 6].

The experiments described above were verified with the latest RTIs of two leading RTI vendors, namely pRTI 5.0.0.0 from Pitch and MÄK RTI 4.3 from MÄK. Both RTIs failed calculating a correct grant time following the use of FQR. In fact, the resulting TAG always delivered a time value of zero.

While this behavior seems to be obviously different from what HLA Time Management intended, feedback from the Pitch support indicates a different view on the issue. They consider the behavior as a correct interpretation of the HLA standard. The main issue at hand here is, which influence the parameter t passed in FQR(t) shall have on GVT calculation.

Currently, it appears, that t is not taken into account at all. This is very unfortunate, as the parameter passed to FQR constitutes a conditional guarantee that the federate will not generate a time stamped message before the next TAG service invocation with a timestamp less than the specified logical time plus the current Lookahead of the joined federate. Only taking this guarantee into account the RTI can perform a correct distributed calculation of grant times.

Further discussion is needed to clarify whether a change in the HLA standard is needed to prevent the interpretation embraced by Pitch.

Beyond this, future work will include more experimentation. We will also investigate the costs associated with state-saving and rollback and identify situations where an optimistic approach will be preferable to conservative synchronization.

6. REFERENCES

[1] Fujimoto, R. M. 1998. Time Management in The High Level Architecture. *SIMULATION* 71, 6, 388–400.

[2] Jefferson, D. 1985. Virtual Time. *ACM Transactions on Programming Languages and Systems* 7, 3, 404–425.

[3] Mustafee, N. and Taylor, S. J. E. 2006. Investigating Distributed Simulation with COTS Simulation Packages: Experiences with Simul8 and the HLA. In *Proceedings of the 2006 Operational Research Society Simulation Workshop (Leamington Spa, UK, March 28-29, 2006). SW06. OR Society, UK, 33-42.*

[4] Simulation Interoperability Standards Organization. 2010. *Standard for Commercial-off-the-shelf Simulation Package Interoperability Reference Models (SISO-STD-006-2010).* http://www.sisostds.org/DigitalLibrary.aspx?Command =Core_Download&EntryId=30829.

[5] Straßburger, S., Schulze, T., Klein, U., and Henriksen, J. O. 1998. Internet-based Simulation using Off-the-shelf Simulation Tools and HLA. In *Proceedings of the 1998 Winter Simulation Conference (Washington D.C., December 13-15, 1998).* IEEE, Piscataway, NJ, 1669–1676.

[6] U.S. Department of Defense. 1996. *HLA Time Management Design Document. Version 1.0.* August 15, 1996.

[7] Wang, X., Turner, S. J., Low, Malcolm Y. H., and Gan, B. P. 2005. Optimistic Synchronization in HLA-Based Distributed Simulation. *SIMULATION* 81, 4, 279–291.

On Energy Consumption in Distributed Simulations

Richard Fujimoto
School of Computational Science and Engineering
Georgia Institute of Technology
Atlanta, Georgia USA 30332
+1 404 894-5615
fujimoto@cc.gatech.edu

Aradhya Biswas
Department of Computer Science and Engineering
India Institute of Technology, Hyderabad
Yeddumailaram, Telangana, India
+91-9652090580
cs11b003@iith.ac.in

ABSTRACT

Power and energy consumption are important concerns in the design of high performance, embedded and mobile computing systems but have not been widely considered in the design of parallel and distributed simulations. The importance of these factors is discussed in the context of mobile online distributed simulations. Preliminary results are reported concerning energy consumption of conservative synchronization algorithms.

Categories and Subject Descriptors

I.6 [**Simulation and Modeling**]: Types of Simulation – *Discrete event; Parallel; Distributed*.

General Terms

Algorithms; Measurement; Performance; Design.

Keywords

Energy consumption; power consumption; distributed simulation.

1. INTRODUCTION

The need to reduce energy consumption in mobile computing applications is clear. Improvements can result in increased battery life or enable the use of smaller batteries thereby reducing the size and weight of devices. In high performance computing (HPC) power is a dominant cost associated with operating large data centers and is a major obstacle to improving supercomputer performance. Despite its importance in computing today, very little attention has focused on understanding and developing techniques to minimize power and energy consumption in parallel and distributed simulations. This paper highlights the need for further research in this area.

Power-aware and *energy-aware* systems are those where power or energy is a principal design consideration. For example, power-aware HPC systems may utilize techniques to change the system's behavior based on the amount of power being consumed. Similarly, energy-aware mobile systems may adapt based the amount of energy remaining in the device's batteries.

Energy use may similarly be an important concern for parallel and distributed simulations. For example, Dynamic Data Driven Application Systems (DDDAS) [4] involve incorporating live data from instrumented systems into executing applications in order to optimize the system and/or steer the measurement process. In such systems predictive distributed simulations may be embedded in a sensor network. Each node of the network collects and processes data concerning its local environment, and may execute a simulation to project future states of its portion of the system. The nodes of the sensor network collectively form an embedded distributed simulation that predicts the future state of the system as a whole. These predictions may then be used to adapt the sensor network to better monitor or optimize the system.

Embedded distributed simulations such as these are described in [5] where a paradigm termed ad hoc distributed simulation was proposed. The system envisioned here differs in that a more traditional approach is used where the system is partitioned into areas, e.g., rectangular grid sectors, and a sensor/simulator node is assigned to each sector. The nodes exchange data and synchronize in much the same way as conventional distributed simulations.

2. RELATED WORK

There is a substantial literature in power- and energy-aware computing systems, and a variety of techniques may be employed. For example, dynamic voltage and frequency scaling (DVFS) is concerned with altering the voltage and/or clock speed of the processor by taking into consideration energy and performance constraints. Other work addresses scheduling algorithms to balance energy saving with meeting real-time deadlines [2], utilizing different modes of operation [1], predictive modeling of energy and power [3] and embedded systems evaluations [6]. To date, work in power and energy aware computing has focused on low-level aspects such as specific hardware capabilities, operating system and compiler issues, and communication protocols such as energy-efficient routing algorithms in sensor and ad hoc networks. To our knowledge energy consumption for distributed simulation synchronization algorithms has not previously been examined.

3. EXPERIMENTAL RESULTS

Several factors impact power and energy consumptions in embedded distributed simulations. These include the level of detail at which the system is modeled, state dissemination and data exchange, and the synchronization algorithm. Here we focus on the synchronization algorithm. Other work considers energy consumption for data dissemination [7].

A central concern here is the amount of additional energy consumed by the parallel/distributed execution that takes into account overheads such as message communication and synchronization. For this purpose we define a metric termed the *energy overhead*. Energy overhead refers to the amount of *additional* energy that is expended in the execution of a particular implementation of a parallel or distributed simulation on some hardware configuration relative to an energy-efficient sequential execution of the same computation.

Initial experiments were conducted to measure the energy overheads of distributed simulations. Two exemplar systems are considered. The first uses a distributed peer-to-peer (P2P) architecture of mobile nodes, each executing a simulation of a portion of the system being monitored. The Chandy/Misra/Bryant (CMB) null message algorithm is used for synchronization. The second utilizes a centralized client-server (CS) approach where the simulations execute in client nodes and synchronization is performed centrally in a server. A simple window algorithm (YAWNS) is used. These approaches represent major classes of conservative synchronization algorithms.

The experimental configuration mimics an embedded distributed simulation application executing on a set of battery-driven mobile processors. The LG Nexus 5 cellular phone with a quadcore Qualcomm MSM8974 Snapdragon 800 processor, 2 GB memory, and 16 GB storage was used as the mobile computing platform. The phone runs the Android version 5.0.1 (Android Lollipop) operating system. All inter-processor communication utilizes the device's 802.11n WiFi network. A private wireless network was established among the devices to avoid interference resulting from Internet traffic. The cellular network capability of the phone is not used in these experiments.

A trace showing power consumption per mobile device for a queueing network simulation is shown in Figure 1. Power for the sequential and distributed simulations are shown. The graphs show a relatively constant amount of power consumed throughout the execution, but exhibit notable spikes at certain points in time. The spikes are due to background tasks that are periodically scheduled for execution on the mobile devices. The distributed simulations utilize a significantly larger amount of power compared to the sequential simulation. The average amount of power consumed was 521 milliWatts (mW) for the sequential simulation compared to 771 mW for CMB, and 770 mW for YAWNS. The power overhead for CMB was therefore 256 mW (or 49%) compared to the sequential execution and 249 mW for YAWNS (48%). Although these results do not provide sufficient data to draw general conclusions, they do illustrate a methodology for power measurement and evaluation and suggest that the power overhead in a distributed simulation can be significant.

4. FUTURE RESEARCH

Power and energy consumption are areas of increasing concern for parallel and distributed simulations. The empirical work presented here represents only an initial evaluation of the energy and power consumed by a distributed simulation. These measurements suggest that distributed execution incurs a significant energy overhead compared to a sequential execution.

Power- and energy- consumption of parallel and distributed simulations opens many unanswered questions. The tradeoffs among execution time, model detail, and energy overheads are not well understood. Deep understandings of the power and energy consumed by distributed simulations, and those aspects that are different relative to other types of computing applications are not available. Accurate, predictive models of energy consumption are needed. A comprehensive examination of synchronization algorithms and their execution on different distributed system architectures is required. Extensive analyses and application of power/energy management techniques for real world applications are needed. Methods to reduce energy use have yet to be developed. Moreover, we believe power- and energy-aware parallel and distributed simulation represents a rich area of future research for the field with many unsolved problems.

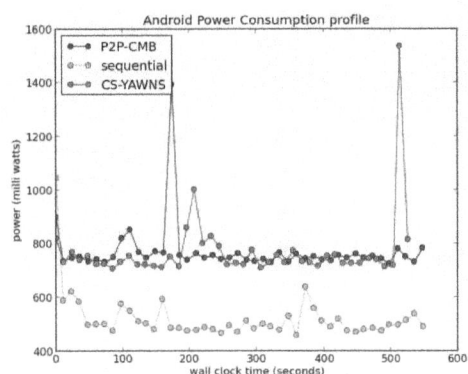

Figure 1. Power consumption of simulations.

5. ACKNOWLEDGMENTS
This research was supported by AFOSR grant FA9550-13-1-0100.

6. REFERENCES
[1] Bhatti, K., C. Belleudy, and M. Auguin. 2010. *Power management in real time embedded systems through online and adaptive interplay of DPM and DVFS policies.* in *Proceedings of the International Conference on Embedded and Ubiquitous Computing.* (Hong Kong, China: Dec. 11-13, 2010). IEEE, p. 184–191.

[2] Cho, K.-M., C.-H. Liang, J.-Y. Huang, and C.-S. Yang. 2011. *Design and implementation of a general purpose power-saving scheduling algorithm for embedded systems.* in *Proceedings of the IEEE International Conference on Signal Processing, Communications and Computing.* (Xi'an, China: Sept. 14-16, 2011). IEEE, p. 1–5.

[3] Czechowski, K. and R. Vuduc. 2013. *A Theoretical Framework for Algorithm-Architecture Co-design.* in *Proceedings of the IEEE International Symposium on Parallel Distributed Processing.* (Boston, MA: May 20-24, 2013). IEEE, p. 791-802.

[4] Darema, F. 2004. *Dynamic Data Driven Applications Systems: A New Paradigm for Application Simulations and Measurements.* in *Proceedings of the International Conference on Computational Science.* (Kraków, Poland: July 6-9, 2004). Springer, p. 662-669.

[5] Fujimoto, R., M. Hunter, J. Sirichoke, M. Palekar, H.-K. Kim, and W. Suh. 2007. *Ad Hoc Distributed Simulations.* in *Proceedings of the Principles of Advanced and Distributed Simulation.* (San Diego, CA: June 12-15, 2007). IEEE, p. 15-24.

[6] Grasso, I., P. Radojkovic, N. Rajovic, I. Gelado, and A. Ramirez. 2014. *Energy Efficient HPC on Embedded SoCs: Optimization Techniques for Mali GPU.* in *Proceedings of the IEEE International Parallel and Distributed Processing Symposium.* (Phoenix, AZ: May 19-23, 2014). IEEE, p. 123-132.

[7] Neal, S., G. Kanitkar, and R.M. Fujimoto. 2014. *Power Consumption of Data Distribution Management for On-Line Simulations.* in *Proceedings of the Principles of Advanced Discrete Simulation.* (Denver, Co.: May 18-21, 2014). ACM, p. 197-204.

Towards a DEVS-based Operating System

Daniella Niyonkuru   Gabriel Wainer
Department of Systems and Computer Engineering
Carleton University 1125 Colonel By Dr, Ottawa, ON, Canada K1S 5B6
{Daniella.Niyonkuru, Gabriel.Wainer}@carleton.ca

ABSTRACT
Embedded systems are becoming increasingly complex and heterogeneous. Formal methods have proven effective in ensuring reliability and safety. However, they are hard to scale up. Modeling and Simulation (M&S)-based methods, on the other hand, deal effectively with scalability issues and provide the benefits of a risk-free testing environment. Yet, they are usually at most semi-formal, and models are not directly executed on the target hardware. To address the above challenges, we present a formal M&S-based kernel that runs on bare-metal and execute the original simulation models on the target hardware.

Categories and Subject Descriptors
C.3 [**Special-Purpose and Application-Based Systems**]: Real-time and embedded systems; D.2.13 [**Software Engineering**]: Reusable Software – Reuse models; D.4.7 [**Operating Systems**]: Organization and Design – *Real-time systems and embedded systems*; I.6.8 [**Simulation and Modeling**]: Types of Simulation – *Discrete event*; B.1.2 [**Control Structure and Microprogramming**]: Control Structure Performance Analysis and Design Aids – *Formal Models*; B.4.4 [**Input/Output and Data Communications**]: Performance Analysis and Design Aids – *Formal Methods*;

General Terms
Design, Experimentation, Theory.

Keywords
Real-Time Embedded Systems; Model Execution Engine; DEVS;

1. INTRODUCTION
Embedded systems are everywhere, and they shape the world. Any device that runs on electricity either already has, or will soon have a computing system embedded within it. An embedded system is generally defined as a combination of computer hardware and software, designed to perform a dedicated function. Real-Time Embedded Systems (RTES) in particular, in addition to producing correct responses, are also required to deliver them within strict timing constraints [11]. Missing these deadlines may lead to significant loss and in some cases catastrophic consequences. Other constraints related to these systems are limited dimensions, low cost, and low power requirements.

SIGSIM-PADS'15, June 10–12, 2015, London, United Kingdom.
© 2015 ACM. ISBN 978-1-4503-3583-6/15/06...$15.00
DOI: http://dx.doi.org/10.1145/2769458.2769465

In addition to dealing with timeliness requirements, RTES design needs to deal with hardware/software partition, and cope with target systems' increasing scalability and complexity. However, there had been a real shortage of effective design and implementation practices. Most design methodologies are ad-hoc based, and therefore hard to scale up for larger systems, and/or require tremendous testing effort with no guarantee of a bug-free software product. Deficiencies come from two main weak areas: the development cycle and system verification. Indeed, disruptions exist in the development cycle since different artifacts and tools are used throughout the various phases [10]. System verification, on the other hand, is hardened by these discontinuities as well as the absence of robust development framework.

Recently, formal methods have shown great potential in dealing with these issues [17], but these methods remain hard to scale up. On the other hand, model-based design techniques handle well heterogeneity but the lack of formal modeling and effective model transformation are major roadblocks. A practical solution to the above problems is the use of formal Modeling and Simulation (M&S), therefore combining the advantages of a simulation based approach with the rigor of a formal methodology [16].

Such a M&S-driven approach must, however, ensure efficient model transformation, and should especially allow the original models to run on the target hardware. In this paper, we will present a kernel based on a formal M&S methodology that enables the user to run models directly on bare-metal. The objective is to be able to execute models directly on the target system hardware without the need of an operating system. The new model execution engine presented here provides functionalities similar to those of a real-time kernel, with formal models operating as system processes. This step narrows further the gap between the simulation and implementation phases. In fact, the same models are used for both simulation and execution on the final target. In order to show the feasibility of the approach, we present a case study of a line tracking robot using the bare metal environment.

A kernel that allows models to run on bare-metal was developed, and tested on ARM Cortex-M boards. As an application, we have modeled, simulated and deployed a line tracking robot. The results obtained using the new environment are compared and validated against another existing embedded environment.

2. BACKGROUND
The proposed approach is based on DEMES (Discrete-Event Modeling of Embedded Systems) [3] that offers a practical method in which models are consistently used throughout the development cycle. DEMES is an M&S based development methodology based on Discrete-EVent Systems specification (DEVS), which is a discrete event simulation formalism for modeling and simulating dynamic systems. The DEVS formalism [15] decomposes complex system designs into basic (behavioral)

models called atomic, and composite (structural) models called coupled. Precise rules are followed to define state changes of the modeled system with regards to input events or time delay triggers. DEVS is especially suitable for RTES since it provides a rich structural representation of components, and formal means for explicit time specification, which is essential to RTES. It has proven to be successful in different complex systems and can also be used alongside with existing real-time techniques such as state-charts, VHDL, Verilog and Timed Automata [17] [18].

2.1 DEMES

DEMES uses M&S for the initial stages, and replaces models incrementally with hardware surrogates without modifying the original models. The transition can be done in incremental steps, incorporating models in the target environment after thorough testing in the simulated platform, allowing model reuse throughout the process.

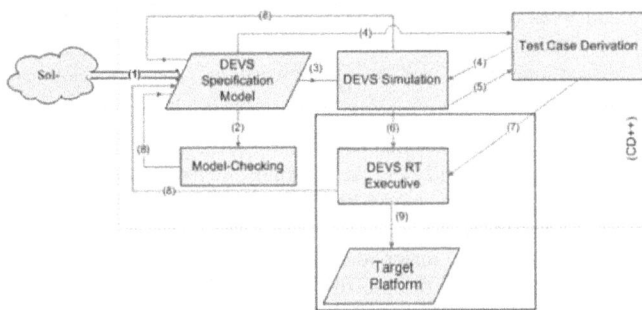

Figure 1. DEMES Development Cycle [17]

A DEMES based development cycle [17] [18] involves Model Specification, Model-Checking, DEVS Simulation, DEVS Real-Time Execution on a Target platform, and Testing. In the **model specification** stage, we define a specification model of the System of Interest (1) using a formal model (using DEVS or alternative techniques translated to equivalent DEVS models). After model specification, **model-checking** (2) can be used for model properties validation. The same models are then used to run **DEVS simulations** (3) of the behavior of the different sub models under specific loads. In brief, we first study system properties analytically, and complement the proofs using simulation, which can also be used for hardware/software co-design (and for training). The same DEVS specification model is used to derive **test cases** (4) (5), which can be also used for the simulation studies. Deriving test cases from both the model and from the simulation results allows us to check that the models conform to the requirements. Once we are satisfied with both analytical and simulated results, the models are incrementally moved into a target platform. A **real-time executive** (6) executes the models on the particular hardware (9). If the hardware is not readily available, the software components can still be developed incrementally and tested (7) against a model of the hardware to verify viability and take early design decisions. As the design process evolves, both software and hardware models can be refined, progressively setting checkpoints in real prototypes. At this point, those parts that are still unverified in the formal and simulated environments are tested, increasing the confidence of the engineer into the implemented system. Any modifications require going back to the same model specifications (8), which ensure that we can provide a consistent set throughout the development. This software lifecycle is cyclic, allowing

refinement following a spiral approach. On each cycle of the spiral, we end with a prototype application consisting of software/hardware components interacting with simulated components.

Other M&S based frameworks and methodologies such as UML-RT, Ptolemy II, ECSL and Matlab/Simulink have been developed but they are semi-formal (which makes more difficult proving valuable properties about the models under development), and do not provide model continuity in the RTES development lifecycle [12]. Instead, formal modeling methods like DEVS provide sound syntax/semantics for structure, behavior, time representation and composition, which lend themselves to well-defined computation. Plus, the DEMES approach offers the following advantages [17]:

- Reliability: logical and timing correctness rely on DEVS system theoretical roots and sound mathematical theory.
- Model Reuse: DEVS has well-defined concepts for coupling of components and hierarchical, modular model composition.
- Hybrid modeling and knowledge reuse: different methods can be used while keeping independence at the level of the executive, using the most adequate technique on each part of system architecture and reusing existing expertise.
- Process Flexibility: hybrid modeling capabilities are transparent for the executive, which is defined by an abstract mechanism that is independent from the model itself.
- Testing: several tests can be carried out and the definition of experimental frames can be automated.

2.2 DEVS-based frameworks

The DEMES concepts have been applied in the development of different tools to offer a unified and consistent development environment. Existing DEVS based development environments for RTES include DEVSJAVA [7], a Java DEVS-based simulator that supports high-level modeling; RTDEVS/CORBA [5], a DEVS implementation based on real time CORBA communication middleware; PowerDEVS [3] a tool for hybrid system modeling and real time simulation; and E-CD++[12][18],an engine for executing DEVS models in embedded systems. The platform limitations remain significant compared to the existing methods: In [7], [5], [9] and [4] where implementation requires Java, the target hardware should be able to support the Java-implemented DEVS real-time execution environment. In [8], the authors presented a DEVS based real-time system on a TINI chip which has limited memory and processing ability. However, this requires Java Virtual Memory and Java class libraries availability on the chip. In [3], Linux RTAI kernel is required for PowerDEVS. In [12], our implementation relied on Xenomai/Linux kernel services. Therefore, although the DEMES approach offers multiple benefits, tools have to be improved to overcome limitations and support different hardware.

The E-CD++ developed by our team [12] was used in various applications and relied on a variant of the Linux kernel. Xenomai provided hard real-time functionality to the Linux kernel. In this paper, we go further with bridging the gap between simulation and implementation (enabling the utilization of the same models) by removing OS limitations while decreasing the embedded application footprint, and increasing efficiency and portability. In the next section, E-CD++ software components will be presented and its implementation explained.

2.3 E-CD++

The DEVS formalism proposes a framework for model construction and defines an abstract simulation mechanism that is independent of the model itself. This mechanism provides a high-level implementation detail for the DEVS framework, and can be feasibly implemented by computer software.

E-CD++ [18] is a real time implementation, based on the CD++ simulator [15] [14] (a DEVS-based framework for M&S), and RT-CD++ [16] (an extension of CD++ for real-time simulation). E-CD++ supports modeling real-time systems by converting the CD++ virtual time-advance function to real-time, and provides an RT simulation platform for verification of such models.

Figure 2 illustrates the E-CD++ development framework. The embedded platform with the external environment is shown in this layered approach representing the cross-platform development of models. The modeller defines models using a high-level DEVS language combined with C++ code if needed, which provides the application layer. These Real-Time models are then interpreted and executed by the DEVS Real-Time (DEVSRT) engine [12].

To allow for direct replacement of models with external entities, the I/O ports of E-CD++ models implement the formal interfacing mechanism of DEVSRT in the Driver Interface layer. The underlying middleware is a real-time kernel and the runtime objects are imported to this platform as RT tasks. In the previous iteration, the E-CD++ execution engine used the Xenomai real-time kernel [12] with multi-tasking services to implement DEVSRT. The user models and the driver objects were merged with the E-CD++ core objects; and the entire combination was compiled to produce an executable.

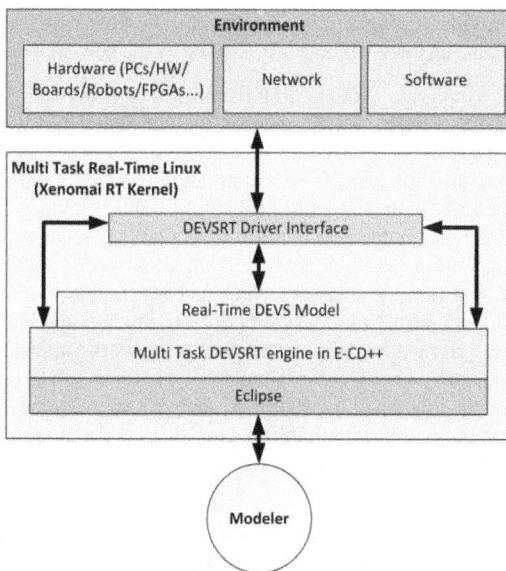

Figure 2. E-CD++ Layers [12]

E-CD++ also include several features also. The Eclipse IDE layer shown in figure 1 also allows for the graphical development of models. Through the IDE, the Generic Graphical Advanced environment for DEVS modeling and simulation (GGAD) [18] allows the developer to use a graph-based representation to specify models hierarchy, interconnections and behaviors to automate model generation. At the execution engine level, various features have been implemented in order to improve the software including DEVSRT simulation algorithms, a Flattened

Coordinator technique and a Time Interval function. The P-DEVS simulation algorithms allows for parallel execution of concurrent events through the implementation of a messaging behaviour for model interaction. The Flattened Coordinator technique improves the efficiency of the DEVSRT messaging behaviour through the removal of superfluous messages that are generated for communication between coupled models. Finally, the Time Interval function enforces real-time constraints through the use of wall-clock time advancement and execution deadline checking.

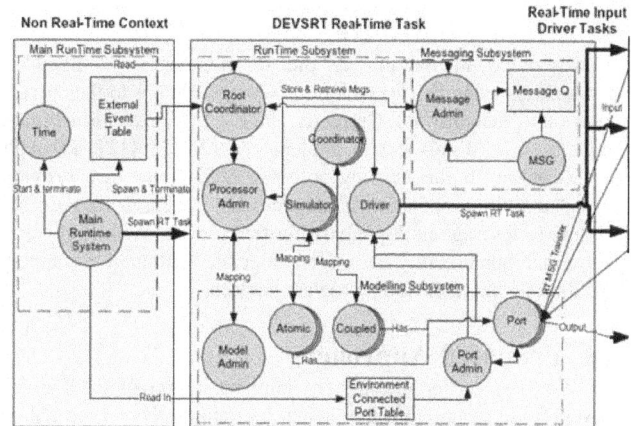

Figure 3. Software Components [12]

CD++ has four main components [Figure 3]: the Main Runtime System, the Modeling Subsystem, the Runtime Subsystem and the Messaging Subsystem [17]. The Main Runtime System manages the overall aspects of the real-time execution and provides timing functions with microsecond precision. The Main Runtime System is the first object that is created in non-real-time context, and it launches the Runtime Subsystem [12]. In general, the Main Runtime System first register Atomic component objects, then the Top coupled component ports that are connected to the external environment, reads in the external events (from an existing event-file) and builds an external event table. After that, the Main Runtime System reads in the model-file and builds the model hierarchy. Finally, it spawns the main real-time task in which the Root Coordinator (RC) is created to start the DEVSRT execution cycle. The Runtime Subsystem consists of Simulators, Coordinators, and the Processor Admin. In E-CD++, the Simulators work on run-time engines that correspond to atomic components, and they perform the main job of executing the internal transition and output function after receiving the proper messages.

The RC is a special Coordinator that manages the real-time event scheduling. It initializes the global Driver object which launches the real-time input driver tasks (associated with input ports of the Top coupled component in the DEVS model hierarchy) declared by the user.

The Modeling subsystem is generated in order to define the atomic and coupled models, as well as the relationships between them. For each of these models, a processor is defined within the Runtime Subsystem in order to manage the behavior of the model and drive the execution. The Messaging subsystem provides the P-DEVS behavior [12].

While this implementation reflects DEMES concepts, it is closely dependent on the Linux kernel and restricts supported devices. We went further and removed this limitation: The new E-CD++

provides a DEVS execution engine that resides in an ARM-based microcontroller, and it is OS independent. Today, the ARM architecture is the most pervasive 32-bit architecture and is found in all types of computing devices from real-time safety systems (automotive braking systems) to smartphones [13]. Besides, since the new E-CD++ does not rely on a particular OS, it becomes applicable to a broader variety of microcontrollers. In order to successfully achieve this objective, several changes were required and will be presented in the next section.

3. A DEVS-based Kernel

As discussed in Section 2, the development of embedded applications using E-CD++ requires several changes to the current iteration of the software. Currently, the E-CD++ execution engine relies on a RT-Linux OS to implement DEVSRT [12]. Through modifications to the existing software architecture, we provide now stand-alone operation, i.e. bare-metal execution. To do so, we had to leverage multiple existing functions as well as develop additional functionality in order to operate without OS support and directly interface with hardware devices.

3.1 Proposed Approach

As described earlier, the current implementation of E-CD++ is based on the assumption that it will be running from a variant of the Linux kernel. This imposes memory capacity, processing, and portability limitations as the target platform must include the memory and processing power necessary for the Linux kernel variant, and there must be a Linux kernel that can be compiled for the target platform and can interface with the available hardware devices.

As a solution to the above challenges, we propose the new architecture shown in figure 4. The modeller defines models using the DEVS formalism and C++ code. Note that an Eclipse IDE can be used in order to make the development task easier. The defined models are then interpreted and executed by the DEVSRT engine which directly rest on bare-metal (target platform) in the new version. Similarly to the previous version, the driver interface layer is used to provide a formal interface for I/O ports. However, this layer has been modified to communicate directly with the underlying hardware without the need of a real-time kernel middleware.

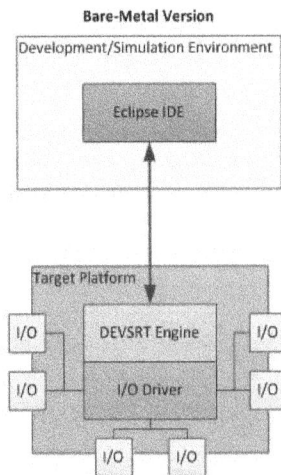

Figure 4. New Layers

Besides, the simulation platform is only used for model development since the DEVSRT execution engine and the I/O drivers are moved to the target platform and run on bare-metal. This is new when compared to the previous platforms where a RTOS was required, and it is especially different from the case where commands were sent through a network interface as shown in figure 2 and in figure 4. With these changes, models execute in real-time on the target platform and model continuity is greatly increased providing therefore higher integrity simulation results.

To develop this DEMES-based design solution that is able to execute directly on the target platform, several updates were made including the reimplementation of a Driver model, and the use of the Flattened Coordinator technique. Plus, the previous implementation of E-CD++ used the Xenomai real-time framework for the Linux kernel; this dependency was removed by interfacing with the hardware clock of the target platform.

E-CD++ has to be implemented as a stand-alone embedded program able to cope with memory limitations of embedded platforms and run independently on the generally limited RAM or ROM available for program storage and execution. Because of this resource limitation, it is necessary to reduce the memory footprint of E-CD++ as much as possible.

More specifically, to implement this novel approach, we have first adapted the Driver model and the Flattened Coordinator technique for direct I/O interfacing as opposed to the transfer of data over a network. The Driver model and Flattened Coordinator concepts have been leveraged in the new E-CD++. Because embedded devices generally lack high memory limits and processing power, the Flattened Coordinator was used to minimize the amount of message passing between models. The driver model, on the other hand, provides a programming construct to be used with hardware components and devices and was adapted to the new architecture.

Second, to migrate E-CD++ to a bare-metal environment, several changes were made. These changes include the removal of the RTOS as well as the reimplementation of various OS kernel function calls. Since E-CD++ will be implemented directly on an embedded platform, the additional functionality provided by the RTOS becomes redundant due to the available low level control of timing and scheduling and as there is only one application running at a time. With these changes, it is possible to move the DEVSRT engine as well as the I/O drivers directly onto the target platform, eliminating the need for a network interface for communication between the simulation platform and the target platform as illustrated in figure 4. Hence, the removal of the Xenomai/Linux RTOS minimizes the size of the program and removes previous Linux dependencies.

Last, as the initial E-CD++ was developed for targets with OS support, there were various system calls made to the Linux kernel in order to handle various functions such as file I/O and memory management. In order to minimize the footprint of E-CD++ to allow for execution in a low memory embedded platform, these functions need to be re-developed with embedded execution in mind. As is discussed later, these calls are largely unnecessary as the embedded platform will not support multi-processing and does not require full file system support; the only file referenced by E-CD++ is the model file which can be loaded directly into memory. The new functions were thus implemented to provide the same functionalities as the original system calls without the overhead of a full OS kernel.

In the following section, the above main changes will be detailed and their implementation further explained.

3.2 Implementation

In a first phase, two main concepts, namely the driver concept and Flattened Coordinator Technique, were adjusted to the new structure. The Run-Time Subsystem and Modelling Subsystem now include a Flattened Coordinator as well as the integration with the Driver model. The Flattened Coordinator has been added to the Run-Time Subsystem where it has replaced the many Coordinators that were previously used. The Flattened Coordinator reduces the number of messages that need to be passed between models. This is accomplished through the removal of Coordinators for Coupled Models which are replaced with a single Flattened Coordinator, which manages the message passing between Atomic models enabling direct communication, reducing the messages needed. This improves processing power and speed, which is a limitation to execution on embedded platforms. In order to increase efficiency, the Flattened Coordinator analyzes the links between models on initialization and generates an influence list, establishing the relationships between models. The Flattened Coordinator is able to identify the recipient of a message and passes the message directly to the Atomic model. In a simple system containing only a few coupled models, this will not have a very large effect on the overall efficiency of the system; however, as the system complexity increases, the increase in performance that is achieved through the implementation of the Flattened Coordinator technique can be seen to improve [18].

Drivers have also been added to the Run-Time Subsystem providing an interface to initialize hardware devices as well as to interact with the Ports that are associated with the model as it will be discussed later. Through the use of the Driver objects, external I/O can be controlled through the encapsulation of hardware specific functionality, made available by accessing the generic functions provided by the Driver model, and not using an embedded RTOS. Using this model, we are able to interface a wide range of devices and greatly improve portability by simply implementing basic hardware drivers that are then accessed by E-CD++. From an implementation point of view, the driver model manages hardware device connections and interfacing through the use of two classes: the Port class, and the Driver class.

Similar to the Models and Processors in the Modelling subsystem and Run-time subsystem (seen in section 2.3.), the Port class resides in the Modelling subsystem while the Driver class is in the Run-time subsystem. Together, they provide a link between the DEVS implementation, and the hardware target platform.

The Port class represents the logical connection between models and hardware devices. Where the previous implementation saw the Port class passing established API commands over a network interface, our implementation of the Port class includes Input and Output low-level functions that are developed to provide the interface directly with the hardware device. In the case of Inputs, the receipt of a signal on a Port will cause the generation of a PDEVS message which is then added to the message queue processed by the Root Coordinator. When configured as an output, the Port will receive the data from a PDEVS message from the Driver class which will then be translated into a signal that can be interpreted by the hardware device. Through bare-metal implementation, it is possible to use the hardware and software

interrupt service routines of the target platform to notify E-CD++ of I/O changes. The specific hardware interrupts associated with each hardware device can then be used to generate PDEVS messages based on the values received from the device. Similarly, software interrupts can be programmed based on a division of the base clock in order to provide periodic polling.

Alternatively, the role of the Driver class is to receive PDEVS messages from the message queue as well as initialize and close hardware devices. As mentioned, when a PDEVS message is retrieved from the message queue, the Driver reads the value from that message and passes it on to its associated Port for interpretation and communication to the device. In the case of initialization or termination, the Driver class includes functions that interface with hardware devices in order to prepare them for operation, or for the end of simulation as required.

In addition to the above, to effectively model real-world inputs, it is necessary to define two types of devices that a Port/Driver may be associated with, the first being *passive* devices. These types of devices include sensors which must be polled at specific intervals to determine their current state. Interfacing with passive devices requires the implementation of a periodic timer interrupt that requests the state of the device. This can be accomplished through the creation of a software interrupt that is tied to a division of the base clock. This allows a software interrupt to be triggered at regular intervals, eliminating the need for real-time tasks. The state that is returned from these interrupts is then passed to the associated Driver which interprets the state, creates, and sends an appropriate PDEVS message to the message bag for further processing. The second type of hardware device that can be seen is an *active* device. An active device is classified as a hardware device that triggers an input event. Active devices can trigger a hardware interrupt at which point, they will pass their states to the Driver for processing.

All operating system dependencies needed to be removed. The original implementation of E-CD++ was developed on a desktop computer for simulation, which would then pass the results of the simulation through the OS to a separate application either on the same platform or over a network to the target platform. With the new version, the DEVSRT execution engine resides directly on the target hardware. As embedded platforms are generally limited to several megabytes of memory and a processor with a clock speed in the megahertz, the OS dependency of the C++ library was removed in order to streamline the performance of the software as well as increase the portability of the overall system. Given that E-CD++ will be the only application that is running on the target platform, there is no need for the extra capabilities available from OS inclusion.

We were able to quickly determine the system calls that were being made. Based on this list, it was possible to identify the purpose and functionality of each of these calls. The functionality of each of these functions could then be reproduced through the creation of functions with the same signature but with a re-designed implementation that takes into accounts the limitations and environment of the target platform. Among these functions, several were deemed unnecessary as they pertained to inter-process communication within a multi-processing system. While they were still required for the compilation of the E-CD++ executable, these functions were re-developed to return constant, known values that are similar to what would be expected when running from within an OS. An example of one of these functions is the *getpid* function. The purpose of this function is to return the process ID of the currently running process. As there is only a single process running, the value returned by this function can be set to an arbitrary integer that meets the constraints of what would be expected from an application launched from an OS. Multi-processing and multi-programming can be implemented directly as a DEVS coupled model, which can be formally verified using model-checking, and building individual kernels for particular purposes.

Although the functions related to inter-process communication could be easily removed, there were still several functions that required significant re-development in order to return appropriate values given the context in which they would be called. Some of these functions relate directly to the programming language that is used, others to the functionality that is provided by the OS. For instance, as E-CD++ is developed in C++, an object-oriented language, dynamic memory allocation is required in order to allow for the instantiation of new objects. While this can be accomplished through the run-time modification of pointers to heap memory allocation, other OS specific functionalities are not so easy to replace, becoming a hurdle to the bare-metal implementation of E-CD++.

We also needed to provide useful functionalities generally provided by the OS. This involved the implementation of several functions that take advantage of the hardware available to replicate the OS functionality. Through the use of hardware devices available on the target platform, such as a real-time clock, on-board memory, and low power modes, the replication of key OS functionalities and complete removal of the OS becomes possible.

In the previous version, Xenomai provided real-time guarantees through the implementation of constrained functions as well as a real-time scheduler. More specifically, while the previous version of E-CD++ used the Xenomai real-time framework for Linux to provide real-time constraints and scheduling, E-CD++ will not have these capabilities available. Instead, timing can now be controlled at the clock level through the creation of periodic software timer interrupts in order to manage scheduling, and at the model level through model specification and model-checking of the timing constraints. As E-CD++ requires microsecond precision, a software timer can be defined that is set to trigger at 1 MHz. By causing this interrupt to commence the next simulation cycle, simulation can occur as it normally would. With this, it is important to note the introduction of a minimum processing speed requirement for the proper execution of E-CD++. Because the simulation cycles are defined as 1 µsec, the clock speed of the microcontroller must be greater than 1 MHz in order to allow the execution of each simulation cycle prior to the next timer interrupt.

Regarding hardware I/O, the implementation of drivers provides hardware I/O interfacing by implementing basic hardware drivers that can be easily accessed by E-CD++. As previously mentioned, this is accomplished through the use of interrupts and hardware polling. Hardware and software interrupts can be used to generate messages from active devices; when the interrupt is triggered, a message can be added to the message bag. One complication that arises in this case is the object-oriented support that is available in C++ but not in C. This is further complicated by the name mangling that occurs with C++ functions. For this reason, it was necessary to generate a wrapper function written in C++ but with a C signature. This function can then call the C++ functions necessary to add the message to the message bag. Passive devices are simpler in that it is only necessary to develop the initial interface functions in C. These functions can be called from C++ whenever input is necessary without any problems.

The only file referenced by E-CD++ during execution (and thus needed on the target platform), is the model file. In fact, models are loaded into E-CD++ at run-time through the reading and interpretation of a model file. This is done by providing E-CD++ with the name and location of the model file from the command line. Since we do not have a directory structure for OS file I/O support, it was necessary to develop a pseudo file system in order to maintain continuity between desktop simulation and target simulation. In order to mimic this behaviour, the model files are loaded directly into memory and the file names are used to populate a file register. The file register then determines the memory address of the text file using a file table which contains the mapping between file names and memory addresses. The file table also provides information about the file that is required by the C++ library, for example, the file size.

In addition, the removal of the Xenomai framework also required redevelopment of the behaviour of the Root Coordinator's handling of done messages. With Xenomai, the Root Coordinator would wait to receive a message from a Xenomai real-time task indicating hardware input. Since this functionality is no longer available, the receipt of the done message will cause the Root Coordinator to sleep until the next internal transition is scheduled, periodically verifying that an external event has not occurred. If an external event occurs, the event will be processed prior to the internal transition and the cycle will repeat. In the case where there are no more internal transitions scheduled, the Root Coordinator will place the microcontroller into a low power mode and await an external event.

Finally, early integration of stand-alone E-CD++ was done using an MCBSTM32F200 evaluation board. Developed by Keil, the board includes the STM32F207IG ARM Cortex-M3 based microcontroller. This microcontroller has a clock speed of 120 MHz and contains 1 MB of ROM and 128 KB of RAM. The clock speed meets the 1 MHz requirement and the memory capacity is great enough to hold the E-CD++ application and associated model files. Through the implementation of drivers for the LEDs and buttons contained on the evaluation board, early integration testing was performed and proved to be successful, demonstrating the feasibility of bare-metal implementation of E-CD++. On the software platform side, Eclipse was used along with the GNU ARM bare metal tool chain to build applications and GDB to debug hardware and software. .

Overall, a high level of portability and model continuity can be achieved, as the DEVS model is not changed throughout development. This design is also portable as the software core of E-CD++ has not changed; all that has changed is the external interfaces. As mentioned, the implementation of the Driver model greatly increases this portability through the encapsulation and generalization of I/O devices allowing for simple addition of new devices.

In the upcoming section, we will illustrate how the new E-CD++ version can be used by implementing a line tracking robot behavior and describing the entire software development process using our DEMES-based approach

4. Case Study: A Line Tracking Robot

In this section we will show an example of the use of the new bare-metal version of E-CD++, by building a case study application for a line tracking robot controller. The Robot is equipped with a light sensor that faces the ground and absorbs the amount of light reflected off a small ground surface. The controller considers a medium percentage of reflected light as a detected path and initiates the robot to move forward. When the robot goes off track and it does not pick up a path trail, it stops, turns counter-clockwise slightly, and then tries to detect a trail again. If a path is detected, the robot will move forward again; otherwise it will continue to turn until it finds a path to follow. The destination is considered to be a wide dark ground surface. At that point, the light sensor would detect a small amount or no light reflection which indicates to the robot's controller that it has reached the destination and causes the robot to stop moving. The robot can also receive manual signals to start and stop.

4.1 System Architecture

The first step in the DEMES-based development cycle is to specify a model of the system of interest using DEVS. Figure 6 illustrates the resulting DEVS model hierarchy for this example.

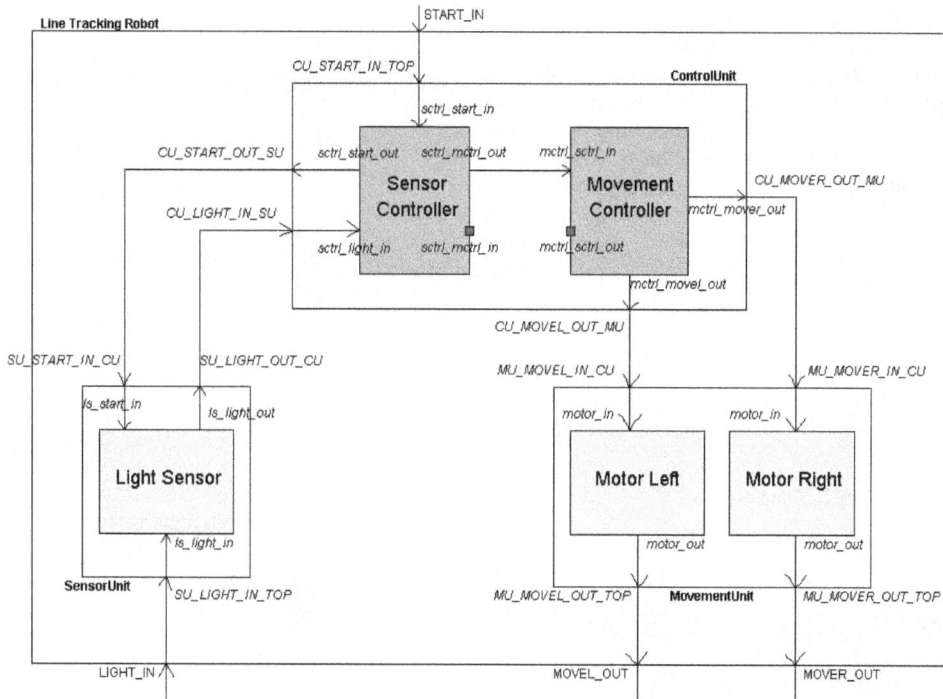

Figure 6. Line Tracking Model Robot Hierarchy Diagram

The top model has one input port, LIGHT_IN, through which the light sensor values are read, and two output ports, MOVEL_OUT and MOVER_OUT, used to send commands to the left and right motors of the robot. Apart from these ports, other input ports are named using the format *ToPort_IN_FromModel* where *ToPort* represents the name of the input port to which a message is sent and *FromModel* is the coupled model from which the message originates. Note that when the signal comes from an atomic model, the *FromModel* part is omitted, and the format becomes therefore *InputPortName_IN*. Hence, *motor_in* is the input port of the motor atomic model. Similarly, for output ports, we use the *FromPort_OUT_ToModel* where *FromPort* is the port through which a message is sent, and *ToModel* is the coupled model the message is adressed to. When the recipient model is atomic, the format is reduced to *FromPort_OUT*. For instance, MU_MOVEL_OUT_TOP is the Movement Unit(MU) output port designed to send messages from the left motor to the TOP model. On the other hand, *mctrl_mover_out* is the mover (move right) Movement Controller(mctrl)'s output port. These formats were used in order to rapidly identify the links among models and the role of each port.

In terms of components, the Line Tracking Robot's top model is a coupled model made of three coupled models: *Sensor Unit*, *Control Unit* and *Movement Unit*. The *Sensor Unit* contains an atomic model: *Light Sensor*. The Light Sensor reads the amount of light reflected off of a ground surface and transmits the readings to the *Control Unit* for processing. The *Control Unit* contains two atomic models: *Sensor Controller* and *Movement Controller*. The *Sensor Controller* activates/stops the light sensor through the *sctrl_start_out* port, receives the light sensor readings through *sctrl_light_in* and sends messages to the movement controller through the *sctr_mctrl_out* output port. These messages specify whether the robot is on-track, off-track or has reached the destination. Indeed, when the light sensor readings indicate a bright surface, the sensor controller sends an off-track signal to the movement controller. Likewise, when the sensor readings indicate a dark surface, it implies that the line tracking robot is properly following the line and an on-track signal is sent instead. When the robot reaches its destination, i.e. the light sensor reads an all dark surface; the sensor controller sends a stop reading command to the light sensor through *sctrl_start_out* and a stop signal to the movement controller. In addition to the above, the sensor controller receives, through the *sctr_start_in* input port, the user signal that starts the line tracking robot and puts the system in motion.

The Movement Controller, on the other hand, receives on/off-track signals from the sensor controller through the *mctrl_sctrl_in* port, and sends appropriate commands to the motors through *mctrl_movel_out* and *mctrl_mover_out*. Therefore, when an on-track signal is received, the movement controller sends a go forward command to both motors in order for the robot to stay on the right path. Correspondingly, when an off-track signal is received, the robot stops and prepares to turn. In this case, a stop signal is sent to all motors; then the right motor is instructed to go forward while the left motor is commanded to go into reverse.

Finally, the *Movement Unit* is made of two atomic models: *Motor Left* and *Motor Right*. It's a collection of the robot's actuators that move in response to commands received from the *Control Unit*. The *Motor* models control the functions of the robot treads. They can only move forward, in reverse or stop according to the signals they receive from the *Control Unit*. A combination of a motor moving forward and the other motor moving in reverse makes the robot turn.

4.2 DEVS Model Specification

Once the hierarchical structures of the model have been established, components are well defined using DEVS formal specification. In this section, we will focus on the Control Unit model specification. As mentioned earlier, this latter is a coupled model that has two atomic models, the sensor and movement controllers.

The Control Unit can be formally defined as:

$$CM = < X, Y, D, \{Md\}, EIC, EOC, IC, select >,$$

Where
X = {(CU_START_IN_TOP, N) ; (CU_LIGHT_IN_SU, N)}
Y = {(CU_START_OUT_SU, N); (CU_MOVEL_OUT_MU, N);(CU_MOVER_OUT_MU, N)}
D = {Sensor Controller, Movement Controller}.
Md = {M(sensor controller), M(movement controller)}
EIC ={((Self, CU_START_IN_TOP), (Sensor Controller, sctrl_start_in));
((Self, CU_LIGHT_IN_SU), (Sensor Controller, sctrl_light_in))}
EOC= {((Sensor Controller, sctrl_start_out), (Self, CU_START_OUT_SU));
((Movement Controller, mctrl_movel_out), (Self, CU_MOVEL_OUT_MU));
((Movement Controller, mctrl_mover_out), (Self, CU_MOVER_OUT_MU))}
IC = { (Sensor Controller, sctrl_mctrl_out); (Movement Controller, mctrl_sctrl_in) }
Select = { Sensor Controller, Movement Controller }.

In the above specification, X represents the set of input events (N being the set of port values), Y the set of output events, D the component name of each model, Md the DEVS basic (atomic or couple) model, EIC the external input coupling, EOC the external output coupling, IC the internal couplings and finally select is the tiebreaker function (refer to Appendix A for more details about this specification).

The DEVS formal specification of the *Sensor Controller* model is as follows and shows how atomic models are defined:

$$M = <X, S, Y, \delta_{ext}, \delta_{int}, \lambda, ta>,$$

Where
X:{(sctrl_light_in,{BRIGHT,DARK,ALL_DARK});(sctrl_start_in,{START_PROC,STOP_PROC});(sctrl_mctrl_in, {Ø})}

S: {"IDLE", "PREP_RX", "WAIT_DATA", "TX_DATA", "PREP_STOP"}

Y: {(sctrl_mctrl_out, {ON_TRACK, OFF_TRACK, STOP_PROC}); (sctrl_start_out, {START_PROC, STOP_PROC})}

δ_{int} (s) {

    switch (s){
        case PREP_STOP: // Stop request
               state = IDLE; ta(state)=infinity;
        case PREP_RX: //Preparing to read data
        case TX_DATA: // Sensor transmitting data
           state = WAIT_DATA; ta(state)=infinity;
    }
}

δ_{ext}(s,e,x){
    if (x.port() == sctrl_start_in){ // A user command is received
        if(state == IDLE && x.value()== START_PROC){
           state = PREP_RX; ta(state)= scRxPrepTime;
        }
        else if (x.value()== STOP_PROC) {
           state = PREP_STOP; ta(state)= ZERO_TIME;
        }
    }
    else if (x.port() == sctrl_light_in){ // Reading from sensor
        if(state == WAIT_DATA) { // Waiting for sensor data
           sensor_input = x.value();
           if(sensor_input == ALL_DARK) {// Destination
               state = PREP_STOP; ta(state)= ZERO_TIME;
           }else {
               state = TX_DATA; ta(state)= scTxTime;
           }
        }
    }
}

λ(s) {
    switch (s){
        case PREP_STOP:
           sendOutput(time, sctrl_start_out, STOP_PROC) ;
           sendOutput(time, sctrl_mctrl_out, STOP_PROC) ;
        case PREP_RX:
           sendOutput(time, sctrl_start_out, START_PROC)
        case TX_DATA: {
           int output_val;
           if(sensor_input == DARK)
            output_val = ON_TRACK;
           else if(sensor_input == BRIGHT)
            output_val = OFF_TRACK;
           sendOutput(time,sctrl_mctrl_out, output_val) ;
        }
    }
}

ta: $S \rightarrow R^+_{0, \infty}$ has been defined in the pseudocode above.

To understand the behavior of the *Sensor Controller* model, the following figure illustrates its state transitions using a state diagram: Fig. 7 illustrates the DEVS Graph representing the sensor controller's behavior. The state diagram summarizes the behavior of a DEVS atomic component by presenting the states, transitions, inputs, outputs and state durations graphically [36]. The circles represent states and the double circle is the initial state. The name and duration of a state is shown in the circle. The continuous edges between the states represent the external transitions, which includes the names of the input ports, the input value and any condition on the input (with format "port?value"). The dotted lines represent the internal transitions and the associated outputs (with format "port!value").

The Sensor Controller starts in the IDLE state and remains in that state until a start command is received. If the user start signal is received, an external transition is triggered and the Sensor Controller state changes to PREP_RX. At this stage, it waits for a defined time ta=scRxPrepTime after which a 'start' output signal is sent to the Light Sensor and an internal transition is triggered changing its state to WAIT_DATA. The Sensor Controller waits in this state until it receives a signal from the Light Sensor. When a signal is received, if the signal indicates that the robot reached the destination (signal value is ALL_DARK), an external transition causes the Sensor Controller to go the PREP_STOP state, at which it will immediately send a stop signal to the Light Sensor and the Movement Controller and then transition back to the IDLE state. However, if the received signal is different, the Sensor Controller will go to the TX_DATA state at which it will wait for a time advance period of ta=scTxTime before it sends an output signal to the Movement Controller indicating whether the robot is on track or not, and transitions back to the WAIT_DATA state. At any point in time, if the Sensor Controller receives a manual stop signal (STOP_PROC), it will execute an external transition to the PREP_STOP state to stop all activities.

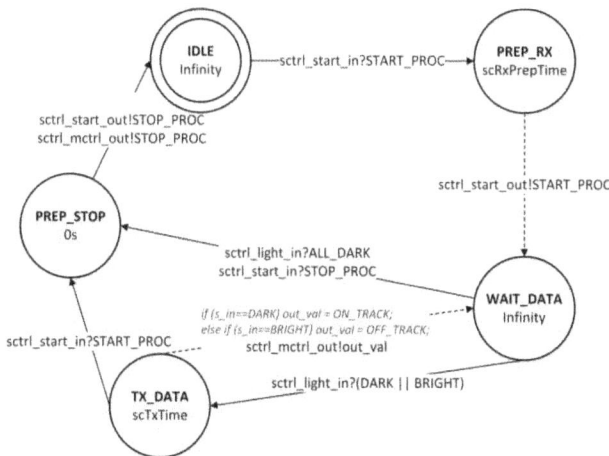

Figure 7. Sensor Controller State Diagram

After the formal specification phase, we implement the models using E-CD++ in order to run simulations, test individual components under different loads, gather results and derive different test cases.

4.3 Implementation in E-CD++

E-CD++ provides a mechanism to program DEVS models' hierarchical structures. The model definitions and couplings are written in a model file following a specific format, and the state

transitions and output function are overwritten in C++, as part of each model's class definition.

The following lines describe the *Sensor* and *Movement Controllers* specification as components of the *Control Unit* in the model file (also called the MA file), in accordance with the model diagram in figure 6:

```
1   [ControlUnit]
2   components : SCtrl@SensorController
    MCtrl@MovementController
3
4   in : CU_START_IN_TOP CU_LIGHT_IN_SU
5   out : CU_START_OUT_SU CU_MOVER_OUT_MU
    CU_MOVEL_OUT_MU
6
7   %input connections
8   Link : CU_START_IN_TOP
    sctrl_start_in@SCtrl
9   Link : CU_LIGHT_IN_SU
    sctrl_light_in@SCtrl
10
11  %output connections
12  Link : sctrl_start_out@SCtrl
    CU_START_OUT_SU
13  Link : mctrl_moveR_out@MCtrl
    CU_MOVER_OUT_MU
14  Link : mctrl_moveL_out@MCtrl
    CU_MOVEL_OUT_MU
15
16  %internal connections
17  Link : sctrl_mctrl_out@SCtrl
    mctrl_sctrl_in@MCtrl
```

The MA snippet starts by defining the Control Unit as a coupled model composed of two instances: *SCtrl* and *MCtrl*, of *Sensor* and *Movement Controller* respectively. Then, the input (CU_START_IN_TOP and CU_LIGHT_IN_SU) and output(CU_MOVEL_OUT_MU and CU_MOVER_OUT_MU) ports of the *Control Unit* are defined. Finally, the input and output connections between the ports of the *Control Unit* and those of *SCtrl* and *MCtrl* are described, as well as the internal connections between *SCtrl* and *MCtrl*. The direction of the connection is read as FROM port → TO port.

The following code describes the transition and output functions of the *Sensor Controller*, in accordance with the state diagram in figure 7:

```
1   Model
    &SensorController::externalFunction(
    const ExternalMessage &msg ) {
2   ...
3   if (msg.port() == sctrl_light_in){
    // Light sensor signal received
4       if(state == WAIT_DATA) {
    // Sensor controller was waiting for data
5          sensor_input= msg.value();
    // Get the light sensor input
6          if(sensor_input==ALL_DARK) {
    // Destination Reached
7             state=PREP_STOP;
    // Prepare to stop immediately
8             holdIn(Atomic::active,ZERO_TIME );
9          } else {
    // Robot is not at destination yet
```

```
10          state = TX_DATA;
    // Sensor goes into transmitting state
11          holdIn(Atomic::active, scTxTime );
    // after scTxTime,send data to MCtrl
12      }
13      }
14  }
15      return *this;
16  }
17
18  Model
    &SensorController::internalFunction(
    const InternalMessage & ) {
19      switch (state){
20          ...
21          case TX_DATA:
    // Just transmitted data to movement
    controller
22              state = WAIT_DATA;
    // Wait for new data from the sensor
23              passivate();
    // stay in this state until new event
24              break;
25      }
26      return *this;
27  }
28
29  Model &SensorController::outputFunction(
    const InternalMessage &msg ) {
30      switch (state){
31          ...
32      case TX_DATA: {
    // in transmitting state
33          int output_val;
34
35          if(sensor_input==DARK)
    // light sensor indicates a dark line
36              output_val = ON_TRACK;
    // output signal to MCtrl is ON_TRACK
37          else if(sensor_input==BRIGHT)
    // light sensor reads a bright surface
38              output_val = OFF_TRACK;
    // send off_track signal to MCtrl
39
    sendOutput(msg.time(),sctrl_mctrl_out,
    output_val); // Output sent to MCtrl
40          break;
41      }
42      };
43      return *this ;
44  }
```

The code snippet first shows a portion of the external transition function that describes the transition from state WAIT_DATA to either TX_DATA or PREP_STOP depending on the value (sensor_input) of the incoming signal from the *Light Sensor* received on port sctrl_light_in. Lines 18 to 28 show a portion of the internal transition function describing the transition from TX_DATA to WAIT_DATA. Finally, lines 29 to 43 show a portion of the output function's behaviour at state TX_DATA. The output function sets the output signal (ON_TRACK or OFF_TRACK) to send to the *Movement Controller* through port sctrl_mctrl_out.

Using these classes and the core components of E-CD++, different scenarios can be tested early on the development platform namely by using event files that generates event for the input ports. Once

the developer is satisfied with the results, the components can be incrementally moved to the target platform. In order to do this, each driver is associated with specific commands related to the hardware component it interacts with.

For the previous version of E-CD++, the Lego's NXT++ library was used to interface the models with hardware i.e. the light sensor and motors. Through a C++ API for Lego NXT robot controller, communication can be established over USB and Bluetooth. Therefore, hardware events can be monitored and events mapped to external transition functions. USB communication was done using Xenomai 2.6 and NXT++ v4.0 since v0.6 does not support Linux. In the same way, the E-CD++ to NXT++ interface can be used for translating hardware commands by having output functions mapped to NXT++ API. However, the NXT robot must be tethered and the DEVS models weren't compiled to the native NXT byte code.

The same models were deployed on the ARM board. This time, the native code was directly downloaded in memory via ST-LINK, an in-circuit programmer for the STM32 microcontroller families. This interface module is enabled with JTAG/serial wire debugging (SWD) interfaces that can be used to communicate with the target platform and debug via an OpenOCD client/server connection. Interfacing E-CD++ with hardware peripherals is made easy by the available port/driver concept and the comprehensive standard peripheral libraries offered by STMicroelectronics in this case. These two elements can be seamlessly integrated, compiled to the native byte code, and result in a DEVS-based firmware able to control the peripherals and respond to diverse external stimuli.

Once the models were implemented, different tests were done by progressively integrating hardware components and testing the entire system. The final deployment was made on the final target and models run on the microcontroller. Section 5 presents the results of our experiments and compares them with the Lego's version.

5. RESULTS
Each model component was first tested using virtual-time simulation. Then, multiple scenarios were simulated in order to observe the behavior of the robot in different environment settings and in real-time. To carry out these experiments, an event file that specifies the event time, input port and its value is used. Table 1 shows the port mapping table and the description of each value.

Table 1: Port Mapping

Port Name	Port Value	Hardware Command	Description
START_IN	10	START	Manual Start Command
	11	STOP	Manual Stop Command
LIGHT_IN	0	BRIGHT	No line detected
	1	DARK	Line detected
	2	ALL_DARK	Destination Reached

MOVER_OUT/ MOVEL_OUT	0	STOP	Stops the motor
	1	FORWARD	Spins Clockwise
	2	REVERSE	Spins Anticlockwise

An example of events that were injected into the system follows:

```
00:00:01:000   START_IN   10
00:00:02:000   LIGHT_IN   1
00:00:02:500   LIGHT_IN   0
00:00:02:700   START_IN   11
00:00:03:000   LIGHT_IN   1
00:00:03:500   LIGHT_IN   0
00:00:05:000   START_IN   10
00:00:05:500   LIGHT_IN   0
00:00:06:000   LIGHT_IN   0
00:00:06:500   LIGHT_IN   1
00:00:07:000   LIGHT_IN   1
00:00:07:500   LIGHT_IN   1
00:00:08:000   LIGHT_IN   2
00:00:08:500   LIGHT_IN   1
00:00:09:000   LIGHT_IN   1
00:00:09:300   START_IN   11
```

After 1s, the system is started by sending an input to the START_IN input port. Then, at 2s, a value of 1, meaning the line is detected, is sent through the LIGHT_IN input port. To illustrate situations when the robot gets off-track, a value of 0 is sent through the LIGHT_IN port. The system is then manually stopped by sending 11 through the START_IN port. Different values are sent through the LIGHT_IN port to test how the system behaves after a manual stop. Afterwards, the system is started again, and bright (0), dark (1) and all dark (2) surfaces are alternately sensed through the LIGHT_IN port. ALL_DARK signals that the robot has reached its destination and acts as an automatic stop signal. More values are sent through the LIGHT_IN port and finally a manual stop signal is sent through the START_IN port.

The resulting behavior is similar to the one defined in the controller models. Indeed, when the robot goes off track and does not detect the line, it stops, turns counter-clockwise slightly, and then tries to detect a trail again. If the line is detected, the robot will move forward again; otherwise it will continue to turn until it finds a path to follow. The destination is considered to be a wide dark ground surface. Once this surface is detected, the robot will stop and go into an idle state.

The same inputs were used on the ARM board. Simulation results are below. Inputs are shown as well as their corresponding results (in bold). The format used is <time> <port> <signal_value>. Microseconds are shown in the logs since we used a 32 bit timer that allows such precision. Inputs are numbered and hardware commands instead of signal value. Output are shown in bold.

1. 00:00:01:000:023 START_IN START
2. 00:00:02:000:030 LIGHT_IN DARK
    00:00:02:200:119 mover_out 1
    00:00:02:200:119 movel_out 1
3. 00:00:02:500:021 LIGHT_IN BRIGHT
    00:00:02:600:115 mover_out 0
    00:00:02:600:115 movel_out 0
    00:00:02:700:115 mover_out 1
    00:00:02:700:115 movel_out 2
4. 00:00:02:700:027 START_IN STOP

00:00:02:700:124 mover_out 0
00:00:02:700:124 movel_out 0
5. 00:00:03:000:019 LIGHT_IN DARK
6. 00:00:03:500:030 LIGHT_IN BRIGHT
7. 00:00:05:000:027 START_IN START
8. 00:00:05:500:021 LIGHT_IN BRIGHT
    00:00:05:700:115 mover_out 1
    00:00:05:700:115 movel_out 2
9. 00:00:06:000:028 LIGHT_IN BRIGHT
10. 00:00:06:500:022 LIGHT_IN DARK
    00:00:06:650:115 mover_out 0
    00:00:06:650:115 movel_out 0
11. 00:00:07:000:029 LIGHT_IN DARK
    00:00:07:200:122 mover_out 1
    00:00:07:200:122 movel_out 1
12. 00:00:07:500:031 LIGHT_IN DARK
13. 00:00:08:000:020 LIGHT_IN ALL_DARK
    00:00:08:050:112 mover_out 0
    00:00:08:050:112 movel_out 0
14. 00:00:08:500:021 LIGHT_IN DARK
15. 00:00:09:000:028 LIGHT_IN DARK
16. 00:00:09:300:027 START_IN STOP
    00:00:09:300:126 mover_out 0
    00:00:09:300:126 movel_out 0

The results of this simulation were found identical within a reason for both the Linux and the bare-metal version.

After running various scenarios to verify the model behavior on the board, the driver interfaces were mapped with the robot sensors and actuators. The START_IN driver is attached to a button for starting/stopping the robot, and acts as an active device in this case. The LIGHT_IN driver is associated with a reflectance sensor for sensing the surface brightness and acts as a passive device since polling is needed to collect the sensor values. The output drivers MOVER_OUT and MOVEL_OUT are connected to two servomotors. The same behavior was observed, and the robot followed the line as expected. It is essential to emphasize here that the same models were used in both the Linux and the bare-metal versions. Only drivers had to be adapted. Videos for the Lego[1] and STM32-based[2] robot are available.

6. CONCLUSION

A new version of E-CD++ was presented. This version allows E-CD++ to run on bare-metal. It also provides a DEVSRT based execution engine that acts as a microkernel while models behave like processes. The main purpose of the new version was to have an OS independent platform that would be fully portable and loadable onto various development boards by removing its Linux dependency. The required system calls have all been replaced with implementation specific to the needs of E-CD++ and the system has proven to execute on target platforms.

A Line Tracking Robot example was developed and E-CD++ used throughout the entire development. The system was decomposed into several atomic and coupled models connected via a well-defined hierarchical scheme, where simply the Robot consisted of three main components: Sensor Unit, Control Unit and Movement Unit. The Sensor Unit receives light reflection readings then sends them to the Control Unit. The Control Unit analyses the data received and determines in whether the Robot is on a valid path or not and sends movement signals to the Movement Unit accordingly. The Control Unit commands the Movement Unit to either move forward, turn or stop. To illustrate our approach, the Sensor Controller was modeled according to DEVS formal specification. Then, a corresponding implementation was presented. Finally, a simulation of the implemented model was run using ECD++. Tests were carried in both virtual and real environments. The results were satisfactory and followed the models' specification.

Based on the case study results, it can be seen that the implementation of E-CD++ as stand-alone software provides results that are identical to those of the simulated system. The case study has demonstrated the full range of abilities of E-CD++ through the use of internal and external transitions, as well as the execution of output functions and the interaction with hardware devices. Through the use of this tool, the simulation and implementation phases are linked as the initial models are deployed on the target hardware. We were also able to execute the engine on bare-metal on different ARM-based boards without the need of middleware RTOS.

The current version still needs to be ported onto a broader variety of platforms. Although the main modules are easy to port onto new platforms, the user will need to find appropriate drivers for the desired platform and be familiar with low-level programming. One of our future objectives is to provide a set of libraries and drivers for multiple microcontrollers to ease development task and only require the definition of DEVS models.

Another goal is to explore IoT applications. Indeed, provided hardware with connectivity capabilities, input/output ports can be associated with a network instead of traditional sensors therefore allowing I/O to be received and sent from any connected device. For instance, data could be sent by the DEVS-based kernel to a cloud based simulator or to any other connected hardware. Our execution engine could be used to connect small data and big data, and build diverse IoT applications.

7. REFERENCES

[1] Advanced Real-Time Simulation Laboratory. 2013. Line Tracking Robot on Lego Hardware. Video. Retrieved March 1,2015 from *https://www.youtube.com/watch?v=mTtlSV7WbuI*

[2] Advanced Real-Time Simulation Laboratory. 2015. Line Tracking Robot on STM32 (Early Debug Version). Video. Retrieved March 1,2015 from *https://www.youtube.com/watch?v=X2itlznkoVw*

[3] Bergero, F. and Kofman, E. 2010. PowerDEVS: a tool for hybrid system modeling and real-time simulation. *Simulation* 87, 1-2 (2010), 113-132.

[4] Cho, S. M. and Kim, T. G. 1998. Real-Time DEVS Simulation: Concurrent, Time-Selective Execution of Combined RT-DEVS Model and Interactive Environment. In *Proceeding of 1998 Summer Simulation Conference* (Reno, NV, USA, July 19 - 22). SCSC '98. Society for Computer Simulation International, Vista, CA. 410-415.

[5] Cho, Y., Hu, X., and Zeigler, B. P. 2003. The RTDEVS/CORBA Environment for Simulation-Based Design of Distributed Real-Time Systems. *Simulation* 79, 4 (2003), 197-210

[6] Edwards, S., Lavagno, L., Lee, E. A., and Sangiovanni-Vincentelli, A. 2001. Design of embedded systems: formal models, validation, and synthesis. In *Readings in hardware/software co-design*, De Micheli G., Ernst R. and Wolf W. (Eds.). Kluwer Academic Publishers, Norwell, MA, USA, 86-107.

[7] Furfaro, A. and Nigro, L. 2009. A development methodology for embedded systems based on RT-DEVS. *Innovations in Systems and Software Engineering* 5, 2 (2009), 117-127.

[8] Hu, X., Zeigler B.P. and Couretas J. 2001. DEVS-On-A-Chip: implementing DEVS in embedded java on a tiny internet interface for scalable factory automation. In *Proceedings of the 2001 IEEE Systems, Man, and Cybernetics Conference* (Tucson, AZ, USA, July 14 - 18, 2001). IEEE, New York, NY, 3051-3056.

[9] Hu, X., and Zeigler, B. 2004. Model Continuity to Support Software Development for Distributed Robotic Systems: A Team Formation Example. *Journal of Intelligent and Robotic Systems* 39, 1 (2004), 71-87.

[10] Hu, X., and Zeigler, B. 2005. Model Continuity in the Design of Dynamic Distributed Real-Time Systems. *IEEE Transactions on Systems, Man, and Cybernetics Part A* 35, 6 (2005), 867-878.

[11] Li, Q., and Yao, C. 2003. *Real-Time Concepts for Embedded Systems*. CMP Books, San Francisco, CA.

[12] Moallemi, M., and Wainer, G. 2013. Modeling and simulation-driven development of embedded real-time systems. *Simulation Modelling Practice and Theory*. 38, 0 (2013), 115-131.

[13] Sloss, A., Symes, D., and Wright, C. 2004. *ARM system developer's guide*. Elsevier/ Morgan Kaufman, San Francisco, CA.

[14] Wainer, G. 2002. CD++: a toolkit to develop DEVS models. *Software: Practice and Experience*. 32, 13 (November 2002), 1261-1306.

[15] Wainer, G. A. 2009. *Discrete-event modeling and simulation: a practitioner's approach*, CRC Press, Boca Raton, FL.

[16] Wainer, G. A., Glinsky E. and MacSween P. 2005. A Model-Driven Technique for Development of Embedded Systems Based on the DEVS Formalism. In *Model-Driven Software Development*, Beydeda S., Book M. and Gruhn, V. (Eds.). Springer, Berlin, Heidelberg, 363-383.

[17] Wainer, G. and Castro, R. 2011. DEMES: a Discrete-Event Methodology for Modeling and Simulation of Embedded Systems. *Modeling and Simulation Magazine*. 2 (April 2011), 65-73.

[18] Yu, H. Y., and Wainer, G. 2007. eCD++: an engine for executing DEVS models in embedded platforms. In *Proceedings of the 2007 Summer Computer Simulation Conference* (San Diego, CA, USA, July 15 - 18, 2007). SCSC '07. Society for Computer Simulation International, Vista, CA, 323-330.

Conjoining Emulation and Network Simulators on Linux Multiprocessors

Jereme Lamps, Vladimir Adam, David M. Nicol, Matthew Caesar
University of Illinois at Urbana-Champaign
{lamps1, adam4, dmnicol, caesar}@illinois.edu

ABSTRACT

Conjoinment of emulation and simulation in virtual time requires that emulated execution bursts be ascribed a duration in virtual time, and that emulated execution and simulation executions be coordinated within this common virtual time basis. This paper shows how an open source tool Time-Keeper for coordinating emulations in virtual time can be integrated with three different existing software emulations/simulations: CORE, ns-3, and S3F. We describe for each of these the modifications made to the tools to support this integration, and examine experiments designed to assess the accuracy of the combined models. Timekeeper permits much tighter sychronization of emulation and simulation than has ever been achieved before.

Categories and Subject Descriptors

C.2.4 [**Computer-Communication Networks**]: Distributed Systems—*distributed applications*; D.4.4 [**Operating Systems**]: Communications Management—*message sending, communication management*; D.4.8 [**Operating Systems**]: Performance—*measurements, simulation*; I.6.3 [**Simulation and Modeling**]: Applications—*Miscellaneous*

General Terms

Experimentation

Keywords

Simulation, Emulation, LXCs, Virtualization, Time Dilation, CORE, ns-3, S3F, Linux Kernel

1. INTRODUCTION

Software emulation involves running executable applications on some virtual platform. Sometimes the operating system is virtualized, sometimes the underlying hardware is virtualized, sometimes the network is virtualized. The main attraction of emulation for model building is that it enables high fidelity execution behavior and traffic generation. However, that fidelity comes with a computational cost. Simulation usually requires fewer resources per unit model, achieved by abstraction. The use of emulation need not exclude simulation, or vice-versa, but to use them simultaneously suggests that the emulated portions of a model operate within the same virtual time coordinates as does the simulated portion. The research applications that motivate our interest call for models with large numbers of simulated and emulated entities, with fairly tight synchrony between them. This drives us towards the lightweight end of the emulation spectrum where as much as possible is shared between co-hosted virtual machines, with mechanisms for tightly integrating the simulation and emulation. Conjoining lightweight emulation and simulation within virtual time, with support for close synchronization, is our objective.

This paper is by no means the first foray into this space. An early effort was motivated by the objective of testing distributed applications [14]. The idea was to have the virtual time within a virtual machine progress more slowly than real time, in order to make the (real) network appear to be performing faster. The technique used (with heavier weight emulators) is simply to rescale the clock time in the virtual machine, essentially with a multiplicative factor called the *time dilation factor* (TDF). A virtual machine (VM) with TDF α is consider to run α times more slowly in the modeled system than on the actual execution platform.

A more controlled approach to transforming real time to virtual time was explored as the lightweight OpenVZ[5] emulation platform and the S3F[20] simulator were integrated and studied [27]. This approach embedded OpenVZ containers in virtual time by the simple expedient of transforming returns of calls to the system clock. A container had a TDF α that modeled the duration of an uninterrupted execution burst that took t units of measured time as a duration of t/α units of virtual time. A key differentiator between this work and prior art was that viewed from a wallclock time perspective, a VM's advancement in virtual time is not continuous. It runs for a burst during which virtual time advances, is paused during which time virtual time is not advanced at all, and advances again when the VM is running again. Modifications to the OpenVZ scheduler allowed OpenVZ to run all its containers through a window of virtual time of size Δ, stop, and exchange traffic with the S3F simulator, which alternatively is also run for Δ units of simulation time.

Follow-on work produced *TimeKeeper*[17], which brings virtual time to general Linux processes using a small modi-

SIGSIM-PADS'15, June 10–12, 2015, London, United Kingdom.
ACM 978-1-4503-3557-7/15/06.
http://dx.doi.org/10.1145/2769458.2769481.

fication to the Linux kernel. The real-to-virtual time translation mechanism is the same as used with OpenVZ, and the scheduling capability is like OpenVZ's. The purpose for TimeKeeper was to use something other than OpenVZ for conjoined emulation and simulation.

In the present paper we take TimeKeeper and show how to integrate it with three different simulators: CORE [7], ns-3 [15], and S3F [20]. The integration with ns-3 and S3F use in particular Linux LXC containers as the emulation envelopes. This work is in the spirit of conjoining OpenVZ and S3F, but is significantly different in that it shows how the generality of TimeKeeper support three different systems, in three different ways. We study the behavior of models using these systems, and assess the realism of the behaviors that are produced. We find that the limiting factor is the granularity of the Linux timer, in the following sense. TimeKeeper schedules a process to run for δ units of wall-clock time as measured by the system clock. The process will run for $\delta + \epsilon$ time, the variation being introduced by operating system overhead. TimeKeeper's ability to control virtual time advancement depends on the magnitude of ϵ relative to the magnitude of δ.

We will show that the integration of TimeKeeper with CORE and with ns-3 is trivial. Integration of TimeKeeper with S3F is likewise trivial if we use the same approach as did the integration of S3F and OpenVZ. Recall however that in this approach there is no interaction between emulated hosts and simulated network while either system is running. We want to explore a tighter coupling where we place the advancement of LXC containers under control of the S3F composite synchronization method. In this approach, from the S3F synchronization point-of-view, an LXC container attached to an S3F "timeline" is a means of advancing that timeline's virtual time, just as executing discrete-event simulation model events are a means of advancing a different timeline's virtual time. The synchronization between timelines is independent of the means by which virtual time advances on those timelines.

The take-away message of this paper is that TimeKeeper can be integrated with various discrete-event simulations, and that in each of the three instances we consider it enables those conjoined systems to model systems with more accuracy than they could before, and/or model larger systems than they could before. This point is important. The applications that motivate our research are embedded real-time systems. We are building a cyber-physical system testbed that brings together actual devices, emulations of large numbers of devices (such as smart meters in the power grid), and simulation of communication networks, including wireless, local area wireline, and wide area wireline. The issues of interest include (a) what are the performance characteristics of this network, e.g., latency, throughput, and packet loss; (b) does the system being modeled still meet real-time constraints as we introduce new technologies to improve security? Our earlier work using OpenVZ forced a granularity of interaction between emulation and simulation where the approximations used for introducing traffic from one system to the other were of a scale larger than interlink latencies seen in actual systems. In order to have the highest possible confidence that the results produced by our testbed reflect those that will be observed in the field, we seek ways to more tightly integrate in virtual time the emulated processes and the simulated processes.

2. TIMEKEEPER

TimeKeeper [17] is a kernel module for Linux that brings the notion of virtual time to Linux processes in general, and LXC containers in particular. TimeKeeper affects the scheduling of processes under its control, and the notion of "time" these processes experience. TimeKeeper modifies the value returned to one of its processes when it calls *getTimeOfDay* to be virtual time. The value returned is a function of the the time dilation factor (TDF) TimeKeeper ascribes to it, and the amount of real execution time that has been allocated and used by the process.

TimeKeeper can

- Ascribe to, and dynamically change the TDF assigned to a process.

- Cause a stopped process to start, immediately.

- Cause a running process to stop, immediately.

- Schedule its processes so that even when different processes have different TDFs, they advance together in virtual time.

With this functionality the interface to TimeKeeper provides an application with the ability to change a process' TDF, and to run a process for a specified duration of virtual time, and know when the processes has stopped at the end of that epoch.

We will use this functionality to integrate emulated execution of hosts within Linux processes with network simulators that carry the traffic they generate.

3. RELATED WORK

The related work falls into one of three categories: virtualization methods, simulation/emulation, and other virtual time systems. Each category will be discussed individually.

3.1 Virtualization Methods

Virtualization grants the ability to allocate system resources such as memory or computing power into separate Virtual Machines (VMs). Each VM will consider itself to be a unique entity, although it runs on the same hardware as the host machine. There are three levels of virtualization: full virtualization, para virtualization, and OS level virtualization. Full virtualization solutions such as VMware [21] and VirtualBox [6] completely abstract out the underlying physical system without needing to modify the guest OS. This solution has the most overhead, but allows for complete isolation, as well as the ability to concurrently run many different operating systems. Para virtualization solutions such as Xen [9] modify the guest VM's kernel to allow direct communication to the host machine. Finally, OS level solutions such as OpenVZ [5] and Linux Containers [2] require all guest VMs to share the same kernel as the host machine. This scenario has the least amount of overhead, but it comes at the cost of flexibility, as you are not able to host VMs with different kernels.

3.2 Simulation/Emulation

In a simulation, the entire experiment is modeled in software. It is considered an attractive solution in research, as the experiments can easily be scaled and repeated. Many popular network simulators exist today, some of the more notable ones are J-Sim [3], OMNeT++ [23], ns-2 [1], and ns-3 [15]. J-Sim is developed in Java, and considers each node, link, and protocol to be a different component. Each component in the experiment has a *component contract* describing how the component should behave if a packet were to arrive on a particular port. OMNeT++ and ns-2 are both discrete event network simulators. Previous research was done comparing the two network simulators [25][16][4]. It was determined that OMNeT++'s hierarchical network model made it both easier to use, as well as more scalable, than ns-2's flat model. Finally, there is ns-3, which was developed to succeed in the areas where ns-2 was lacking. It is a completely independent project from ns-2, and aims to be modular and scalable. Previous studies have found ns-3 to be more efficient than both OMNeT++ and ns-2 [25].

In contrast to simulation, emulation utilizes a testbed or physical network to run an experiment. This provides more realism, as physical packets are being sent across an actual network. However, there are two fundamental drawbacks to consider when using emulation. First, scalability may be limited, as your experiment can not be larger than the testbed itself. Second, it may be hard to reproduce the results from an experiment, as some physical conditions may change. Two very popular emulation testbeds are Emulab [26] and PlanetLab [22]. In Emulab, the experimenter creates the desired network, then is granted access to the nodes within the testbed for a specific period of time. The experimenter is given root access and may install any OS on each node. On the other hand, PlanetLab consists of connected machines around the world. PlanetLab is continually growing, with 1343 nodes at 657 sites to date. Unlike Emulab which gives you sole access to the machine, PlanetLab gives you a Linux LXC container on each machine in the experiment. Therefore, you will not be able to run a custom OS. You get the same Linux as every other processon the machine.

Finally, there exist hybrid solutions which attempt to bring the benefits of both simulation and emulation in one package. Some popular hybrid solutions are the Common Open Research Emulator (CORE) [7], ns-3 [15] and S3F [20] with OpenVZ [5]. We integrated TimeKeeper with these simulators, and we will discuss them at greater depths in later sections.

3.3 Virtual Time Systems

Bringing virtual time to a computer system is not a new idea, as many recent papers have explored this concept [27, 12, 13, 11, 24, 18]. SVEET! [11] and DieCast [13] both make modifications to the Xen hypervisor in order to give each VM a notion of virtual time. The modification changes the rate at which interrupts are sent from the Xen hypervisor to each VM. SVEET! is considered a performance evaluation testbed and introduces a static TDF which will slow down both the VMs and the simulator. This will help the experiment if it had been previously overloaded. DieCast is able to scale the perceived performance of various hardware components. This is useful if you need to create a large experiment, where the number of required experiment nodes is larger than the number of nodes in your testbed. TimeKeeper is different from both DieCast and SVEET! in three ways. First, our solution supports the dynamic change of TDFs, instead of a static TDF. Next, TimeKeeper can run multiple LXCs with different TDFs simultaneously, while synchronizing their virtual times. Finally, TimeKeeper supports lightweight LXCs and minor Linux Kernel modifications instead of a Xen-based approach. Our solution is most similar to the work done by Zheng et al. [27], who developed a virtual time system for emulation and simulation using OpenVZ for virtualization. Similar to our solution, they modified certain system calls to change the VM's perception of time. However, there are key differing distinctions. Our solution uses a more lightweight virtualization method, and has demonstrated the ability to run much larger experiments [17].

4. CORE

CORE is considered a hybrid emulator/simulator, as it uses lightweight virtualization to emulate the networking stack of end hosts and routers, while simulating the links between these devices. The proceeding sections will give a brief overview of how CORE works under the hood, followed by a list of the required changes to fully integrate TimeKeeper with CORE. The section will conclude with some CORE specific experiments we have conducted.

4.1 CORE Overview

CORE uses network namespaces to divide a process into a logically separate networking entity (each process will have its own routing tables, network adapters, and so forth). Internally, LXCs also use network namespaces to achieve the same goal; however, LXCs provide additional features which are not necessary for CORE's functionality. For this reason, CORE bypasses LXCs entirely and uses network namespaces directly.

To illustrate what CORE does behind the scenes, consider a simple 2-router topology. The network will be modeled with CORE's basic on/off wireless connectivity model. If the two routers are close enough (as determined by the distance from one another in the CORE GUI), they will be able to communicate. If the routers are too far away from one another they will not be able to communicate. When an experiment is started, a *vnoded* daemon is spawned for every node in the topology. Each *vnoded* daemon is responsible for creating its own network namespace [8]. To establish the network connectivity, CORE uses a combination of virtual Ethernet pair drivers (*veth*), Linux Bridging, and Ethernet Bridging Tables (*ebtables*). A *veth* is simply a Ethernet-like device, where one end is installed on the host while the other end is installed in the *vnoded* daemon. When a packet is sent to one end device, it will simply come out the other end. The necessary *veths* will then be tied together with Linux bridges. Finally, appropriate *ebtable* rules will be applied to the bridge. The rules will determine if packets should be dropped or not, and are modified as the distances between the routers change. See Figure 1.

4.2 TimeKeeper with CORE

Only a few changes needed to be made to the CORE source code to allow TimeKeeper's functionality to be fully integrated with CORE. Specifically, modifications were needed to allow both CORE's GUI and each *vnoded* daemon to communicate with TimeKeeper. It is worth noting CORE does not use LXCs directly; however, TimeKeeper was still easily integrated with CORE. This attests to a flexible API capable of assigning TDFs to not just LXCs, but any process

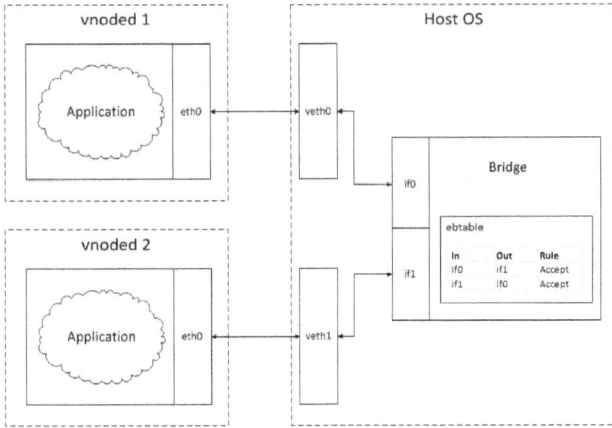

Figure 1: Core Networking Internals

on the Linux system. The necessary changes to the CORE source code are as follows:

1. First, CORE's GUI was modified in order to support additional topology information for each node. If a user double clicks on a node, the option is provided to set that node's TDF. In addition, the user has the ability to set the TDF for every node in the experiment at once, reducing setup time.

2. As mentioned above, when the CORE experiment is started a *vnoded* daemon is created for every host and router. This daemon will create the network namespace via a *clone()* system call. Once the newly created process is spawned in its own network namespace, a message is sent to TimeKeeper to give it the appropriate TDF.

3. After a short time, all of the time-dilated *vnoded* daemons will be initialized, and the CORE experiment will begin. At this point, all *vnoded* daemons will progress in time with respect to their TDFs. From here, the user may tell TimeKeeper to start a synchronized experiment, in which all *vnoded* daemon's virtual times will progress uniformly through time. This was done by adding an additional button to CORE's GUI, which will send the start message to TimeKeeper when it is clicked.

4.3 CORE Experiments

Here, we will investigate CORE specific experiments. Unless otherwise specified, experiments were conducted on a Dell Studio XPS Desktop, with 24 GB of RAM, and 8 Intel Core i-7 CPU X 980's @ 3.33GHz. The machine is running 64-bit Ubuntu with a modified 3.10.9 Linux Kernel.

The basic idea of the experiments is to show that the conjoined emulation and simulation give the sort of results one expects from the system being modeled. The specific experiment involves measurement of the maximum bandwidth that can be squeezed out of a network using TCP (alternatively, using UDP). The Unix tool *iperf* is executed to make this measurement. We set up within CORE models with clients and servers, running *iperf* to measure the bandwidth achieved with a *simulated* network. The maximum network bandwidth is independent of the speed of the processors attached to it, and so we tested the sensitivity of

iperf measurements as a function of changing TDF factors in processes used to make and interpret those measurements.

Within TimeKeeper's synchronized experiment, some containers may be frozen for periods of time to allow other container's virtual times to catch up. For example, when one container has a TDF of 1 and another has a TDF of 2, the container with the TDF of 1 will only be given 1/2 the amount of CPU time as the container with a TDF of 2. Thus, it is important for the fidelity of the experiment that this synchronization of the container's virtual time does not interfere with the packet flow of the application, and hence the measurements made by *iperf*. The experiment consisted of a 3-node topology, with one switch, one server, and one client. We used *iperf* to measure the bandwidth between the client node and the server node. The experiment was repeated numerous times and the average bandwidth, CPU utilization, and length of experiment was recorded. This process was repeated across many different TDFs, and the results are collected in Figures 2 and 3. Figure 2 displays the resulting bandwidth across time with various time dilation factors.

As one expects, regardless of whether the experiment was running in realtime, or much slower than realtime (as in the case where the TDF was 50), the resultant bandwidth was approximately the same. The bandwidth is the same because TimeKeeper is forcing the process to run for the same amount of CPU time, but over a longer period of time. This increases our confidence that a time dilated experiment will give us similar results as if it were run without TimeKeeper in realtime. Next, Figure 3 explores how the TDF affects both CPU utilization and the physical time required to run an experiment. Without a TDF, *iperf* takes approximately 10 seconds to complete, and in that time *iperf* demands 100% of a CPU. The default case is not displayed on the graph in order to show more detail as to what is going on in a synchronized experiment. As the TDF of an experiment increases, the amount of time a process spends on the CPU is throttled back; however, this comes at the cost of increased experiment runtime. As Figure 3 demonstrates, when the TDF of the experiment was 50, the *iperf* process spends only roughly 2% of the time on the CPU. However, the time required to actually run *iperf* for a 10 second long analysis now took 500 seconds to complete. This tradeoff is beneficial and being able to advance time more slowly will allow us to run more complex experiments, which is further explored in Section 5.3.

We extended this experiment by more processes, to convince ourselves that TimeKeeper will still function properly even while synchronizing the virtual times of a large number of containers. We spawned an additional 100 containers, each running a script that sends traffic with randomly chosen destinations. This is done concurrently with *iperf*, and once again the experiment was run with many different TDFs. As before, we found the maximum measured bandwidth to be consistent across all runs. The additional containers did not affect TimeKeeper's ability to maintain a consistent bandwidth, it only caused the experiment to take longer due to the additional overhead. The overall bandwidth of this new experiment was lower than the previous one, but is only due to the extra background traffic saturating the network while *iperf* was executing.

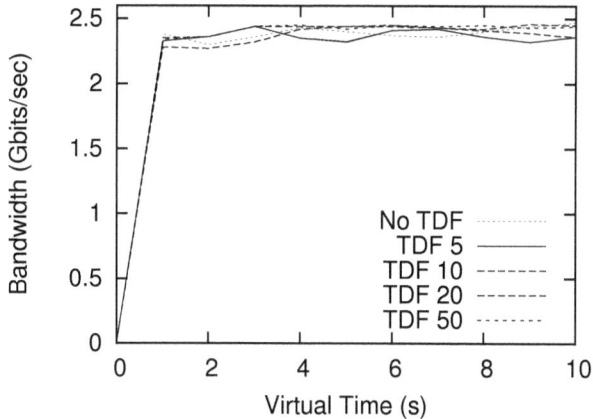

Figure 2: Average Bandwidth Across Various TDFs

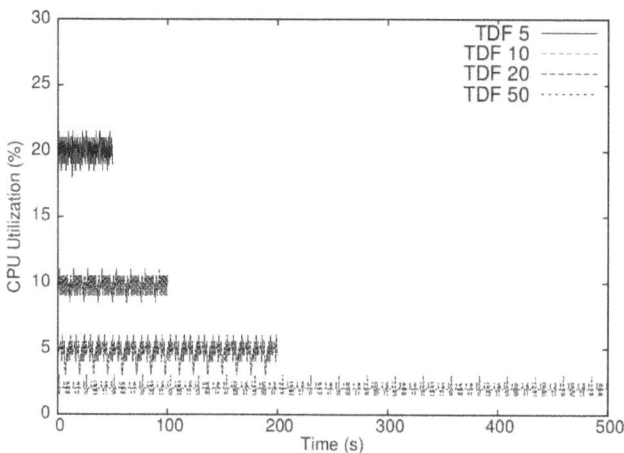

Figure 3: Relationship Between CPU Utilization and Experiment Time

5. NS-3

Ns-3 is a very popular discrete-event network simulator, designed primarily for research and educational use. It consists of numerous 'network' models, such as LANs or Wi-Fi. With respect to TimeKeeper, we are interested in ns-3's ability to interact with real systems, e.g., 'simulation-in-the-loop' experiments. This can be done with ns-3's Realtime Scheduler option. The following sections will give a brief overview of how ns-3 works, followed by necessary changes to support the TimeKeeper integration, and concluding with some ns-3 experiments that were conducted once TimeKeeper was integrated.

5.1 ns-3 Overview

Describing all of the components in ns-3 would be out of the scope of this paper. Instead, we will focus on the two components that allow us to connect LXCs to the ns-3 simulator: the TapBridge Model and the RealTime Scheduler. They will be discussed individually.

- **TapBridge Model**
  The TapBridge Model was created to allow real internet hosts (LXCs) to interact with an ns-3 simulation. Essentially, it works by connecting the inputs and out-

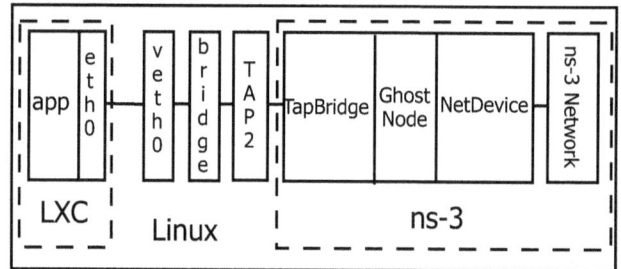

Figure 4: LXCs and ns-3

puts of a Linux TAP device with the inputs and outputs of an ns-3 NetDevice. A Linux TAP device allows a user space program to send and receive packets without needing to traverse physical media. The Linux TAP acts as the glue connecting an LXC with the ns-3 simulation. An ns-3 NetDevice is an abstraction which covers the simulated hardware as well as the software driver. When a NetDevice is installed on a ns-3 *Node*, it will be able to communicate with other *Nodes* in the simulation. For every LXC we wish to integrate with the ns-3 simulation, the TapBridge Model will create a *Ghost Node*. A *Ghost Node* is simply a *Node* in the ns-3 experiment that represents an external entity (where the upper levels of the network stack are not being simulated). For every *Ghost Node* there is a corresponding NetDevice acting as the connection to the simulation. Every time an LXC sends a packet, the Tap Device will bring the packet to user-space to the corresponding *Ghost Node*, which will push it to the NetDevice. This setup allows an LXC to interact with the ns-3 simulator. See Figure 4.

- **RealTime Scheduler**
  By default, the ns-3 scheduler is not real-time. Rather, when an event is processed, the simulator's time will jump to the time of the next scheduled event. Obviously, this technique will not work if ns-3 is tied to an external entity, as the entity may send a network packet at any time. Thus, the RealTime Scheduler was implemented, which attempts to keep ns-3's simulation time synchronized with respect to an external time source (commonly the wall clock). The RealTime Scheduler works as follows: When the next event in the simulation is ready to be processed, the scheduler will compare the system time with the scheduled time of the event. If the scheduled time of the event is in the future, the simulator will sleep until the system clock catches up to the scheduled time of the event, then execute the event. It is possible for the simulator to fall behind the system clock (if the simulator can not process a sequence of events fast enough). When this happens, the RealTime Scheduler has two options which is set by the user: *BestEffort* or *HardLimit*. If the scheduler is running in *BestEffort* mode, the simulator will repeatedly process events to the best of it's ability in an attempt to catch up to the system clock. However, this may never happen if the packets are continuously sent. The *HardLimit* option will also try to

catch up to the system clock, but will terminate the simulation if the difference between the system clock and simulation clock becomes too large.

5.2 TimeKeeper with ns-3

Integrating TimeKeeper with ns-3 was actually surprisingly simple. In fact, no changes were necessary to the ns-3 source code. This is because ns-3's RealTime Scheduler utilizes the *gettimeofday()* system call to determine how far away the simulation time is from the system time. Recall that TimeKeeper implements a modified version of the *gettimeofday()* system call, which will return a modified virtual time based on the TDF of the process. With this knowledge, you can can place ns-3 and all of its LXC containers under control of TimeKeeper scheduling set the TDF of the ns-3 process in order to make it progress more slowly in time (allowing more time to process events) and in synch with the TDF of the LXC containers holding its emulated hosts. Therefore, all that was necessary was to add the ns-3 process and its containers to TimeKeeper's concept of a synchronized experiment and assign them TDF values. When this is done, ns-3's notion of simulation time will progress at the same rate as the other LXCs in the experiment, and keep the LXCs synchronized in virtual time.

5.3 ns-3 Experiments

Here we discuss experiments applied to the conjoined ns-3 and TimeKeeper system.

5.3.1 Measuring Jitter

In ns-3, *jitter* is defined as the difference between when an event should leave the simulator and when it actually does. With respect to the RealTime Scheduler, minimizing the jitter is important to increase the fidelity of the experiment. When the scheduler is running in *HardLimit* mode, the experiment will abruptly stop if the jitter becomes too large. To investigate how TimeKeeper can help reduce jitter, we ran a series of experiments. First, we created a ns-3 network using the WiFi network model and performed an *iperf* test between two LXCs. Throughout the test we measured the jitter of every single event, and repeated this experiment using different TDFs. This setup will not overload the ns-3 simulator. The results are found in Figure 6. The jitter was always below the default 100ms *HardLimit*. The average jitter in the non time-dilated experiment was 40ms. When the experiment was repeated with TDFs of 2, 3, and 4, the resulting jitters were 18.7ms, 12.2ms, and 9.1ms respectively. This makes sense, as the TDF specifies how long an experiment will take to run, and the average jitter is reduced by the factor of the TDF.

Next, we look at how the jitter is affected when the simulator is overloaded. From the previous CORE experiments, we know a high TDF will slow down the experiment and reduce the stress on the simulator. Therefore, a previously overloaded simulation should be able to complete if it is given a sufficiently large TDF. For the overloaded experiment, we create a ns-3 network using the CSMA network model, and performed an *iperf* test between two LXCs. Once again we measured the jitter of every event, and repeated the experiment with different TDFs. The results are found in Figure 7.

This setup originally overloads the ns-3 simulator, because the CSMA network model tries to provide higher bandwidth

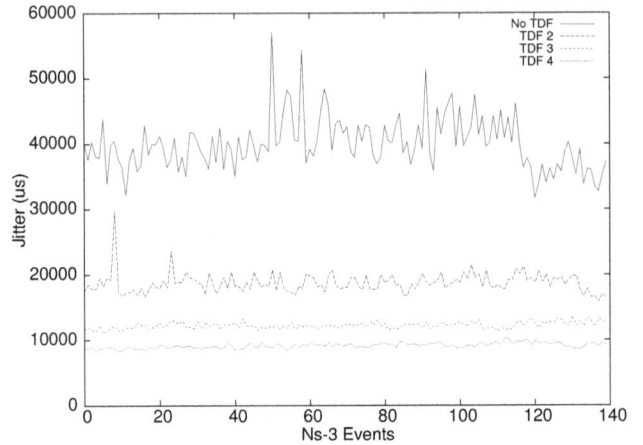

Figure 5: Measuring Jitter When Simulator Is Not Overloaded

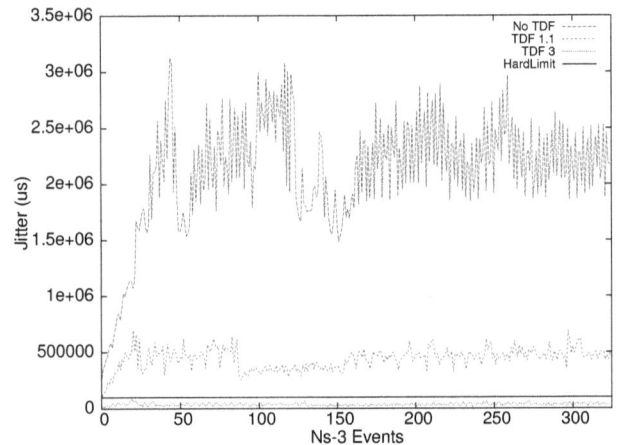

Figure 6: Measuring Jitter When Simulator Is Overloaded

than the WiFi model, and the additional packet events bog down the simulation. When the simulator is overloaded, the average jitter is hurt dramatically. With no TDF, the average jitter was 2,108ms, or 20x greater than the RealTime Scheduler's default *HardLimit*. A little improvement is seen when the experiment is slowed down with a TDF of 1.1, resulting in a average jitter of 441ms. Increasing the experiment's TDF to 3 further reduces the average jitter, this time to 35.5ms. This is a successful experiment, as the jitter never exceeds the *HardLimit*.

5.3.2 Increasing ns-3 Complexity

While we demonstrated that increasing the experiment TDF will increase jitter, we wanted to ensure this held true for more complicated ns-3 experiments as well. We constructed a network topology consisting of 100 ns-3 nodes which communicate with one another over the WiFi 802.11b model in order to create background traffic. In addition, we tied in two LXCs who were connected to the same network model, and performed a bandwidth test. This more complicated network was able to overload the simulator, unlike in the previous WiFi example. We ran this experiment with

TDF	Runtime
None	1700ms
2	738ms
3	312ms
4	101ms
5	30ms
10	4.25ms

Table 1: Average Jitter with Large ns-3 WiFi Model

varying TDFs, and calculated the average jitter. The results can be found in Table 1.

Similar to the previous experiment, as the TDF of the simulator increased, the average jitter decreased. When the TDF of the simulator was either 5 or 10, the jitter stayed under the default *HardLimit* of the RealTime Scheduler, and would be able to finish successfully. We are able to run more complicated experiments while keeping the jitter low, but this comes at the cost of the overall experiment runtime.

6. S3F

6.1 S3F and Synchronization

The S3F system was developed after ten years of experience with the Scalable Simulation Framework (SSF) [10]. A prime objective was to make the system simpler to understand and maintain. S3F eschews use of any libraries other than those which are standard with C++, and it backs away from direct support of process oriented simulation. It shares SSF's notion of Entities, inChannels and outChannels, and communication through those channels.

Timeline is an important concept in S3F; one thinks of it as a construct that advances simulation time. Every S3F Entity is aligned to exactly one timeline; entities on the same timeline are synchronized with each other using an ordinary discrete event simulation event-list. Channels where the in-Channel side is bound to a timeline different than that of the entity to which the out-channel side is bound expose communication that must be synchronized using parallel simulation time synchronization techniques. S3F requires that any channel which has its inChannel and outChannel in different timelines must have also declared a minimum latency time. This minimum time is a lower bound on the time between when the first bit of a communication enters the channel, and when the entity receiving the message can be affected by the arrival of the message. In network-oriented models minimum latencies are typically derived from network characteristics. Figure 8 illustrates the S3F architecture.

S3F uses *composite synchronization* [19], which works as follows. Given some threshold τ, every cross-timeline channel is categorized as being "fast" or "slow', depending on whether its minimum latency is no greater than τ (in which case it is fast), or otherwise. Composite synchronization defines a synchronization window of size τ, and does a global barrier among timelines every τ units of virtual time. No communication that crosses a slow channel will affect the recipient within the same window as the message is sent. This means that the simulation can wait to physically pass that message between timelines until all timelines are stopped at the end-of-window barrier. In contrast, interactions that use fast channels have to be synchronized dynamically during the concurrent execution of timelines within a window. If a channel extends from an entity E_s on one timeline T_s to

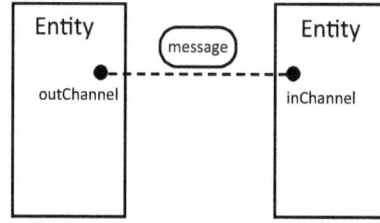

(a) Entities communication with Messages through Channels

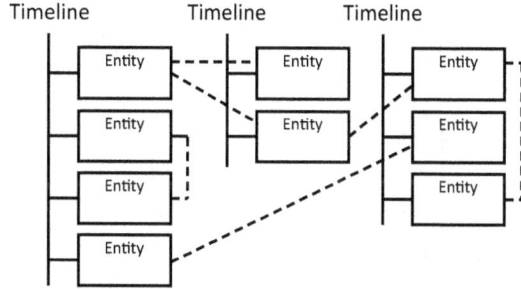

(b) Entities aligned on Timelines, expose cross-Timeline Channels

Figure 7: S3F Logical Architecture

an entity E_d on another timeline T_d, and this channel has a minimum latency of $\gamma < \tau$, then the two timelines involved synchronize with each every γ units of simulation. This means that at times $k\gamma$ (for $k = 1, 2, \ldots$) T_d does not advance beyond time $k\gamma$ until it learns that T_s has reached that time, and has passed to T_d any message it created within virtual time window $[(k-1)\gamma, k\gamma)$. These synchronization points are called *appointments*. The timeline action by T_s associated with indicating to a potential recipient T_d that the timeline's virtual time has reached an appointment time is placed in T_d's event list. Likewise, the action by timeline T_d associated with waiting for a sending timeline T_d to reach the next appointment time is likewise placed in T_d's event list.

Messages received either at appointments or at barriers all have virtual receive-times that are in the future, and so the actions associated with receiving and processing each message can be scheduled in the recipient timeline's event-list.

Clearly the alignment of entities to timelines greatly affects performance. The objective of the alignment algorithm is to balance workload, while keeping entities that share channels with small (or zero) minimal latencies aligned on the same timeline (thereby synchronizing those entities extremely efficiently through an event list rather than a cross-timeline synchronization algorithm). For a given alignment, the choice of τ can also impact performance. At one extreme one might choose τ equal to the smallest minimum latency among all cross-timeline channels. In this case every channel is a slow one, and *all* synchronization and message exchange occurs at barrier. Alternatively, one could choose τ to be so large that every cross-timeline channel is fast, in which case all synchronization and message exchange occurs at appointments. Situations where the former extreme is attractive include when an entity is connected to many many others. In such a case the cost of appointment synchronization is se-

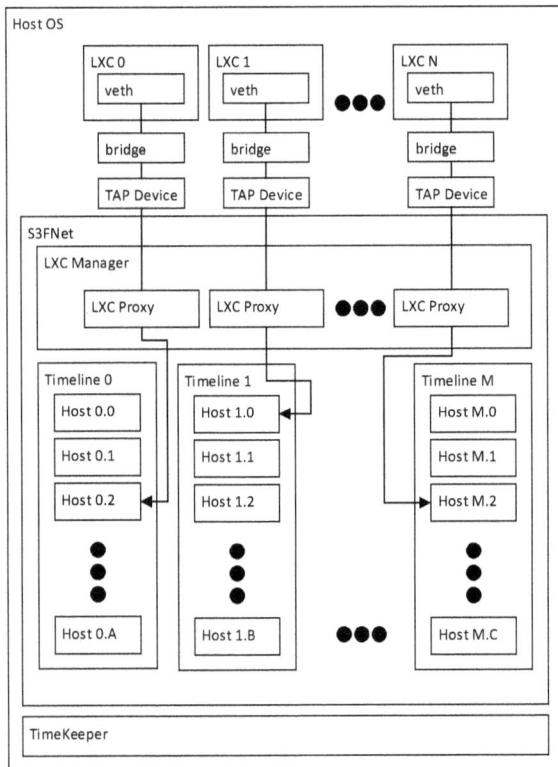

Figure 8: S3F Conjoined with LXC Containers

rialized over the number of channels, but this is avoided by a barrier because the cost of synchronization is insensitive to the communication topology. Situations where the latter case is attractive include when the minimum cross-timeline latency is very small relative to the average cross-timeline latency, which means that overly many barrier synchronizations are called for just to deal with the synchronization requirements of a few channels with small minimum latencies. Implementation of composite synchronization can dynamic alter τ and search for the sweet spot that gives the best performance [19].

6.2 S3F and TimeKeeper

The integration of S3F and OpenVZ limited communication between OpenVZ and S3F to be at barrier synchronizations points; appointments were not used. Messages between S3F and OpenVZ were exchanged only at the end of the synchronization window, using application level communication mechanisms. As we have seen in the discussions of CORE and ns-3, more sophisticated kernel-level functionality is available (TAPs and bridges) to support concurrent generation, delivery, and receipt of traffic between LXC containers and a discrete-event simulator. This observation led us to re-architect integration of emulation with S3F. The new architecture is shown in Figure 9. Here the mechanism for trapping LXC traffic and conveying it to S3F, and vice-versa is the same as used in ns-3: the LXC interacts with what looks like a normal interface to it, and linkages involving virtual interfaces, bridges, and TAP devices connect the LXC with another application. The S3F/LXC interface is

managed by an entity we call the LXC Manager. This has a list of data structures called LXC Proxies, with one for each managed LXC. As with the SF3/OpenVZ integration and similar to ns-3, the simulation has a node that represents the LXC host, which for consistency here we will also call a *ghost*. One can think of the LXC as being an application that sends traffic to the network simulator and receives traffic from the network simulator. The LXC's ghost has S3F model code for the simulated network at the bottom of the stack, and exchanges packets with the LXC at the highest layer of the stack.

The LXC Manager has a thread which is responsible for noticing when any LXC has done a write, and conveys the packet written to the timeline to which the LXC's ghost is aligned. The receive time will be in the future, and so the action is to insert an event into the timeline's event list. Packets bubbling up from an LXC's ghost are written into the LXC proxy's outgoing queue and are written out to the recipient LXC at the packet's receive time. The LXC Manager interacts with the kernel's Timekeeper module (which is not shown). The LXC Manger can query TimeKeeper for the virtual time of any specific LXC, and can instruct TimeKeeper to cause a stopped LXC to advance a specific interval of time, and stop again. TimeKeeper is implemented with multiple kernel threads, to allow for many timelines to interact with it concurrently (through the LXC Manager module).

The architecture of trapping traffic at the TAP has the benefit of not requiring any modification to the executing code within the LXC, but has a consequence of a certain amount of inaccuracy in virtual time measurement. This occurs because the LXC will write a message to the network interface *and keep executing*, while the virtual time associated with that transmission is measured by the LXC Manager, when it notices the write, at which point it queries the LXC for the the virtual time. Conceptually it would be possible to measure the virtual time at the point of transmission, but this would require further modification to the kernel and to the packet to carry the time-stamp along. This is illustrated in Figure 10. We have determined by instrumentation that the delay between when the packet is sent and when the clock returns a value for the send time is close to 16 μs. This obviously impacts the granularity of accuracy we can expect, but note that this depends on the time dilation factor, for the lag in *virtual time* is on the order of $(16/TDF)$ μs. We will see the impact of this in our experiments.

With this architecture and an appropriate interface with TimeKeeper, we are able integrate LXC execution behavior more deeply with the virtual time synchronization structure than has ever before been accomplished. We are able to view an S3F entity as something that holds state, that generates messages, that receives messages, and that synchronizes with other entities *regardless of whether that entity's behavior is simulated or emulated.*

The LXC Manager plays the role of an event-list manager for an LXC. When an LXC ghost's timeline knows that it is safe to advance to time t, it asks the LXC Manager to advance the LXC to time t, and then stop. At time t the LXC Manager may deliver a packet to the stopped LXC, or possibly just wait until additional synchronization information makes it clear that it is safe to advance the LXC even further.

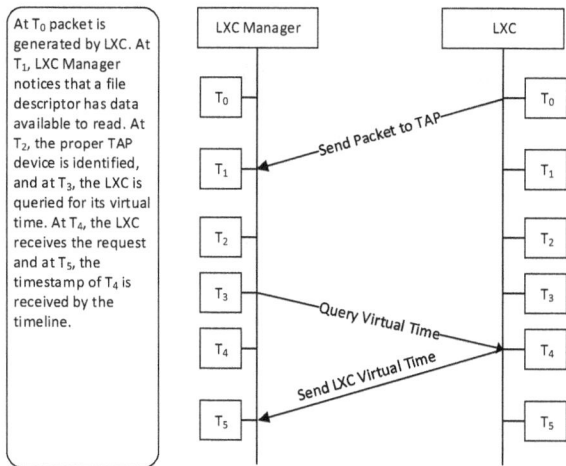

At T_0 packet is generated by LXC. At T_1, LXC Manager notices that a file descriptor has data available to read. At T_2, the proper TAP device is identified, and at T_3, the LXC is queried for its virtual time. At T_4, the LXC receives the request and at T_5, the timestamp of T_4 is received by the timeline.

Figure 9: Determining Timestamp of LXC Generated packet.

We cannot emphasize this contribution strongly enough. Prior to this work, simulators only interacted with emulators by attempting to continuously track observed passage of time (e.g., ns-3 and CORE), or at fixed points in time (e.g., S3F/OpenVZ). Fine-grained synchronization based on directed commands such as "run for 540 μs and then stop" are new. That said, control over LXC execution is not exact. TimeKeeper uses a timer to govern when it signals an LXC to stop. The precise firing of that timer, and the precise point in the code execution when that LXC responds is non-deterministic. Furthermore, we observe that the magnitude of that non-determinism suggest we not try to control an LXC with time intervals much smaller than 10 wall-clock μs. Our approach includes buffering advancement requests. The LXC's manager has an accumulator of advancement requests. When a request comes in to advance by δ wallclock time, the accumulated value and δ are added together. If that sum is less than 10 μs, then the accumulated value becomes the sum, the LXC's clock is advanced by the virtual time corresponding to δ, but the LXC is not run. If instead that sum exceeds 10 μs, the LXC is run for a wallclock time equal to the sum, the accumulator is cleared, and when the LXC completes its virtual clock is advanced by the amount to virtual time corresponding to δ units of wallclock time.

6.3 Experiments

We conclude this section by evaluating the accuracy and practicality of S3FNet's integration with TimeKeeper. One experiment highlights the most significant source of inaccuracy, and shows how models with high TDF are largely unaffected by it. The second experiment demonstrates that this integration is capable of handling models with thousands of containers, and measures the overhead as a function of overload model activity.

6.3.1 Accuracy

Accuracy experiments were conducted on a desktop running a modified 3.10.9 Linux Kernel with 8 Intel Core i7-2600s @3.40GHz. Since the motivation behind virtual time is to artificially scale performance of LXCs, we explored how varying TDF affects results of a simulation, specifically by bouncing a message between containers. In the first experiment, we repeat the following experiment 3000 times: a container sends a minimally sized UDP packet to the other, which on receipt immediately returns a minimally sized UDP response. The virtual time at the point of transmission is measured by the process running in the LXC, as is the virtual time at the point of receipt. Note that these virtual times are different from the virtual times ascribed to the UDP packets by S3F, because they are made from within the container, and are not the times acquired by the LXC manager. The channel delay between the 2 LXCs is 100 μs and the transmission time is 271 μs, which means the "perfect" round-trip time between LXCs should be $(100 \cdot 2 + 217 \cdot 2) = 634$ μs.

Table 2 reports statistics from this experiment, varying the time-dilation factor. The reduction in error with increasing TDF is largely (but not exactly) explained by the lag between actual send/receive time and queried send/receive time.

TDF	Mean RTT	ρ RTT	Mean Error
1	704.57	11.5	70.57
5	647.03	2.5	13.03
10	642.21	1.9	8.21
20	638.86	1.5	4.86
30	637.66	1.2	3.66
40	636.70	1.1	2.70
50	635.95	0.8	1.95
100	634.54	0.7	0.54

Table 2: Accuracy of simulation with varying TDFs, sampled from 3000 round-trips. Time units are μs, mean and standard deviation ρ are shown.

6.3.2 Large Scale Model

This experiment measures the overhead incurred on a larger network model that fully exercises composite synchronization, and compares the overhead of managing LXCs under conditions of no traffic, and under conditions of heavy traffic. Figure 11 illustrates the topology. The upper half of the figure shows the subnetwork that is aligned to a timeline. It is compromised of 200 hosts that are joined by a router that has a fast (50 μs) connection to a gateway router, and 200 hosts that are joined by a router that has a slow (1 ms) connection to that same router. There are 10 timelines, with 10 gateways, with the gateways being joined in a ring. The traffic pattern has randomly chosen pairs of hosts performing the UDP back-and-back experiment described earlier. Under composite synchronization, the fast channels (including those between gateways) use appointments while the traffic that crosses the slow channels are exchanged at barrier synchronization points.

These experiments were run on an enterprise server with 24 Intel Xeon X5650s running at 2.67 GHz, with 24 GB of RAM. For any given experiment we can measure the time spent in LXC management in a timeline by subtracting the measured time executing the emulations from the total running time. We did this in two scenarios, one in which there was no traffic at all generated by the containers, the other in which the back-and-forth UDP messaging was constant. As Table 3 and 4 show, the simulation with traffic has higher overhead, on the order of 10%. This happens because the communication between the LXC Manager and Timekeeper greatly increases as LXCs advance more frequently with smaller intervals. Without traffic, an LXC advances from virtual time $T_1 \rightarrow T_2$ by a single interval. However, with traffic, an LXC may advance (unfreeze and freeze) multiple times when going from $T_1 \rightarrow T_2$, yielding greater overhead.

Two things are revealed by this experiment. First, that S3FNet with Timekeeper support is capable of advancing at least 4000 containers using less than half the resources of an ordinary enterprise server. This experiment was not designed to see where the system breaks, the upper bound is yet to be discovered. The second lesson is that traffic load increases overhead, but not overwhelmingly so. This also speaks to the practicality of the system.

TL	Total (s)	Emulation (s)	Overhead (%)
1	1200.43	1199.52	0.076
2	1200.2	1199.52	0.057
3	1199.93	1199.52	0.034
4	1200.18	1199.52	0.055
5	1200.65	1199.52	0.094
6	1200.44	1199.52	0.077
7	1200.52	1199.52	0.083
8	1200.36	1199.52	0.07
9	1199.95	1199.52	0.036
10	1200.1	1199.52	0.048

Table 3: 4000 LXCs Aligned on 10 Timelines With No Traffic

7. CONCLUSION

We have shown that emulation can be conjoined with simulation in Linux multiprocessors, using a kernel module TimeKeeper. To emphasize the generality of the approach, we have shown how to bring TimeKeeper's capabilities to three simulation/emulation systems: CORE, ns-3, and S3F. In each case TimeKeeper brings new capabilities to conjoined models. It makes CORE's behavior more accurate by synchronizing the execution of its emulation modules in virtual time, something CORE did not do before. It makes ns-3 able to simulate/emulate larger models than it currently can, by moving the common basis for coordination between ns-3 and emulation from the wallclock to the potentially slower

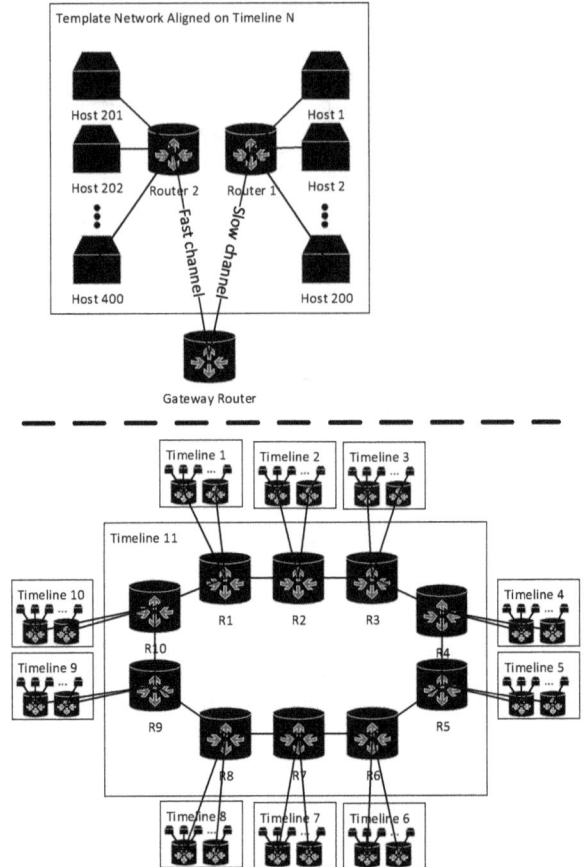

Figure 10: Topology supporting 4000 LXCs

virtual clock. Finally, it showed for the first time how to integrate fine-grained control of emulated hosts within a parallel simulation synchronization algorithm. From the point of view of synchronization, it removes the distinction between emulated and simulated hosts.

There is no free lunch however. LXC containers are controlled by timers whose firings cause an LXC to halt. There is inescapable variation in the behavior of a timer—telling it to fire in T units of time will result in it firing in $T + \epsilon$ units of time, where ϵ will vary with every execution. The number of instructions executed by a container within a given interval of time will vary also, depending on things like cache hits/misses, page faults, and other variation induced by the operating system. Likewise, in the current implementation, inaccuracy creeps in because of a difference between when a container sends or receives a packet and when a time-stamp is ascribed to that event. Both causes of inaccuracy are inaccuracies in physical time, and so decrease in *in virtual time* as the time-dilation factor increases.

The experiments we provide show that conjoined emulation/simulations using TimeKeeper behave as would be hoped for, illustrate the magnitude of the the variation due to non-determinism, and the overhead of managing many many LXCs concurrently. We believe TimeKeeper will be a valuable tool for bringing emulation capabilities to other

TL	Total (s)	Emulation (s)	Overhead (%)
1	1353.31	1199.52	11.364
2	1456.51	1199.52	17.644
3	1385.29	1199.52	13.41
4	1318.87	1199.52	9.049
5	1371.41	1199.52	12.534
6	1340.93	1199.52	10.546
7	1377.82	1199.52	12.941
8	1404.09	1199.52	14.57
9	1313.71	1199.52	8.692
10	1314.11	1199.52	8.72

Table 4: 4000 LXCs Aligned on 10 Timelines With Heavy Traffic

simulators, and to bring virtual time to other Linux applications.

Acknowledgments

This material is based upon work supported in part by the Boeing Corporation, in part by the Department of Energy under Award Number DE-OE0000097, and in part by the Maryland Procurement Office under Contract No. H98230-14-C-0141 [1].

8. REFERENCES

[1] The network simulator - ns-2. http://www.isi.edu/nsnam/ns/, 1997. Accessed: 2015-02-03.

[2] Lxc: Linux containers. https://linuxcontainers.org/, 2009. Accessed: 2015-02-30.

[3] J-sim official. https://sites.google.com/site/jsimofficial/, 2014. Accessed: 2015-02-03.

[4] Omnet++ vs ns-2: A comparison. http://ctieware.eng.monash.edu.au/twiki/bin/view/Simulation/OMNeTppComparison, 2014. Accessed: 2015-03-06.

[5] Openvz: a container-based virtualization for linux. http://openvz.org/Main_Page, 2014. Accessed: 2015-01-30.

[6] Virtualbox. https://www.virtualbox.org/, 2014. Accessed: 2015-02-15.

[7] J. Ahrenholz, C. Danilov, T. R. Henderson, and J. H. Kim. Core: A real-time network emulator. In *Military Communications Conference, (San Diego, CA, Nov 16-19, 2008)*, pages 1–7. IEEE, 2008.

[8] J. Ahrenholz, T. Goff, and B. Adamson. Integration of the core and emane network emulators. In *MILITARY COMMUNICATIONS CONFERENCE, (Baltimore, MD, Nov 7-10, 2011)*, pages 1870–1875. IEEE, 2011.

[9] P. Barham, B. Dragovic, K. Fraser, S. Hand, T. Harris, A. Ho, R. Neugebauer, I. Pratt, and A. Warfield. Xen and the art of virtualization. In *Proceedings of the 19th ACM Symposium on Operating System Principles, (Bolton Landing, New York, Oct 19-22, 2003)*. ACM, 2003.

[10] J. Cowie, D. Nicol, and A. Ogielski. Modeling the global internet. *IEEE Computing in Science and Engineering*, 1(1):42–50, Jan.-Feb. 1999.

[11] M. A. Erazo, Y. Li, and J. Liu. Sveet! a scalable virtualized evaluation environment for tcp. In *Testbeds and Research Infrastructures for the Development of Networks & Communities and Workshops, 2009. TridentCom 2009. 5th International Conference, (Washington, DC, April 6-8, 2009)*, pages 1–10. IEEE, 2009.

[12] A. Grau, S. Maier, K. Herrmann, and K. Rothermel. Time jails: A hybrid approach to scalable network emulation. In *Principles of Advanced and Distributed Simulation, 2008. PADS'08. 22nd Workshop, (Rome, Italy, June 3-6, 2008)*, pages 7–14. IEEE, 2008.

[13] D. Gupta, K. V. Vishwanath, M. McNett, A. Vahdat, K. Yocum, A. Snoeren, and G. M. Voelker. Diecast: Testing distributed systems with an accurate scale model. *ACM Transactions on Computer Systems (TOCS)*, 29(2):4, 2011.

[14] D. Gupta, K. Yocum, M. McNett, A. C. Snoeren, A. Vahdat, and G. M. Voelker. To infinity and beyond: time warped network emulation. In *Proceedings of the twentieth ACM symposium on Operating systems principles, (San Jose, CA, May 8-10, 2006)*, pages 1–2. ACM, 2005.

[15] T. R. Henderson, S. Roy, S. Floyd, and G. F. Riley. ns-3 project goals. In *Proceeding from the 2006 workshop on ns-2: the IP network simulator*, page 13. ACM, 2006.

[16] M. Koksal. A survey of network simulators supporting wireless networks. In *Middle East Technical University (Ankara, Turkey)*, pages 1–11, 2008.

[17] J. Lamps, D. M. Nicol, and M. Caesar. Timekeeper: a lightweight virtual time system for linux. In *Proceedings of the 2nd ACM SIGSIM/PADS conference on Principles of advanced discrete simulation, (Denver, CO, May 18-21, 2014)*, pages 179–186. ACM, 2014.

[18] H. W. Lee, D. Thuente, and M. L. Sichitiu. Integrated simulation and emulation using adaptive time dilation. In *Proceedings of the 2nd ACM SIGSIM/PADS conference on Principles of advanced discrete simulation, (Denver, CO, May 18-21, 2014)*, pages 167–178. ACM, 2014.

[1] Disclaimer: Any opinions, findings and conclusions or recommendations expressed in this material are those of the author(s) and do not necessarily reflect the views of the Maryland Procurement Office. This report was prepared as an account of work sponsored by an agency of the United States Government. Neither the United States Government nor any agency thereof, nor any of their employees, makes any warranty, express or implied, or assumes any legal liability or responsibility for the accuracy, completeness, or usefulness of any information, apparatus, product, or process disclosed, or represents that its use would not infringe privately owned rights. Reference herein to any specific commercial product, process, or service by trade name, trademark, manufacturer, or otherwise does not necessarily constitute or imply its endorsement, recommendation, or favoring by the United States Government or any agency thereof. The views and opinions of authors expressed herein do not necessarily state or reflect those of the United States Government or any agency thereof.

[19] D. Nicol and J. Liu. Composite synchronization in parallel discrete-event simulation. *Parallel and Distributed Systems, IEEE Transactions on,* 13(5):433–446, May 2002.

[20] D. M. Nicol, D. Jin, and Y. Zheng. S3F: The scalable simulation framework revisited. In *Proceedings of the Winter Simulation Conference, (Phoenix, AZ, Dec 11-14, 2011),* pages 3288–3299. Winter Simulation Conference, 2011.

[21] M. Rosenblum. Vmware's virtual platform. In *Proceedings of hot chips, (Stanford, CA, Aug 15-17, 1999),* volume 1999, pages 185–196, 1999.

[22] A. Vahdat, K. Yocum, K. Walsh, P. Mahadevan, D. Kostić, J. Chase, and D. Becker. Scalability and accuracy in a large-scale network emulator. *ACM SIGOPS Operating Systems Review,* 36(SI):271–284, 2002.

[23] A. Varga et al. The omnet++ discrete event simulation system. In *Proceedings of the European simulation multiconference, (Prague, Czech Republic, June 6-9, 2001),* volume 9, page 65. ESM, 2001.

[24] E. Weingärtner, F. Schmidt, H. Vom Lehn, T. Heer, and K. Wehrle. Slicetime: A platform for scalable and accurate network emulation. In *NSDI, (Boston, MA, March 30-April 1, 2011),* 2011.

[25] E. Weingartner, H. Vom Lehn, and K. Wehrle. A performance comparison of recent network simulators. In *Communications, 2009. ICC'09. IEEE International Conference, (Dresden, Germany, June 14-18, 2009),* pages 1–5. IEEE, 2009.

[26] B. White, J. Lepreau, L. Stoller, R. Ricci, S. Guruprasad, M. Newbold, M. Hibler, C. Barb, and A. Joglekar. An integrated experimental environment for distributed systems and networks. *ACM SIGOPS Operating Systems Review,* 36(SI):255–270, 2002.

[27] Y. Zheng, D. Nicol, D. Jin, and N. Tanaka. A virtual time system for virtualization-based network emulations and simulations. *Journal of Simulation,* 6(3):205–213, 2012.

Keynote Talk

Enabling Distributed Simulations Using Big Data and Clouds

Peter Kacsuk
MTA SZTAKI
Victor Hugo u. 18-22
Budapest, 1132,
Hungary
kacsuk@sztaki.hu

ABSTRACT

Large scientific simulation projects should enable the collaboration of large scientific consortia where members are located in different countries and even continents storing their usually very large data set in different kind of storages. Therefore state-of-the-art simulations should process very large set of data stored in a distributed way in different kind of storages located in all over the world. As the data is big its processing time can be intolerably long. To reduce processing time we have to use large infrastructure that enables the exploitation of parallel processing wherever it is possible in the simulation process. Clouds provide the required large set of computing resources and hence we need simulation environments that enable the easy exploitation of cloud resources.

This keynote speech introduces a cloud-oriented simulation platform that enables the exploitation of large cloud resources as well as accessing all the major data storage types. This platform called as WS-PGRADE/gUSE is intensively used in many EU FP7 projects among them in CloudSME where the main target is to enable particularly small and medium-sized manufacturing and engineering companies (SMEs), to use state of the art simulation technology as a Service (SaaS, one-stop-shop, pay-per-use) in the cloud.

In this talk we will show the main features of WS-PGRADE/gUSE that enable the use of cloud and large data resources to conduct distributed simulations. First, the workflow creation and execution mechanism will be explained. Then the DCI Bridge service will be shown that enables the exploitation of many independent cloud resources in parallel. Finally, the Data Avenue service that enables the access and transfer of large data among various types of data storages will be described. These services together enable the creation of simulation workflows that are easily portable among different distributed computing and data infrastructures including various types of clouds and cloud storages. At the end of the talk some concrete examples from the CloudSME project (www.cloudsme.eu) will highlight the main advantages of using the platform.

Categories and Subject Descriptors

I.6.0 [**Simulation and Modelling**]: General

General Terms

Algorithms.

Keywords

Simulation, Distributed Simulation, Big Data

An Agent-Based Simulation Model to Evaluate the Efficiency of a Synthetic Biology System

Fernando Cea-Olvera, Adrian Ramirez-Nafarrate, Begoña Albizuri-Romero

Instituto Tecnológico Autónomo de México

{fernando.cea, adrian.ramirez, albizuri}@itam.mx

ABSTRACT

In this paper, we present an agent-based simulation (ABS) model of a synthetic biology system that captures substrates and transfers them amongst a group of enzymes until reaching an acceptor enzyme, which generates a substrate-channeling event (SCE). In particular, we analyze the number of simulation cycles required to reach a pre-specified number of SCEs varying the system composition, which is given by the number of enzymes of two types: donor and acceptor. The results show an efficient frontier that generates the desired number of SCEs with the minimum number of cycles and the lowest acceptor:donor ratio for a given density of enzymes in the system. This frontier is characterized by an exponential function to define the system composition that would minimize the number of cycles to generate the desired SCEs. The output of the ABS confirms that compositions obtained by this function are highly efficient.

Categories and Subject Descriptors

I.6.3 [**SIMULATION AND MODELING**]: Applications; I.6.5 [**SIMULATION AND MODELING**]: Model Development – *Modeling methodologies*; I.6.8 [**SIMULATION AND MODELING**]: Types of Simulation – *Discrete event.*

General Terms

Algorithms, Performance, Design, Experimentation.

Keywords

Agent-based simulation, synthetic biology, substrate-channeling events.

1. INTRODUCTION

The sustainable production of fossil fuel alternatives is a critical challenge for the scientific community. Current day-to-day activities are highly dependent on non-renewable resources (e.g., petroleum derivatives), which do not promote sustainable processes. The emerging area of synthetic biology is well positioned to address the need for new green technologies, through the combination of many characterized natural processes and structures.

SIGSIM-PADS '15, June 10 - 12, 2015, London, United Kingdom
© 2015 ACM. ISBN 978-1-4503-3583-6/15/06...$15.00
DOI: http://dx.doi.org/10.1145/2769458.2769466

Synthetic biology combines biology and engineering methods to construct systems to accomplish a defined goal (e.g., produce energy in a sustainable manner) [17]. However, the design of novel pathways (metabolic processes triggered by enzymes) and architectures through synthetic biology is hindered in part by the vast amount of biological parts and their possible combinations. Thus, computer models may help the planning process of design-build-test-learn (DBTL) cycle of synthetic biology, for example, as shown for the design of novel metabolic pathways [14, 17]. The DBTL cycle is an engineering-based process used for the development of new technology. It consists of designing the new system (defining objectives, components, structure and interrelationships), building a model and testing it to analyze its performance and learning from the gaps between the actual and desired performance to refine system through multiple iterations. The cycle has been widely used for devising new technology in areas such as synthetic biology [16] and high-performance computing [10].

Enzymes are the catalytic component of a metabolic pathway. In nature, enzymes of a pathway may be bounded to proteins that form a structure where the metabolic process takes place (scaffold). For example, three-dimensional (icosahedral) protein architectures (i.e., bacterial microcompartments, hereafter BMCs) compartmentalize metabolic pathways to increase their reaction efficiency, encapsulate toxin intermediates, etc. [9]. Enzyme scaffolding is a promising strategy for the development and optimization of bioinspired devices for biotechnological purposes. These complex structures can be generated through the combination of interchangeable protein building blocks [8]. Scaffolding of proteins has been shown to be effective in controlling and improving the efficiency of synthetic metabolic reactions [5], whether by substrate channeling (the efficient transfer of molecules produced by one enzyme to a different enzyme when they are found in close vicinity) [4] or by modulation of the stoichiometry (the relative quantities of every enzyme in a metabolic pathway) of the reaction components.

In this paper, we present a proof-of-concept using an agent-based simulation model of a hypothetical biological system whose objective is to generate synthetic metabolic reactions by means of substrate channeling. We inspired our agent-based simulation model on BMC architectures similar to the one observed by Lassila et al. [11]. They showed that proteins with specific characteristics (sequence of amino acids) might interact with proteins from a BMC shell to form a bidimensional layer.

The model presented in this paper consists of a hypothetical 2-dimensional scaffold in form of a grid. Two types of enzymes, donor and acceptor, are modeled so that they can interact with the scaffold. The donor and acceptor enzymes are part of a metabolic pathway. We consider that only one enzyme can occupy one square of the grid and that the enzymes can move freely throughout the scaffold. Substrate channeling will occur when both donor and acceptor are found in proximity. In other words, we simulate the arrival of substrates to a grid populated with donors and acceptors, the donors and acceptors move around the grid over time and the substrate is transferred from donor to donor until reaching an acceptor enzyme, which triggers a metabolic reaction (substrate channeling event). While donor-to-donor transfers may not occur in nature, they were considered as a proxy for inefficiencies in the donor enzyme in the hypothetical scaffold system.

The objective of the paper is to study the number of cycles required to generate a pre-specified number of substrate-channeling events (SCE) varying the total number of enzymes in the system (density) and the ratio acceptor:donor. Furthermore, we want to characterize the most efficient configuration of the system, which produces the desired number of SCE with the lowest number of cycles and the minimum number of enzymes. A cycle is defined from the arrival of a substrate to the active site of the donor enzyme until the transfer of the substrate to the acceptor enzyme. The experiments shown in this paper confirm the existence of an efficient frontier in the density-ratio space to generate a pre-specified number of SCEs with a minimum number of simulation cycles.

Computational models in synthetic biology have been discussed in the literature published in recent years. In [17] the opportunities of using computational tools for designing large-scale complex systems based on synthetic biology are identified. Despite of not being perfect and not including all the features in complex biological systems, computational models can help during an iterative process, similar to the DBTL cycle, to refine the system. In particular, the authors discuss about the capability of computational models to perform sensitivity analysis. A list of computational tools for the design and analysis of genetic networks is available in [17].

Current simulation approaches of synthetic biology systems include systems dynamics to model growth of cells [15] and BioBrick-based models to design synthetic biological circuits. BioBricks represent blocks of DNA that are assembled together to construct system with special properties, similar to Lego blocks that can be assembled in different ways. BioJade is an example of a Java-based tool to simulate BioBrick-based systems [7].

Another simulation paradigm that is suitable for modelling biological systems is Agent-based Simulation (ABS) due to its capability to model complex system [13]. ABS framework enables interactions amongst agents and can implement decision rules based on environmental conditions.

ABS has been used to model a wide variety of natural systems. For example, a traditional problem analyzed with ABS is the "game of Life" [1, 6]. This problem simulates the evolution of cells located in a grid using simple rules to turn on or turn off the cells based on the state of the neighbors. The simulation shows that the system evolves from a random distribution of cells to well-defined patterns that depend on the complexity of the rules [2, 3].

Another application of ABS for modeling natural processes is presented in [18]. In that paper, the authors used ABS to model molecular self-organization process. They used a grid structure with 25 types of molecular agents. The algorithm includes rules that allow the agents to move, merge or split based on

deterministic, stochastic and learning processes. The results show that the implemented algorithm produces more ordered and uniformed clusters than Monte Carlo simulation.

The model presented in this paper consists of an ABS. The basic structure of the model also consists of a grid (scaffold) populated with agents (enzymes). Differently from previous works, the analysis on this paper is based on the substrate transference until reaching an acceptor enzyme that triggers a metabolic reaction. The simulation experiments are followed by an analysis of the results to characterize the best configuration of the system to obtain the desired number of SCE. The model and the analysis are similar to other studies using ABS (e.g., pray-predator models), but it is oriented to an area of increasing opportunity for applications, such as synthetic biological systems. The analysis presented in this paper is aligned with the DBTL cycle applied to a hypothetical synthetic biological system and can be used to teach the potential of ABS in this field.

The remaining sections in this paper are organized as follows: Section 2 presents a description of the simulation model; Section 3 describes the experimentation process and presents the results. Finally, Section 4 presents the concluding remarks and future research directions.

2. DESCRIPTION OF THE SIMULATION MODEL

The main outcome in the simulation model is the SCE, which in biological systems may represent a generation of a product or metabolic intermediate. As in [4], we defined a SCE when the close vicinity of an acceptor enzyme and a donor enzyme does not allow the substrate to diffuse out of the system but rather to be transferred between enzymes.

The basic biological process begins when a donor enzyme receives a newly arriving substrate. The enzymes of the system move randomly over the physical space and through time such that the substrate is transferred to other enzymes in the neighborhood. When the substrate is transferred from a donor to an acceptor, one SCE is generated.

The composition of the system, defined as the amount of donor and acceptor enzymes, has an effect on the efficiency of the system. Thus, the number of cycles required to generate the desired SCEs depends on the population of enzymes and the ratio acceptor:donor. Understanding the effect of the composition of the system on the efficiency of the biological process may allow researchers to design better artificial systems in terms of cost-effectiveness.

Therefore, the objective of this paper is to present an initial effort on simulating a synthetic biology process to determine the most efficient composition to generate SCEs.

2.1 Agent-based Simulation Model

The process described above implies that all the enzymes move randomly and simultaneously across the space. Since computing processes are executed in a discrete manner, simulating the biological system requires a random-based modeling methodology to overcome this issue.

The model environment presented in this paper is reduced to 2 dimensions. The system consists of a 28x28 grid with an initial random location of e enzymes, divided in d donor enzymes and a

acceptor enzymes ($e = d + a$). After initializing the location of enzymes, the simulation process is divided in cycles that comprise the following steps:

1. A new substrate arrives to the system. A donor enzyme receives the substrate, randomly.

2. All the enzymes in the grid randomly move to an available location in the neighborhood. The neighborhood is defined by the eight spaces surrounding a cell (neighborhood size is less than eight for cells in the edge of the grid).

3. The substrates in the system are randomly transferred from one enzyme to another enzyme in the neighborhood. If there is exactly one acceptor enzyme in the neighborhood, then the substrate is transferred to the acceptor. If there is more than one acceptor enzyme in the neighborhood, the substrate is randomly transferred to one of them. If there are only donor enzymes in the neighborhood, the substrate is transferred to another donor, randomly. If there are no enzymes in the neighborhood, the substrate remains with the current enzyme. This process is assumed for a specific synthetic biology system. Natural processes and engineer biosynthetic systems may transfer substrate using different rules.

4. If the substrate is transferred to an acceptor enzyme, the SCE is generated (SCE count increases by one) and the substrate is removed from the system.

The execution of cycles repeats until a pre-specified number of SCEs has been generated. The steps in the cycle are executed in evenly distributed instants through time. In order to overcome the limitations of the discrete nature of computing processes for modeling simultaneous movement of enzymes and substrates, the simulation moves the enzymes and substrates one at a time, but the sequence of the movement is randomly defined. Thus, every time that steps two and three are executed, a different sequence of movement is considered. All random processes are uniformly distributed. Figure 1 shows a graphic representation of the system.

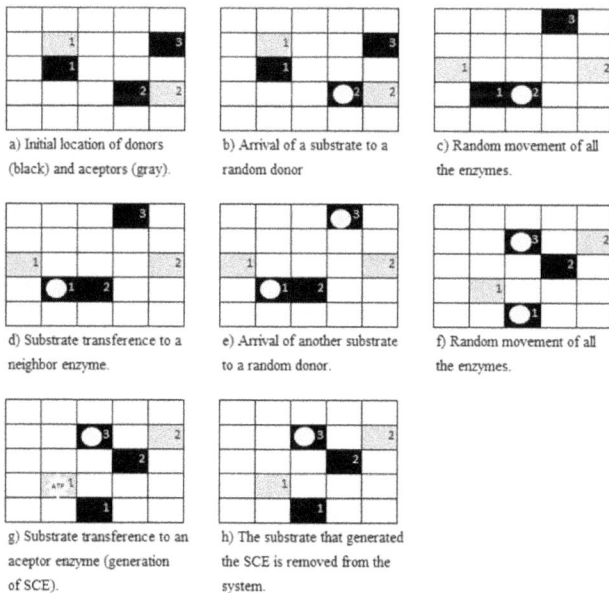

a) Initial location of donors (black) and aceptors (gray).

b) Arrival of a substrate to a random donor

c) Random movement of all the enzymes.

d) Substrate transference to a neighbor enzyme.

e) Arrival of another substrate to a random donor.

f) Random movement of all the enzymes.

g) Substrate transference to an acceptor enzyme (generation of SCE).

h) The substrate that generated the SCE is removed from the system.

Figure 1. Representation of the simulation. Two cycles are shown (figures b-d and e-h) with one SCE generated.

The system may be saturated if there are no donor enzymes available to receive a new substrate. In this case, the simulation stops and reports that the current composition of donor and acceptors is not efficient (infeasible).

The simulation model is coded in C++ with three types of classes: 1) *Location* with attributes defined by coordinates (X, Y) to represent the grid; 2) *Enzyme* to represent donor and acceptor enzymes with attributes defined by the location, hosting level (Boolean) and type (donor or acceptor defined as Boolean); 3) *Substrate* to represent the substrates in the system with attributes defined by arrival time and index of the enzyme host. The simulation implements the object-oriented pseudo-random number generator proposed in [12].

3. EXPERIMENTS
3.1 Exploratory Experiments
The objective of the exploratory experiments is to analyze the efficiency of the generation of SCE varying the density of enzymes in the system, defined by the proportion α and the ratio acceptor:donor, defined by the proportion β, as shown in Equations 1 and 2, respectively.

$$\alpha = e/28^2 \qquad (1)$$

$$\beta = a/d \qquad (2)$$

For the initial set of experiments, e is evaluated in the range from 20 ($\beta = 0.025$) to 780 ($\beta = 0.994$) in steps of 20. For each value of e, each combination of d and a such that $d > a$ is evaluated. Thus, for a given e, $a = 1, 2, ..., (e/2 - 1)$ and $d = e - a$. For instance, Table 1 shows the values of d and a evaluated when $e = 20$. We assume that $d > a$ as it is expected that the donor enzyme would be the limiting factor on the metabolic reaction (i.e. the acceptor enzymes can only receive substrate from the donor enzymes).

Each system composition is evaluated with the number of cycles required to complete the generation of γ SCEs. For the initial set of experiments, γ is set between 10 and 280 in steps of 10. Each combination of α, β and γ is simulated 500 replications. Furthermore, the compositions given by α and β that achieve the best efficiency score (cycles = γ) are recorded for analysis. Figure 2 shows the most efficient compositions for $\gamma = 20$ and 200 SCEs. The characteristics of the figures for the omitted values of γ are similar to these plots.

Table 1. System compositions evaluated when $e = 20$

e	d	a	α	β
20	19	1	0.0255	0.053
20	18	2	0.0255	0.111
20	17	3	0.0255	0.176
20	16	4	0.0255	0.250
20	15	5	0.0255	0.333
20	14	6	0.0255	0.429
20	13	7	0.0255	0.538
20	12	8	0.0255	0.667
20	11	9	0.0255	0.818

Figure 2 suggests that a density value lower than 10% is not efficient to generate SCEs. In addition, this figure shows that the efficiency of the system increases as the density and the ratio acceptor:donor increase. Thus, given the characteristics of the system described in this paper, the number of cycles to generate γ SCEs decreases when the number of enzymes in the system increases and/or the number of acceptor enzymes increases. This conclusion is trivial since a system with high density and high ratio acceptor:donor facilitate finding and transferring substrates to an acceptor enzyme and generating SCE. However, the cost of generating SCE increases with the number of enzymes that has to be synthesized. Therefore, in order to design a cost-effective artificial photosynthetic system, the minimum number of enzymes and the best ratio must be defined.

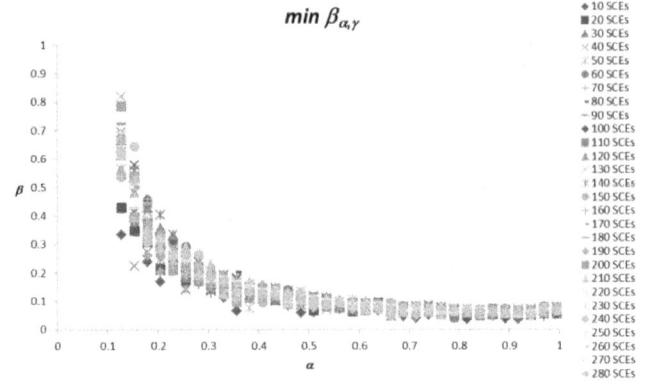

Figure 3. *min $\beta_{\alpha,\gamma}$* for each value of γ.

In order to model the efficient frontier and analyze its performance for generating different values of γ, we compute the average *min $\beta_{\alpha,\gamma}$* across all the values of γ, denoted as $\bar{\beta}_\alpha$ for all α, as shown in Equation 3.

$$\bar{\beta}_\alpha = \frac{\Sigma_{\forall\gamma} \min \beta_{\alpha,\gamma}}{k} \qquad \forall \alpha \tag{3}$$

where k is the number of different values tested for γ. In this paper, $k = 28$. Figure 4 shows the values of $\bar{\beta}_\alpha$.

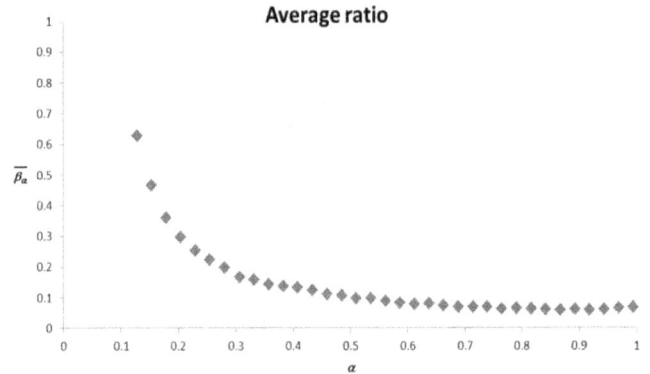

Figure 4. Average ratio ($\bar{\beta}_\alpha$) for different values of α.

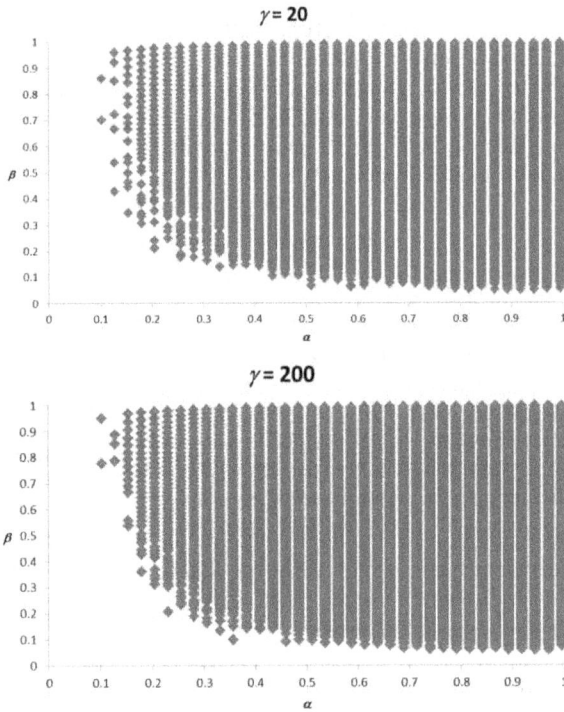

Figure 2. Efficient compositions (α and β) to generate 20 and 200 SCEs.

3.2 Definition of the Efficient Frontier

Figure 2 suggests that an efficient frontier defined by the smallest values of β (smallest ratio) for each value of α exists to generate γ SCEs. In order to analyze this efficient frontier, the smallest value of β is obtained for each combination of α and γ defined as *min $\beta_{\alpha,\gamma}$* and presented in Figure 3. This figure suggests that the smallest number of acceptor enzymes to generate γ SCEs increases as α decreases. Thus, the lower the density the larger the ratio acceptor:donor is. In addition, the smallest ratio acceptor:donor to generate a specified number of SCEs depends also on γ. Moreover, the variability on the values of *min $\beta_{\alpha,\gamma}$* decreases as α increases. In general, for small values of α, the larger γ is, the larger β has to be for the system to be efficient.

Each value of the efficient frontier shown in Figure 4, which is defined by $\bar{\beta}_\alpha$, is tested with another set of experiments to generate between 5 SCEs and 280 SCEs, in steps of 5. In total, 1960 different scenarios, defined by the combinations of (α, β, γ), are simulated with 500 replications for each of them. The efficiency of the frontier defined by $\bar{\beta}_\alpha$ is then evaluated with the number of additional cycles required to generate γ SCEs, defined by δ as:

$$\delta = C - \gamma \tag{4}$$

where C is the minimum number of cycles required to generate γ SCEs across the replications. Table 2 shows the relative frequency of scenarios that observed each value of δ.

The results show that the number of cycles required to generate γ SCEs is the minimum (i.e., $C = \gamma$) in 16.89% of the scenarios and only one additional cycle is required in 61.53% of the scenarios. Furthermore, in 99.9% of the different scenarios, 2 or less additional cycles are needed to generate γ SCEs. Therefore, the frontier defined by $\bar{\beta}_\alpha$ can assess on the value that β must be set for a given α due to its high efficiency in terms of cycles required to generate a specified number of SCEs.

Table 2. Performance of the efficient frontier defined by $\bar{\beta}_\alpha$ using the number of additional cycles to generate γ SCEs ($\gamma = 5, 10, 15, \ldots, 280$)

δ	Relative Frequency (%)	Cumulative Relative Frequency (%)
0	16.89	16.89
1	61.53	78.42
2	21.48	99.9
3	0.10	100

In order to determine the appropriate value of β for a value of α that is not included in the exploratory experiments, the efficient frontier given by $\bar{\beta}_\alpha$ can be approximated by $\hat{\beta}_\alpha$, which is the least squares fit of an exponential function [19], as shown in Equation 5.

$$\hat{\beta}_\alpha = 0.568 e^{-2.87\alpha} \qquad (5)$$

Figure 5 shows the efficient frontier defined by the actual averages $\bar{\beta}_\alpha$ and the predicted average $\hat{\beta}_\alpha$.

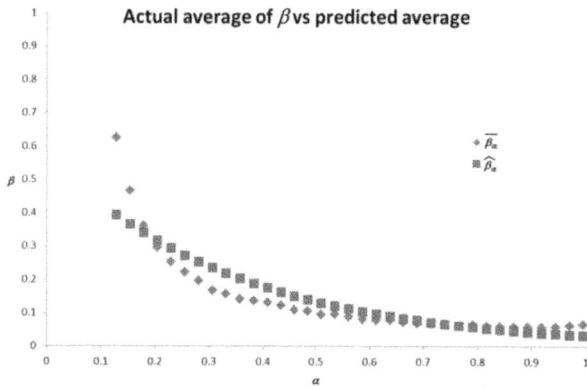

Figure 5. Actual average of β computed for each value of α vs. predicted average.

In order to evaluate the predicted frontier, a new set of experiments is designed to obtain the number of additional cycles required after the minimum to generate a specified number of SCEs. The new scenarios consider a density value not evaluated in the exploratory experiments. Thus, the new scenarios vary the number of enzymes e from 110 to 770 in steps of 20. Therefore, the resulting values of α are located in the middle of each consecutive pair of α shown in Figures 3-5. The ratio acceptor:donor is set to $\hat{\beta}_\alpha$. For each pair $(\alpha, \hat{\beta}_\alpha)$, γ varies between 5 and 280 in steps of 5, which produces a total of 1960 different scenarios, each of them simulated with 500 replications. Figure 6 shows the cumulative relative frequency of scenarios that

observed each value of δ with the ratio acceptor:donor defined by $\hat{\beta}_\alpha$.

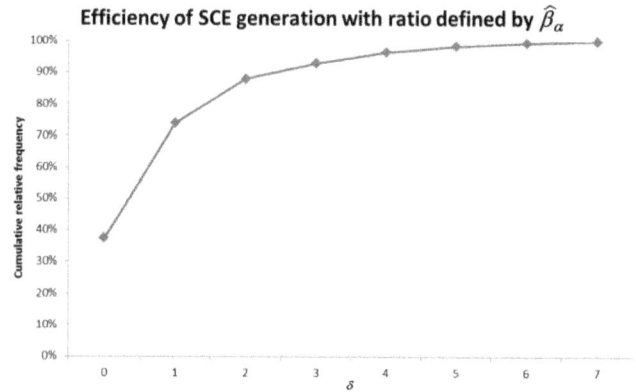

Figure 6. Performance of the efficient frontier defined by $\hat{\beta}_\alpha$ through the number of additional cycles to generate γ SCEs ($\gamma = 5, 10, 15, \ldots, 280$).

This figure shows that 37.34% of the scenarios achieved the minimum the number of cycles to generate γ SCEs. Moreover, 92.91% of the scenarios required 3 or less cycles to generate the desired SCEs and the maximum number of additional cycles is only 7. Therefore, the frontier modeled by $\hat{\beta}_\alpha$ can help to decide on the ratio acceptor:donor given a specified density of enzymes to produce an efficient system in terms of cycles required to generate a desired number of SCEs with a relative low number of acceptor enzymes to synthesize.

4. CONCLUSIONS

This paper presents an ABS model for simulating a synthetic biological system that may allow researchers (e.g. biologists, biotechnology engineers, etc.) to analyze the effect of the system composition on its efficiency. Synthetic biology can have multiple applications with significant benefits and applications. The manipulation of metabolic functions and architectures found in nature as building blocks of novel pathways and synthetic modules can help address the technical challenges frequently faced by new biotechnologies. For example, by understanding the effect of the density of enzymes and the ratio acceptor:donor on the system, and optimizing its composition, one can decrease the cost of enzyme synthesis or increase industrial feasibility by improving product yields.

The analysis of the model presented in this paper suggests that an efficient frontier could exist for generating a specified number of SCEs with the minimum number of cycles and low cost in terms of density of enzymes and number of acceptors. Furthermore, the efficient frontier may be modeled by a function, such as an exponential function for the system analyzed in this paper, which can assess on the system design. The simulation model and analysis of this paper is a proof-of-concept to support the design stage in synthetic biology. The next step is to include differentiated synthesis cost for both types of enzymes considering economies of scale and a scrap cost to penalize for underutilization of enzymes.

Future research lines, from the perspective of synthetic biological systems, include analyzing multidimensional systems with structures and functions that closely resemble the biological counterparts (e.g., a scaffold comprised by hexamers, instead of squares). From the computing perspective, the analysis can be extended to develop the simulation model with parallel processing to enable simultaneous movements of enzymes and substrates.

5. ACKNOWLEDGMENTS

This work has been supported by Asociación Mexicana de Cultura A.C. We thank the assessment of Dr. Raul González Esquer, Mario Sanchez Dominguez and Ricardo Munguia Diaz for the development of the model.

6. REFERENCES

[1] Berlekamp, E. R., Conway , J. H., and Guy, R. K. 2003. *Winning Ways for Your Mathematical Plays*. 2nd Edition. AK Peters Ltd., Natick, MA.

[2] Chan, W. K. V. 2010. Foundations of simulation modeling. In *Encyclopedia of Operations Research and Management Science*, J. J. Cochran, Ed. John Wiley & Sons, Inc. New York, NY

[3] Chan, W. K. V., Son, Y.-J., and Macal C. M. 2010. Agent-based simulation tutorial-simulation of emergent behavior and differences between agent-based simulation and discrete-event simulation. In *Proceedings of the Winter Simulation Conference* (Baltimore, MD, December 05-08, 2010). IEEE, Piscataway, NJ. 135-150. DOI= http://dx.doi.org/10.1109/WSC.2010.5679168.

[4] Conrado, R. J., Varner, J. D., and DeLisa, M. P. 2008. Engineering the spatial organization of metabolic enzymes: mimicking nature's synergy. *Curr. Opin. Biotech.* 19, 5, 492-499. DOI= http://dx.doi.org/10.1016/j.copbio.2008.07.006.

[5] Dueber, J. E., Wu, G. C., Malmirchegini, G. R., Moon, T. S., Petzold, C. J., Ullal, A. V, Prather, K. L. J., and Keasling, J. D. 2009. Synthetic protein scaffolds provide modular control over metabolic flux. *Nat. Biotech.* 27, 8, 753-759. DOI= http://dx.doi.org/10.1038/nbt.1557.

[6] Gardner, M. 1970. The fantastic combinations of John Conway's new solitaire game "Life", *Sci. Am.* 223, Oct 1970, 120-123.

[7] Goler, J.A. 2002-2004. BioJade: MIT Synthetic Biology Working Group. URL: http://web.mit.edu/jagoler/www/biojade/. Last access: May 6, 2015.

[8] Gradišar, H., and Jerala, R. 2014. Self-assembled bionanostructures: proteins following the lead of DNA nanostructures. *J. Nanobiotechnology* 12, 4, 1-9. DOI= http://dx.doi.org/10.1186/1477-3155-12-4.

[9] Kerfeld, C. A., and Erbilgin, O. 2015. Bacterial microcompartments and the modular construction of microbial metabolism. *Trends Microbiol.* 23, 1, 22-34. DOI= http://dx.doi.org/10.1016/j.tim.2014.10.003.

[10] Kettunen, P., and Moilanen, S. 2012. Sensing high-performing software teams: Proposal of an instrument for self-monitoring. In *Agile Processes in Software Engineering and Extreme Programming,* C. Wohli, Ed. Springer Berlin Heidelberg.

[11] Lassila, J. K., Bernstein, S. L., Kinney, J. N., Axen, S. D., and Kerfeld, C. A. 2014. Assembly of robust bacterial microcompartment shells using building blocks from an organelle of unknown function. *J. Mol. Biol.* 426, 11, 2217-2228. DOI= http://dx.doi.org/10.1016/j.jmb.2014.02.025.

[12] L'ecuyer, P., Simard, R., Chen, E.J., and Kelton, W.D. 2002. An object-oriented random-number package with many long streams and substreams. *Oper. Res.* 50, 6, 1073-1075. DOI= http://dx.doi.org/ 10.1287/opre.50.6.1073.358.

[13] Macal, C.M., and North, M. J. 2006. Tutorial on agent-based modeling and simulation part 2: how to model with agents. In *Proceedings of the Winter Simulation Conference* (Monterey, CA, December 03-06, 2006). IEEE, Piscataway, NJ. 73-83. DOI= http://dx.doi.org/10.1109/WSC.2006.323040.

[14] Medema, M. H., van Raaphorst, R., Takano, E., and Breitling, R. 2012. Computational tools for the synthetic design of biochemical pathways. *Nat. Rev. Micro.* 10, 3, 191-202. DOI= http://dx.doi.org/10.1038/nrmicro2717.

[15] Miller, M., Hafner, M., Sontag, E., Davidsohn, N., Subramanian, S., Purnick, P. E., Lauffenburger, D., and Weiss, R. 2012. Modular design of artificial tissue homeostasis: robust control through synthetic cellular heterogeneity. *Plos Comput. Biol.* 8, 7, e1002579. DOI= http://dx.doi.org/10.1371/journal.pcbi.1002579.

[16] Poust, S., Hagen, A., Katz, L., and Keasling, J. D. 2014. Narrowing the gap between the promise and reality of polyketide synthases as a synthetic biology platform. *Curr. Opin. Biotech.* 30, Dec 2014, 32-39. DOI= http://dx.doi.org/ 10.1016/j.copbio.2014.04.011.

[17] Purnick, P.E., and Weiss, R. 2009. The second wave of synthetic biology: from modules to systems. *Nat. Rev. Mol. Cell Bio.* 10, 6, 410-422. DOI= http://dx.doi.org/ 10.1038/nrm2698.

[18] Troisi, A., Wong, V., and Ratner, M. 2005. An agent-based approach for modeling molecular self-organization. *P. Natl. Acad. Sci. USA* 102, 2, 255-260. DOI= http://dx.doi.org/10.1073/pnas.0408308102.

[19] Weisstein, E. W. 2002. Least squares fitting. From *MathWorld--A Wolfram Web Resource*. URL: http://mathworld.wolfram.com/LeastSquaresFitting.html. Last access: May 6, 2015.

Syntax and Semantics of a Multi-Level Modeling Language

Tom Warnke, Tobias Helms, Adelinde M. Uhrmacher
Institute of Computer Science
University of Rostock, Germany
first.lastname@uni-rostock.de

ABSTRACT

The domain specific modeling and simulation language ML-Rules makes it possible to describe cell biological systems at different levels of organization. A model is formed by attributed and dynamically nested species, with reactions that are constrained by functions on attributes. In this paper, we extend ML-Rules to also support constraints using functions on multi-sets of species, i.e., solutions. Further, we present the formal syntax and semantics of ML-Rules, we define its stochastic simulator and we illustrate its expressiveness based on a model of the cell cycle and proliferation.

Categories and Subject Descriptors

I.6.2 [**Simulation and Modeling**]: Simulation Languages;
I.6.5 [**Simulation and Modeling**]: Model Development—
Modeling methodologies

General Terms

Languages, Theory

Keywords

Rule-Based Modeling, Computational Biology, Formal Semantics, Continuous-time Markov Chain

1. INTRODUCTION

General modeling formalisms like DEVS and stochastic Petri Nets aim at modeling and simulating entire classes of dynamic systems, i.e., discrete event systems and continuous-time Markov chains (CTMCs), respectively. Due to their underlying modeling metaphor — in DEVS reactive systems and in stochastic Petri Nets reaction networks — they are more or less suitable for describing specific systems. For cell biological systems it is argued that a reactive systems metaphor lends itself to describe the behavior of entire cells and their interactions whereas the reaction

metaphor appears more suitable to describe biochemical reaction networks [10]. Thus, among many other application areas, DEVS as well as stochastic Petri Nets have been used for cell biological systems. However, domain specific modeling languages exist which focus on this particular application domain [34], e.g., rule-based modeling languages for cell biology. Due to this focus, such domain specific modeling languages are typically more suitable to be used by domain experts than general modeling formalisms.

1.1 Rule-based approaches, attributes, and functions on attributes

Rule-based modeling languages exploit the notation of chemical reactions, e.g., like $A + B \rightarrow AB$ (species A and species B react to species AB). Typically, rule-based approaches make it possible to equip species with attributes as well as rules with reactant patterns, e.g., Kappa [8], BioNetgen [3], React(C) [18], or ML-Rules [22]. Thereby, they relieve the user from listing all reaction rules manually. For example, let us assume species A being a typical signaling protein which possesses two interaction sites to bind to a species B and a species C. Thus, species A can be in four states: $A(free, free)$, $A(free, bound)$, $A(bound, free)$, and $A(bound, bound)$ and four reaction rules are needed to describe the binding process. Instead, in a rule-based language which supports reactant patterns, only two rules are needed:

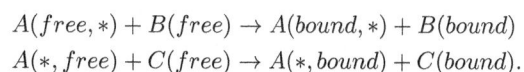

$$A(free, *) + B(free) \rightarrow A(bound, *) + B(bound)$$
$$A(*, free) + C(free) \rightarrow A(*, bound) + C(bound).$$

The usage of variables within rules leads to rules being instantiated based on the current state of the model, i.e., the current solution. For example, if the current solution comprises the species $[2A(1) + 4A(2)]$, the rule $A(x) \rightarrow B$ will be instantiated into the following two rules: $A(1) \rightarrow B$ and $A(2) \rightarrow B$. Accessing attributes and supporting functions on these attributes allows us to calculate within rules and to constrain reactions. For example, to express an increase of volume due to a reaction, we can use a function defined on the attribute which binds to the volume v: $A(v) \rightarrow A(inc(v))$; to state that a reaction can only happen if two molecules are sufficiently close, we can introduce a guard on the reaction: $A(pos_A) + B(pos_B) \rightarrow AB(pos_A)$ if $dist(pos_A, pos_B) < \epsilon$. Due to specifying molecules with attributes and constraining reactions based on these attributes, rule-based approaches are generally acknowledged to allow a succinct compact description of biochemical systems [3]. One should note though, that using attributes for constraining biochemical reactions is not reserved to rule-based approaches; it has been and is being exploited in process algebras, e.g., [31, 17] and in colored Petri nets [27] as well. Also variations in expressiveness between the different approaches exist, see e.g., the discussion in [18].

1.2 Compartments and dynamic nesting structures

In the context of rule-based approaches, *compartmental dynamics* like merging of two compartments or endocytosis are supported inherently, e.g., by ML-Rules [21], CSMMR [25], ML-Space [2], and Bigraphs [20] and have also been suggested as extensions of other rule-based languages, e.g., for Kappa [6]. Endocytosis is a process by which cells absorb molecules by engulfing them; it might be used to transport larger molecules into the cell or to recycle receptors. For example, let us assume that the signalosome LRP6 would be engulfed in a cell by endocytosis, which could be described in ML-Rules as

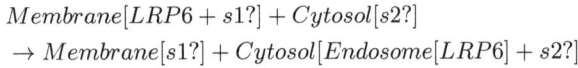

$$Membrane[LRP6 + s1?] + Cytosol[s2?]$$
$$\rightarrow Membrane[s1?] + Cytosol[Endosome[LRP6] + s2?]$$

Thereby, an endosome, which contains the signalosome of LRP6 receptors, is created. The variables $s1?$ and $s2?$ bind to the entire content minus the endosome of the membrane and the entire content of the cytosol, respectively. Thus, neither the "rest" solution of the membrane (all the other species in the membrane) nor those species already in the cytosol are affected. Whereas we use round brackets to specify attributes of species, we use squared brackets to represent compartmental structures. For example, given the current solution $[2A + D[A]]$, the rule $A \rightarrow B$ will be instantiated into the following two reactions: $A \rightarrow B$ and $D[A \rightarrow B]$ ($A \rightarrow B$ applied in the context of D). With attributed species, the ability to apply arbitrary functions to denote the result of the reaction plus the dynamic nesting structures, ML-Rules provides a quite powerful modeling language, see also [9]. However, to effectively support multi-level modeling in cell biology, an additional feature is needed in ML-Rules, i.e., *functions on solutions*.

1.3 Motivating functions on solutions - the cell division cycle

We illustrate the problem with some extracts from a *cell division cycle model* that we defined in ML-Rules (see Figure 8 for full model) adopting a simple but highly influential cell cycle model, published in 1991 [33]. Since then, a large number of models have been developed to analyze how the cell cycle is regulated at various levels of detail [5]. The cell cycle comprises a sequence of phases that leads to the duplication of cells. During the S-phase, a cell replicates its DNA. During the M-phase, i.e., mitosis, it distributes the two copies of the DNA into two daughter nuclei. Gap phases (G1 and G2) are introduced between the phases to ensure that the cell synchronizes growth and DNA replication in a correct manner. The interplay of CdK and cyclin regulates the phase transitions. CdK and cyclin generate inactive MPF (maturation promotion factor), whose activation happens in an autocatalytic manner. The amounts of inactive and active MPF guard the transitions between the phases. The cell changing rules are shown in Figure 1. Here, the first attribute of the cell species represents the volume of a cell. The second attribute is used to describe the cur-

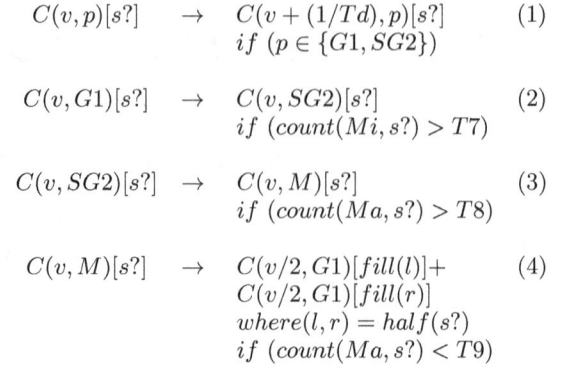

$$
\begin{aligned}
C(v, p)[s?] &\rightarrow C(v + (1/Td), p)[s?] & (1) \\
& \quad if\ (p \in \{G1, SG2\}) \\[4pt]
C(v, G1)[s?] &\rightarrow C(v, SG2)[s?] & (2) \\
& \quad if\ (count(Mi, s?) > T7) \\[4pt]
C(v, SG2)[s?] &\rightarrow C(v, M)[s?] & (3) \\
& \quad if\ (count(Ma, s?) > T8) \\[4pt]
C(v, M)[s?] &\rightarrow C(v/2, G1)[fill(l)]+ & (4) \\
& \quad C(v/2, G1)[fill(r)] \\
& \quad where(l, r) = half(s?) \\
& \quad if\ (count(Ma, s?) < T9)
\end{aligned}
$$

Figure 1: Cell division rules of the cell cycle model.

rent phase of a cell: $G1$ (gap), $SG2$ (synthesis/gap), and M (mitosis). The rules can be explained as follows:

(1) In the phases $G1$ and $SG2$ the volume v of cells increases.

(2) A cell in phase $G1$ can enter the phase $SG2$ if it contains more than $T7$ inactive MPF complexes.

(3) A cell in phase $SG2$ can enter the phase M if it contains more than $T8$ active MPF complexes.

(4) The division of a cell in state M can happen if it contains less than $T9$ active MPF complexes. The contents of the created daughter cells are dependent on the contents of the dividing cell.

Already this small example shows that functions on solutions are needed: to check whether the cell is ready to change the state and to determine how the content of a cell is divided when it splits. Functions on solutions help us constrain reactions and define the outcome of reactions. To express examples like the one above in a convenient manner, we need to extend ML-Rules to integrate functions on solutions. In the following, we will present this extension of ML-Rules. Therefore, we will introduce the abstract syntax of ML-Rules and develop a formal operational semantics for ML-Rules taking functions on solutions into account.

1.4 CTMC Semantics

A formal description of the *semantics* of a modeling language allows us to have a clear understanding of what is meant by a model and how the implemented execution algorithm should execute the model. Formally defining the semantics of new modeling approaches is crucial in addressing the credibility crises that simulation is facing by bringing together conceptual and formal model concepts [1] and in addressing a more general uneasiness referring to the many custom-oriented simulation systems that emerge to support scientists [19]. So far, formal approaches in the area of simulation have often only been associated with modeling formalisms, e.g., like DEVS [26]. However, this attitude is slowly changing, e.g., being reflected in current efforts to equip not only new domain-specific modeling languages like [8, 18, 25], but also well established simulation formalisms like SimuLink with a formal semantics [4].

$$C(v, p)[s?] \quad \rightarrow \quad C(v + (1/Td), p)[s?] \qquad @ \; if \; (p \in \{G1, SG2\}) \; then \; k_6 \; else \; 0 \qquad (1)$$

$$C(v, G1)[s?] \quad \rightarrow \quad C(v, SG2)[s?] \qquad @ \; if \; (count(Mi, s?) > T7) \; then \; k_7 \; else \; 0 \qquad (2)$$

$$C(v, SG2)[s?] \quad \rightarrow \quad C(v, M)[s?] \qquad @ \; if \; (count(Ma, s?) > T8) \; then \; k_8 \; else \; 0 \qquad (3)$$

$$C(v, M)[s?] \quad \rightarrow \quad C(v/2, G1)[fill(l)] + C(v/2, G1)[fill(r)] \qquad @ \; if \; (count(Ma, s?) < T9) \; then \; k_9 \; else \; 0 \qquad (4)$$
$$where(l, r) = half(s?)$$

Figure 2: Cell division rules with rates from the cell cycle model in ML-Rules.

Biochemical models are often interpreted as CTMCs as this has proven a suitable abstraction for modeling such systems. Following this interpretation in ML-Rules, one state of our system corresponds to the current well mixed solution which can be encoded as a multi-set of chemical species, e.g., $\{5A, 4B, 2C\}$ where A, B and C are chemical species. Further, reactions are labeled with rate equations, e.g., realizing mass action kinetics so that the rate of a reaction is defined as the product of a rate constant multiplied with the number of possible reactant combinations. For example, if a reaction

$$A + B \xrightarrow{k \cdot \#A \cdot \#B} C$$

with rate k has been defined, the system will exit state $\{5A, 4B, 2C\}$ to enter state $\{4A, 3B, 3C\}$ with the rate $k \cdot 5 \cdot 4$ ($\#A$ and $\#B$ represent the number of existing species A and B). Adding further assumptions, e.g., using the deterministic limit of a CTMC, a set of coupled ordinary differential equations can be derived to compute a simulation of the model. However, systems are often characterized by small sample sizes so that the stochastic effects should not be ignored, e.g., see [23]. In such cases, stochastic simulation algorithms (SSAs) exist to compute CTMCs in a stochastic manner [11]. Our operational semantics will interpret ML-Rules models as CTMCs, and its execution algorithms will sample trajectories from the CTMC based on an SSA.

Coming back to our example of the cell cycle above, we can now add the kinetic information to our rules, see Figure 2. For example, k_7 denotes the rate with which a cell is entering the synthesis/growth phase once it contains enough Mi. Rules are instantiated based on the species in our solution. Thus, if ten cells are in the $G1$ phase, rule (2) will be instantiated ten times. Depending on the volume, the waiting time until this rule fires will be either ∞ (in case the rate is zero) or drawn from an exponential distribution with average $1/k_7$. Intuitively, the more cells in phase $G1$ have enough Mi, the more likely it is to observe a cell moving from phase $G1$ to phase $SG2$ within the near future. For the other cells being in different phases, e.g., $SG2$ or M, waiting times will be determined as well, depending on the rates k_8 and k_9. The smallest waiting time will win and the corresponding rule will fire, being selected by a stochastic race. This describes in a nutshell the execution of the model with a typical SSA [11].

After introducing the relevant concepts for extending ML-Rules, i.e., rule-based languages, compartments, a small motivating example for functions on solutions, and the intended semantics, we can now progress to present the extended rule-based multi-level modeling and simulation language ML-Rules. In the following, we describe the abstract syntax of ML-Rules, its operational semantics, and its exe-

cution algorithm. Further, we discuss its expressiveness in comparison to other formalisms and the impact of this expressiveness on the efficiency of the simulation algorithms.

2. ABSTRACT SYNTAX

Our abstract syntax describes the syntax of ML-Rules abstracting from concrete representations to focus on the structure of the language. For example, in the abstract syntax we do not distinguish between attributes and compartments by using different parentheses nor do we care how rest solutions are represented. These questions are addressed in the concrete syntax of ML-Rules. In the following, we write $\tilde{e}$ for a tuple of expressions like $(e_1, \ldots, e_n)$. Notations like $(\tilde{e}, p)$ mean that the tuple $\tilde{e}$ will be expanded by the expression p to the tuple $(e_1, \ldots, e_n, p)$. Tuples of values $\tilde{v}$ and types $\tilde{\tau}$ are handled analogously. The abstract syntax of ML-Rules is described in Figure 3. For specifying the syntax of ML-Rules we rely on:

- $\mathcal{S} = \{S : \tilde{\tau}, \ldots\}$ is a set of typed species names. The last attribute of each species always has the type $\mathtt{sol}$ and denotes its sub-solution. It is always the only attribute with type $\mathtt{sol}$. The number of attributes of a species S is written as $ar(S)$, whereas $ar(S) \geq 1$, because every species has a (possibly empty) subsolution.

- $\mathcal{C} = \{c : \tau, \ldots\}$ is a set of typed n-ary constants. This set may contain basic operations, e.g., arithmetic operations for natural numbers and the if-then-else construct. We say that the arity of $c : \tau$ is n for the type definition $\tau = \tau_1 \rightarrow \ldots \rightarrow \tau_n \rightarrow \tau'$, i.e., $ar(c) = n$. For every constant $c : \tau_1 \rightarrow \cdots \rightarrow \tau_n \rightarrow \tau' \in \mathcal{C}$, there exists a function $[[c]] : Vals(\tau_1) \times \cdots \times Vals(\tau_n) \rightarrow Vals(\tau')$. $Vals(\tau)$ denotes the set of values of type τ.

- $\mathcal{V} = \{x : \tau, \ldots\}$ is an infinite set of typed variables. Another infinite set $\mathcal{R} = \{y : \mathtt{sol}, \ldots\}$ of variables of type $\mathtt{sol}$ is used for rest solutions. $\mathcal{V} \cap \mathcal{R} = \emptyset$ holds. A function $\sigma : \mathcal{V} \cup \mathcal{R} \mapsto Vals$ maps variables to a value of the corresponding type: $\forall (x : \tau) \in dom(\sigma) : \sigma(x) \in Vals(\tau)$.

- $\mathcal{L} = Vals(\mathtt{link})$ is an infinite set of link names. Species sharing a link name are linked. The set $\mathcal{L}^U$ contains all unused link names; the ν-operator is used to obtain values from this set.

Base types for natural and real-valued numbers are provided, as well as the functional type $\tau \rightarrow \tau$ to construct new types. The type $\mathtt{sol}$ is used for solutions, i.e., multi-sets

Types	τ	$::=$	$\tau \to \tau \mid$ `nat` $\mid$ `real` $\mid$ `sol` $\mid$ `link`	
Values	v	$::=$	$c\, v_1 \ldots v_n \mid \lambda x.e \mid s$	where $c \in \mathcal{C}, x \in \mathcal{V},\ n = ar(c)$
Expressions	e	$::=$	$x \mid c \mid \lambda x.e \mid e_1\, e_2 \mid S(\tilde{e}) \mid e_1 + e_2 \mid 0$	where $c \in \mathcal{C},\ x, x_1, x_2, x_3, f \in \mathcal{V},\ S \in \mathcal{S}$
			$\mid$ `caseSol` e_1 `of` $x_1{}^{x_2} + x_3$ `then` e_2 `else` e_3	
			$\mid$ `letrec` $f = e_1$ `in` $f\, e_2$	
Solutions	s	$::=$	$S(\tilde{v}) \mid s_1 + s_2 \mid 0$	where $S \in \mathcal{S}$
Patterns	p	$::=$	$S(\tilde{e}, p_r)^e \rhd x \mid p_1 + p_2 \mid 0$	where $S \in \mathcal{S},\ x \in \mathcal{V}$
Patterns with rest	p_r	$::=$	$p + y$	where $y \in \mathcal{R}$
Rules	r	$::=$	$p_r \xrightarrow{e_1} (\nu\tilde{x})e_2$	where $\tilde{x} = (x_1, \ldots, x_n), \{x_1, \ldots, x_n\} \subseteq \mathcal{V} \wedge$
				$fv(r) = fv(p_r) \wedge fv(e_1) \subseteq fv(p_r) \wedge$
				$fv(e_2) \subseteq \{x_1, \ldots, x_n\} \cup fv(p_r)$

Figure 3: Abstract syntax of ML-Rules.

of species. The type `link` is used for the linking between species. Values can originate from the application of an n-ary constant on n values, a λ-abstraction or a solution. By allowing λ-abstractions as values, they can again be input to constant functions, i.e., higher-order functions are supported. Expressions consist of variables, constants, λ-abstractions, (partial) applications of functions, species, and solutions. The symbol 0 is used for the empty solution. The language constructs `caseSol` e_1 `of` $x_1{}^{x_2} + y$ `then` e_2 `else` e_3 and `letrec` $f = e_1$ `in` $f\, e_2$ can be used together to iterate over solutions. Solutions are multi-sets of species, which are concatenated with the $+$ operator. Each species has a defined name $S \in \mathcal{S}$ and a fixed tuple $\tilde{v}$ of typed values as attributes. Our type system (see Figure 7) requires that the last attribute value of each species is of type `sol` which describes the sub-solution of this species. This solution can also be 0 in case of a species that does not contain other species. All other attributes are not allowed to be of type `sol`. The last part of the ML-Rules syntax are reaction rules and patterns. Rules describe how to transform solutions into new solutions by specifying a pattern. A pattern consists of multiple species patterns $S(\tilde{e}, p_r)^e \rhd x$. A species matches a pattern if its attributes equal the evaluated expressions $\tilde{e}$ and its subsolution matches the subsolution pattern p_r. The variable x of the pattern binds to a matched species. The expression e, which has to evaluate to a natural number, describes the number of a matched species which is relevant for the corresponding rule. The variable y of patterns with rest is bound to the subsolution of the enclosing matched species excluding the species matched to the patterns p.

We use the usual notion of free variables of the Lambda-Calculus [28], i.e., all variables that are not bound by a λ are considered *free* and denoted by $fv(\cdot)$. However, due to combining the Lambda-Calculus with other concepts such as pattern matching, we have to make some adjustments. For example, x is a free variable in the pattern $A(x, 0)^1 \rhd a$ as usual. The variable a, in contrast, is bound to a pattern and not free as it cannot have arbitrary values. a is a *dependent* variable that receives a value from the pattern it is bound to. This distinction is important: Dependent variables receive

a value as a "side effect" of the pattern matching process, i.e., they occur on the left-hand rule side exactly once in a way that allows to unambiguously infer their value. On the other hand, the values for all free variables in a rule must be obtainable *directly* through pattern matching of the left-hand rule side. An exception are free link variables on the right-hand side whose values can also be generated by the ν-operator. For example, consider the rule:

$$A(x, 0)^1 \rhd a + B(f(x), 0)^1 \rhd b + y \xrightarrow{\#a \cdot \#b} C(0) + y$$

Here, values for x can be found by matching an A species with an empty subsolution. When a value for x is chosen, the values for a, $f(x)$, b, and y are directly determined. Thus, x is the only free variable; a, b and y are dependent variables.

3. SEMANTICS OF ML-RULES

We provide a formal definition of the semantics of ML-Rules. Therefore, we adopt an operational semantics, i.e., a collection of rules specifying how values, expressions and patterns are evaluated or executed. The operational semantics defines how a possible implementation of the modeling and simulation language should operate. The semantics of ML-Rules will be presented as a structured operational semantics, based on reductions with evaluation context, and the big step operator. Figure 5 defines the evaluation of all syntactic elements excluding the rules; the semantics of rules, i.e., the construction of CTMC state transitions, is then described in Figure 6.

The left-hand side of every rule is a pattern that is matched onto the current solution. As semantically equivalent solutions can have multiple syntactic representations, we define some congruence relations on solutions. The operator $+$, used for constructing solutions, is associative and commutative with the neutral element 0 as described by the precongruence definition $\approx$ from Figure 4, i.e. solutions are order-independent under $\approx$. The congruence relation $\equiv$ additionally describes the irrelevance of concrete link names for two solutions. Two solutions are defined as $\equiv$-congruent if they can be transformed into each other through renaming

$$(1)\frac{c \in \mathcal{C} \quad ar(c) = n}{c\ v_1\ \dots\ v_n \Downarrow_{s,\sigma} [[c]](v_1, \dots, v_n)} \qquad (2)\frac{x \in \mathcal{V} \quad \sigma(x) = v}{x \Downarrow_{s,\sigma} v} \qquad (3)\frac{y \in \mathcal{R} \quad \sigma(y) = v}{y \Downarrow_{s,\sigma} v}$$

$$(4)\frac{c \in \mathcal{C} \quad ar(c) = n \quad e_1 \Downarrow_{s,\sigma} v_1 \quad \dots \quad e_n \Downarrow_{s,\sigma} v_n}{c\ e_1\ \dots\ e_n \Downarrow_{s,\sigma} c\ v_1, \dots, v_n} \qquad (5)\frac{e_1 \Downarrow_{s,\sigma} \lambda x.e \quad e_2 \Downarrow_{s,\sigma} v_2 \quad e[v_2/x] \Downarrow_{s,\sigma} v}{e_1\ e_2 \Downarrow_{s,\sigma} v}$$

$$(6)\frac{\tilde{e} \Downarrow_{s,\sigma} \tilde{v}}{S(\tilde{e}) \Downarrow_{s,\sigma} S(\tilde{v})} \qquad (7)\frac{e_1 \Downarrow_{s,\sigma} s_1 \quad e_2 \Downarrow_{s,\sigma} s_2}{e_1 + e_2 \Downarrow_{s,\sigma} s_1 + s_2} \qquad (8)\frac{}{0 \Downarrow_{s,\sigma}}$$

$$(9)\frac{f \in \mathcal{V} \quad G = \lambda f.e_1 \quad Y = \lambda g.(\lambda z.(g\ z\ z)\ (\lambda z.(g\ z\ z))) \quad (Y\ G)\ e_2 \Downarrow_{s,\sigma} v}{\texttt{letrec}\ f = e_1\ \texttt{in}\ f\ e_2 \Downarrow_{s,\sigma} v}$$

$$(10)\frac{x_1, x_2 \in \mathcal{V}, y \in \mathcal{R} \quad e_1 \Downarrow_{s,\sigma} s_1 \quad s_1 \approx \sum_{i=1}^n a_i^{m_i} \quad s_1 = a_1^{m_1} + s_2 \quad s_2 \approx \sum_{i=2}^n a_i^{m_i} \quad e_2[a_1/x_1][m_1/x_2][s_2/y] \Downarrow_{s,\sigma} v}{\texttt{caseSol}\ e_1\ \texttt{of}\ x_1^{x_2} + y\ \texttt{then}\ e_2\ \texttt{else}\ e_3 \Downarrow_{s,\sigma} v}$$

$$(11)\frac{x_1, x_2 \in \mathcal{V} \quad y \in \mathcal{R} \quad e_1 \Downarrow_{s,\sigma} 0 \quad e_3 \Downarrow_{s,\sigma} v}{\texttt{caseSol}\ e_1\ \texttt{of}\ x_1^{x_2} + y\ \texttt{then}\ e_2\ \texttt{else}\ e_3 \Downarrow_{s,\sigma} v}$$

$$(12)\frac{x \in \mathcal{V} \quad S \in \mathcal{S} \quad \tilde{e} \Downarrow_{s,\sigma} \tilde{v} \quad e \Downarrow_{s,\sigma} v \quad s \approx \sum_{i=1}^v S(\tilde{v}, s_1) + s_2 \quad p_r \Downarrow_{s_1,\sigma} s_1 \quad a = S(\tilde{v}, s_1)}{S(\tilde{e}, p_r)^e \triangleright x \Downarrow_{s,\sigma \cup (x \mapsto a)} \sum_{i=1}^v a}$$

$$(13)\frac{p_1 \Downarrow_{s,\sigma} s_1 \quad p_2 \Downarrow_{s,\sigma} s_2}{p_1 + p_2 \Downarrow_{s,\sigma} s_1 + s_2} \qquad (14)\frac{y \in \mathcal{R} \quad p \Downarrow_{s,\sigma} s_1 \quad s \approx s_1 + s_2}{p + y \Downarrow_{s,\sigma \cup (y \mapsto s_2)} s_1 + s_2}$$

Figure 5: Big-step evaluator for ML-Rules

Precongruence:
$$(s_1 + s_2) + s_3 \approx s_1 + (s_2 + s_3), s_1 + s_2 \approx s_2 + s_1, s + 0 \approx s$$

Congruence:
$$\frac{s \approx s' \quad \pi : \mathcal{L} \to \mathcal{L}\ \text{injective}}{s \equiv s'\pi}$$

Figure 4: Precongruence and congruence on solutions

and reordering. The full big-step evaluator for the syntactic elements forming rules is shown in Figure 5.

Most of the definition ((2)-(11)) refers to the very powerful expressions, with some further rules describing the matching of patterns ((12) - (14)). Each evaluation takes the current context s and the variable assignments (substitutions) already done σ into account. The context refers to the part of the model state that represents the surrounding of the currently considered species. As ML-Rules allows explicit nesting of species in other species, this facilitates the evaluation of rule parts in a subsolution of nested species. (1) defines the application of a function, given that c is a constant with a arity n and n values are supplied as arguments. (2) shows the evaluation of variables to the values they are bound to. The special case of a rest-solution variable y is given in (3). (4) defines the application of an n-ary constant with n expressions as arguments. (5) shows the application of a lambda function on an argument as usual:

The function $\lambda x.e$ with an argument e_2 (that evaluates to v_2) is replaced with e, where all occurrences of x are replaced by v_2. The resulting expression $e[v_2/x]$ is further evaluated to v. (6) describes that if the expressions that denote the attributes and the subsolution of a species can be evaluated to values, they are replaced by these values. (7) shows how expressions that evaluate to solutions can be composed to describe the composition of solutions. (8) defines that the symbol for the empty solution 0 is evaluated to nothing.

In (9) the evaluation of $\texttt{letrec}\ f = e_1\ \texttt{in}\ f\ e_2$ is shown. As the lambda-calculus does not allow recursion, this expression can be used to define a function whose definition contains a call to itself[1]. The Y-Combinator is used to find a fixpoint $Y\ G$ of the function $G = \lambda f.e_1$. As f is a function here, the fixpoint is a function, too. This function fixpoint $Y\ G$ is applied to the argument e_2 to obtain v, which is then the result of the whole $\texttt{letrec}$-expression.

The evaluation of the $\texttt{caseSol}$ operator is shown in (10) and (11). The expression e_1 is evaluated to a solution. If that solution is empty (11), the else branch expression e_3 is evaluated and returned. Otherwise (10), it is evaluated to s_1 and split into m_1 instances of some species a_1 and the solution s_2 with the remaining species. In e_2 substitutions for x_1, x_2 and y with the name a_1 and the number m_1 of the chosen species and the rest solution y are done. The whole $\texttt{caseSol}$ is then evaluated to the value of e_2. In this form, $\texttt{caseSol}$ only takes into account one species of a solution. The $\texttt{caseSol}$ operator can be combined with the $\texttt{letrec}$

---

[1]For example, a letrec expression for the factorial of 5 could look like this: $\texttt{letrec}\ f = \lambda n.if(n = 0)\ then\ 1\ else\ n \cdot f(n-1)\ \texttt{in}\ f\ 5$.

$$\text{(INST)} \quad \frac{\begin{array}{cc} \sigma : (fv(p+y)) \mapsto Vals \text{ type preserving} & \sigma' : \tilde{x} \mapsto \mathcal{L}^U \text{ injective} \\ p+y \Downarrow_{s,\sigma} s \qquad e_1 \Downarrow_{s,\sigma} r \qquad\qquad e_2 \Downarrow_{s,\sigma\cup\sigma'} s_2 \end{array}}{p+y \xrightarrow{e_1} (\nu\tilde{x})e_2 \Downarrow_{s,\sigma} s \xrightarrow{r} s_2}$$

$$\text{(SUM)} \quad \frac{s_1 \equiv s_1' \quad \left(\left(\sum_{R\in\text{Rules}} \sum_{\{(r',\sigma) \ | \ R \Downarrow_{s_1',\sigma}\rho, \ \rho \vdash s_1' \xrightarrow{r'} s_2' \equiv s_2\}} r' \right) + \sum_{\{(r',k) \ | \ s_1' \xrightarrow[k]{r'} s_2' \equiv s_2\}} r' \right) = r}{\text{Rules} \vdash s_1 \xrightarrow{r} s_2}$$

$$\text{(SUB)} \quad \frac{k \in \{1,\dots,n\} \qquad a_k = S(\tilde{v},s) \qquad \text{Rules} \vdash s \xrightarrow{r} s'}{\sum_{i=1}^n a_i \xrightarrow[k]{r} \left(\sum_{i=1}^{k-1} a_i + S(\tilde{v},s') + \sum_{i=k+1}^n a_i \right)}$$

Figure 6: Stochastic semantics of ML-Rules

expression to iterate through a solution. For example, a function counting all species in a solution can be realized like this:

$$countAll \triangleq \lambda s.\texttt{letrec } f =$$
$$\lambda s'. \texttt{ caseSol } s' \texttt{ of } x^z + y \texttt{ then } z + (f\ y) \texttt{ else } 0$$
$$\texttt{in } f\ s$$

Similarly, a function to only count a specific species in a solution can be defined:

$$countSpecies \triangleq \lambda spec.\lambda s.\texttt{letrec } f =$$
$$\lambda s'. \texttt{ caseSol } s' \texttt{ of } spec^z + y \texttt{ then } z + (f\ y) \texttt{ else } f\ y$$
$$\texttt{in } f\ s$$

(12) defines how a pattern expression with multiplicity and a variable to bind to is matched with the correct number of matching species in the current solution, binding the given variable in the process. The pattern attributes $\tilde{e}$ as well as the multiplicity e (given as exponent) are evaluated to values $\tilde{v}$ and v. The current solution s is separated into the required number of species given in the pattern (with the same attribute values and a subsolution s_1 to which p_r, the subsolution pattern, evaluates) and the remaining solution s_2. The evaluated pattern $S(\tilde{v},s_1)$ is referred to as a for convenience. The pattern expression can then be evaluated to v instances of a, whereas the pattern variable x is bound to a. In the process of pattern matching, no information about the number of possible matchings with the same σ is given. This implies that the application of Mass action kinetics requires counting of possible matches in the rate expression of rules (see Section 4). However, this also facilitates the use of alternative kinetics, e.g., Michaelis-Menten or Hill kinetics [24].

(13) denotes that patterns composed with the $+$ operator have to be matched together as well. Also, bindings from one pattern instantiation are made visible in other pattern instantiations by using the same σ. This implies that a variable bound to a value in one pattern expression can be used in other pattern expressions to access its value. (14) describes how the rest solution variable y is bound to the rest solution s_2, consisting of all species that are not matched by patterns. Here σ already contains the binding for variables bound in the patterns p.

For the big step evaluation semantics of expressions in ML-Rules as defined in Figure 5, some definitions could be adopted from the semantics defined for React(C) in [18]. However, React(C) does not support explicit nesting, and thus also the concept of rest solutions which has been shown to be valuable for realizing an explicit dynamic nesting is not supported. The above big-step evaluator defines how a current solution can be transformed, in the following we will describe how rules are instantiated, applied, and the rate (of a CTMC) is determined.

The rule (INST) describes the instantiation of rules depending on the bindings σ and σ'. σ maps the free variables in the pattern to values of the correct type. σ' maps all new link variables required by the ν-operator to unused link names. While the mappings in σ' can be arbitrarily chosen as long as the selected link names are previously unused, the contents of σ are restricted by the big-step evaluation in Figure 5. Instances of reaction rules are fully identified by binding σ, i.e. two instances of a reaction rule that only differ in σ' (the concrete names for the new links) are considered to be the same. Also, the instantiation shows how the rate expression of a rule (once evaluated, see above) is replaced by the concrete rate r of a reaction. The pattern $p+y$ evaluates to the *whole* solution s, so that the resulting instantiated rule $s \xrightarrow{r} s_2$ transforms the whole context to s_2. To only change the part of the solution referred to by p, the rest solution of the left-hand side y will typically be re-added on the right-hand side e_2.

The rules (SUM) and (SUB) describe how the propensities of state transitions are calculated. For those it is essential to calculate how often a reaction is applicable within a solution. As illustrated above, only reactions with different variable bindings σ are differentiated here. An example of this calculation is given in Section 4. ML-Rules is a language for the stochastic modeling of biochemical systems and its semantics is defined in terms of continuous-time Markov chains (CTMC). Solutions, i.e. $s = s_1 + \dots + s_n$ need therefore to be mapped to states of the CTMC. This is done by identifying an equivalence class $[s]_\equiv$ of a solution s w.r.t. congruence $\equiv$ with one state. In other words, all solutions that only differ in order of the species and concrete link names are subsumed in a CTMC state. The transitions between states in the CTMC are obtained by applying reaction rules to solutions in all ways possible. The semantics have to account for each of a reaction rule's possible instantiations

$$(\text{T-Spec})\ \frac{\Gamma \vdash \tilde{e} : (\tilde{\tau}, \mathtt{sol}) \quad S : (\tilde{\tau}, \mathtt{sol}) \in \mathcal{S}}{\Gamma \vdash S(\tilde{e}) : \mathtt{sol}} \qquad (\text{T-App})\ \frac{\Gamma \vdash e_1 : \tau_1 \to \tau_2 \quad \Gamma \vdash e_2 : \tau_1}{\Gamma \vdash e_1\, e_2 : \tau_2}$$

$$(\text{T-Let})\ \frac{\Gamma, f \vdash e_1 f \tau_1 \to \tau_2 \quad \Gamma \vdash e_2 : \tau_1}{\Gamma \vdash \mathtt{letrec}\ f = e_1\ \mathtt{in}\ f\ e_2 : \tau_2} \qquad (\text{T-Func})\ \frac{\Gamma, x : \tau_1 \vdash e : \tau_2}{\Gamma \vdash \lambda x.e : \tau_1 \to \tau_2}$$

$$(\text{T-Case})\ \frac{\Gamma \vdash e_1 : \mathtt{sol} \quad \Gamma, x_1 : \mathtt{sol}, x_2 : \mathtt{nat}, y : \mathtt{sol} \vdash e_2 : \tau \quad \Gamma \vdash e_3 : \tau}{\Gamma \vdash \mathtt{caseSol}\ e_1\ \mathtt{of}\ x_1^{x_2} + y\ \mathtt{then}\ e_2\ \mathtt{else}\ e_3 : \tau}$$

$$(\text{T-Const})\ \frac{\Gamma \vdash v_1 : \tau_1 \ldots \Gamma \vdash v_n : \tau_n \quad c : (\tau_1, \ldots, \tau_n) \in \Gamma}{\Gamma \vdash c\, v_1\ \ldots\ v_n : \tau'} \qquad (\text{T-Var})\ \frac{x : \tau \in \Gamma}{\Gamma \vdash x : \tau}$$

$$(\text{T-Rule})\ \frac{\begin{array}{c} dom(\Gamma) = fv(p_r) \cup \{x_1, \ldots, x_n\} \\ \Gamma \vdash p_r : \mathtt{sol} \quad \Gamma \vdash e_1 : \mathtt{real} \quad \Gamma, \tilde{x} \vdash e_2 : \mathtt{sol} \end{array}}{\vdash p_r \xrightarrow{e_1} (\nu \tilde{x}) e_2} \qquad (\text{T-Rules})\ \frac{\forall r \in \text{Rules} \quad \vdash r}{\vdash \text{Rules}}$$

$$(\text{T-Pat})\ \frac{\Gamma \vdash \tilde{e} : \tilde{\tau} \quad \Gamma \vdash p_r : \mathtt{sol} \quad S : (\tilde{\tau}, \mathtt{sol}) \in \mathcal{S} \quad \Gamma \vdash e : \mathtt{nat}}{\Gamma \vdash S(\tilde{e}, p_r)^e \triangleright x : \mathtt{sol}}$$

$$(\text{T-Sol})\ \frac{\Gamma \vdash e_1 : \mathtt{sol} \quad \Gamma \vdash e_2 : \mathtt{sol}}{\Gamma \vdash e_1 + e_2 : \mathtt{sol}}$$

Figure 7: Type-system for ML-Rules

(reactions) that can be applied to a solution. Rule instances that lead to the same state are considered to contribute to the same transition. Thus, the sum of the rates of all reaction rule instances that can be applied to a state $[s_1]_\equiv$ and lead to the successor state $[s_2]_\equiv$ yields the rate of the transition from $[s_1]_\equiv$ to $[s_2]_\equiv$ (SUM). The instantiation of rules to reactions is dependent on the variable assignment σ and the current solution s. Instances of a reaction rule are fully identified by the mapping σ, since we wish to abstract from the (infinitely many) specific choices of link names as introduced by ν-operators on the right-hand side of reaction rules. We therefore sum up for each reaction rule R over all tuples (r', σ), where σ identifies an instantiation ρ of R that can be applied to state $[s_1]_\equiv$ and leads to state $[s_2]_\equiv$ with a rate r'.

The first part of our rule (SUM) is similar to the rule SUM of the semantics of React(C) [18, Fig.13]. However, to obtain the transition rate from state $[s_1]_\equiv$ to $[s_2]_\equiv$, not only reactions operating directly on solutions in $[s_1]_\equiv$ are taken into account. Additionally, rates for reactions that lead from $[s_1]_\equiv$ to $[s_2]_\equiv$, but take place in a subsolution of a species in $[s_1]_\equiv$ are added up. This demonstrates a central feature of ML-Rules: Rules are not only matched on the uppermost hierarchy level, i.e., the root of the nesting tree. Instead, rules are applicable in every subsolution that matches their reactant pattern. This is done by recursively traversing the nesting tree in the second part of the (SUM) rule. For all species in the solution s_1' the (SUB) rule is invoked. As the order of the species in the solution s_1' is fixed, the index variable k can be used to iterate over them. (SUB) then shows how the reaction rate for this k-th subsolution is obtained: Whereas all species a_i with an index $i \neq k$ are left unchanged, the subsolution of a_k is transformed according to rule instances, which leads to an invocation of (SUM) again. By reciprocal invocations of (SUM) and (SUB) all possible

ways of applying rules in the nested hierarchy of species are taken into account. For every solution in an equivalence class the same possible transitions and the same transition rates are obtained, as all $\equiv$-congruent solutions differ only in order and concrete link names and these differences are not influencing the evaluation of rules. To complete the formal definition of ML-Rules, Figure 7 shows the type system for all syntactic elements.

4. EXAMPLE

Before we describe the implications of the semantics for the implementation of a simulation algorithm, we illustrate the formal definitions by continuing with the cell division cycle example. In the earlier version of ML-Rules, the model looked slightly different because no functions on solutions were supported at that time [22]. As already stated in Section 1, the model describes the sequence of events that leads through the cell division cycle in dependence on the active and inactive form of the MPF, and the interplay of cdc2 (D) and cyclin (Y). The complete model definition is listed in Figure 8.

When comparing the concrete syntax with the abstract syntax, we introduced some syntactic sugar and simplifications. First, the subsolution of a species is separated from the attributes and written in brackets. For species with no attributes and an empty subsolution the parentheses and brackets can be omitted. It is not mandatory to write down the rest solution in the uppermost level of a pattern. If it is omitted, it is assumed to be unchanged, i.e., it is added on both sides of the rule. The rate expression is written after the products, denoted by an @. Finally, the operator # denotes the count function, i.e., evaluates to the number of possible equivalent matches for a variable.

In our concrete example, the rates constitute Mass action kinetics. The functions `half` and `fill` operate on solutions

```
// PARAMETERS
Dtot:1000; k1:0.015*Dtot; k2:200; k3:180; k3prime:0.018; k4:4.5; k5:0.6;
k6:1.0; k7:1e6; k8:k7; k9:k7; T7:250; T8:70; T9:20; Td:116;


// SPECIES DEFINITIONS
C(2); Y(); Yp(); D(); Mi(); Ma();


// INITIAL SOLUTION
>>INIT[ 2 C(1.0,'G1')[(Dtot) D] ];


// RULES
// (1) cyclin synthesis
C(v,p)[s?]:c -> C(v,p)[Y + s?] @ k1*#c;
// (2) formation of inactive MPF complex
Y:y + D:d -> Mi @ k2*#y*#d;
// (3) activation of MPF complex
C(v,p)[Mi:i + s?]:c -> C(v,p)[Ma + s?] @ (k3prime+(k3*((count('Ma', s?)/Dtot)^2)))*#i*#c;
// (4) breakage of activated MPF complex
C(v,p)[Ma:a + s?]:c -> C(v,p)[Yp + D + s?] @ (k4/v)*#a*#c;
// (5) cyclin degradation
Yp:y -> @ k5*#y;
// (6) cell growth
C(v,p)[s?]:c -> C(v+(1/Td),p)[s?] @ if (p=='G1') || (p=='SG2') then k6*#c else 0;
// (7) cell cycle transition from G1->S/G2
C(v,'G1')[s?]:c -> C(v,'SG2')[s?] @ if (count('Mi', s?)>T7) then k7*#c else 0;
// (8) cell cycle transition from S/G2->M
C(v,'SG2')[s?]:c -> C(v,'M')[s?] @ if (count('Ma', s?)>T8) then k8*#c else 0;
// (9) cell division (transition from M->G1)
C(v,'M')[s?]:c -> C(v/2,'G1')[fill(l)] + C(v/2,'G1')[fill(r)] where (l,r) = half(s?)
                  @ if (count('Ma', s?)<T9) then k9*#c else 0;
```

Figure 8: A simple cell cycle model.

and can be defined in the functional style of ML-Rules (Figure 9). `half` splits a solution into two parts and guarantees that the sum of both parts is exactly the solution that was split. This is an advantage over simpler rounding approaches that would duplicate or lose species when splitting odd numbers. `fill` takes a solution and fills it up with D so that the sum of Ma, Mi and D is Dtot. Function definitions of this kind correspond to constant functions in the abstract syntax.

```
half :: sol -> tuple
half []        = ([],[])
half s + rest = (numl s + restl, numr s + restr)
                where numl = round(#s * 0.5)
                      numr = #s - numl
                      (restl,restr) = half(rest)


fill :: sol -> sol
fill s        = s + (Dtot - num) D
                where num = count('Ma', s)
                          + count('Mi', s)
                          + count('D', s)
```

Figure 9: Function definitions in ML-Rules

We will now show how a CTMC can be derived from the rules. For now, let us focus on the rules (3), (4) and (9).

In rule (3) the activation of an MPF (maturation promotion factor) is described as a reaction that transfers an inactive MPF (Mi) into an active one (Ma). This happens in the context of a cell. It is modeled as an autocatalytic reaction, i.e., dependent on the number of Ma already existing. To realize this, a function count that operates on the solution $s?$, similar to the one introduced in Section 3, is used to obtain the number of Ma present in the cell. Rule (4) describes the breakage of active MPF complexes. Here the propensity of the breakage is inversely proportional to the volume of the cell. This is due to the fact that this reaction depends on an enzyme whose concentration decreases with growing cell volume. In rule (9), the division of a cell into two daughter cells is modeled. Each daughter cell has half the volume and half the contents of the original cell. However, as in this model it is assumed that in each cell the cdc2 protein is continuously synthesized to maintain a constant concentration of cdc2 subunits, each of the daughter cells is filled up with $d_{tot} - (\#M_i + \#M_a)$ many D, afterward. Again, this can be naturally realized using functions on solutions (`fill`).

To see how these rules are applied, let us consider two cells in phase G1 that each contain $500D$, $200Ma$, $300Mi$ and $10Y$. This model state $[2C(1.0, G1)[500D + 200Ma + 300Mi + 10Y]]$ and its possible successor states are visualized in Figure 10. The state transitions are labeled with the number of the corresponding rule from Figure 8 and the rate of the transition. The matching of rules and instan-

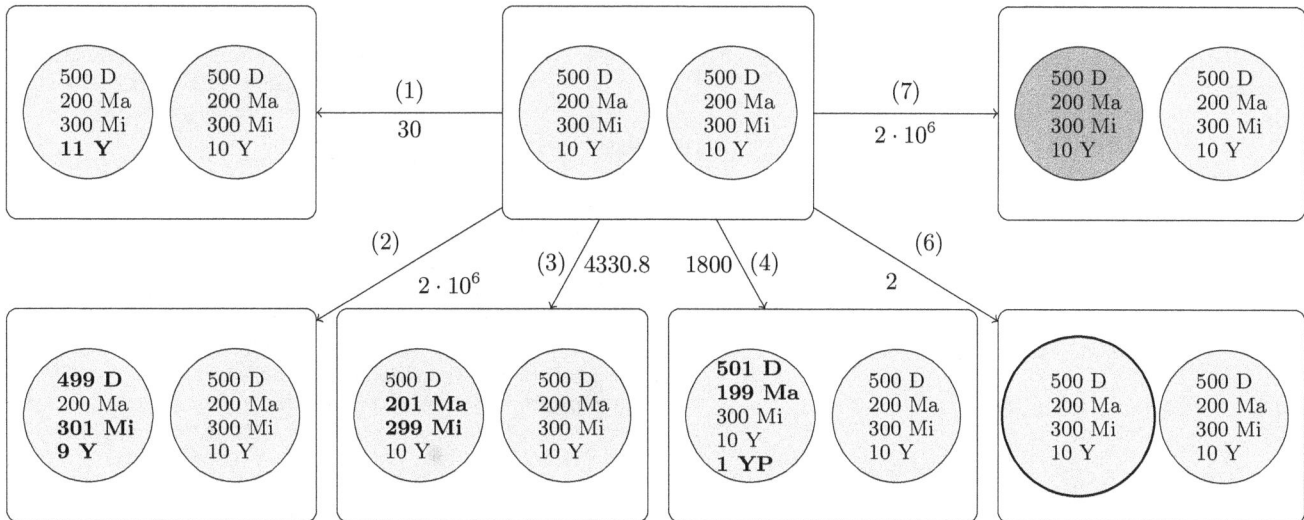

Figure 10: Illustration of states and state transitions. Cells are darkened according to their phase in the cell cycle: light gray for $G1$, dark gray for $SG2$.

tiation of reactions depends on the current state. For example, for rule (1) only one variable assignment $\sigma = \{v \mapsto 1.0, p \mapsto G1, s? \mapsto [500D + 200Ma + 300Mi + 10Y], c \mapsto C(1.0, G1)[500D + 200Ma + 300Mi + 10Y]\}$ is possible in the given state. The reaction instantiated in such a way leads to the successor state $[C(1.0, G1)[500D + 200Ma + 300Mi + 11Y] + C(1.0, G1)[500D + 200Ma + 300Mi + 10Y]]$. Note that in this case it is irrelevant which of the two cells c is assigned to. As both cells are completely equivalent, the successor state is the same in both cases. However, the number of these equivalent choices for c is crucial for determining the transition rate. This is reflected in the rate expression $k1 * \#c$. Two equivalent choices for c in the variable assignment σ exists, thus $\#c$ evaluates to 2. The rate is then $15 * 2 = 30$. Rule (2) is instantiated in the context of a cell, as its reactants Y and D can only be found there. The variable assignment is $\sigma = \{y \mapsto Y, d \mapsto D\}$. For this one σ, there are two contexts (cells) in which it can be applied. However, in both contexts the reaction leads to the same successor state $[C(1.0, G1)[499D + 200Ma + 301Mi + 9Y] + C(1.0, G1)[500D + 200Ma + 300Mi + 10Y]]$. Consequently, the rate $k2 * \#y * \#d$ is doubled to obtain the rate for the transition to this state. The final rate is then $2 * 200 * 10 * 500 = 2 \cdot 10^6$. This shows how Mass action kinetics can be implemented using the language constructs provided by ML-Rules. Alternative kinetics can naturally be realized the same way. By evaluating and instantiating rules as shown, from a given model state the set of possible successor states as well as the corresponding transition rates are obtained. This way CTMC semantics are established. We will now elaborate on implementation details of our simulator for ML-Rules.

5. SIMULATOR IMPLEMENTATION

The rules (SUM), (SUB), and (INST) of the stochastic semantics shown in Figure 6, together with all states of an ML-Rules model, describe a complete CTMC containing all states and all transition rates between states and their successor states. Since the number of states is probably large

or even infinite, the simulation algorithm of ML-Rules does not compute this state transition network, but it computes traces within this network in an SSA-based manner [11]. The basic simulation algorithm is shown in Figure 11. Initially, the method `inst` is called with the current solution and rules, see step (1). This method returns a set of quadruples $(s, \sigma, r, (\nu \tilde{x})e_2)$ representing reaction templates, where s is the matched solution, σ is the set of variable assignments, r is the reaction rate, and $(\nu \tilde{x})e_2$ is the expression to calculate the product solution of the corresponding reaction based on the variable assignments σ. Thus, one quadruple represents a reaction template, which contains all information to execute the corresponding reaction. Within loop (6), all quadruples are computed for each rule and the given solution sol by following the (INST) rule of the stochastic semantics in Figure 6. Within loop (7), all quadruples for each species of the given solution sol are computed recursively according to the recursion within the (SUB) and (SUM) rule of the stochastic semantics. The `inst` method explicitly does not calculate the product solution of a reaction directly, because it is not needed for the reaction selection procedure. Instead, a product is only computed if the corresponding reaction is selected to be executed. In step (2), the rate sum r_{sum} of all reaction templates is computed. This sum is needed in step (3) to sample the time advance from an exponential distribution with rate r_{sum}. The sum is also needed in step (4) to select the reaction template to be executed, i.e., a reaction template $(sol, \sigma, r, (\nu \tilde{x})e_2)$ is chosen with probability r/r_{sum}. Finally, in step (5) the selected reaction template $(sol, \sigma, r, (\nu \tilde{x})e_2)$ is executed by removing sol from its compartment, computing the product solution with $(\nu \tilde{x})e_2$ and σ according to the (INST) rule of the stochastic semantics, and adding the product solution to the corresponding compartment.

The crucial part of the algorithm is the evaluation of the term $p + y \Downarrow_{sol, \sigma} sol$ within loop (6), i.e., finding all valid instantiations of the left hand side $p + y$ of a rule within the given solution sol. A simple approach to find these instantiations works as follows. Initially, all mappings from patterns of p to species of the solution sol are created. The maximum

```
nextstep (sol, rules, t) {
    reactions  :=  inst (sol, rules)                                    (1)
    r_sum      :=  ∑_{(_,_,r,_)∈reactions} r                            (2)
    t          :=  t + Exp(r_sum)                                       (3)
    reaction   :=  select (reactions, r_sum)                           (4)
    sol        :=  execute (reaction, sol)                              (5)
}

inst (sol, rules) {
    rs  :=  ∅
    for  (p + y --e₁--> (νx̃)e₂ ∈ rules)                                (6)
        rs  :=  rs ∪
            {(sol, σ, r, (νx̃)e₂)|p + y ⇓_{sol,σ} sol, e₁ ⇓_{sol,σ} r}
    for  (S(ṽ, sol_sub) ∈ sol)                                         (7)
        rs  :=  rs ∪ inst (sol_sub, rules)
    return rs
}
```

Figure 11: Pseudo-Code for the ML-Rules simulation algorithm

number of mappings is $|sol|^{|p|}$, where $|sol|$ is the number of species of sol including all sub solutions and $|p|$ the number of patterns of p including all sub patterns. Afterward, the validity is checked for each mapping. To check whether a species matches the expressions $\tilde{e}$ of a pattern $S(\tilde{e}, p_r)^e$, all constants within $\tilde{e}$ must be evaluated and checked. Since arbitrary complex constants can be defined by the modeler in ML-Rules, the evaluation of constants can be arbitrary complex. Thus, the complexity of the simulation algorithm depends significantly on the complexities of the used constants. However, the complexity of reasonable constants is typically not worse than linear, e.g., the *count* constant as well as the *fill* constant have a linear complexity. Altogether, the complexity to find all valid instantiations of the left hand side $p + y$ of a rule within the given solution sol is the complexity to check each pattern of each mapping, i.e., $O(c \cdot |p| \cdot |sol|^{|p|})$, where c is the complexity of the used constants.

To improve the runtime performance of the simulation algorithm, we applied several adaptations. For example, the algorithm follows a population-based handling of species, i.e., an amount value is added to species, identical species are merged and the amount value is adapted accordingly. Further, the algorithm filters possible mappings during the instantiation as early as possible, i.e., the species type and primitive attribute values of a pattern are checked immediately and if they do not match the pattern, the corresponding mapping is discarded directly. Similar to [7], we added mechanisms to consider only influenced solutions after a reaction execution, so that it is not necessary to execute the complete instantiation process after each step. Furthermore, we added multi-key data structures and different hash algorithms to efficiently access and compare species with specific properties. We also applied an adaptive simulation algorithm on top of the ML-Rules simulator to change its configuration during runtime to improve its performance [13]. Besides these implementation optimizations, we developed approximate variants of the simulation algorithm

based on τ-leaping [14] and hybrid algorithms. All source code referring to ML-Rules is open source [22]. A sandbox tool to create and simulate ML-Rules models is available at *http://wwwmosi.informatik.uni-rostock.de/software/*.

6. EXPRESSIVENESS AND EFFICIENCY

As already stated in [22], ML-Rules bears similarities to a couple of other rule-based modeling formalisms. Among the different rule-based languages, ML-Rules is most closely related to React(C) [18]. It has been shown that React(C) can encode arbitrary models defined in attributed π [17], i.e., it can express attributed π. The attributed π-calculus represents an extension of the stochastic π-calculus [29]. It equips processes with attributes defined by a language $\mathcal{L}$ and constrains reactions due to these attributes. It might not be surprising that React(C) expresses attributed π: it has been instrumental in developing React(C), as well as in developing ML-Rules. However, it is of relevance that React(C) can express attributed π: attributed π can express a variety of different variants of the stochastic π calculus, including the stochastic π calculus itself [17, 16]. Rather than relating the expressiveness of ML-Rules to attributed π or stochastic π, "the usual yardstick for the expressiveness of concurrent languages" [18], we will relate the expressiveness of ML-Rules to that of React(C). The syntax of ML-Rules and the syntax of React(C) look rather similar on first glance, the differences become evident in the semantics. These differences are most notable in the SUM and SUB functions that invoke each other mutually in ML-Rules to correctly count among all the different compartments, whereas in React(C) a simple summation (similarly, like in attributed π) does suffice: the reason for this is that in contrast to ML-Rules, React(C) has no true concept of compartments and dynamic nesting. Thus, if changes in hierarchies or reactions on lower levels need to be expressed, rules in React(C) have to be defined from the top-most level of the hierarchy. Consequently, e.g., the following rule $A()[s?] \rightarrow A()[A()[s?]]$ to generate arbitrarily deeply nested species during simulation cannot be expressed in React(C). Furthermore, given a solution that contains a species A at different levels, in ML-Rules a degradation rule $A() \rightarrow$ is applicable in every context in $C()[B()[5A()] + 10A()]$, whereas in React(C) to have the same effect one would have to write one rule for each hierarchy level. Due to their similarity, it is simple to show that any model encoded in React(C) can be encoded in ML-Rules, i.e., by adding a root context to the ML-Rules model, putting all species inside this root context and forcing each rule in the ML-Rules model to describe their hierarchy starting from the root context. Being able to encode arbitrary React(C) models in ML-Rules implies that also attributed π models can be encoded in ML-Rules, and also models of many other modeling languages like BetaBinders [30], BioAmbients [32] and the stochastic π calculus [29].

Nevertheless, due to the expressiveness of ML-Rules, the simulation algorithm becomes more complex compared to other modeling languages and specific improvements are more difficult to be applied. For example, the rigidity property for connected patterns of the κ calculus, which is important for the simulation algorithm implementation described in [7], does not hold for ML-Rules. Basically, this property implies that after matching one pattern of a connected pattern, the remaining matching process becomes clearly determined, i.e., only one valid mapping of patterns to species containing the specified matching exists [7]. This means, e.g., that after adding a single new species to the current solution in the κ calculus, at most one new rule instantiation per rule is possible. However, due to compartmental connections of species in ML-Rules — representing hyperedges between species — this property does not hold, see also [18]. For example, the pattern $A(x) + B(y)$ is connected in ML-Rules due to the needed compartmental link of matched species. After matching a species A to the pattern $A(x)$, it is still possible to match various species B to the pattern $B(y)$. Consequently, by adding a single new species to the current solution in ML-Rules, several new reaction instantiations per rule are possible.

The simulation algorithm for stochastic bigraphs described in [15] is another example for an algorithm which cannot simply be applied to ML-Rules. Within stochastic bigraphs, it is not possible to define internal states of species. Further, all instantiations of a rule have the same reaction rate. Due to these two properties, the number of instantiable reactions of a rule can be used to compute the rate sum of all instantiations by multiplying this number with the reaction rate constant. On the one hand, this is typically easier than summing the rates of all rule instantiations. On the other hand, more importantly, this can be helpful if the number of instantiable reactions of some rules can be computed easily without computing the reactions themselves. For example, the number of reactions of a rule

$$A(x) + B(y) \xrightarrow{k \cdot \#A \cdot \#B} C(x+y)$$

within a specific compartment can be computed easily by multiplying the amount of all $A(x)$ with the amount of all $B(y)$ inside the chosen compartment. Thus, it is not necessary to compute all reactions, because the rate sum can be used to decide whether a reaction of this rule should be executed. Only after the rule is chosen, one instantiation is computed stochastically and it is executed. In ML-Rules, however, the rates of reactions typically depend on reactant attributes and solution properties, so that in these cases all reactions must be computed before the rate sum can be computed.

These examples show that the expressiveness of ML-Rules does come with a cost. It is more difficult to apply specific performance improvements and some of these might not even be applicable for all ML-Rules models. However, despite these issues, ML-Rules has been already successfully used within complex modeling and simulation studies, e.g., [12].

7. CONCLUSIONS

A formal semantics of a modeling language facilitates the unambiguous interpretation and well-defined execution of models. Up until now, there was no formal definition of the semantics of ML-Rules. With the work presented in this paper, we have not only closed this gap, but also extended ML-Rules by functions on solutions. Furthermore, we related our simulation algorithm to the formal semantics and elaborated on implications for the algorithm, but also on performance improvements and omissions the implementation benefits from while still being semantically correct.

We illustrated that ML-Rules with functions on solutions is able to express every React(C) model. However, the expressiveness of ML-Rules impedes some typical improvements used by simulation algorithms for comparable, less expressive modeling languages. We are therefore planning to continue our work on efficient simulation algorithms.

8. ACKNOWLEDGMENTS

For their contributions to ML-Rules, we would like to thank Mathias John, Carsten Maus and Sebastian Nähring. This research is partly supported by the German Research Foundation (DFG) via research grants ESCeMMo (UH-66/14) and MoSiLLDe (UH-66/15-1).

9. REFERENCES

[1] J. Banks and L. Chwif. Warnings about simulation. *Journal of Simulation*, 5(4):279–291, 2011.

[2] A. T. Bittig, F. Haack, C. Maus, and A. M. Uhrmacher. Adapting Rule-based Model Descriptions for Simulating in Continuous and Hybrid Space. In *Proceedings of the 9th International Conference on Computational Methods in Systems Biology, CMSB 2011*, pages 161–170, New York, NY, USA, 2011. ACM.

[3] M. L. Blinov, J. R. Faeder, B. Goldstein, and W. S. Hlavacek. BioNetGen: Software for Rule-based Modeling of Signal Transduction Based on the Interactions of Molecular Domains. *Bioinformatics*, 20(17):3289–3291, 2004.

[4] O. Bouissou and A. Chapoutot. An Operational Semantics for Simulink's Simulation Engine. In *Proceedings of the 13th ACM SIGPLAN/SIGBED International Conference on Languages, Compilers, Tools and Theory for Embedded Systems 2012, LCTES '12*, pages 129–138, New York, NY, USA, 2012. ACM.

[5] A. Csikasz-Nagy. Computational systems biology of the cell cycle. *Briefings in Bioinformatics*, 10(4):424–434, 2009.

[6] T. C. Damgaard, E. Højsgaard, and J. Krivine. Formal Cellular Machinery. *Electronic Notes in Theoretical Computer Science*, 284:55–74, 2012.

[7] V. Danos, J. Feret, W. Fontana, and J. Krivine. Scalable Simulation of Cellular Signaling Networks. In *Proceedings of the 5th Asian Symposium on Programming Languages and Systems, APLAS 2007*, pages 139–157, Berlin, Heidelberg, 2007. Springer-Verlag.

[8] V. Danos and C. Laneve. Formal molecular biology. *Theoretical Computer Science*, 325(1):69–110, 2004.

[9] J. R. Faeder. Toward a comprehensive language for biological systems. *BMC Biology*, 9(1):68, 2011.

[10] J. Fisher and T. A. Henzinger. Executable cell biology. *Nature Biotechnology*, 25(11):1239–1249, 2007.

[11] D. T. Gillespie. Exact stochastic simulation of coupled chemical reactions. *The Journal of Physical Chemistry*, 81(25):2340–2361, 1977.

[12] F. Haack, H. Lemcke, R. Ewald, T. Rharass, and A. M. Uhrmacher. Spatio-temporal Model of Endogenous ROS and Raft-Dependent WNT/Beta-Catenin Signaling Driving Cell Fate Commitment in Human Neural Progenitor Cells. *PLoS Computational Biology*, 11(3):e1004106, 2015.

[13] T. Helms, R. Ewald, S. Rybacki, and A. M. Uhrmacher. A Generic Adaptive Simulation Algorithm for Component-based Simulation Systems. In

Proceedings of the ACM SIGSIM Conference on Principles of Advanced Discrete Simulation, SIGSIM-PADS '13, pages 11–22, New York, NY, USA, 2013. ACM.

[14] T. Helms, M. Luboschik, H. Schumann, and A. M. Uhrmacher. An Approximate Execution of Rule-Based Multi-level Models. In *Proceedings of the 11th International Conference on Computational Methods in Systems Biology, CMSB 2013*, pages 19–32, Berlin, Heidelberg, 2013. Springer-Verlag.

[15] E. Højsgaard and J. Krivine. Towards Scalable Simulation of Stochastic Bigraphs. Technical Report TR-2011-148, IT University of Copenhagen, 2011.

[16] M. John. *Reaction Constraints for the Pi-Calculus - A Language for the Stochastic and Spatial Modeling of Cell-Biological Processes*. PhD thesis, Universität Rostock, 2010. *http://tel.archives-ouvertes.fr/tel-00825257* [Accessed 7 May 2015].

[17] M. John, C. Lhoussaine, J. Niehren, and A. Uhrmacher. The Attributed Pi Calculus with Priorities. *Transactions on Computational Systems Biology*, 5945(12):13–76, 2010.

[18] M. John, C. Lhoussaine, J. Niehren, and C. Versari. Biochemical Reaction Rules with Constraints. In *Proceedings of the 20th European Symposium on Programming, ESOP 2011*, pages 338–357, Berlin, Heidelberg, 2011. Springer-Verlag.

[19] L. Joppa, G. McInerny, R. Harper, L. Salido, K. Takeda, K. O'Hara, D. Gavaghan, and S. Emmott. Troubling trends in scientific software use. *Science*, 340(6134):814–815, 2013.

[20] J. Krivine, R. Milner, and A. Troina. Stochastic Bigraphs. *Electronic Notes in Theoretical Computer Science*, 218:73–96, 2008.

[21] C. Maus. *Toward Accessible Multilevel Modeling in Systems Biology: A Rule-based Language Concept*. PhD thesis, Universität Rostock, 2013. *http://rosdok.uni-rostock.de/resolve/id/rosdok_disshab_0000001060* [Accessed 7 May 2015].

[22] C. Maus, S. Rybacki, and A. M. Uhrmacher. Rule-based multi-level modeling of cell biological systems. *BMC Systems Biology*, 5(166), 2011.

[23] O. Mazemondet, M. John, S. Leye, A. Rolfs, and A. M. Uhrmacher. Elucidating the Sources of β-Catenin Dynamics in Human Neural Progenitor Cells. *PLoS ONE*, 7(8), 2012.

[24] O. Mazemondet, M. John, C. Maus, A. M. Uhrmacher, and A. Rolfs. Integrating Diverse Reaction Types into Stochastic Models: A Signaling Pathway Case Study in the Imperative π-calculus. In *Proceedings of the 2009 Winter Simulation Conference, WSC 2009*, pages 932–943, Austin, Texas, 2009. Winter Simulation Conference.

[25] N. Oury and G. D. Plotkin. Multi-level modelling via stochastic multi-level multiset rewriting. *Mathematical Structures in Computer Science*, 23(2):471–503, 2013.

[26] E. H. Page. *Simulation Modeling Methodology: Principles and Etiology of Decision Support*. PhD thesis, Virginia Polytechnic Institute and State University, 1994. *www.thesimguy.com/articles/simModMeth.pdf* [Accessed 7 May 2015].

[27] O. Parvu, D. Gilbert, M. Heiner, F. Liu, N. Saunders, and S. Shaw. Spatial-temporal modelling and analysis of bacterial colonies with phase variable genes. *Transactions on Modeling and Computer Simulation*, 25(2):13:1–13:25, 2015.

[28] B. C. Pierce. *Types and programming languages*. MIT Press, Cambridge, Mass., 2002.

[29] C. Priami. Stochastic π-Calculus. *The Computer Journal*, 38(7):578–589, 1995.

[30] C. Priami and P. Quaglia. Beta Binders for Biological Interactions. In *Proceedings of the International Conference on Computational Methods in Systems Biology, CMSB 2004*, pages 20–33, Berlin, Heidelberg, 2005. Springer-Verlag.

[31] C. Priami, P. Quaglia, and A. Romanel. BlenX Static and Dynamic Semantics. In *Proceedings of the 20th International Conference on Concurrency Theory, CONCUR 2009*, pages 37–52, Berlin, Heidelberg, 2009. Springer-Verlag.

[32] A. Regev, E. M. Panina, W. Silverman, L. Cardelli, and E. Shapiro. BioAmbients: an abstraction for biological compartments. *Theoretical Computer Science*, 325(1):141–167, 2004.

[33] J. J. Tyson. Modeling the cell division cycle: cdc2 and cyclin interactions. *Proceedings of the National Academy of Sciences*, 88(16):7328–7332, 1991.

[34] A. van Deursen, P. Klint, and J. Visser. Domain-specific Languages: An Annotated Bibliography. *SIGPLAN Notices*, 35(6):26–36, 2000.

Exploring the Relationship between Adherence to Treatment and Viral Load through a New Discrete Simulation Model of HIV Infectivity

Ela R. Rana
Department of Computer
Science, Troy University
Troy, Alabama 36082, USA
(+1)334-670-3409
erana@troy.edu

Philippe J. Giabbanelli
School of Clinical Medicine
University of Cambridge
Cambridge, CB2 0QQ, UK
(+44) 01223-330315
pg438@medschl.cam.ac.uk

Naga H.
Balabhadrapathruni,
Xiaoyu Li, Vijay K. Mago
Dept. of Computer Science,
Troy University, Troy, AL, USA
{nbala,xli130586,vmago}@troy.edu

ABSTRACT

Human immunodeficiency virus (HIV) has been a major health problem throughout the world for decades. This paper introduces a new discrete simulation model for the growth of HIV infection within a host body. The model is developed incrementally, and compared at each stage for congruence with real-world observations of disease dynamics. We used the model to get a better understanding of how HIV-infected cells behave, and particularly to assess the importance of medication adherence for effectiveness of treatment. We found that a small lack of adherence could have a proportionally much larger impact on infection as well as trigger negative effects on health sooner. Consequently, improving adherence can be very beneficial (particularly for those whose adherence is already high), and small issues in adherence should be addressed early on. Our work is one step in the development of detailed discrete simulations for HIV dynamics. However, much work remains to be done in order to accurately capture adherence as well as medication schedule, viral resistance, or multiple medication types.

Categories and Subject Descriptors

I.6.5 [**Simulation and modeling**]: Model Development; I.6.8 [**Simulation and modeling**]: Types of simulation— *Discrete event*; J.3 [**Computer Applications**]: Life and medical sciences—*Health*

General Terms

Experimentation

Keywords

Antiretroviral therapy; Cellular automata; Discrete simulation; HIV

SIGSIM-PADS'15, June 10–12, 2015, London, United Kingdom.
© 2015 ACM. ISBN 978-1-4503-3583-6/15/06 ...$15.00.
DOI: http://dx.doi.org/10.1145/2769458.2769477.

1. INTRODUCTION

The Human Immunodeficiency Virus (HIV) has been a major health problem throughout the world for decades. Data from the World Health Organization (WHO) shows that in 2013, 1.5 million people died of HIV and the number of people infected reached 35 million [47]. Research in HIV continues to be a very active field, prompted by the need to better understand the context in which the infection occurs, as well as to develop treatment methods (e.g., antiretroviral therapy) that can decrease the progression of HIV and its mortality. Simulations have played a key role in many aspects of HIV research, utilizing a variety of methods. Several of these methods have been reviewed in [36, 34]. Methods can be broadly divided as either continuous or discrete simulations. Continuous simulations offer several influential examples regarding HIV and public policies. These include the recent work of Granich *et al.*, whose system dynamics model assessed the consequences of universal testing for HIV followed by immediate antiretroviral therapy [15], and the early findings from Kaplan that HIV prevalence among injection drug users could be reduced by needle exchange programs [21]. Discrete simulations also have a rich history in understanding the dynamics of the disease between and within hosts. For example, both social network models and discrete Markov chains have been used to examine the spread of HIV among injecting drug users [11, 24], while cellular automata research has shed light on the dynamics of HIV within the human body [10, 43, 27]. In this paper, we focus on designing a discrete model of HIV dynamics within the host body, and on using the model to understand the consequences of issues in treatment adherence.

HIV requires treatment for life, thus resembling a chronic disease [12]. This raises a number of long-term issues, of which two are of particular interest in this paper. First, there is long-term toxicity. For example, antiretroviral drugs used to treat HIV, such as nucleoside reverse transcriptase inhibitors (NRTIs), can seriously affect the liver (e.g., causing hepatic failure) and can also produce mitochondrial toxicity [28, 46]. Toxicity can necessitate drug switching, or even stopping therapy. Consequently, alternatives to triple therapy (also known as tri-therapy) include dual therapy as well as mono-therapy [6]. Our models include dual therapy as well as mono-therapy. Second, there is the issue of maintaining long-term adherence, which is influenced by a wide array of individual (e.g., perceived severity of side-effects, feeling better on treatment, being away from home) and societal factors (e.g., cost of the drugs) [9]. A (conservative) metric for adherence is the Proportion of Days Covered (PDC), which measures the number of days 'covered' by the treatment and divides by the number of days in the measurement period. Full-adherence to treatment would be a PDC of 100%. Observational cohort studies have reported that only about 20% to 35% of patients may have PDC>80% for HIV antiretroviral regimens [31]. Defining a 'sufficient' level of adherence is difficult [9]. For example, it depends on the class of medication: unboosted protease inhibitors (PIs) need over 95% while 80% may be sufficient for boosted PIs, and non-nucleoside reverse transcriptase inhibitors (NNR-TIs) may work with even lower rates [23]. This paper sheds light on the consequences of adherence to the dynamics of HIV within the host, using new advanced discrete simulation models of dual- and mono-therapy.

The main contributions of this paper are twofold:

- We develop discrete simulation models for the dynamics of HIV within the human body in the presence of dual- and mono-therapy, using the technique of cellular automata.

- We use these models to investigate how issues in adherence to the antiretroviral regimen may impact the dynamics of HIV.

The organization of this paper is as follows: in Section 2, we provide a background on the key stages and factors in the dynamics of HIV. We also review how these dynamics have been previously captured using cellular automata. In Section 3, we develop a series of cellular automata models of HIV, going from a model with no therapy to mono-therapy and finally dual therapy. The calibration of each model is discussed, and rules are gradually added as the model becomes more advanced. In Section 4, we show that the key results obtained by this series of models are in accordance with real-world observations. In Section 5, we investigate how adherence to treatment relates to the spread of HIV within the host. Finally, key findings from the models and simulations are discussed, together with limitations and suggestions for future work.

2. BACKGROUND

2.1 Biological background

To understand the mathematical modeling of HIV, we first need to understand the virus itself. HIV is a virus that attacks cells that are important for immune defense, primarily T cells. CD4 is one type of T cell that the virus infects, and its count is thus used by medical professionals to examine immune functioning in an infected person [2]. When HIV infects a large enough number of T cells, the immune system becomes unable to replenish the loss of healthy T cells. Without a well-functioning immune system, the human body cannot fight against minor infections and illnesses. This is called Acquired Immunodeficiency Syndrome (AIDS), and it is the last and most harmful stage of the disease brought on by HIV infection [8].

HIV has a complex disease process, which is divided into three phases. In the first few weeks after acquiring the virus, HIV-infected individuals experience an acute phase of the infection. They can develop flu-like symptoms or be asymptomatic. During this phase, the virus is most active. It replicates by infecting and using the CD4 cells of the host to make many copies of itself. Thus at this stage there is a rapid rise in the viral load, which is the amount of HIV in the host blood [2]. As the immune system begins to detect the virus at the end of this phase, a viral load set point is achieved that in essence represents a temporary ability of the host immune system to control the virus. This is followed by the next stage of HIV, which is called the latent stage. In this stage, which can last many years, infected individuals are generally asymptomatic. During this phase, the virus replicates much slower. However, the virus does keep growing, and over time, it will have infected enough CD4 cells to reach the next and final stage, which is the AIDS stage. When the CD4 cell count is less than 200 $cells/mm^3$ of blood, the patient is considered to be in the AIDS stage [8]. In this stage, patients are severely immunocompromised, and can thus develop multiple types of infections and tumors [8].

To prevent the worsening of the host's condition to AIDS, the chief form of treatment used is antiretroviral therapy (ART). One or multiple types of ART medications are used to prevent specific phases in virus replication. HIV replicates by a series of steps, which include binding, fusion, reverse transcription, integration, transcription, assembly, and budding [1]. Each ART medication is generally designed to prevent one of these steps in the virus lifecycle, often by inhibiting enzymes that facilitate the process [33].

2.2 Modeling background

Intuitively, a cellular automaton (CA) is a collection of coloured cells on a grid that updates over a period of discrete, fixed timesteps based on certain rules defined around neighbouring cells [26]. CA grids and cells can be of different types and shapes. Square and hexagonal cells are most common. CA models are generally one-dimensional (1D), two-dimensional (2D), and three-dimensional (3D), but can have more dimensions as well. There is a vast quantity of research using CA, as it can be applied to study any situation where individual units or cells affect others surrounding them [38]. One such use of CA is to study biological systems [20]. In this paper, we are interested in the use of CA to create discrete simulations representing the environment of the HIV-infected cells within the host body. In this context, cellular automata allow us to simulate and observe the spread of the virus as a simplification of how it works in the real-world [43].

Among the earlier works on cellular automata modeling of HIV, Santos & Coutinho [10] used a model that took into consideration the global features of the immune response to the HIV pathogen, the fast mutation rate of the virus, and spatial localization. In this seminal research, they used CA to reproduce the three-stage dynamics of HIV infection, and kept the parameter set unchanged during simulation. The results indicated that the clinical latency was not a steady state but a long transient when compared to the ordinary differential equation models. The importance of the lymph nodes, the spatial localization, and the local interactions of HIV were found. They succeeded in describing the three-stage dynamics, which was not as well captured in previous methods that did not consider local interactions.

Shi *et al.* [43] proposed a novel cellular automata model for HIV dynamics. The model, based on realistic conditions, showed the replication cycle of HIV. Precharattana *et al.* [39] developed a CA model that described the situation of HIV infection with different simulation environments. Through the model algorithm and the control parameters, this research compared the simulation results with and without leukapheresis treatment. Another model proposed by Precharattana & Triampo [40] considered the HIV infection dynamics by incorporating the cells such as CD4 cells, dendritic cells (DCs), and CD8 cells into the model and observed the interaction between the host immune response and the infected T cells in the lymph nodes. Gonzalez *et al.* [14] investigated the dynamics of human immunodeficiency virus infection under antiretroviral therapy treatment. While the focus of CA research on HIV infection is typically on the lymph tissue, research by Moonchai *et al.* [29, 30] also considered infection in blood compartments. The CA grid was used to represent lymph cell and blood compartment to show the infection of HIV in each location, making it a two-compartment model of HIV infection.

3. MODEL DESIGN

Along with the biology of HIV summarized in section 2.1, we utilize 2-dimensional cellular automata as reviewed in section 2.2. The host body environment is discretized as a 2-dimensional grid, where each (square) cell corresponds to one host body cell which may or may not be infected with HIV. We created a series of three models, where rules of the CA are gradually introduced starting with no therapy, and going to mono- and dual therapy. Specifically, the first model provides a simplified view of how HIV-infected cells convert the body's CD4 cells from healthy to infectious (divided as acute and latent), eventually resulting in cell death. The second model builds on this to add antiretroviral therapy treatment. This addition is captured by dividing the healthy stage into two (depending on whether the healthy cell receives treatment) and by creating rules specifying which cells receive treatment and whether cells can be infected while on treatment. Finally, the third model adds another therapy. In this situation, a cell can not only receive therapy but can also change from one therapy to another or receive both, depending on certain parameters.

This section focuses on formally specifying the design of the models, their assumptions, and how they relate to previous work. Simulations to validate the model are provided in the next section. Models are introduced by providing a list of their states. The transitions between these states are visually provided as flowcharts, and mathematically specified. These transitions are applied at every timestep, where one timestep represents 1 week as in the work of Precharattana *et al.* [39]. The mathematical specification of the transitions consists of a set of rules. Each rule is composed of two parts: the states through which to move, and the condition to move. For example, we denote by $A \leftarrow B : \mathcal{P}_i$ a transition from state B to state A with probability $\mathcal{P}_i$. Our conditions primarily include delays (denoted as τ), probabilities (denoted as $\mathcal{P}$), and counts (denoted as $\mathcal{N}$) which represent the number of cells of a certain type immediately adjacent to a given cell. For example, $\mathcal{N}_{I_1}$ denotes the number of cells of type I_1 immediately touching. It should be noted that each cell is surrounded by 8 neighbours, thus the count is always at most 8. When a condition has different parts, these parts are combined by multiplying in the probability ($\times$) and with logical *or* ($\|$) operators. For example,

$A \leftarrow B : (\mathcal{P}_i \times (\mathcal{N}_{I_1} \geq 1)) \| \mathcal{P}_v$ states that a cell goes from state B to A either with probability $\mathcal{P}_i$ and at least one neighbour in state I_1, or with probability $\mathcal{P}_v$. For all of the models, if a rule or every part of a rule is not met, then the cell simply remains in the state it was previously in.

3.1 Model 1 - No antiretroviral therapy

Each cell of the CA represents a CD4 cell in lymph tissue, which is the primary location for CD4 cells [10]. The cell can be in four possible states:

- *Healthy state (H)*: regular CD4 cell that has not been infected by HIV.

- *Acute Infected state (I_1)*: infected CD4 state with the virus in an acute (more active) stage. At this stage, the virus has not been detected by the immune system yet, and thus infects neighbours easily.

- *Latent Infected state (I_2)*: infected CD4 state with the virus in latent (less active) stage. Here, the immune system has detected the virus, making it more difficult for the virus to grow and spread.

- *Dead cell (D)*: CD4 cell that was infected and was attacked by the immune system.

The set of rules is specified in Ruleset 1, while the states and transitions involved in these rules are depicted in Figure 1. The rules for the CA are based on the model originally developed by Santos & Coutinho in 2001 [10], which we will refer to as 'the original rules' from here on. We added parameters to these rules, to reflect recent work surveyed in Section 2.2. The list of parameters together with the works they are derived from is provided in Table 1.

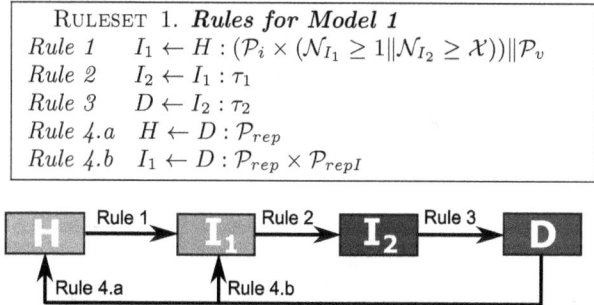

RULESET 1. *Rules for Model 1*

Rule 1 $I_1 \leftarrow H : (\mathcal{P}_i \times (\mathcal{N}_{I_1} \geq 1 \| \mathcal{N}_{I_2} \geq \mathcal{X})) \| \mathcal{P}_v$
Rule 2 $I_2 \leftarrow I_1 : \tau_1$
Rule 3 $D \leftarrow I_2 : \tau_2$
Rule 4.a $H \leftarrow D : \mathcal{P}_{rep}$
Rule 4.b $I_1 \leftarrow D : \mathcal{P}_{rep} \times \mathcal{P}_{repI}$

Figure 1: **Flow Diagram of Model 1 Rules**

Rule 1 is called the 'basic infection constraint': it provides the two possible conditions in which a healthy cell can become (acute) infected. First, it can be an infection from neighbouring cells. Specifically, infection can occur when there is at least one acute infected neighbour ($\mathcal{N}_{I_1} \geq 1$) or $\mathcal{X}$ latent infected neighbours ($\mathcal{N}_{I_2} \geq \mathcal{X}$); this was specified in the original rules [10]. We added the parameter $\mathcal{P}_i$ to the original rule to reflect the probability that neighbours can successfully pass on the infection. Second, there is a probability that a cell travels through blood and hence infect other cells beyond its original neighbourhood. This was captured in the work of Moonchai *et al.* [30, 29] via a parameter $\mathcal{P}_v$ as the probability of infection from outside the neighbourhood.

Rule 2 states that an acute infected cell may grow and spread undetected for τ_1 timesteps, until the immune system finds it and it becomes latent [10, 44, 39]. Rule 3 states that

Rule 1.a $H_T \leftarrow H : \mathcal{P}_T \times (timestep \geq Th_{start})$

Rule 1.b $I_1 \leftarrow H : (1 - (\mathcal{P}_T \times (timestep \geq Th_{start}))) \times ((\mathcal{P}_i \times (\mathcal{N}_{I_1} \geq 1 \| \mathcal{N}_{I_2} \geq \mathcal{X})) \| \mathcal{P}_v)$

Rule 5.a $I_1 \leftarrow H_T : \mathcal{P}_{infT} \times ((\mathcal{P}_i \times (\mathcal{N}_{I_1} \geq 1 \| \mathcal{N}_{I_2} \geq \mathcal{X})) \| \mathcal{P}_v)$

Rule 5.b $H \leftarrow H_T : (1 - \mathcal{P}_T) \times (1 - (\mathcal{P}_{infT} \times ((\mathcal{P}_i \times (\mathcal{N}_{I_1} \geq 1 \| \mathcal{N}_{I_2} \geq \mathcal{X})) \| \mathcal{P}_v)))$

after τ_2 timesteps, the immune system destroys the infected cell [10, 44, 39]. Finally, Rule 4 determines how a dead cell is replaced. Generally, the immune response replaces dead cells with new CD4 cells. However, this may take time, and the new cell may also become infected. These two phenomena are captured by rules 4.a and 4.b respectively, where $\mathcal{P}_{rep}$ is the probability to replace a dead cell, and $\mathcal{P}_{repI}$ is the probability that the new replaced cell is infected [10, 44, 39]. If neither condition is met, no replacement occurs, which is captured in the model by maintaining that cell location in the dead state. Note that rule 4.b has priority over rule 4.a. That is, if the probabilistic conditions ($\mathcal{P}_{rep}$ and $\mathcal{P}_{repI}$) are both met, then a new replaced cell is infected (rule 4.b).

3.2   Model 2 - Single antiretroviral therapy

Model 2 adds to Model 1 a single therapy treatment. This type of model has previously been developed either to observe differences in virus growth with mono-therapy, or to observe the effect of a multiple combination therapy (e.g., highly active antiretroviral therapy (HAART)) by treating it as a single treatment group with a combined estimate of the CA parameters. This model subdivides the one healthy state from Model 1 into two states: healthy cell H without therapy (identical to a healthy cell in model 1) and healthy cell H_T with therapy.

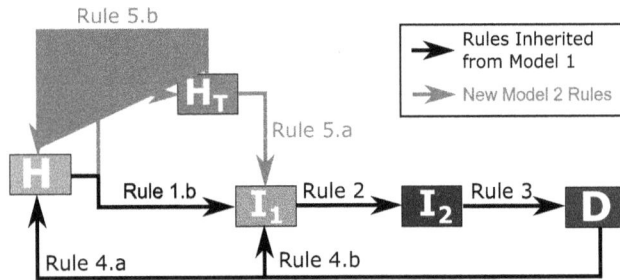

Figure 2: **Flow Diagram of Model 2 Rules**

We adapted additional rules in this model from the dual therapy model by Shi *et al.* and Gonzalez *et al.* [43, 14]. Shi *et al.* and Gonzalez *et al.* used a medication effectiveness parameter to determine the fraction of the healthy cells that receive therapy. In a similar manner, our model utilizes a probabilistic parameter $\mathcal{P}_T$ to determine the number of healthy cells that are receiving therapy. However, one feature that was not previously accounted for by discrete simulation models of HIV was that a healthy cell with therapy should have a decreased ability to become infected. Various studies have shown that HIV infectivity is significantly lowered in a person that is taking medication therapy [37, 7]. To incorporate this feature for each medicated cell, we have introduced a new parameter, $\mathcal{P}_{infT}$. $\mathcal{P}_{infT}$ is the (small) probability that a healthy cell that is receiving therapy may become infected.

Another parameter that is added to this model is the starting week of the therapy, which is denoted by Th_{start}. We chose to set one specific value of Th_{start} in order to keep this constraint constant for all models. This helps us to better note the effect of variations in adherence and number of medications on the healthy and infected cells. Furthermore, since the earlier a therapy is started, the more effectiveness is seen [16, 22], and since most professional organizations also recommend that treatment be started early [18], we chose an early treatment start week for the models. This also allows us to more clearly see the difference made by therapy in virus progression. Although our therapy is started quite early, we do not begin it until the second phase of HIV has started. The reason for this is that most people who have HIV do not immediately find out that they are infected in the acute phase [13]. The new parameters introduced in model 2 and their values are given in Table 1. The rules for model 2 are detailed in Ruleset 2 and depicted in Figure 2.

Rule 1.a states that if therapy has started, there is a probability for a healthy cell to receive that therapy. Rule 1.b states that if the healthy cell remains without therapy, then it can become acute infected provided that the basic infection constraint is met (in a similar manner to Rule 1 of model 1). Rule 1 and Rule 5 of this model are based in part from the dual therapy rules of Gonzalez *et al.* [14]. Rule 5.a states that a cell receiving therapy may still become infected with a (small) probability $\mathcal{P}_{infT}$ and provided that the basic infection constraint is met. Rule 5.b represents the wearing off of therapy. Cells that contain medication at one point may later return to a drug-free state [14]. Rule 5.b states that if the cell did not get infected and is not receiving therapy, then it returns to a healthy state without therapy. Rules 2, 3, and 4 of this model are the same as in model 1.

3.3   Model 3 - Dual antiretroviral therapy

HIV-infected individuals are often prescribed a combination of two medications to better restrict the virus, as explained in section 2.1. Model 3 further builds on model 2 by adding rules to include a combination of two medications. This model, like model 2, is derived from the works of Shi *et al.* and Gonzalez *et al.* [43, 14]. However, these works did not fully describe all the possible state changes of a cell that is receiving therapy. We incorporated these changes and added parameters to make a more complete model for dual therapy of HIV medication. In model 2, there was a single therapy, hence there were 2 states for healthy cell (with/without therapy). Model 3 has two therapies, that lead to 4 situations for a healthy cell: no therapy (H), the first therapy (H_{T1}), the second therapy (H_{T2}), and both therapies (H_{Tb}).

The probabilities associated with the new stages are also changed. $\mathcal{P}_{T1}$ and $\mathcal{P}_{T2}$ are the probabilities of a cell receiving therapy 1 and therapy 2 respectively. $\mathcal{P}_{infT1}$ and $\mathcal{P}_{infT2}$ are new parameters not previously used in HIV CA research. They introduce the probabilities of a cell that is on therapy 1 and 2 respectively of becoming infected. Dual therapy models in previous research utilized different values for $\mathcal{P}_{T1}$ and $\mathcal{P}_{T2}$ to view the changes in simulation with different levels of virus effectiveness. However for this study, we utilize a moderate effectiveness value for these parameters and keep them constant, while adherence values are modified. The values of $\mathcal{P}_{infT1}$ and $\mathcal{P}_{infT2}$ are kept very low, similar to $\mathcal{P}_{infT}$ parameter of model 2. In addition to that, we also utilize the parameter Th_{start} from model 2. Ruleset 3 lists the rules of model 3 while states and transitions are shown in Figure 3. The new parameters and their values are given in Table 1.

Rule 1 describes the transition from a healthy cell to receiving one of the possible combinations of treatment (starting at step Th_{start}), or getting infected. Given that the probabilities to receive therapies 1 and 2 are denoted as $\mathcal{P}_{T1}$ and $\mathcal{P}_{T2}$ respectively, a cell receives both therapies (H_{Tb}) with probability $\mathcal{P}_{T1} \times \mathcal{P}_{T2}$ or receives a single one with the corresponding probability. If the cell does not receive therapy, it can remain in a healthy state or become infected per the basic infection constraint introduced in model 1. Rules 2, 3 and 4 are the same as model 1.

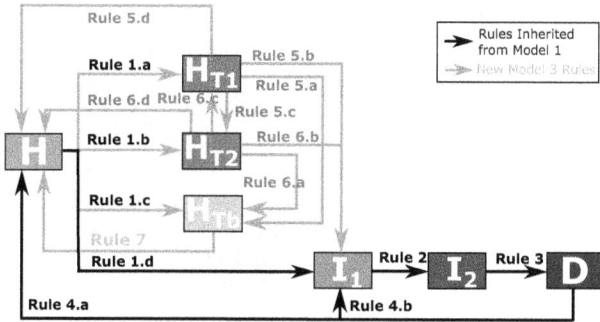

Figure 3: **Flow Diagram of Rules of Model 3**

Rule 5 and 6 show some similarities to the first rule, but describe the transition from a cell receiving treatment (H_{T1} or H_{T2}) rather than from a healthy cell without treatment. If a cell is on a single treatment, it may switch to receiving both with probability $\mathcal{P}_{T1} \times \mathcal{P}_{T2}$ (Rule 5.a and 6.a), or if it is only receiving one or no therapy, then it may become infected with a small probability ($\mathcal{P}_{infT1}$ for Rule 5.b or $\mathcal{P}_{infT2}$ for Rule 6.b) and provided the basic infection constraint is met.

This rule utilizes the assumption made by Gonzalez *et al.* that if a cell is on both therapies, it cannot be infected [14]. Gonzalez *et al.* also assumed the ability of H_{T1} and H_{T2} to be infected to be the same as H cell. However, since the cell is on therapy, the chances of infection should be greatly decreased. To lower this chance, we multiply the basic infection constraint by $\mathcal{P}_{infT1}$ or $\mathcal{P}_{infT2}$, which are newly introduced parameters in CA research of HIV therapy.

Just as the presence of both $\mathcal{P}_{T1}$ and $\mathcal{P}_{T2}$ would cause the single therapy cell to become H_{Tb}, we introduce another rule not used in previous research, which is that if the cell only has the probability of receiving the therapy other than the one it currently has, then it will change from one therapy state to the other (Rule 5.c, 6.c). Finally, if none of the other parts of Rule 5 or 6 is implemented, the cell returns to a healthy with no therapy state, provided that there is no probability of either therapy (Rule 5.d, 6.d). We may observe that in the 4 parts of Rules 5 and 6, the earlier parts take priority over the lower parts. For instance, if both rules 5.b and 5.d apply, 5.b will be implemented.

Rule 7 states that a cell that is on both therapies will eventually transition back to healthy state, after τ_3 time. We assume that H_{Tb} cell cannot become infected, since the presence of both therapies makes it even more difficult for the HIV to infect it, just as seen in Rules 5 and 6. [14].

4. MODEL VALIDATION

The three models were implemented using MATLAB version R2014b. A grid of $n \times n$ square cells was used to simulate each of the three models, where n was set to 100 [41, 39]. Each run of the simulation started with all cells in healthy state. Then, they were randomly infected by HIV with probability $\mathcal{P}_{HIV} = 0.05$ [41, 39]. The value for the parameter $\mathcal{P}_v$ was modified from what was found in previous research. We found that the value 0.0001 [30] for $\mathcal{P}_v$ used for the two compartment model of HIV by Moonchai *et al.*, as discussed in section 2.1, was too large. At this value, the second phase of the virus was shorter by a few years than what is seen in biological research [35]. Thus, we used a smaller value of 0.00001 for this research, which better reflected the biological timeline of the disease. The value for $\mathcal{P}_i$ ($\mathcal{P}_i$=0.997) was determined from constants for infectibility, r_1 and r_2, used in Moonchai *et al.* [30]. After all parameter values were set, we implemented the models with the CA rules.

In order to support replications of the experiment, the simulation code for all models can be freely accessed at using the corresponding parameters summarized in Table 1.

In this section, each model is assessed in two ways. First, a single simulation is performed to view how the states of cells change over time. Second, the simulation is repeated 1000 times and values are averaged to graphically examine the mean trajectories over time (e.g., number of healthy cells, number of infected cells), along with standard deviations of the graph represented as error bars. Both are compared to current knowledge about the dynamics of HIV.

4.1 Model 1 - No antiretroviral therapy

We first simulate HIV without therapy. One full simulation is performed for 600 weeks (approx. 11.5 years) and the change of states of each cell from one timestep to the next is viewed. The simulation is performed for 11.5 years in order to capture the entire first and second phase of the virus. Cell states, represented by different colours, can be viewed at specific timesteps in Figure 4. Figure 5 graphically displays the average of a 1000 runs, showing the total number of cells in each state at each timestep. At every 15 timesteps, vertical lines are shown above and below the state's value to represent the standard deviation for the graph.

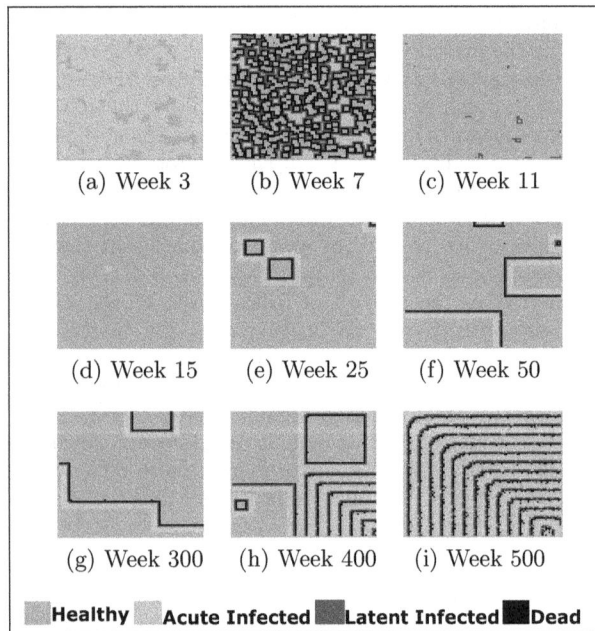

Figure 5: **Simulations for model 1 averaged across 1000 runs, with standard deviation shown as a bar across data points.**

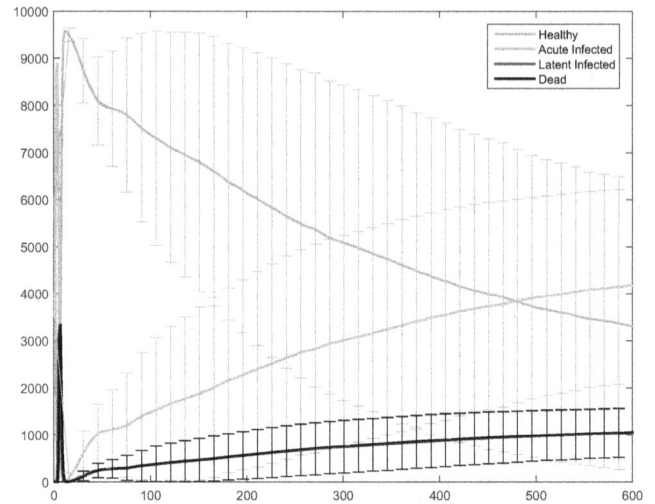

Figure 4: **Sample simulation run for model 1 over 500 weeks, showing the first (a-c) and second phases (d-i) of HIV dynamics in the host.**

Cells are coloured according to their state. The simulation starts with a grid containing mostly healthy cells (green), and a few acute infected cells (light blue). In the first few weeks, the virus grows undetected by the immune system: acute infected cell regions spread rapidly, infecting surrounding neighbours (Figure 4a). After τ_1 time (τ_1 = week 4 [10]), infected cells start to become detected by the immune system and thus begin to go into the latent infected stage. After τ_2 time (1 week), the latent cells are killed by the immune system. We see this in Figure 4b where the acute infected cells (light blue) have begun to turn into latent infected cells (dark blue) and then dead ones (black). Dead cells

are replaced with healthy cells, returning the body back to a healthy state with very few infected cells (Figure 4c). This first phase of HIV dynamics is also depicted in weeks 4-8 of Figure 5, whose trend match the dynamics of HIV seen in biological research [35].

Following this begins the second phase of HIV growth [35]. This phase begins with the infected cells at a very low count (Figure 4d). Now, the virus grows at a much slower rate over many years, as depicted by the small infected regions in Figures 4e, 4f, and 4g. Nonetheless, the virus count continues to gradually increase, as seen in Figure 5. Also note that the latent infected cells and dead cells almost always overlap in the graph, as they grow at the same rate throughout the simulation. Additionally, we see that the healthy cell count gradually decreases over the course of many years, as seen in Figure 5, or through the decrease in green regions over time in Figures 4h and 4i.

The second phase represents how long a person lives with HIV until they reach the AIDS stage. Generally a patient remains in phase 2 of HIV for an average of 10 years [33]. However this timeline may vary by many years from patient to patient. Research has indeed found "a large between-subject variation in estimated viral dynamic parameters [...] even after accounting for variations in drug exposure and drug susceptibility" [48]. This is well captured by our simulations: the standard variation (depicted as bars around the averaged graph in Figure 5) is large to account for the huge heterogeneity of that phase, but the trajectories are clear.

4.2 Model 2 - Single antiretroviral therapy

In the second model, we observe the changes in HIV growth when a single medication therapy is added. The simulation is initially the same as for model 1, since the therapy does not start until week Th_{start}. We use the beginning part of phase 2 (Th_{start}=20) as the treatment start time, and maintain the same value for all models in this paper. We may note that since this start time for therapy is earlier than in many real-life cases, the effectiveness shown may be a little higher than what is often encountered in the real-world. We did not investigate the consequences of changes in therapy

Table 1: **Simulation parameters for all three models**

Parameter	Description	Value	Source
n	size of each dimension of our square cellular automata grid	100	[41]
$\mathcal{X}$	Number of I2 cells in the neighbourhood of an H cell that can cause it to become infected	4	[10]
$\mathcal{P}_{HIV}$	Fraction (probability) of cells initially infected by virus	0.05	[43, 41]
$\mathcal{P}_i$	Probability of healthy cell becoming infected by neighbouring cells	0.997	[30, 41]
$\mathcal{P}_v$	Probability of healthy cell becoming infected by a random virus from outside neighbourhood	0.00001	[30],estimated
$\mathcal{P}_{rep}$	Probability of a dead cell becoming replaced by a healthy cell	0.99	[10]
$\mathcal{P}_{repI}$	Probability of a replaced dead cell of becoming infected	0.00001	[10]
τ_1	Time taken for an acute infected cell to become latent	4	[10]
τ_2	Time taken for a latent infected cell to become dead	1	[10]
τ_3	Time taken for a healthy cell with dual therapy to return to healthy state	1	[14]
$totalsteps$	Total number of steps of the CA (the total number of weeks of simulations)	600	[33],estimated
Th_{start}	Week on which therapy is initiated	20	[13],estimated
$\mathcal{P}_T$	Probability of presence of mono-therapy medication in cell	0.70	[14]
$\mathcal{P}_{infT}$	Probability of infection while being on mono-therapy	0.07	estimated
$\mathcal{P}_{T1}$	Probability of presence of therapy 1 medication in cell	0.70	[14]
$\mathcal{P}_{infT1}$	Probability of infection while being on therapy 1	0.07	estimated
$\mathcal{P}_{T2}$	Probability of presence of therapy 2 medication in cell	0.5	[14]
$\mathcal{P}_{infT2}$	Probability of infection while being on therapy 2	0.05	estimated

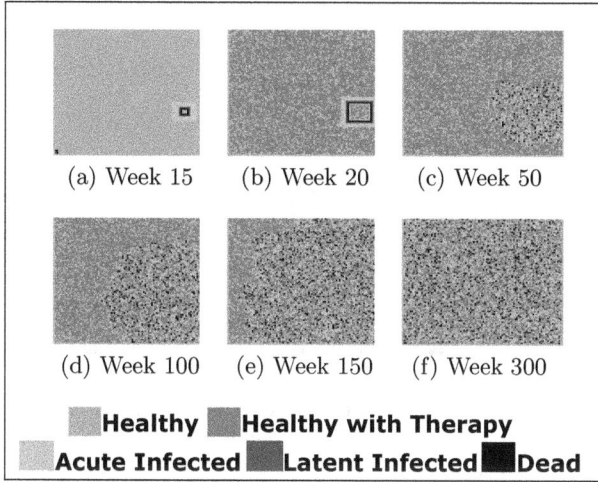

(a) Week 15   (b) Week 20   (c) Week 50

(d) Week 100   (e) Week 150   (f) Week 300

Healthy   **Healthy with Therapy**
Acute Infected   **Latent Infected**   **Dead**

Figure 6: **Sample simulation run for model 2 over 300 weeks, showing an infection starting at the bottom right and sparsely growing.**

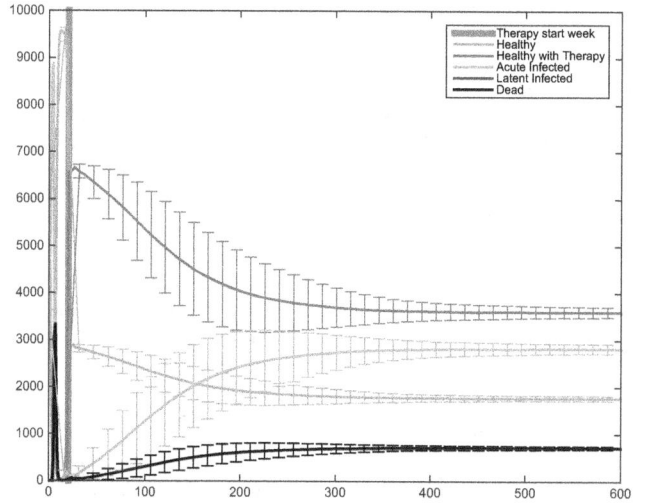

Figure 7: **Simulations for model 2 averaged across 1000 runs, with standard deviation shown as a bar across data points.**

start times on treatment effectiveness as this has been done in details elsewhere [14].

In model 2, the first phase (rise and fall of infected cells) is the same as in model 1 (Figures 4a-4d). However, once therapy is initiated, we begin to see a change in the trend for phase 2 (Figures 6b, 7). The beginning of therapy is depicted by a light-brown vertical line in Figure 7. As therapy starts, healthy cells are divided to either green (no therapy) or red (therapy) state. Cells receive therapy with a probability $\mathcal{P}_T$, which is determined by the effectiveness of the medication therapy. For this model we use a moderate effectiveness value of 0.7, and the same value is used again for one of the therapies in the dual therapy model in section 4.3, as well as in the different adherence simulations discussed in section 5. Since, the value of $\mathcal{P}_T$ is 0.7, we observe that the healthy cells are split to a larger number of H_T cells (70%)

and fewer H cells (30%). This is the reason for the red line to be plotted much higher than the green one in the graph, and for the simulation grid to be populated with more red cells than green ones.

We also introduce the new parameter $\mathcal{P}_{infT}$, which is the probability that a cell receiving medication becomes infected. This value was estimated after running the simulation for many different values of $\mathcal{P}_{infT}$. We utilized the value 0.07 for $\mathcal{P}_{infT}$, keeping the value very small to reflect decreased ability of a medicated cell to become infected.

Once the therapy starts, we observe that the infection continues to grow over many years, but at a slower pace compared to the situation without therapy. This is reflected in Figure 6a where the infection started at the bottom right on week 20, and it become more sparsely distributed even as it is growing on week 50 (Figure 6c). Although this infected region continues to grow as seen in week 100, 150, and 300, it does not create dense clusters as in model 1. This is because, in the neighbourhood of the infected cells, there are now more medicated cells that are less likely to become infected. Another confirmation is provided by Figure 7, which shows that the average count of healthy cells $(H + H_T)$ throughout the therapy is higher than it was in model 1. Thus, simulations confirm that adding therapy extends the second phase of the HIV process, causing the patient to live many years longer without immune system failure, as is expected in the real-world.

4.3 Model 3 - Dual antiretroviral therapy

In the third model, we add a second therapy in addition to the therapy from model 2, and observe the changes in HIV growth when the medication effects are combined. Just as in the second model, we begin therapy at week $Th_{start} = 20$, and start to see changes in the simulation. This is reflected in Figure 8-b and Figure 9. The different healthy states are represented in red (H_{T1}), magenta (H_{T2}), yellow (H_{Tb}) and green (H). Figure 9 shows the beginning of therapy at week 20 as a brown vertical line. As therapy begins, healthy cells either get into one of the three medication states (depending on the probability of receiving either or both types of therapy), or remain as healthy cells. This trend can be seen on week 20 when the healthy count (green line) reduces to a much lower number as it is replaced by the newly entering therapy states (red, magenta, and yellow).

The red count is much higher than the magenta count because different probabilities were associated with the two medication ($\mathcal{P}_{T1}$=0.7 versus $\mathcal{P}_{T2}$=0.5). Also note that, once all transitions are taken into account, the probability to transition to state H_{Tb} is 0.7, which is the same as $\mathcal{P}_{T1}$. This is shown in Figure 9, where the red H_{T1} count and the yellow H_{Tb} count overlap throughout the graph.

The results of the graph show that with dual combination therapy, the virus' growth is significantly slowed, causing the patient to have a low enough infection count for many more years than in the case of single or no therapy.

5. ADHERENCE SIMULATION

In the previous sections, we established a model of mono- and dual therapy whose dynamics were found to satisfactorily replicate real-world observations. In this section, we use these models to investigate the consequences of variations in adherence to treatment.

A significant issue with antiretroviral therapy treatment of HIV-infected individuals is that most do not take their medication at all times [31]. This can result in an increased viral load, but there is currently a limited understanding of the relationship between adherence and viral load [9, 23]. Creating models that take adherence into account has thus been an important endeavour for HIV research, as reviewed in [17]. This section contributes to that line of research by exploring the relationship between adherence and viral load.

We introduce adherence as a new probability $\mathcal{P}_{adh}$, which is the fraction of medication that is taken by the patient. That is, the larger the value, and the more the patient follows the treatment. This is also known as *taking compliance*, and it is one of several measures of adherence; others include checking for the correct number of doses (*correct dosing*) or taking doses following the schedule (*timing compliance*) [45]. Using compliance as a measure of adherence in HIV dynam-

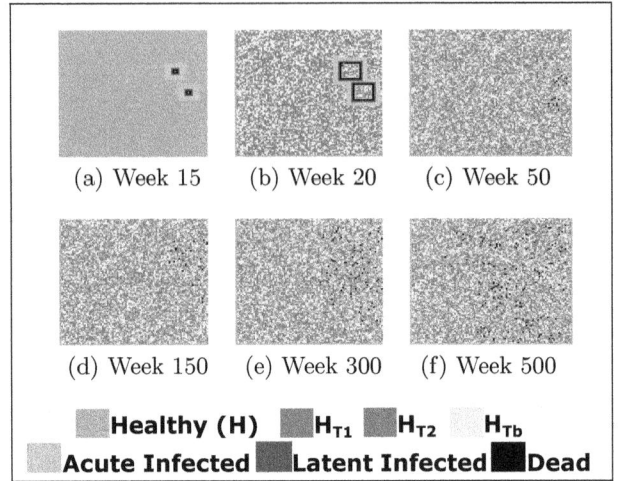

Figure 8: **Sample simulation run for model 3 over 500 weeks, showing a very slow growth for HIV.**

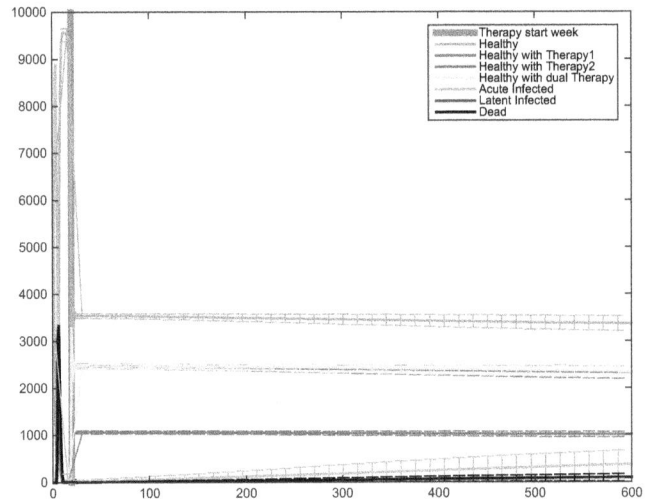

Figure 9: **Simulations for model 3 averaged across 1000 runs, with standard deviation shown as a bar across data points.**

ics was previously done in Huang *et al.*, although they took a macro-level perspective which did not explicitly represent cells and their neighbourhoods [19]. For example, they used a rate to represent how fast cells became infected, whereas we account for the fact that proximity with an infected cell results in a higher likelihood of infection.

We ran simulations for model 3 with different values of $\mathcal{P}_{adh}$. The relationship between the adherence $\mathcal{P}_{adh}$ and the total number of cells in each state (healthy, infected, dead) at 600 weeks is provided in Figure 10. A comparison of different levels of adherence over the course of the treatment is also provided in Figure 12 for an adherence of 90% (Figure 12a), 70% (Figure 12b), and 50% (Figure 12c).

As expected, Figure 10 shows that the number of acute infected cells increases as adherence decreases. What was unknown however was the shape of this relationship. We find that the relationship is non-linear: the number of acute infected cells picks up sharply as we move slightly away from full-adherence, whereas going from a low adherence to an even lower adherence has much less impact on the infec-

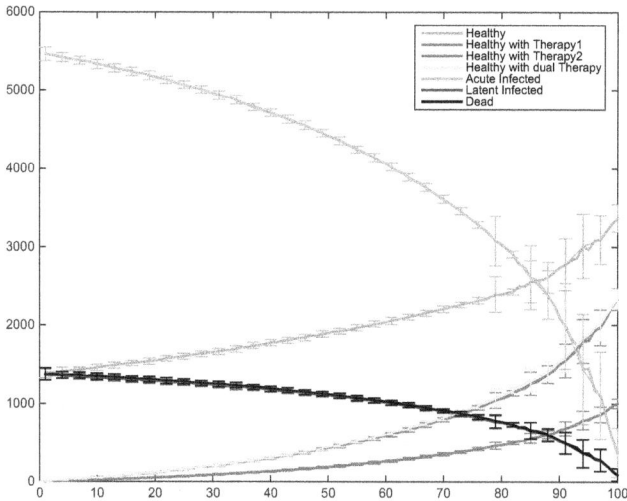

Figure 10: **Simulations for dual therapy with adherence averaged across 100 runs, with standard deviation shown as a bar across data points. Adherence goes from 0% (never takes medication; left) to 100% (always takes medication; right). Values are shown for week 600.**

tion. Consequently, an improvement in adherence by a few percentage points could have a very beneficial impact particularly for those who already have 80% adherence or above.

The relationship between dead cells and adherence has small but noteworthy differences with the relationship between acute infected cells and adherence, discussed above. While this relationship is still non-linear and a small improvement in adherence can still have a larger impact on cells' states, we note that the number of dead cells does not increase as fast with a decreasing adherence. Therefore, maintaining a high-level of adherence is still important but the impact of missing some medication is not as marked as could have been expected from the previous relationship.

Due to the structure of the model, the relationship between cells on treatment and adherence mirrors that of infected cells and adherence. To better understand the relationships, we investigated how the course of the virus changes for different levels of adherence (Figure 12). The final values of the different states were already provided in Figure 10: for example, we see a higher level of acute infected cells as the adherence decreases. Figure 12 informs us about *how* these values were reached: we observe that the time to reach a stable value decreases with a decreasing adherence. For example, the level of acute infected cells stabilized around week 200 for a 90% adherence (Figure 12a) whereas it stabilized around week 100 for an adherence of 50% (Figure 12c). This has an important consequence: individuals with lower adherence will not only experience adverse effects, but they will also experience them sooner.

While the simulations in Figures 10 and 12 were based on model 3 (dual therapy), we also performed the simulations using model 2 (mono-therapy). Results are shown in Figure 11. The results for adherence simulations for both model 2 and 3 confirm that a decreasing adherence leads to having more infected cells sooner, which can lead to faster progression of the disease.

Note that, in Figure 10, results (y-axis) represent the *final* values for the simulations at week 600 using different levels

of adherence (x-axis). Thus, each data point requires the full simulation to be performed. In contrast, in all other figures, results (y-axis) represent *intermediate* values for the simulation at each week (x-axis). Consequently, generating the results for Figure 10 can take up to an order of magnitude longer than any other figure. This resulted in computing the average and standard deviation across 100 runs of the simulation for Figure 10, while using 1000 runs for all other figures. Suggestions to speed-up the simulations are provided as part of the discussion section.

6. DISCUSSION

The Human Immunodeficiency Virus (HIV) has been a major health problem throughout the world for decades. Several discrete simulation models such as cellular automata have been developed to better understand the dynamics of the disease within the host [10, 43, 27]. In this paper, we used these previous models as a point of departure to incrementally develop a new detailed model. The model was developed to replicate the dynamics of HIV in the absence of therapy as well as with mono- and dual therapy. The dynamics of the model matched our expectations based on current knowledge about HIV.

While previous discrete models focused on the dynamics of HIV in response to treatment, we went one step further in linking the dynamics to the adherence to treatment. Adherence is indeed an important issue, as only about 20% to 35% of patients may have over 80% adherence for HIV antiretroviral regimens [31]. Defining 'sufficient' level of adherence has been a challenging question [9], which we set out to investigate using our new discrete simulations for HIV. We found non-linear relationships between adherence and prevalence of infected or dead cells, such that missing only a few medication could have a proportionally much larger impact on prevalence. This suggests that small improvements in adherence can be very beneficial, particularly for those whose adherence is already high. We also observed that a lack of adherence not only results in a higher prevalence of infected and dead cells, but also triggers these effects sooner. It is interesting to note that the same observation was made by Huang *et al.*, where a lack of adherence created an earlier rebound of the viral load [19]. While their observation was based on consecutive missed doses, our conclusion suggests that the same effect is found when doses are missed independently. Overall, this suggests that finding solutions to a lack of adherence early on could be very beneficial. The simulations performed in this research are thus important in giving us a practical tool to investigate the behavior of HIV, which is exemplified by studying antiretroviral therapy management for HIV-infected individuals.

There are several limitations to the new discrete simulations developed here, both at the conceptual and implementation stages. From a conceptual viewpoint, our models assume that drug efficacy was constant over time, which has been a common assumption in previous models of HIV [36]. However, there is considerable genetic diversity with HIV, and drug resistant mutations can emerge [19]. Consequently, real-world dynamics may be less favorable for the individual than depicted in our models. Our model also focused on capturing the first and second phases of the disease. We did not include the (final) third phase, which is when the immune system can no longer fight the infection (i.e., AIDS stage). Our emphasis on the first two phases results from

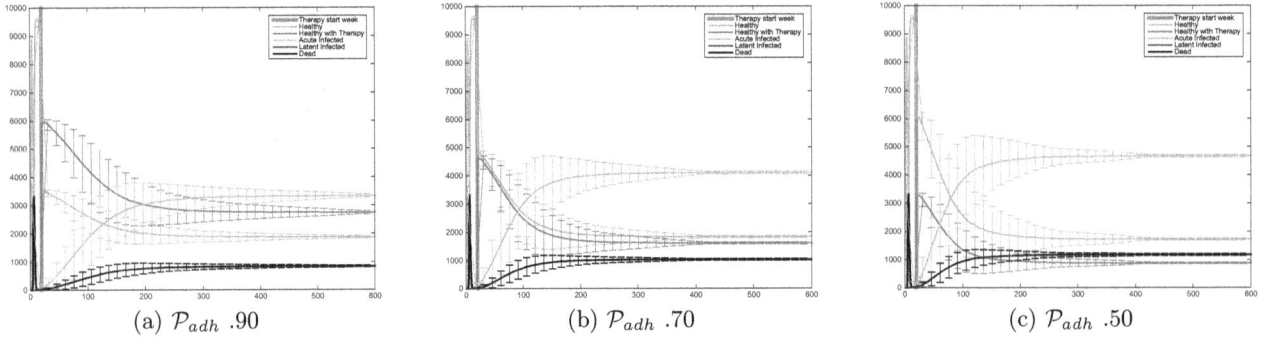

(a) $\mathcal{P}_{adh}$ .90   (b) $\mathcal{P}_{adh}$ .70   (c) $\mathcal{P}_{adh}$ .50

Figure 11: **Graphs of mono-therapy with adherence averaged over 1000 runs for different adherence values,** $\mathcal{P}_{adh}$

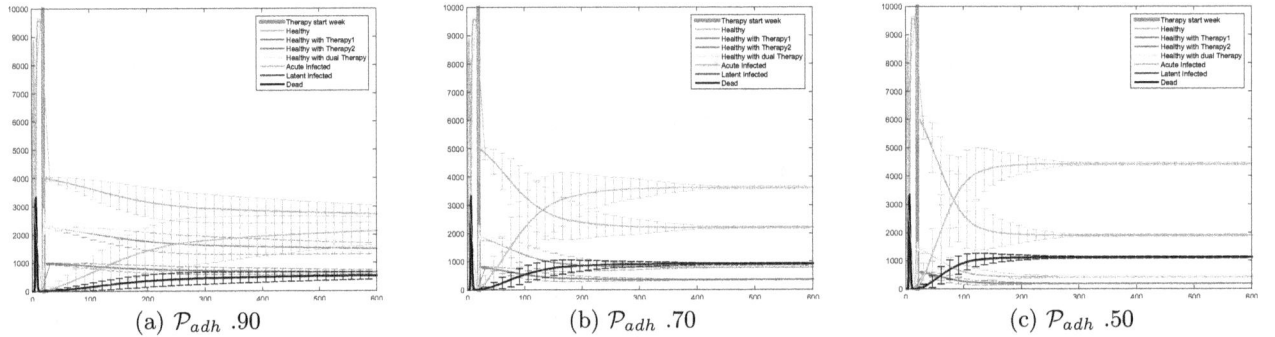

(a) $\mathcal{P}_{adh}$ .90   (b) $\mathcal{P}_{adh}$ .70   (c) $\mathcal{P}_{adh}$ .50

Figure 12: **Graphs of dual therapy with adherence averaged over 1000 runs for different adherence values,** $\mathcal{P}_{adh}$

our focus on therapies. Models interested in following individuals from infection onto death would need to extend our work to account for the final phase.

We conceptualized adherence as a constant probability throughout the simulation. In practice, adherence is known to decrease over time [5], which could be modelled by adjusting the probability as the simulation unfolds. In addition, it would be possible that an individual who does not take medication on one occasion is more likely to take it the next occasion. Thus, the probability at a given time may depend on the history. Finally, individuals who feel well may skip some medication, but have increased adherence when they start feeling unwell, which would require connecting the probability to the viral load. There is thus a range of possible scenarios in which the probability would depend on its previous values and other variables. Better capturing these scenarios is an interesting area for future work.

Another area of interest could be to improve the accuracy of the simulation in terms of the exact numbers of healthy, infected, or medicated cells. Similarly to previous research using cellular automata to investigate for the dynamics of HIV, our goal was to obtain a realistic timeline and trends for HIV. However, going beyond trajectories and being able to accurately report the exact number of cells in a specific state could be very valuable for clinical decision-making. For example, these numbers are used to make decisions such as when to start treatment. Different thresholds exist, from initiating treatment when the CD4 count cells under 350 cells/mm^3 [32], or earlier, when the count falls under 350 cells/mm^3 [25]. Being able to capture the consequences of these different thresholds in the simulation could contribute to research on the impact of guidelines to initiate treatment.

From an implementation viewpoint, our model relied on a 2-dimensional cellular automaton where each cell was represented as a grid. This has typically been the approach used in previous cellular automata models. However, HIV naturally spreads in a volume (3 dimensions). In addition, using square cells creates a further restriction. Consequently, future models could be designed in 3 dimensions with more degrees of freedom. One solution would be to replace the traditional square grid by a Face Centered Cubic (FCC) arrangement. The neighbourhood of a cell is represented in Figure 13a while the overall configuration is shown in Figure 13b. The same sets of rules could then be run on this new structure [3]. In addition to changing the structure, the implementation can also be improved. Cellular automata can parallelize well [4] but the rules play an important role as to which way of parallelizing is most efficient (e.g., multi core, GPU-based) [42]. While our simulation do not have information flows between distant cells (hence facilitating a parallel implementation), storing all states at each time step limits the improvement from a parallel solution (c.f. [42] for a comparison of a GPU solution with and without readback).

Most discrete simulation studies have looked into specific features of HIV treatment. However, there is currently no model that can account for multiple types of medications, and incorporate medication scheduling, adherence, viral resistance to medication, as well as decreased ability of immune response in the late-stage of the disease. Since all these features occur together, such comprehensive discrete model would be ideal in observing all these aspects of antiretroviral therapy and their combined effects on the host body. While our models are one more step in this direction,

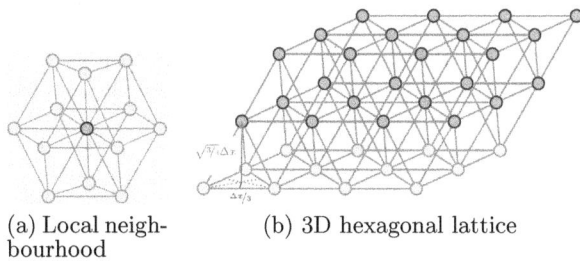

(a) Local neighbourhood   (b) 3D hexagonal lattice

Figure 13: **A 3-dimensional structure that could be used to show the spread of HIV within a volume.**

a lot of work still remains in tying the biological dynamics to the complexity of therapies.

7. ACKNOWLEDGMENTS

The authors would like to thank Hongyu Ma, Sushrutha Kanuganti and Amit Kumar from the Department of Computer Science at Troy University (Troy, AL) for assistance in idea formulation. The authors also benefited from the feedback of Dr Ralph Pantophlet from the Faculty of Health Sciences at Simon Fraser University (Burnaby, BC). As part of the Centre for Diet and Activity Research (CEDAR), a UKCRC Public Health Research Centre of Excellence, PJG acknowledges partial funding from the British Heart Foundation, CRUK, ESRC, MRC, NIHR, and the Wellcome Trust, via the UK Clinical Research Collaboration.

8. REFERENCES

[1] AIDS.gov. HIV lifecycle, 2009. URL: `https://www.aids.gov/hiv-aids-basics/just-diagnosed-with-hiv-aids/hiv-in-your-body/hiv-lifecycle/` [cited April 10, 2015].

[2] AIDS.gov. CD4 count, 2014. URL: `https://aids.gov/hiv-aids-basics/just-diagnosed-with-hiv-aids/understand-your-test-results/cd4-count` [cited April 10, 2015].

[3] L. Bakker and A. Poelstra. Calculating hyphal surface area in models of fungal networks. *Biomath*, 2(1):1309087, 2013.

[4] S. Bandini, G. Mauri, and R. Serra. Cellular automata: from a theoretical parallel computational model to its application to complex systems. *Parallel Comput*, 27(5):539–553, 2001.

[5] J. Bartlett. Addressing the challenges of adherence. *J. Acquir. Immune Defic. Syndr.*, 29(S1):2–10, 2002.

[6] J. Burgos, M. Crespo, et al. Simplification to dual antiretroviral therapy including a ritonavir-boosted protease inhibitor in treatment-experienced HIV-1-infected patients. *J Antimicrob Chemother*, 67(10):2479–2486, 2012.

[7] J. Castilla, D. Romero, et al. Effectiveness of highly active antiretroviral therapy in reducing heterosexual transmission of HIV. *J. Acquir. Immune Defic. Syndr.*, 40(1):96–101, 2005.

[8] CDC. About HIV/AIDS, 2014. URL: `http://www.cdc.gov/hiv/basics/whatishiv.html` [cited April 10, 2015].

[9] M. Dahab, S. Charalambous, R. Hamilton, K. Fielding, G. Churchyard, and A. Grant. 'That is why i stopped the ART': patients' & providers' perspectives on barriers to and enablers of HIV treatment adherence in a south african workplace programme. *BMC Public Health*, 18(8):63, 2008.

[10] R. M. Z. dos Santos and S. Coutinho. Dynamics of HIV infection: A cellular automata approach. *Phys Rev Lett*, 87(16):168102, 2001.

[11] C. Eslahchi, H. Pezeshk, M. Sadeghi, P. Giabbanelli, F. Movahedi, and V. Dabbaghian. A probabilistic model for the spread of HIV infection among injection drug users. *WJMS*, 6(4):267–273, 2010.

[12] G. Friedland and A. Williams. Attaining higher goals in hiv treatment: the central importance of adherence. *AIDS*, 13(S1):61–72, 1999.

[13] C. Gay, O. Dibben, et al. Cross-sectional detection of acute hiv infection: timing of transmission, inflammation and antiretroviral therapy. *PLoS One*, 6(5):e19617, 2011.

[14] R. E. Gonzalez, S. Coutinho, R. M. Zorzenon dos Santos, and P. H. de Figueire. Dynamics of the HIV infection under antiretroviral therapy: A cellular automata approach. *Physica A*, 392(19):4701–4716, 2013.

[15] R. M. Granich, C. F. Gilks, C. Dye, K. M. de Cock, and B. G. Williams. Universal voluntary HIV testing with immediate antiretroviral therapy as a strategy for elimination of HIV transmission: A mathematical model. *The Lancet*, 373(9657):48–57, 2009.

[16] B. Grinsztejn, Hosseinipour, et al. Effects of early versus delayed initiation of antiretroviral treatment on clinical outcomes of hiv-1 infection: results from the phase 3 hptn 052 randomised controlled trial. *Lancet Infect Dis*, 14(4):281–290, 2014.

[17] J. M. Heffernan and L. M. Wahl. Treatment interruptions and resistance: a review. In W.-Y. Tan and H. Wu, editors, *Deterministic and stochastic models of AIDS epidemics and HIV infections with intervention*. World Scientific, Singapore, 2005.

[18] HHS. Guidelines for the use of antiretroviral agents in HIV-1-infected adults and adolescents, 2015. URL: `http://aidsinfo.nih.gov/guidelines/html/1/adult-and-adolescent-treatment-guidelines/0` [cited April 10, 2015].

[19] Y. Huang, S. L. Rosenkranz, and H. Wu. Modeling hiv dynamics and antiviral response with consideration of time-varying drug exposures, adherence and phenotypic sensitivity. *Math Biosci*, 184(2):165–186, 2003.

[20] R. M. Jafelice, B. Bechara, L. C. Barros, R. C. Bassanezi, and F. Gomide. Cellular automata with fuzzy parameters in microscopic study of positive HIV individuals. *Math Comput Model*, 50(1):32–44, 2009.

[21] E. H. Kaplan. Needles that kill: modeling human immunodeficiency virus transmission via shared drug injection equipment in shooting galleries. *Rev Infect Dis*, 11(2):289–298, 1989.

[22] M. M. Kitahata, S. J. Gange, et al. Effect of early versus deferred antiretroviral therapy for hiv on survival. *NEJM*, 360(18):1815–1826, 2009.

[23] A. Kobin and N. Sheth. Levels of adherence required for virologic suppression among newer antiretroviral medications. *Ann Pharmacother*, 45(3):372–379, 2011.

[24] M. Kretzschmar and L. G. Wiessing. Modelling the spread of HIV in social networks of injecting drug users. *AIDS*, 12(7):801–811, 1998.

[25] B. Lebouche, K. Engler, et al. HIV experts on the decision to use early art for prevention in france: are we there yet? *Retrovirology*, 9(S1):95, 2012.

[26] V. K. Mago, L. Bakker, E. I. Papageorgiou, A. Alimadad, P. Borwein, and V. Dabbaghian. Fuzzy cognitive maps and cellular automata: An evolutionary approach for social systems modelling. *Appl Soft Comput*, 12(12):3771–3784, 2012.

[27] Y. Mo, B. Ren, W. Yang, and J. Shuai. The 3-dimensional cellular automata for HIV infection. *Physica A*, 399:31–39, 2014.

[28] J. S. Montagner, H. C. Cote, et al. Nucleoside-related mitochondrial toxicity among HIV-infected patients receiving antiretroviral therapy: Insights from the evaluation of venous lactic acid and peripheral blood mitochondrial dna. *Clin Infect Dis*, 38(S2):S73–S79, 2004.

[29] S. Moonchai, Y. Lenbury, and W. Triampo. Multiple latticed cellular automata: HIV dynamics in coupled lymph node and peripheral blood compartments. In *Proceedings of the 2nd WSEAS Conf on ACS (Iwate, Japan, October 4–6, 2010)*. WSEAS, 56–61, 2010.

[30] S. Moonchai, Y. Lenbury, and W. Triampo. Cellular automata simulation modeling of HIV infection in lymph node and peripheral blood compartments. *Int. J. Math. Comp. Sim*, 4(4):124–134, 2010.

[31] R. E. Nelson, J. R. Nebeker, C. Hayden, L. Reimer, K. Kome, and J. LaFleur. Comparing adherence to two different HIV antiretroviral regimens: An instrumental variable analysis. *AIDS Behav*, 17(1):160–167, 2013.

[32] NIH. Guidelines for the use of antiretroviral agents in hiv-1-infected adults and adolescents, 2014. URL: `http://aidsinfo.nih.gov/guidelines/html/1/adult-and-adolescent-arv-guidelines/10/initiating-art-in-treatment-naive-patients` [cited April 10, 2015].

[33] NIH. The HIV life cycle, 2015. URL: `http://aidsinfo.nih.gov/education-materials/fact-sheets/19/73/the-hiv-life-cycle` [cited April 10, 2015].

[34] M. Nowak and R. M. May. *Virus dynamics: mathematical principles of immunology and virology*. Oxford University Press, Oxford, 2000.

[35] G. Pantaleo, C. Graziosi, and A. S. Fauci. The immunopathogenesis of human immunodeficiency virus infection. *NEJM*, 328(5):327–335, 1993.

[36] A. Perelson and P. Nelson. Mathematical analysis of HIV-1 dynamics in vivo. *SIAM Rev*, 41(1):3–44, 1999.

[37] T. C. Porco, J. N. Martin, et al. Decline in HIV infectivity following the introduction of highly active antiretroviral therapy. *AIDS*, 18(1):81, 2004.

[38] S. F. Pratt, P. J. Giabbanelli, P. Jackson, and V. K. Mago. Rebel with many causes: A computational model of insurgency. In *Proceedings of the IEEE Int Conf on ISI (Washington DC, USA, June 11–14, 2012)*. IEEE, 90–95, 2012.

[39] M. Precharattana, A. Nokkeaw, W. Triampo, D. Triampo, and Y. Lenbury. Stochastic cellular automata model and monte carlo simulations of CD4+ t cell dynamics with a proposed alternative leukapheresis treatment for HIV/AIDS. *Comput Biol Med*, 41(7):546–558, 2011.

[40] M. Precharattana and W. Triampo. Modeling dynamics of HIV infected cells using stochastic cellular automaton. *Physica A*, 407:303–311, 2014.

[41] M. Precharattana, W. Triampo, C. Modchang, D. Triampo, and Y. Lenbury. Investigation of spatial pattern formation involving CD4+ T cells in HIV/AIDS dynamics by a stochastic cellular automata model. *Int. J. Math. Comp. Sim*, 4(4):135–143, 2010.

[42] S. Rybacki, J. Himmelspach, and A. M. Uhrmacher. Experiments with single core, multi core, and gpu-based computation of cellular automata. In *Proceedings of the 1st Int Conf on SIMUL (Porto, Portugal, September 20–25, 2009)*. IEEE, 62–67, 2009.

[43] V. Shi, A. Tridane, and Y. Kuang. A viral load-based cellular automata approach to modeling HIV dynamics and drug treatment. *J Theor Biol*, 253(1):24–35, 2008.

[44] P. M. Sloot, P. V. Coveney, G. Ertaylan, V. Mueller, C. Boucher, and M. Bubak. HIV decision support: from molecule to man. *Phil. Trans. R. Soc. A*, 367(1898):2691–2703, 2009.

[45] B. Vrijens and E. Goetghebeur. Comparing compliance patterns between randomized treatments. *Control Clin Trials*, 18(3):187–203, 1997.

[46] A. White. Mitochondrial toxicity and HIV therapy. *Sex Transm Infect*, 77(3):158–173, 2001.

[47] WHO. HIV/AIDS fact sheet, 2014. URL: `http://www.who.int/mediacentre/factsheets/fs360/en/` [cited April 10, 2015].

[48] H. Wu, Y. Huang, et al. Modeling long-term hiv dynamics and antiretroviral response: Effects of drug potency, pharmacokinetics, adherence, and drug resistance. *J. Acquir. Immune Defic. Syndr.*, 39(3):272–283, 2005.

NTW-MT: a Multi-threaded Simulator for Reaction Diffusion Simulations in NEURON

Zhongwei Lin[*]
National University of Defense Technology
Changsha, Hunan, China
zwlin@nudt.edu.cn

Carl Tropper
School of Computer Science
McGill University
Montreal, Quebec, Canada
carl@cs.mcgill.ca

Mohammand Nazrul Ishlam Patoary
School of Computer Science
McGill University
Montreal, Quebec, Canada
nazrul.eis@gmail.com

Robert A. McDougal
Department of Neurobiology
Yale University
333 Cedar St. New Haven, Connecticut, USA
robert.mcdougal@yale.edu

William W. Lytton
SUNY Downstate Medical Center
Brooklyn, NY, 11203, USA
blytton@downstate.edu

Michael L. Hines
Department of Neurobiology
Yale University
New Haven, Connecticut, USA
michael.hines@yale.edu

ABSTRACT

This paper describes a parallel discrete event simulator, Neuron Time Warp-Multi Thread (NTW-MT), developed for the simulation of reaction diffusion models of neurons. The simulator was developed as part of the NEURON project and is intended to be included in NEURON. It relies upon a stochastic discrete event model developed for chemical reactions. NTW-MT is optimistic and thread-based, in which communication latency among threads within the same process is minimized by pointers. We investigate the performance of NTW-MT on a reaction-diffusion model for the transmission of calcium waves in a neuron. Calcium plays a fundamental role in the second messenger system of a neuron. However, the mechanism by which calcium waves are transmitted is not entirely understood. Stochastic models are more realistic than deterministic models for small populations of ions such as those found in apical dendrites. To be more precise, we simulate a stochastic discrete event model for calcium wave propagation on an unbranched apical dendrite of a hippocampal pyramidal neuron. We examine the performance of NTW-MT on this calcium wave model and compare it to the performance of (1) a process based optimistic simulator and (2) a threaded simulator which uses a single priority (SQ) queue for each thread. Our multi-threaded simulator is shown to achieve superior performance to these simulators.

Categories and Subject Descriptors

D.1.3 [**Programming Techniques**]: Concurrent Programming—*parallel programming*; I.6.8 [**Simulation and Modeling**]: Types of Simulation—*parallel, distributed, discrete event*

General Terms

Algorithms, Design, Performance

Keywords

Stochastic Neuronal Simulation, PDES, Multiple Thread

1. INTRODUCTION

The human brain may be viewed as a sparsely connected network of neurons [3] containing approximately 10^{14} neurons. Each neuron receives inputs from thousands of dendrites and sends outputs to thousands of neurons by means of its axon.

The membrane of a neuron contains channels which selectively control the flow of ions (primarily sodium, potassium, and calcium) through the membrane. Movements of ions through these channels is by (1) diffusion from a higher concentration of ions or (2) by pumps which are dependent on the voltage drop across the membrane. Electrical models for neurons [14] can be constructed using the well-known laws of electricity (Ohm, Kirchhoff, capacitance). However, these electrical models only provide a limited view of neuronal activity since there are ions (notably calcium) which

[*]This author is affiliated with State Key Laboratory of High Performance Computing at National University of Defense Technology.

function as information messengers. In order to develop realistic models of a neuron, it is necessary to develop models which account for the movement and functioning of these messengers.

The combination of chemical reactions within a cell with the diffusion of ions through the membrane can be modelled as a reaction diffusion system and simulated by (parabolic) partial differential equations [3, 14]. However, a continuous model is not appropriate for a small number of molecules. Stochastic model is a far more realistic and accurate representation [23, 20] for this sort of situation.

It is well known that a system consisting of a collection of chemical reactions can be represented by a chemical master equation, the solution of which is a probability distribution of the chemical reactants in the system [23]. In general, it is very difficult to solve this equation. In [9] a Monte Carlo simulation algorithm called the Stochastic Simulation Algorithm (SSA) is described. Under the assumption that the molecules of the system are uniformly distributed, the algorithm simulates a single trajectory of the chemical system. Simulating a number of these trajectories then gives a picture of the system. The Next sub-volume Method (NSM) [8] is an extension of the SSA which incorporates the diffusion of molecules into the model. The NSM partitions space into cubes called sub-volumes, and it can be applied to PDES by representing sub-volumes as Logical Processes (LP) [24]. Diffusion of ions between neighboring sub-volumes is represented as events. NTW-MT relies on the NSM algorithm.

NEURON [4, 3] is a widely used simulator in the neuroscience community. It makes use of deterministic simulators for the reaction diffusion model [15] and for electrical models. We are collaborating with the NEURON group; our intention is to develop parallel discrete event simulators suitable for simulating the reaction diffusion models. It is intended that our simulators will be integrated into NEURON. We previously developed a process based simulator, NTW [18], which makes use of a multi-level queue. We verified and examined its performance on a Calcium buffer model and a predator prey [21] model. The queueing structure described in this paper and the one in [18] are outgrowths of the multi-level queue described in XTW [27].

The remainder of this paper is organized as follows. Section 2 describes the related work, section 3 is devoted to the architecture and algorithms of our simulator, section 4 describes our experimental results. The conclusion and future work are presented in section 5.

2. RELATED WORK

[6] points out that a conservative synchronization algorithm for parallel simulation will perform poorly because of the zero-lookahead property of the exponential distribution and the fact that a dependency graph of the reactions is likely to be highly connected and filled with loops. This indicates that an optimistic synchronization algorithm such as Time Warp is preferable. [25] presents an experimental analysis of several optimistic protocols for the parallel simulation of a reaction-diffusion system. [13] uses NSM in an optimistic simulation along with an adaptive time window. [12] compares the performance of spatial τ-leaping with that of NSM and Gillespie's Multi-particle Method (GMPM) in terms of speedup and accuracy.

There are two main schemes for the storage of the pending events for each thread, a global queue and separated (dis-

tributed) queue. In a global queue, a number of threads (Processing Elements, PE) share a single priority queue. This achieves load sharing at the expense of contention at the queue, e.g. threaded WARPED [16]. The main drawback of this scheme is too much contention on the global queue [5]. In a separated queue, each worker thread has its own priority queue and only processes events from this queue. However, there are still concurrent operations on the priority queue arising from other threads in the same process. In order to avoid locking the contents of individual LPs, each LP is mapped to only one specific thread. This may lead to a load imbalance, so it is necessary to balance the workload for threads and processes. [5] uses a separated queue and proposes a global scheduling mechanism to balance the workload between the threads in the same process. A global scheduling mechanism was employed for load balancing, decreasing the contention and improving performance. However, a global schedule still allows simultaneous processing of events at individual LPs, necessitating a locking mechanism. ROSS-MT [10] also employs a separated queue and uses an input queue to store the events sent from other threads. Contention on the input queue remains high. A hybrid scheme combines the above two schemes by creating several priority queues within one process and mapping a subset of the threads to a single queue, as described in [7].

3. ARCHITECTURE

We employ a separated priority queue scheme in our architecture. The simulator architecture is depicted in figure 1. One of the processes is a controller, exercising global control functions (GVT computation (Mattern's algorithm) and load balancing). The remaining processes are worker processes which process the events at the LPs which reside in the process. Each worker process contains a *communication thread* and several *processing threads*. All of the worker processes have the same number of threads.

The communication thread sends and receives messages for a process. Processing threads cannot send or receive messages. After initialization, the communication thread receives messages from shared memory, in which case the the message is from a *family process* residing in the same node (see section 3.3) or via MPI from remote nodes. Control messages are the first messages to be processed. LPs then schedule external events by placing them into the send buffer of the communication thread. To avoid contention for this buffer, it is partitioned into m segments, where m is the number of processing threads. The ith processing thread can write only into the ith segment. The communication thread scans the segments in the buffer and then sends out the messages. At present, the communication thread sends only one message per segment (a fairness policy).

LPs are partitioned into $m \times n$ subsets, where n is the number of worker processes and m is the number of processing threads. Each subset is mapped to a processing thread. Each processing thread includes a *LP List* which stores the LPs associated with the thread, a *Thread Event Queue* (TEQ), a *Thread Memory Allocator* which is involved in the Memory Management and a *Thread Function*. The Thread Function is responsible for processing the events, and is portrayed in figure 2.

An event has two timestamps, the receive time and the send time [11]. The events in the priority queue are sorted by their receive time. There are two types of events: *internal*

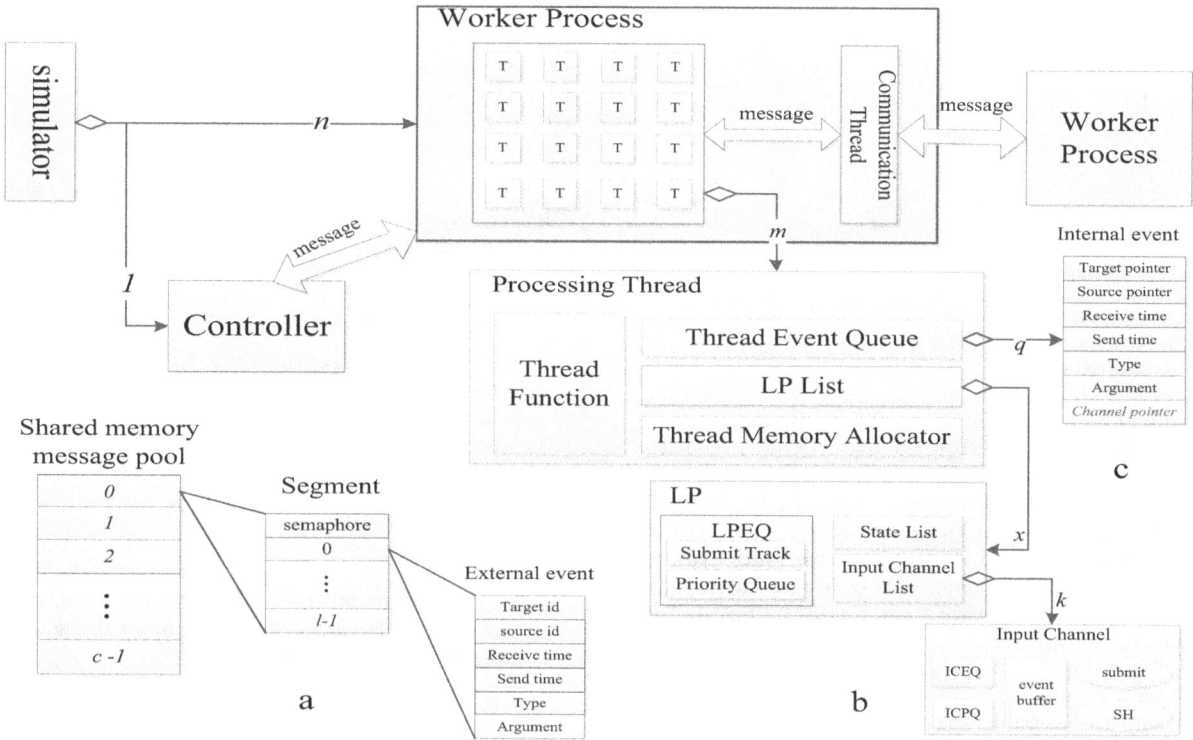

Figure 1: Architecture of NTW-MT simulator.

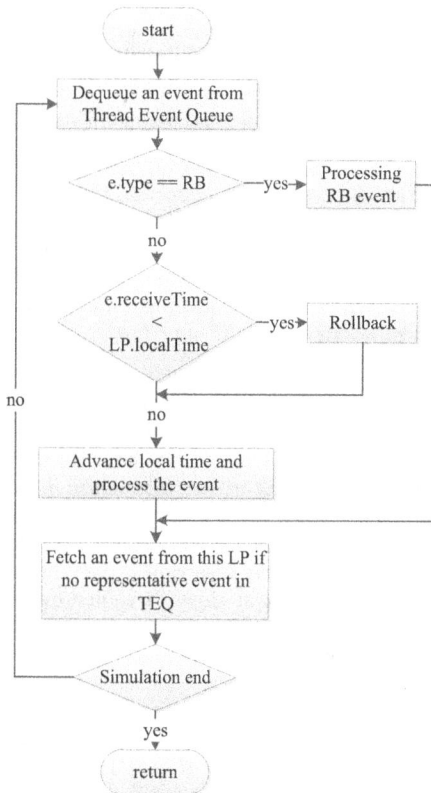

Figure 2: Processing sequence of a PE.

events which are scheduled by internal processing threads and *external events* from external processing threads. As the processing threads share the same memory space, internal events use a pointer to identify LPs. A PE can use this pointer to access the LP directly. External events use an integer identifier to represent LPs. They are converted into internal events upon receipt by a communication thread and are then inserted into LPs.

3.1 Multi-Level Queuing

Every thread in a process can access any priority queue in the same process, which can cause excessive contention [7]. To further aggravate matters, during a roll-back processed events with a timestamp greater than the receive time are re-enqueued in the priority queue. Two ways are used to alleviate this contention (1) decreasing the probability by which a few threads can access the same queue and (2) decreasing the cost of a single operation on a queue.

Consider the example in figure 3. In a stochastic neuronal simulation, the virtual time increment can vary from 0 to a large value. The diagram in figure 3 depicts 6 LPs (rounded rectangles) which are distributed over three processes (dashed rectangles). The number in each LP is the Local Virtual Time (LVT) of the LP (also used to identify the LP). Each arrow represents an event. The number on each arrow is the timestamp of the event (receive time, send time).

In figure 3 event (12,10) is a straggler at LP 15, and the dashed-lined-events at LP 16 are pending events. LP 16 has four pending events which would be stored in a queue. One may notice that it is not necessary to store and sort all four events in the TEQ- only event (18,14) needs to stay in the

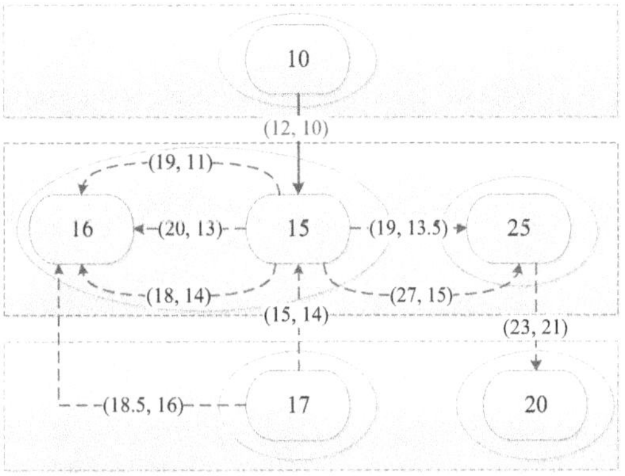

Figure 3: This example shows 6 LPs (rounded rectangles) which are distributed over three processes (dashed rectangles). Some are located in the same processing thread(an ellipse). The number in each LP is the local virtual time of the LP, and is also used to identify the LP. Each arrow indicates an event.The number on each arrow is the timestamp of the event (receive time, send time). Some LPs and events are omitted.

TEQ. There are several reasons for this: (1) some insertions in the TEQ can be omitted, decreasing the probability of contention. (2) the size of the TEQ can be controlled and the cost of an operation eliminated. Events (20,13) and (18,14) would be cancelled due to the roll-back of LP 15, hence sorting them is wasteful. (3) to cancel an event which would not access the TEQ decreases the probability of contention. Suppose that (1) a PE holds x LPs, numbered from 0 to $x-1$ (2) S_i is the Pending Event Set (PES) of LP_i and that the events in S_i are in non-decreasing order in receive time. The minimum pending event of LP_i is $minPE_i$. It is easy to prove that $minPE$ in PES is equal to the $min\{minPE_i, i = 0, 1, \cdots, x-1\}$. Therefore the PE only needs to compare each $minPE_i$ to find $minPE$. This indicates that any LP only needs to have one representative event in TEQ. The remaining events are stored in the LP Event Queue (LPEQ). Each LP has a LPEQ and all the LPEQs are linked to the corresponding TEQ.

In a three-dimensional environment, space is partitioned by a mesh grid, resulting in a maximum of 6 neighbors for each LP. Molecules diffuse through channels between these neighbors. We use an input channel to receive events from a neighbor and store them in an Input Channel Event Queue (ICEQ). All of the ICEQs are linked to the corresponding LPEQ.

To control the size of a queue, a lower level queue can only submit an *urgent event* (definition 1 below) to an upper level queue. A lower level queue records the unprocessed events which have been submitted to an upper level queue, and checks to see if an event is urgent when it receives it. Every input channel has a variable *submit* of event pointer which refers to the lower bound of unprocessed events which have been submitted to the LPEQ. Every LPEQ has a stack structure *submitTrack* which traces the unprocessed events which have been submitted to its TEQ. At the input channel level, urgency is checked by comparing the receive time of event e_x and *submit* of this channel. Because the LPEQ receives events from several input channels, it may submit

several events to the TEQ, and there may be several pointers in *submitTrack*, hence urgency is checked by comparing the receive time of event e_x and the *top* element of this stack. In a reaction-diffusion simulation an event can have smaller receive time then a predecessor, thereby leading to the creation of an urgent event (see the example below).

Definition 1. An event e_x^i in a queue q_x^i at level i is urgent if its receive time is less than the receive time of any events e_y^j in its upper level queue q_y^j at level j ($j > i$).

At this point, we have three level queuing architecture, as shown in part b of figure 1. The queuing works as follows.

- In the initialize phase, the TEQ, LPEQ and input channels are constructed, *submitTrack* of LPEQ is empty and *submit* of input channel is set to 0. Each LP schedules an *initial* event to itself and adds it to its TEQ and then add the *initial* event to *submitTrack*.

- Any processing thread and communication thread can insert events into a LP. To insert an event e, a thread first identifies the target LP_x by routing and checks if it is located in the same process. If not, this event will be added to the send buffer of the communication thread. If so it is inserted in the target LP as follows.

  1. Apply memory, find the target LP LP_x, fill in the *Targetpointer* field of this event by the pointer to LP_x.
  2. Determine the input channel $channel_x$, fill in the *Channel Pointer* field of this event by the pointer to $channel_x$, check whether it is urgent. If it is not urgent, insert it into ICEQ. Otherwise submit it to the LPEQ and update *submit*.
  3. At the LPEQ level, check urgency. If it is not urgent, insert it into LPEQ. Otherwise submit it to TEQ and insert its pointer to the *top* of *submitTrack*.
  4. At the TEQ level, insert this event into the TEQ.

- After processing an event from input channel $channel_s$, a PE fetches an event from $channel_s$ to make sure that there is a representative in the LPEQ, updates *submit* of $channel_s$, then inserts the new event in the LPEQ. At the level of the LPEQ, this PE checks *submitTrack* and the smallest event in LPEQ at that time to determine whether to submit an event to the TEQ or not.

In the example in figure 3, LP 16 has two neighbors LP 15 and 17. Event (19, 11) comes from LP 15, arriving at channel [16, 15] (a channel is marked in the format [host LP, source LP]), finds *submit* of this channel to be 0, and is submitted to the LPEQ of LP 16, *submit* is set to (19, 11); *submitTrack* of LPEQ 16 is empty. Then this event is submitted to TEQ, the pointer to (19, 11) is pushed at the *top* of *submitTrack* and the insertion of (19, 11) now ends. It is in the TEQ, where it at time $T1$. Then event (20, 13) arrives at channel [16, 15]. It is not urgent and thus stays in ICEQ. This insertion ends at time $T2$. Event (18, 14) arrives, and is found to be urgent for channel [16, 15], then it is submitted to the LPEQ; it is also urgent for LPEQ 16, and is submitted to the TEQ. The *top* of *submitTrack* becomes the pointer to event (18, 14) at time $T3$. Event (18.5, 16) from LP 17 arrives at channel [16, 17], finds *submit* to be 0, and is submitted to LPEQ 16. *submit* is set as a pointer to (18.5, 16) at time $T4$. The successive insertions depend upon the relationship of the above time points.

160

- $T4 < T1$, this implies this event arrives before any events from LP 15. (18.5, 16) will be submitted to TEQ, (19, 11) will stay at LPEQ 16, (18, 14) will be submitted to TEQ, (20, 13) stays at ICEQ [16, 15]. *top* of *submitTrack* is pointer to (18, 14) followed by pointer to (18.5, 16).

- $T1 < T4 < T2$, event (18.5, 16) is urgent and will be submitted to TEQ. Event (18, 14) is also urgent when it arrives at LPEQ 16. In this case, there are three events, (18, 14), (18.5, 16) and (19, 11), in TEQ.

- $T2 < T4$, event (18.5, 16) is not urgent when it arrives at LPEQ 16, thus stays at LPEQ 16. Two event, (19, 11) and (18, 14) are submitted to TEQ.

3.2 RB-Message

XTW [27] uses one RB-message to cancel incorrect events instead of sending a series of anti-messages, eliminating the need for an output queue at each LP thereby reducing the overhead of a roll-back.

When a LP receives a straggler, it rolls back to a point in time prior to the time of the straggler and then processes the straggler, as shown in figure 4. A LP does not store the processed events which were scheduled by itself. Processed events scheduled by other LPs are stored in the appropriate Input Channel Processed Queue (ICPQ). Note that the straggler may be not the processed event with smallest event because a processed event may have been sent from the TEQ.

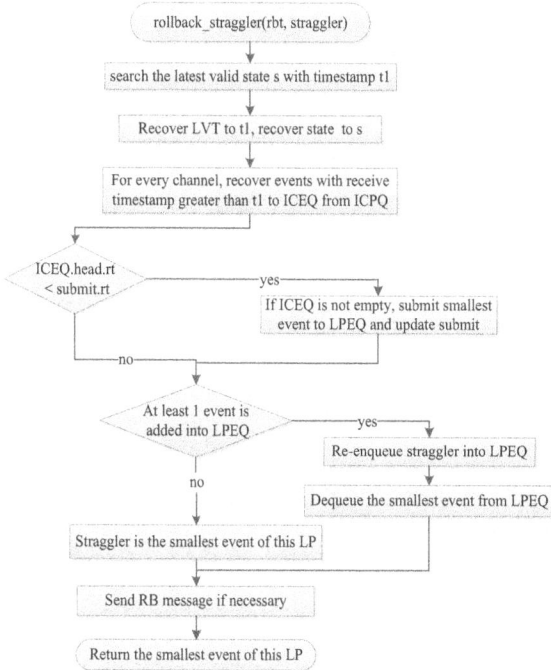

Figure 4: Steps for roll-back caused by straggler, *head* is the smallest event in any queue. rt(st) is receive time (send time).

In the above example, the message (12, 10) sent by LP 10 to LP 15 is a straggler, so LP 15 should roll back to a point in time before time 12. Suppose a state at 11.5 is found, and the states with timestamp greater than 11.5 are released. After that, LP 15 recovers processed events

with timestamp greater than 11.5, finds the smallest event and sends RB-messages to its neighbors, LP 16 and LP 25. However, it is not really necessary to send a RB message to every neighbour; we use a variable *ScheduleHistory* (SH) [18] in the input channel in figure 1. SH records the upper bound of the send times of events sent to a LP. The use of SH can avoid sending unnecessary RB messages. For example, the local virtual time of LP i is 100, its input channel[0].SH is 80 (this indicates that it did not schedule any event to this neighbour after 80) and input channel[1].SH is 90. Assume that LP i receives a straggler and needs to roll back to 88. It is easy to assert that a RB message should be sent to the neighbour related to input channel[1] whereas there is no need to send a RB message to the neighbour related to input channel[0].

RB-messages has a higher priority $RB\_PRIORITY$, a negative real constant, than other normal events, the send time of RB-message is set as the present LVT of the LP which sends it. A RB-message ($RB\_PRIORITY$, t_{rb}) sent from LP x to LP y announces that LP x has rolled back to t_{rb}, then the pre-sent events with send time greater than t_{rb} becomes invalid. LP y follows the steps in figure 5 to process RB-messages.

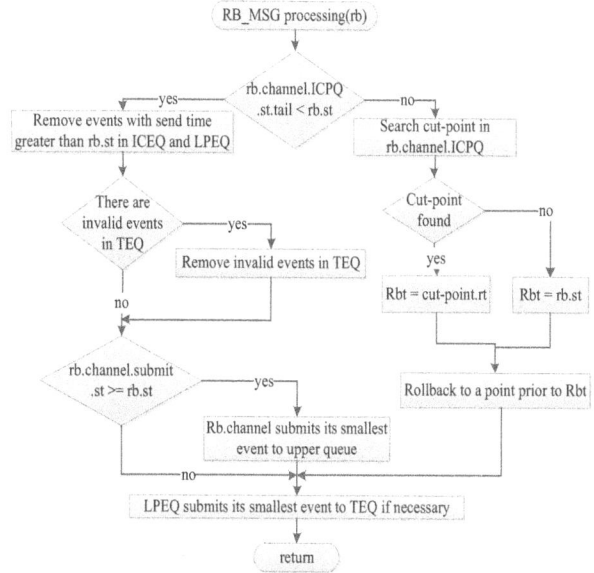

Figure 5: Steps for processing a RB-message, *tail* refers to the element with the greatest timestamp in the queue.

The processing of a RB-message depends upon whether or not invalid events have been processed.

- Left branch. The invalid events have not been processed. These events are removed and submit event to upper level queue if necessary. In the above example, a RB-message ($RB\_PRIORITY$, 12) will sent by LP 15 to LP 16. Events (20, 13) and (18, 14) become invalid, while event (19, 11) is valid. The invalid events are removed from the queue in LP 16. This kind of RB-message does not interfere other LPs, for no successive roll-back will be triggered, thus we call it *friendly* RB-message.

- Right branch. The invalid events have been partly or totally processed. A roll-back is triggered. The send time of the RB-message is used to find the $cut - point$ in the ICPQ, such that all events with a send time larger than the send time of the RB-message are after the cut-point. The LP sets the $rollbacktime$ equal to the receive time of the first event after the $cut - point$. In the above example, a RB-message ($RB\_PRIORITY$, 12) will be sent by LP 15 to LP 25, the events (19, 13.5) and (27, 15) become invalid while (19, 13.5) has been processed. A secondary roll-back is triggered and LP 25 follows steps in figure 6 to handle the roll-back.

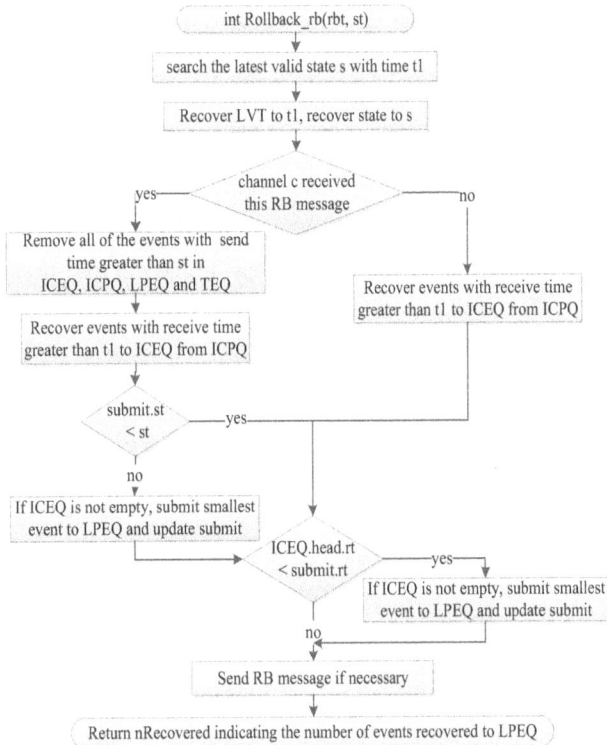

Figure 6: Steps for roll-back triggered by a RB-message.

The basic operation of RB-rollback is the same as that of a roll-back triggered by a straggler, except for the recovery of processed events. The channel which received the RB-message removes all of the events with a send time greater than the send time of the RB-message. Otherwise it moves the processed events with receive time greater than $rollback$ $time$ from ICPQ to ICEQ. Sending a RB-message is necessary for either type of roll-back. The $ScheduleHistory$ of channel [25, 20] is 21. Suppose that the first event after the $cut - point$ is (22, 10.5). LP 25 will roll back to time 22, because $22 > 21$ and no RB-message will be sent from LP 25 to LP 20. If the $rollback$ $time$ is 19, a RB-message ($RB\_PRIORITY$, 19) will be sent to LP 20 by LP 25, and LP 20 applies the above steps to process this RB-message again. Our use of multi-level queue and RB-message is an extension of [27].

3.3 Hybrid Communication

We employ shared memory to shorten the delay of message passing because communication is the main performance

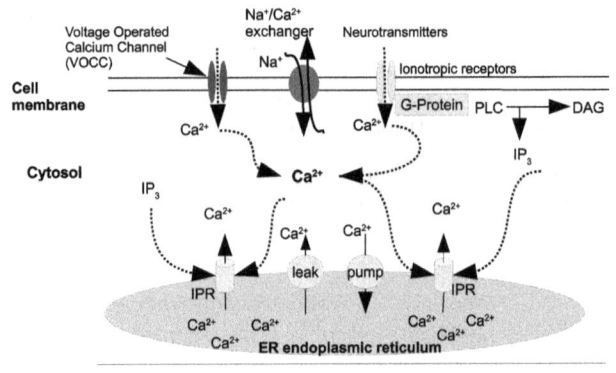

Figure 7: Intracellular calcium dynamics.

bottleneck for PDES applications. We call the worker processes located in the same node a family. As shown in part a of figure 1, suppose there are c processes in a node, the shared memory is partitioned into c segments, numbered by $0, 1, \cdots, c-1$, each family process uses one of the segments as its receive buffer. Each segment employs a semaphore to control the access to it. For example, when process 0 is about to send data to its family member process 2, process 0 needs to hold the semaphore for process 2, then find room to write the data, after which it releases the semaphore when writing is finished. When receiving data, process 0 must first hold the semaphore and then receive the data, after which it releases the semaphore.

Together, we have three-level communication mechanism, communication between threads within same process is completed by pointers, by shared memory for processes in the same node, and by MPI for remote processes.

4. EXPERIMENTAL STUDY

4.1 Model

As previously mentioned, Calcium plays an important role in regulating a great variety of neuronal processes. A notable example of intracellular calcium dynamics is the Ca^{2+}-induced-Ca^{2+}-release (CICR) [2, 19] which controls a diverse array of cellular processes including fertilization, gene transcription, muscle contraction and even cell death. Figure 7 describes the CICR flow.

There is high level of calcium stored in the endoplasmic reticulum (ER) of a neuron. Inositol 1,4,5-triphosphate (IP_3) receptors are distributed on the surface of the ER. These receptors can be activated when the Ca^{2+} and IP_3 in the cytosol reaches a certain concentration. The IP_3 receptor acts to open a channel, and the ER then releases Ca^{2+} into the cytosol through this channel, thereby elevating the concentration of Ca^{2+}. Both the IP_3 and Ca^{2+} can diffuse freely. Generally the concentration of cytosolic Ca^{2+} and IP_3 are low and the channels are closed. If a neuron receives a signal from adjacent neurons, the G-protein on the cell membrane releases IP_3 into cytosol, some receptors are activated, leading to a local elevation of cytosolic Ca^{2+}. The IP_3 and the newly-generated Ca^{2+} diffuse to an adjacent region and activate the IP_3 receptor channels there. The concentration of cytosolic Ca^{2+} increases, and a wave begins to spread. Because of a difference in the concentration (the concentration gradient) of calcium along the ER, calcium ions leak into the cytosol at a low rate, increasing the concentration of calcium in the cytosol. There are pumps on the surface of the ER (known as SERCA pumps) which pump the calcium back into ER at a rate related to the concentration gradient, causing the opened channels to close.

A deterministic model has been developed in NEURON [17]. Based on this model we developed a discrete event model and simulated it. In our experiments we only take the IP_3 and Ca^{2+} into account. As the real CICR model is complex we simplified it by assuming (1) the $IP3$ receptor opens when the concentration of $IP3$ and Ca^{2+} are both higher than some respective threshold (2) an opening $IP3$ receptor channel will close for a period of time determined by an exponential distribution. The reactions include:

$$ER\ Release:\ Ca^{2+}_{er} \xrightarrow{k_{release}} Ca^{2+}_{cyt},$$
$$k_{release} = \nu_{IP3R}\, m^3\, n^3\, ([Ca^{2+}_{er}] - [Ca^{2+}_{cyt}])$$
$$ER\ Leak:\ Ca^{2+}_{er} \xrightarrow{k_{leak}} Ca^{2+}_{cyt},$$
$$k_{leak} = \nu_{leak}\, ([Ca^{2+}_{er}] - [Ca^{2+}_{cyt}])$$
$$SERCA\ Pump:\ Ca^{2+}_{cyt} \xrightarrow{k_{pump}} Ca^{2+}_{er},$$
$$k_{pump} = \frac{\nu_{SERCA}\,[Ca^{2+}_{cyt}]^2}{k^2_{SERCA}+[Ca^{2+}_{cyt}]^2}$$

where Ca^{2+}_{er} refers to Ca^{2+} in ER, Ca^{2+}_{cyt} refers to Ca^{2+} in cytosol, [•] refers to the concentration of the corresponding species •, $m = \frac{[IP_3]}{[IP_3]+k_{IP_3}}$, $n = \frac{[Ca^{2+}]}{[Ca^{2+}_{cyt}]+k_{act}}$, k_{IP_3}, k_{act}, ν_{IP3R}, ν_{leak}, ν_{SERCA} and k_{SERCA} are given constant parameters, the value can be found in [17]. Ca^{2+}_{er} can only diffuse within ER, cytosolic Ca^{2+} and IP_3 can only diffuse within cytosol.

We made use of the following scenario. At first, both cytosolic Ca^{2+} and IP_3 concentrations are low. Hence most of the IP_3 channels are inactive, and only leaks and SERCA pumping take place. IP_3 molecules are injected into some sub-volumes in the middle of a dendrite. The cytosolic Ca^{2+} concentration achieves a threshold level due to the leak, the IP_3 receptor channels begin to open and the ER release is triggered.

4.2 Geometry

We simulate the intracellular Ca^{2+} wave in an unbranched apical dendrite of a hippocampal pyramidal neuron (length: 1000 μm, diameter: 1 μm). An introduction to pyramidal neurons can be found in [22], Watanabe et al. modulate the calcium wave propagation in the dendrites and to the soma of rat hippocampal pyramidal neurons [26]. The hippocampus is a small region of the brain that resembles a seahorse and plays a role in learning and memory, figure 8 shows a three-dimensional view of the neuron. The neuron is partitioned into mesh grids, and each grid is taken to be a sub-volume. We select 14749 sub-volumes with a distance of less than 50 μm from the middle, and the length of each sub-volume to be 0.5 μm. The sub-volumes are evenly distributed among the processing threads.

4.3 Platform

We use two platforms. One machine (PEPI) is a cluster with 4 Intel(R) Xeon(R) E7 4860 2.27 GHz, 10 cores per processor, 1 TB memory, with Linux 2.6.32-358.2.1.el6.x86_64,

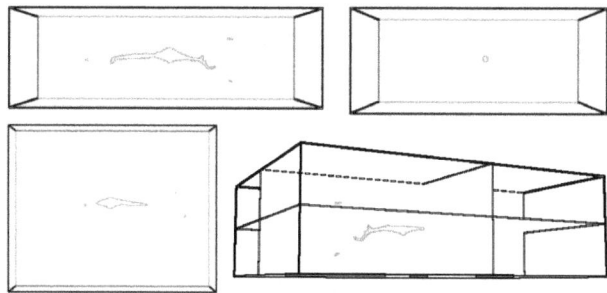

Figure 8: Pyramidal neuron in a three-dimensional view.

Red Hat Enterprise Linux Server release 6.4 (Santiago). The other is the SW2 node (of Guillimin), consisting of two Dual Intel(R) Sandy Bridge EP E5-2670 2.6 GHz CPUs, 8 cores per processor, 8 GB of memory per core, and a Non-blocking QDR InfiniBand network with 40 Gbps between nodes. The node runs Linux 2.6.32-279.22.1.el6.x86_64 GNU/Linux.

4.4 Performance

The performance of NTW-MT is compared to two other simulators. One is a process-based parallel simulator which uses a controller process to calculate GVT. Memory operations employ the standard *new* and *delete* mechanism. A thread+SQ version uses threads but does not use the MLQ algorithm. Each thread uses a single priority queue to hold the pending events. We know from [27] that RB messages result in superior performance when compared to anti-messages and do not compare the simulator to one with anti-messages.

We use an STL multi-set as the implementation of the priority queue. The mean access time to this multi-set is proportional to its size.

In the Thread+SQ case, when 32 processing threads are used, a roll-back avalanche occurs. This phenomenon is much more serious for the process-based version, which essentially cannot get beyond 8 processes. We consider these results inaccurate in terms of performance and do not include them.

The placement of processing threads is an important issue, it affects the memory usage and communication. We consider three placements- (1) *within process* in which all of the processing threads are in the same process, thereby no interprocess events; (2) *within node* in which processes exchange messages via shared memory; (3) *hybrid* respectively which makes use of MPI for remote processes and the preceding techniques otherwise.

4.4.1 within Process Mode

We run this experiment in the PEPI machine by starting up two processes, one *controller* and one *worker* process, and creating the *processing* threads within the *worker* process.

From figure 9, we can see that the execution time decreases with an increase in the number of processing threads. The process-based version is slowest because each process receives and sends events in the main processing loop and communication is time-consuming.

When fewer then 8 processing threads are involved in the simulation, the thread+MLQ version is slower then the thread+SQ version. The greatest difference (about 13%)

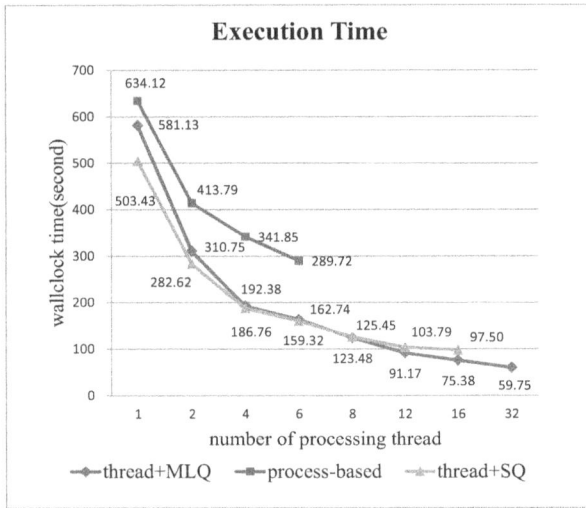

Figure 9: Execution time with all of the processing threads running within one process in the PEPI machine.

occurs when one processing thread is used. Because the essence of MLQ is the dispersion of contention on a single queue, it is of no use if there is no contention.

Consider the 1 processing thread case-almost all of the insertion of events end at the TEQ level, figure 12 illustrates this. Checking urgency in the input channel and the LPEQ level cause unnecessary overhead. When more threads are used, contention for the TEQ takes place. One LP may receive more than one event, the probability of contention at the SQ increases and the MLQ becomes more efficient. The thread+MLQ version is superior to the thread+SQ version when more than 8 processing threads are used, and finally achieves a speedup of 9 with 32 processing threads used, compared to the 1 processing thread case.

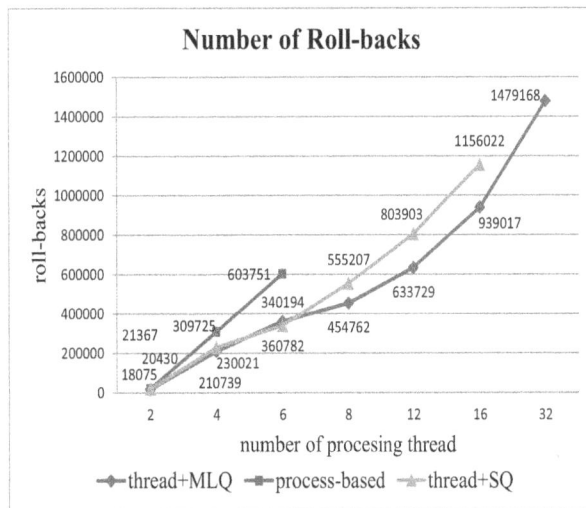

Figure 10: Roll-backs in within process mode in the PEPI machine.

Roll-backs increase for all of the versions in figure 10. The process-based version suffers more roll-backs (25%-35%)

than the other two versions. The roll-back of the two thread version is almost same in the few thread cases, while the MLQ version experienced fewer (around 18%) roll-backs than the SQ version. The events are inserted into thread queue directly in the SQ version resulting in a greater delay.

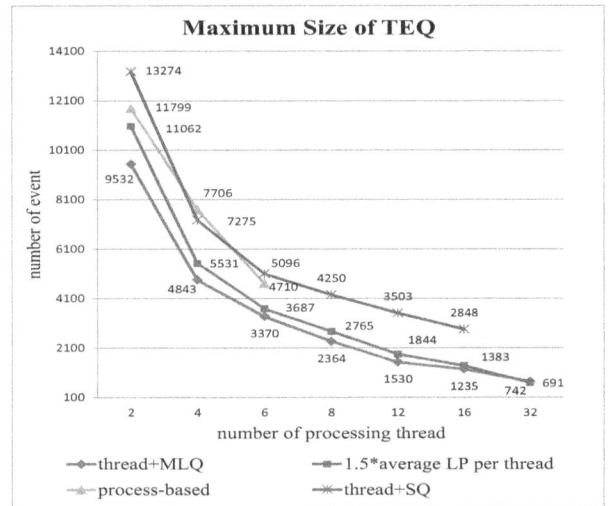

Figure 11: Maximum size of TEQ in within process mode in the PEPI machine.

The size of the TEQ scales well-it contains no more than 1.5 times the average number of LPs per processing thread. Hence the access time for the TEQ is well controlled, see figure 11.

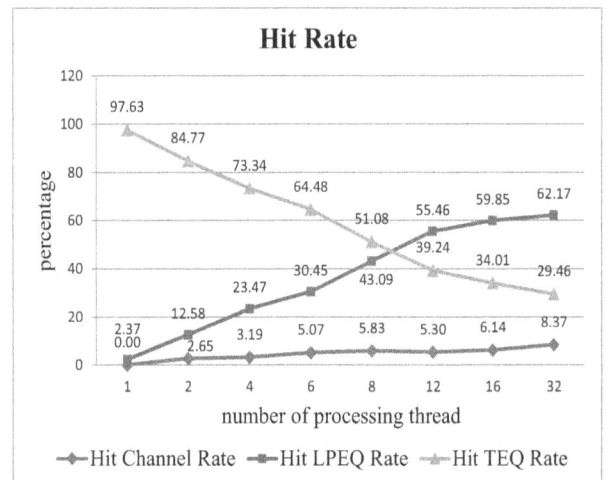

Figure 12: Hit rate in within process mode in PEPI machine.

In the MLQ algorithm, an event insertion may end at different levels of the queuing system-the input channel, the LPEQ and the TEQ. Define the hit rate of a level to be the proportion of insertions ending at each level. In the process-based and thread+SQ version, all of the events are inserted into the thread queue. From figure 12, we can see that most insertions end at the LPEQ when more than 8 threads are used, suggesting that the contention is dispersed.

4.4.2 within Node Mode

We assume that each worker process has the same number of processing threads, and vary the total number of processing threads in the simulation by starting up variant number of worker processes. All of the processes reside in the same node, they transfer external messages via shared memory. This experiment was done in the PEPI machine.

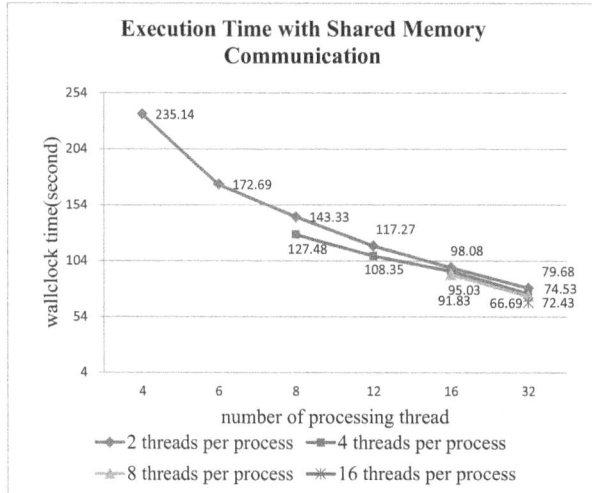

Figure 13: Execution time with shared memory communication in within node mode in the the PEPI machine.

From figure 13 and 14, we see that placing more threads in the same process results in better performance, this is reasonable for less interprocess communication is used. However, comparing these results to those obtained by placing all of the processing threads in the same process, we do not see a great difference. The combination of communication threads and shared memory results in a short latency.

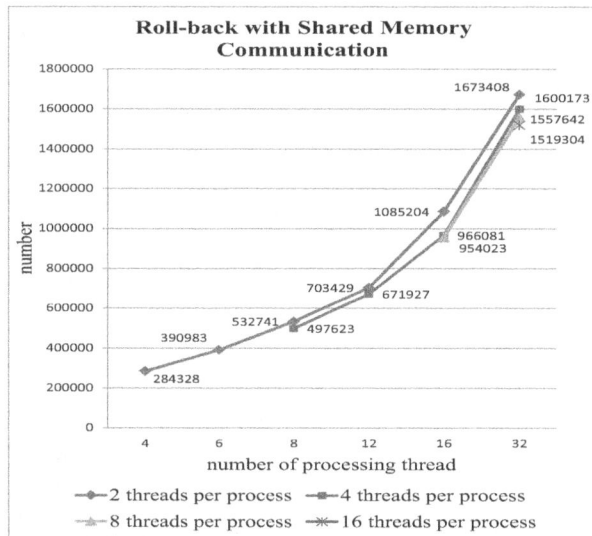

Figure 14: Roll-back with shared memory communication in within node mode in the PEPI machine.

4.4.3 Hybrid Mode

The number of threads is limited by the number of physical cores in a node, and the number of threads should not exceed the number of physical cores [1], which indicates employing several nodes to have large scale simulation is inevitable. We had this experiment in the Guillimin machine and used the MPI option ppn (process per node) to dispatch *worker* processes to nodes.

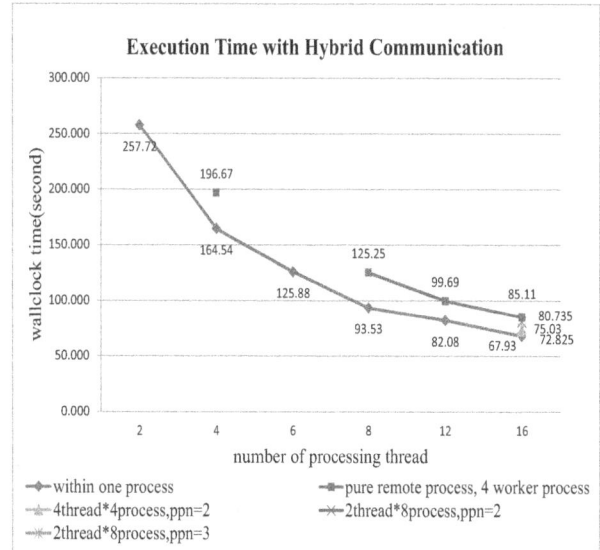

Figure 15: Execution time with hybrid communication in the Guillimin machine, ppn refers to process per node.

The Guillimin machine uses a well-optimized infiniBand for remote communication. From the results in figure 15 and 16, we again see that placing all of the processing threads in the same process results in the best performance. Once when the remote communication is involved in, the performance goes down without any surprise, the roll-back increases sharply, the execution time is enslaved to the longest latency.

In the purely remote communication case, the send buffer of the communication thread overflows when more than 8 threads are in the same process. One communication thread cannot accommodate 8 processing threads and more. This indicates the hybrid mode is the general mode for large scale simulation, and the number of processing threads in one worker process should be properly determined.

5. CONCLUSION AND FUTURE WORK

This paper is concerned with the development of a parallel discrete event simulator for reaction diffusion models used in the simulation of neurons. The research was done as part of the NEURON project (www.neuron.yale.edu). It is our intention to include NTW-MT in NEURON for use by the general neuroscience community.

We simulate a discrete event model for calcium wave propagation on an unbranched apical dendrite of a hippocampal pyramidal neuron. It is known that calcium plays a fundamental role in the second messenger system of a neuron. However, the mechanism by which calcium waves are transmitted is not completely understood. Our model is based

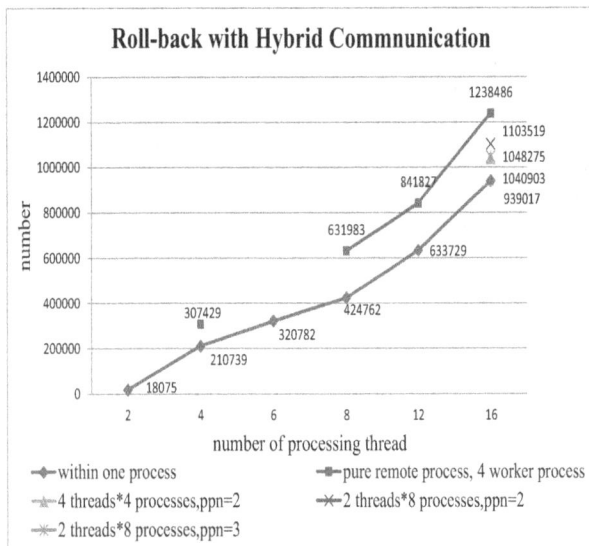

Figure 16: Roll-back with hybrid communication in the Guillimin machine.

on a deterministic calcium wave model described in [17]. Because stochastic models are more realistic than deterministic models for small populations, it may be possible to shed more light on the transmission mechanism.

Our parallel simulator is optimistic and thread based. It makes use of the NSM algorithm [8]. The use of threads is an attempt to capitalize on multicore architectures used in high performance machines, communication latency among threads within the same process is minimized by pointers. It makes use of a multi-level queue for the pending event set and a single rollback message in place of individual antimessages. We examined its performance on the calcium wave model and compared it to the performance of (1) a process based optimistic simulator and (2) a threaded simulator which uses a single priority queue for each thread. The multi-level queue simulator exhibited a superior performance when all of the threads were placed in the same process. The effects of shared memory and MPI based communication were also investigated; the multi-level queue simulator proved to be scalable. However, the need for load balancing algorithms was very clear in our experiments.

Our future work on the calcium wave model includes (1) implementing a more detailed model and larger reaction diffusion model and examining the performance of the multi-level queue algorithm on this model (2) developing load balancing algorithms for NTW-MT. A hybrid (deterministic-stochastic) model is another future effort.

6. ACKNOWLEDGMENTS

This work is funded by China Scholarship Council and in part by the National Natural Science Foundation of China (No. 61170048), Research Project of State Key Laboratory of High Performance Computing of National University of Defense Technology (No. 201303-05) and the Research Fund for the Doctoral Program of High Education of China (No. 20124307110017). This work is also funded by NIH R01MH086638 and NIH T15LM007056.

7. REFERENCES

[1] S. R. Alam, R. F. Barrett, J. A. Kuehn, P. C. Roth, and J. S. Vetter. Characterization of scientific workloads on systems with multi-core processors. In *Proceedings of the 2006 IEEE International Symposium on Workload Characterization*, pages 225–236, San Jose, California, USA, October 25-27 2006. IEEE.

[2] M. J. Berridge. Neuronal calcium signaling. *Neuron*, 21(1):13–26, 1998.

[3] N. T. Carnevale and M. L. Hines. *The NEURON book*. Cambridge University Press, New York, USA, 2006.

[4] N. T. Carnevale and M. L. Hines. Neuron, for empirically-based simulations of neurons and networks of neurons. http://www.neuron.yale.edu, 2009-2013. Last access on May 1st 2015.

[5] L.-l. Chen, Y.-s. Lu, Y.-p. Yao, S.-l. Peng, and L.-d. Wu. A well-balanced time warp system on multi-core environments. In *Proceedings of the 2011 IEEE Workshop on Principles of Advanced and Distributed Simulation*, pages 1–9, Nice, France, June 14-17 2011. IEEE Computer Society.

[6] L. Dematté and T. Mazza. On parallel stochastic simulation of diffusive systems. In M. Heiner and A. M. Uhrmacher, editors, *Computational methods in systems biology*, volume 5307 of *Lecture Notes in Computer Science*, pages 191–210. Springer Berlin Heidelberg, 2008.

[7] T. Dickman, S. Gupta, and P. A. Wilsey. Event pool structures for pdes on many-core beowulf clusters. In *Proceedings of the 2013 ACM SIGSIM Conference on Principles of Advanced Discrete Simulation*, SIGSIM-PADS '13, pages 103–114, New York, NY, USA, 2013. ACM.

[8] J. Elf and M. Ehrenberg. Spontaneous separation of bi-stable biochemical systems into spatial domains of opposite phases. *Systems biology*, 1(2):230–236, 2004.

[9] D. T. Gillespie. Exact stochastic simulation of coupled chemical reactions. *The journal of physical chemistry*, 81(25):2340–2361, 1977.

[10] D. Jagtap, N. Abu-Ghazaleh, and D. Ponomarev. Optimization of parallel discrete event simulator for multi-core systems. In *Proceedings of the 26th IEEE International Parallel & Distributed Processing Symposium (IPDPS)*, pages 520–531, Shanghai, China, May 21-25 2012.

[11] D. R. Jefferson. Virtual time. *ACM Transactions on Programming Languages and Systems (TOPLAS)*, 7(3):404–425, 1985.

[12] M. Jeschke, R. Ewald, and A. M. Uhrmacher. Exploring the performance of spatial stochastic simulation algorithms. *Journal of Computational Physics*, 230(7):2562–2574, 2011.

[13] M. Jeschke, A. Park, R. Ewald, R. Fujimoto, and A. M. Uhrmacher. Parallel and distributed spatial simulation of chemical reactions. In *Proceedings of the 22nd Workshop on Principles of Advanced and Distributed Simulation*, PADS '08, pages 51–59, Washington, DC, USA, 2008. IEEE Computer Society.

[14] W. W. Lytton. *From Computer to Brain*. Springer-Verlag, New York, USA, 2002.

[15] R. A. McDougal, M. L. Hines, and W. W. Lytton. Reaction-diffusion in the neuron simulator. *Frontiers in Neuroinformatics*, 7(28), 2013.

[16] R. J. Miller. *Optimistic parallel discrete event simulation on a beowulf cluster of multi-core machines*. PhD thesis, University of Cincinnati, 2010. http://secs.ceas.uc.edu/p̃aw/research/theses/ryan_miller.pdf.gz, last access on May 1st 2015.

[17] S. A. Neymotin, R. A. McDougal, M. A. Sherif, C. P. Fall, M. L. Hines, and W. W. Lytton. Neuronal calcium wave propagation varies with changes in endoplasmic reticulum parameters: A computer model. *Neural Computation*, 27(4):898–924, Mar. 2015.

[18] M. N. I. Patoary, C. Tropper, Z. Lin, R. McDougal, and W. W. Lytton. Neuron time warp. In *Proceedings of the 2014 Winter Simulation Conference*, WSC '14, pages 3447–3458, Piscataway, NJ, USA, 2014. IEEE Press.

[19] H. Roderick, M. J. Berridge, and M. D. Bootman. Calcium-induced calcium release. *Current Biology*, 13(11):R425, 2003.

[20] W. N. Ross. Understanding calcium waves and sparks in central neurons. *Nat Rev Neurosci*, 13(3):157–168, Mar. 2012.

[21] R. B. Schinazi. Predator-prey and host-parasite spatial stochastic models. *The Annals of Applied Probability*, 7(1):1–9, 1997.

[22] N. Spruston. Pyramidal neuron. *Scholarpedia*, 4(5):6130, 2009.

[23] D. Sterratt, B. Graham, A. Gillies, and D. Willshaw. *Principles of computational modelling in neuroscience*. Cambridge University Press, New York, USA, 2011.

[24] B. Wang, B. Hou, F. Xing, and Y. Yao. Abstract next subvolume method: A logical process-based approach for spatial stochastic simulation of chemical reactions. *Computational biology and chemistry*, 35(3):193–198, 2011.

[25] B. Wang, Y. Yao, Y. Zhao, B. Hou, and S. Peng. Experimental analysis of optimistic synchronization algorithms for parallel simulation of reaction-diffusion systems. In *Proceedings of the 2009 International Conference on High Performance Computational Systems Biology*, pages 91–100, Trento, Italy, October 14-16 2009.

[26] S. Watanabe, M. Hong, N. Lasser-Ross, and W. N. Ross. Modulation of calcium wave propagation in the dendrites and to the soma of rat hippocampal pyramidal neurons. *The Journal of Physiology*, 575(2):455–468, 2006.

[27] Q. Xu and C. Tropper. Xtw, a parallel and distributed logic simulator. In *Proceedings of the 19th Workshop on Principles of Advanced and Distributed Simulation*, pages 181–188, Monterey, California, USA, June 1-3 2005. IEEE Computer Society.

Management of Ubiquitous Systems with a Mobile Application Using Discrete Event Simulations

Souhila Sehili
University of Corsica
SPE UMR CNRS 6134
Campus Grimaldi, 20250
Corte (France)
sehili@univ-corse.fr

Laurent Capocchi
University of Corsica
SPE UMR CNRS 6134
Campus Grimaldi, 20250
Corte (France)
capocchi@univ-corse.fr

Jean-François Santucci
University of Corsica
SPE UMR CNRS 6134
Campus Grimaldi, 20250
Corte (France)
santucci@univ-corse.fr

ABSTRACT

Discrete-event simulation plays an increasingly important role in the management of ubiquitous systems. This working progress proposes a cross-platform mobile application dedicated to the management of ubiquitous systems using discrete-event simulation. The mobile application aims to perform the simulation of models specified with discrete-event system specifications (DEVS). Web services are invoked by the mobile application in a generic way in order to load, set and simulate models defined using the DEVSimPy software and stored on a web server. The propose approach has been validated on an ubiquitous system defined from an interconnection of physical computing platforms including microcontrollers, switches and sensors.

Categories and Subject Descriptors

I.6.8 [**Simulation and Modeling**]: Types of Simulation—*Discrete event*; D.2.6 [**Software Engineering**]: Programming Environments—*Graphical environments*

General Terms

Theory

Keywords

Discrete event modeling, Simulation, Ubiquitous system, DEVSimPy, Mobile application

1. INTRODUCTION

Ubiquitous systems [4] necessary lean on an interaction between virtual objects and users. Discrete-event simulation can offer a way to control such systems according to real time constraints [5, 3]. The paper deals with a mobile application aimed to manage discrete-event simulations obtained from DEVS (Discrete EVent system Specification) models associated with connected objects such as board computers, sensors, controllers or actuators.

SIGSIM-PADS'15, June 10–12, 2015, London, United Kingdom.
ACM 978-1-4503-3583-6/15/06.
http://dx.doi.org/10.1145/2769458.2769490.

The interest of the propose working progress is to strongly associate simulations, mobile applications and connected objects. The result will be the ability to manage connected objects (sensors, computer boards, actuators, controller) from a mobile application while providing intelligent decisions based on simulations. The user of the proposed mobile application DEVSimPy-Mob will first have to connect to a board computer through the cloud. This connection will offer the user a list of DEVS models that can be simulated. These models are based on the DEVS formalism and involved a set of DEVS models in order to manage sensors, actuators, board computers or controller. One of the main interests of such an approach is the possibility to associate DEVS models of connected objects with classical DEVS models (such as prediction models, decision models, etc.) allowing to propose the management of connected objects from a mobile application integrating intelligent decisions based on simulations.

The DEVS modeling aspects are implemented using the DEVSimPy Framework [1]. The connected objects features are based on Phidgets [2]. Phidgets offer a set of low-cost electronic components and sensors that are controlled by a personal computer. The integration of Phidgets interface with DEVS is necessary for two reasons: (i) to simulate real time systems with data coming from Phidgets sensors; (ii) to exploit simulation results to control in real time Phidgets actuators; (iii) to enrich the use of Phidgets interfaces by coupling them with DEVS models specialized in decision making (neural network, fuzzy logic, optimization via simulation, etc.). The rest of the paper is organized as follows: the next section deals with the Modeling and Simulation methodologies that have been developed in the framework of the presented work. The implementation and results are presented in section 3 while the the future work and conclusion sare detailed in section 4 and 5.

2. M&S METHODOLOGIES

DEVS (Discrete EVent system Specification) [6] has been introduced as an abstract formalism for the modeling of discrete event systems, and allows a complete independence from the simulator using the notion of abstract simulator. DEVS defines two kinds of models: atomic models and coupled models. An atomic model is a basic model with specifications for the dynamics of the model. It describes the behavior of a component, which is indivisible, in a timed state transition level. Coupled models tell how to couple several component models together to form a new model. This kind of model can be employed as a component in a larger coupled model. As in general systems theory, a DEVS model contains a set of states and transition functions that are triggered by the simulator. DEVSimPy [1] is an open Source project supported by the SPE team of the university of Corsica. This aim is to provide a GUI for the modeling and simulation of PyDEVS models. PyDEVS is an Application Programming Interface (API) allowing the implementation of the DEVS formalism in Python language.

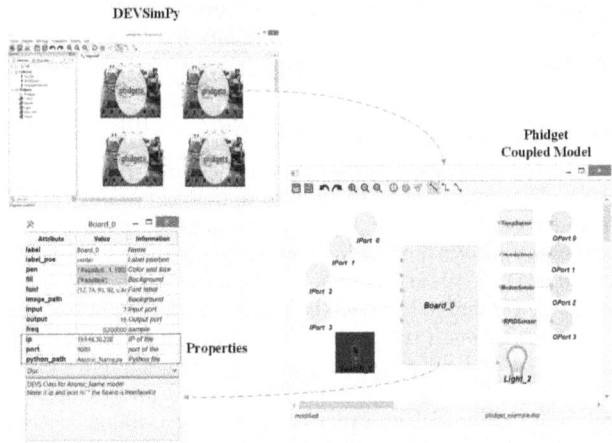

Figure 1: The DEVSimPy Phidget Library.

From a M&S aspects the following tasks have been performed: (i) Development of a DEVSimPy Phidget component library for manipulating Phidget board computers, sensors and actuators. The Figure 1 illustrates the definition and use of the Library (with components "Board", a To-disk corresponding to a "Lamp" component and a "RandomGenerator" component corresponding to a "Switch" component). Figure 1 points out how a Phidget DEVSimPy model is automatically associated with sensors, actuators and boards through the IP address of the Phidget. (ii) Implementation of a Web Server in order to run the simulations involving components of the DEVSimPy Phidgets library which allows to manage connected objects and provision of web services allowing to dynamically interact from the mobile application with the DEVSimPy framework (from the Web Server).

3. IMPLEMENTATION AND RESULTS

The implementation has involved two parts: (i) the development of the mobile application and (ii) the M&S features. The chosen technologies concerning the development of the mobile application are summarized as follows: (i) Technology choice: PhoneGap, JavaScript for the communication with the DEVSimPy WebServices; (ii) Tools: Bookstore, JointJS, CSS: ratchet framework. The technical aspects of the implementation DEVSimPy library and DEVSimPy Web Server are listed below: (i) Development of nogui DEVSimPy version; (ii) Implementation of a python Web Server: Python, HTML5, CSS3, MySQL; (iii) Servers: Web Server, File server and SVN server. The capabilities of the mobile application DEVSimPy-Mob are summarized below: (i) Multi-Platform (IOS, Android, etc.); (ii) Access to the Web Server Services DEVSimPy; (iii) Launch simulations (interactions with the simulation); (iv) Graphically

visualization of DEVS models; (v) Visualization of the results (as sensors data, the activity of actuators as the state of a lamp managed by the mobile application).

4. FUTURE WORK

During a short term period, we plan to improve the visualization of the results and to develop a set of web-services to better communicate with the DEVSimPy web server. In a longer term research, we plan to deal with complex applications involving the interconnections connected objects such as sensors, actuators, board computers and DEVS models specialized with artificial intelligent features such as neural networks, fuzzy inductive modeling, etc.

5. CONCLUSIONS

The proposed work in progress concerns the development of an approach for managing ubiquitous systems from a mobile application using DEVS. We have proposed a library of DEVSimPy components allowing to model and simulate the behavior of connected objects. Since the DEVSimPy models are associated with the real objects through the IP address, we are able to manage connected objects through DEVS simulations. Furthermore DEVS models are accessible through the Internet using a DEVSimPy Web server. We have also developed a generic mobile application allowing to: (i) select a DEVS model to be simulated, (ii) performs the simulation and (iii) visualizes the obtained results.

6. REFERENCES

[1] Capocchi, L., Santucci, J.-F., Poggi, B. and Nicolai, C. 2011. DEVSimPy: A Collaborative Python Software for Modeling and Simulation of DEVS Systems, In *Proc. of 20th IEEE International Workshops on Enabling Technologies: Infrastructure for Collaborative Enterprises* (Paris, France, 27-29 June, 2011). IEEE, 170-175. DOI=10.1109/WETICE.2011.31.

[2] Greenberg, S. and Fitchett, C. 2001. Phidgets: Easy Development of Physical Interfaces Through Physical Widgets, In *Proc. of the 14th Annual ACM Symposium on User Interface Software and Technology* (Orlando, Florida, 2001). ACM, New York, NY, USA, 209-218. DOI=10.1145/502348.502388.

[3] Jeffery, A., Panke, J., Jonathon, E., Eaket, N. and Wainer, G. 2013. Mobile Simulation with Applications for Serious Gaming, In *Proc. of the Summer Computer Simulation Conference* (Toronto, Ontario, Canada 2013). Society for Modeling & Simulation International, Vista, CA, Art. 27, 8 pages. ISBN=978-1-62748-276-9.

[4] Kindberg, T. and Fox, A. 2002. System software for ubiquitous computing. *IEEE Pervasive Computing 1*, 1 (January 2002), 70-81. DOI=10.1109/MPRV.2002.993146.

[5] Sarjoughian, H. S., Gholami, S., Jonathon, E. and Jackson, T. 2013. Interacting Real-time Simulation Models and Reactive Computational-physical Systems, In *Proc. of the Winter Simulation Conference: Simulation: Making Decisions in a Complex World* (Washington, D.C., 8-11 Dec, 2013). IEEE, 1120-1131. DOI=10.1109/WSC.2013.6721501.

[6] Zeigler, B., Praehofer, H. and Kim, T.G. 2000. *Theory of Modeling and Simulation, Second Edition*. Academic Press, Inc., Orlando, FL, USA.

An Application of Distributed Simulation for Hybrid Modeling of Offshore Wind Farms

Navonil Mustafee
University of Exeter
CISR, Business School
+44 (0) 1392725661
n.mustafee@exeter.ac.uk

M'Hammed Sahnoun
IRISE Laboratory - CESI
Rouen, France
+33 (0) 673642966
msahnoun@cesi.fr

Andi Smart, Phil Godsiff
University of Exeter
CISR, Business School
p.a.smart@exeter.ac.uk
phil.godsiff@exeter.ac.uk

ABSTRACT

The work in progress paper presents a case study on M&S of offshore wind farms. Two simulation models have been developed, an agent-based model and a discrete-event model, with the former modeling turbine failures using a degradation function and the latter modeling the Maintenance, Repair and Operations (MRO) strategies. The models have been implemented in *NetLogo* and *Simul8* respectively. In this paper we present ongoing work in hybrid simulation which uses the IEEE 1516 HLA standard for distributed simulation for synchronized model execution and dynamic information exchange between the agent-based and the discrete-event models.

Categories and Subject Descriptors

I.6.3 [**Simulation and Modeling**]: Applications; I.6.5 [**Simulation and Modeling**]: Model Development - *modeling methodologies*; I.6.8 [**Simulation and Modeling**]: Types of Simulation - *discrete event, distributed*.

General Terms

Management, Design, Experimentation

Keywords

Hybrid Simulation; Distributed Simulation; Maintenance, Repair and Operations; Offshore Wind Farm.

1. INTRODUCTION

Modelling & Simulation (M&S) techniques have their underlying theoretical and methodological foundations which make them relevant for application in specific problem context. However, as the system being modelled increases in complexity it is arguable that researchers need to explore opportunities for the combined application of simulation techniques, or hybrid simulation, to potentially enable synergies across techniques and provide greater insights to problem solving. A profiling study consisting of 525 papers published in the journal *Simulation: Transactions of the SCS* identified only thirteen studies that have applied

SIGSIM-PADS '15, June 10-12, 2015, London, United Kingdom
ACM 978-1-4503-3583-6/15/06.
http://dx.doi.org/10.1145/2769458.2769492

multiple techniques to the problem context; the number of M&S studies in which the techniques were applied symbiotically were only eight [2]. Our work in progress (WIP) is on the application of hybrid M&S in the domain of Maintenance, Repair and Operations (MRO) in offshore wind farms. The remainder of our WIP paper is structured as follows. In the next section we provide a definition of hybrid simulation looking at it from both discrete and continuous paradigms. We provide a short description of our application area and the Agent-based Simulation (ABS) and the Discrete-Event Simulation (DES) models that have been developed; we outline the inter-model interaction that will be required to enable hybrid simulation. The following section present a short review on the approaches considered for enabling such simulation using models developed in commercial software packages, and argues for the use of the IEEE 1516 HLA standard for distributed simulation. The final section of the paper describes future work.

2. HYBRID SIMULATION

How do we define hybrid simulation? Indeed, the combination of continuous and discrete models has been referred to as hybrid in several studies. We take a wider view of hybrid simulation to also include the methodological aspects of modeling techniques and the advantages gained through the symbiosis of such techniques. For example, ABS and DES are discrete-event but they are also an example of hybrid when they are applied together for the purposes of systems' enquiry. DES relies on the concept of queues and servers, ABS relies on the interaction between individual agents and patterns and behaviors emerge which were not explicitly programmed. Each methodology has its strengths and our definition of hybrid simulation includes investigation of systems which have used multiple simulation techniques, and is thus wider than the notion of only discrete and continuous time. Similarly, the use of System Dynamics (SD; continuous time) with ABS or DES is also an example of hybrid simulation since the application of SD-DES, SD-ABS or indeed SD-DES-ABS will combine the advantages associated with both continuous and discrete models.

3. M&S OF OFFSHORE WIND FARMS

An offshore wind farm is defined as a collection of wind turbines and associated equipment to generate electricity from wind power. In terms of installed capacity, in 2011 Europe had more than 90% of the world's installed capacity in offshore wind energy (European Wind Energy Association; http://www.ewea.org/). A major obstacle to the ongoing development of this source of energy is the high cost of installation, operation and maintenance compared with other sources of energy [4]. As a result, it is estimated that the cost of maintaining offshore wind turbines makes up between 25%-40% of the total kWh cost of electricity, compared with 10%-15% of onshore terrestrial sites. Reducing maintenance costs through intelligent MRO strategies is a key step in establishing the future of offshore wind farms. Further, modeling of turbine degradation is equally important as factors such as wind speed, events like lightning strike on a turbine, etc. determine the health of the assets and consequently the frequency of maintenance.

3.1 Modeling Turbine Degradation using ABS

Through the use of ABS the modeler can model each agent in the system independently, and subsequently add the interactions and relationships between the different parts of the system [1]. The purpose of our ABS model is to consider each wind turbine as an independent agent that is able to interact with its environment, which is composed of the other agents (turbines) and the maintenance and production facilities. Each agent is characterized by variables which represent the state of the turbine it models, its *Equipment Health Factor (EHF)* and the energy that it produces. Each agent follows two rules – turbine degradation and turbine production - which are influenced by several internal variables (e.g., regular maintenance performed on a turbine will lower turbine degradation, random mechanical outages will not only degrade the performance but also affect energy production) and external variables (e.g., wind speed will determine the energy that is being produced; weather conditions will have a direct bearing to whether maintenance operations can be performed, which in turn is related to turbine degradation). Our ABS model is implemented in *NetLogo*.

3.2 Modeling MRO strategies using DES

Maximization of turbine capability time through intelligent MRO strategies is a crucial operations management activity for both operators of the wind farms (to maximize return on investment) and the turbine manufacturers (to understand turbine performance under actual conditions). The MRO strategies should take into consideration the fact that maintenance activities are dependent on weather windows being available, for example, permissible wave height, wind speed, visibility are all important factors since that determine whether offshore maintenance can take place. The purpose of our DES model is to experiment with various MRO strategies which increase up-time of the wind turbines, while also trying to reduce costs associated with such operations. Our model has been developed using *Simul8*. The model simulates the operational processes starting from specific faults being reported by individual turbines (includes preventive maintenance) and through until the faults have been rectified and the resources are released for subsequent maintenance operations. The resources in question are the parts for maintenance, the availability of technicians/engineers who would carry out the MRO activities, the availability of the right size of boat (for example, a large boat is required if the maintenance requires the transportation of large spare parts) and the correct mix of these resources for specific MRO tasks.

3.3 ABS-DES Model Interaction

Our models have been developed such that the ABS model feeds information on turbine *EHF* (refer to section 3.1) through simulating a degradation model of individual turbines to the DES model. The DES will then use this information to prioritize maintenance operations in the wind farm; it will simulate several MRO strategies and feed data back to the ABS model to inform that maintenance operations have taken place on specific turbines. The ABS model will then receive this information and will change

the EHF for the turbines in question to the maximum permissible value (as good as new). This process repeats itself through the entire simulation timeframe.

4. EXISITNG APPROACHES

In a previous study [3] the authors identified three predominant approaches for enabling interaction between models developed using different M&S methodologies. The first strategy is the manual execution of the models, with the modeler being responsible for transferring variables between them. The second strategy is similar to the previous in respect of the models running independent of each other and demonstrating a similar throttled execution behavior (non-synchronized). However, it is different compared to the first case because this process is now automated. The third strategy of hybrid model execution involves the use of a simulation package like *AnyLogic* which has built-in support for multi-paradigm M&S. We have also reviewed wider literature on modelling methodology and have identified the field of distributed simulation to hold promise for our hybrid model execution [3]. Distributed simulation implements well-known time management algorithms to achieve synchronization between individual running simulations. Like our hybrid model, in a distributed simulation the system being modelled may be composed of a number of sub-models, each of which may be mapped to a specific simulation package (in our case this is *NetLogo* and *Simul8*). This has been our preferred option.

5. FUTURE WORK

The execution strategy for our hybrid M&S study requires the application of the IEEE1516 HLA standard and the RTI software that implements this standard. The authors are presently implementing a distributed simulation federation which comprises of the ABS and the DES federate, thus also realizing hybrid simulation. The use of the RTI middleware, together with integration software being coded by the authors, will enable our two federates to execute concurrently and without causality and serve as a platform for data exchange.

6. ACKNOWLEDGEMENTS

Acknowledgement is made to European Union for the support of this research through the European Program INTERREG IVA France-Channel-UK by funding project entitled MER Innovate.

7. REFERENCES

[1] Dimeas, A.L. and Hatziargyriou, N.D. 2005. Operation of a multiagent system for microgrid control. *IEEE T. Power Syst.* 20, 3, 1447-1455.

[2] Mustafee, N., Katsaliaki, K., Fishwick, P., and Williams, M.D. 2012. SCS – 60 years and counting! A time to reflect on the society's scholarly contribution to M&S from the turn of the millennium. *Simul-T. Soc. Mod. Sim.* 88, 9, 1047-1071.

[3] Mustafee, N., Sahnoun, M., Smart, A., et al. 2015. Investigating Execution Strategies for Hybrid Models developed using Multiple M&S Methodologies. In *Proceedings of the 2015 Spring Simulation Multi-Conference* (Alexandria, VA, April 12-15, 2015). ACM.

[4] Pineda, I., Azau, S., Moccia, J., and Wilkes, J. 2014. *Wind in power – 2013 European statistics*. The European Wind Energy Association, 1–12.

Cloning Agent-based Simulation on GPU

Xiaosong Li, Wentong Cai, Stephen John Turner
Parallel and Distributed Computing Center
School of Computer Engineering
Nanyang Technological University, Singapore 639798
xli15@e.ntu.edu.sg, aswtcai@ntu.edu.sg, steve@pmail.ntu.edu.sg

ABSTRACT

Simulation cloning is an efficient way to analyze multiple configurations in a parameter exploration task. This paper presents a generic approach to perform incremental agent-based simulation cloning and discusses its implementation on GPU. Compared with the incremental cloning of parallel and distributed simulation (PADS), cloning agent-based simulation (ABS) has new challenges due to the unique way how ABS is executed. In this paper, to support incremental cloning, mechanisms for both actively and passively cloning agents are proposed. A scheme to maintain the correct context of each cloned ABS instance is developed. In addition, a strategy to restrain the propagation of passive cloning in order to maximize computation sharing amongst cloned ABS instances is also investigated. The implementation of our proposed approach on GPU supports concurrent execution of agents within each simulation instance as well as concurrent execution of multiple simulation instances. Performance of the proposed approach is evaluated and analyzed using a case study of an agent-based evacuation simulation on a NVIDIA Quadro 2000 GPU. Our experiment results demonstrate that cloning can significantly speed up the overall parameter exploration task. The proposed approach achieves 2.4 to 5.1 times speedup for parameter exploration tasks containing 8 to 125 simulation instances that evaluate different parameter configurations.

Categories and Subject Descriptors

I.6.8 [**SIMULATION AND MODELING**]: Types of Simulation - *parallel*; C.1.2 [**PROCESSOR ARCHITECTURES**]: Multiple Data Stream Architectures (Multiprocessors) - *single-instruction-stream, multiple-data-stream processors (SIMD)*; I.2.11 [**DISTRIBUTED ARTIFICAL INTELLIGENCE**]: Multiagent systems

Keywords

Agent-based simulation; Cloning; GPU; Speedup

1. INTRODUCTION

One of the main applications of simulations is analyzing systems. A simulation model usually contains a set of tunable parameters for exploring different configurations of a system. To carry out a parameter exploration task or to evaluate different design alternatives, multiple simulation instances need be launched, each evaluating a different parameter configuration. It is possible that different simulation instances may share some common execution paths. So, computation can be saved by processing the common execution paths shared by multiple simulation instances only once. Simulation cloning technique is therefore proposed. The performance gain of cloning can be promising if common execution paths are of high ratio. To clone parallel discrete-event simulation, an incremental cloning strategy has been proposed in [15]. It has also been subsequently applied to clone HLA-based distributed simulation in [8]. A summary of the existing work on simulation cloning can be found in Section 2.

Agent-based simulation (ABS) is a technique with growing popularity for analyzing complex adaptive systems. To study complex group or global phenomena, ABS allows researchers to instead model individual behaviors which are easier to observe, extract and summarize. The global phenomena are revealed through agent interactions. In addition to evaluate different design alternatives (and to answer "what-if" questions), parameter space exploration is also required in ABS for sensitivity analysis of simulation parameters [11], calibrating model parameters [3, 24], and identifying simulation models which exhibit emergent system behaviors of interest [29, 27]. However, cloning techniques for ABS have been rarely studied in the literature. In this paper, we investigate how the incremental cloning technique can be applied to ABS. Cloning ABS is different from cloning parallel and distributed simulation (PADS) in many aspects. The challenges of cloning ABS will be elaborated in Section 3. A generic approach for incrementally cloning ABS is also described in the same section.

The motivation of carrying out the cloning-based parameter exploration task for ABS on GPU is that ABS is suitable for parallel processing due to agent's autonomy and self-containedness. Furthermore, GPU is commodity hardware that provides hundreds to thousands of parallel threads. Executing a large-scale ABS may take considerable amount of time. Exploring parameter space for such a large-scale ABS will take even longer time. If each ABS instance as well as different simulation clones can be executed in parallel on GPU, the total execution time of the parameter space exploration task will be significantly reduced. However, GPU is not spontaneously efficient because of the following reasons: i) Compared with multi-core CPU, GPU provides much more parallel threads but the clock rate of each thread is much slower; ii) Execution on GPU is only efficient if single instruction issued on GPU can be executed by all threads simultaneously; iii) GPU memory access pattern has determinant effect on the overall performance; and iv) Cloning agents requires frequent memory allocation during run-time, however GPU does not provide an efficient support for dynamic memory allocation. In this paper, we also present a strategy to efficiently implement our proposed cloning approach for agent-based simulation on GPU. Details can be found in Section 4.

In addition to the generic approach of incremental cloning of ABS and its implementation on GPU, experiments to evaluate the approach and its implementation using a case study on agent-based evacuation simulation will be described in Section 5. Finally, Section 6 concludes the paper and points out several directions for future work.

2. RELATED WORK

Replication is initially proposed by von Neumann [26] decades ago to provide fault tolerance, and is realized by duplicating processes, data, transactions, and services. Later it is used to improve throughput by placing replicas in the proximity where a service is needed [13] and to increase the concurrency of access by replicating databases [2]. In the area of simulation, replications are used to gain statistically meaningful simulation results [12, 1]. While replication refers to the execution of multiple simulation instances with the same set of parameter configuration, cloning is used to generate multiple simulation instances with different parameter configurations. It is generally used to explore different design alternatives or to answer "what-if" questions [9].

Cloning of PADS has been well studied. In [15], an incremental cloning technique for parallel discrete event simulation is proposed. It allows exploration of multiple execution paths concurrently. The main idea of the proposed technique is to incrementally clone part of the simulation instead of creating a copy of an entire simulation on a decision point. To support incremental cloning, the concept of virtual logical process (LP) and virtual message is proposed. A series of work investigating how incremental cloning can be applied to HLA-based distributed simulation is reported in [8, 7, 4, 6, 5]. Particularly, a scenario tree is proposed in [8] for defining the routing space of each cloned simulation instance in order to isolate the interactions among different cloned simulation instances that are running in the same simulation federation. With the routing space correctly defined, using the data distribution management (DDM) service provided by HLA/RTI, when a federate sends a message, it will be sent only to the federates belonging to the same cloned simulation instance. In our approach discussed later, a clone tree is proposed. But, it is constructed in a different way and used for different purpose.

Besides investigating strategies for cloning agent-based simulation, we also aim at their efficient implementation on GPU. Simulation parameter space exploration using GPU has been investigated in [16]. Data structures and mechanisms are proposed to support intra simulation instance and inter simulation instance parallelism on GPU. However, they are not specifically designed for agent-based simulations and

incremental cloning technique is not considered either. Implementing incremental cloning of agent-based simulation on GPU is challenging. For example, cloning agent-based simulation may require frequent memory allocation during run-time. However, dynamic memory allocation is not well supported on GPU. The key problem is that native allocation and deallocation require global synchronization which may become a severe performance bottleneck when the number of threads increases [28]. Besides, as reported in [22], allocation and deallocation using CUDA's dynamic memory allocation solution are prone to fault under a heavy load. To solve the problem, some techniques are proposed in the literature. In [20, 21], each thread is given a piece of preallocated memory space for adding new elements. To prevent a single thread quickly filling up its own reserved space, this strategy is further improved in [23]. However, all the existing approaches deal with a single copy of simulation instance. The memory allocation problem on GPU becomes much more complicated when multiple cloned simulation instances are executed concurrently.

3. CLONING AGENT-BASED SIMULATIONS

A simulation model inherently has a multitude of configurable parameters (e.g., dispatching rules in manufacturing simulation and environment settings in evacuation simulation). A *simulation scenario* is defined by a combination of parameter values. To explore the simulation parameter space, *stand-alone simulation instances* can be created for every combinations of parameter values. Alternatively, simulation cloning techniques can be used. A *cloned simulation instance* (in short, *clone*) is created when a decision point is reached. Simulation can be cloned in its entirety or incrementally. In *entire cloning*, all simulation components (e.g., toolsets in manufacturing simulation and agents in evacuation simulation) are cloned at one time; whereas in *incremental cloning*, simulation components are cloned incrementally when necessary. To maximum sharing of computation amongst clones, in this paper we consider incremental cloning only.

3.1 Issues in cloning agent-based simulations

Cloning is usually triggered under two circumstances, at decision point or through interaction. In PADS, a decision point represents the start of an LP's execution path divergence. An LP reaches a decision point and actively clone itself when certain condition is satisfied (e.g., queue length of a toolset is greater than a predefined threshold level as in manufacturing simulation). Other LPs are further passively cloned when communicating with the cloned LP.

In ABS, agents are typically situated in an environment. An agent may move in the environment and its behavior can be influenced by some other surrounding agents (that is, agents in its *neighborhood*). An agent-based simulation is usually executed in a time-stepping manner. In each time-step, an agent will perform a *sense-think-act* cycle. In the sense stage, the agent gets information from the environment and other surrounding agents. In the think stage, the agent processes the obtained information. Lastly, in the act stage, the agent modifies its own states based on the results of thinking. So, an agent reaches a decision point, evaluating a cloning decision, only when a configurable environmental setting is within its sensing range. For example, in our case study we use cloning to evaluate different combinations of gate sizes in an evacuation simulation. The size of each gate is a configurable parameter and active cloning occurs when the distance between agent and the gate is within a certain predefined range. Since environment settings affect agent's behavior (e.g., gate size affects agent's movement in evacuation simulation), the cloned agent and its original copy will have different states.

Similar to passive cloning in PADS, agents are passively cloned when they interact with a cloned agent. However, unlike direct interaction between LPs in PADS by message-passing, interaction in ABS is usually indirect through state sharing. Different from PADS where LPs are loosely coupled by communication links, agents in ABS can be tightly coupled if they are situated closely in the environment (this is especially true for evacuation simulation). Tight coupling may cause passive cloning progress rapidly and thus diminishing the benefit of incremental cloning (that is, sharing of computation).

Compared with the LPs in PADS, the number of agents in ABS is much larger. The state of an agent-based simulation is defined as the set of states of all agents in the environment. A reference to the simulation state is referred to as *world*. In incremental cloning, a cloned simulation instance may contain agents that belong to different clones. So, in order to obtain the correct world of a clone, an execution ordering of clones must be determined and an efficient mechanism for world creation and update must be developed.

Executing agents in each clone in parallel as well as different clones in parallel on GPU brings additional challenges. This will be further discussed in Section 4.

3.2 Incremental cloning of agent-based simulations

Our proposed mechanism for ABS cloning allows exploring the entire parameter space with one session of execution. $P_j^{(i)}$ represents i^{th} parameter's j^{th} value choice. $P_0^{(i)}$ is the default value choice of parameter $P^{(i)}$ when the space exploration task is launched; while $P_j^{(i)}$, $j > 0$, represents other value choices of parameter $P^{(i)}$ to be evaluated. For each parameter $P^{(i)}$, there is a corresponding rule for agents to determine whether or not they reach the decision point $D^{(i)}$. The clone evaluating a parameter combination

$$\{P_{j_1}^{(1)}, P_{j_2}^{(2)}, \ldots, P_{j_{N_P}}^{(N_P)}\}$$

is denoted as

$$C(\{P_{j_1}^{(1)}, P_{j_2}^{(2)}, \ldots, P_{j_{N_P}}^{(N_P)}\}),$$

where $0 \leq j_i < N_V^{(i)}$ and $1 \leq i \leq N_P$. $N_V^{(i)}$ is the number of value choices of parameter $P^{(i)}$ and N_P is the number of parameters. $C(\{P_0^{(1)}, P_0^{(2)}, \ldots, P_0^{(N_P)}\})$ is the default simulation instance (or *root clone*). The number of clones is determined by the number of parameters (i.e., N_P) and the number of each parameter's value choices (i.e., $N_V^{(i)}$). So, the space exploration task contains $\prod_{i=1}^{N_P} N_V^{(i)}$ clones in total.

Consider a parameter exploration task evaluating two parameters, each having three value choices (i.e., $P_j^{(i)}$, where $i \in \{1, 2\}$ and $j \in \{0, 1, 2\}$). In this example, agents are considered to firstly hit $D^{(1)}$ followed by $D^{(2)}$. The entire parameter space has nine parameter configurations in total as shown in Figure 1. For simplicity, we use notation

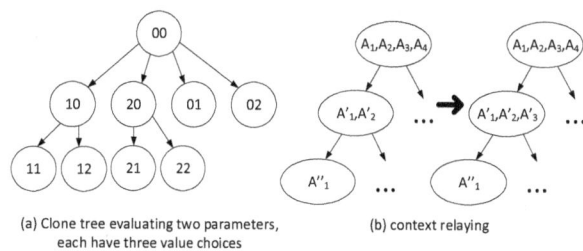

(a) Clone tree evaluating two parameters, each have three value choices

(b) context relaying

Figure 1: Clone tree

$C(ab)$ to represent $C(\{P_a^{(1)}, P_b^{(2)}\})$. The exploration task starts with the default clone $C(00)$. As the simulation goes on, some agents hit $D^{(1)}$. To evaluate two additional value choices of $P^{(1)}$, two clones $C(10)$ and $C(20)$ are generated. When agents from clones $C(j0)$, $j \in \{0, 1, 2\}$, hit $D^{(2)}$, each clone forks out another two clones $C(j1)$ and $C(j2)$ to evaluate the combined value choices of parameters. Based on the order of hitting decision points, clones evaluating all parameter combinations form a tree as shown in Figure 1(a). Clearly, this approach can be generalized to evaluate combinations of more parameters, each with more value choices.

Each node in the clone tree represents a cloned simulation instance exploring a parameter value combination. The root clone evaluates default combination. Child clone inherits the parameter value combination of the parent clone and alters the value choice of one of the parameters. For the example shown in Figure 1(a), $C(20)$ differs from $C(00)$ by altering $P_0^{(1)}$ to $P_2^{(1)}$, and $C(21)$ differs from $C(20)$ by altering $P_0^{(2)}$ to $P_1^{(2)}$.

3.2.1 Agent execution

To facilitate active and passive cloning, each agent maintains two sets of flags: *cloning flags* and *cloned flags*. Cloning flags indicate to which cloned simulation instances the agent should be cloned; and cloned flags keep track of the cloned simulation instances of which the agent has already been cloned. For both sets of flags, there is one flag for each cloned simulation instance. Taking the parameter exploration task in Figure 1(a) as an example, there are nine flags in the sets of cloning flags and cloned flags, respectively, for each agent.

Two sets of flags are needed because ABS is executed in time-stepping manner. In the current time-step, agents that will be cloned in the next time-step are identified by setting their corresponding cloning flags. When the agents are actually cloned in the next time-step, their cloning flags will be cleared and the corresponding cloned flags will be set to true accordingly.

For detecting active cloning conditions, an agent checks its own state against the rule associated with each parameter. Assuming the current cloned simulation instance is

$$C(\{P_{j_1}^{(1)}, P_{j_2}^{(2)}, \ldots, P_0^{(i)}, \ldots\}),$$

if the rule associated with parameter $P^{(i)}$ is satisfied (i.e., the decision point $D^{(i)}$ is reached), the agent will set its cloning flags corresponding to the child clones,

$$C(\{P_{j_1}^{(1)}, P_{j_2}^{(2)}, \ldots, P_j^{(i)}, \ldots\}), 0 < j \leq N_V^{(i)},$$

to true. This is to indicate that the agent will be cloned in the next time-step in order to evaluate other value choices of the parameter. For the example shown in Figure 1(a), when an agent in C(00) hits $D^{(1)}$, it will set its cloning flags corresponding to C(10) and C(20) to true so that it will be cloned to evaluate other two values of parameter $P^{(1)}$.

For detecting passive cloning conditions, an agent checks all its neighbors' cloned flags. If a neighbor's cloned flag is set for a child clone, the agent will set its own cloning flag for the corresponding child clone to true. This is to indicate that the state of this agent may be influenced by a cloned neighbor in the child clone and so it needs to create a copy of itself to participate in the execution of the child clone. Again, for the example shown in Figure 1(a), assuming agents A_1 and A_2 have been actively cloned to C(10) (i.e., its cloned flag corresponding to C(10) is set), when A_3 detects A_1 in its neighborhood, A_3 will set its cloning flag corresponding to C(10) to true.

It is necessary to perform interaction based cloning (i.e., passive cloning) to maintain the correctness of simulation. However, interaction also makes the passive cloning quickly propagate to agents which have not yet been impacted by the variation of parameter values. A throttling mechanism to refrain cloning propagation is therefore proposed. It involves an extra round of *compare-and-eliminate* in each time-step. To be specific, state difference between an agent A' in the current clone and its counterpart A in the parent clone is evaluated. If the difference lies within a predefined threshold T, A' will be removed from the current clone. This is feasible because the difference is so small that the state of A in the parent clone is sufficient to ensure the correctness of the execution of the current clone.

ALGORITHM 1: Modified sense-think-act cycle

Function step()
    cloneItself();
    performSensing();
    checkActivePassiveCloningConditions();
    performThinking();
    performActing();
    compareAndEliminate();
end

Agent's sense-think-act cycle is typically implemented in a *step()* function that is executed in every time step. To incorporate the cloning mechanisms described above, the *step()* function is modified as shown in Algorithm 1.

3.2.2 Clone management

To support incremental cloning, each cloned simulation instance maintains two data structures: *agent pool* to keep the actual agent data belonging to the clone and *world* to maintain the interaction context of the clone. The actual agent data are kept in the agent pool. The world only contains references to agents and it may contain references to agents in agent pools belonging to different clones.

Agent pool of a clone is updated by scanning through agents in the agent pool of its parent clone. If an agent in the parent agent pool has cloning flag set, a clone of the agent is created by copying its data from the parent's agent pool.

To correctly capture the simulation state of a cloned simulation instance, a world needs to be created (and updated). An agent will use the world to perform sensing and update its state accordingly. The clone tree structure facilitates the creation (and update) of the world as well as computation sharing. Processing on agents that have not been influenced

by the parameter variation yet is not required in the child clone. The states of these agents can be directly inherited from parent and ancestor clones. Hence, the world is created in a top-down manner by following a path in the clone tree. A child clone first copies the world of its parent, and then uses the references of agents in its own agent pool to replace the references of the corresponding agents in the world.

For the example shown in Figure 1(b), originally there are four agents in C(00), A_1, A_2, A_3 and A_4. Suppose at time t_1, both A_1 and A_2 reach the decision point $D^{(1)}$. Their copies, A_1' and A_2', are then created in clone C(10) (i.e., they are actively cloned). At a later time t_2, $t_2 > t_1$, agent A_1' reaches decision point $D(2)$. So, a copy of it, A_1'', is created in clone C(11). Assume at this time, both agents A_1 and A_2 are nether actively nor passively cloned. The agent pools and worlds for clones C(00), C(10), and C(11) are shown in Table 1. The world of C(00) is $\{A_1, A_2, A_3, A_4\}$. C(10) copies the world of C(00) and uses A_1' and A_2' to replace A_1 and A_2 to create its own world. Similarly, the world of C(11) is created by copying the world of C(10) and replacing A_1' by A_1''. Clearly, in this way the computation of agents that have not yet cloned in the parent clone needs not to be repeated in the child clone. In the above example, clones C(10) and C(11) can get the state of agents A_3 and A_4 directly from clone C(00).

Table 1: Agent pool and world

clone	agent pool	world
C(00)	$\{A_1, A_2, A_3, A_4\}$	$\{A_1, A_2, A_3, A_4\}$
C(10)	$\{A_1', A_2'\}$	$\{A_1', A_2', A_3, A_4\}$
C(11)	$\{A_1''\}$	$\{A_1'', A_2', A_3, A_4\}$

The world is updated in a similar manner. For the example shown in Figure 1(b), assume at time t_3, agent A_3 in clone C(00) is passively cloned. A copy of it, A_3', is created in clone C(10). The contexts of C(10) and C(11) will be updated to $\{A_1', A_2', A_3', A_4\}$ and $\{A_1'', A_2', A_3', A_4\}$ respectively. However, this mechanism for clone world creation and update stipulates a specific ordering of clone execution. Child clones can only be processed when its parent clone finishes processing. But, the execution of sibling clones can be potentially concurrent.

4. GPU IMPLEMENTATION

4.1 GPU programming model

GPU is chosen as the execution platform because of the potential speedup achieved by concurrently processing agents with numerous GPU threads. Figure 2(a) shows the architecture of an NVIDIA CUDA enabled GPU in comparison with CPU. Physically, a GPU consists of a DRAM and many stream multi-processors (SMs). Each SM has multiple stream processors (SPs) with equivalent capability of an arithmetic logic unit (ALU) of a CPU. Each SM can support up to 2048 concurrent threads through context switching. Programming model on GPU follows the single-instruction-multiple-thread (SIMT) paradigm. Every 32 threads forming a warp will be assigned the same instruction. The execution context (program counters, registers, etc) is maintained on-chip during the entire lifetime of the warp. Therefore, switching from one execution context to another incurs no cost.

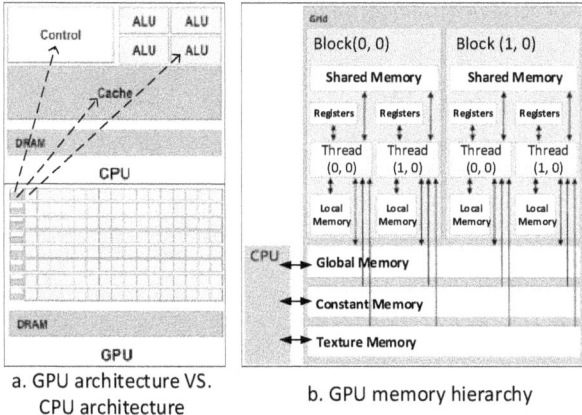

a. GPU architecture VS. CPU architecture

b. GPU memory hierarchy

Figure 2: GPU architecture [19]

The NVIDIA CUDA GPU has an hierarchical memory design as shown in Figure 2(b). The global memory is accessible by all threads. The per-block shared memory can only be accessed within a thread block and is of limited size, up to 48 kilobytes per block. However, it has about seven times higher bandwidth than that of the global memory under full utilization [25].

Neighbor accessing is a critical issue to deploy ABS on GPU. Detecting and accessing neighbors is a memory intensive operation, which often becomes a major bottleneck in an agent-based simulation. In our previous work [17], a strategy is proposed to efficiently utilize the GPU shared memory to cache neighbors of agents accessed by one thread block. Because of its limited size, neighbors are loaded into the shared memory batch by batch. Finishing interactions with one batch of neighbors, the shared memory is overwritten by the next batch of neighbors. Consequently, the frequent slow global memory access can be replaced by faster shared memory access. In this paper, we adopted the same neighbor accessing strategy, which makes cloning the only variant that impacts the performance.

4.2 Dynamic memory allocation

Cloning requires frequent dynamic memory allocation to place newly cloned agents. Native dynamic memory allocation on GPU is supported but not efficient [28]. To accommodate our design requirements, we have designed our own mechanism, *AgentPool*, to manage memory space required for each cloned simulation instance. An instance of *AgentPool* is initiated with a fixed capacity, *numAgentMax*, specified by users. Spaces for several arrays, as shown in Figure 3(a), are pre-allocated on GPU global memory with *cudaMalloc* API. *agentArray[]* holds the actual agent data. *agentPtrArray[]* keeps pointers to the entries in *agentArray[]* (i.e., *agentPtrArray[i]* contains an index of *agentArray[]*). Initially, *agentPtrArray[i]* is set to *i*. For each element in *agentPtrArray[]*, there is a corresponding element in *delMark[]* array which indicates whether the *agentArray[]* entry pointed by *agentPtrArray[]* element is free or occupied (e.g., *delMark[i]* = 0 indicates the entry agentArray[agentPtrArray[i]] is free). All the entries in *delMark[]* are initialized to '0', meaning that agent pool is initially empty.

Two functions, *remove()* and *add()*, are provided for deleting and adding agents in agent pool. To remove an agent in agent pool, the corresponding element in *delMark[]* array is simply changed from '1' to '0' (see Figure 3(b)). For efficiency, at end of each simulation time-step, a generalized sorting operation will be performed on *agentPtrArray[]* and *delMark[]* together so that the first *numAgent* elements in *delMark[]* array contain '1' and the remaining elements contain '0' (see Figure 3(c)). *numAgent* is the current number of agents in agent pool, which can be easily obtained using a parallel prefix operation on *delmark[]*. In this way, the next free entry in *agentArray[]* can be easily identified by *agentPtrArray[numAgent]*. Note that the general sort operation needs to be performed only on *agentPtrArray[]* and *delMark[]*, not on *agentArray[]* where actual agent data are stored.

Add() will create an agent using the next available entry in *agentArray[]* (Figure 3(d)). Since multiple threads may create new agents at the same time during the simulation, an important issue in implementing *add()* is to obtain a conflict-free index of a free entry in *agentArray[]*. For this purpose, an atomic operation *freeEntry()* is implemented, which returns the index of next available entry in *agentArray[]*.

Using agent pools, the *World* of each cloned simulation instance can be easily constructed as explained in Section 3.2.2.

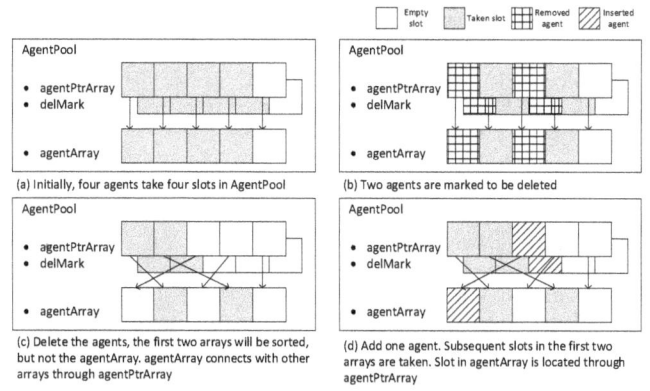

Figure 3: AgentPool manipulation

(a) Initially, four agents take four slots in AgentPool

(b) Two agents are marked to be deleted

(c) Delete the agents, the first two arrays will be sorted, but not the agentArray. agentArray connects with other arrays through agentPtrArray

(d) Add one agent. Subsequent slots in the first two arrays are taken. Slot in agentArray is located through agentPtrArray

4.3 Cloning agents on GPU

Given the massive number of threads a GPU can support, each agent in the agent pools is implemented using a thread. As mentioned above, each agent keeps two sets of flags: cloning flags and cloned flags. With a large number of agents and clones, storing these two sets of flags requires a large memory space. In our implementation, these flags are compressed into bits. Taking cloning flags as an example, in a 32 bit machine, they are stored as an array of 32-bit integers. The size of the array is determined by the number of parameters (i.e., N_P), one integer per parameter. Thus, each parameter is allowed to have 32 value choices in addition to the default one. By default, all bits are set to '0'. When an agent will be either actively or passively cloned because of parameter value choice $P_j^{(i)}$, the jth bit of *cloningFlags[i]* will be set to '1'. Each clone also has a *cloneMasks[]* array with N_P integers. It is used to represent parameter value choices evaluated by the current clone. For example, in a parameter exploration task with two parameters, *cloneMasks[]* array of clone $C(ab)$ should have a^{th} bit of the first integer and b^{th} bit of the second integer set to '1'.

177

Assume the parameter value combinations of parent and child clones differ at parameter $P^{(i)}$. To determine whether or not a copy of an agent in the parent clone needs to be created in the child clone, a bitwise AND operation needs to be performed between agent's $cloningFlags[i]$ and child clone's $cloneMasks[i]$[1]. For example, given a clone $C(ab)$ and its parent clone $C(a0)$, suppose we want to know if a copy of an agent in $C(a0)$ needs to be created in $C(ab)$. This can be done by simply perform a bitwise AND operation between $cloningFlags[2]$ and $cloneMasks[2]$. If the result is greater than 0, it indicates that b^{th} bit of $cloningFlags[2]$ is set to 1 and a copy of this agent needs to be created in the child clone. The pseudo-code of this procedure is given in Algorithm 2.

ALGORITHM 2: Performing actual cloning

Function clone($parentClone$, $childClone$, $P^{(i)}$)
    idx := getGPUThreadId();
    agent := parentClone.AgentPool.get(idx);
    // Child and parent are different at $P^{(i)}$
    cloneMask := childClone.cloneMasks[i];
    isClone := cloneMask;
    isClone &= agent.cloningFlags[i];
    isClone &= ~agent.clonedFlags[i];
    if *isClone > 0* **then**
        agent.cloningFlags[i] &= ~cloneMask;
        childAgent := genChildAgent(agent);
        childAgent.origin := agent;
        childClone.AgentPool.add(childAgent);
    end
end

ALGORITHM 3: Checking active and passive cloning conditions

Function checkActivePassiveCloningConditions($AgentPool$, $World$, $Params$)
    idx := getGPUThreadId();
    agent := AgentPool.get(idx);
    foreach *param $\in$ Params* **do**
        // active cloning condition
        if *agent.matchRule(param)* **then**
            agent.cloningFlags[i] := 0xffffffff;
        end
    end
    neighbors := getNeighbors(agent, World);
    foreach *neighbor $\in$ neighbors* **do**
        // passive cloning condition
        for $i := 0 \to N_P$ **do**
            agent.cloningFlags[i] |= neighbor.cloningFlags[i];
        end
    end
end

For decision point detection (i.e., active cloning), each agent compares its own state with each parameter's decision point detection rule. If the rule specified for $P^{(i)}$ is satisfied, all bits of $cloningFlags[i]$ are set '1', indicating that multiple clones of the agent will be generated to evaluate all value choice of the target parameter. For cloned neighbor detection (i.e., passive cloning), each agent performs a bitwise OR operation between its $cloningFlags[]$ and neighbors' $clonedFlags[]$. This will set the corresponding bits in agent's $cloningFlags[]$ to '1' if it encounters cloned neighbors.

---

[1]It assumes that the array index starts from 1.

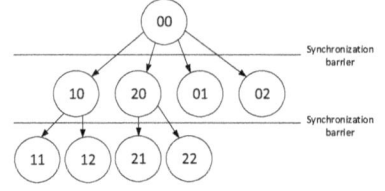

Figure 4: Group of concurrent clones and synchronization barrier

Efficient neighbor searching strategy as discussed in work [17] requires hashing and sorting of agent references in the world according to their geographical locations in the environments, which can be performed rather efficiently on GPU. As explained in Section 3.2.1, setting cloning flags only indicates that agents will be cloned in the next time-step. Copies of agents whose cloning flags are set will be actually created at the beginning of the next time-step. The procedure for checking active and passive cloning conditions is shown in Algorithm 3.

To refrain passive cloning propagation, a throttling mechanism is implemented as shown in Algorithm 4. If the difference between an agent in the child clone and its counterpart in the parent clone is within threshold T, the former will be removed and the latter's corresponding bit in $clonedFlags[i]$ is cleared (i.e., changed to '0'). Since the $clonedFlags[i]$ may be modified by threads corresponding to agents in multiple child clones concurrently at different bits, the bitwise AND operation needs to be performed atomically.

ALGORITHM 4: Refraining passive cloning propagation

Function compareAndEleminate($childClone$, $P^{(i)}$, T)
    idx := getGPUThreadId();
    agent := childClone.AgentPool.get(idx);
    cloneMask := childClone.cloneMasks[i];
    // corresponding agent in the parent clone
    parent := agent.origin;
    diff := compareDiff(agent, parent);
    if *diff < T* **then**
        childClone.AgentPool.remove(agent);
        atomicAnd(parent.clonedFlags[i], ~cloneMask) ;
    end
end

4.4 Optimization

4.4.1 Concurrent clone execution

In our implementation, each agent is implemented using a thread. For each cloned simulation instance, agent's $step()$ function is implemented as a kernel function which is called on the host and executed on GPU by all the threads belonging to the same clone in parallel. To increase concurrency, multiple clones' step() kernel can actually be launched asynchronously and executed concurrently by scheduling each to a CUDA stream. Execution of kernels scheduled to different streams can be overlapped. Kernels scheduled to the same stream are executed according to call order.

Clones at the same height in the clone tree are either child clones of the same parent clone or of different parent clones. They are independent and can be processed in parallel. However, processing of child clone depends on the execution results of parent clone (as explained in Section 3.2.2). So. clones are grouped by height in the clone

178

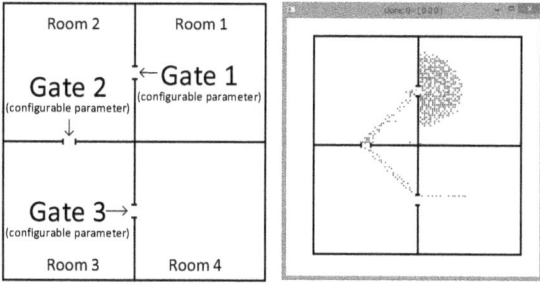

Figure 5: Environment

tree. A synchronization barrier is placed between upper and lower groups, as shown in Figure 4. The synchronization barrier is implemented with the CUDA API *cudaStream-Synchronize*. This API takes parent clone's stream as a parameter, meaning that child clones wait for its parent clone finishing its processing.

4.4.2 Sequential operation aggregation

As explained above, removing holes in agent pool and pre-processing world for efficient neighbor searching require sorting operations. Although `Thrust` library[2] is adopted to carry out highly optimized GPU based sorting algorithm, this part of processing is still very time consuming and accounts for a big percentage of the total execution time. Besides, each sorting operation occupies the entire GPU, which prevents the use of streams to achieve concurrent processing. Sorting must be done sequentially one clone at a time and sorting on data set of each clone individually under-utilizes GPU.

To tackle such inefficiency, a mechanism is proposed to aggregate data sets of all the clones and then sorting is performed on the aggregated data set. Each clone copies the data into its reserved segment of a bigger array. Then each data element is labeled with the clone id. During actual sorting, the clone id is also included as a key. Consequently, data of the same clone are still grouped together after sorting, and can be conveniently copied back to the correct clone for later processing.

5. EXPERIMENTS AND RESULTS

A case study to demonstrate the performance gain obtained through ABS cloning is conducted. The test case is a pedestrian evacuation under social force. In this case study, agents are initiated in room 1 and will be evacuated to room 4 through three gates, as shown in Figure 5. The size of each gate is a configurable parameter to be evaluated with the cloning mechanism. The social force model [14] is used in the simulation. The detail of experiment setups is given in Table 2.

The experiment is performed on a 1.25GHz Fermi-based NVIDIA Quadro 2000 GPU with 1024 MB of main memory and 192 cores distributed over 4 SMs. Each SM has 48 SPs and supports at most 1536 concurrent threads under full GPU utilization. This Fermi-based GPU has 64 KB of fast memory per SM that is split between the L1 data cache and the shared memory. All SMs share an L2 cache of 768 KB. The CUDA programs are compiled with nvcc v6.0 and `-O3` `-arch=sm_20` flags.

---

[2]https://developer.nvidia.com/Thrust

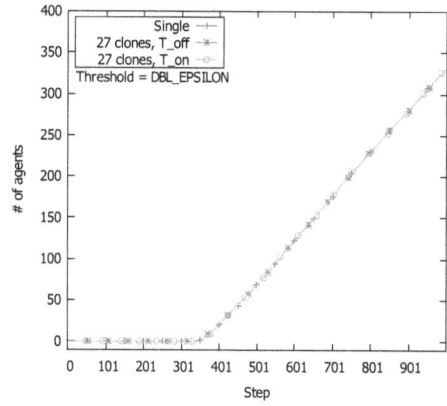

Figure 6: Correctness verification

Table 2: Experiment setups

Description	Value
Environment dimension (unit)	128 * 128
Gate 1, 2, and 3 size choices (unit)	2, 3, 4
Max agent speed (unit per step)	3
Number of time steps	1000
Threshold value in throttling mechanism	DBL_EPSILON (2.22e-16)

5.1 Verification

Simulation cloning reduces computation but should guarantee the correctness. The correctness is defined as that the cloned execution should generate the same result as the stand-alone execution. To show the correctness, the results of clones in ABS cloning and their stand-alone counterparts are compared both with and without the throttling mechanism. Since there are three parameters (i.e., gates), each with three different value choices, the total number of clones is 27. Only the result of the 27th clone, which takes the last value choice of each parameter, is used to compare against the execution result of its stand-alone counterpart. This clone is chosen because it has fewest agents of its own and thus its correctness highly depends on all its ancestor clones. To verify the correctness of our cloning mechanism, the number of agents in the passing through the last gate at each simulation time-step is used as a metric. Randomness is removed to guarantee different runs of the simulation with the same parameter configuration generate identical result.

The test case with 1024 agents running 1000 steps shows that the per step difference between the two execution results are 0, as shown in Figure 6. The state of each agent (location, velocity, etc.) in every simulation time-step is also the same between the two executions. In particular, the cloned simulation using throttling mechanism with threshold value of DBL_EPSILON (i.e., T_on in Figure 6) also generates the same result. This small threshold makes the correctness of simulation remain intact. As shown by lines 1 and 2 in Figure 7, the throttling mechanism significantly improves execution performance.

5.2 Benefit of optimization

This part of experiments shows the performance enhancement obtained through the two optimization techniques, i.e., concurrent clone execution (denoted as *opt 1*) and sequential processing aggregation (denoted as *opt 2*). Similar to the

179

last subsection, the test case with 1024 agents running 1000 steps is used in the experiments. Throttling mechanism is also used in the experiments. NVIDIA NSight Profiler v4.5 is used to collect the profiling data during the execution. Table 3 shows the profiling results of time taken by the default clone (i.e., the simulation instance that takes the first value choice of each parameter) per time-step and the total time taken by all clones of one time-step. Note that for the time-step shown in Table 3, all 27 clones have agents in their agent pools.

In all three cases, the step function of the default clone takes almost the same time to finish ($\sim$4 ms). When both optimization techniques are not used, all clones are processed sequentially and individually. The total execution time of the step is about $\sim$120 ms. When concurrent clone execution is turned on, all 27 clones are processed using different CUDA streams. The synchronization barriers are set between the child and parent clones and processing of clones at the same level of clone tree are overlapped. As a result, the total execution time of the step is reduced to $\sim$100 ms (i.e., 1.2 times speed up). When both optimization techniques are used, the total execution time of the step is further reduced to $\sim$49 ms, resulting 2 times speed up.

Table 3: Profiling results of optimizations

Cases	Execution Time Per Step	
	Default Clone	All Clones
Opt 1 off, Opt 2 off	4.145 ms	120.235 ms
Opt 1 on, Opt 2 off	4.352 ms	100.180 ms
Opt 1 on, Opt 2 on	4.346 ms	49.259 ms

Figure 7 shows the per-step execution time of four cases, i.e., the three cases shown in Table 3 plus the case without using the throttling mechanism and optimization techniques. Jumps in curves correspond to the decision points. The computation load in each simulation time-step is determined by two factors: i) the total number of agents in the agent pools of all the cloned simulation instances; and ii) the amount of processing per agent. Without using the throttling mechanism, agents will be cloned rapidly to all the cloned simulation instances and the total number of agents will reach the maximum before simulation time-step 400. As shown in Figure 5, in the test case used in the experiments, the execution time per step of each clone will decrease as simulation progresses since the density of the crowd surrounding gate 1 decreases. This results in the decreasing trend of per step execution time, after it reaches the maximum, for the case where the throttling mechanism is not used. In all other cases, the throttling mechanism is on and the total number of cloned agents gradually increases and never reaches the maximum.

The results shown in Figure 7 are consistent with that in Table 3. For the case where both optimization techniques are used, it does not perform well at the beginning when most of the agent pools are empty. However, it significantly outperforms all other cases as simulation progresses.

5.3 Overall performance gain

In this part of experiments, the overall performance of the proposed ABS cloning technique is evaluated. All optimizations are turned on. The number of value choices per gate varies from 1 to 5, resulting 1, 8, 27, 64, and 125 clones. The execution time of a stand-alone simulation is used as a

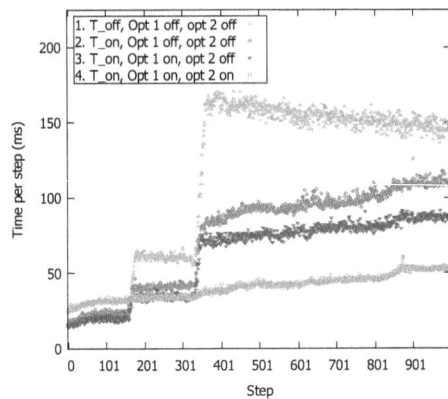

Figure 7: Performance of optimization

baseline for comparison. It takes the default value choices of all the parameters. Speedup is computed as follows:

$$speedup = \frac{Time_{standalone} \times Num_{clones}}{Time_{sim\_cloning}}$$

The total execution time of all stand-alone simulations can be estimated by simply multiplying the execution time of one stand-alone simulation by the number of clones because for the test case used in the experiments, the variation of parameter combinations does not have significant effect on the simulation time.

Figures 8(a) and (b) show the per step execution time and speed up of multiple clones with 1024 agents running for 1000 steps. When the number of clones increases, the execution time increases accordingly. The maximum per step speedup is obtained at the beginning of the simulation, because agents are not yet cloned. The computation performed by the parent clone is shared by all child clones. However, this computation sharing will decrease when the number of cloned agents increases, resulting in the decrease of per step speedup. The average speedups computed based on the total execution time (see Figure 8(c)) are shown in Figure 8(d). The best speedup of 5.1 is achieved when cloning technique is used to evaluate 125 parameter configurations.

Experiments are also conducted to see how the cloning technique responds to the scale of simulation. Figure 9 shows that our proposed cloning mechanism is suitable to process both small scale simulation and relatively large scale simulation. Speedups of 27 clones compared to the stand-alone execution are all above 3 when the number of agents changes from 128 to 2048.

6. CONCLUSIONS AND FUTURE WORK

To conclude, in this paper we present a generic approach for incrementally cloning agent-based simulation and its implementation on GPU. Simulation cloning can be used to accelerate the task of simulation parameter exploration. Existing work mainly focuses on cloning of discrete-event simulation on conventional parallel and distributed computing platforms (e.g., multi-core clusters). Due to the unique way how ABS is executed, cloning agent-based simulation faces new challenges. To support incremental cloning of ABS, mechanisms for both actively and passively cloning agents are proposed. A scheme to maintain the correct context for each cloned ABS instance is developed. In addition, a strategy to restrain the propagation of passive cloning in or-

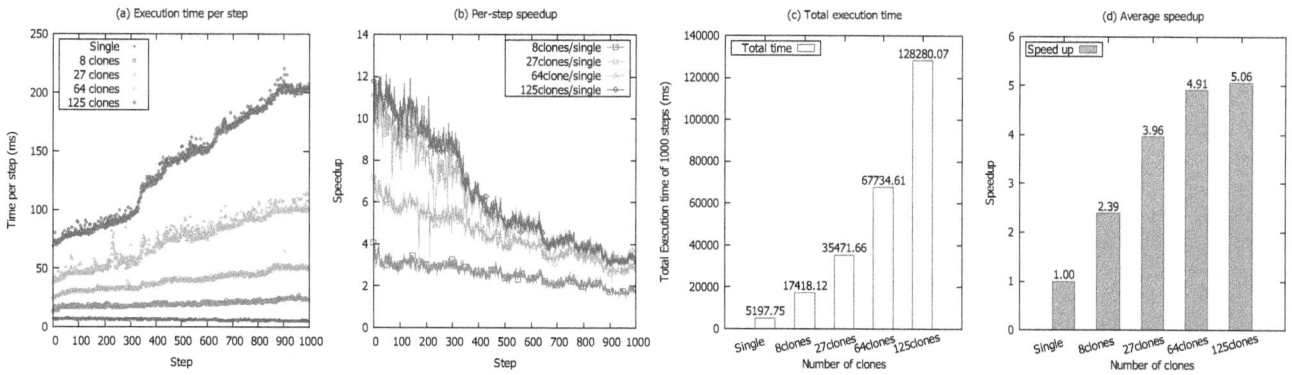

Figure 8: Execution time and speedup vs. number of clones

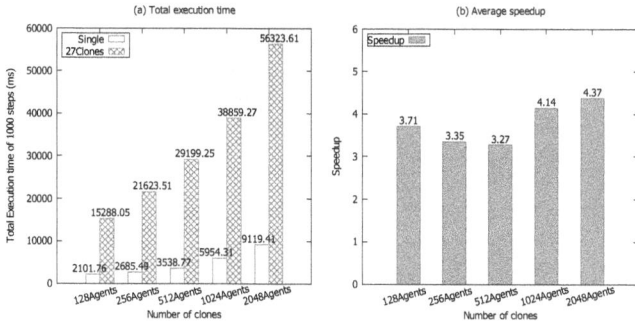

Figure 9: Execution time and speedup vs. number of agents

der to maximize computation sharing amongst cloned ABS instances is also investigated. To efficiently implement the proposed solutions on GPU, a dynamic memory allocation technique is developed. In addition, the implementation is further optimized using concurrent clone execution and sequential operation aggregation techniques. Experiments are conducted on a NVIDIA Quadro 2000 GPU using an agent-based evacuation simulation to demonstrate the correctness and performance advantages of our approach. Particularly, the cloning approach achieves 5.1 times speedup, compared to the stand-alone executions, when evaluating totally 125 parameter configurations. Speedups of the parameter exploration task with 27 configures are all above 3 when the number of agents changes from 128 to 2048.

There are several directions for future work. Firstly, the test case used in the experiments is rather simple, mainly because our current focus is on the development of cloning approach for agent-based simulation and its efficient implementation on GPU. To thoroughly evaluate the proposed approach, more realistic and complex test cases will be used. Secondly, the ultimate goal of simulation cloning is to speedup the evaluation of multiple simulation parameter configurations. In our future work, we will use multiple GPUs to further speedup this evaluation process. Thirdly, we will explore the possibility of integrating our simulation cloning mechanisms with an evolutionary algorithm based optimization engine (e.g., ECJ [18] or CASE [10]) to holistically speed-up the task of parameter space exploration for agent-based simulations.

7. REFERENCES

[1] C. Alexopoulos. A comprehensive review of methods for simulation output analysis. In *Proceedings of the 38th conference on Winter simulation, (Monterey, CA, USA, December 03-06, 2006)*, pages 168–178. IEEE, 2006.

[2] A. Bestavros and B. Wang. Multi-version speculative concurrency control with delayed commit. Technical report, Boston University Computer Science Department, 1993.

[3] B. Calvez and G. Hutzler. Parameter space exploration of agent-based models. In *Proceedings of the 9th international conference on Knowledge-Based Intelligent Information and Engineering Systems, (Melbourne, Australia, September 14-16, 2005)*, pages 633–639. Springer, 2005.

[4] D. Chen, S. J. Turner, W. Cai, B. P. Gan, and M. Y. H. Low. Incremental HLA-based distributed simulation cloning. In *Proceedings of the 36th conference on Winter simulation, (Washington, DC, USA, December 5-8, 2004)*, pages 386–394. Winter Simulation Conference, 2004.

[5] D. Chen, S. J. Turner, W. Cai, B. P. Gan, and M. Y. H. Low. Algorithms for HLA-based distributed simulation cloning. *ACM Transactions on Modeling and Computer Simulation (TOMACS)*, 15(4):316–345, 2005.

[6] D. Chen, S. J. Turner, B. P. Gan, and W. Cai. HLA-based distributed simulation cloning. In *Proceedings of 8th IEEE International Symposium on Distributed Simulation and Real-Time Applications, (Budapest, Hungary, October 21-23, 2004)*, pages 244–247. IEEE, 2004.

[7] D. Chen, S. J. Turner, B. P. Gan, W. Cai, and J. Wei. A decoupled federate architecture for distributed simulation cloning. In *Proceedings of the 15th European Simulation Symposium, (Delft, the Netherlands, October 26-29, 2003)*, pages 131–140. SCS European Publishing House, 2003.

[8] D. Chen, S. J. Turner, B. P. Gan, W. Cai, J. Wei, and N. Julka. Alternative solutions for distributed simulation cloning. *Simulation*, 79(5-6):299–315, 2003.

[9] W. J. Davis. On-line simulation: Need and evolving research requirements. In *Handbook of simulation*, pages 465–516. Wiley-Interscience, 1998.

[10] J. Decraene, M. Y.-H. Low, F. Zeng, S. Zhou, and W. Cai. Automated modeling and analysis of agent-based simulations using the CASE framework. In *Proceedings of 11th International Conference on Control Automation Robotics & Vision (ICARCV) (Singapore, Singapore, December 7-10, 2010)*, pages 346–351. IEEE, 2010.

[11] A. L. Espindola, D. Girardi, T. J. Penna, C. T. Bauch, A. S. Martinez, and B. C. Cabella. Exploration of the parameter space in an agent-based model of tuberculosis spread: emergence of drug resistance in developing vs developed countries. *International Journal of Modern Physics C*, 23(06):1–9, 2012.

[12] P. W. Glynn and P. Heidelberger. Analysis of parallel replicated simulations under a completion time constraint. *ACM Transactions on Modeling and Computer Simulation (TOMACS)*, 1(1):3–23, 1991.

[13] A. P. Goldberg. Virtual time synchronization of replicated processes. In *Proceedings of the 6th Workshop on Parallel and distributed simulation (Newport Beach, CA, USA, January 20-22, 1992)*, pages 107–116. SCS Simulation Series, 1992.

[14] D. Helbing and P. Molnar. Social force model for pedestrian dynamics. *Physical review E*, 51(5):4282, 1995.

[15] M. Hybinette and R. M. Fujimoto. Cloning parallel simulations. *ACM Transactions on Modeling and Computer Simulation (TOMACS)*, 11(4):378–407, 2001.

[16] G. Kunz, D. Schemmel, J. Gross, and K. Wehrle. Multi-level parallelism for time-and cost-efficient parallel discrete event simulation on gpus. In *Proceedings of the 2012 ACM/IEEE/SCS 26th Workshop on Principles of Advanced and Distributed Simulation, (Zhangjiajie, China, July 15-19, 2012)*, pages 23–32. IEEE, 2012.

[17] X. Li, W. Cai, and S. J. Turner. Efficient neighbor searching for agent-based simulation on GPU. In *Proceedings of 18th IEEE International Symposium on Distributed Simulation and Real-Time Applications, (Toulouse, France, October 1-3, 2014)*, pages 87–96. IEEE/ACM, 2014.

[18] S. Luke. The ECJ Owner's Manual. Technical report, ECJ Evolutionary Computation Library, George Mason University, 2010.

[19] NVIDIA. NVIDIA CUDA programming guide. Technical report, `http://docs.nvidia.com/cuda/cuda-c-programming-guide/index.html`. [Online, last accessed: March 2015].

[20] H. Park and P. A. Fishwick. A GPU-based application framework supporting fast discrete-event simulation. *Simulation*, 86(10):613–628, 2009.

[21] H. Park and P. A. Fishwick. An analysis of queuing network simulation using GPU-based hardware acceleration. *ACM Transactions on Modeling and Computer Simulation (TOMACS)*, 21(3):1–22, 2011.

[22] M. Steinberger, M. Kenzel, B. Kainz, and D. Schmalstieg. Scatteralloc: Massively parallel dynamic memory allocation for the GPU. In *Proceedings of Innovative Parallel Computing, (San Jose, CA, USA, May 13-14, 2012)*, pages 1–10. IEEE, 2012.

[23] W. Tang and Y. Yao. A GPU-based discrete event simulation kernel. *Simulation*, 89(11):1335–1354, 2013.

[24] T. Terano. Exploring the vast parameter space of multi-agent based simulation. In *Proceedings of the 2006 international conference on Multi-agent-based simulation (Hakodate, Japan, May 8-12, 2006)*, pages 1–14. Springer, 2006.

[25] V. Volkov. Better performance at lower occupancy. In *Proceedings of the GPU Technology Conference (San Jose, CA, USA, September 20-23, 2010)*, volume 10. NVIDIA, 2010.

[26] J. Von Neumann. Probabilistic logics and the synthesis of reliable organisms from unreliable components. *Automata studies*, 34:43–98, 1956.

[27] M. Wagner, W. Cai, and M. H. Lees. Emergence by strategy: flocking boids and their fitness in relation to model complexity. In *Proceedings of the 2013 Winter Simulation Conference (Washington, DC, USA, December 8-11, 2013)*, pages 1479–1490. IEEE, 2013.

[28] S. Widmer, D. Wodniok, N. Weber, and M. Goesele. Fast dynamic memory allocator for massively parallel architectures. In *Proceedings of the 6th Workshop on General Purpose Processor Using Graphics Processing Units*, pages 120–126. ACM, 2013.

[29] F. Zeng, J. Decraene, M. Y. H. Low, S. Zhou, and W. Cai. Evolving optimal and diversified military operational plans for computational red teaming. *Systems Journal*, 6(3):499–509, 2012.

Efficient Inter-Process Synchronization for Parallel Discrete Event Simulation on Multicores

Pavol Bauer, Jonatan Lindén, Stefan Engblom and Bengt Jonsson

Dept. of Information Technology, Uppsala University

{pavol.bauer,jonatan.linden,stefane,bengt}@it.uu.se

ABSTRACT

We present a new technique for controlling optimism in Parallel Discrete Event Simulation on multicores. It is designed to be suitable for simulating models, in which the time intervals between successive events between different processes are highly variable, and have no lower bounds. In our technique, called *Dynamic Local Time Window Estimates (DLTWE)*, each processor communicates time estimates of its next inter-processor event to (some of) its neighbors, which use the estimates as bounds for advancement of their local simulation time. We have implemented our technique in a parallel simulator for simulation of spatially extended Markovian processes of interacting entities, which can model chemical reactions, processes from biology, epidemics, and many other applications. Intervals between successive events are exponentially distributed, thus having a significant variance and no lower bound. We show that the DLTWE technique can be tuned to drastically reduce the frequency of rollbacks and enable speedups which is superior to that obtained by other works. We also show that the DLTWE technique significantly improves performance over other existing techniques for optimism control that attempt to predict arrival of inter-process events by statistical techniques.

Categories and Subject Descriptors

I.6.8 [**Simulation and Modeling**]: Types of simulation—*Discrete Event,Parallel*

Keywords

Parallel Discrete-Event Simulation, PDES, Optimism control, Multicore, Spatial Stochastic Simulation

1. INTRODUCTION

Discrete Event Simulation (DES) is an increasingly important tool for evaluating system models in all fields of science and engineering. To improve the capacity and performance of DES simulators, several techniques for Parallel DES (PDES) were developed in the 90's [26, 20, 25, 15]. Parallelization made it possible to simulate large system models, but it was challenging to achieve good speedup corresponding to the number of employed processors. A major difficulty was that PDES requires fine-grained synchronization between processing elements, which was not easy to realize efficiently on multiprocessors at that time, given the comparatively long communication delays between processing elements. With the current advent of multicore processors, these delays have decreased, triggering the development of new techniques for PDES targeting multicores (e.g., [7, 27, 35]).

In PDES, the simulation model is partitioned onto logical processes (LPs), each of which evolves its sub-model along a local simulation time axis. LPs exchange timestamped events to incorporate inter-LP dependencies. Each LP must ensure that the processing of incoming events is correctly interleaved with local events. The problem with incoming events that violate an LP's local timestamp ordering (so-called *stragglers*) can in principle be handled in two ways: *conservative* approaches allow an LP to process an event only when it is guaranteed that no straggler will later arrive [26]; *optimistic* approaches allow stragglers by invoking suitable corrective action (rollback) [20, 25]. In purely conservative approaches, local execution of LPs may be blocked excessively unless inter-LP events can always be predicted long in advance (e.g., when simulating networks with long communication latencies), which most often is not possible. On the other hand, in optimistic approaches, performance may be damaged by excessive numbers of rollbacks. Many approaches to PDES therefore allow stragglers, but control the optimism by various heuristic techniques, based on, e.g., observed frequency of rollbacks [29, 8], patterns of past inter-LP messages [14], etc.

In this paper we present a new technique for controlling optimism in PDES. It is particularly designed for high efficiency when simulating models in which the time intervals between successive inter-LP events are highly variable and have no lower bounds. Such models pose severe difficulties for both conservative and existing variants of optimistic approaches. Our technique, called *Dynamic Local Time Window Estimates (DLTWE)*, exploits the opportunities for fast multicore inter-LP communication. DLTWE assumes that an LP can reasonably estimate timestamps of its next k outgoing inter-LP events, where k is a tuneable parameter of our technique. Each LP continuously communicates these estimates to its corresponding neighboring LPs, which use the estimates as bounds for advancing their local simulation time. Since the communicated timestamps are merely estimates, DLTWE does not rule out the occurrence of stragglers, meaning that each LP must perform rollbacks when needed. If the estimates are sufficiently accurate, then the number of rollbacks should be small, allowing the simulator to operate with high efficiency.

We have developed the DLTWE technique in the context of stochastic spatial simulation of models governed by the mesoscopic reaction-diffusion master equation (RDME) [4]. Here the model's geometry is discretized into small subvolumes (a.k.a., voxels), each of which contains a discrete number of species (e.g., molecules). In each subvolume the species obey prescribed stochastic reaction laws and the species may move (by diffusion) to other neighboring subvolumes. When simulating an RDME model using PDES, the subvolumes are partitioned onto LPs. Hence, a diffusion event between two boundary subvolumes causes inter-LP communication. By the Markovian nature of the model, the waiting time of any event is an exponentially distributed random variable; thus the waiting time has a significant variance and no lower bound.

In the present paper we show that the DLTWE technique has small overhead when implemented on a shared-memory multicore processor. In our simulator, each LP maintains a list of future events, whose occurrence times have already been sampled; this is already a component of our technique for simulating RDME models [3]. We show how the DLTWE technique can be tuned by limiting how far into the future DLTWE estimates will be provided: The cost of providing more accurate DLTWE estimates further into the future can be tuned, both against the cost of rollbacks caused by poor estimates and against achieving limited optimism in contexts where rollbacks are relatively inexpensive.

In the paper, we also demonstrate the effect of a technique to limit the cost of rollbacks by reversing only those processed events that are causally dependent on the straggler that caused the rollback in the first place. Less costly rollbacks also allow more optimism in the simulation, thereby limiting waiting and increasing overall simulation efficiency.

In our evaluation, we show how our implementation of the DLTWE technique enables speedups in parallel simulation of RDME models, which is superior to that obtained by other works. We support this comparison by a detailed profiling of the simulator behavior, which shows how DLTWE significantly reduces both the cost of unnecessary blocking and of excessive rollbacks. In particular, we compare the DLTWE technique against other existing techniques for optimistic control, such as the Probabilistic Adaptive Direct Optimism by Ferscha [14], and show that employing the DLTWE results in at least a doubling of parallel efficiency.

After reviewing related work in the next section, we review the class of spatial stochastic simulation models considered by our simulator in Section 3. A detailed description of our parallelization algorithm, including the DLTWE technique, is given in Section 4. Section 5 contains a detailed evaluation of the performance of our parallelization technique, including a detailed breakdown of the simulation effort, and a comparison with other techniques for optimism control. Section 6 contains conclusions and directions for future work.

2. RELATED WORK

Numerous methods for synchronization in PDES have been proposed. Extensive surveys are provided in [15, 9, 18]; here we can only review a selection.

Synchronization methods can be coarsely classified into *conservative* [26] and *optimistic* [20, 25]. Each approach has its drawbacks, which subsequently proposed techniques aim to mitigate. For instance, *conservative time windows* [1] are used to increase parallelism in a purely conservative approach: this assumes that there is always a guaranteed lower bound on the delay until the next inter-LP event, which does not exist in stochastic simulations that we consider.

Optimistic approaches [20, 25] have the potential to achieve higher parallelism, but performance may be damaged by excessive rollbacks. Many techniques have been developed for controlling the optimism and limiting the frequency of rollbacks. One idea is to employ dynamically moving *time windows* that bound how far each LP can advance its local time (e.g., [31, 33]). Synchronization between time windows typically assumes frequent calculation of *global virtual time* (GVT), which is an expensive global calculation, for which a special high-speed network is recommended. A further development of these approaches is the class of "near-perfect" state information (NPSI) protocols, including the *elastic time algorithm* [32]. Here, the bound is based on GVT and information about future messages to neighboring LPs, which is computed and communicated over a special high-speed network. Our DLTWE approach is also based on controlling optimism by information propagated between LPs; however, we show how such an idea can be realized on a modern multicore without using such a high-speed network.

There are also approaches where optimism control can be performed by LPs based on locally available information, not requiring a special high-speed network. In some of these techniques, each LP autonomously regulates its event processing speed against parameters, such as frequency of rollbacks [29, 8]. Another approach is to use the pattern of past incoming inter-LP messages [14] to predict the time of the next incoming message by statistical techniques, thereby obtaining a bound for advancement of local time. We compare this approach to our technique in Section 5.5. A study where model-specific information has been used to extract additional synchronization information (in the form of an extended lookahead) is presented in [24]. In our approach we also make use of model-specific knowledge; we extract relevant entries from the event queue and communicate them to neighbors as DLTWEs.

Other performance-enhancing techniques in optimistic PDES include to avoid rollbacks due to out-of-timestamp-order when this is possible. Chen and Szymanski [6] introduce a "lookback", a limited history of recent events. When a straggler event arrives, it is checked against the history, and if no causality error is found, the event is processed as if arriving in order. Leong et al. [23] view the processes in the simulator as objects of abstract data types, and messages as operations being performed on the objects. Some of the operations commute with each other, and hence rollbacks can be avoided. Recently, techniques for PDES that specifically target multicores have been developed. One approach is to allow each subdomain to be accessed by several cores (e.g., [7, 27]), thereby achieving better load balancing.

We conjecture that for our work, this benefit would be more than outweighed by the cost needed for synchronizing accesses to shared data. Wang et al. [35] present a multicore NUMA-aware modification of the general optimistic simulator ROSS [5]. We believe that our simulator would gain from being optimized for a NUMA architecture as well, such an improvement is however orthogonal to what we present here.

Parallel simulation of RDME models using exact numerical methods was previously addressed by [21, 34, 10]. The simulators are implemented in MPI, where each LP is mapped to an MPI process. Each LP simulates a subvolume [10, 34] or a larger subdomain [21]. As discussed by Dematté and Mazza [10], conservative simulation of RDME models is infeasible due to the lack of precise lookahead. Hence, simulators rely on optimistic protocols. A reduction of rollback cost for RDME models was previously implemented by a static time window from the GVT [21] or adaptive protocols, such as Breathing Time Warp [34]. A more general class of diffusive systems can also be represented in Cell-DEVS, parallel simulation of such models has been studied by Jafer et al. [19].

3. SPATIAL STOCHASTIC SIMULATION

In this section, we review the class of spatial stochastic simulation models considered by our simulator.

The reaction-diffusion master equation (RDME) is a framework to describe the dynamics of spatially extended Markovian processes of interacting entities. As the name suggests, the RDME is a suitable model for chemical reactions in a diffusive environment, but processes from biology, epidemics, and many other applications may also be successfully treated. In particular, the RDME is particularly suitable for systems where discrete effects (due to small populations) and thermal noise should not be neglected.

The spatial domain of interest is divided into *subvolumes*, each of which maintains a *copy number* (discrete count) of all participating *species*. The dynamics of the model is then a continuous-time Markov chain over the state space consisting of all copy numbers in all subvolumes. The state transitions fall in one of two categories, (i) a *reaction event* acts in a *single* subvolume by removing a combination of species and replacing it with a different combination, (ii) a *diffusion event* moves a single unit of one species from one subvolume to a neighboring subvolume, and hence changes the state of *two* subvolumes. The waiting time for each transition is exponentially distributed with an intensity that is proportional to the product of the copy numbers of the involved species.

As a concrete example, a reaction from the Lotka-Volterra predator-prey model described in Section 5.1 reads

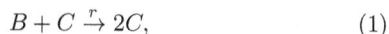

$$B + C \xrightarrow{r} 2C, \qquad (1)$$

that is, in a particular subvolume one unit of B (prey) is consumed and one unit of C (predator) is produced. The intensity for this event is proportional to the product of the number of B's and C's, where r is the constant of proportionality, later referred to as the reaction rate constant. At any time t, the waiting time to the next event is exponentially distributed with this intensity.

In a *spatial* context, prey in one subvolume can escape by moving to another subvolume. If B_i and B_j denote the population of preys in neighboring subvolumes i and j, then

$$B_i \xrightarrow{q_{ij}} B_j, \qquad (2)$$

expresses the event that one unit of prey in the ith subvolume moves to the jth. The waiting time for this event is equal to the product of B_i and the transport rate constant q_{ij}. Depending on the scaling of this constant versus the spatial units, different types of transport may in principle be modeled. In this work we consider the *diffusive scaling regime*, in which $q_{ij} \propto h^{-2}$, with h a length-scale (e.g., a radius) of the subvolumes. Notably, with a finer discretization (i.e., $h \to 0$), the number of diffusion events will increasingly dominate the Markov chain.

It was Gillespie [17] who popularized simulating independent samples from master equations in general. For RDMEs one of the first practical sampling algorithms was proposed in [12], the Next Subvolume Method (NSM). The NSM is a spatial extension of Gillespie's Direct Method, incorporating features of the Next Reaction Method [16], which was the first sampling algorithm using a sorted event queue for efficiency.

In this work we consider a related method, the All Events Method (AEM) [3]. The algorithm generates next event times for each reaction and diffusion in all subvolumes and stores them in an *event queue*. It proceeds by repeatedly selecting the event with the smallest time from the event queue, processes it by updating the state, and finally updates the event queue by sampling the next time for the event just processed. Also, at this stage, those rates which have changed due to the state update need to be rescaled (see [3] for details).

Being essentially a spatial extension of the Common Reaction Path method [28], the AEM has the benefit of defining a consistent stochastic *flow* in the sense of dynamical systems. This means that the result from different simulation runs, e.g., with slightly different model parameters, using the same stream of random numbers will be comparable in a path-wise sense. Besides implying a much reduced variance in statistical estimators, this is also required when evaluating the effect of small perturbations or coefficient uncertainties in a path-wise sense (e.g., root-mean-square, see [3]).

Of relevance to the current application, the AEM stores the waiting times for the next instance of each reaction or diffusion event such that it is possible to estimate with reasonable precision when specific events will happen, notably including diffusion events between subvolumes. Another feature of more practical nature is that, by seeding the random number generators in an identical way, the parallel simulations yield identical results independently on the number of LPs, thus ensuring correctness. These features come at a certain cost, however, as the AEM requires to store more entries in the event queue compared to, e.g., the NSM.

4. PARALLEL IMPLEMENTATION

In this section we detail our parallelization of the All Events Method (PAEM), which implements the DLTWE for a general class of RDME models.

In our parallel simulator, the subvolumes of the simulation model are partitioned into subdomains, each of which is assigned to an LP. Each LP evolves the state of its subdomain while maintaining three main data structures: (i) the *subdomain state*, i.e., for each subvolume, the number of entities of each species (the copy number) as well as the timestamp of the last event affecting the subvolume, (ii) a time-sorted *event queue*, containing the next occurrence of each event type (reaction or diffusion) for each subvolume in its subdomain, and (iii) a *rollback history*, which is a time-sorted sequence of events already processed by this LP.

Each LP advances the simulation by processing events that affect its subdomain. The LP repeatedly finds the next event for processing, either in its event queue or in a message from another LP, and processes it by (i) updating the states of affected subvolumes, (ii) adding the event to its rollback history, and (iii) adding the next event of the same type and subvolume to its event queue. If the event is a diffusion event which crosses a subdomain boundary, then a message is transmitted to the neighboring LP; each pair of LPs is connected by a FIFO channel in each direction.

Whenever an LP receives a diffusion message that causes a causality violation (i.e., it is a *straggler*), it must perform a *rollback* to the time immediately before the straggler's timestamp, using its rollback history. We have implemented two different versions of the rollback operation: a more costly simple rollback and a less costly selective rollback. The selective rollback is described further below. In the *simple rollback*, the local time of the LP is reset to the time immediately preceding the timestamp of the straggler, and the events in the rollback history that occur after this timestamp are processed "backwards". All diffusion messages that had been sent by the LP during the rollback interval must be undone by sending corresponding *anti-messages* to the corresponding LPs. An anti-message *cancels* any event that was sent earlier with the same or a later timestamp. The receipt of an anti-message triggers rollbacks at the receiving LPs if it cancels a message that has already been processed.

Since rollbacks triggered by stragglers hurt performance, an LP should try not to advance its local simulation time past the timestamp of any diffusion message that will be received in the future. For this purpose, we have developed the DLTWE (Dynamic Local Time Window Estimate) technique, whereby each LP communicates to a subset of its neighboring LPs an estimate of the timestamp of the next diffusion to respective LP; these estimates are obtained from the current contents of the event queue. An LP does not advance its local simulation past the time of the earliest incoming time estimate. The optimism of the simulation is controlled by the tuning of the DLTWE computation, as described in more detail in Section 5.4.

To reduce the impact of rollbacks, we have developed a technique for *selective rollback*. An LP that receives a straggler or an anti-message performs a refined analysis before executing a rollback. Rather than merely comparing the timestamp of the incoming diffusion message with its local simulation time, the receiving LP finds the causality violations that are incurred by the incoming message. The LP finds the processed events that are causally dependent on the straggler or anti-message using the trace. Only these events are rolled back. The cost of selective rollback is typically significantly lower than the cost of simple rollback.

4.1 The simulator main loop

Algorithm 1 is a pseudocode description of the main loop executed by each LP. Lines 2 through 6 define the main data structures. These are

- *EventQueue* is a time-sorted priority queue containing the scheduled local events;

- *SubvolumeState* represents the state of each subvolume in the subdomain, i.e., the number of entities of each species in each subvolume, as well as the timestamp of the last event affecting the subvolume,

- *History* is a time-sorted sequence of events already processed by the LP; old events are regularly removed from the history by fossil collection, which we do not further describe here,

- *Channels* contains an incoming message channel for each neighboring LP, and

- $Dltwe_{j,i}$ consists of a DLTWE estimate from LP_i to LP_j, defined for each pair of neighboring LPs.

For an event e, we let $e.time$ denote its timestamp; for a diffusion event e, we let $e.dest$ denote its destination subvolume. For a subvolume s, we let $dom(s)$ denote the index of the LP to which s belongs.

The main simulator loop consists of two phases. The first phase (lines 8–18), finds the next event to be processed, as follows. First, for each incoming channel, the first message that is not canceled by a later anti-message in the channel, is retrieved by means of the function RETRIEVEMSG. Intuitively, the retrieved message is the first one in the channel that should be processed after all rollbacks induced by anti-messages have been performed. The earliest of these messages is assigned to e_{msg}. If e_{msg} is a straggler which violates causality in its destination subvolume (checked at line 9) then a rollback is performed. Second, the earliest event e_{local} in the event queue is read. If e_{msg} is earlier than e_{local} (line 12), then e_{msg} is assigned to e for processing. Otherwise, the event e_{local} is assigned to e for processing, but only if no DLTWE estimate is violated (line 15). If a DLTWE estimate is violated, the LP blocks until the expected message or a message from another neighbor is received, at which time the main loop is restarted, in order to process the message (line 17).

The second phase (lines 19–30) updates the subdomain state of the LP by processing the event e that was selected in the first phase. It starts by checking whether e is a "local straggler", i.e., a local diffusion event (between subvolumes of the same LP) that would cause a local causality error (line 19), in which case a rollback is necessary. Thereafter, e is processed by adding it to the event history (line 21), updating the states of affected subvolumes, and updating the times of future events in the event queue that are affected by the state change(s) (lines 22 through 26). If e is a diffusion to another subdomain, a message is sent (line 28) to the appropriate LP. After that, the DLTWEs are updated (line 30) to inform the neighboring LPs of the estimated times of the next diffusion events.

DLTWEs are computed based on outgoing diffusion events that can be found in a prefix of the event queue, thus not considering diffusion events that are scheduled far into the future. If no relevant diffusion events for a specific LP are found in the prefix, the corresponding DLTWE is set to infinity. The length of the considered prefix is a tuneable parameter of our approach. A short prefix induces less effort for DLTWE computation, but will generate DLTWE estimates for only a subset of neighboring LPs, inducing more optimism in the simulation; too much optimism may result in high cost for rollbacks. A long prefix, on the other hand, costs more effort for DLTWE computation, and will avoid excessive cost of rollbacks, but may in some context also in-

---

Algorithm 1: Main loop of Parallel AEM Simulator, executed by each LP.

1: LPs are indexed $1 \ldots N$, Subvolumes of LP_i are indexed $1 \ldots n_i$.
   Each LP contains:

2:      $EventQueue$ ▷ *Time-sorted priority queue of scheduled events*

3:      $SubvolumeState[1 \ldots n_i]$ ▷ *Current state of subdomain*

4:      $History$ ▷ *Event history, used for rollbacks*

5:      $Channels[\text{neighbor } LP_j s]$ ▷ *Incoming message channels, one for each neighboring LP*

   Additionally, LPs communicate via global DLTWEs:

6:      $Dltwe_{j,i}$ ▷ *A DLTWE from LP_j to LP_i (defined for each pair of neighboring LPs)*

7: **while true do**

     ▷ *First phase: find the next event to process*

8:      $e_{\text{msg}} \leftarrow$ earliest message in $\{\textsc{RetrieveMsg}(\text{chan}) \mid \text{chan} \in Channels\}$ ▷ *Retrieve, but do not pop, the earliest process-*

9:      **if** $e_{\text{msg}}.\text{time} < SubvolumeState[e_{\text{msg}}.\text{dest}].\text{time}$ **then**   ▷ *able incoming message.*

10:          $\textsc{SelectiveRollback}(e_{\text{msg}})$ ▷ *If e_{msg} is a straggler, then a rollback must be performed.*

11:      $e_{\text{local}} \leftarrow$ earliest event in $EventQueue$

12:      **if** $e_{\text{msg}}.\text{time} \leq e_{\text{local}}.\text{time}$ **then**   ▷ *If m precedes any local event*

13:          $e \leftarrow$ pop e_{msg} from its message channel   ▷ *The event e to be processed is from the incoming channels*

14:      **else**

15:          **while** $\exists$ neighboring LP_j s.t. $Dltwe_{j,i} < e_{\text{local}}.\text{time}$ **do** ▷ *If next event is later than some DLTWE*

16:              **if** $\exists e_{\text{new}} \in Channels[LP_j]$ **or**
                     exists message in other channel earlier than $Dltwe_{j,i}$ **then**

17:                  **goto** 8   ▷ *restart loop from line 8*

18:          $e \leftarrow$ pop e_{local} from event queue   ▷ *Otherwise the event to be processed is the next local one*

     ▷ *Second phase: process selected event*

19:      **if** e is a local diffusion event and $SubvolumeState[e.\text{dest}].\text{time} > e.\text{time}$ **then**

20:          $\textsc{SelectiveRollback}(e)$

21:      add e to $History$

22:      update state of $SubvolumeState[e.\text{subvol}]$

23:      update timestamps of affected future reactions/diffusions in $EventQueue$

24:      **if** e is a diffusion **then**

25:          **if** $e.\text{dest}$ is local **then**

26:              update $SubvolumeState[e.\text{dest}]$

27:          **else**

28:              send diffusion message to owner of $e.\text{dest}$

29:      **for each** neighbor LP_j **do**

30:          $Dltwe_{i,j} \leftarrow \min(\{e_{\text{diff}}.\text{time} \mid e_{\text{diff}} \in \text{prefix}(EventQueue) \text{ and } e_{\text{diff}}.\text{dest} \text{ is in the domain of } LP_j\} \cup \infty)$

---

duce too little optimism. How to tune the prefix length to make this trade-off is examined in Section 5.4.

As an optimization, the updates of the DLTWEs at line 30 are performed only when necessary, i.e., when the estimated time of some future inter-LP diffusion event is updated. The DLTWE estimates are communicated using a single memory cell per direction and neighboring LP-pair, which is only written to when this results in a new value, to avoid unnecessary coherence traffic.

4.2 The SelectiveRollback function

The function $\textsc{SelectiveRollback}(e_{\text{cause}})$, shown in Algorithm 2, reverses the effect of all events processed by an LP at or after time $e_{\text{cause}}.\text{time}$, that are causally dependent on e_{cause}. If a causally dependent event has been sent to a neighbor, a corresponding anti-message will be sent. Different subvolumes may be rolled back to a different timestamp. First, we let H contain the part of the history that may be rolled back (line 2). After that we define a set D of subvolume timestamp pairs, $\langle \text{subvolume}, \text{timestamp} \rangle$. Each pair $\langle s, t \rangle$ defines the time t to which subvolume s has to be rolled back. Initially, if e_{cause} is a straggler, D must at least contain $\langle e_{\text{cause}}.\text{dest}, e_{\text{cause}}.\text{time} \rangle$ (line 4). If e_{cause} is an anti-message,

D instead contains all destination subvolumes of messages received from $\text{dom}(e_{\text{cause}})$ after time $e_{\text{cause}}.\text{time}$, and their respective time (line 6). Thereafter, D is completed to contain all $\langle \text{subvolume}, \text{timestamp} \rangle$ pairs that are causally dependent on e_{cause}. More precisely, for every diffusion event between any two subvolumes s, s' of this LP at time t'', we have that if $\langle s, t \rangle \in D$ and $t < t''$, there exists $\langle s', t' \rangle \in D$ such that $t' \leq t''$ (line 7). In the main **while** loop, the subset of the history H is traversed backwards in time, event by event (line 8). Each event being incident on some subvolume occurring in D, after the corresponding time t, is rolled back. An event e is reverted by reversing the state changes of the affected subvolumes, and updating the intensity of the corresponding reaction or diffusion accordingly. If the rollback was initiated by an anti-message, and e is an incoming diffusion originating from a neighbor LP that did not send this anti-message, then e will be pushed back to the top of its originating message channel (checked at line 12). If one or more diffusion events have been sent to a neighbor LP_j during the rollback interval, a single anti-message will be sent, containing the timestamp of the earliest message sent to LP_j after t (starting at line 14).

Algorithm 2: Rollback events at or after time t.

1: **function** SELECTIVEROLLBACK(event e_{cause})
2:     $H \leftarrow \{e \mid e \in History \text{ and } e.\text{time} \geq e_{\text{cause}}.\text{time}\}$
3:     **if** e_{cause} is straggler **then**
4:         $D \leftarrow \{\langle e_{\text{cause}}.\text{dest}, e_{\text{cause}}.\text{time}\rangle\}$
5:     **else** $\triangleright$ e_{cause} *is an anti-message*
6:         $D \leftarrow \{\langle e.\text{dest}, e.\text{time}\rangle \mid e \in H, \text{dom}(e.\text{subvol}) = $
                                $\text{dom}(e_{\text{cause}}.\text{subvol})\}$
7:     $D \leftarrow$ extend D under causal dependence
8:     **while** $e \leftarrow$ pop latest event in H **do**
9:         **if** $\exists \langle s, t \rangle \in D$ s.t.
                $e.\text{subvol} = s$ and $e.\text{time} \geq t$ **then**
10:            revert e
11:            Pop e from *History*
12:            **if** $e.\text{subvol} \in LP_j$ and not $(\text{isanti}(e_{\text{cause}})$ and
                $\text{dom}(e_{\text{cause}}.\text{subvol}) = LP_j)$ **then**
13:                push e back to front of $Channels[LP_j]$
14:     **for each** neighbor LP_j **do** $\triangleright$ *send anti-messages*
15:         $e_{\text{diff}} \leftarrow$ earliest rolled back diffusion to LP_j
16:         send anti-message with time $e_{\text{diff}}.\text{time}$ to LP_j

4.3 The RetrieveMsg function

The function RETRIEVEMSG(*chan*) returns the first message in the incoming channel *chan* that can be meaningfully processed, i.e., it is not undone by a corresponding anti-message already present in *chan*. The function starts by finding the timestamp of the earliest anti-message in the channel (line 3). Thereafter, messages are popped and discarded from the channel, until either the first message preceding the earliest anti-message is encountered, or until the anti-message itself is encountered (lines 4–7). In the former case, the function returns the message immediately without popping it from *chan*. In the latter case, a rollback corresponding to the anti-message is performed (line 8) and the procedure is repeated. Thus, there are two possible states of the channel after the completion of the function: *a*) either there are no anti-messages left in the channel, or *b*) the first message in the channel is a diffusion event and has a time earlier than the time of the earliest anti-message in the channel.

Algorithm 3: Locating the first processable message.

1: **function** RETRIEVEMSG(channel *chan*)
2:     **while** *chan* contains anti-messages **do**
3:         $e_{\text{anti}} \leftarrow$ earliest anti-message in *chan*
4:         **for** $e \leftarrow$ first message in *chan* **do**
5:            **if** $e.\text{time} < e_{\text{anti}}.\text{time}$ **then return** e
6:            pop e from *chan*
7:            **if** $e = e_{\text{anti}}$ **then goto** 8
8:         SELECTIVEROLLBACK($e_{\text{anti}}.\text{event}$)
9:     **return** first message in *chan*

5. PERFORMANCE EVALUATION

In this section, we evaluate the performance of our parallelization technique. The aim is to answer the following questions.

- *How does our technique scale with the number of LPs?* In Section 5.2 we determine the speedup obtained on benchmarks, and investigate the dependency on model parameters.
- *How does the parallelized simulator behave?* In Section 5.3 we describe how the computation effort is spent on different activities, exposing potential bottlenecks.
- *How should the DLTWE technique be tuned?* In Section 5.4 we describe how to tune the cost for the computation of the DLTWE estimate against the gain in reduced rollback frequency.
- *How does the DLTWE technique compare to other techniques?* In Section 5.5, we compare the DLTWE technique to adaptive optimism control techniques, that are based on local history. In Section 5.6, we compare our parallel simulator to other existing simulators for RDME models.

The performance was evaluated on three sets of benchmarks, described in more detail in Section 5.1. All experiments were run on a 4-socket Intel Sandy Bridge E5–4650 machine, each socket having 8 cores and a 20 MB shared L3-cache. Hyperthreading was used, resulting in a total of 16 hardware threads per processor. An LP is always assigned to a single thread. Speedup is defined as the wall-clock time of the sequential algorithm (AEM) over the wall-clock time of parallel algorithm (PAEM). Three-dimensional geometries were constructed using Comsol Multiphysics 4.3 and converted to computational models using the URDME framework [11]. The two-dimensional structured meshes used in the spatial predator and prey model were constructed using custom Matlab scripts. The resulting meshes were divided into subdomains using the multilevel k-way partitioning method provided by the Metis library [22]. Metis optimizes the partitioning for minimal number of diffusions crossing subdomain boundaries, while maintaining an equal number of subvolumes in each subdomain. The partitioning provides a balanced simulator workload, which we believe has an impact on the parallel performance.

5.1 Benchmarks

We investigated the behavior of our simulator on three benchmarks. In the first benchmark we evaluated the scaling as a function of the geometry and the ratio of diffusion to reaction events (D:R). The D:R was measured during a sequential profiling run. The second benchmark is a spatial predator and prey model in two dimensions, which was previously used for performance evaluation by others [34]. The last benchmark is the simulation of the Min-protein system in a three-dimensional model of the *E. Coli* bacterium.

5.1.1 Reversible isomerization

We created spatial models from different three-dimensional geometries, namely a *sphere*, a *disc*, and a *rod*, all of equal volume. The RDME model considered consists of two freely diffusing species, A and B, each with initial copy numbers of 1000 per subvolume. We prescribed the simplest possible reversible isomerization

$$A \xrightarrow{c} B, \qquad B \xrightarrow{c} A, \qquad (3)$$

where the reaction rate c is selected such that the D:R is 1 when both species diffuse at a diffusion rate of 1. The diffusion rates of both species were varied in $\{1, 100\}$, thereby increasing the D:R. We also varied the volume of the geometries in $\{1, 10, 100\}$. For the sphere and the disc we did this by increasing the radius, keeping the height of the disc at the constant value 0.2. For the rod, the radius was kept at the value 0.2 while the length was increased. As all discretization parameters remained the same for all model configurations, the number of subvolumes in each model grew to approximately $\{1500, 15000, 150000\}$. In the following, we refer to the specific model configurations as $[vx, dy]$, denoting that the model has a volume of x and that the diffusion rates for both species are y.

5.1.2 Spatial predator-prey model

This benchmark is the spatial extension of the Lotka-Volterra model, proposed by Schinazi [30]. We use the model parameters proposed by Wang et al. [34]. The system contains three species, A, B, and C, where the initial copy number for each is set to 1000 per subvolume. The model reads

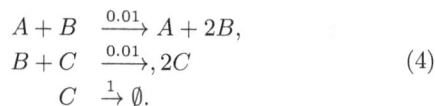

$$
\begin{aligned}
A + B &\xrightarrow{0.01} A + 2B, \\
B + C &\xrightarrow{0.01} 2C \\
C &\xrightarrow{1} \emptyset.
\end{aligned}
\tag{4}
$$

Note that the count of species A is not changed in the first reaction, but A is a factor of the total reaction intensity. The geometry is a two-dimensional square with a varying side of length $\{64, 200, 400\}$ units and with square subvolumes of unit area. The diffusion rates of species B and C are either $d_B^1 = 2.5$ and $d_C^1 = 5$, or $d_B^2 = 5$ and $d_C^2 = 10$, while $d_A = 0$ in all cases. In the first case, the D:R is approximately 1, and about 2 in the second.

5.1.3 A model of the Min-protein system

As a rather challenging benchmark we used a model of a Min-protein system in a three-dimensional model of an *E. Coli* bacterium [13]. The model contains five chemical species interacting in a system of five reactions. The geometry is pill-shaped, resulting from the union of a cylinder with two spheres (Figure 1). The complete set of reaction- and diffusion-rates can be found in [13], and the model is also available for download in the current release of URDME [2]. We simulated the model at two different mesh resolutions, hence at two different ratios of reaction to diffusion events since the diffusion rate is inversely proportional to the square of the subvolume length. The *coarse mesh* (Figure 1A) contained 1555 subvolumes and the D:R was approximately 250. In the *fine mesh* (Figure 1B) the system consisted of 13307 subvolumes, and the D:R was about 1400.

5.2 Scalability

In this section, we evaluate how the simulator performance scales with increasing LP-count, and how the scaling depends on the particular model. In order to relate the models better to the measured performance we identify four potential performance indicators:

- *Subvolume count*: The number of subvolumes in the model.
- *The diffusion to reaction ratio (D:R)*: The ratio of simulated diffusion to reaction events.
- *Average degree*: The average number of neighbors of each LP.
- *Inter-LP diffusion ratio (Inter-LPD)*: The number of diffusions crossing subdomain boundaries over the total number of diffusions. We also tried including the

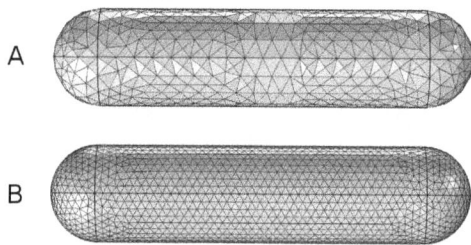

Figure 1: The spatial discretization of the *E. coli* bacterium geometry; coarse-grained (A) and fine-grained (B) tetrahedral meshes.

reactions into the ratio, but this yielded a worse indicator. We discuss the impact of reactions separately under the D:R.

In Table 1 we present an overview of the benchmark configurations together with the introduced indicators. As the indicators *inter-LP diffusion ratio* and the *average degree* depend on the number of partitions, the values are listed for the partitioning to 16, 32 and 64 subdomains. We also list the sequential and parallel wall-clock time measured for all model configurations. Note that to measure the sequential time we used the sequential version of the algorithm (AEM), thus no parallelization overhead is included in the measurement. Moreover, the simulated time range was freely varied for each configuration, thus no direct relationship exists between wall-clock times shown in different rows.

Lastly, we list the *parallel efficiency* for all experiments and the same set of partitions. The parallel efficiency calculates as $T_1(T_N * N)^{-1}$, where T_1 is the sequential simulation time and T_N the parallel simulation time using N LPs.

We investigated the relationship of the introduced indicators to the measured parallel efficiency. To study the influence of the *inter-LP diffusion ratio* (inter-LPD) we observe the scaling of the rod, disc and sphere models at the [d1] configuration shown in Figures 2a, 2b and 2c. We see that large models (v100) scale significantly better than models of medium (v10) and small size (v1). As shown in Table 1, a large model size leads to a high private work-load per LP and thus a low inter-LPD. Furthermore, large models with a lower inter-LPD (e.g., rod) achieve a higher parallel efficiency than models with a higher inter-LPD (e.g., sphere). The inter-LPD increases at an increasing LP-count, as the average subdomain size and the number of internal diffusions decreases. This noticeably affects the scaling of small models (v1), where doubling the LP-count significantly reduces the parallel efficiency. Hence, we find that the inter-LPD is an accurate indicator for the parallel performance of our simulator.

To study the impact of an increasing *diffusion to reaction ratio* (D:R) we present the scaling of the sphere model at configurations [d1] and [d100] shown in Figure 4. Here we find that the difference in parallel performance due to the increased D:R is small ($< 10\%$). Furthermore, for large models (v100) we observe that the parallel performance is independent of the D:R, as shown in Table 1. This is an unexpected finding, as we assumed that the D:R has a stronger influence on the scaling due to its effect on private workload.

To study how the parallel efficiency depends on the *average degree* in isolation, we compare different configurations

Model	Conf.	#Subvol.	D:R	Avg. Degree			Inter-LPD.%			Time [s]				Efficiency		
				16	32	64	16	32	64	Seq.	16	32	64	16	32	64
Sphere	[v1,d1]	1437	1	7.6	8.8	10.3	24	32	42	198.7	34.7	29.9	21.9	0.36	0.21	0.14
	[v1,d100]	1437	105	7.6	8.8	10.3	24	32	42	216.4	45.5	40.5	37.9	0.3	0.17	0.09
	[v10,d1]	13575	1	7.8	8.8	10.8	12	15	21	259.8	37.7	23.1	13.7	0.43	0.35	0.3
	[v10,d100]	13575	107	7.8	8.8	10.8	12	15	21	293.7	43.3	28.2	17.1	0.42	0.33	0.27
	[v100,d1]	135228	1	7.9	9.8	10.8	6	8	10	545.1	64.1	31.1	12.6	0.53	0.55	0.68
	[v100,d100]	135228	109	7.9	9.8	10.8	6	8	10	476.1	53.3	24.5	11.6	0.56	0.61	0.64
Disc	[v1,d1]	1555	1	4.1	5	5.7	15	22	33	186.9	31.3	23.7	23.1	0.37	0.25	0.13
	[v1,d100]	1555	91	4.1	5	5.7	15	22	33	190.2	33.5	26.8	30	0.36	0.22	0.1
	[v10,d1]	13452	1	4.4	4.7	5.2	5	8	11	203.4	27.3	14.9	8.8	0.47	0.43	0.36
	[v10,d100]	13452	85	4.4	4.7	5.2	5	8	11	204.4	26.8	15.9	9.7	0.48	0.4	0.33
	[v100,d1]	125537	1	4.2	4.6	5.1	2	3	4	376.9	45.7	20.1	7.4	0.52	0.59	0.8
	[v100,d100]	125537	82	4.2	4.6	5.1	2	3	4	282.7	34.2	14.9	5.5	0.52	0.59	0.8
Rod	[v1,d1]	1429	1	1.9	1.9	2.8	13	27	54	174.7	27.1	22.9	27.1	0.4	0.24	0.1
	[v1,d100]	1429	90	1.9	1.9	2.8	13	27	54	177.6	31.1	30.1	33.8	0.36	0.19	0.08
	[v10,d1]	14000	1	1.9	1.9	2	1	2	5	224.2	28	14.7	8.3	0.5	0.48	0.42
	[v10,d100]	14000	90	1.9	1.9	2	1	2	5	232.6	27.7	15.6	9.3	0.53	0.47	0.39
	[v100,d1]	139139	1	1.9	1.9	2	0	0	0	325.5	40.1	18	6.4	0.51	0.56	0.79
	[v100,d100]	139139	91	1.9	1.9	2	0	0	0	357	42.2	19.7	6.9	0.53	0.57	0.81
Pred.-Prey	[n64,d1]	4096	1	4.1	4.7	4.9	6	10	14	203.5	29.2	22.8	12.2	0.44	0.28	0.26
	[n64,d2]	4096	2	4.1	4.7	4.9	6	10	14	324.6	51.6	41.2	33.4	0.39	0.25	0.15
	[n200,d1]	40000	1	4.1	4.6	5	2	3	5	371.2	44.2	22.7	11	0.53	0.51	0.53
	[n200,d2]	40000	2	4.1	4.6	5	2	3	5	592.6	72.3	34.6	20.9	0.51	0.54	0.44
	[n400,d1]	160000	1	4	4.6	5.1	1	2	2	286.1	31.5	13.8	5.8	0.57	0.65	0.78
	[n400,d2]	160000	2	4	4.6	5.1	1	2	2	387.1	50.5	22.2	9.1	0.48	0.54	0.67
Min-System	[coarse,–]	1555	304	5.2	7.5	8.7	20	27	38	126	29.7	23	24	0.27	0.17	0.08
	[fine,–]	13307	1517	4.9	7.3	8.9	10	14	20	539.9	80.4	53.1	34.1	0.42	0.32	0.25

Table 1: Overview of benchmark characteristics and results.

of geometries with the same Inter-LPD. Namely, the models disc [v10,d1] and sphere [v100,d1], both of which have a Inter-LPD of 8% at the partitioning on 32 LPs. We find that the sphere model has a higher average degree than the disc model and the parallel efficiency is likewise increased. Nonetheless, as the models are of different subvolume sizes, we can not rule out the influence of unknown factors that correlate with the average degree.

Lastly, we observe the effect of the *subvolume count* indicator. It can be seen in Table 1 that a correlation with the Inter-LPD and thus the parallel efficiency exist. Furthermore, the efficiency for simulation of large models (v100) increases at increasing LP-count, which is not the case for small or medium size models. We suspect that this outcome is attributable to cache effects, as the partitioned model may fit better into core-local cache levels.

To visualize the correlation of the *inter-LP diffusion ratio* and *subvolume count* indicators to the parallel efficiency we applied least-squares curve fitting to the data for all [d1] models simulated on 64 LPs, as shown in Table 1. In Figure 3 we see the inter-LPD to parallel efficiency data fitted with a negative exponential function, and the subvolume count to parallel efficiency correlation fitted by a log-linear relationship.

5.3 Detailed Behavior

In this section, we study in detail how the effort of the simulator is allocated. The DLTWEs were tuned to achieve

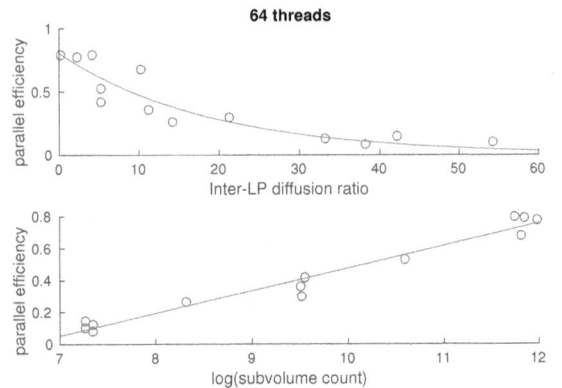

Figure 3: Curve fitting of the inter-LPD and subvolume-count indicators to the parallel efficiency for all [d1] models simulated on 64 LPs.

the best performance for each model; hence the degree of optimism varies, and as a consequence the allocation of effort may be distributed differently. To measure the different parts of the effort, a lightweight instrumentation of the simulator was performed. The instrumentation allows us to break down the execution time into six parts of interest (line numbers refer to Algorithm 1):

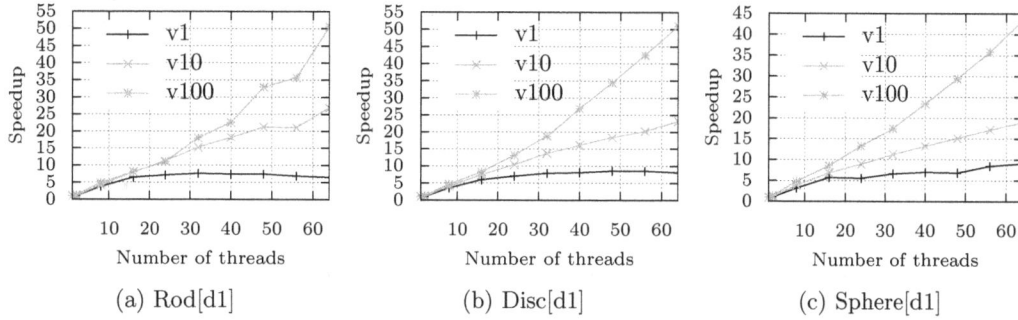

(a) Rod[d1]　　　　(b) Disc[d1]　　　　(c) Sphere[d1]

Figure 2: Speedup for different configurations of the geometries rod, disc and sphere, the size is varied.

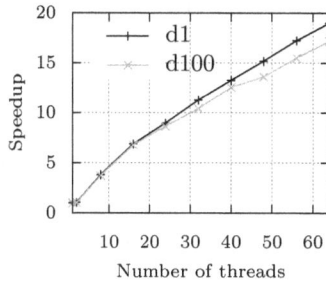

Figure 4: Speedup for the sphere[v10] model, D:R d1 and d100.

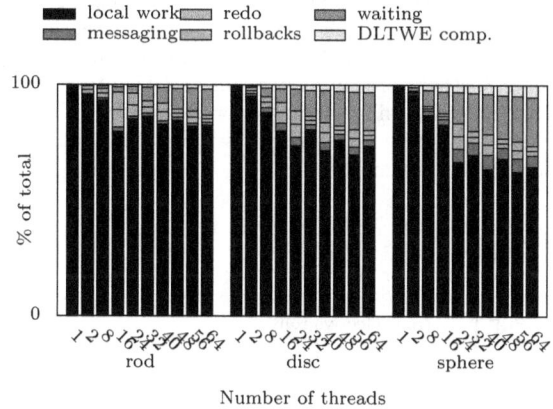

Figure 5: Breakdown of the execution time for the rod, disc and sphere models, size v100 and D:R d1.

- **Waiting:** Time spent on blocking due to DLTWEs. (lines 15–17)
- **Rollbacks:** Time spent on processing anti-messages and rollbacks. (lines 8,9 and 20).
- **Redo:** Time spent on redoing work that has been undone by a preceding rollback. We estimate that the forward processing time is roughly equal to the backward processing time of an event, thus we estimate this value to be the same as Rollbacks.
- **Local work:** Time spent on processing of local events, other than events that could be attributed to Redo. (roughly lines 21–28, when e originates from the local event e_{local} at line 18)
- **Messaging:** Time spent on processing of diffusion messages other than anti-messages and messages that could be attributed to Redo. (roughly lines 21–28, when e originates from the message m at line 13)
- **DLTWE computation:** Time spent on computing new DLTWEs, including scanning of the event queue. (line 30)

Of the above, Local work and Messaging are considered useful work, and the other parts are referred to as non-work.

The results of the breakdown analysis for the rod[d1], disc[d1] and sphere[d1] models, large size (v100), are shown in Figure 5. We see that the non-work part is completely dominated by blocking due to DLTWEs. Only a lesser part of the time is spent on rollbacks. Hence, the DLTWEs lead to a largely conservative execution for these models. For the sphere model, more time is spent on the processing of messages in relation to the other models. This difference is explained by the increased connectivity of the sphere model,

whose average degree is the double of that of the disc model, and five-fold in comparison to the rod.

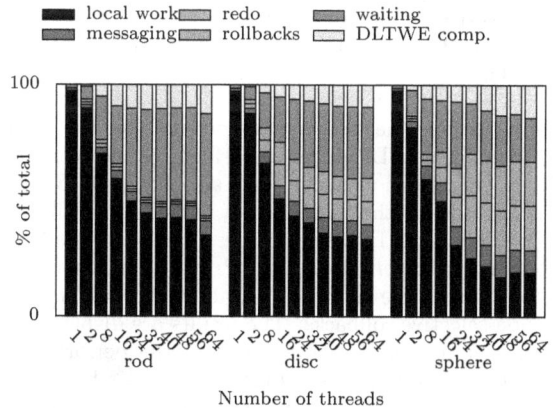

Figure 6: Breakdown of the execution time for the rod, disc and sphere models, size v1 and D:R d1.

In Figure 6, a corresponding breakdown analysis for the small models (v1) is shown. Here we see that a much larger portion of the non-work time is spent on rollbacks, for the disc and the sphere models. The DLTWEs have been tuned for optimal performance in each case. For the small models (v1), we see that for the best performance, a more optimistic (i.e., allowing for more rollbacks) simulation is better. Overall, more time is spent on parallel overhead for small models, which is in line with our expectation, as the amount of private work per LP is very small.

5.4 Tuning the DLTWE Computation

In this section, we discuss how to tune the DLTWE computation, and we show how the selective rollback technique affects the performance in comparison to using non-selective rollbacks.

The *EventQueue* of Algorithm 1 is implemented as two separate queues, one for reactions and one for diffusions. The diffusion queue contains both local and inter-LP diffusion events. The DLTWEs are produced by scanning the events in the diffusion queue (line 30 in Algorithm 1). The length of the prefix being scanned is a tunable parameter of our simulator, that affect the number of neighbors of each LP for which the DLTWEs are updated. Scanning a longer prefix of the diffusion queue results in a greater fraction of the DLTWEs being updated, and thus a more conservative simulation; furthermore, it requires more effort to update the DLTWEs. Scanning a shorter prefix results in fewer DLTWEs being updated (and thus set to infinity), and a more optimistic simulation.

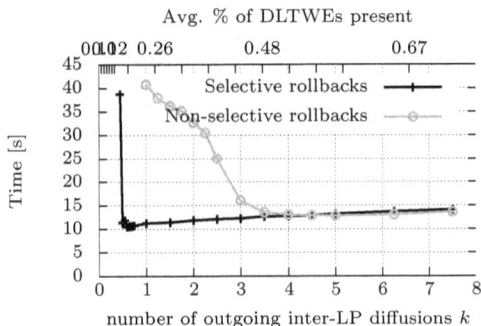

Figure 7: **Total execution time for varying number of outgoing inter-LP diffusion events** k **being scanned, and average percentage of DLTWEs computed on the Predator-Prey[n200,d1] benchmark, on 64 threads.**

We analyze how the performance depends on the number of outgoing inter-LP diffusions k found while scanning a prefix of the diffusion queue, and also how this dependency is affected by the total cost of performing rollbacks during a simulation. For this, we run simulations under a range of scan prefix lengths, on the Predator-prey[n200,d1] model, both using the selective rollback technique and using the non-selective rollbacks. The results are displayed in Figure 7. On the x-axis above the plot, the performance is related to the average percentage of DLTWEs being updated. On the x-axis below, the performance is related to the number of outgoing inter-LP diffusions k. The execution time of the simulation using selective rollbacks and using non-selective rollbacks are shown for different lengths of the scan prefix (and hence for different k). For a smaller k, the performance of the non-selective rollback starts to decline when the percentage of the DLTWEs being updated passes below 50%. For the selective rollback, the performance does not start to decline until 5%.

We see that in general the selective rollback technique always results in a superior or similar performance in compari-

son to the non-selective rollbacks. The optimal k is different for the two techniques, using selective rollbacks it is substantially shorter. This is because the effort of rollbacks is much smaller, and thus the performance improves, as optimism increases, even though the number of stragglers increase. We also see that in general, the best performance is achieved when quite a modest percentage of the DLTWEs between the LPs are known.

5.5 Comparison to other techniques.

In this part we compare the DLTWE-synchronization technique to an adaptive protocol guided by the LP's local history, namely the Probabilistic Adaptive Direct Optimism Control (PADOC) proposed by Ferscha [14]. PADOC was implemented in our simulator, replacing the DLTWE synchronization. We have used non-selective rollbacks in this comparison, as it was more efficient when using the PADOC algorithm.

The PADOC algorithm relies on message arrival statistics that are continuously collected on each LP. At each advance of the local simulation time, the LP computes an estimate of the next message arrival time based on the statistics and the last arrival time. Depending on the distance from the current simulation time to the estimate, the LP decides to block for a constant amount of real time or or to proceed with optimistic execution of local events. To be exact, the decision is made by sampling of a sigmoidal probability density function described by a mean at the estimated future arrival time. The steepness of the probability distribution function is scaled with a constant in the range [0 1], where a value closer to 1 implies a stronger confidence in the estimator. In our experiments PADOC obtained the best performance at a scaling constant of 0.1. This suggest a large variance of the message arrival times in the simulations. We used the arithmetic mean as the estimator of message arrival statistics.

We evaluated PADOC on two benchmarks; the spatial predator and prey model at the [n400,d1] configuration, and the Min-system at the [fine] configuration. The speedup for both models simulated using the PADOC or DLTWE protocol is shown in Figure 8a, 8c. For both models, the DLTWE outperforms PADOC by a large margin. The breakdown of the execution time is shown in Figure 8b and 8d. For each LP-count, the execution time is normalized to the DLTWE time, the left bar. We see that in general, DLTWE keeps the time spent on rollbacks at a very modest level. It should be noted that in the breakdown figures, the relative portion of the waiting time is slightly bigger for the DLTWE than if selective rollbacks would have been used. For PADOC, waiting for neighbors and performing rollbacks takes up a greater part of the total execution time. As the number of LPs increases, the failure to accurately predict arrivals of messages carries an increasingly significant cost.

5.6 Relation to other works

In this section we discuss the performance of our simulator using the DLTWE technique in relation to other works. We would like to point out that is difficult to make a fair comparison to other approaches, as previously used methods differ from our approach (e.g., other numerical algorithms or distributed instead of shared-memory). The single previously published RDME benchmark that can be found in the literature for the amount of LPs considered by us was

(a) Speedup Predator-Prey

(b) Breakdown Predator-Prey

(c) Speedup Min-System

(d) Breakdown Min-System

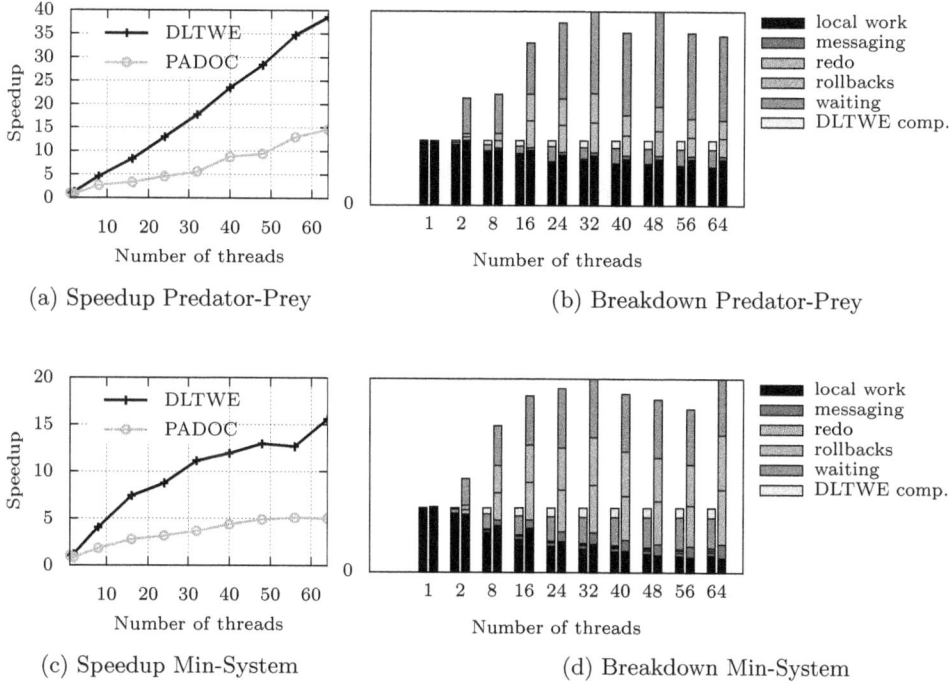

Figure 8: Comparison of DLTWE and PADOC on the Predator-Prey[n400,d1] and Min-System[fine] models. In (a) and (c) the speedup of the DLTWE and the PADOC method is shown. In (b) and (d) a breakdown of how the time is spent is shown.

the spatial predator and prey model presented by Wang et al. [34]. The parallel simulator used in the study is the Abstract Next Subvolume Method (ANSM), a distributed-memory implementation of the NSM using the Breathing Time-Warp protocol for synchronization. Our speedup and the ANSM speedup taken from [34], Figure 2b, are shown in Table 2.

Simulator (Protocol)	8 LPs	16 LPs	32 LPs	64 LPs
ANSM (BTW)	4x	6x	11x	20x
PAEM (DLTWE)	4.5x	8.4x	16.4x	33.9x

Table 2: Speedups obtained on the spatial predator prey model on a 200 x 200 grid using the ANSM and PAEM simulators.

6. CONCLUSION

We have presented a new technique for inter-LP synchronization in PDES. It is designed to be suitable when simulating models in which the time intervals between successive inter-LP events are highly variable and have no lower bounds, as in the spatial stochastic simulation that we have considered. Our DLTWE technique enables a detailed control of the amount of optimism in the simulation, which can be tuned to achieve desired accuracy of information communicated between LPs. We have shown how using a technique for selective rollbacks, the cost of optimism decreases, thus making it beneficial to allow for more optimism in the simulation.

With our implementation we have shown that the DLTWE technique is well suited to the setting of spatial stochastic simulations, and that it performs well on realistic problems in a shared memory environment. Notably, the DLTWE enables a parallel scaling which compares favorably to other inter-LP synchronization techniques described in the literature, as well as other parallelization efforts that have been reported in the literature.

7. ACKNOWLEDGMENTS

This work was supported in part by the Swedish Foundation for Strategic Research through the CoDeR-MP project as well as the Swedish Research Council within the UP-MARC Linnaeus centre of Excellence.

8. REFERENCES

[1] R. Ayani and H. Rajaei. Parallel simulation using conservative time windows. In *Proceedings of the 24th Winter Simulation Conference*, pages 709–717, Arlington, VA, USA, December 13-16 1992. ACM.

[2] P. Bauer, B. Drawert, S. Engblom, and A. Hellander. Urdme v. 1.2: User's manual. Technical Report 2012-036, Uppsala University, 2012.

[3] P. Bauer and S. Engblom. Sensitivity estimation and inverse problems in spatial stochastic models of chemical kinetics. volume 103 of *Lecture Notes in Computational Science and Engineering*, pages 519–527. Springer Switzerland, 2015.

[4] D. Bernstein. Simulating mesoscopic reaction-diffusion systems using the gillespie algorithm. *Phys. Rev. E*, 71(4):041103, 2005.

[5] C. Carothers, D. Bauer, and S. Pearce. ROSS: a high-performance, low memory, modular time warp system. In *Proceedings of the 14th Workshop on Parallel and Distributed Simulation*, pages 53–60, Bologna, Italy, May 28-31 2000. IEEE.

[6] G. Chen and B. Szymanski. Lookback: a new way of exploiting parallelism in discrete event simulation. In *Proceedings of the 16th Workshop on Parallel and Distributed Simulation*, pages 138–147, Los Alamitos, CA, USA, May 12-15 2002. IEEE.

[7] L. Chen, Y. Lu, Y. Yao, S. Peng, and L. Wu. A well-balanced time warp system on multi-core environments. In *Proceedings of the 25th Workshop on Parallel and Distributed Simulation*, pages 1–9, Nice, France, June 14-17 2011. IEEE.

[8] S. H. D. Ball. The adaptive time-warp concurrency control algorithm. In *Proceedings of the SCS Multiconference on Distributed Simulation*, pages 174–177, San Diego, CA, USA, Jan. 17-19 1990. SCSI.

[9] S. R. Das. Adaptive protocols for parallel discrete event simulation. *J. Oper. Res. Soc.*, 51(4):385–394, 2000.

[10] L. Dematté and T. Mazza. On parallel stochastic simulation of diffusive systems. volume 5307 of *Lecture Notes in Computer Science*, pages 191–210. Springer Berlin Heidelberg, 2008.

[11] B. Drawert, S. Engblom, and A. Hellander. URDME: a modular framework for stochastic simulation of reaction-transport processes in complex geometries. *BMC Syst. Biol.*, 6(1):76, 2012.

[12] J. Elf and M. Ehrenberg. Spontaneous separation of bi-stable biochemical systems into spatial domains of opposite phases. *Syst. biol.*, 1(2):230–236, 2004.

[13] D. Fange and J. Elf. Noise-Induced Min Phenotypes in E. coli. *PLoS Comput. Biol.*, 2(6):e80, 2006.

[14] A. Ferscha. Probabilistic adaptive direct optimism control in time warp. In *Proceedings of the 9th Workshop on Parallel and Distributed Simulation*, pages 120–129, Lake Placid, NY, USA, June 13-16 1995. IEEE.

[15] R. M. Fujimoto. Parallel discrete event simulation. *Comm. of the ACM*, 33(10):30–53, 1990.

[16] M. A. Gibson and J. Bruck. Efficient exact stochastic simulation of chemical systems with many species and many channels. *J. Phys. Chem. A*, 104(9):1876–1889, 2000.

[17] D. T. Gillespie. Exact stochastic simulation of coupled chemical reactions. *J. Phys. Chem.*, 81(25):2340–2361, 1977.

[18] S. Jafer, Q. Liu, and G. A. Wainer. Synchronization methods in parallel and distributed discrete-event simulation. *Simul. Model. Pract. Th.*, 30:54–73, 2013.

[19] S. Jafer and G. Wainer. Conservative vs. optimistic parallel simulation of DEVS and cell-DEVS: A comparative study. In *Proceedings of the 2010 Summer Computer Simulation Conference*, pages 342–349, Ottawa, Canada, July 11-14 2010. SCSI.

[20] D. R. Jefferson. Virtual time. *ACM Trans. Program. Lang. Syst.*, 7(3):404–425, 1985.

[21] M. Jeschke, R. Ewald, A. Park, R. Fujimoto, and A. M. Uhrmacher. A parallel and distributed discrete event approach for spatial cell-biological simulations. *SIGMETRICS Perform. Eval. Rev.*, 35(4):22–31, 2008.

[22] G. Karypis and V. Kumar. A Fast and High Quality Multilevel Scheme for Partitioning Irregular Graphs. *SIAM J. Sci. Comput.*, 20(1):359–392, 1998.

[23] H. Leong, D. Agrawal, and J. Agre. Using message semantics to reduce rollback in the time warp mechanism. volume 725 of *Lecture Notes in Computer Science*, pages 309–323. Springer Berlin Heidelberg, 1993.

[24] J. Liu and D. M. Nicol. Lookahead revisited in wireless network simulations. In *Proceedings of 16th Workshop on Parallel and Distributed Simulation*, pages 79–88, Arlington, VA, USA, May 12-15 2002. IEEE.

[25] B. D. Lubachevsky. Efficient parallel simulations of dynamic ising spin systems. *J. Comput. Phys.*, 75(1):103–122, 1988.

[26] J. Misra. Distributed discrete-event simulation. *ACM Comput. Surv.*, 18(1):39–65, 1986.

[27] A. Pellegrini, R. Vitali, S. Peluso, and F. Quaglia. Transparent and efficient shared-state management for optimistic simulations on multi-core machines. In *Proceedings of the 20th International Symposium on Modeling, Analysis Simulation of Computer and Telecommunication Systems*, pages 134–141, Arlington, VA, USA, August 7-9 2012. IEEE.

[28] M. Rathinam, P. W. Sheppard, and M. Khammash. Efficient computation of parameter sensitivities of discrete stochastic chemical reaction networks. *J. Chem. Phys.*, 132(3):034103, Jan. 2010.

[29] P. L. Reiher, F. Wieland, and D. Jefferson. Limitation of optimism in the time warp operating system. In *Proceedings of the 21st Winter Simulation Conference*, pages 765–770, Washington, D.C., USA, Dec. 4-6 1989. ACM.

[30] R. B. Schinazi. Predator-prey and host-parasite spatial stochastic models. *Ann. Appl. Probab.*, 7(1):1–9, 1997.

[31] L. M. Sokol, D. P. Briscoe, and A. P. Wieland. MTW: A strategy for scheduling discrete simulation events for concurrent execution. In *Proceedings of the SCS Multiconference on Distributed Simulation*, pages 34–42, San Diego, CA, USA, Feb. 3-5 1988. SCSI.

[32] S. Srinivasan and P. F. R. Jr. Elastic time. *ACM Trans. Model. Comput. Simul.*, 8(2):103–139, 1998.

[33] J. S. Steinman. Breathing time warp. In *Proceedings of the 7th Workshop on Parallel and Distributed Simulation*, pages 109–118, San Diego, CA, USA, May 16-19 1993. ACM.

[34] B. Wang, B. Hou, F. Xing, and Y. Yao. Abstract next subvolume method: A logical process-based approach for spatial stochastic simulation of chemical reactions. *Comput. Biol. Chem.*, 35(3):193–198, 2011.

[35] J. Wang, D. Jagtap, N. B. Abu-Ghazaleh, and D. Ponomarev. Parallel discrete event simulation for multi-core systems: Analysis and optimization. *IEEE Trans. Parallel Distrib. Syst.*, 25(6):1574–1584, 2014.

Improving Computational Performance of Simulation-based Heuristic Algorithms for Job Sequencing

Shell Ying Huang and Ya Li
School of Computer Engineering, Nanyang Technological University
Nanyang Avenue
Singapore 639798
(65) 67904932
{assyhuang,liya}@ntu.edu.sg

ABSTRACT

In many simulation-based optimization algorithms, substantial amount of time is often required in the simulation experiments to evaluate the solutions to the problem. In some heuristic or metaheuristic algorithms a significant number of revisits to the same solutions are made when the search converges. We use the ATCRSS heuristic for job sequencing problems as an example to investigate two ways of implementing a dictionary to memorize the simulation results. The objective is to eliminate repeated simulations to improve the computational performance of the algorithm. Our experiments show that the saving in computational time is comparable between hash table and TRIE. For sequencing 10 to 60 jobs the saving is between 20% and 30%. In addition, hash table is more efficient in memory usage than TRIE in our tested cases. We also suggest that hash table is a more general way of implementing the dictionary for other heuristic algorithms.

Categories and Subject Descriptors

F.2.2 [**Analysis of Algorithms and Problem Complexity**]: Nonnumerical Algorithms and Problems – *sequencing and scheduling*.

General Terms

Algorithms, Management, Measurement, Performance.

Keywords

Simulation-based optimization, heuristics, computational performance, memorization.

1. INTRODUCTION

Many NP-hard optimization problems rely on heuristic or metaheuristic algorithms to compute a near optimal solution so that they may be solved in a reasonable amount of computational time. These algorithms very often have a main control flow as shown in Figure 1. It is an iterative process consisting of three main steps: (i) generating new solution(s) according to the heuristic search strategy; (ii) conducting simulation experiments to evaluate the

SIGSIM-PADS '15, June 10-12, 2015, London, United Kingdom.
ACM 978-1-4503-3583-6/15/06.
http://dx.doi.org/10.1145/2769458.2774213

performance of the generated solution(s). In many algorithms, substantial amount of time is required in the simulation experiments to evaluate the solutions to the problem.

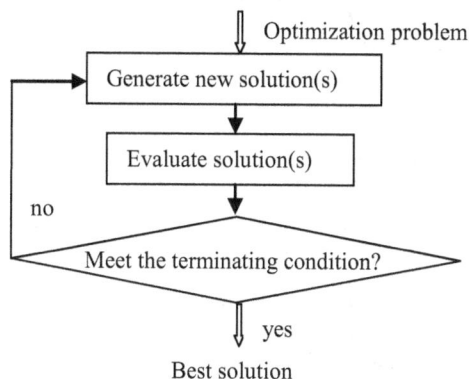

Figure 1. Control flow of heuristic/metaheuristic algorithm.

When a candidate solution is built incrementally in an optimization algorithm for deterministic problems, two methods to reduce simulation cost by incremental evaluation are investigated in [1]. A TREE data structure is used to save the performance of solutions and system status. One of the methods is able to cut more than 50% of the computational times.

For some heuristic or metaheuristic algorithms a significant number of revisits to the same solutions are made when the search converges. ATCRSS heuristic [3] is known to efficiently reduce tardiness for many machine scheduling problems for single machine scheduling with separable sequence dependent setup time. Such problems are found in petroleum production plants, printing plants, car spraying facilities, metallurgical industries, and textile dying plants. Huang and Li [2] proposed to use a TRIE dictionary to memorize the simulation results so that each unique sequence is simulated once only. Around 20% improvement in computational time is achieved for sequencing a set of 28 jobs. In this paper, we investigate the use of hash tables and compare its effectiveness with using a TRIE [2] in improving the computational performance of simulation-based heuristics for job sequencing problems.

2. REDUCING COMPUTATIONAL COSTS USING A HASH TABLE

The advantages of a hash table over a TRIE are (1) it still works for solutions with no common prefixes; (2) it supports constant access time to insert and retrieve data entries on average. (2) is important because the time taken to store and retrieve data is the overhead to be paid in the attempt to reduce computational cost in re-evaluating solutions. Each entry in the hash table is a pair (k, p) where k = a (partial) solution, p = performance of the solution, that is, the result of the simulation. The issues to be resolved include (1) how a solution should be represented as the key k for efficient hashing; (2) which hash function or does it matter.

The job sequence computed by a heuristic algorithm will be a sequence of job identifiers. This is usually a sequence of integers. A hash function that computes from all the integers in the sequence like the folding method proves to be computationally very expensive in our preliminary study. We encode a sequence of job identifiers as a string of characters. (1) This method consumes less memory space than a list of integers; (2) Conversion between a sequence of integers and a string of characters is a very simple operation; (3) Hash functions based on shift and exclusive-or operators on a string of characters are very efficient in computational time. This encoding method allows a job set as large as the number of characters (128 for ASCII character encoding, 256 for Unicode encoding). This is enough for job sequencing problems in most applications.

```
Code = length of Key
For each character of Key
    Code = (Code<<4)^(Code>>28)^Key[i]
HashCode = Code%TABLE_SIZE
```

Figure 2. Hash Function.

The choice of the hash function is critical in the success of algorithm after choosing an efficient encoding of the key. The hash function we choose after a few preliminary experiments is shown in Figure 2. Open addressing is used to resolve collisions in hash. So the hash table itself is an array of linked lists. A node in a list is a character string representing the key and the simulation result of the (partial) job sequence.

3. PERFORMANCE COMPARISON AND ANALYSIS

We use the same method to generate job scheduling problems as [3]. Jobs with different characteristics (job severity, due date tightness, due date range, job availability and ready time) are generated. Experiments for job sequences of 10, 20, 30, 40, 50 and 60 jobs respectively are conducted. For each setup, 30 problems are generated randomly. The original ATCRSS algorithm without the dictionary and the ATCRSS algorithm with the hash table/TRIE dictionary are evaluated. All algorithms produce the same optimization result so they are not presented.

The computational times used by the three algorithms and the percentage improvement over the original algorithm are presented in Table 1. Significant saving of computational times of 20-30% is achieved with the use of the hash table/TRIE dictionary to eliminate the repeated simulations of the same job sequence. Even though in absolute terms, the ATCRSS algorithm only takes seconds to compute the final solution for one scheduling problem thus the time saved may not seem important, the saving will be considerable in a manufacturing environment with hundreds of machines. However, there is no real difference between the effectiveness between using a hash table and using a TRIE.

The memory space used by hash table is also compared with that used by TRIE in Table 2. To facilitate fast multi-way access to child nodes, a node in TRIE is an array whose size is the size of the job set. Each element in the array is for storing the simulation result of a (partial) sequence and the reference to another node of TRIE. In the hash table a node stores the simulation result of a (partial) job sequence together with the character string which represents the sequence. Therefore, a node in the hash table is smaller than a node in the TRIE. The difference in node size increases as the job set increases in size. It should be noted that the hash table needs the additional space for the table itself but compared with the total space for the lists of nodes, the space of the table is not significant. As shown in the fourth row of Table 2, TRIE uses 2 to 5 times the memory space of that of hash table.

Table 1. Computational times and percentage improvement of computational times made by the ATCRSS algorithm with the hash table/TRIE dictionary: (1) without dictionary; (2) using hash; (3) using TRIE.

	10	20	30	40	50	60
(1)	1.26 (0.0%)	3.02 (0.0%)	5.58 (0.0%)	8.64 (0.0%)	12.46 (0.0%)	16.63 (0.0%)
(2)	1.05 (20.0%)	2.52 (20.5%)	4.44 (27.2%)	6.70 (30.0%)	9.37 (33.9%)	12.69 (32.7%)
(3)	1.05 (19.9%)	2.51 (20.0%)	4.38 (25.5%)	6.65 (29.0%)	9.31 (33.1%)	12.53 (31.0%)

Table 2. Memory space used by dictionary implemented as a hash table and a TRIE (Kbytes) for problems of different number of jobs.

	10	20	30	40	50	60
hash	3.482	29.88	105.8	252.4	489.3	827.2
TRIE	6.942	89.78	392.7	1071.2	2278.6	4126.6
trie/hash	1.99	3.00	3.71	4.24	4.66	4.99

4. CONCLUSIONS

The ATCRSS dispatching rule is an example of a heuristic algorithm where the search strategy generates many solutions repeatedly that leads to repeated simulation of the same solutions. Our study shows that using a dictionary can save computational time. There is no real difference in computational time between using a hash table or a TRIE. However, the memory space used by a TRIE is much more than that of a hash table. Future work includes other types of optimization problems.

5. REFERENCES

[1] Huang S. Y. and Guo, X. 2013. Reducing Simulation Costs of Embedded Simulation in Yard Crane Dispatching in Container Terminals. In *Proceedings of SIGSIM-PADS'13* (Montreal, Canada, 19-22 May, 2013). ACM. 305-314.

[2] Huang S. Y. and Li, Y. 2014. Reducing Simulation Costs in ATCRSS Algorithm for Job Scheduling Problems. In *Proceedings of 2014 European Simulation and Modelling Conference* (Porto, Portugal, 22-24 October, 2014). EUROSIS. 291-295.

[3] Xi, Y. and Jang, J. 2013. Minimizing total weighted tardiness on a single machine with sequence-dependent setup and future ready time. *International Journal of Advanced Manufacturing Technology*, 67(1-4): 281-294.

Agent-based Modeling of Large-scale Complex Social Interactions

Mingxin Zhang, Alexander Verbraeck
Delft University of Technology
Jaffalaan 5
2628BX Delft, The Netherlands
m.zhang-1@tudelft.nl,
a.verbraeck@tudelft.nl

Rongqing Meng, Xiaogang Qiu
National University of Defense Technology
College of IS&M
410073, Changsha, China
meng.rongqing.nudt@gmail.com,
michael.qiu@139.com

ABSTRACT

Modeling complex human social interactions is an important part in agent-based social simulation research. For example, results of interactions (negotiations) for scheduling joint social activities could influence the future plans of the involved individuals, which has a great impact on the researches such as activity-based travel demand analysis and agent-based epidemic models. To describe these interactions is a rather difficult task than it may seem, in particular when the system has a very large scale (millions of individuals). Current research efforts ignore or simplify the negotiation/coordination part of the social interactions in order to reduce complexity, either by using fixed and predefined human daily schedules as input or by constraining the joint social activities (interaction purposes) into several specific types (e.g. eating out). In this paper, we describe an agent-based approach to model large-scale complex social interactions, by which individuals can discuss the duration and location of the coming social activities and make decisions about their attendance. We conducted a simulation experiment including nearly 20 million agents with complex social interactions on the basis of dynamic generation of friendship networks to realize this approach, and the simulation results comply with some social interaction phenomena.

Categories and Subject Descriptors

I.6.8 [**Modeling and simulation**]: Simulation types and techniques-*agent/discrete models*

General Terms

Design

Keywords

social simulation, social networks, large-scale social interactions

SIGSIM-PADS'15, June 10–12, 2015, London, United Kingdom.
ACM 978-1-4503-3583-6/15/06.
http://dx.doi.org/10.1145/2769458.2773790.

1. INTRODUCTION

Modeling complex social interactions received much research attention for epidemic and pandemic predictions [4] due to the fact that social interactions provide a perfect fabric for fast disease propagation while they can be dramatically altered when people respond to the crisis and interventions [1]. Another research area that social interactions could have great impacts on is activity-based travel demand analysis. Results of social interactions for negotiating about social activities can influence a significant amount of travel [3]. However, the ways of modeling interactions in both epidemic predictions and traffic demand analysis have difficulties to be perfectly applied to large-scale complex social interactions. To be precise, this paper constrain the complex social interactions into the scope of planing-negotiating-executing joint social activities.

2. AGENT-BASED MODEL

Typical agent-based models for traffic demand analysis or epidemic predictions [4] are activity-based where all activities for the whole simulation existed in the input data source or were generated before the simulation run which consumed a lot of memory. To reduce memory consumption, we design an agent as activity pattern based.

Firstly, each agent is given a social role(infant, student, worker, elder, unemployed) and family role (child, parent, grandparent) in this research. Then, we distinguish the social roles by different week patterns. For instance, an university student will be assigned an university student pattern. Likewise, a worker will be assigned a worker pattern. To increase the heterogeneity and richness of the agents in the same role, we design different week patterns for every social role. A week pattern is made up of seven day patterns.

A day pattern is a sequence of linked activities. Typical activities are such as sleeping, staying at home, working, shopping, eating in a restaurant, going to school, and visiting a doctor, etc.

3. MODELING SOCIAL INTERACTIONS

Social networks play an important role for social interactions as they provide the contact information. There are three types of social networks modeled in this research, which are family, colleagues/classmates and friendships.

Compared with family and colleagues/classmates relations, friendship is more difficult to model as it is impossible to get the entire topology of friends connections on a large scale.

Thus, egocentric networks are dynamically generated to represent friendship connections. In this research, friendships will only be generated before planing and negotiating social activities based on an algorithm.

This algorithm calculates the possibility of being friends between two agents based on a newly proposed concept 'social similarity', which calculates the correlation between two agents. The considered variables include age, social role (week pattern), family role and the number of friends of an agent. In this research, the correlation is evaluated by Weighted Euclidean distance which is shown is in Equation 1, where a represents age, s represents social role (converted to an index), f represents family role, n represents the agent's friends size and μ represents the weight for different variables.

$$S(A, B) = 1 - \sqrt{\sum_{i=a,s,f,n} \mu_i (A_i - B_i)^2} \qquad (1)$$

The interaction mechanism in this research contains two stages. The first stage is equation based, by which agents calculate how much intention they have to join in proposed social activities.

For every agent I_i, it calculates the attendance possibility after receiving a social activity proposal according to Equation 2, where N is the total number of agents involved in the planned social activity, I_o is the organizer of this activity, $S(I_i, I_j)$ calculate the link weight between the two agents according to Equation 1. $A(d, E)$ calculates the interest degree of the activity to the agent, where d is the distance between agent's current location and proposed activity location, E gives out the degree that the agent is interested in the activity and σ is a corrective coefficient.

$$P(i, o, N) = e^{\sum_{j=1, j \neq o}^{N} S(I_i, I_j) - N} \times A(d, E) \qquad (2)$$
$$A(d, E) = \frac{\sigma E}{d}$$

The second stage is decision-tree based, by which agents make decisions according to social norms, sanctions and try to avoid conflicts with their own schedules. The decision can be a fully agree with a proposal, a decline or propose a new location or postpone the starting time.

Executing joint social activities is the last phase of social interactions. Dynamically generated Group Agents are designed to help execute the social activities in modeling practice.

4. SIMULATION ANALYSIS

To test the above design, we constructed a large-scale artificial city model of Beijing with 19.6 million population and 8 million geo-referenced locations(like households, schools, offices, hospitals, stations, etc.).

By implementing this large-scale artificial city model using a simulation package[2], we run this simulation on a PC(Intel Core i7-2620M CPU, 16.0 GB RAM) for a simulation period of 30 days.

One of the simulation results indicates that university students have the shortest time and the fewest opportunities for family activities. This is caused by two reasons. First is the fact that most university students come from other cities which make them impossible to join in family social activity

(decline in the decision tree process). The second is that, when they receive proposals from family members, most of them already have noncancelable friendship social activity schedules in their daily pattern.

Figure 1 shows how the number of agents in different social activities changes in a typical week day.

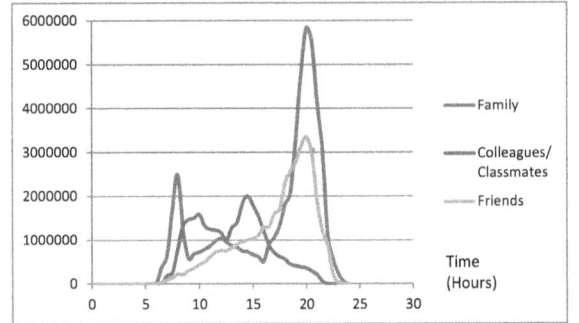

Figure 1: Number of people in social activities

Take family social activity as an example, there are three peaks in the Figure 1 and it reaches the highest point in the evening. This indicates that people in the society are more willing to plan activities with their families, which conforms to reality.

5. CONCLUSIONS

The research is considered as a proof of concept that complex social interactions on a large-scale can be modeled by agent-based method. By combining diverse data sets, an agent-based city model with 19611800 population are modeled and all of these individuals can schedule social activities and join in other social activities dynamically. The decision-making process for joining in social activities is at individual level, which contains two stages.

As for future research, two more efforts are required to refine the model. The first is adding more optional week patterns by further surveying people's activity patterns. The other is to conduct experimentations on epidemic propagation to investigate the effect of this research.

6. REFERENCES

[1] K. R. Bisset, X. Feng, M. Marathe, and S. Yardi. Modeling interaction between individuals, social networks and public policy to support public health epidemiology. In *Proceedings of the 2009 Winter Simulation Conference (WSC)*, pages 2020–2031, Austin, TX, USA, 13–16 Dec. 2009. IEEE.

[2] P. H. Jacobs, N. A. Lang, and A. Verbraeck. D-SOL: A Distributed JAVA based Discrete Event Simulation Architecture. In *Proceedings of the 2002 Winter Simulation Conference*, pages 793–800, San Diego, California, USA, 8–11 Dec. 2002. IEEE.

[3] N. Ronald, T. Arentze, and H. Timmermans. Modeling social interactions between individuals for joint activity scheduling. *Transportation Research Part B: Methodological*, 46(2):276–290, 2012.

[4] P. Stroud and S. D. Valle. Spatial dynamics of pandemic influenza in a massive artificial society. *Journal of Artificial Societies and Social Simulation*, 10(4):1–18, 2007.

FatTreeSim: Modeling Large-scale Fat-Tree Networks for HPC Systems and Data Centers Using Parallel and Discrete Event Simulation

Ning Liu, Adnan Haider, Xian-He Sun, Dong Jin
Illinois Institute of Technology
10 West 31st Street
Chicago, IL 60616
{nliu8,ahaider3}@hawk.iit.edu,{sun,dong.jin}@iit.edu

ABSTRACT

Fat-tree topologies have been widely adopted as the communication network in data centers in the past decade. Nowadays, high-performance computing (HPC) system designers are considering using fat-tree as the interconnection network for the next generation supercomputers. For extreme-scale computing systems like the data centers and supercomputers, the performance is highly dependent on the interconnection networks. In this paper, we present FatTreeSim, a PDES-based toolkit consisting of a highly scalable fat-tree network model, with the goal of better understanding the design constraints of fat-tree networking architectures in data centers and HPC systems, as well as evaluating the applications running on top of the network. FatTreeSim is designed to model and simulate large-scale fat-tree networks up to millions of nodes with protocol-level fidelity. We have conducted extensive experiments to validate and demonstrate the accuracy, scalability and usability of FatTreeSim. On Argonne Leadership Computing Facility's Blue Gene/Q system, Mira, FatTreeSim is capable of achieving a peak event rate of 305 M/s for a 524,288-node fat-tree model with a total of 567 billion committed events. The strong scaling experiments use up to 32,768 cores and show a near linear scalability. Comparing with a small-scale physical system in Emulab, FatTreeSim can accurately model the latency in the same fat-tree network with less than 10% error rate for most cases. Finally, we demonstrate FatTreeSim's usability through a case study in which FatTreeSim serves as the network module of the YARNsim system, and the error rates for all test cases are less than 13.7%.

Categories and Subject Descriptors

I.6.4 [**Computing methodologies**]: Modeling and simulation

General Terms

Design, Experimentation, Performance, Measurement

SIGSIM-PADS'15, June 10–12, 2015, London, United Kingdom.
© 2015 ACM ISBN 978-1-4503-3583-6/15/06 $15.00.
DOI: http://dx.doi.org/10.1145/2769458.2769474.

Keywords

Fat-tree networks; Parallel discrete event simulation; Blue Gene/Q; Datacenter interconnection network; Supercomputer interconnection networks

1. INTRODUCTION

The growing demands of Internet Services have greatly propelled the development and deployment of data centers in the past decade. According to [4], the total number of data centers deployed will reach 8.6 million by the year 2017 and then start to decline. But the total capacity of the data center will continue to increase, which indicates the size of individual data centers will continue to grow. Today's leading data centers usually take up millions of square feet, host sub-millions of physical servers and consume million watts of energy. Communication network is a key component in data centers. According to the report from Cisco[2], the total amount of data processed in data centers is 3.8 Zettabytes in 2014 and will reach 8.6 Zettabytes in 2018, of which, around 75% is internal traffic. Therefore, we need an efficient data center communication network that is capable of running at extreme-scale and processing large volumes of application data. Fat-tree has been the mainstream networking topology adopted in data centers and will continue to dominate in the near future.

In the HPC community, there is a growing interest in understanding how parallel programs, including system software like MPI/OpenMP and scientific applications, scale in extreme large scale architectures. One key performance impact factor is also the interconnection communication network. In the past decades, torus network is widely adopted in HPC systems because of its low cost and high delivered performance. For example, the Blue Gene/L and P series and the CrayXT series use a 3-D torus network and the newly delivered Blue Gene/Q system uses a 5-D torus network. However, the torus network is inherently a blocking network, meaning the total number of available paths is smaller than the total demand, which can significantly exacerbate the network performance in communication bursts such as the MPI All-to-All and the Reduce communication. A fat-tree can provide the non-blocking feature with the 1:1 subscription ratio and keep the total cost within a reasonable level [7]. Oak Ridge National Laboratory has recently announced that the next generation OLCF supercomputer, SUMMIT, will adopt a fat-tree as its interconnection network [8].

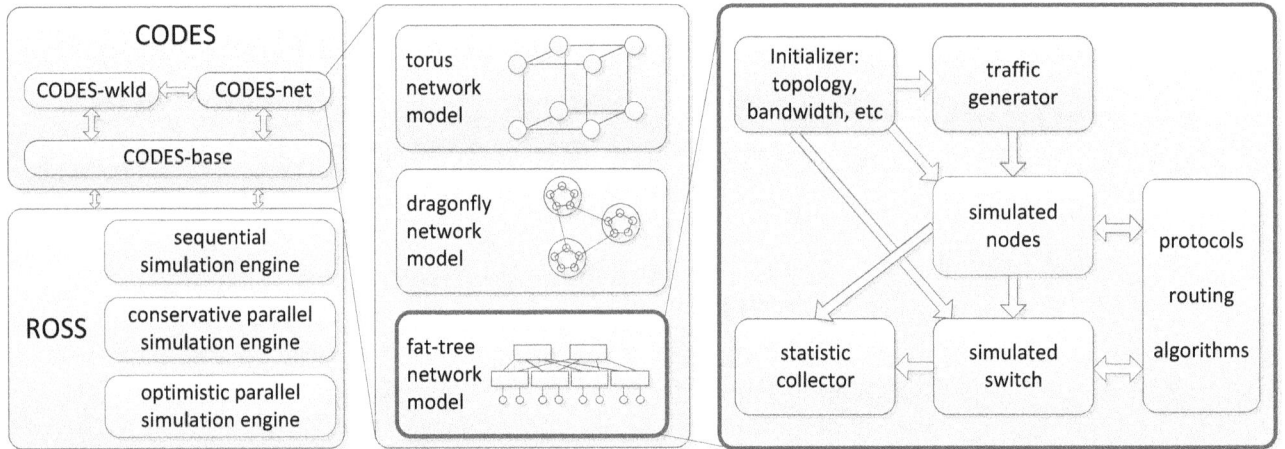

Figure 1: FatTreeSim system architecture in CODES ecosystem. CODES is based on ROSS and is comprised of multiple modules: CODES-base, CODES-workload and CODES-net. CODES-net is comprised of multiple network models. FatTreeSim is designed to be part of the CODES-net module and is the fat-tree network model illustrated in this Figure. FatTreeSim is comprised of multiple components: Initializer, Traffic Generator, Nodes, Switches, Protocols & Routing Algorithms and Statistic Collectors.

In order to quantify the performance and design trade-offs of extreme-scale systems, such as a multi-million node communication network, many researchers resort to parallel and discrete-event simulation (PDES). PDES can provide a scalable and cost-efficient alternative for evaluating systems whose architecture is still in the research stage, or systems that are economically infeasible to deploy.

In this paper, we present a parallel simulation toolkit, Fat-TreeSim, for supporting the design and evaluation of large-scale data center and HPC communication networks, as well as the applications running on those networks. FatTreeSim is based on two parallel simulation packages: the Rensselaer Optimistic Simulation System (ROSS) [14] and the Co-Design of Exascale Storage System (CODES) [15]. Fig. 1 illustrates the architecture of CODES.The CODES-workload [31] module provides the functionalities to model and simulate HPC and Cloud workload traces and directly applying existing traces to drive the underlying models. The CODES-net module provides multiple PDES-based networking models as well as a unified user interfaces that facilitate the use of the underlying networking models. The CODES-net includes four submodules: a torus network model [23], a dragonfly network model [28], a loggp[13] model, and a simple-net model. To date, many simulation systems [25, 32] that are based on CODES have successfully leveraged the functionalities provided by CODES-net. In this work, our contribution is to develop a highly scalable PDES-based fat-tree model, abbreviated as *FatTreeSim*, as shown in Fig 1. Fat-TreeSim has been incorporated as a submodule in CODES and has been used by the aforementioned simulation systems. We highlight the features of FatTreeSim as follows:

1. To the best of our knowledge, FatTreeSim is the first simulation system that is capable of modeling and simulating a fat-tree network with sub-million nodes in a time efficient manner. FatTreeSim has demonstrated a close-to-linear scalability on the Blue Gene/Q system and has achieved a peak event rate of 305 M/s. The task

of simulating a sub-trillion events test case can be accomplished within minutes instead of days as compared with the sequential discrete event simulation.

2. FatTreeSim models the protocol-level granularity in a fat-tree network with an ECMP routing algorithm. Its performance accuracy is validated through comparisons with the real system developed in Emulab, and results show that errors are all within 10% bounds.

3. We demonstrate the functionalities and compatibilities of FatTreeSim through a case study. We run YARNsim [25] with FatTreeSim and show that the network model can effectively capture the network traffic characteristics and enable the scalable simulation of MapReduce benchmark applications.

The remainder of the paper is organized as follows. We discuss the background and motivation in Section 2. We describe the fat-tree model in Section 3. Section 4 presents the validation experiments of the fat-tree model, and Section 5 discusses the related work. Closing remarks and future works are presented in Section 6.

2. BACKGROUND & MOTIVATION

In this section, we present the background information and motivation of developing FatTreeSim. Then we discuss two related systems, including the knowledge and techniques, used by FatTreeSim.

2.1 HPC & Data Centers and the Interconnection Networks

The design, evaluation and deployment of data center and HPC system is a systematic and time-consuming process. As the key component, the communication network has a significant impact on system performance. Large-scale data center and HPC system network architecture need to support a wide range of applications, each with different communication and I/O requirements. This paper concentrates on discussing an interconnection network candidate for HPC

200

and date centers: the fat-tree network, and its model and simulation in large-scale. In distributed computing community, it is projected that a single data center can scale out to host millions of virtual machines or even physical servers and serve multi-millions jobs/tasks. The requirements for building a data center network at such a scale also differ with that of the traditional data centers. The communication network must guarantee the high availability and reliability, desirable bisection bandwidth, and support for multi-tenancy. To quantify the design trade-offs of a network at a scale, it is desirable to build a large scale simulation toolkit that is capable of evaluating different design points in an efficient and cost-effective manner. A fat-tree or folded-Clos topology is the conventional and yet still the most prevalent design choice for data center communication networks [2].

2.2 Hadoop

In 2003, Google first proposed the MapReduce system [17] and since then it has become the most well accepted programming models in the distributed computing community because of its simplicity and efficacy. While Google kept its MapReduce system proprietary, Apache Hadoop [1] is the most popular open-source implementation of MapReduce framework. According to a report from Gartner [3], 65% of the packaged data analytic applications will be built on Hadoop by 2015. Thus, it is necessary to evaluate the large-scale network performance under a wide range of Hadoop applications.

Because of Hadoop's popularity, we have built YARN-sim [25]: a Hadoop YARN simulation system. Compared to other MapReduce simulation system [33, 26, 18, 9, 5], YARNsim is advantageous in that it is a parallel simulation system that is potentially capable of simulating extreme-scale Hadoop YARN systems. Similar systems are constrained, for example, MRperf uses ns-2 as its network module. While ns-2 has a rich set of functionalities that can simulate the network at fine-granularity, it lacks the mechanism to run in parallel, thus is constrained in terms of modeling large-scale system. YARNsim includes a comprehensive model for HDFS, which can mimic the I/O system behaviors of Hadoop YARN. However, YARNsim's capabilities are limited in that it lacks the support of a detailed parallel network model. We are motivated to develop Fat-TreeSim to support YARNsim in modeling and simulating Hadoop YARN at extreme-scale with minimal cost and good accuracy. We expect YARNsim and FatTreeSim to help the community to better understand the advantages and disadvantages of Hadoop system and quantitatively measure the trade-offs between different design points.

2.3 ROSS & CODES

FatTreeSim is based on two parallel simulation packages: ROSS and CODES. ROSS is a massively parallel discrete-event simulator that has demonstrated the ability to process billions of events per second by leveraging large-scale HPC systems. A parallel discrete-event simulation (PDES) system consists of a collection of logical processes (LPs), each modeling a distinct component of the system (e.g., a server). LPs communicate by exchanging time stamped event messages (e.g., denoting the arrival of a new I/O request at that node). The goal of PDES is to efficiently process all events in a global timestamp order while minimizing any processor synchronization overheads. Two well-established

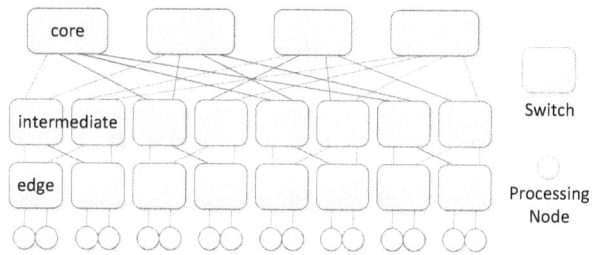

Figure 2: A fat-tree network with the total number of processing nodes equals to 16, the fat-tree height equals to 3, the number of edge switch equals to 8, and the number of core switch equals to 4.

approaches toward this goal are broadly called conservative processing and optimistic processing. ROSS supports both approaches. As shown in 4.2, FatTreeSim reaches the performance peak using the optimistic approach.

CODES [15] is a simulation system based on ROSS. Its goal is to enable the exploration and co-design of exascale storage systems by providing a detailed, accurate, and highly parallel simulation toolkit for exascale storage systems. Besides the two modules illustrated in Fig. 1, CODES also includes two modules CODES-bg and CODES-lsm. As seen in Fig 1, the current CODES-net toolkit includes two important submodules, the torus network model [29], and the dragonfly network model [28]. CODES is capable of simulating complex large-scale systems, e.g. FusionFS [36, 35], a distributed file system for both HPC and Cloud computing. The metadata in FusionFS is managed by ZHT [21], a zero hop distributed hash table service. Researchers from Illinois Institute of Technology have build models for the two systems and evaluated the performance at exascale. Tang et. al build a resource scheduler for multicloud workflows [32]. YARNsim [25] is the Hadoop YARN simulation system that aims to model and simulate extreme-scale Hadoop systems. However, current CODES-net module doesn't include a model for fat-tree network, which is the prevailing network topology used in current data centers. FatTreeSim targets the fat-tree network and is built in the CODES-net module. Therefore, it is compatible with any existing simulation systems built on CODES.

3. SIMULATING FAT-TREE NETWORK

In this section, we present the details related to the design, implementation and simulation of FatTreeSim. Specifically, we discuss the network topology and parameters, the simulated network traffic, routing algorithms and design considerations, and the discrete-event model.

3.1 Fat-Tree Topology

We illustrate a simple topology of the fat-tree network in Fig. 2, and it describes precisely how switches and hosts are interconnected. In graph representation, vertices represent switches or hosts, and links are the edges that connect them. The network topology is central to both the performance and the cost of the interconnection network. The topology affects a number of design tradeoffs, including performance, redundancy, and path diversity, which, in turn, affect the network's cost, resilience to faults, and average cable length.

A fat-tree can be described using the number of ports

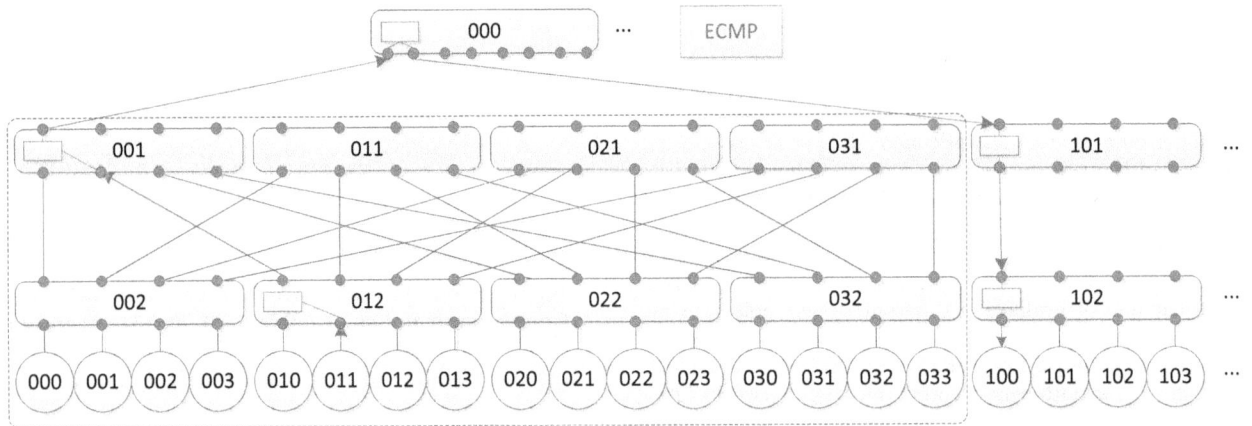

Figure 3: A packet routing in a 128 node fat-tree network. Fat-tree setup: m=8 n=3. The total number of switches is 80. The source node is 011, and the destination node is 100.

and the tree height. In general, a m-port n-tree fat-tree have the following characteristics [22, 11]: the height of the tree is $n + 1$; m is a power of 2; the tree consists of $m \cdot (m/2)^{(n-1)}$ processing nodes and $(2n - 1) \cdot (m/2)^{(n-1)}$ switches; each switch has m communication ports. Thus m and n determines the size of the fat-tree network. A 4-port 3-tree fat-tree network is given in Fig. 2. Here, the tree height is 3 which means there are 3 levels of switches. The switch that connects directly to the processing nodes are called edge switch, and the topmost level switch is called the root switch. The rest switches are named intermediate switch.

3.2 Fat-Tree Traffic

The traffic within the network of data center or HPC system is often bursty, meaning a large volume of packets will be injected into the network within a short period of time. In HPC system, defensive checkpointping often happens after the computation phase and usually starts with a synchronization [24]. In data centers, the network traffic exhibits a high degree of variability and is usually non-Gaussian [27]. In fact, a network that is only 10 percent utilized can see a lot of packet drops when running a web-search application [10].

In HPC and data centers, the communication pattern can be categorized as follows: 1) N to 1; 2) 1 to N; 3) N to N; 4) 1 to 1. In the first two scenarios, the application performs a global reduction or broadcast, which is a common traffic. This patterTo represent and validate a variety of traffic patterns and test the scalability of FatTreeSim, we pick two traffic patterns: random destination traffic and nearest neighbor traffic [24, 28]. With the random destination traffic pattern, each source node randomly picks a destination node and generates a packet stream with the intervals apply to the exponential distribution. In fact, the generated packet is a Poisson stream. With nearest neighbor traffic pattern, each source node picks the nearest-neighboring node or the second-nearest-neighboring node as the destination node. This traffic pattern generates packets at a fixed time interval and the ratio of packets passing through the core routers is also fixed. It is challenging to simulate ran-

dom destination traffic in discrete event simulation because the generated packet flows have very low locality. ROSS optimistic simulation mode can handle this scenario in an efficient manner. The nearest neighbor traffic is more balanced and thus is more amenable to parallel simulation performance.

3.3 Fat-Tree Routing Algorithm

The routing algorithm determines the route a packet traverses through the network. Non-blocking fat-tree network provides abundant path diversity in which multiple possible egress ports exist. To take the advantage of the paths multiplicity, equal-cost multi-paths routing algorithm (ECMP) is the widely used [11]. ECMP is a load balancing routing protocol based on RFC 2991 [19] that optimizes flows over multiple best paths to a single destination. ECMP applies load balancing routing on flows such as TCP or UDP, and can potentially increase the bandwidth between two endpoints by spreading the traffic over multiple paths. Path selection is based on hashing of the packet header. In recent years, networking researchers have pointed the limitations of ECMP routing and proposed dynamic routing algorithm like Hedera [12]. A path through the network is called minimal path if no shorter path, less number of hops, exists. Different from other network topology, e.g. dragonfly, a fat-tree has multiple minimal paths. In Fig. 3, we illustrate an exemplar packet routing procedure in a 8-port 3-tree fat-tree network. The total number of processing nodes equals to 128 and total number of switches equals to 80. Here, the packet starts from the source node 011 and tries to reach the destination node 100. As we can see, the packet reaches a different level at each hop, thus the maximum number of hops for the complete route is 2 times the tree height. In each step, the ECMP routing algorithm is used to determine the next hop node. In FatTreeSim, we model ECMP routing and focus on minimal path. Network flow control is also key to the network model. It dictates how the input buffers at each switch or router are managed. FatTreeSim buffers currently use the store-and-forward technique, thus the delay can be described using equation 1.

$$T = H \cdot (D/B + T_p) + T_s \tag{1}$$

```
procedure GT                    ▷ generate packet stream
    t = processing delay
    τ = rng(I)
    if RandomDestinationTraffic then
        dst = rng(maxnodeID)
        Generate packet (header contains dst )
    else if NearestNeighborTraffic then
        dst = neighborID
        Generate packet (header contains dst )
    else
        Unsupported traffic
    end if
    Call NSP procedure with t
    Call GT procedure with τ
end procedure
```

Figure 4: Procedure GT

```
procedure NSP                    ▷ node send packet
    t = D/B + T_p
    dst = my connected router
    Call flit generates procedure with t and dst
end procedure
```

Figure 5: Procedure NSP

```
procedure RFR                    ▷ router receives flit
    t = processing delay
    Check flit dst
    Call RFS procedure with t
end procedure
```

Figure 6: Procedure RFR

Here, H is the number of hops the packet takes in its entire route. In fat-tree network this number usually equals to the number of hops in a minimal path. D is the packet size. B is the link bandwidth. Equation 1 assumes the bandwidth are equal between nodes or switches. In FatTreeSim, the link bandwidth is configurable through a customized configuration file. Thus equation 1 can be slightly modified so as to represent the most accurate cost. T_p is the average propagation delay on links. This parameter is also configurable in FatTreeSim.

3.4 Simulating the Fat-Tree Network

The key components in a fat-tree network system are switches and processing nodes. In FatTreeSim, we use LP to model switch and processing nodes. FatTreeSim only focuses on the network topology and its related features and simplifies the hardware components such as I/O system, CPU and memory. The processing node LP can be considered as a network interface card (NIC) in CODES system where detailed hardware models are provided. We also use an additional LP (App LP) type to model an application software, e.g. a MPI process or MapReduce task. The purpose is to accurately capture the application layer behavior and thus quantitatively model its effects on the network layer. For example, a group of MPI processes running on terminals can issue a collective communication call which generates a burst of packets in the network layer. In FatTreeSim, switch LPs are classified as a core switch LP, intermediate-switch LP and edge switch LP. This resembles a real fat-tree network system. Edge-switch LP connects to processing-node LP. The same group of switch LP and processing-node LP share the same address prefix. For the convenience of presentation, we use procedures to describe the typical events used in FatTreeSim and illustrate them in Figures 4 to 7.

The packet routing in FatTreeSim is based on the addressing system. A m-port n-tree fat-tree network has a total of $m \cdot (m/2)^{(n-1)}$ processing nodes and $(2n-1) \cdot (m/2)^{(n-1)}$ switches. Each node LP is assigned a unique n-bit address. The first bit indicates the group number. $m$port means the total number of groups is m. The rest $n - 1$ bits vary from 1 to $(m - 1)/2$. Thus the total number of processing nodes inside each group is $(m/2)^{(n-1)}$. A switch LP is also assigned a unique n-bit address. The first bit also indicates the group number. The last bit of the address indicates the layer number, where 0 represents the core layer and $n - 1$ represents the edge layer. The rest $n - 2$ bits vary from 1 to $(m - 1)/2$. Thus the total number of switches in each layer is $2 \cdot (m/2)^{(n-1)}$ with the exception that the core layer has $(m/2)^{(n-1)}$ switches. The routing starts at the edge switch LP and iterates through all the layers. At any layer, if the first k bits of the destination node address matches the first k bits of the address of the current switch, then the packet starts to go down to the lower layer of the switch or the processing node. Otherwise, the packet continues to go to upper layer switch. When packets go up, there are multi-paths to choose from. ECMP algorithm hashes the packet header and find the corresponding egress port based on the hash value. In [22], the authors validated the routing algorithms with analytical proof and experiments. With the aforementioned scheme, the packet routing is based on table look-up rather than pre-allocation, which could save memory for storing LP state variables in FatTreeSim.

In ROSS and CODES, the LP is addressed through a global ID in the form an unsigned long integer. This is different from the bit-format address assigned to the LP in routing. Thus, we convert addresses between the two formats and guarantee the events are forwarded to the correct LPs.

The most important event in an App LP is the packet generation event. We describe this event in Fig. 4. GT procedure models the communication patterns of an application. As described in 3.2, FatTreeSim support two types of traffic: random destination and nearest neighbor. GT procedure calls itself with an random interval. The intervals applies to exponential distribution, therefore, the GT procedure is capable of generating a Poisson input stream.

The NSP procedure illustrates a packet has been generated in an App LP and is injected into the fat-tree network. NSP further triggers the flits generation event that models the protocol level details of network traffic. Users can customize the flit sizes to evaluate how different network configurations can affect the performance. When a switch receives a flit, it parses the flit header and calls the ADDRESS procedure to get the exact next-hop address. Routing algorithms such as ECMP is implemented in ADDRESS procedure. In this study, we only implemented and evaluated the ECMP. It is our future work to develop models for other routing algorithms and evaluate the performance

```
procedure RFS                          ▷ router sends flit
    Parse flit dst
    nextHop =ADDRESS(dst,flit)
    t = D/B + T_p
    Call RFR procedure with t and nextHop
end procedure
```

Figure 7: Procedure RFS

```
procedure ADDRESS                      ▷ find next hop node
    Parse flit dst
    Get my address adr
    Find gcp address greatest common prefix (dst,adr)
    if gcp == L_c then
        Route down, hash packet header
        nextHop =ECMP()
    else if gcp < L_c then
        Route up, hash packet header
        nextHop =ECMP()
    else
        Error
    end if
    return nextHop
end procedure
```

Figure 8: Procedure ADDRESS

under different applications at large scale.

At the processing node LP, the flits that belong to the same packet are assembled and then further forwarded to the destination App LP. We use additional events to model this process and the details are omitted in the discussion.

4. EXPERIMENTAL EVALUATION

We evaluate FatTreeSim from three aspects: its accuracy, scalability and usage. To verify that FatTreeSim can accurately model the real-world network traffic, we conducted extensive experiments on Emulab and compare the results against the simulation results. The detailed discussion is provided in section 4.1. To further demonstrate the scalability, we run FatTreeSim on Blue Gene/Q supercomputer with a variety of configurations. The details are presented in 4.2. Lastly, we demonstrate the usage of FatTreeSim through a use case study and its discussion is in section 4.3.

4.1 Fidelity Evaluation on Emulab

Emulab is a network testbed that allows users to flexibly allocate the physical devices as well as virtual devices to build the desired networking experiment environment [16]. Throughout the duration of the experiment, a user has complete control of the devices and thus is capable to configure the system with the desired parameters. We choose Emulab for FatTreeSim accuracy tests because we can configure the fat-tree network in a flexible manner. The maximum number of physical links an Emulab router can have is 4, thus we configured a 4-port 3-tree fat-tree network topology, in which we have full control of the physical nodes and links. We used the MPI Ping-Pong benchmark for the experiments. Here, the message size is set as 1,024 bytes because we want to use and verify the MPI eager protocol. Similar to UDP,

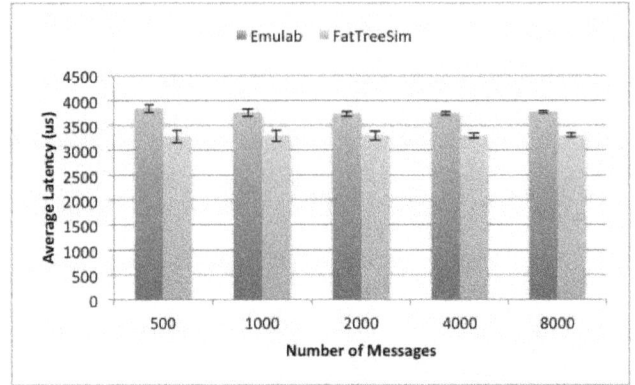

Figure 9: Latency comparison between Emulab measurements and FatTreeSim results using MPI Ping-Pong benchmark. The message size is 1,024 bytes. The total number of nodes is 16, and the total number of switches is 20. The traffic pattern is Nearest Neighbor.

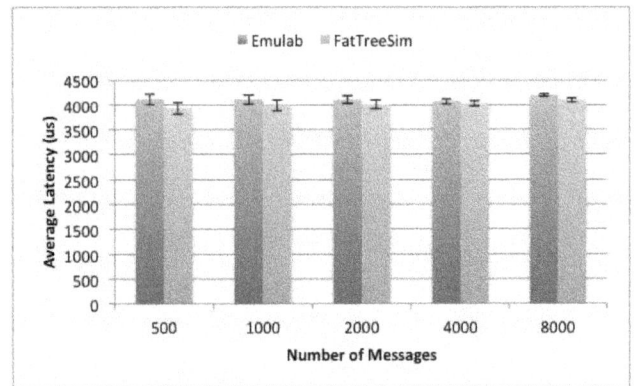

Figure 10: Latency comparison between Emulab measurements and FatTreeSim results using MPI Ping-Pong benchmark. The message size is 1,024 bytes. The total number of nodes is 16, and the total number of switches is 20. The traffic pattern is Random Destination.

The eager protocol features a fire-and-forget communication pattern in which no acknowledgment message is generated. An MPI message smaller than 2,048 bytes will automatically trigger the eager protocol. This experiment setting guarantees that FatTreeSim has the correct configurations for each node, link and switch.

We used two traffic patterns, nearest neighbor and random destination, in the experiments. For each traffic pattern, we vary the number of outgoing messages from 500 to 8,000, and we repeat the test 10 times and calculated the standard deviation. In FatTreeSim, we set up an exact 4-port 3-tree fat-tree network with identical configurations. We repeat the experiments 10 times and calculate the average for each configuration. The experimental results for the nearest neighbor test is reported in Figure 9. As we can see, the standard deviation decreases with the increase of the number of messages and its maximum value is 2.86% in a 500-message test. This demonstrates that the system noise has minimal impact on the experiments. We conducted identical

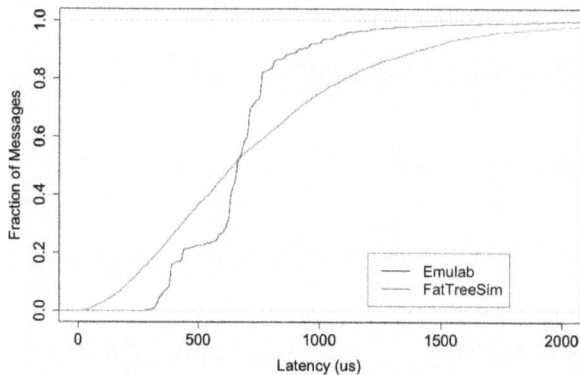

(a) CDF of Message Latency. The number of processing nodes is 8. The number of switches is 6. The traffic pattern is Nearest Neighbor.

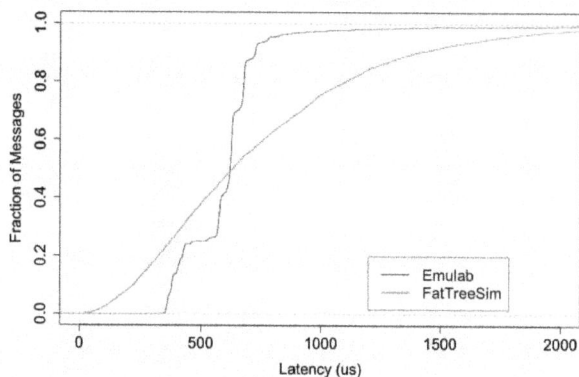

(b) CDF of Message Latency. The number of processing nodes is 8. The number of switches is 6. The traffic pattern is Random Destination.

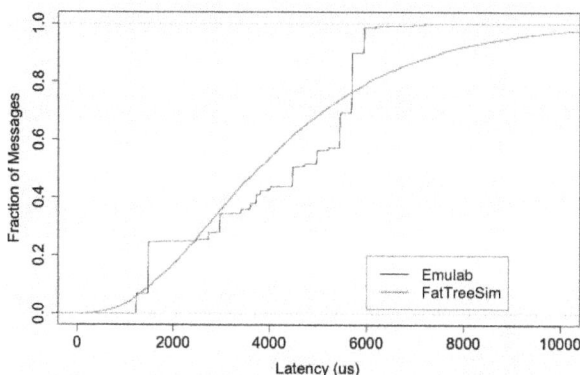

(c) CDF of Message Latency. The number of processing nodes is 16. The number of switches is 20. The traffic pattern is Nearest Neighbor.

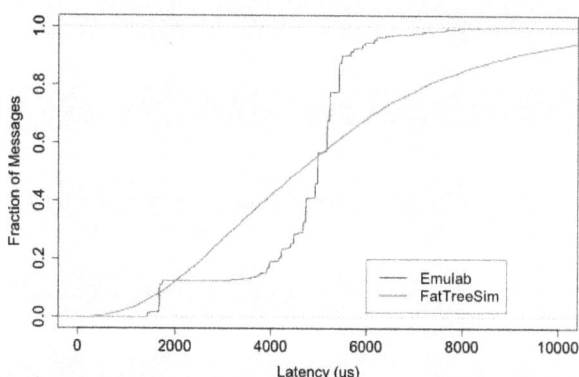

(d) CDF of Message Latency. The number of processing nodes is 16. The number of switches is 20. The traffic pattern is Random Destination.

Figure 11: CDF of MPI Ping-Pong Test Message Latency. The message size is 1,024 bytes. The number of messages is 1,000.

experiments on FatTreeSim in which we manually introduce random noise to match the real system. There are, however, around 10-13% error in FatTreeSim for all test cases. In Figure 10, we report the experimental results for random destination traffic. Here, simulation can achieve a better accuracy and the error range is within 3% for all test cases.

To further evaluate the accuracy of FatTreeSim, we record the latency for each message from both the Emulab cluster and FatTreeSim and report the results in the CDF plots. We used two different configurations: a 4-port 2-tree and a 4-port 3-tree. The message size is 1,024 bytes and the number of messages is 1,000 per node. In all experiments, we observed that the curve for simulation is much smoother than the curve for Emulab. This is attributed to the fact that we model only one outgoing buffer in each outgoing port. If multiple messages are sent through this port, congestion will occur and this single point queuing effect lead to a unique waiting time for each packet. Another observation is that there is a gap between the two CDF curves in the high latency zone in Figure 11a. We attribute this to the congestion model overuse in FatTreeSim. This gap explains the average latency error in Figure 9. In the 4-port 3-tree

test, we observed better CDF curve match. However, Fat-TreeSim cannot generate the steep increase or plateau observed in the Emulab real system tests. As discussed earlier, one way to model this effect is to introduce the multi-thread and multi-channel model.

4.2 Validation on BG/Q

We conduct the strong-scaling experiment of FatTreeSim on Mira, a Blue Gene/Q supercomputing system in Argonne National Laboratory. As of Nov. 2014, Mira ranks 4_{th} in the top 500 lists. Mira consists of a total of 48 racks and 786,432 processors and is capable of 10 quadrillion calculations per second. The total memory of Mira is 768 terabytes. Each rack consists of 1,024 nodes and each node consists of 16 cores with a total of 16 gigabytes of shared memory. Users can choose to run on different modes, thus allocating different size of memory for each MPI process. The interconnection network is a 5-D torus which provides a fast collective communication for global reduce operations. This is ideal for ROSS to perform the optimistic synchronization algorithm. FatTreeSim leverages the fast 5-D torus interconnection network and achieves a performance of 305 million events per

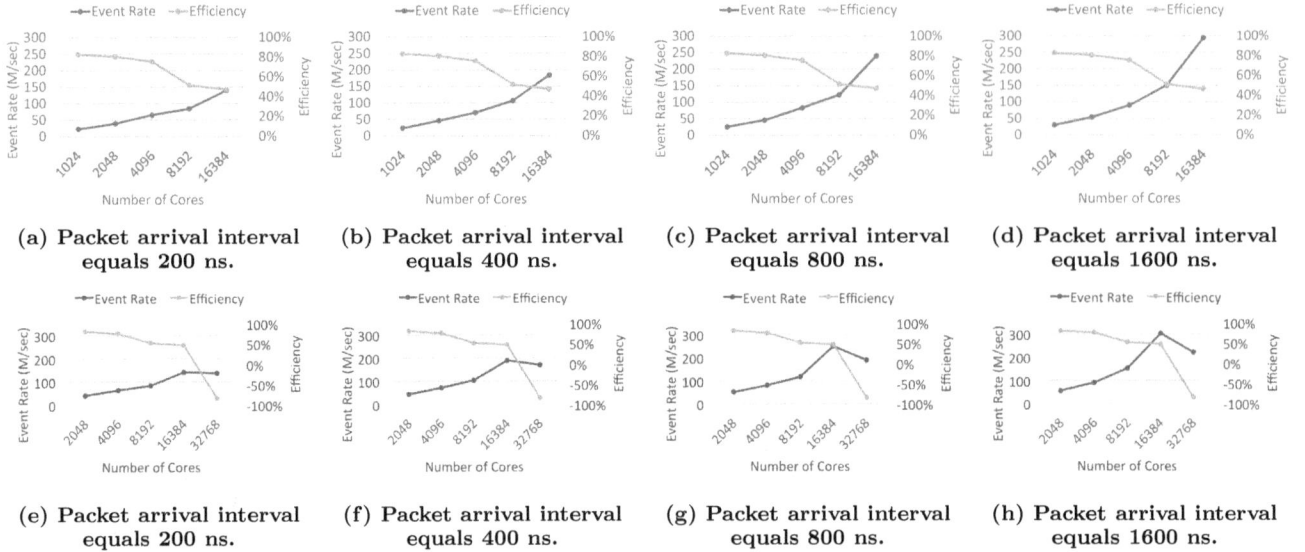

(a) Packet arrival interval equals 200 ns.

(b) Packet arrival interval equals 400 ns.

(c) Packet arrival interval equals 800 ns.

(d) Packet arrival interval equals 1600 ns.

(e) Packet arrival interval equals 200 ns.

(f) Packet arrival interval equals 400 ns.

(g) Packet arrival interval equals 800 ns.

(h) Packet arrival interval equals 1600 ns.

Figure 12: FatTreeSim Scalability Experiment on Blue Gene/Q. The fat-tree model consists of 524,288 processing nodes and 20,480 switches. The total number of committed events is 567 billion. In each top subfigure, we vary the number of cores from 1,024 to 16,384 through running experiments on c1, c2, c4, c8 and c16 modes. From top-left subfigure to top-right subfigure, we vary the packet arrival interval from 200 ns to 1,600 ns. Experiments on the top subfigures are conducted using 1 Blue Gene/Q rack. In each bottom subfigure, we vary the number of cores from 2,048 to 32,768 through running experiments on c1, c2, c4, c8 and c16 modes. From top-left subfigure to top-right subfigure, we vary the packet arrival interval from 200 ns to 1600 ns. Experiments on the top subfigures are conducted using 2 Blue Gene/Q racks. The traffic pattern is random destination.

second using 32,768 cores.

We use two metrics: the committed event rate and the event efficiency to evaluate the simulation performance of FatTreeSim. In ROSS, the event efficiency determines the amount of useful work performed by the simulation. It is defined in Equation 2 [14]:

$$efficiency = 1 - \frac{rolled\_back\_event}{total\_committed\_events} \quad (2)$$

The simulation efficiency is inversely proportional to the number of rollbacks and is a rigorous indicator of the performance of a simulation system. The higher the efficiency, the faster the simulation performs. Another factor that affects the efficiency is the percentage of remote events, which is defined as the event transmitted between physical processes. The delay of remote event is unpredictable and can cause the logically erroneous events. The percentage of remote event is inherent to the model and usually increases with the increase of the number of physical processes when performing the scaling experiment. Global synchronization can effectively reduce the number of rollbacks, however, this global communication is usually expensive, especially in large-scale systems like Mira. There is a tradeoff in determining how frequently the simulation system performs the synchronization. ROSS uses gvt-interval and batch to control the frequency of global virtual time computation. FatTreeSim leverages the functionalities provided by ROSS and can achieve its peak performance in large-scale through parameters tuning and system configuration. The strategy for obtaining the optimal gvt-interval and batch size for the Dragonfly network module is discussed in [28].

Specifically, we configured a 128-port 3-tree fat-tree net-

work in FatTreeSim. The total number of processing-node LP and App LP is 524,288 respectively, and total number of switch LP is 20,480. We select random destination traffic as it can generate the worst case scenario for parallel simulation for its large percentage of remote event. Each node continuously generates a packet stream and each packet randomly selects a destination. The time interval between two packets applies to the exponential distribution, thus the packet is a Poison stream. The author in [24] has pointed out that the interval also has an impact on the simulation performance. To perform the strong scaling experiment, we fixed the simulation size through setting the number of packets to 5,000 on each node. The total committed event is 567 billion.

We perform the experiments on Mira using 1 rack and 2 rack of nodes respectively. Each Blue Gene/Q node has 16 processors and 16 gigabytes of shared memory, the job can run on 6 different modes in which the each node can host 1, 2, 4, 8, 16, 32, and 64 MPI processes. In the last two modes, an MPI process runs as a hyper-thread and 32/64 threads share 16 physical cores. We focus on the first 5 modes because, a parallel simulation is usually memory intensive rather than CPU intensive. Thus, each MPI process can get more memory. We vary the modes and packet arrival intervals and report the performance of FatTreeSim on Mira in details in Figure 12. In the tests that use 1 rack of nodes, FatTreeSim nearly achieves a linear speedup up to 16,384 cores, the peak event rate is 297 million per second. The efficiency decreases as the number of cores increases, this is because of the increase of remote event percentage. The maximum percentage we observed is 37%. Comparing horizontally, we can see that the event rate increases with the enlarged packet arrival interval. This is because the intensive packet arrivals can cause the simulation engine to generate more out of order events which contributes to the total rollbacks. The takeaway here is that the performance of FatTreeSim will decrease on simulating a burst of communication or I/O operations. On the experiments that use 2 racks of nodes, we start to observe negative efficiency when the scale reaches 32,768 cores. This phenomenon is inherent in the model. The efficiency will increase if we: a) use the nearest neighbor traffic instead of random destination traffic; b) increase the problem size of the simulation, e.g. total number of LPs; c) tune the gvt-interval and batch parameter in a fine-grained manner; d) perform a better mapping of LPs to MPI processes so as to better balance the wordload. We have yet to use experiments to corroborate the above assertions. The gvt-interval and batch used in the experiments are 32 and 8 respectively. The peak event observed in this set of experiments is 305 million per second using 16,384 cores.

4.3 Case Study: YARNsim

YARNsim [25] is a comprehensive Hadoop YARN simulation system that is capable of evaluating both the hardware and software stack performance under a wide range of applications. YARNsim is built on CODES and ROSS and leverage the fast 5-D torus network provided by Blue Gene/Q system for global reduction and synchronization. In [25], the performance of YARNsim is evaluated through comprehensive Hadoop benchmarks and a bioinformatic application study. The details regarding the design, implementation and usage of YARNsim are beyond the scope of this paper. In this experiment, we want to demonstrate the usability of FatTreeSim through running YARNsim using FatTreeSim. We perform the Hadoop application simulation in YARNsim. Here, FatTreeSim serves as the network layer module in CODES and helps YARNsim in evaluating Hadoop benchmarks and application. We record the YARNsim performance and compare it against the results collected from HEC. HEC is a 51-node Sun Fire Linux- based cluster, in which there are one head node and 50 computing nodes. The head node was Sun Fire X4240, equipped with dual 2.7 GHz Opteron quad-core processors, 8GB memory, and 12 500GB 7200RPM SATA-II drives configured as RAID5 disk array. The computing nodes were Sun Fire X2200 servers, each node with dual 2.3GHz Opteron quad-core processors, 8GB memory, and a 250GB 7200RPM SATA hard drive. All 51 nodes are connected through Gigabit Ethernet. We use Hadoop YARN 2.5.0 for all experiments.

We choose Terasort and Wordcount benchmarks for the experiments because they are widely accepted and can represent a class of Hadoop applications. To further analyze the application performance, we decompose each job to three phases, the map phase, shuffle phase and reduce phase, assuming map phase and reduce phase contains the merge-sort operations. In HEC, we use a total of 16 nodes and vary the input data size from 128MB to 16GB. To accurately record the performance of each phase in the real system, we leverage the job history service provided by Hadoop, in which the detailed performance of each phase is reported. We collect and report these numbers and compare them against the numbers collected from the YARNsim system. In YARNsim, we use the same configuration as in HEC for configuring the simulated clusters

We report the results of Terasort benchmark experiment

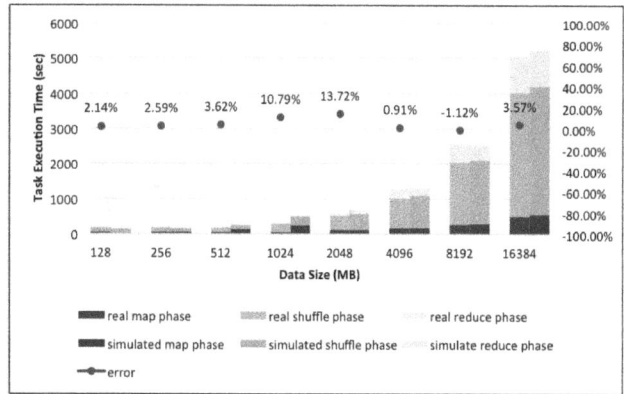

Figure 13: Performance Comparison of Terasort Benchmark between real system and simulation. The simulation uses FatTreeSim as the network module: input data size varies from 128MB to 16GB; number of nodes is 16. Blue stacks are the reported performance of each MapReduce phase on HEC, red stacks are the reported performance of each MapReduce phase on YARNsim.

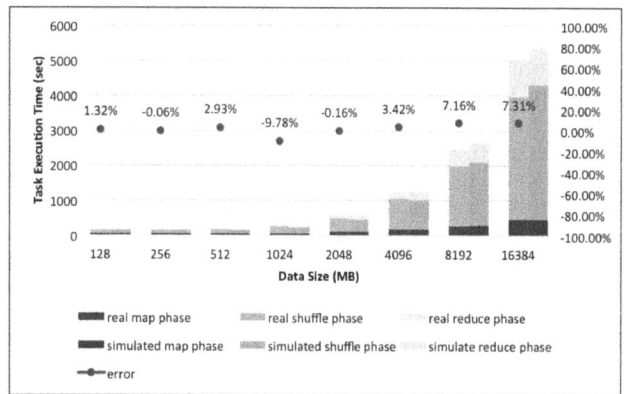

Figure 14: Performance Comparison of Wordcound Benchmark between the real system measurements and simulation results. The Simulation uses FatTreeSim as the network module: the input data size varies from 128MB to 16GB; the number of nodes is 16. The blue stacks are the reported performance of each MapReduce phase on HEC, and the red stacks are the reported performance of each MapReduce phase on YARNsim.

in Figure 13. Here we compare the performance results from both HEC and YARNsim. In most test cases the error of the accumulated performance is within 5%. YARNsim can achieve a good accuracy in modeling Terasort benchmark and the Hadoop system with the FatTreeSim network module deployed. In Figure 14, we report the Hadoop Wordcount benchmark performance results on both HEC and YARNsim. As we can see, YARNsim can also achieve a good accuracy in modeling Wordcount benchmark and the Hadoop system with the FatTreeSim network module deployed. The observed error rate is within 10% for all test cases.

In the field of bioinformatics, large dataset clustering is a

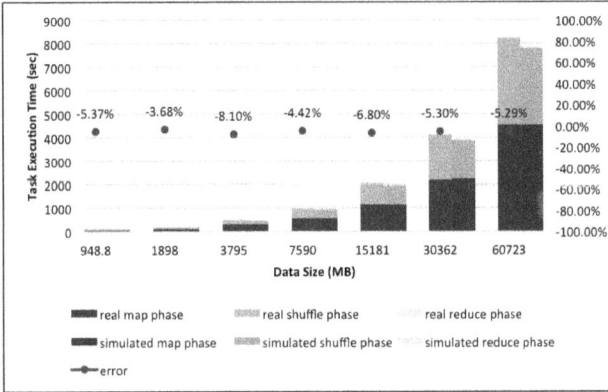

Figure 15: Performance Comparison of Bio-application between real system measurements and simulation results. The Simulation uses FatTreeSim as the network module: the input data size varies from 128MB to 16GB; the number of nodes is 16. The blue stacks are the reported performance of each MapReduce phase on HEC, and the red stacks are the reported performance of each MapReduce phase on YARNsim.

challenging problem. Many biological scientists resort to Hadoop MapReduce for large scale and parallel processing solutions. In [34], researchers from the University of Delaware have developed an octree based clustering algorithm for classifying protein-ligand binding geometries. The proposed method is implemented in Hadoop MapReduce and is divided into a two-phase MapReduce job. The geometry reduction and key generation are the first phase MapReduce job where large datasets are read by the map tasks. The output of the first phase is the input of the second phase MapReduce job. Here, iterative octree based clustering algorithm is implemented as a chain of MapReduce jobs representing the search has iterated to the deep level of the search tree. In the first phase, the output data size is about 1% of the input data size. Thus the MapReduce job spends most of the time on the map and the shuffle phase. To effectively model this application, we identify the sizes and locations of all data blocks in each phase and use them as input to the modeled MapReduce jobs. We vary the input file of protein geometry data from 948MB to 60GB and run the experiments on HEC using 16 nodes. We also build a model for this clustering application and run it on YARN-sim with different configuration. The performance on HEC and YARNsim are reported in Fig 15. Here, FatTreeSim also serves as the underlying network topology. The performance results show that the error is within 10% for all test cases. With FatTreeSim, we are capable of building a large-scale model of the data centers where the Hadoop system is deployed. Thus, it is potentially possible to evaluate and optimize a large-scale Hadoop application from a simulation perspective. It is our future work to continue on this topic.

5. RELATED WORK

There exists a plethora of works in modeling and simulating large scale systems, each with a different focus. As part of the exascale co-design process, there is a growing interest in understanding how parallel systems software such as MPI/OpenMP and the associated supercomputing appli-

cations scale on extreme-scale computing systems. To this end, researchers have turned to parallel discrete-event simulation. For example, Perumallas $\mu\pi$ [30] system allows MPI programs to be transparently executed on top of the MPI modeling layer and simulate the MPI messages. Each MPI task is realized as a thread in the underlying μsilk simulator. Thus, $\mu\pi$ captures the true direct execution behavior across millions of MPI tasks that are part of a massively parallel application. Similar systems, such as BigSim [37], have not achieved such a level of scaling. The Structural Simulation Toolkit (SST) uses a component-based parallel discrete-event model built on top of MPI. SST models a variety of hardware components including processors, memory and networks under different accuracy and details. To the best of our knowledge, neither of these systems performs packet-level simulations of the underlying network at scale. Instead, the focus of their research is application computation performance with the hardwares abstracted away.

Wang et al. have built the Hadoop simulator MRperf [33]. MRperf use NS2 [20] as the network module. NS2 is a well established network simulator in the community due its rich set of functionalities, however, NS2 cannot run in parallel and thus is constrained in terms of modeling large-scale network. The new NS3 [6] project uses the conservative parallel simulation and its performance on large-scale has yet to be evaluated.

Researchers have focused on modeling large-scale network model for topologies like torus [24] and dragonfly [28]. These network models also leverage the functionalities provided by ROSS platform and have already been ported to the CODES [15] platform. Currently, the network models can support a wide range of application models that run on CODES. For example, Tang et al. [32] build a data-aware resource scheduler on CODES. YARNsim [25] is the Hadoop YARN system simulator that runs on CODES. However, to the best of our knowledge, there is no large-scale model for fat-tree networks. FatTreeSim targets the fat-tree network, which has already been widely used in the distributed computing community and is being considered as a network candidate for the next generation HPC system.

6. CONCLUSIONS AND FUTURE WORK

In this paper, we present FatTreeSim, a fat-tree network simulation system built on ROSS and CODES. We discuss the design and implementation of FatTreeSim and validate its accuracy, scalability and usability through extensive experiments. Specifically, we run FatTreeSim on the Argonne Leadership Computing Facility's Blue Gene/Q system, Mira, and demonstrates a close-to-linear scalability up to 32,768 cores. We also configured a 4-port 3-tree fat-tree network in EmuLab and compared with FatTreeSim results using the MPI Ping-Pong benchmark. The experimental results show that the error rate of average latency is within 10%. Finally, we run YARNsim, a Hadoop YARN simulation system with FatTreeSim to test the Terasort and Wordcount benchmarks and a bio-application. The experimental results show that FatTreeSim can help YARNsim to accurately model Hadoop benchmarks as well as real system applications.

Fat-tree is an important network topology that has been widely used in the community of parallel and distributed computing. Nowadays, fat-tree networks face new challenges with the advent of the era of extreme-scale computing, when systems feature millions of physical cores and the potential billion-way concurrency. FatTreeSim is a timely work to equip system designers with the right tools to cope with deploying large-scale fat-tree networks. We plan to focus on the following issues in the future: a) To increase the accuracy of FatTreeSim, we plan to augment the existing system with a multi-channel model and a buffer management mechanism; b) to conduct extensive experiments on a Blue Gene supercomputer at even larger scale to find the optimal system configuration to maximize the model scalability; c) to test YARNsim on FatTreeSim with large-scale Hadoop applications, whose results can be used for large-scale Hadoop system optimization.

Acknowledgements

The authors would like to thank Dr. Misbah Mubarak, Dr. Jonathan Jenkins, and Dr. Robert Ross from Argonne National Laboratory for their valuable suggestions and help throughout this work. This material is based upon work supported byt the Maryland Procurement Office under Contract NO. H98230-14-C-0141. This also research used resources of the Argonne Leadership Computing Facility at Argonne National Laboratory, which is supported by the Office of Science of the U.S. Department of Energy under contract DE-AC02-06CH11357[1].

7. REFERENCES

[1] Apache Hadoop. http://hadoop.apache.org. [Last accessed May 2015].

[2] Cisco Global Cloud Index: Forecast and Methodology, 2013-2018. http://cisco.com/c/en/us/solutions/collateral/service-provider/global-cloud-index-gci/Cloud_Index_White_Paper.html. [Last accessed November 2014].

[3] Gartner Report. http://www.gartner.com/newsroom/id/2313915. [Last accessed May 2015].

[4] IDC: Amount of World Data Centers to Start Declining in 2017. http://www.datacenterknowledge.com/archives/2014/11/11/idc-amount-of-worlds-data-centers/-to-start-declining-in-2017/. [Last accessed November 2014].

[5] Mumak: Map-Reduce Simulator. https://issues.apache.org/jira/browse/MAPREDUCE-728. [Last accessed May 2015].

[6] ns-3. https://www.nsnam.org/. [Last accessed May 2015].

[7] Real Cost Comparison of Fat-tree and Torus Networks | ClusterDesign.org. http://clusterdesign.org/2013/01/real-cost-comparison-of-fat-tree-and-torus-networks/. [Last accessed May 2015].

[8] Summit. Scale new heights. Discover new solutions. http://www.olcf.ornl.gov/summit/. [Last accessed May 2015].

[9] Yarn Scheduler Load Simulator (SLS). http://hadoop.apache.org/docs/r2.4.1/hadoop-sls/SchedulerLoadSimulator.html. [Last accessed May 2015].

[10] D. Abts and B. Felderman. A guided tour through data-center networking. Queue, 10(5):10:10–10:23, May 2012.

[11] M. Al-Fares, A. Loukissas, and A. Vahdat. A scalable, commodity data center network architecture. ACM SIGCOMM Computer Communication Review, 38(4):63–74, Oct. 2008.

[12] M. Al-Fares, S. Radhakrishnan, B. Raghavan, N. Huang, and A. Vahdat. Hedera: Dynamic flow scheduling for data center networks. In Proceedings of the 7th USENIX Conference on Networked Systems Design and Implementation, NSDI'10, pages 19–19, Berkeley, CA, USA, Apr. 2010. USENIX Association.

[13] A. Alexandrov, M. F. Ionescu, K. E. Schauser, and C. Scheiman. LogGP: Incorporating Long Messages into the LogP Model&Mdash;One Step Closer Towards a Realistic Model for Parallel Computation. In Proceedings of the Seventh Annual ACM Symposium on Parallel Algorithms and Architectures, SPAA '95, pages 95–105, New York, NY, USA, July 1995. ACM.

[14] C. Carothers, D. Bauer, and S. Pearce. ROSS: a high-performance, low memory, modular time warp system. In Fourteenth Workshop on Parallel and Distributed Simulation, 2000. PADS 2000. Proceedings, pages 53–60, Bologna, Italy, May 2000.

[15] J. Cope, N. Liu, S. Lang, P. Carns, C. D. Carothers, and R. Ross. CODES: Enabling co-design of multilayer exascale storage architectures. In Proceedings of the Workshop on Emerging Supercomputing Technologies (WEST), Tuscon, AZ, June 2011.

[16] C. Cutler, M. Hibler, E. Eide, and R. Ricci. Trusted disk loading in the emulab network testbed. In Proceedings of the 3rd International Conference on Cyber Security Experimentation and Test, CSET'10, pages 1–8, Berkeley, CA, USA, Aug. 2010. USENIX Association.

[17] J. Dean and S. Ghemawat. Mapreduce: Simplified data processing on large clusters. Communications of the ACM, 51(1):107–113, Jan. 2008.

[18] S. Hammoud, M. Li, Y. Liu, N. Alham, and Z. Liu. MRSim: A discrete event based MapReduce simulator. In 2010 Seventh International Conference on Fuzzy Systems and Knowledge Discovery (FSKD), volume 6, pages 2993–2997, Yantai, China, Aug. 2010.

[19] C. E. Hopps and D. Thaler. Multipath Issues in Unicast and Multicast Next-Hop Selection. https://tools.ietf.org/html/rfc2991. [Last accessed May 2015].

[20] T. Issariyakul and E. Hossain. Introduction to Network Simulator NS2. Springer Publishing Company, Incorporated, 1 edition, 2008.

[21] T. Li, X. Zhou, K. Brandstatter, D. Zhao, K. Wang, A. Rajendran, Z. Zhang, and I. Raicu. ZHT: A light-weight reliable persistent dynamic scalable zero-hop distributed hash table. IPDPS '13, pages 775–787, Boston, MA, May 2013.

[22] X.-Y. Lin, Y.-C. Chung, and T.-Y. Huang. A multiple

[1]Disclaimer: Any opinions, findings and conclusions or recommendations expressed in this material are those of the author(s) and do not necessarily reflect the views of the Maryland Procurement Office.

LID routing scheme for fat-tree-based InfiniBand networks. In *Parallel and Distributed Processing Symposium, 2004. Proceedings. 18th International*, pages 11–, Santa Fe, New Mexico, Apr. 2004.

[23] N. Liu, C. Carothers, J. Cope, P. Carns, and R. Ross. Model and simulation of exascale communication networks. *Journal of Simulation*, 6(4):227–236, Nov. 2012.

[24] N. Liu and C. D. Carothers. Modeling Billion-Node Torus Networks Using Massively Parallel Discrete-Event Simulation. In *Proceedings of the 2011 IEEE Workshop on Principles of Advanced and Distributed Simulation*, PADS '11, pages 1–8, Washington, DC, USA, 2011. IEEE Computer Society.

[25] N. Liu, X. Yang, X.-H. Sun, J. Jenkins, and R. Ross. Yarnsim: Simulating hadoop yarn. In *15th IEEE/ACM International Symposium on Cluster, Cloud and Grid Computing*, CCGrid '15, Shenzhen, China, May 2015.

[26] Y. Liu, M. Li, N. K. Alham, and S. Hammoud. HSim: A MapReduce Simulator in Enabling Cloud Computing. *Future Generation Computer Systems*, 29(1):300–308, Jan. 2013.

[27] T. Mori, M. Uchida, R. Kawahara, J. Pan, and S. Goto. Identifying elephant flows through periodically sampled packets. In *Proceedings of the 4th ACM SIGCOMM Conference on Internet Measurement*, IMC '04, pages 115–120, New York, NY, USA, Nov. 2004. ACM.

[28] M. Mubarak, C. Carothers, R. Ross, and P. Carns. Modeling a Million-Node Dragonfly Network Using Massively Parallel Discrete-Event Simulation. In *2012 SC Companion: High Performance Computing, Networking, Storage and Analysis (SCC)*, pages 366–376, Washington, DC, USA, Nov. 2012.

[29] M. Mubarak, C. D. Carothers, R. B. Ross, and P. Carns. A case study in using massively parallel simulation for extreme-scale torus network codesign. In *Proceedings of the 2Nd ACM SIGSIM/PADS Conference on Principles of Advanced Discrete Simulation*, SIGSIM-PADS '14, pages 27–38, New York, NY, USA, 2014. ACM.

[30] K. S. Perumalla and A. J. Park. Simulating billion-task parallel programs. In *Performance Evaluation of Computer and Telecommunication Systems (SPECTS 2014), International Symposium on*, pages 585–592, Monterey, CA, USA, July 2014.

[31] S. Snyder, P. Carns, J. Jenkins, K. Harms, R. Ross, M. Mubarak, and C. Carothers. A case for epidemic fault detection and group membership in hpc storage systems. In *the 5th International Workshop on Performance Modeling, Benchmarking and Simulation of High Performance Computer Systems (PMBS14).*, pages 237–248, New Orleans, LA, USA, Nov. 2014. Springer International Publishing.

[32] W. Tang, J. Jenkins, F. Meyer, R. B. Ross, R. Kettimuthu, L. Winkler, X. Yang, T. Lehman, and N. L. Desai. Data-aware resource scheduling for multicloud workflows: A fine-grained simulation approach. In *2014 IEEE 6th International Conference on Cloud Computing Technology and Science (CloudCom)*, pages 887–892, Singapore, Dec. 2014.

[33] G. Wang, A. Butt, P. Pandey, and K. Gupta. A simulation approach to evaluating design decisions in MapReduce setups. In *IEEE International Symposium on Modeling, Analysis Simulation of Computer and Telecommunication Systems*, MASCOTS '09, pages 1–11, London, UK, Sept. 2009.

[34] B. Zhang, D. T. Yehdego, K. L. Johnson, M.-Y. Leung, and M. Taufer. Enhancement of accuracy and efficiency for RNA secondary structure prediction by sequence segmentation and MapReduce. *BMC Structural Biology*, 13(Suppl 1):S3, Nov. 2013.

[35] D. Zhao, D. Zhang, K. Wang, and I. Raicu. Exploring reliability of exascale systems through simulations. In *Proceedings of the High Performance Computing Symposium*, HPC '13, pages 1:1–1:9, San Diego, CA, USA, 2013. Society for Computer Simulation International.

[36] D. Zhao, Z. Zhang, X. Zhou, T. Li, K. Wang, D. Kimpe, P. Carns, R. Ross, and I. Raicu. Fusionfs: Toward supporting data-intensive scientific applications on extreme-scale high-performance computing systems. In *2014 IEEE International Conference on Big Data*, pages 61–70, Washington, DC, Oct 2014.

[37] G. Zheng, G. Gupta, E. Bohm, I. Dooley, and L. V. Kale. Simulating Large Scale Parallel Applications using Statistical Models for Sequential Execution Blocks. In *Proceedings of the 16th International Conference on Parallel and Distributed Systems,*

Transparently Mixing Undo Logs and Software Reversibility for State Recovery in Optimistic PDES

Davide Cingolani, Alessandro Pellegrini, Francesco Quaglia
DIAG – Sapienza, University of Rome
Via Ariosto 25, 00185 Rome, Italy
cingodvd@gmail.com, {pellegrini, quaglia}@dis.uniroma1.it

ABSTRACT

The rollback operation is a fundamental building block to support the correct execution of a speculative Time Warp-based Parallel Discrete Event Simulation. In the literature, several solutions to reduce the execution cost of this operation have been proposed, either based on the creation of a checkpoint of previous simulation state images, or on the execution of negative copies of simulation events which are able to undo the updates on the state. In this paper, we explore the practical design and implementation of a state recoverability technique which allows to restore a previous simulation state either relying on checkpointing or on the reverse execution of the state updates occurred while processing events in forward mode. Differently from other proposals, we address the issue of executing backward updates in a fully-transparent and event granularity-independent way, by relying on static software instrumentation (targeting the x86 architecture and Linux systems) to generate at runtime *reverse update code blocks* (not to be confused with *reverse events*, proper of the reverse computing approach). These are able to undo the effects of a forward execution while minimizing the cost of the undo operation. We also present experimental results related to our implementation, which is released as free software and fully integrated into the open source ROOT-Sim (ROme OpTimistic Simulator) package. The experimental data support the viability and effectiveness of our proposal.

Categories and Subject Descriptors

I.6.8 [**Simulation and Modeling**]: Types of Simulation—
Discrete Event, Parallel; D.3.4 [**Programming Languages**]:
Processors—*Code Generation*

General Terms

Algorithms, Performance

Keywords

PDES; Speculative Processing; Code Instrumentation; Reversibility

1. INTRODUCTION

In Parallel Discrete Event Simulation (PDES) [11], Time Warp [12] has been proven to be an effective synchronization protocol, which has been shown to be relatively independent (in terms of its run-time dynamics) of both the the simulation model's lookahead and the communication latency for exchanging data across threads/processes involved in the simulation platform. All these peculiarities allow it to guarantee high performance even in systems that are not tightly coupled and/or possibly entail up to millions of processors [3]. According to classical PDES, in Time Warp the simulation model is partitioned into distinct simulation objects, which are mapped to Logical Processes (LPs). The latter are in charge of handling the execution of impulsive events, which ultimately produce state updates (hence transitions) in the actual simulation model state.

Time Warp is a speculative protocol, hence it allows simulation events to be processed at any LP optimistically. This means that they are processed independently of their safety (or causal consistency). If an event is a-posteriori detected to be violating causality, its effects on the simulation state are undone, via the *rollback operation*. Correctly and efficiently rolling back the simulation state is therefore a fundamental building block for an effective optimistic simulation platform.

In the literature, this operation has been thoroughly studied. Different approaches have been proposed, which provide benefits in differentiated scenarios. All these solutions can be mainly grouped into two separate families, namely *checkpoint-based* [12] and *reverse computing-based* [6], depending on the algorithmic technique which is used to bring one simulation state to a previous (consistent) snapshot.

The checkpoint-based rollback operation grounds on the possibility, for a simulation engine, to know the location (in main memory) of each simulation object's state. By exploiting this information, the engine can therefore create a copy of the simulation state after the execution of one (or a group of) operations which have produced state updates. In this context, different possibilities have been presented, all aiming at reducing the cost (both in terms of memory and CPU usage) paid to create a state snapshot, which will be (possibly) used for a later state restore. Among the various research lines, we find two main different approaches, which have been often combined together. On the one hand, we find solutions to reduce the frequency according to which a simulation object's state is inspected to create a copy—the so-called *sparse* or *periodic state saving* [15, 4, 16, 26, 9, 28, 24]—with a focus on detecting which is the best-suited checkpointing interval to minimize unfruitful work (e.g., taking checkpoints which are never used for a rollback operation). On the other hand, we find solutions which try to reduce the amount of data copied into a state snapshot, ensuring anyhow that no meaningful piece of information is lost at any time—the so-called *incremental state saving* [35, 19]. A mixture of these approaches has been proposed as well in [21], trying to modify at runtime the execution mode of the state saving operation, depending on the current execution dynamics, in order to capture different execution phases of the simulation models.

At different scales, all these solutions suffer from the high cost associated with making a (logically) complete copy of the simulation state, which is either proportional to the size of the state (in case of full state saving) or to the number of update operations related to the execution of one or more events (in case of incremental state saving).

The reverse computing-based rollback operation, on the other hand, tries to cancel the non-negligible memory footprint produced by the state saving technique. This solution grounds on the availability (either on a manual [6] or automatic [14] basis) of reverse copies of simulation events, such that if the execution of a forward event e on a simulation state S produces a state transition $e(S) \rightarrow S'$, then the execution of the reverse event r associated with e on S' produces the inverse transition $r(S') \rightarrow S$. Overall, while the reverse computing approach is able to strongly reduce the impact of memory usage from which state saving may suffer, the execution cost of the rollback operation is directly proportional to the execution time of simulation events. This cost could become predominant in case of events with a high granularity, and in case the rollback length is non-minimal.

By mixing the different philosophies standing behind the above state recoverability techniques, we present a new approach which is based on the combination of undo-logs with software reversibility. Particularly, in our proposal, the data that are typically recorded by undo-log systems are used to generate so called *update undo code blocks*. The latter can be used to squash the memory side effects (namely updates) generated by a non casually-consistent portion of the computation.

To achieve our goal, we rely on ad-hoc software instrumentation, which allows us to capture the *effects* on memory of an event's forward execution. This information is then used to build at runtime the update undo code blocks, which are basically compact undo logs of actual operations. They are compact because they are specifically encoded directly as a set of subsequent machine instructions which are able to cancel the overall effects of the execution of forward events. This is different from the reverse computing technique, as our approach is independent of the actual event granularity. In fact, the execution cost of an update undo code block is only proportional to the amount of memory areas touched in write mode during the forward execution.

Further, our approach is different from classical undo logs used in, e.g., the context of fault tolerance. In fact, undo log architectures are not based on dynamic generation of reversibility code. Also, contrarily to incremental state saving, our solution is specifically designed to avoid the (high)

cost paid by incremental state saving when executing a rollback operation. In fact, while the latter generally requires to inspect some (arbitrarily complex) metadata to determine where each portion of the incremental log should be placed in memory, our update undo code blocks can be simply executed with no additional overhead associated with metadata management, as they are specifically generated so as to keep all the relevant information already packed together.

Another important aspect in our proposal is that it can be combined with classical checkpointing methods (both incremental and non-incremental). Particularly, by taking infrequent checkpoints, we can generate checkpoint intervals where some passed-through snapshots are not coverable by update undo code blocks, while others are. Hence state restoration can be executed by either reloading a previous checkpoint and executing a classical coasting forward phase, or by applying the update undo code from the current state snapshot (or from a conveniently selected checkpointed snapshot). While the former case occurs for restoration to a snapshot uncovered by the update undo facility, the latter occurs for snapshots covered by the update undo scheme. In other words, a single checkpoint interval can be optimized by the combination of the two techniques, in terms of the tradeoff between overhead for recoverability tasks and actual recovery costs. Other proposals do not have such a fine-grained mixture of different recoverability supports. In fact, most mixed-based solutions either switch between different recoverability modes along different phases of the simulation model execution (i.e., not in a single checkpoint interval) [21], or are exclusively based on incremental vs non-incremental checkpointing, thus not relying on the update undo code block technique.

Finally, borrowing from the results in [7], we present an analytic model that allows to determine how to partition each single checkpoint interval in terms of recoverability support, thus optimizing the decision on the length of the interval, as well as the decision on what are the snapshots which will be reconstructed (in case of a rollback operation) by relying on the coasting forward operation or on update undo code blocks.

We again remark that our proposal is fully application transparent, and has been released as free software and integrated into the open source ROOT-Sim package [18, 20].

The remainder of this paper is structured as follows. In Section 2 we discuss related work. Section 3 presents the design choices below our proposal, and its implementation. Experimental data to assess the viability and effectiveness of our proposal are finally reported in Section 4.

2. RELATED WORK

As already pointed out, due to the fundamental role of the rollback operation in the context of optimistic synchronization for PDES, the literature on this topic is extremely wide. In the state saving-based context, several solutions have been introduced for logging the whole state of a simulation object (at each event execution or after an interval of executed events) [9, 22, 25, 26], or incrementally logging modified state portions [27, 31, 35], or supporting a mix of the two approaches [10, 29]. These solutions either ask the application-model developer to implement callbacks which are explicitly invoked when the simulation environment determines that a state log is necessary, or require the modeler to issue a call to some specific API used to identify the simulation state location in memory, or request to statically identify (e.g. at compile-time) which portions of the address space need to be considered part of the state. The works in [8, 30] address the management of dynamic memory maps to store simulation objects' states, and in [32] the management of dynamic memory is additionally tackled in a completely transparent way, by proposing a memory manager specifically targeted at optimistic PDES environments, which allows to transparently manage a dynamically scattered memory map of simulation objects' states. Our proposal is complementary to all the aforementioned ones, as we integrate traditional state saving with the runtime generation of update undo code blocks.

In the context of reverse computing-based state restore, a recent work [14] presents a software-instrumentation based approach (at the level of LLVM IR) to automatically generate the code associated with negative events. This work is similar in spirit to ours, as one of our final goals is to relieve the user from the burden of implementing the negative version of the events as well. Nevertheless, in the approach in [14], binary instrumentation is used to generate at compile time exact negated versions of code blocks, while we generate at runtime the instructions which undo the effects of the execution of one event in memory. Therefore, our solution's cost (in terms of recovery latency) is not proportional to the granularity of the events, rather to the amount of memory locations which are updated during the execution in forward mode. On the other hand, the final tradeoff by our solution is different from the one in [14] also because our instrumentation scheme operates at run-time, thus inducing some cost for the dynamic generation of update undo code blocks.

The work in [19], similarly to what we do, relies on static binary instrumentation to track memory updates during the forward execution of the events. Nevertheless, the goal in [19] is to use this information to generate periodic incremental checkpoints. Contrarily, we use tracked memory updates to build update undo code blocks. This is similar, as well, to the proposal in [35], but rather than packing the undo log in linked data structures, we pack on the fly assembly instructions which are later executed consecutively, so as to reduce to the highest extent the execution time of the restore operation.

Our approach shares underlying principles with the works in [7, 21]. In [21], an autonomic system to determine at runtime the best suited checkpointing mode (incremental vs full) is presented. Efficiency is ensured by relying on a dual-version executable technique, which allows to switch between the two execution modes changing only a couple of function pointers. We keep the same ability to change the support for state recoverability (using the same software dual-version technique), but we do this within each single checkpoint interval (by covering a subset of the states passed through in the interval by update undo code blocks). Hence we are able to optimize dynamics at smaller granularity levels (single events within a checkpoint interval). With respect to [7], we propose a similar model. However, in that work no support for application transparency of recoverability tasks is presented, while our proposal is fully application transparent.

Our proposal is also related to a number of works in the field of program execution tracing (see, e.g., [1, 2, 23, 36]) for debugging, vulnerability assessment and repeatability. These approaches provide detailed analysis of changes in the state of the program, and of the execution flow. However, this is achieved via performance-intrusive techniques relying on dynamic instrumentation and/or kernel-level services, unsuited for contexts where performance cannot be sacrificed (e.g., parallel simulation). Debugging supports showing basic operating modes comparable to ours (namely, the employment of trap mechanisms based on code insertion and/or replacement to detect memory write accesses) are those addressing data watch points (see, e.g., [34]). However they have performance targets different from ours since optimizations mostly cope with search techniques for verifying whether a memory reference falls inside a region that is currently subject to a watch point. In other words, aspects related to the identification of areas that have been modified and to log/restore operations are not considered.

3. THE STATE RECOVERABILITY ARCHITECTURE

Our architecture to manage state recoverability relies on static software instrumentation to transparently modify the application-level code, in order to let the simulation engine track at runtime what are the *effects* of the forward execution of events on the simulation model's state. This information is used to build a packed version of negative instructions which only undo the effects of the forward execution, allowing for a reverse execution of events (in terms of state updates) which is independent of the actual forward event granularity. This technique is complemented with an analytic model which determines, during the forward phase, whether the next event updates will be guaranteed to be recoverable either through classical coasting forward, or via the execution of update undo code blocks. The model decisions are aimed at minimizing an overhead function that expresses the tradeoff between the cost of recoverability tasks and actual recovery operations. The whole approach will be based on the coexistence of dual executable modes (inspired to [21]). This allows to quickly switch from an instrumented version of the simulation model's code (which allows to track memory updates and to generate update undo code blocks) to the "plain" one (where no actual tracking is performed). In this section, we will describe the various design choices which have driven the implementation of our proposal.

3.1 Instrumentation Technique

To statically instrument the application-level code, we rely on Hijacker [17], an open-source static instrumentation tool specifically targeted at HPC applications. Hijacker has been developed on the first instance to support incremental state saving in optimistic PDES systems [19], but has later been extended to support differentiated tasks. For the proposal in this paper, we have augmented the set of operations which this tool can perform. The basic support provided by Hijacker is to let the user specify (by using simple xml-based rules) what are the operations to perform on the original application code. Hijacker is conceived to be part of the compiling tool-chain, placing itself as a pre-linking stage. This allows our state recoverability architecture to be easily integrated into different simulation engines.

Hijacker works on *relocatable object files*. Specifically, it operates on the Executable and Linkable Format (ELF). The rules interpreted by Hijacker allow to perform instrumentation at different scopes, namely executable-wide or at the

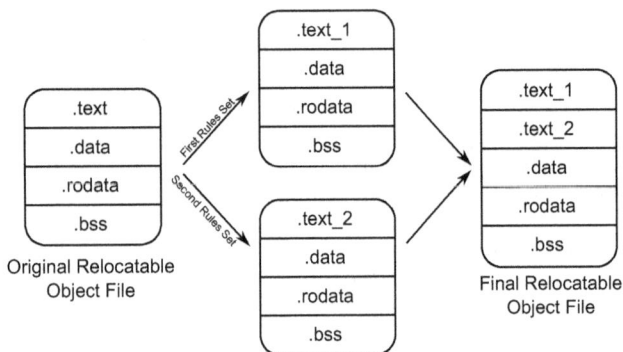

Figure 1: Code multiversioning

level of single functions/instructions. Additionally, the rules allow to instruct Hijacker to create multiple copies of the same executable, but differently instrumented. This technique, known as *multi-coding*, creates different versions of the code which nevertheless share the same data sections within the virtual address space. Hijacker transparently allows to change the name of all the (instrumented) functions when it comes to generate multiple versions of the software, by simply appending a user-defined suffix to them. This allows the simulation engine to exactly identify which copy of the application-level function is instrumented in a specific way. Overall, after the generation of multiple versions of the code, the final memory organization of the executable complies with the scheme shown in Figure 1.

To reach our target, we have specified the rules reported in Figure 2 and implemented the specific modules that apply them to the original executable. This configuration file instructs Hijacker to generate a modified application-level relocatable object which has two different versions (as pointed out, sharing the same data). Specifically, by using the rules in the first `<Executable>` tag (which generates the first version, associated with the `memtrack` suffix), Hijacker scans the whole simulation model's code to find instructions belonging to the `I_MEMWR` family, namely assembly instructions which have a memory address as the destination operand. Among the various ones, the most significant instructions for the x86 architecture (which represents our target) are `mov`, `movs`, and `cmov` instructions. These different instructions are handled internally in a different way by Hijacker, nevertheless before each of them (in the whole original program's image) a call to a specific internal trampoline is placed, along with some instructions which generate an invocation context for it, therefore allowing to identify the characteristics of the original instruction which caused the invocation. This is done via the `<AddCall>` tag, with the `arguments` attribute set to `target`.

The goal of this instrumentation rule is to let Hijacker generate a cache of disassembly information, which can be used at runtime. This step is important to address the efficiency of the runtime execution of our tracking scheme, as it allows us to avoid costly disassembly of instructions at runtime. More specifically, Hijacker extracts from the memory-write instruction the information related to the *size* of the memory write, and the *destination address*. According to the addressing mode of the x86 architecture, each memory address is identified by the expression *base address* + (*index* ∗ *scale*) + *displacement*. While the parameters *scale*

and *displacement* are already encoded in the instruction binary representation, *base address* and *index* refer to the content of registers, which can be evaluated only at runtime. Therefore, Hijacker packs this information retrieved at compile time in a structure named `insn_entry` which will be directly placed on the stack at runtime, along the execution flow of the running thread. This operation is done by injecting a set of ad-hoc `mov` instructions in the original executable, right before the memory-writing instruction which caused the activation of this procedure, as depicted in Figure 3. To create space for this packed data, Hijacker places as well a `sub` instruction before the `mov` instructions, and a related `add` instruction after the original memory-write instruction, which operate on the stack-pointer. This is to retrieve, during the execution of the instrumented executable, the parameters required to reconstruct the target address (and the size) of the memory update. The `insn_entry` structure is composed of the following fields:

```
struct insn_entry {
        char flags;
        char base;
        char idx;
        char scale;
        int  size;
        long long offset;
}
```

where `flags` tells which are the relevant fields of `insn_entry` to recompute the target address, or to identify the class of data-movement instructions, as we will explain later in details; `base` keeps the (3 or 4 bits) base register binary representation; `idx` keeps the (3 or 4 bits) index register binary representation; `scale` is used to store the scale factor of the addressing mode; `size` holds the size (in bytes) of the memory area being affected by the memory-write instruction (when available at disassemble time); `offset` keeps the displacement of the addressing mode[1].

Additionally to this information, Hijacker places (again, using a couple of ad-hoc `mov` instructions) the address of the function specified in the `function` attribute of the `<AddCall>` tag, `reverse_generator` in our case. This function is defined as `reverse_generator(void *address, size_t size)`, and represents our entry point in the state recoverability manager to build the actual negative instruction which will undo the effect of the memory-write instruction on the simulation state. Since this function could not be present in the original executable[2], Hijacker simply creates a *relocation entry* in the final relocatable object file, leaving to the final linker the task of identifying the correct address.

As mentioned, the actual value for `address` in the most general case can be retrieved only at runtime, as it may depend on the content of the base and/or index registers. Therefore, Hijacker, after having placed the `mov` instructions which put on stack the `insn_info` record associated with the information concerning the current memory-write instruction, inserts a `call` instruction to an internally-defined trampoline which is used to compute the final address. This

---

[1] We provide 64-bits space in the `insn_entry` structure due to the fact that the x86_64 assembly language allows one single instruction, namely `movabs`, to directly use a 64-bits addressing mode. In all the other cases, only 32 bits of the `offset` field are actually used.

[2] This is exactly our case, in fact the module is part of the state recoverability manager, not of the simulation model, which is transparently injected in the original model's code via the `<Inject>` tag specified in the xml-based rules.

```
<hijacker:Rules xmlns:hijacker="http://www.dis.uniroma1.it/~hpdcs/">

        <hijacker:Inject file="mixed-state-saving.c" />

        <hijacker:Executable suffix="memtrack"> <!-- First code version -->

                <hijacker:Instruction type="I_MEMWR">
                        <hijacker:AddCall where="before" function="reverse_generator" arguments="target" />
                </hijacker:Instruction>

        </hijacker:Executable>

        <hijacker:Executable suffix="notrack"> <!-- Second code version -->
        </hijacker:Executable>
</hijacker:Rules>
```

Figure 2: Hijacker rules to instrument application-level code

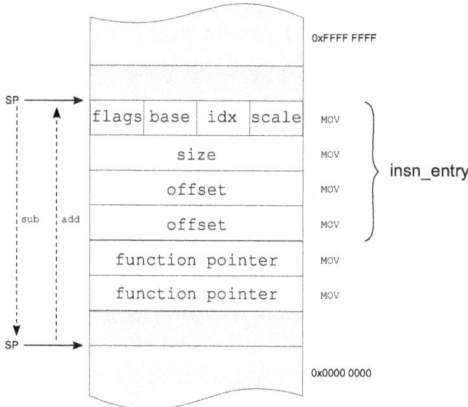

Figure 3: Trampoline call stack frame

trampoline exploits the `flags` field of the `insn_info` structure to determine which, among the four parameters *base address*, *index*, *scale*, and *displacement*, determine the memory write address. After having determined this, the trampoline computes the final address and places it either on the stack or in the `rdi`, `rsi` registers, depending on the calling convention of the system (namely, 32-bits vs 64-bits x86). At this point, it retrieves from stack the 4 or 8 bytes composing the address of the function (`reverse_generator` in our case), places it in a general purpose register and performs an indirect call.

To ensure the correctness of the overall original executable, the trampoline is used as well to save the CPU context of the application before executing the final function, and then restores it before giving control back to the original software. Nevertheless, due to the fact that a `sub`/`add` couple of instructions is placed around the original memory-write instruction, Hijacker must as well save the status register of the CPU, namely the `flags` register, in order to leave the flow of execution untouched, so as to let the software continue its execution as if no additional operation was performed. To this end, we place a couple of `pushfw`/`popfw` instructions before and after all the operations on the stack, just to save and restore the status register.

The other two aforementioned types of memory-write instructions have been dealt with in two different ways. On the one hand, the `cmov` instruction is managed directly by the Hijacker's trampoline. Specifically, in case the instrumentation is triggered by a `cmov` instruction, we use 4 bits in the `flags` field of `insn_info` to record what is the actual check to be emulated in order to determine if the memory

update will be executed or not. Specifically, the trampoline checks whether the bits are different from zero, and in the positive case the corresponding status bits are checked to determine whether the condition is met or not. Nevertheless, by the above discussion, the values of status bits might have been already altered during the execution of the previous injected operations (namely, before the trampoline takes control). To this end, the trampoline's code looks on the application stack for the old value, as stored by the previously-executed `pushfw` instruction. In case the values of these bits, according to the code stored in the `flags` field, tell that the memory-update instruction will be executed, then the control is passed to the `reverse_generator` function, exactly as in the previous scenario. In the negative case, the control is simply returned back to the application. This check is performed right after the trampoline has taken control, in order to avoid the cost of computing the target address in case this information is not useful, thus trying to reduce the cost of this operation.

Concerning the `movs` instruction, we use one bit of the `flags` field to let the trampoline know whether its invocation is related to such an instruction. In this specific case, the `size` flag tells only the size of one single iteration of the `movs` instruction. Therefore, to compute the total size, the trampoline's code checks the value of the `rcx` register, and multiplies it by `size`. The starting address of the write is then computed by first checking the *direction flag* of the `flags` register. In case this flag is cleared, the destination starting address is already present in the `rdi` register. If the flag is set, then the `movs` instruction will make a backwards copy, and therefore the (logical) initial address of the move is computed as `rdi - rcx * size`.

In all cases, the trampoline is able to compute the tuple $\langle address, size \rangle$, which is passed to the function specified in the xml configuration file (`reverse_generator` in our case). In this way, Hijacker is able (by using the internal trampoline module) to hide the complexity of the underlying hardware architecture and pass the relevant information to the module which will perform the generation of the update undo code blocks. We emphasize that the trampoline has been developed directly in x86 assembly, in a very efficient way, so as to reduce as much as possible the overhead to compute the target address. Additionally, using cached disassembly information allows the trampoline to access all the relevant information very quickly, avoiding the need for costly runtime disassembly, which is more proper of dynamic instrumentation approaches. Moreover, this instrumentation technique allows us to keep, in the same executable, two different versions of the original code, one instrumented to track memory accesses, and one which simply executes the original code. Since by using Hijacker we are able to differentiate these versions by the name of all the functions (namely, one version has all function names with the `memtrack` suffix, the other with the `notrack` suffix), we are able to give control to the two versions of the code very easily. This facility will be exploited later, when this architecture will be coupled with the analytic model to decide which support for the rollback operations should be activated on a very fine grain (e.g. per event) basis.

3.2 Runtime Generation of Update Undo Code Blocks

The instrumentation architecture described so far allows, at runtime, to activate the `reverse_generator(void *address, size_t size)` API just before any memory-update operation is performed. At this point, the state recoverability manager is notified of the application code's will to update the simulation model state, and therefore negative instructions (to restore the state in case of a rollback operation) can be built on-the-fly.

Specifically, in case the invocation of `reverse_generator` is related to the execution (in the forward event) of a `mov` or a `cmov` instruction, the negative instruction is simply built by accessing memory at `address` and by reading `size` bytes. This value, since the invocation of `reverse_generator` happens right before the execution of the original memory-write instruction, allows the module to retrieve the "old" value of the simulation model's state. This value is then placed within a data movement instruction as the source (immediate) operand. Of course, the destination of this negative instruction is `address`, as the ultimate goal of this operation is to restore the state by placing back at the same addresses the originally-kept value.

If the activation of `reverse_generation` is due to a `movs` instruction, this can be easily determined by `size`, as it could be higher than the largest representable immediate[3]. In this case, the negative instruction could be only another `movs` instruction. Therefore, `reverse_generator` allocates a memory buffer and creates a copy of the memory pointed by `address`. Then, a set of instructions which place back the same memory content is generated. Of course, this operation is more costly than the generation of a single negative `mov` instruction, but is nonetheless necessary to allow for the correct restoration of the simulation state.

We emphasize that the generation of negative instructions by `reverse_generator` is not a costly operation, except for the `movs` case where a memory buffer must be explicitly copied. In fact, since the set of instructions to be generated is very limited (namely, some variants of `mov` instructions), the opcodes are known beforehand. This allows us to use pre-compiled tables of instructions, where only the relevant parameters should be packed within, namely the old memory value and the destination memory address. With this approach, we are paying an instrumentation overhead which is similar to that of incremental state saving solutions (see, e.g., [19]), but we are completely avoiding any generation of

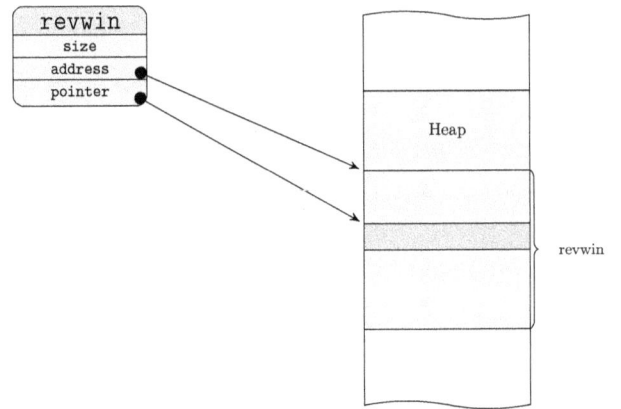

Figure 4: Revwin descriptor

metadata, thus reducing the overhead for the installation of a previous snapshot during the execution of a rollback.

The runtime generation module of update undo code blocks offers an additional API, namely `initialize_event(int LP)` which is used to let the simulation engine inform that a new simulation event (during the forward execution phase) is about to be delivered to some LP[4]. Whenever the `initialize_event` API is called, the reverse code generator module allocates on the heap a private region space to dynamically store generated instructions. These instructions are packed into the *reverse window* structure, which is depicted in Figure 4. In this way, both multi-process and multi-thread simulation engines can rely on the reverse generator module, as each LP (and therefore any possible thread executing the LP's code) has its own (private) reverse window, thus easily supporting re-entrant execution. When the reverse window is created, the reverse generator module places at the end of this space a `ret` instruction. This allows to let the execution of the undo event return control to the caller function after the end of the reverse window has been reached. Additionally, the `pointer` field of the `revwin` structure is set to the address of this `ret` instruction.

Each time the `reverse_generator` module is called, a new negative instruction is generated, which is inserted right before the address of `pointer`, whose value is then updated accordingly. In this way, negative instructions are placed within a reverse window (which is associated with one specific simulation event) in the reverse order with respect to the forward execution, which is a fundamental prerequisite for building correct update undo code blocks. In fact, this allows to undo all the effects of a forward event by simply issuing a `call` to the first instruction in the reverse window (i.e., the one pointed by `pointer`).

In case one event requires the generation of a large number of negative instructions, the reverse window's space could get exhausted. In this case, the reverse generator module doubles the size of the reverse window. This operation could be costly, as it requires shifting the content of the current reverse window (namely, all the negative instructions) to the end of the newly allocated memory area, and updating `pointer` accordingly. To reduce the frequency of this opera-

---

[3]We note that, by using this approach, a `movs` instruction involving few bytes of memory is negated using a standard `mov` instruction, which is nevertheless correct, and possibly more efficient.

[4]In our architecture, each LP is associated with a unique numerical ID in the range $[0, N-1]$. Any simulation engine using a different identification strategy can, nevertheless, rely on some mapping function to integer values.

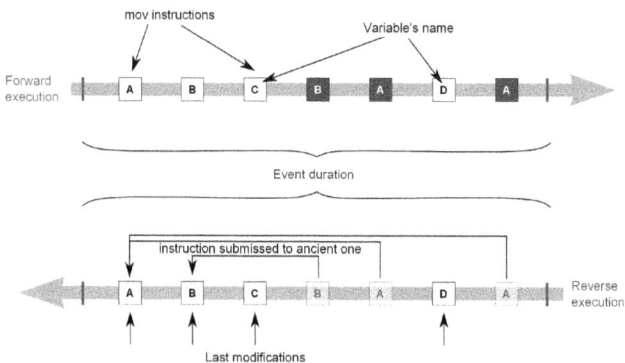

Figure 5: Instruction predominance

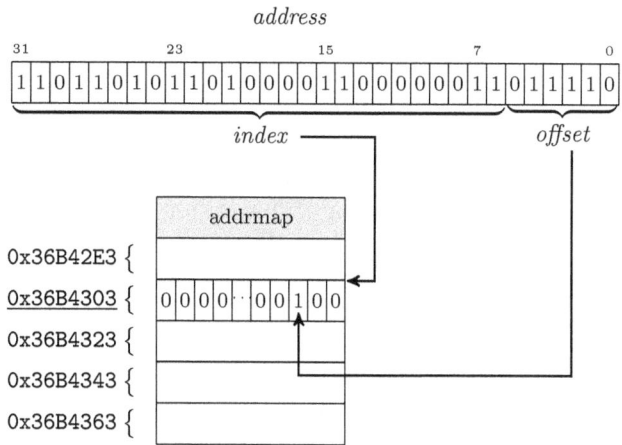

Figure 6: The `index` and `offset` bitmasks of revwin's hashmap

tion, the initial size of a reverse window can be specified at compile time according to conservative (size overestimation) approaches.

To reduce the amount of negative instructions which are stored into a reverse window, we have explicitly addressed the case where, during the execution of an event in forward mode, the same memory location is touched multiple times in write mode. Due to the impulsive nature of discrete events, these multiple updates should be all undone during a rollback operation. Therefore, generating multiple negative instruction for a same memory target into the update undo code blocks would be both a waste of space in the reverse window and an additional non-necessary cost when executing the actual update undo instructions. This scenario is depicted in Figure 5.

We therefore employ an ad-hoc data structure to keep track of referenced addresses, namely a fast hashmap. Whenever `reverse_generator` is activated, this hashmap is queried to determine whether (within the same event's execution) the destination address was already involved in a negative instruction generation. Basically, this hashmap exploits a two-level bitmap to coalesce multiple addresses within a single word, so as to optimize space requirement for address mapping. A toggle bit is used to indicate if an address is already referenced by some memory-write instruction or not. The structure is a linear array of elements treated as a bi-dimensional matrix. Each element of the array is a quad-word of 64 bits used as basic storage unit for a single range of family's addresses[5]. To access the map, the following two values are needed: (i) an *index* providing the address family range, and (ii) the *offset* which identifies the address' bit within the storage unit (i.e. the quadword). These are computed by properly masking the address value. A family range is therefore composed by all the addresses whose value starts with the same prefix. The length of this prefix depends on the number of flags the storage unit can contain, namely a quadword in our case. This can store up to 64 flags. Given the address, the *offset* is computed by extracting the least $n - 1$ significant bits, while *index* is computed as the result of a bitwise-AND with the remainder of most significant bits. Figure 6 shows an example of address' binding for a 32-bit architecture.

To correctly keep a per-event reverse window, whenever the simulation engine invokes the `initialize_event` API,

[5]This allows us to handle both 64-bits x86 architectures and 32-bits ones, at the cost of wasting some space if running on older CPUs.

the hashmap's content is flushed, so as to allow the new reverse window to store all the negative instructions, even though previously-executed events touched the same memory addresses.

3.3 Model-based Optimization of the Recoverability Support

As for models aimed at optimizing the parameters driving the execution of recoverability (and actual recovery) tasks in optimistic PDES, the one presented in [7] can be used as a basis for optimizing the configuration of the specific recoverability support we are presenting. Particularly, in this work the authors consider a scenario where full and incremental logs (in the form of before images) are mixed in a same checkpoint interval. A full log is taken each χ event executions, and then the LP executes a number μ of events without saving before-images of updated memory locations, then for the remaining $\nu = \chi - 1 - \mu$ events in the same checkpoint interval, before-images of the state variables are logged. In this way a state can be recovered by reloading an older checkpoint and the coasting forward, or by reloading a later checkpoint and applying the incremental changes in backward mode. A final equation is achieved that describes the trade-off between recoverability tasks and actual recovery, namely:

$$\frac{(\delta_s + \nu\delta_{bi})}{\chi} + F_r \left[\frac{\chi - \nu}{\chi} \left(\delta_r + \frac{\chi - \nu - 1}{2} \delta_e \right) + \frac{\nu}{\chi} \left(\delta_r + \frac{\nu}{2} \delta_b \right) \right]$$

where:

δ_s is the average time to take a full log of the LP state;

δ_{bi} is the average time for saving the before-images of the state variables during the execution of an event;

δ_r is the average time to reload a full checkpoint from the log;

δ_e is the base execution time of the event (not including the cost for saving before images in case of memory updates);

δ_b is the latency for one backward recovery operation that reloads the before images for a specific event execution to be undone;

217

F_r is the frequency of rollback of the LP (classically evaluated as the number of rollbacks over the total number of event executions).

The minimization of this equation vs the tunable parameters χ and ν (as depicted in [7]) leads to the optimal combination of coasting forward based recovery, and backward recovery. This same equation can be applied to our architecture when considering that δ_{bi} will correspond to the time for running the injected code that traps memory accesses and builds (packs) the update undo code blocks, and δ_b is the average time for running the undo update code block associated with a specific event.

Let us again stress that reusing the above model for optimization purposes of the configuration of the recoverability support based on update undo code blocks does not reduce the level of innovation by our proposal, given that the original solution in [7] had no support for application level transparency, rather all the checkpoint operations (incremental and non-incremental) were demanded to the application level code. Full application transparency is instead guaranteed in our approach.

3.4 Final Integration

Once the execution of a simulation event is completed, the reverse code generation module ensures that all the relevant negative instructions have already been assembled in the current reverse window. We have therefore augmented the set of API functions offered by the reverse code generation module including `void *get_last_window()`, which allows to retrieve a pointer to the just packed `revwin` data structure. This pointer can be therefore stored by the simulation engine directly in the event queue (specifically, in the just processed event node), so as to allow for a fast retrieve in case the event should be undone due to a rollback operation.

Once the simulation engine detects that an out-of-order event e associated with timestamp T_e has been received, the rollback operation is actually executed according to the following algorithmic steps:

1. The event e is incorporated into the event queue of the destination LP. The next event e_{next} in the queue if found;

2. If this event has a pointer to a reverse window, then by the actual operating mode of the recoverability support that combines coasting forward and update undo code blocks (namely, the one whose analytic model for its optimization has been discussed in Section 3.3) we can execute a reverse reconstruction. If the pointer is not set, then a traditional state restore (possibly involving a coasting forward operation) is executed;

3. If a reverse window is present, then the log queue is scanned in order to find a checkpoint C_{next} associated with timestamp $T_{C_{next}}$ such that $T_{e_{next}} \leq T_{C_{next}}$, if any;

4. If this checkpoint does not exist, then it means that we are rolling back to a recent simulation time, so we can simply start executing update undo code blocks. If C_{next} is found, then the simulation engine restores this state, and sets e_{rev} to the last event executed before C_{next} was taken;

5. All update undo code blocks between e_{rev} and e are executed in reverse order.

The execution of an update undo code block is left to the state recoverability architecture, via the `undo_event(void *)` API function. This function takes a pointer to a reverse window, determines the value of the associated `pointer` fields and issues an indirect call to that address. The presence of a `ret` instruction at the end of the reverse window ensures that, after having undone the event, control is given back to the rollback algorithm of the simulation engine. A similar procedure as the one depicted above is executed in case of a rollback caused by an anti-message.

To recover memory, the logic associated with the traditional fossil collection operation should be augmented. Specifically, during the fossil collection, when the input queue of some LP is pruned from older events, the simulation engine is offered the `release_window(void *)` API function, which allows to release all the memory used for the update undo instructions of one event. In this way, we are able to recollect memory, which can be used again during forward execution to maintain reverse instructions related to the execution of additional simulation events.

4. EXPERIMENTAL RESULTS

4.1 Test-bed Environment

We have integrated the presented state recoverability manager within the ROOT-Sim simulation platform [18, 20]. This is a C-based open source simulation package targeted at POSIX systems, which implements a general-purpose simulation environment based on the Time Warp synchronization paradigm. It offers a very simple programming model relying on the classical notion of simulation-event handlers (both for processing events and for accessing a committed and globally-consistent state image upon GVT calculations), to be implemented according to the ANSI-C standard, and transparently supports all the services required to parallelize the execution. More in detail, we have integrated our innovative state recoverability support in the symmetric multithreaded version of ROOT-Sim[6] that has been presented in [33].

This platform has been run on top of a 32-core HP ProLiant server equipped with 64GB of RAM and running Debian 6 on top of the 2.6.32-5-amd64 Linux kernel.

Our integration has been carried out following two steps. On the one hand, we have altered the final executable generation chain proper of ROOT-Sim, adding one step which involves the actual invocation of Hijacker to instrument the application-level code. On the other hand, we have added some logic to the simulation kernel in order to execute the rollback operation adopting our update-undo-based recoverability support.

As for the first step, ROOT-Sim relies on the `rootsim-cc` custom compiler to generate the final simulation model's executable, carrying out several steps in order to correctly link to the set of static libraries proper of the simulation engine. In particular, during the compilation of a simulation model, `rootsim-cc` performs the following steps:

1. All the sources from the model are compiled using the standard `gcc` compiler, and one single relocatable object file is produced.

---

[6]The source of the multi-threaded version of ROOT-Sim, along with the presented state recoverability support, can be found at `http://github.com/HPDCS/ROOT-Sim`.

2. This relocatable object file is then incrementally linked via `ld` to the DyMeLoR static library. In this process, all the calls to the `malloc` standard library are redirected to the proper DyMeLoR allocator (see [21] for a thorough description of DyMeLoR and this compilation step).

3. Then, the produced incrementally-linked relocatable object is again incrementally linked to an additional static library (called `libwrapper`) which allows for the redirection of all stateless library functions proper of the `C` standard library to a set of wrappers which allow for a correct integration with the DyMeLoR library.

4. Finally, this new relocatable object is linked to the final `librootsim` library.

We have altered this compilation process by inserting an additional step right after Step 1 in the previous list. In particular, during this additional step we explicitly call Hijacker, passing the configuration-rule set shown in Figure 2. This allows us, as discussed, to generate a model relocatable object file which is already integrated with the innovative state recoverability support.

As a note, we emphasize that calling Hijacker before linking the model with DyMeLoR does not pose any issue regarding memory management, as the reverse generation module relies on `mmap` to allocate memory to keep reverse instructions, which is not redirected by DyMeLoR itself, and therefore allows to keep these buffers away from the LPs' simulation state.

4.2 Test-Bed Application Model

We have run experiments to assess the overall performance and behavior of the presented state recoverability architecture by relying on the Personal Communication System (PCS) benchmark, which models a mobile network adhering to GSM technology. Each LP models the state's evolution of an individual hexagonal cell, and the whole set of cells provides wireless coverage on a square region of variable size. Each cell handles a parameterizable number N of wireless channels, which are modeled in a high fidelity fashion via explicit simulation of power regulation and interference/fading phenomena, according to the results in [13].

The event types which can occur at any LP are: *Start Call*, which simulates a new call installation on a target cell; *End Call* which simulates a call termination; *Handoff Leave* which simulates the leave of an on-going call from the current residence cell; *Handoff Receive* which simulates the installation of a call handed off from an adjacent cell; *Recompute Fading*, which simulates the effects of weather variations onto the fading (and consequently interference) phenomena for ongoing calls.

Upon the start of a call, a call-setup record is instantiated via dynamically-allocated data structures, which is linked to a list of already active records within that same cell. Each record is released when the corresponding call ends or is handed off towards an adjacent cell. In the latter case, a similar call-setup procedure is executed at the destination cell. Upon call setup, power regulation is performed, which involves scanning the aforementioned list of records for computing the minimum transmission power allowing the current call setup to achieve the threshold-level Signal-to-Interference Ratio (SIR) value. Data structures keeping track of fading coefficients are also updated while scanning the list, and on a periodic basis, according to a

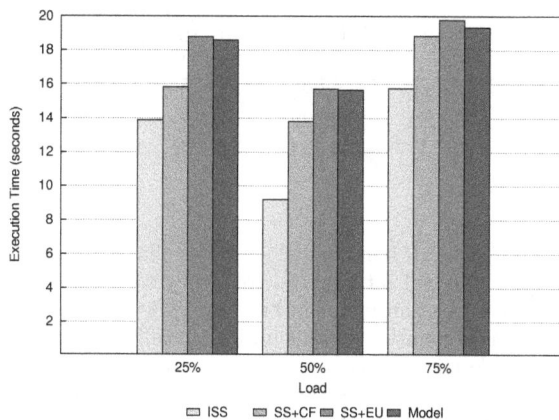

Figure 7: PCS execution time with 64 LPs

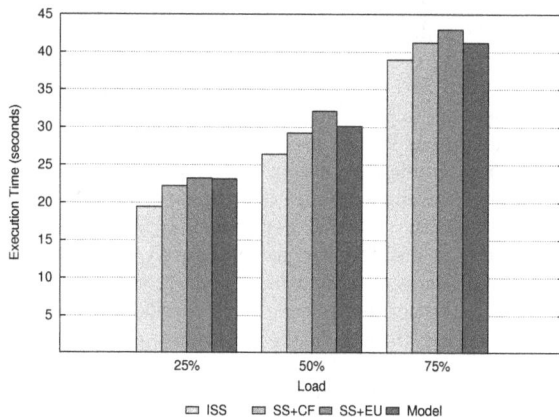

Figure 8: PCS execution time with 256 LPs

meteorological model defining climatic conditions (and related variations).

This application is highly parameterizable. Beyond the already mentioned number N of wireless channels per cell, the set of configurable parameters entails: (i) τ_A, which expresses the inter-arrival time of subsequent calls to any target cell; (ii) $\tau_{duration}$, which expresses the expected call duration; (iii) τ_{change}, which expresses the residual residence time of a mobile device into the current cell. These parameters affect the *utilization factor* of available channels, expressed as $\tau_{duration}/(\tau_A * N)$. This impacts the granularity of the events since the more channels are busy, the more power-management records are allocated and consequently scanned/updated during the processing of different events. On the other hand, higher values of the channel utilization factor lead to higher memory requirements for the state image of individual LPs. Both the above dependencies (namely, CPU demand and memory) are anyhow bounded depending on the total number N of per-cell managed channels.

4.3 Experimental Data

To study the effects of our state recoverability architecture when considering differentiated execution and memory access patterns for the application layer, we have run experiments varying the actual size of the model, setting the number of simulated cells (and thus, of LPs) in the interval

Table 1: Sequential execution time (seconds)

Load	64 LP	256 LP	576 LP	1024 LP
25%	68.249	188.821	412.830	847.429
50%	80.256	310.822	716.359	1266.089
75%	117.117	433.494	1058.123	1772.595

[64, 1024]. Each cell handles 1000 wireless channels, and we have varied the call inter-arrival frequency so as to obtain an average utilization factor in between 25% and 75%. We have run the simulation models until each cell has managed 10000 completed calls, assessing the overall execution time (and therefore the performance) of different configurations of the simulation engine. Specifically, we compare the traditional rollback technique based on state saving and coasting forward (referred to as SS+CF), the rollback technique relying on incremental state saving as presented in [21] (referred to as ISS), the rollback technique based on the execution of our update undo code blocks (referred to as SS+EU) and the interleave of SS+CF and SS+EU based on the analytic model presented in [7]. For completeness, we also report the execution times for the case of a serial execution of the same identical configurations on top of a calendar queue-based sequential scheduler [5], to confirm that this study refers to competitive parallel performance. All the results are averaged over 5 different runs, configured with the same initial pseudo-random seeds used by the random number generators. All experiments have been carried out using 32 concurrent worker threads in the simulation engine, and in all configurations the checkpointing interval χ has been set to 10, so as to allow for an even comparison between the differentiated approaches (i.e., there is no actual benefit by the checkpointing interval for any of the presented configurations). In fact, since the various techniques that we are comparing in this study can rely on different approaches to fine tune χ (let them be iterative, analytic, hill-climbing-based, ...), we have decided to set this parameter to a fixed value, so as not to create any bias favoring any approach. Given this selection, the model based approach presented in [7], which we have exploited in Section 3.3, has been used to derive the optimal value ν, starting from this fixed value of χ.

In Figures 7–10, we present the overall execution time of our simulations in the aforementioned configurations. We can see that the parallel runs offer a speedup with respect to the sequential execution (as reported in Table 1) ranging from 5 (in case of 64 LPs) to 14 (in case of 1024 LPs). Therefore, this experimentation allows us to assess the behavior of our proposed architecture in scenarios with a high degree of parallelism and a somewhat limited efficiency of the parallel run, and scenarios where the efficiency is much higher.

By the results, we can see that when the number of LPs is limited (Figures 7 and 8), independently of the load of the system the best performance is provided by ISS. This is related to the fact that, although the operations required by ISS to mark a portion of the simulation state as modified require scanning complex metadata, all the tables are already allocated in memory. On the contrary, in the case of SS+EU each event requires allocating a new reverse window. When the load is limited (namely, 25%), by the configuration of our benchmark application, the amount of write operations

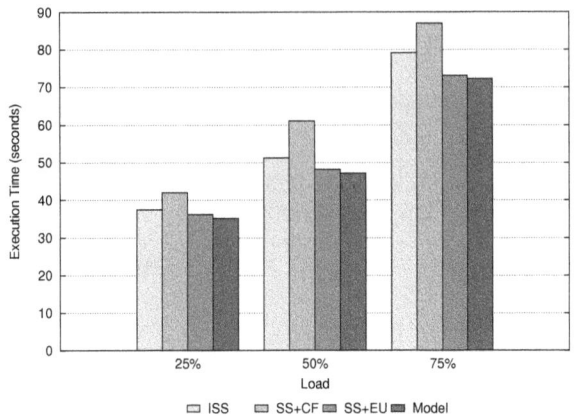

Figure 9: PCS execution time with 576 LPs

per each event is reduced. Therefore, the cost of allocating the reverse window and the cost of generating negative instructions at runtime are not amortized by the events' duration. Furthermore, concerning the rollback operation, the amount of data touched in write mode by the model with a low load is reduced. Thus, this configuration can be regarded as mostly an assessment of the overhead produced by our state recoverability architecture. Overall, the slowdown of SS+EU with respect to ISS is on the order of 30%, while with respect to SS+CF is on the order of 15%. Conversely, when the load of the system is higher, namely 75%, the amount of data touched in write mode is higher. Therefore, the ratio between the number of created reverse windows and the amount of generated negative instructions is lower. This reduces the relative overhead by our state recoverability architecture, due to a better exploitation of data locality in the undo log (namely, the update undo code block) by the rollback operation. In this configuration, the maximum slowdown by SS+EU with respect to ISS is on the order of 15%. In all the configurations, the model-based scheme allows to reduce the overhead by SS+EU, with a performance increase on the order of 5%.

When the number of LPs involved in the simulation is larger (namely, as reported in Figures 9 and 10), the situation changes. When the workload is reduced, SS+EU provides a performance increase on the order of 5% with respect to ISS, and on the order of 25% with respect to SS+CF. This is mainly related to the fact that this scenario offers a lower degree of parallelism, and thus the number of rollback operations is reduced. Therefore, this configuration allows us to assess that the overhead to generate a log by ISS and SS+CF is higher than the overhead by SS+EU to generate the update undo code blocks. When the workload increases, namely it reaches 75%, this phenomenon is exacerbated. In fact, similarly to the configurations with 64 and 256 LPs, the number of negative instructions per undo event is higher, which compensates for the cost of allocating memory and setting up the associated data structures. In this context, the performance gain of SS+EU with respect to ISS is on the order of 10%, while it is on the order of 20% with respect to SS+CF. Analogously to the configurations with 64 and 256 LPs, the model-based approach allows for an even higher performance increase, up to 32%.

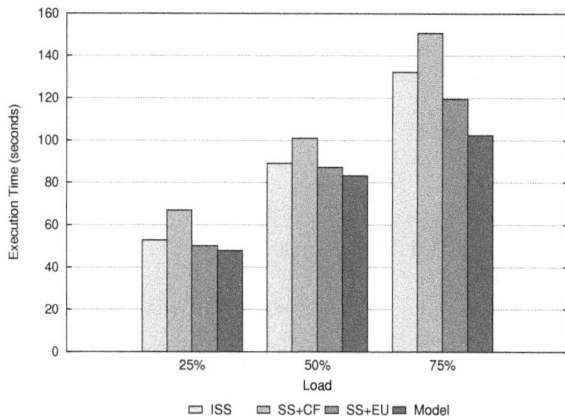

Figure 10: PCS execution time with 1024 LPs

Overall, the data show our state recoverability solution to be the most effective one in larger configurations of the test-bed application, exhibiting heavier workloads, which are, after all, the key scenarios where (optimistic) parallel simulation is considered to be of wide usage.

5. CONCLUSIONS

In this paper we have presented the design and implementation of a practical state recoverability manager for optimistic PDES that mixes undo logs and software reversibility techniques. Our proposal is completely transparent to the application-level developer, by relying on static binary instrumentation to detect what are the assembly instructions which perform memory updates during the execution of an event in the speculative forward phase. By exploiting this information, we have proposed an approach to generate at runtime update-undo code blocks, which are able, when executed, to revert the effects of the execution of an event on the LP's state. We have shown this solution, as well, to lie as a practical support for the transparent implementation of decision models, which can be used to determine at runtime what is the most effective (forward) execution mode, in terms of its recoverability support.

Our experimental assessment highlights that relying on update undo code blocks to put in place rollback operations can provide benefits on execution timeliness, when compared to other traditional supports.

6. REFERENCES

[1] GDB: The GNU Project Debugger. *http://www.gnu.org/software/gdb/* (last accessed: May 11th, 2015).

[2] V. Bala, E. Duesterwald, and S. Banerjia. Dynamo: A transparent dynamic optimization system. *ACM SIGPLAN Notices*, 35(5):1–12, 2000.

[3] P. D. Barnes, Jr., C. D. Carothers, D. R. Jefferson, and J. M. LaPre. Warp speed: executing Time Warp on 1,966,080 cores. In *Proceedings of the 2013 ACM SIGSIM Conference on Principles of Advanced Discrete Simulation* (SIGSIM-PADS), pages 327–336. ACM Press. Montréal, Canada – May 19–22, 2013.

[4] S. Bellenot. State skipping performance with the Time Warp operating system. In *Proceedings of the 6th*

Workshop on Parallel and Distributed Simulation* (PADS), pages 53–64. Society for Computer Simulation International. Newport Beach, California – January 20–22, 1992.

[5] R. Brown. Calendar queues: a fast O(1) priority queue implementation for the simulation event set problem. *Communications of the ACM*, 31(10):1220–1227, 1988.

[6] C. D. Carothers, K. S. Perumalla, and R. M. Fujimoto. Efficient optimistic parallel simulations using reverse computation. *ACM Transactions on Modeling and Computer Simulation*, 9(3):224–253, 1999.

[7] V. Cortellessa and F. Quaglia. A checkpointing–recovery scheme for Time Warp parallel simulation. *Parallel Computing*, 27(9):1226–1252, 2000.

[8] S. R. Das, R. M. Fujimoto, K. Panesar, D. Allison, and M. Hybinette. GTW: a Time Warp system for shared memory multiprocessors. In *Proceedings of the Winter Simulation Conference* (WSC), pages 1332–1339. Society for Computer Simulation International. Orlando, FL, USA – December 11–14, 1994.

[9] J. Fleischmann and P. A. Wilsey. Comparative analysis of periodic state saving techniques in Time Warp simulators. In *Proceedings of the 9th Workshop on Parallel and Distributed Simulation* (PADS), pages 50–58. IEEE Computer Society. Lake Placid, NY, USA – June 13–16, 1995.

[10] S. Franks, F. Gomes, B. Unger, and J. Cleary. State saving for interactive optimistic simulation. In *Proceedings of the 11th Workshop on Parallel and Distributed Simulation* (PADS), pages 72–79. IEEE Computer Society. Lockenhaus, Austria – June 10–13, 1997.

[11] R. M. Fujimoto. Parallel discrete event simulation. *Communications of the ACM*, 33(10):30–53, 1990.

[12] D. R. Jefferson. Virtual Time. *ACM Transactions on Programming Languages and System*, 7(3):404–425, 1985.

[13] S. Kandukuri and S. Boyd. Optimal power control in interference-limited fading wireless channels with outage-probability specifications. *IEEE Transactions on Wireless Communications*, 1(1):46–55, 2002.

[14] J. M. LaPre, E. J. Gonsiorowski, and C. D. Carothers. Lorain: A step closer to the PDES 'holy grail'. In *Proceedings of the 2nd ACM SIGSIM Conference on Principles of Advanced Discrete Simulation* (SIGSIM-PADS), pages 3–14. ACM Press. Denver, CO, USA – May 18–21, 2014.

[15] Y.-B. Lin and E. D. Lazowska. Reducing the state saving overhead for Time Warp parallel simulation. *Tech. Rep. 90-02-03, Department of Computer Science and Engineering, University of Washington, Seattle, Feb. 1990*.

[16] A. C. Palaniswamy and P. A. Wilsey. An analytical comparison of periodic checkpointing and incremental state saving. In *Proceedings of the 7th Workshop on Parallel and Distributed Simulation* (PADS), pages 127–134. ACM Press. San Diego, CA, USA – May 16–19, 1993.

[17] A. Pellegrini. Hijacker: Efficient static software instrumentation with applications in high performance computing. In *Proceedings of the 2013 International*

Conference on High Performance Computing & Simulation (HPCS), pages 650–655. IEEE Computer Society. Helsinki, Finland – July 1–5, 2013.

[18] A. Pellegrini and F. Quaglia. The ROme OpTimistic Simulator: A tutorial. In *Proceedings of the 1st Workshop on Parallel and Distributed Agent-Based Simulations* (PADABS). LNCS, Springer-Verlag Berlin Heidelberg. Aachen, Germany – August 26–30, 2013.

[19] A. Pellegrini, R. Vitali, and F. Quaglia. Di-DyMeLoR: Logging only dirty chunks for efficient management of dynamic memory based optimistic simulation objects. In *Proceedings of the 23rd Workshop on Principles of Advanced and Distributed Simulation* (PADS), pages 45–53. IEEE Computer Society. Lake Placid, NY, USA – June 22–25, 2009.

[20] A. Pellegrini, R. Vitali, and F. Quaglia. The ROme OpTimistic Simulator: Core internals and programming model. In *Proceedings of the 4th International ICST Conference on Simulation Tools and Techniques* (SIMUTools), pages 96–98. ICST. Barcelona, Spain – March 22–24, 2011.

[21] A. Pellegrini, R. Vitali, and F. Quaglia. Autonomic state management for optimistic simulation platforms. *IEEE Transactions on Parallel and Distributed Systems (preprint available)*, May 2014. doi: 10.1109/TPDS.2014.2323967.

[22] B. R. Preiss, W. M. Loucks, and D. MacIntyre. Effects of the checkpoint interval on time and space in Time Warp. *ACM Transactions on Modeling and Computer Simulation*, 4(3):223–253, 1994.

[23] F. Qin, C. Wang, Z. Li, H.-s. Kim, Y. Zhou, and Y. Wu. LIFT: A low-overhead practical information flow tracking system for detecting security attacks. In *Proceedings of the 39th Annual IEEE/ACM International Symposium on Microarchitecture* (MICRO), pages 135–148. IEEE Computer Society. Orlando, FL, USA – December 9–13, 2006.

[24] F. Quaglia. A cost model for selecting checkpoint positions in Time Warp parallel simulation. *IEEE Transactions on Parallel and Distributed Systems*, 12(4):346–362, 2001.

[25] F. Quaglia and A. Santoro. Non-blocking checkpointing for optimistic parallel simulation: Description and an implementation. *IEEE Transactions on Parallel and Distributed Systems*, 14(6):593–610, 2003.

[26] R. Rönngren and R. Ayani. Adaptive checkpointing in Time Warp. In *Proceedings of the 8th Workshop on Parallel and Distributed Simulation* (PADS), pages 110–117. Society for Computer Simulation. Edinburgh, Scotland – July 6–8, 1994.

[27] R. Rönngren, M. Liljenstam, R. Ayani, and J. Montagnat. Transparent incremental state saving in Time Warp parallel discrete event simulation. In

Proceedings of the 10th Workshop on Parallel and Distributed Simulation (PADS), pages 70–77. IEEE Computer Society. Philadelphia, PA, USA – May 22–24, 1996.

[28] S. Skold and R. Rönngren. Event sensitive state saving in Time Warp parallel discrete event simulation. In *Proceedings of the Winter Simulation Conference* (WSC), pages 653–660. Society for Computer Simulation. Coronado, CA, USA – December 8–11, 1996.

[29] H. Soliman and A. Elmaghraby. An analytical model for hybrid checkpointing in Time Warp distributed simulation. *IEEE Transactions on Parallel and Distributed Systems*, 9(10):947–951, 1998.

[30] J. S. Steinman. SPEEDES—a multiple-synchronization environment for parallel discrete-event simulation. *International Journal in Computer Simulation*, 2:251–286, 1992.

[31] J. S. Steinman. Incremental state saving in SPEEDES using C plus plus. In *Proceedings of the Winter Simulation Conference* (WSC), pages 687–696. Society for Computer Simulation. Los Angeles, CA, USA – December 12–15, 1993.

[32] R. Toccaceli and F. Quaglia. DyMeLoR: Dynamic Memory Logger and Restorer library for optimistic simulation objects with generic memory layout. In *Proceedings of the 22nd Workshop on Principles of Advanced and Distributed Simulation* (PADS), pages 163–172. IEEE Computer Society. Rome, Italy – June 3–6, 2008.

[33] R. Vitali, A. Pellegrini, and F. Quaglia. Towards symmetric multi-threaded optimistic simulation kernels. In *Proceedings of the 26th Workshop on Principles of Advanced and Distributed Simulation* (PADS), pages 211–220. IEEE Computer Society. Zhangjiajie, China – July 15–19, 2012.

[34] R. Wahbe, S. Lucco, and S. L. Graham. Practical data breakpoints: Design and implementation. In *Proceedings of the ACM SIGPLAN Conference on Programming Language Design and Implementation* (PLDI), pages 1–12. ACM Press. Albuquerque, NM, USA – June 21–25, 1993 .

[35] D. West and K. Panesar. Automatic incremental state saving. In *Proceedings of the 10th Workshop on Parallel and Distributed Simulation* (PADS), pages 78–85. IEEE Computer Society. Philadelphia, PA, USA – May 22–24, 1996.

[36] Q. Zhao, R. Rabbah, S. Amarasinghe, L. Rudolph, and W.-F. Wong. How to do a million watchpoints: Efficient debugging using dynamic instrumentation. In L. Hendren, editor, *Compiler Construction*, LNCS, Springer-Verlag Berlin Heidelberg. Budapest, Hungary – March 29 - April 6, 2008.

Model-Based Concurrency Analysis of Network Simulations

Philipp Andelfinger and Hannes Hartenstein
Steinbuch Centre for Computing and Institute of Telematics
Karlsruhe Institute of Technology
76131 Karlsruhe, Germany
{philipp.andelfinger, hannes.hartenstein}@kit.edu

ABSTRACT

To achieve highest performance, parallel simulation of networks on modern hardware architectures depends on large numbers of independent computational tasks. However, the properties determining a network model's concurrency are still not well understood. In this paper, we propose an analytical model that enables concurrency estimations based on model knowledge and on statistics gathered from sequential simulation runs. In contrast to an automated concurrency analysis of event traces, the analytical approach enables insights into the relationship between the topology and communication patterns of the simulated network, and the resulting concurrency. We consider three fundamentally different network models as implemented in the network simulators PeerSim and ns-3: a large-scale application-layer peer-to-peer network, IP-based routing in a fixed topology, and a wireless ad-hoc network. For each model, we conduct an in-depth analysis, exposing the relationships between model characteristics and concurrency. Our analysis is validated by comparing estimated concurrency values to reference results of a trace-based analysis. The identification of key factors for concurrency forms a step towards a classification of network models according to their potential for parallelization.

Categories and Subject Descriptors

C.4 [**Computer Systems Organization**]: Performance of Systems—*Modeling Techniques*; I.6.1 [**Computing Methodology**]: Simulation Theory—*Model Classification*; I.6.8 [**Computing Methodology**]: Types of Simulation—*Parallel, Distributed, Discrete Event*

General Terms

Performance

Keywords

concurrency, parallelism, simulation, parallel, distributed, discrete-event, network simulation, network models

1. INTRODUCTION

The benefit of parallelization of a discrete-event network simulation model depends on properties of the considered network. Due to the complex interactions between the network topology, the communication patterns and the simulator realization, there is still a lack of guidelines to decide upon the suitability of different classes of network models for parallel simulation.

In the past years, there has been a renewed interest in parallel simulation due to the diminishing increases in single-core performance of processors. In addition to traditional approaches in CPU-based multi-core or supercomputing environments, the increasing prevalence of parallel hardware architectures such as graphics processing units and CPU-based many-core accelerators has led researchers to consider simulator designs for parallel execution on hundreds or thousands of tightly coupled cores [1, 5, 15, 18]. The novel simulator designs enable an efficient execution of network models previously considered unsuitable for parallel simulation due to their fine-grained computations and the need for frequent synchronization between cores. However, to occupy the enormous numbers of available cores, large numbers of independent computational tasks are required. Hence, the *concurrency* of simulation models, i.e., the maximum number of simulation events that can be executed in parallel while still maintaining simulation correctness, comes into focus as a key property for efficient parallel simulation. We distinguish concurrency from *parallelism*, i.e., the number of events executed in parallel in a real-world simulation run, as well as from the resulting real-world simulation *performance*, both of which are subject to the simulator realization.

In this paper, we conduct an analysis of network simulation models to expose the relationships between the models' network topologies and communication patterns, and their concurrency. We analyze three network models representing distinct classes of networks and show how the parameters required for analytical concurrency estimation can be calculated. We expect the presented results to facilitate the analysis of further network models with similar topologies and communication patterns, so that our analysis forms a step towards a classification of network models according to their concurrency, i.e., according to their aptness for parallelization. We validate the concurrency estimations by comparison with reference values gathered from event traces of sequential simulation runs. In addition to guiding parallelization decisions, the analysis enables a closer understanding of differences in concurrency between models of different classes of networks.

Our main contributions are as follows:

1. Estimation Model: We present an analytical model to estimate the concurrency of network models based on model knowledge and on statistics gathered from sequential simulation runs. The analytical approach enables an understanding of the causes of a network model's degree of concurrency. Our validation shows that reasonably accurate estimations can be achieved even when abstracting from the network model's topology to a large degree.

2. Network Model Analysis: We apply the estimation model to three fundamentally different network models as implemented in popular simulators: a large-scale peer-to-peer network, IP-based routing in a fixed topology, and a wireless ad-hoc network. The analysis uncovers the relationship between network model properties and concurrency.

The remainder of the paper is structured as follows. In Section 2, we give a brief overview of our approach to the construction of our analytical concurrency model. In Section 3, we discuss related approaches to concurrency evaluation. In Section 4, we present our methodology and our analytical model for concurrency estimation. In Section 5, we analyze three network models' event patterns, conduct a sensitivity analysis and estimate the models' concurrency. In Section 6, we evaluate the accuracy of our concurrency estimation. In Section 7, we discuss challenges of the analytical approach. Section 8 gives a summary of our results and concludes the paper.

2. OUR APPROACH

Our goal is to provide an analytical model to *estimate* a network simulation model's concurrency in a white-box fashion, i.e., while enabling insights into the causes of the network model's concurrency. A network model's *exact* concurrency can be determined using *critical path analysis*, a well-known black-box approach that will be introduced in Section 3. Critical path analysis provides reference values that our analytical model will be validated against. However, the properties of critical path analysis render it a difficult target for mathematical analysis.

Instead, we construct our analytical model by analyzing *YAWNS* (cf. Section 3), a second black-box concurrency evaluation approach that lends itself to mathematical modeling and whose results are close to critical path analysis. Our analytical model successfully approximates the results of YAWNS, and hence, the reference results gathered using critical path analysis.

Our analysis applies to simulations under *conservative* synchronization, where the synchronization algorithm ensures correctness prior to each event execution. *Optimistic* synchronization may potentially enable larger concurrency, but is out of the scope of our work.

3. RELATED WORK

In this section, we give a brief summary of two classes of methods for concurrency evaluation: trace-based approaches determine the concurrency in a network model by a programmatic analysis of event traces generated during sequential simulation runs. These approaches determine the concurrency in the model accurately under their stated assumptions, but are performed in a black-box fashion that limits insights into the sources of the identified concurrency. Analytical approaches require more manual effort and usually

determine a rough estimation of concurrency, yet may allow for an understanding of concurrency potentials and limitations, as is the intention of the analytical model and results presented in this paper.

3.1 Trace-Based Concurrency Evaluation

In discrete-event network models, communication activities are modeled as timestamped *events* representing instantaneous state changes of the simulated nodes. The communication patterns in a given network model define a precedence relation governing the event execution order. For instance, subsequent message arrivals at a single node must be simulated in timestamp order to maintain the correctness of the node state. An event can safely be executed as soon as no remaining precedence relationships demand the prior execution of other events. An additional constraint is given by the *lookahead*, which defines an upper bound for the delta between the current simulation time and the timestamp of events that can be executed safely. The magnitude of valid lookahead values depends on network model properties, e.g., on the link latencies between simulated nodes. In synchronous simulation approaches, processor cores can be considered to execute safe events in lock-step. The concurrency of the network model is the average number of events executed at the same time, disregarding simulation overheads and limitations in the number of cores.

Critical path analysis [4, 9] is a method to determine the concurrency in a simulation model by traversing a dependency graph reflecting the precedence relationships between the events of a previous sequential simulation run of the considered model. In the dependency graph depicted in Figure 1, events are represented by circles. An arrow between events e_1 and e_2 reflects the precedence relationship "e_1 before e_2". There are two causes of precedence relationships: first, events cannot be processed prior to their creation in the course of the simulation. Hence, there is an edge reflecting the precedence of an event e over any new events created by e. Second, to enforce timestamp ordering of events in each node, there is an edge between an event and its direct predecessor w.r.t. simulated time pertaining to the same node. Critical path analysis can be performed in an iterative fashion: events that are safe to be executed according to the precedence relation are removed, allowing further events to be removed in the next execution. In Figure 1, dashed rectangles indicate groups of events that can be processed at the same time, i.e., concurrently. If equal processing time for all events is assumed, the total number of executions, divided by the number of events in the simulation in total, is the average concurrency of the simulation model assuming an unlimited number of processor cores, infinite lookahead, and no overheads for synchronization and communication. In Figure 1, nine events are processed in a total of six executions. Hence, the concurrency is $9/6 = 1.5$.

YAWNS [13] is a well-known synchronous synchronization algorithm for parallel and distributed simulation. A simulation iteration using YAWNS is illustrated in Figure 2. In each iteration, the timestamp t_{min} of the earliest event is determined. A fixed lookahead value l determined according to model properties gives a lower bound on the timestamp delta between an event and its creation. Given t_{min}, $l \in \mathbb{N}$, all events in the *lookahead window* $[t_{min}, t_{min} + l]$ are guaranteed to create no events with timestamps below $t_{min} + l$. As the lookahead window is a closed interval, its

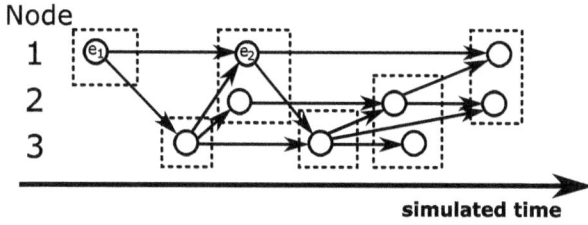

Figure 1: Critical path analysis of a dependency graph.

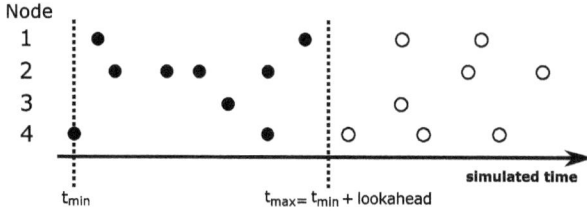

Figure 2: A simulation iteration using YAWNS: events in the interval $[t_{min}, t_{max}]$ create no events with timestamps below t_{max} and are thus safe to be executed in parallel.

width is $l + 1$. Events pertaining to different nodes within each lookahead window can be processed concurrently without allowing for violations of timestamp order per node. The number of executions required to process a lookahead window is the largest number of events pertaining to a single node. In the example, nine events in the lookahead window can be processed in four executions. Hence, the concurrency within the shown lookahead window is $9/4 = 2.25$. Due to its conceptual simplicity, YAWNS has been used as a basis for analytical concurrency estimation in previous works [13, 17]. Here, we employ YAWNS in two ways: first, we analytically estimate the expected YAWNS concurrency on the basis of key parameters of network models. Second, we show that the results between a concurrency analysis using critical path analysis and YAWNS are sufficiently close to use these approaches interchangeably when evaluating the potential of network models for parallelization.

3.2 Analytical Concurrency Estimation

Existing works proposed a multitude of approaches to performance estimation of parallel and distributed simulations. In this paragraph, we limit our brief summary of previous works to approaches that focus on allowing for insights in the causes of the concurrency available in simulation models, disregarding black-box approaches based on simulative models or event traces.

In 1993, Nicol [13] studied the concurrency of simulations based on YAWNS. Using a stochastic model, it is shown that synchronization overheads relative to event processing costs decrease with larger simulation activity. Calculated bounds are evaluated for a number of example models. Similar to our work, concurrency analysis is performed by estimating the number of events in each lookahead window. However, contrary to Nicol, we focus on specific network models implemented in popular simulators and show how concurrency estimations can be derived with relative ease based on network model properties readily available to modelers.

In 1999, Liu et al. [7] presented back-of-the-envelope calculations to estimate the runtime of parallel simulations. However, while the costs for communication in the execution environment are taken into account, load imbalances,

which determine the model's concurrency, are not considered. Hence, the proposed approach is not applicable if we are interested in the concurrency of the network model.

In 2003, Varga et al. [20] proposed an efficiency criterion for conservative parallel simulation using the null-message algorithm. Their approach relates the number of events per lookahead window to the communication costs in the execution environment, allowing for rough estimations of simulation efficiency. Since differences in the workload for different groups of nodes in the simulated network are not considered, estimation errors will be large if there are substantial load imbalances. Improvements in estimation accuracy of their approach may be possible by conducting a manual network model analysis as presented in our paper, and relating the resulting estimation to the expected communication costs.

In 2013, Pienta et al. [17] analyzed the concurrency of scale-free networks. Based on an assumed communication pattern within the network, their analysis provides an estimation of the expected concurrency under YAWNS-based synchronization. To determine the stationary distribution of events among the simulated nodes, an iterative calculation is performed until a steady-state is reached. Again, our work differs in the consideration of specific network models as implemented in real-world simulators. Further, an analysis of the communication patterns in the studied network models allows us to base our estimation on expected numbers of events within a single lookahead window without the need for an iterative model.

4. ESTIMATING CONCURRENCY

In this section, we first describe the building blocks and assumptions of our concurrency estimation methodology. We then propose an analytical concurrency model as a basis for the analysis of specific network models.

4.1 Methodology

Critical path analysis allows for a trace-based calculation of the concurrency in the network model assuming infinite lookahead. However, typically, parallel simulation is performed under a fixed lookahead value that restricts the concurrency that is visible to the simulator. Thus, the results given by critical path analysis are not sufficient to determine the effective maximum concurrency.

To gather more realistic estimates, we adapt critical path analysis by limiting the lookahead during each analysis iteration. The adapted critical path analysis determines an upper bound for the average number of events that can realistically be executed in parallel given unlimited processor cores and assuming no overhead for synchronization and communication between cores. In addition, we apply the common assumption of identical computational costs for all events. In effect, the adapted critical path analysis coincides with an analysis of event traces similar to YAWNS, with the difference that a new lookahead window is calculated after each execution of events. Hence, a YAWNS-based analysis will typically determine lower concurrency values than the upper bound calculated by critical path analysis.

Ideally, we would derive an analytical model to estimate critical path analysis results directly. However, we are not aware of a method to analytically estimate critical path analysis without relying on an iterative, i.e., numerical approach. As critical path analysis allows for overlapping lookahead windows, each iteration depends on the results of the previous iteration. However, our aim is a concurrency estimation that enables insights beyond the sheer concurrency values determined by iterative approaches.

In contrast, when analyzing YAWNS, each lookahead window can be considered separately. Therefore, the analytical model that will be presented in Section 4.2 estimates concurrency according to YAWNS. For the analytical results to be meaningful, it is important that the estimations are close to the reference results from critical path analysis. In Section 6, we show that for all considered network models, the deviations between the results of critical path analysis, YAWNS and our analytical model are sufficiently low so that the methods can be used interchangeably to guide decisions on the parallelization of network models.

Further, the benefit of the analytical approach hinges on the simplicity of acquiring the necessary inputs to the analytical model from the given network model. In Section 4.2, we will detail the information required to gather estimations for three network models with fundamentally different characteristics. We argue that for the considered network models, the required inputs to the analytical model can be determined with relative ease.

4.2 Analytical Model

Our fundamental approach to concurrency estimation is to determine the characteristics of an average lookahead window. In Section 3.1, we have seen that the concurrency within a single lookahead window of a YAWNS-based simulation is the total number of events e_{total} in the lookahead window, divided by the largest number m of events pertaining to a single simulated node. Hence, given estimates of m and e_{total}, the estimated concurrency of the network model is

$$Y_{est} := \frac{e_{total}}{m}$$

While e_{total} can easily be estimated based on the communication activity in a network model, we need to derive m from an estimate of the distribution of events to simulated nodes. As we will see in Section 5 on the example of concrete network models, simulated nodes can be grouped into a small number of categories, each category being assigned a distinct number of events total. As an approximation, events assigned to each category are assumed to be distributed uniformly among the nodes in the category. The *number of nodes in each category* and the *number of events assigned to each category* are the inputs from which our analytical model derives m.

More formally, we divide the nodes of the simulated network into c categories so that all n_i nodes in a single category i share the same estimated number of events e_i per lookahead window. Within each category, we consider the assignment of events to nodes as a sequence of Bernoulli trials with probability $p_i = 1/n_i$ each. The probability for a *single* node of category i being assigned $\leq k$ events follows the binomial distribution:

$$F_i(k) = \sum_{j=0}^{k} \binom{e_i}{j} p_i^{\ j} (1 - p_i)^{e_i - j}$$

The probability for *all* nodes of category i being assigned $\leq k$ events is then:

$$G_i(k) = F_i(k)^{n_i}$$

By considering all node categories, we arrive at the probability for all nodes *of all categories* being assigned $\leq k$ events:

$$G(k) = \prod_{i=1}^{c} G_i(k)$$

We are interested in the expectation of random values distributed according to G, i.e., the expected largest number of events any single node is assigned in a lookahead window [3]. The expectation is:

$$m = \sum_{k=1}^{\infty} k g(k)$$

Here, m is the expected number of parallel event executions required to process a single lookahead window. Now, given the expected total number of events in a lookahead window e_{total}, the estimated YAWNS concurrency is: $Y_{est} := e_{total}/m$

In the following, we show how the node categories and event counts can be determined for concrete network models.

5. NETWORK MODEL ANALYSIS

In this section, we study the concurrency of three network models. For each model, we first analyze the event patterns resulting from the communication patterns in the simulated network. Second, we conduct a sensitivity analysis to find the key factors determining the model's concurrency. Third, we determine the parameters required to analytically estimate the model's concurrency.

5.1 Peer-to-Peer Overlay Network

As our first example, we study a model of a Kademlia-based network. Kademlia [11] is a protocol used to form a distributed hash table (DHT) enabling the efficient storage and retrieval of key-value pairs in a peer-to-peer network. We have previously shown that models of Kademlia-based networks contain substantial concurrency and can benefit strongly from parallelization using SMP clusters or many-core architectures [1, 2]. We analyze the Kademlia model with reference to an implementation in the PeerSim network simulator[1]. As is common with peer-to-peer networks, the model abstracts from all OSI layers but the application layer, i.e., the physical topology is reflected by link latencies drawn from a random distribution. The application-layer itself is modeled accurately in accordance with the BitTorrent DHT specification [10].

5.1.1 Event Patterns

There are two sources of traffic in Kademlia: communication triggered actively by users of the DHT, and routing table maintenance. The latter comprises both operations for refreshing bucket contents as well as operations for checking the responsiveness of specific peers.

The event patterns representing the communication activities in the Kademlia model are shown in Figure 3. The building block fundamental to all communication in Kademlia is the remote procedure call (RPC), a sequence of three events representing the following interaction:

A. Peer 1 sends a request

B. Peer 2 receives the request and creates a response

C. Peer 1 receives the response.

[1]http://peersim.sourceforge.net/

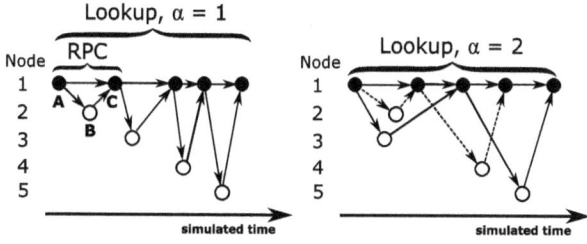

Figure 3: Event patterns in the Kademlia model: lookups are composed of α overlapping sequences of RPCs. Node 1 performs a lookup with $\alpha = 1$ (left) and $\alpha = 2$ (right).

So-called *lookups* are used to perform storage and retrieval operations. Each lookup consists of a sequence of RPCs where step C generates a new request until the lookup terminates. A parameter α specifies the number of concurrent RPCs during a lookup. Lookups with $\alpha > 1$ can be regarded as a superposition of multiple sequences of RPCs.

From the event pattern, we can easily deduce the number of events associated with a lookup. One initial event triggers the lookup, and each subsequent RPC is associated with two events: a request and its response. If the number of RPCs r per lookup is known, the total number of events per lookup is $e_{per\_lookup} = 2r + 1$, independently of α. Of these, $r + 1$ events pertain to the peer performing the lookup, and r events pertain to other peers.

The remaining traffic in the Kademlia model is created by pings triggered if the responsiveness of a peer is to be checked. If a peer's routing table is fully populated and a peer becomes aware of a new remote peer, peers of unknown responsiveness in the routing table are checked using ping RPCs. The receiver of a ping request may then recursively trigger new pings to further peers.

When creating the inputs to the analytical model, we consider the events created by lookups in detail, while treating ping events as uniformly distributed noise.

Concurrency in the Kademlia model results from two independent parameters:

1. λ independent lookups running concurrently

2. α concurrent RPCs performed during each lookup

Since events pertaining to each individual peer must be executed sequentially in timestamp order, the resulting concurrency is limited by the number n of peers in the network.

5.1.2 Sensitivity Analysis

We study the sensitivity of the Kademlia model to the number n of peers in the network, the number λ of concurrent lookups, and the number α of concurrent RPCs per lookup. To set a fixed λ accurately, we require an estimate of the average lookup duration d, which can be gathered from a brief initial simulation run. Then, the rate r at which lookups must be generated to achieve the desired number of λ concurrent lookups follows Little's law: $r = \frac{\lambda}{d}$.

For runs with $\lambda = 100$ and $\lambda = 1,000$, we triggered the generation of event traces after 1,000s of simulated time to allow the network to reach a steady state. Using the adapted critical path analysis according to Section 4.1, we analyzed events executed within 10s of simulated time. However, since the results differed only slightly with shorter runs, we configured the computationally expensive runs for $\lambda =$

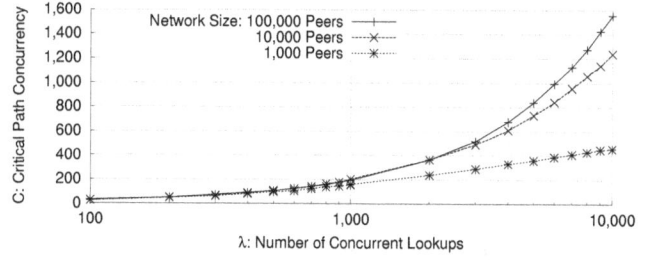

Figure 4: Results of sensitivity analysis of the Kademlia model with $\alpha = 8$, varying the number λ of concurrent lookups.

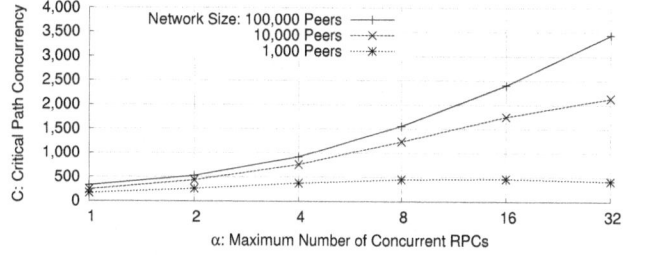

Figure 5: Results of sensitivity analysis of the Kademlia model with $\lambda = 10,000$, varying the number α of concurrent RPCs per lookup.

10,000 with only 300s of warm-up time. Since link latencies in ms are drawn from a uniform distribution on $[10, 200]$, a fixed lookahead value of 10ms was used. From the results depicted in Figures 4 and 5, we can see that, as expected, larger numbers of concurrent lookups result in larger concurrency. Furthermore, larger α provides an increase in concurrency. In both figures, we can see that concurrency is limited by the network size. The results provide an upper bound for the speedup by parallelization of the network model. Depending on the costs of communication and synchronization during simulation, many of the considered parameterizations suggest the parallel execution of the model on hundreds or thousands of processor cores. Hence, as shown on the example of a GPU-based simulator in [1], the results indicate that the Kademlia network model can benefit substantially from execution on many-core devices.

5.1.3 Analytical Concurrency Estimation

In the following, we describe how, based on key metrics of the Kademlia model, we determine the inputs required for the analytical concurrency estimation. The inputs to the analytical model are printed in boldface.

We differentiate between two categories of peers: active *peers that are currently executing a lookup, and* passive *peers that respond to incoming requests only.* We assume that the number λ of concurrent lookups is a scenario parameter, and that the initiations of lookups are distributed uniformly over the peers in the simulated network. The average number λ_{rt} of additional concurrent lookups created for routing table maintenance can be gathered from a sequential simulation run of the given configuration and subsequently be included in our consideration:

$$\lambda' = \lambda + \lambda_{rt}$$

Then, the ratio of active peers of all peers is:

$$r_{active} = 1 - (1 - \frac{1}{n})^{\lambda'}$$

The absolute numbers of active and passive peers are thus:

$$n_{active} = n \times r_{active}$$

$$n_{passive} = n - n_{active}$$

Given the width of the lookahead window $l + 1$, the average number r of RPCs per lookup, and the average lookup duration d, the total number of events generated for all lookups per lookahead window is:

$$e_{lookups} = (l + 1) \times \lambda' \times \frac{2r + 1}{d}$$

Finally, we consider the number p of ping RPCs per unit of simulated time generated for checking the online status of peers, each generating two events, to obtain the total number of events per lookahead window:

$$e_{total} = (l + 1) \times (\lambda' \times \frac{2r + 1}{d} + 2p)$$

Now, we consider active and passive peers separately. In each lookup, active peers generate one initial event and one event for each RPC. The number of these events for all active peers is:

$$e_{active,lookup} = (l + 1) \times \lambda' \times \frac{r + 1}{d}$$

Active peers also receive some of the requests generated in lookups of other peers. The number of request events for all active peers is:

$$e_{active,request} = (l + 1) \times \lambda' \times r_{active} \times \frac{r}{d}$$

Finally, a proportion of ping events targets active peers:

$$e_{active,ping} = (l + 1) \times p \times r_{active}$$

Now, the total number of events expected to be generated per lookahead window for all active peers is:

$$e_{active} = e_{active,lookup} + e_{active,request} + e_{active,ping}$$

The remaining events pertain to passive peers:

$$e_{passive} = e_{total} - e_{active}$$

Using the estimated number of events for the two categories of active and passive peers, we can now determine the expected largest number m of events per lookahead window to be processed by a single peer in the simulation according to the calculations described in Section 4.2. The estimated concurrency is then e_{total}/m.

Discussion: In the simulated network, each lookup creates a sequence of RPCs targeting a sequence of peers according to the dynamic contents of the routing tables of peers on the path to the target of the lookup. Nevertheless, in the analysis, we consider the events pertaining to each peer category as uniformly distributed among the peers in the respective category, ignoring the network topology created by the Kademlia protocol completely. In Section 6 we will see that our estimations are reasonably accurate. Hence, we can conclude that the impact of the exact topology of the considered Kademlia-based network on the concurrency of the network model is relatively low. Instead, the concurrency is dominated by the raw message counts per peer category as well as by the overall network size.

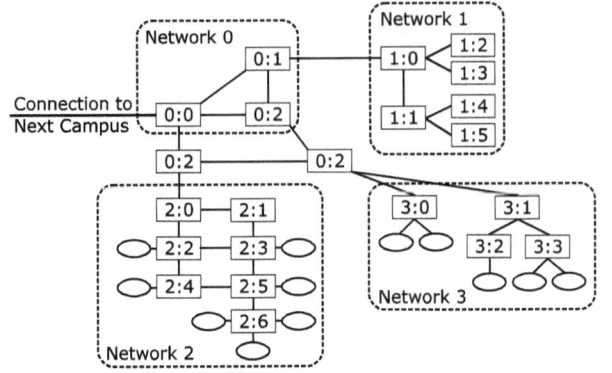

Figure 6: A single campus network of the topology from the NMS program (Fig. adapted from [14]).

5.2 TCP/IP in a Fixed Topology

Our second example is a network model created in the context of the DARPA "Network Modeling and Simulation" (NMS) program. The model is commonly used to benchmark parallel simulators [6, 14, 19] and was selected for its strong impact of the network topology on concurrency.

The basic building block of the topology is the campus network depicted in Figure 6. On each campus, there are three subnetworks. In Network 0 and Network 1 and between Network 0, 1 and 3, there are nodes representing servers and routers interconnected by a 1 Gbps link with 5ms latency. In Network 2 and 3, there are local area networks containing a configurable number of nodes representing user workstations connected to a switch using 100 Mbps links with 1ms latency. A configurable number of campus networks is connected in a ring using links with a latency of 200 ms. For each of the LAN nodes, a TCP stream with a constant data rate of 500 kbps is transmitted by one of the nodes 1:2, 1:3, 1:4 or 1:5 of the neighboring campus network.

Since all messages pass through the nodes connecting individual campus networks, we study the effects of varying the bandwidth between these nodes between 1 Mbps and 1,000 Mbps. In the following, we refer to the nodes connecting the individual campus networks as *hubs*. In addition, we differentiate between two types of bottlenecks: *network bottlenecks* are nodes that due to their position in the network and their limited bandwidth restrict the overall throughput in the network. *Simulation bottlenecks* are nodes for which disproportionally large numbers of events must be processed per unit of simulated time, so that these nodes limit the concurrency of the simulation model.

An implementation of the network model in the popular network simulator ns-3[2] uses an accurate representation of the network and transport layer, whereas the lower layers are modeled by the fixed link latencies specified above. In our analysis, we apply the common approach of using a fixed lookahead value of 1ms that is applicable to all nodes in the network. It may be possible to extract larger concurrency with a dedicated lookahead value for each link at the cost of higher complexity of the synchronization scheme (e.g., [12]).

5.2.1 Event Patterns

Since it is not always possible to transmit messages created by a simulated application instantaneously, in ns-3,

[2]http://www.nsnam.org/

228

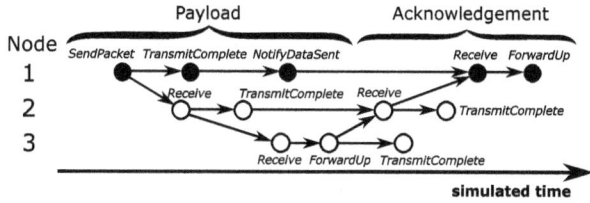

Figure 7: Event patterns in the TCP/IP model: a single packet is transmitted from node 1 to 3 via node 2. Node 3 replies with an acknowledgement.

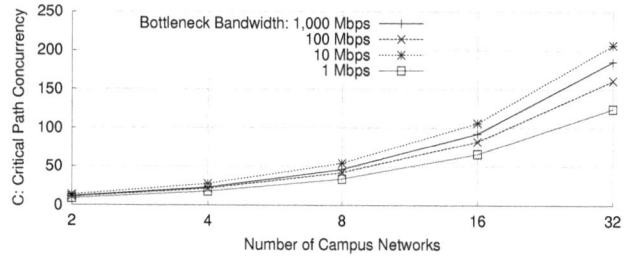

Figure 8: Results of sensitivity of the TCP/IP model varying the number of campus networks.

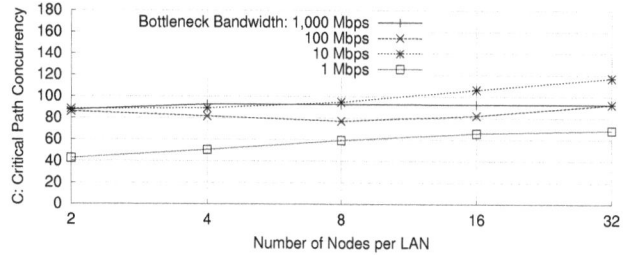

Figure 9: Results of sensitivity analysis of the TCP/IP model varying the number of receiving nodes per LAN.

creation of messages and their transmission is modeled separately. Hence, the transmission of a single message holding a payload via a linear sequence of nodes is reflected by the events and precedence relationships depicted on the left hand side of Figure 7: the sender generates one event for the message's creation (`SendPacket`), one for the message's successful transmission on the link layer (`TransmitComplete`), and one notifying the transport layer that a packet was sent (`NotifyDataSent`). Each node on the path to the receiver generates two events for reception (`Receive`) and successful forwarding (`TransmitComplete`) of the message. Finally, the receiving node generates two events representing reception: one for reception on the link layer (`Receive`), and one for forwarding the message to the upper layers of the network stack (`ForwardUp`).

Additional messages are created by TCP on the receiver side. We use the New Reno implementation of TCP, wherein by default, for every second message, an acknowledgement is transmitted from the receiver to the sender. As depicted on the right hand side of Figure 7, each acknowledgement generates one event for the receiver of the payload (`TransmitComplete`), two events for each hop on the path to the sender (`Receive`, `TransmitComplete`) and two events for the original sender (`Receive`, `ForwardUp`).

5.2.2 Sensitivity Analysis

In the analysis of the sensitivity of the model's concurrency to model parameters, we used 60s of warm-up time. Since the results were virtually independent of the considered span of simulated time, it was sufficient to analyze events executed within 1s of simulated time. The results in Figure 8 show the sensitivity of the model's concurrency to the number of campus network and the hub bandwidth for a fixed number of 16 LAN nodes. Since campus networks communicate only with their direct neighbors, larger numbers of campus networks do not increase the amount of traffic handled by individual hubs. Hence, irrespective of the hub bandwidth, there is a linear relationship between the number of campus networks and the critical path concurrency. A comparison between the curves for different hub bandwidths shows initially surprising results: the concurrency does not simply increase with larger hub bandwidth: even though a hub bandwidth of 1,000 Mbps allows for far fewer messages transmitted per unit of simulated time than a bandwidth of 10 Mbps, the larger number of messages crossing the hubs limits the concurrency of the simulation.

Figure 9 shows the concurrency when varying the number of LAN nodes and the hub bandwidth for a fixed number of 16 campus networks. With 2 LAN nodes, only 2,000 kbps of traffic crosses each hub, i.e., there is a network bottleneck in the run with 1 Mbps only. Accordingly, the results with

hub bandwidths of 10 Mbps and above are nearly identical. For 4 and more LAN nodes, the magnitudes of the results do not simply follow the hub bandwidth. Instead, the resulting concurrency depends on three factors: the rate of message generation by the senders, the rate at which the messages pass through the network as dictated by the hub bandwidth, and the total number of message flows. With 1,000 Mbps, the concurrency is nearly independent of the LAN node count. The reason is that, since there are no network bottlenecks, each doubling of the LAN node count doubles the total number of messages per unit of time, but at the same time doubles the number of messages at each hub, i.e., double the original number of events is processed in double the number of executions.

When disregarding the costs of synchronization and communication during a simulation run, the concurrency with 32 campus networks suggests the use of up to about 200 cores for execution of the model. As the concurrency depends strongly on the number of campus networks, efficient parallel execution on many-core devices requires a large number of campus networks in relation to the number of cores.

5.2.3 Analytical Concurrency Estimation

For the analysis, we first assume that there are no network bottlenecks. Then, the total number e_{total} of events per TCP flow and simulated second in the steady-state can be estimated as follows:

$$m_{app} = r_{app}/s_m$$

$$e_{payload} = m_{app}(3 + 2n_{fw} + 2)$$

$$e_{ack} = \frac{m_{app}}{2}(1 + 2n_{fw} + 2)$$

$$e_{total} = e_{payload} + e_{ack}$$

Here, r_{app} is the desired bitrate of each application that generates a TCP flow. s_m is the size of each message including headers. In our example, TCP and IP add 20 bytes

229

of header data each to a payload of 512 bytes. m_{app} is the message rate per flow. n_{fw} is the average number of forwarding nodes between a sender and a receiver. Using these values, the total event rate is given by the sum of the payload and acknowledgement event rates. This calculation can be repeated for each TCP flow to determine the total event rate of the simulation.

Up to this point, we did not consider network bottlenecks. We model these by considering two message rates: as above, m_{app} is the target message rate of the application. m_{tm} is the number of messages actually transmitted per second when considering network bottlenecks. Of course, network bottlenecks must be identified first. For complex topologies, an approximation can be calculated using common flow algorithms. In the topology considered here, hubs with low bandwidth are obvious network bottlenecks. All other forwarding nodes handle substantially smaller numbers of events.

When considering network bottlenecks, the event rate estimation must be based on the rate of actually transmitted messages m_{tm} per flow according to the maximum message rate m_{hubs} of the hubs resulting from their bandwidth:

$$m_{app} = r_{app}/s_m$$

$$m_{tm} = min(m_{hubs}, m_{app})$$

$$e_{payload} = m_{tm}(2 + 2n_{fw} + 2) + m_{app}$$

$$e_{ack} = \frac{m_{tm}}{2}(1 + 2n_{fw} + 2)$$

$$e_{total} = e_{payload} + e_{ack}$$

The estimation makes the simplifying assumption that the combination of all TCP flows fully saturates the capacity of network bottlenecks. Since TCP only approximates the channel capacity, the average number of messages in flight will be somewhat lower than our estimation. In Section 6, we evaluate how strongly network bottlenecks affect the accuracy of the concurrency estimation.

We now explicitly consider the event rates of two categories of nodes: hubs and senders. Each of the n_{cns} campus networks holds a single hub and four senders:

$$n_{hubs} = n_{cns}$$

$$n_{senders} = 4n_{cns}$$

Since each campus network contains both senders and receivers, the number of TCP flows crossing each hub is $2 \times n_{lan\_nodes} \times n_{cns}$.

The total event rate for the hubs is thus:

$$e_{hubs} = 2n_{hubs} \times (m_{tm} + \frac{m_{tm}}{2})$$

Again, each forwarded message generates one event for reception and one for transmission and there is one acknowledgement for every other message.

The total event rate for the senders is:

$$e_{senders} = n_{flows} \times (m_{app} + 2m_{tm} + 2 \times \frac{m_{tm}}{2})$$

As before, for the concurrency estimation, we assume that e_{hubs} events are placed in the lookahead window with the same per-event probability for each hub. The corresponding assumption is made for the senders. Using our analytical model, we can now estimate the largest expected number of events in each lookahead window for a single node in either

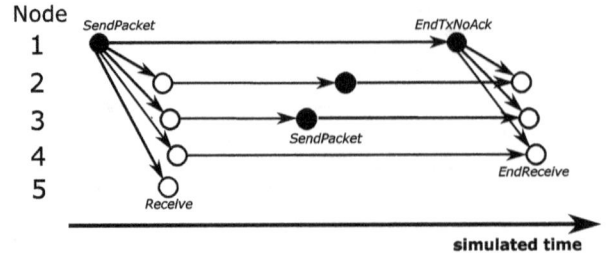

Figure 10: Event patterns in the wireless model.

the hub or the sender group. The result m is the number of parallel event executions required to process a single lookahead window. The estimated concurrency is then e_{total}/m.

Discussion: From the analysis, we can gather relationships between properties of the considered network model and the model's concurrency: first, since parallel simulation progress is determined by the simulation bottlenecks, a large number of events for non-bottleneck nodes is beneficial for high concurrency. Hence, given the fact that each hop forwarding a message generates two events, longer path lengths increase concurrency. Second, m_{tm} decreases if there are network bottlenecks, whereas m_{app} is independent of network bottlenecks. Therefore, it is possible that the total event rate is dominated by events generated at senders, even though all traffic passes through the hubs. Because of this, there is an inverse relationship between network and simulation bottlenecks: *hubs that* do not *limit the message rate are simulation bottlenecks, but no network bottlenecks, whereas hubs that* do *limit the message rate are network bottlenecks, but no simulation bottlenecks.*

5.3 Wireless Ad-Hoc Communication

As a third example, we study the concurrency of a model of a wireless ad-hoc network. The model's analysis forms a counter-example to the approach used to determine the concurrency of the previous two models: due to the broadcast nature of the wireless medium and the avoidance of message collisions, we can express the concurrency directly based on an analysis of individual transmissions, without reliance on the statistical approach presented in Section 4.2.

Ad-hoc networks are frequently studied in the context of car-to-car communication, where cars establish a mutual awareness by periodic transmission of *beacon* messages holding, e.g., the sender's current position. The mutual awareness can be leveraged by applications to increase road safety and efficiency. A frequent focus of simulation studies in this area lies in investigating the channel load resulting from the beacon traffic.

In the scenario considered here, a configurable number of nodes are positioned randomly on a linear 100m road segment. The nodes broadcast beacons at a configurable rate, each beacon comprising 400 bytes of data including headers. Communication is performed with a data rate of 6 Mbps over a wireless channel using a CSMA-based MAC layer, i.e., nodes check for activity on the channel and delay their transmissions if necessary.

5.3.1 Event Patterns

We study the event patterns resulting from the described model by reference to ns-3. A single transmission comprises the following sequence of events (cf. Figure 10): given no ongoing transmission on the channel, a `SendPacket` event of the transmitting node represents the start of a transmission and creates a `Receive` event for every remaining node as well as a single `EndTxNoAck` event reflecting the completion of the transmission. For each receiver that successfully detects the beacon, the `Receive` event creates a corresponding `End-Receive`. In total, each successful transmission is reflected by a minimum of $1 + (n-1) + 1 = n+1$ and a maximum of $1 + (n-1) + 1 + (n-1) = 2n$ events.

A CSMA-based MAC layer aims to reduce the probability of collisions. In case the channel is busy, the initial `SendPacket` event creates a single `AccessTimeout` event that takes the role of a `SendPacket` at a later point in simulated time. In the following, we refer to `SendPacket` events only, since `AccessTimeout` events are handled identically during simulation. We refer to `SendPacket` events by which a busy channel is detected as `Probe` events.

There are two situations in which interactions between multiple transmission attempts affect concurrency. First, collisions occur in the case of two nodes starting to send at the same time. Second, a `SendPacket` event will detect a busy channel and delay the corresponding transmission, so that no `Receive` events are created until the next attempt. The occurrence probabilities of both situations depend on the channel load. Our concurrency estimation disregards overlapping transmissions, but does consider `Probe` events.

5.3.2 Sensitivity Analysis

The sensitivity of the network model's concurrency to the beacon rate and the number of nodes was analyzed using event traces covering 10s of simulated time after a warm-up time of 30s. Figure 11 shows that the concurrency increases close to linearly with the number of nodes in the network. For extremely large channel loads, collisions increase the concurrency substantially. Further, slight differences in concurrency for lower beacon rates are caused by varying numbers of *Probe* events.

In the considered parameter combinations, we measured concurrency values below 100 even for large node densities. Due to the limited spatial extent of 100m of the network, larger node counts lead to unrealistically large channel load. Parallel execution on many-core devices should hence be considered when studying scenarios with larger spatial extent that support larger numbers of nodes under realistic channel loads.

5.3.3 Analytical Concurrency Estimation

To estimate the concurrency in the model analytically, we need to be aware of the lookahead that will be available in a simulation run. Simulations of wireless networks are well-known to exhibit only small amounts of fixed lookahead. Due to the broadcast nature and limited spatial extent of wireless networks, transmissions pertain to all nodes in proximity of the sender, and the time delta between transmission and reception is quite small. Hence, a fixed lookahead value considering the minimum latency between any two nodes of the network can be insufficient for high concurrency. The literature proposes the use of model knowledge regarding OSI layers 2 and above to enable larger lookahead values [8, 16]. If it is known at simulation runtime that according to the current state of, e.g., the MAC or application layer of the nodes, new events up to a certain point in time can be ruled out, the lookahead can be extended to this point.

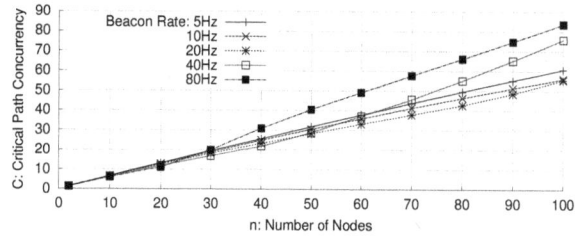

Figure 11: Results of sensitivity analysis of the wireless network model, varying the number of nodes and the beacon rate.

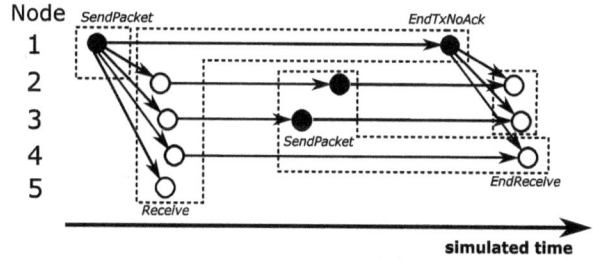

Figure 12: Concurrency in a single transmission in the wireless model. Sets of events surrounded by dashed lines can can be executed concurrently.

For the analysis, we consider the case where model knowledge provides sufficient lookahead to cover all events that have no pending precedence relationships. Figure 12 depicts the event patterns in the model, grouping concurrent events. The initial `SendPacket` event creates $n-1$ `Receive` events as well as a single `EndTxNoAck` event. Since execution of the `SendPacket` event triggers the creation of all other events, it cannot be executed in parallel with any further events. Now, all `Receive` events can be executed in parallel together with the `EndTxNoAck`, n events in total. Next, all remaining `SendPacket` events are executed concurrently with `EndReceive` events of nodes that execute no `Probe` events and receive the current packet successfully.

We now consider the number of parallel event executions required to process the `Probe` events. Since events for each node must be executed in timestamp order, up to n events can be executed at the same time. For a given simulation run of T transmissions with f_t `Probe` events during transmission t, the average number of event executions required to process all `Probe` events is $r_p = \frac{1}{T} \sum_{t=1}^{T} \lceil \frac{p_t}{n} \rceil$, the value of which can be determined from a sequential simulation run.

Now, we estimate the model's concurrency by dividing the number of events per transmission by the number of executions required. The estimated concurrency is

$$C_{est} = \frac{1 + (n-1) + 1 + s(n-1) + p}{3 + r_p} = \frac{n + 1 + s(n-1) + p}{3 + r_p}$$

Discussion: The simplicity of the analysis reflects the simplicity of the event precedence relation in the wireless model: the available concurrency results from the independent reception events evenly distributed among all receivers. Hence, in contrast to the previous two network models, we can estimate the critical path concurrency directly without estimating YAWNS concurrency first.

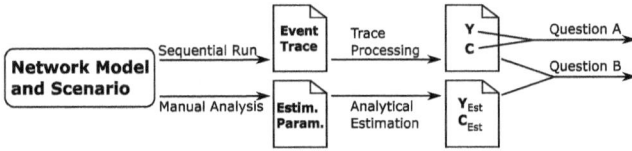

Figure 13: Validation of analytical concurrency estimations with reference to trace-based results.

6. EVALUATION

In this section, two questions are addressed:

Question A: Are the concurrency values determined by YAWNS-based analysis and critical path analysis sufficiently close to use these methods interchangeably? Our analytical model estimates concurrency according to YAWNS. However, since critical path analysis determines the largest possible concurrency, it must be considered the reference for concurrency estimation.

Question B: Does our analytical model estimate critical path concurrency of the considered network models with sufficient accuracy? A correspondence between the estimation and the critical path analysis results is an indication that our network model analysis captured the key influencing factors for the models' concurrency, clarifying the relationship between properties of the simulated networks and the resulting concurrency.

Figure 13 depicts the general work flow for validation of the concurrency estimation results for the parameterizations of each network model. Based on knowledge of the network model and, if necessary, on a sequential simulation run, the inputs required by the generic analytical model are determined. Event traces generated during the sequential run are processed programmatically using YAWNS-based analysis and critical path analysis. To answer question A, the results of the YAWNS-based analysis and critical path analysis are compared. To answer question B, the analytical estimate is compared to the critical path analysis result.

We first consider question A and focus on the results for the Kademlia and TCP/IP models, as the concurrency of the wireless network model was estimated directly with reference to critical path analysis. The parameters of the Kademlia model were varied as follows:

- $n \in \{1,000; 10,000; 100,000\}$

- $\lambda \in \{100; 1,000; 10,000\}$

- $\alpha \in \{1; 2; 4; 8; 16; 32\}$

In addition, we configured the probability of packet loss as 0%, 25%, 50% and 75%.

The TCP/IP model was configured as follows:

- Number of CNs $\in \{2; 4; 8; 16; 32\}$

- Number of nodes per LAN $\in \{2; 4; 8; 16; 32\}$

- Bottleneck bandwidth $\in \{1; 10; 100; 1,000\}$ Mbps

Figures 14 and 15 compare the results of YAWNS-based analysis to critical path analysis results. In both cases, YAWNS-based analysis determines lower concurrency values than critical path analysis. The deviation increases slightly with larger concurrency. However, even for very large concurrency values, YAWNS determines concurrency values be-

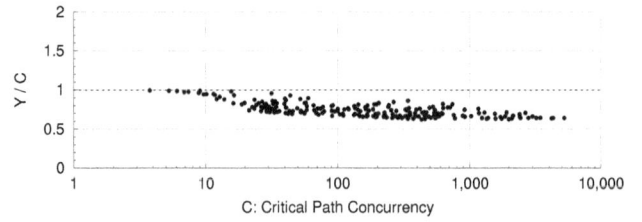

Figure 14: Comparison of YAWNS concurrency (Y) with critical path concurrency (C) of the Kademlia model.

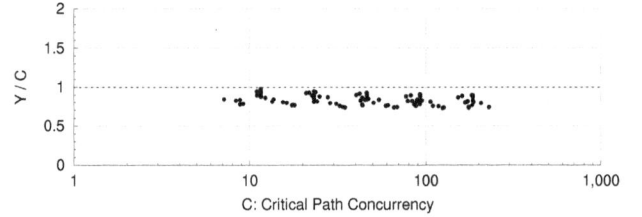

Figure 15: Comparison of YAWNS (Y) with critical path concurrency (C) of the TCP/IP model.

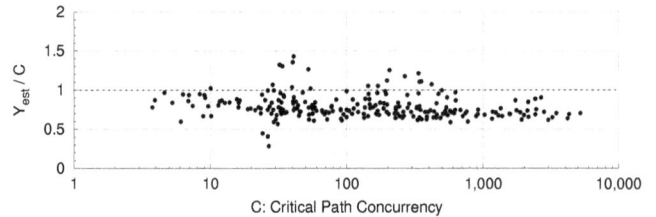

Figure 16: Comparison of our analytical estimate (Y_{est}) with critical path concurrency (C) of the Kademlia model.

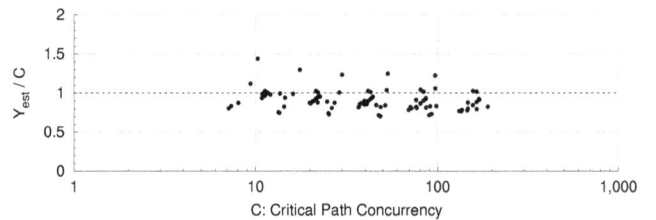

Figure 17: Comparison of our analytical estimate (Y_{est}) with critical path concurrency (C) of the TCP/IP model.

tween a factor of 0.6 and 1 of critical path analysis. We consider the correspondence sufficiently close to evaluate the parallelization potential of network models.

Now, we address question B and compare the analytical estimate with the critical path analysis results. Figure 16 shows the results for the Kademlia network model. As in the comparison of YAWNS and critical path analysis, a slight underestimation between the analytical model and critical path analysis can be observed in many cases. However, the model captures critical path analysis sufficiently so that, apart from few outliers, the model determines a factor between 0.5 and 1.5 of the reference value over a vast range of model parameters and resulting concurrency values.

Similarly, the results for the TCP/IP model depicted in Figure 17 show a close correspondence between the analyt-

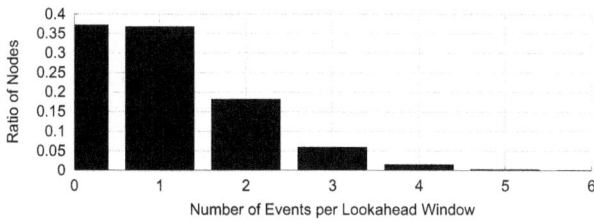

(a) Binomial distribution B(296, 1/300)

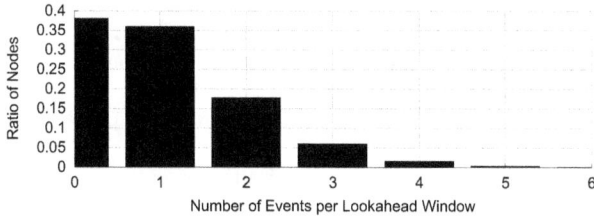

(b) Results from simulation run.

Figure 18: Expected and observed distribution of the number of events per node in the *active* category in each lookahead window for a run of the Kademlia model with $n = 1,000$, $\lambda = 300$, $\alpha = 8$, and 0% packet loss.

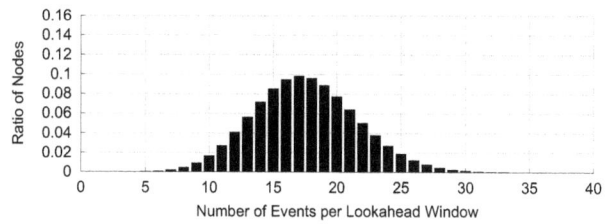

(a) Binomial distribution B(281, 1/16)

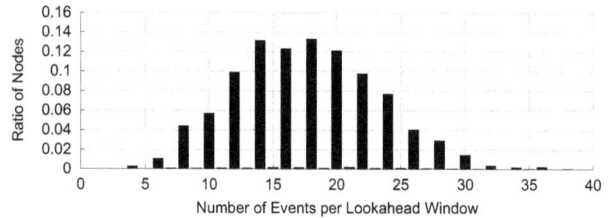

(b) Results from simulation run.

Figure 19: Expected and observed distribution of the number of events per node of the *hub* category in each lookahead window for a run of the TCP/IP model with 16 campus networks, 1 node per LAN, and 1Gbps of hub bandwidth.

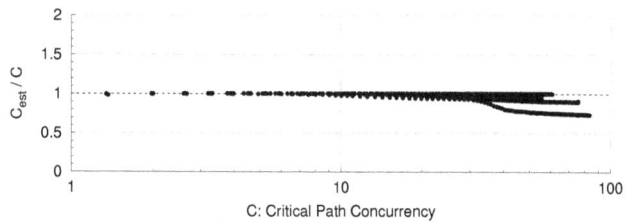

Figure 20: Comparison of our analytical estimate (C_{est}) with critical path concurrency (C) of the wireless model.

ical estimate and critical path analysis results. Here, a repeating pattern emerges in the plotted results: our network model analysis assumed a full utilization of the channel capacity in the simulated network. With decreasing hub bandwidth, the simulated network deviates increasingly from full utilization, leading to an overestimation of concurrency.

The analytical approach used to estimate the concurrency of the Kademlia and TCP/IP network models makes the assumption of a uniform distribution of events within each lookahead window over the nodes of each of the identified categories. If the assumption of a uniform distribution of events to nodes holds, we expect a binomial distribution of the number of events assigned to each node in each lookahead window. Since this section already shows the validity of the concurrency estimations of our analytical model, we limit our illustration of the validity of our assumption of uniform distribution to two example scenarios. We determined the appropriate parameters for the binomial distribution according to the observed number of events per lookahead window, and the number of nodes in the considered node category. Figure 18 compares the expected binomial distribution with the number of events per node of the *active* category (cf. Section 5.1) actually observed in an exemplary simulation run of the Kademlia network model. We can see that in the considered scenario, the simulation results are matched closely by the binomial distribution. Figure 19 compares the expected binomial distribution with the number of events per node of the *hub* category (cf. Section 5.2) in an example run of the TCP/IP network model. Here, a deviation in the distributions is caused by the fact that in the network model, groups of two events each are scheduled with only a small delta in simulated time. Hence, in almost all cases, an even number of events is assigned to an individual node in each lookahead window.

For validation of the estimations for the wireless network model, we varied the number of nodes in the network between 2 and 100. Figure 20 relates the estimated concurrency C_{est} to the results from critical path analysis of event

traces. For small networks, the estimation is nearly identical to the critical path results. The estimation becomes too pessimistic only in cases of extreme channel load, where collisions, which are not considered by the analytical estimate, are frequent. The largest deviation was measured in a scenario with 100 nodes and a beacon rate of 80Hz, where the estimation amounts to 73.5% of the concurrency determined using critical path analysis.

7. DISCUSSION

Our estimation approach requires the identification of simulation bottlenecks and a classification of nodes according to the number of assigned events. These requirements expose a fundamental challenge in performance estimation of simulations: simulation is typically applied when studying systems whose behavior cannot be easily modeled in a static form, such as by mathematical equations. If it is possible to model the runtime behavior of the model a priori, simulation is unnecessary. Hence, in case the aspects of the model's runtime behavior that are to be determined using simulation are also critical to the performance of the simulation, performance estimation is non-trivial.

Depending on the network model under study, it is possible to approximate the required statistics by performing brief sequential simulation runs. For instance, if the lookup duration is the desired metric when studying the Kademlia model, yet the lookup duration is critical to the model's concurrency, a brief sequential simulation run can be performed to approximate the average lookup duration. In the cases considered here, such an estimation was sufficient to achieve a reasonable level of estimation accuracy.

8. CONCLUSION

We presented an analytical model to estimate and understand the concurrency of network simulation models. A sensitivity analysis and investigation of event patterns showed the factors determining the concurrency of three network models and the differences in their potential for parallelization. Given a modest amount of knowledge of the network model and information from sequential simulation runs, the analytical approach estimates concurrency with high accuracy over a large range of scenario parameter settings.

The key relationships between the properties of the considered network models and their concurrency are as follows: the concurrency of the considered peer-to-peer network model is strongly dependent on the number of nodes actively initiating traffic and limited by the total number of nodes, whereas the exact network topology has only little impact on concurrency. The peer-to-peer network model suggests the use of hundreds of cores for simulation. In the considered model of TCP/IP in a fixed topology, concurrency increases with larger numbers of hops between senders and receivers and, to a moderate degree, with larger bandwidth of bottleneck routers. The concurrency of a wireless network model was shown to scale in proportion to the number of nodes in the network, but is limited by the spatial extent of the scenario.

In future work, we aim to move towards a more general classification of network models by identifying recurring event patterns in models with similar topologies and communication patterns.

9. REFERENCES

[1] P. Andelfinger and H. Hartenstein. Exploiting the Parallelism of Large-Scale Application-Layer Networks by Adaptive GPU-based Simulation. In *Proceedings of the 2014 Winter Simulation Conference*, WSC '14, pages 3471–3482. IEEE, 2014.

[2] P. Andelfinger, K. Jünemann, and H. Hartenstein. Parallelism Potentials in Distributed Simulations of Kademlia-based Peer-to-Peer Networks. In *Proceedings of the Conference on Simulation Tools and Techniques (SIMUTools)*, pages 41–50. ICST, 2014.

[3] B. C. Arnold, N. Balakrishnan, and H. N. Nagaraja. *A First Course in Order Statistics*, volume 54. Siam, 1992.

[4] O. Berry and D. Jefferson. Critical Path Analysis of Distributed Simulation. In *Proceedings of the 1985 SCS Multiconference on Distributed Simulation*, pages 57–60. SCS, 1985.

[5] G. Kunz, D. Schemmel, J. Gross, and K. Wehrle. Multi-Level Parallelism for Time- and Cost-Efficient Parallel Discrete Event Simulation on GPUs. In *Proceedings of the 26th Workshop on Principles of Advanced and Distributed Simulation*, pages 23–32. IEEE Computer Society, 2012.

[6] J. Liu, Y. Li, and Y. He. A Large-Scale Real-Time Network Simulation Study Using PRIME. In *Proceedings of the 2009 Winter Simulation Conference (WSC)*, pages 797–806. IEEE Press, Dec 2009.

[7] J. Liu, D. Nicol, B. J. Premore, and A. L. Poplawski. Performance Prediction of a Parallel Simulator. In *Proceedings of the Workshop on Parallel and Distributed Simulation (PADS)*, pages 156–164. IEEE Computer Society, 1999.

[8] J. Liu and D. M. Nicol. Lookahead Revisited in Wireless Network Simulations. In *Proceedings of the 16th Workshop on Parallel and Distributed Simulation*, pages 79–88. IEEE Computer Society, 2002.

[9] M. Livny. A Study of Parallelism in Distributed Simulation. In *Proceedings of the 1985 SCS Multiconference on Distributed Simulation*, pages 94–98. SCS, 1985.

[10] A. Loewenstern. BitTorrent Enhancement Proposal 5: DHT Protocol. http://www.bittorrent.org/beps/bep_0005.html, 2008. [Online; accessed 05-05-2015].

[11] P. Maymounkov and D. Mazieres. Kademlia: A Peer-to-Peer Information System Based on the XOR Metric. In *Peer-to-Peer Systems*, pages 53–65. Springer, 2002.

[12] R. A. Meyer and R. L. Bagrodia. Path Lookahead: a Data Flow View of PDES Models. In *13th Workshop on Parallel and Distributed Simulation*, pages 12–19. IEEE, 1999.

[13] D. M. Nicol. The Cost of Conservative Synchronization in Parallel Discrete Event Simulations. *Journal of the ACM (JACM)*, 40(2):304–333, 1993.

[14] J. Pelkey and G. Riley. Distributed Simulation with MPI in ns-3. In *Proceedings of the Conference on Simulation Tools and Techniques (SIMUTools)*, pages 410–414. ICST, 2011.

[15] K. S. Perumalla. Discrete-Event Execution Alternatives on General Purpose Graphical Processing Units (GPGPUs). In *Proceedings of the 20th Workshop on Principles of Advanced and Distributed Simulation*, pages 74–81. IEEE Computer Society, 2006.

[16] P. Peschlow, A. Voss, and P. Martini. Good News for Parallel Wireless Network Simulations. In *Proceedings of the 12th ACM International Conference on Modeling, Analysis and Simulation of Wireless and Mobile Systems*, pages 134–142. ACM, 2009.

[17] R. S. Pienta and R. M. Fujimoto. On the Parallel Simulation of Scale-Free Networks. In *Proceedings of the Conference on Principles of Advanced Discrete Simulation (PADS)*, pages 179–188. ACM, 2013.

[18] C. Roth, S. Reder, G. Erdogan, O. Sander, G. Almeida, H. Bucher, and J. Becker. Asynchronous Parallel MPSoC Simulation on the Single-Chip Cloud Computer. In *2012 International Symposium on System on Chip (SoC)*, pages 1–8. IEEE, Oct 2012.

[19] B. P. Swenson, J. S. Ivey, and G. F. Riley. Performance of Conservative Synchronization Methods for Complex Interconnected Campus Networks in ns-3. In *Proceedings of the 2014 Winter Simulation Conference*, WSC '14, pages 3096–3106. IEEE, 2014.

[20] A. Varga, Y. A. Sekercioglu, and G. K. Egan. A Practical Efficiency Criterion for the Null Message Algorithm. In *ESS 2003: 15th European Simulation Symposium*. SCS, 2003.

A Virtual Time System for Linux-container-based Emulation of Software-defined Networks

Jiaqi Yan
Illinois Institute of Technology
10 West 31st Street
Chicago, IL, United States
jyan31@hawk.iit.edu

Dong Jin
Illinois Institute of Technology
10 West 31st Street
Chicago, IL, United States
dong.jin@iit.edu

ABSTRACT

Realistic and scalable testing systems are critical to evaluate network applications and protocols to ensure successful real system deployments. Container-based network emulation is attractive because of the combination of many desired features of network simulators and physical testbeds . The success of Mininet, a popular software- defined networking (SDN) emulation testbed, demonstrates the value of such approach that we can execute unmodified binary code on a large- scale emulated network with lightweight OS-level virtualization techniques. However, an ordinary network emulator uses the system clock across all the containers even if a container is not being scheduled to run. This leads to the issue of temporal fidelity, especially with high workloads. Virtual time sheds the light on the issue of preserving temporal fidelity for large-scale emulation. The key insight is to trade time with system resources via precisely scaling the time of interactions between containers and physical devices by a factor of n, hence, making an emulated network appear to be n times faster from the viewpoints of applications in the container. In this paper, we develop a lightweight Linux-container-based virtual time system and integrate the system to Mininet for fidelity and scalability enhancement. We also design an adaptive time dilation scheduling module for balancing speed and accuracy. Experimental results demonstrate that (1) with virtual time, Mininet is able to accurately emulate a network n times larger in scale, where n is the scaling factor, with the system behaviors closely match data obtained from a physical testbed; and (2) with the adaptive time dilation scheduling, we reduce the running time by 46% with little accuracy loss. Finally, we present a case study using the virtual-time-enabled Mininet to evaluate the limitations of equal-cost multi-path (ECMP) routing in a data center network.

Categories and Subject Descriptors

C.2.4 [**Computer-Communication Networks**]: Distributed Systems—*Distributed Applications*; C.2.1 [**Computer Sys-**

tems **Organization**]: Computer - Communication Networks—*Network Communications*; I.6.3 [**Simulation and Modeling**]: Application—*Miscellaneous*; D.4.8 [**Operating Systems**]: Performance—*Measurement, Simulation*

General Terms

Emulation

Keywords

Virtual Time; Network Emulation; Software-defined Networking; Mininet; Time Dilation; Linux Container

1. INTRODUCTION

Researchers conducting analysis of networked computer systems are often concerned with questions of scale. What is the impact of a system if the communication delay is X times longer, the bandwidth is Y times larger, or the processing speed is Z times faster? Various testbeds have been created to explore answers to those questions before the actual deployment. Ideally, testing on an exact copy of the original system preserves the highest fidelity, but is often technically challenging and economically infeasible, especially for large-scale systems. Simulation-based testbeds can significantly improve the scalability and reduce the cost by modeling the real systems. However, the fidelity of modeled systems is always in question due to model abstraction and simplification. For example, large ISPs today prefer to evaluate the influence of planned changes of their internal networks through tests driven by realistic traffic traces rather than complex simulations. Network emulation is extremely useful for such scenarios, by allowing unmodified network applications being executed inside virtual machines (VMs) over controlled networking environments. This way, scalability and fidelity is well balanced as compared with physical or simulation testbeds.

A handful of network emulators have been created based on various types of virtualization technologies. Examples include DieCast [24], TimeJails [23], VENICE [34] and dONE [18], which are built using full or para-virtualization (such as Xen [14]), as well as Mininet [26,33], CORE [15] and vEmulab [28]. using OS-level virtualization (such as OpenVZ [10], Linux container [4] and FreeBSD jails [2]). All those network emulators offer functional fidelity through the direct execution of unmodified code. Xen enables virtualization of different operating systems, whereas lightweight Linux container enables virtualization at the application level with two orders of magnitude more of VM (or container) instances,

SIGSIM-PADS'15, June 10–12, 2015, London, United Kingdom.
ⓒ 2015 ACM ISBN 978-1-4503-3583-6/15/06$15.00.
DOI: http://dx.doi.org/10.1145/2769458.2769480.

i.e., emulated nodes, on a single physical host. In this work, we focus on improving the Linux container technology for scalable network emulation, in particular with the application of software-defined networks (SDN). Mininet [33] is by far the most popular network emulator used by the SDN community [20,31,37]. The linux-container-based design enables Mininet users to experiment "a network in a laptop" with thousands of emulated nodes. However, Mininet cannot guarantee fidelity at high loads, in particular when the number of concurrent active events is more than the number of parallel cores. For example, on a commodity machine with 2.98 GHz CPU and 4 GB RAM providing 3 Gb/s internal bandwidth, Mininet is only capable to emulate a network up to 30 hosts, each with a 100 MHz CPU and 100 MB RAM and connected by 100 Mb/s links [26]. Emulators cannot reproduce correct behaviors of a real network with large topology and high traffic load because of the limited physical resources. In fact, the same issue occurs in many other VM-based network emulators, because a host *serializes* the execution of multiple VMs, rather than in parallel like a physical testbed. VMs take its notion of time from the host system's clock, and hence time-stamped events generated by the VMs are multiplexed to reflect the host's serialization.

Our approach is to develop the notion of virtual time inside containers to improve fidelity and scalability of the container-based network emulation. A key insight is to trade time for system resources by precisely scaling the system's capacity to match behaviors of the target network. The idea of virtual time has been explored in the form of time-dilation-based [25] and VM-scheduling-based [40,41] designs, and has been applied to various virtualization platforms including Xen [24], OpenVZ [41], and Linux Container [32]. In this work, we take a time-dilation-based approach to build a lightweight virtual time system in Linux container, and have integrated the system to Mininet for scalability and fidelity enhancement. The time dilation factor (TDF) is defined as the ratio between the rate at which wall-clock time has passed to the emulated host's perception of time [25]. A TDF of 10 means that for every ten seconds of real time, applications running in a time-dilated emulated host perceive the time advancement as one second. This way, a 100 Mbps link is scaled to a 1 Gbps link from the emulated host's viewpoint.

Our contributions are summarized as follows. First, we have developed an independent and lightweight middleware in the Linux kernel to support virtual time for Linux container. Our system transparently provides the virtual time to processes inside the containers, while returns the ordinary system time to other processes. No change is required in applications, and the integration with network emulators is easy (only slight changes in the initialization routine). Second, to the best of our knowledge, we are the first to apply virtual time in the context of SDN emulation, and have built a prototype system in Mininet. Experimental results indicate that with virtual time, Mininet is capable to precisely emulate much larger networks with high loads, approximately increased by a factor of TDF. Third, we have designed an adaptive time dilation scheme to optimize the performance tradeoff between speed and fidelity. Finally, we have demonstrated the fidelity improvement through a realistic case study about evaluation of the limitations of the equal-cost multi-path (ECMP) routing in data center networks.

The remainder of the paper is structured as follows. Section 2 discusses the related work. Section 3 presents the virtual time system architecture design. Section 4 illustrates the implementation of the system and its integration with Mininet. Section 5 evaluates the virtual-time-enabled Mininet, with a case study of ECMP routing evaluation in Section 6. Section 7 concludes the paper with future works.

2. RELATED WORK

2.1 Virtual Time System

Virtual time has been investigated to improve the scalability and fidelity of virtual-machine-based network emulation. There are two main approaches to develop virtual time systems. The first approach is based on time dilation, a technique to uniformly scale the virtual machine's perception of time by a specified factor. It was first introduced by Gupta et al. [25], and has been adopted to various types of virtualization techniques and integrated with a handful of network emulators. Examples include DieCast [24], SVEET [19], NETbalance [22], TimeJails [23,35] and TimeKeeper [32]. The second approach focuses on synchronized virtual time by modifying the hypervisor scheduling mechanism. Hybrid testing systems that integrate network emulation and simulation have adopted this approach. For example, our previous work [30] integrates an OpenVZ-based virtual time system [41] with a parallel discrete-event network simulator by virtual timer. SliceTime [40] integrates ns-3 [27] with Xen to build a scalable and accurate network testbed.

Our approach is technically closest to TimeKeeper [32] through direct kernel modifications of time-related system calls. The differences are (1) we are the first to apply virtual time in the context of SDN emulation, (2) our system has a wider coverage of system calls interacting in virtual time, and (3) our system has an adaptive time dilation scheduler to balance speed and fidelity for emulation experiments.

2.2 Adaptive Virtual Time Scheduling

The key insight of virtual time is to trade time with system resources. Therefore, a primary drawback is the proportionally increased execution time. To determine an appropriate TDF, VENICE [34] proposes a static management scheme to forecast the recourse demand. One problem of static time dilation management is that we often assume the maximum load to ensure fidelity and thus overestimate the scaling factor.

TimeJails [23] presents a dynamic management scheme [21] to adjust TDF in run-time based on CPU utilization. We take a similar approach with two differences: the target platform and communication overhead. TimeJails is a Xen-based platform extended to a 64-node cluster for scalability, while our system supports more scalable experiments on a single machine with Linux container. TimeJails requires a special protocol to prioritizing TDF request message in local area networks, while the communication overhead of our system is much lower, either through synchronized queues or method invocations among extended modules in the emulator.

2.3 SDN Emulation and Simulation

OpenFlow [36] is the first standard communications interface defined between the control and forwarding planes of an SDN architecture. Examples of OpenFlow-based SDN emulation testbeds include Mininet [33], Mininet-HiFi [26], EstiNet [39], ns-3 [27] and S3FNet [29]. Mininet is currently the most popular SDN emulator, which uses process-based virtualization technique to provide a lightweight and inexpensive testbed. Ns-3 [27] has an OpenFlow simulation model and also offers a realistic OpenFlow environment through its generic emulation capability, which has been linked with Mininet [3]. S3FNet [29] supports scalable simulation/emulation of OpenFlow-based SDN through a hybrid platform that integrates a parallel network simulator and a virtual-time-enabled OpenVZ-based network emulator [13].

3. SYSTEM ARCHITECTURE DESIGN

3.1 System Overview

Figure 1 depicts the architecture of our virtual time system within a Linux-container-based network emulator. Linux container [4] is a lightweight virtualization technique that enables multiple instances of Linux OS sharing the kernel. Linux container has less overhead than full or para-virtualization platforms, such as Xen, QEMU, or VMware, in which separated kernels are required for each VM, and therefore, has been applied in the area of scalable network emulation. For example, Mininet [5] is a Linux-container-based emulation platform supporting SDN research.

Mininet creates containers to virtualize network hosts, and each container has its own private network namespace and interface. Applications (such as web services) are encapsulated in the containers. The containers are connected by software switches (typically kernel-model Open vSwitch [9]) with virtual interfaces and links as shown in Figure 1, and are multiplexed onto the physical machine. Like many other network emulators, Mininet is also vulnerable to the temporal fidelity issue in large-scale network experiments. Containers use the same system clock of the physical machine, but the execution of the containers is scheduled by the OS in serial. This leads to incorrect perception of time in a container, because the container's clock keeps advancing even if it is not running (e.g., idle, waiting, suspended). Such errors are particularly severe when emulating high workload network experiments.

To improve the temporal fidelity, we build a virtual time system as a lightweight middleware in the Linux kernel (see Figure 1). We employ the time dilation technique to provide the illusion that a container has as much processing power, disk I/O, and network bandwidth as a real physical host in a production network despite the fact that it shares the underlying resources with other containers. The basic idea is to make time appear to be slower than the wall-clock time, so that the emulated network appears faster.

A capable virtual time system for scalable network emulation needs to have the following requirements: (1) lightweight design with low system overhead, (2) transparent virtual time provision to applications in containers, i.e., no code required modification, (3) universal virtual time support within the emulator and invisible to other processes on the same machine, and (4) ease of integration to the emulator. Accurate and positive emulation results can improve the confidence that any changes (e.g., a transformation from a traditional network to an SDN-based architecture) to the target production network will be successfully deployed.

3.2 Virtual Time Management

Our virtual time system, as shown in Figure 1, is designed to meet all the requirements. The time dilation manager is responsible for computing and maintaining the virtual time, according to a given TDF for all the containers. It can offer per-container virtual time or the global virtual time for the emulator. The per-container virtual time is useful to support synchronized emulation (in virtual time) and facilitates the integration with network simulators. We have made a small set of changes in the kernel, in particular, a modified data structure to present virtual time, and a new algorithm to convert the elapsed wall-clock time to the dilated virtual time, with no dependency on third-party libraries.

We attach each container an integer-valued TDF, which could also be shared among all containers. A TDF of k slows down a container's time advancement rate by a factor of k, thus re-scales a container's notion of time with reference to a physical network. This way, Mininet can emulate a seemingly k times faster network owing to the accelerated rate of interaction between the containers and the virtual network Note that our design cannot scale the capacity of hardware components such as main memory, processor caches, and disk, firmware on network interfaces.

The integration with Mininet, and potentially other container-based software is straightforward. We provide a set of simple APIs to (1) initialize containers with virtual time, and (2) inquire virtual time at run time. The system returns precise virtual time to container processes and transparently to all their child processes while returning the ordinary system time to other processes. We have integrated the system with Mininet. The implementation details are discussed in Section 4, and we plan to make our code base available to public on GitHub soon.

3.3 Adaptive Time Dilation

The key insight of virtual time is to trade time with available system resources. The execution time can be unnecessarily long with an overestimated TDF. It is difficult to avoid that with a fixed TDF when the resource demands vary substantially during the emulation. Therefore, we investigate means to adaptively adjust TDF in run-time with the goal of well balancing the execution speed and accuracy. We take a similar epoch-based approach described in [21], and develop two modules, Emulation Monitor and Time Dilation Adaptor (see Figure 1), to achieve the dynamic TDF adjustment.

Emulation Monitor periodically collects the process-related information (not necessarily coincides with the epoch duration) and computes the run-time emulation load statistics, such as CPU utilization, number of waiting processes, or average process waiting time. Time Dilation Adaptor takes the inputs from Emulation Monitor, and adaptively computes the TDF for the next epoch based on a heuristic algorithm, whose details are presented in Section 4. Currently we only use the CPU utilization as the feedback control indicator, and will leave the exploration of other control algorithms as future works.

4. IMPLEMENTATION

The implementation of the virtual time system and its integration with Mininet-Hifi (the latest version of Mininet) is composed of three parts. First, we built a lightweight and

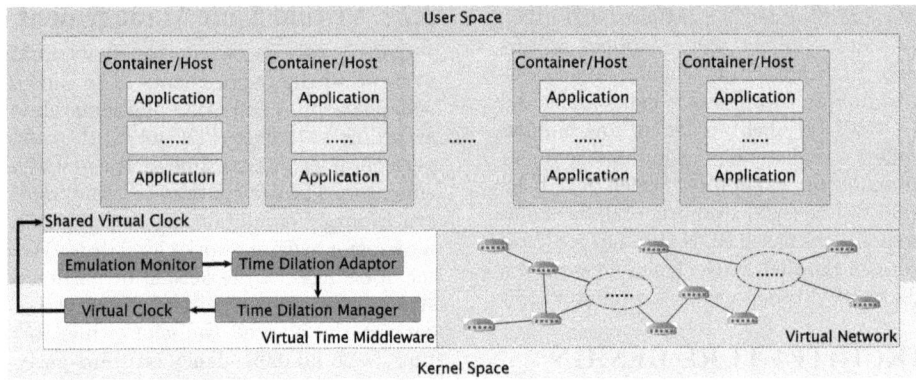

Figure 1: **Architecture of the Virtual Time System in a Container-based Network Emulator. Note that a typical container-based network emulator can be presented by this figure without the Virtual Time Middleware.**

independent middleware in the Linux kernel to provide virtual time support to user-space software. Second, we slightly modified the initialization procedure of Mininet with two additional python modules to realize (adaptive) virtual time in Mininet. Third, we discuss our design to enable transparent support of virtual time for applications running in the containers.

4.1 Linux Kernel Modifications

Our implementation is based on a recent Linux kernel 3.16.3 with no third-part library dependency.

4.1.1 Timing-related Kernel Modifications

To make a process have its own perception of time, we added the following four new fields in the `task_struct` struct type.

- `virtual_start_nsec` represents the starting time that a process detaches from the system clock and uses the virtual time, in nanoseconds

- `physical_past_nsec` represents how much physical time has elapsed since the last time the process requested the current time, in nanoseconds

- `virtual_past_nsec` represents how much virtual time has elapsed since the last time the process requested the current time, in nanoseconds

- `dilation` represents the TDF of a time-dilated process

Algorithm 1 gives the details about how we implement the time dilation. To preserve an accurate virtual clock in the kernel, we added a private function `do_dilatetimeofday` in the Linux's timekeeping subsystem to keep tracking the dilated virtual time based on the physical time passed and TDF. Based on process's `virtual_start_nsec`, the system determines the type of time to return, i.e., the physical system clock time or the virtual time.

`virtual_start_nsec` in `INIT_VIRTUAL_TIME` should first be initialized to zero so that the next gettimeofday always returns the undilated time to compute and record the exact physical time that a process starts to use virtual time. To return the accurate virtual time upon requests, the duration since the last call to `do_dilatetimeofday` is calculated and precisely scaled with TDF. To enable virtual time support for a wide range of timing-related system calls, we extensively traced the routines in Linux's subsystems that request

timing information (such as `getnstimeofday`, `ktime_get`, `ktime_get_ts`, etc.), and modified them to properly invoke `do_dilatetimeofday`.

4.1.2 Process-related Kernel Modifications

To enable the virtual time perception to processes running in a network emulator, we added the following new system calls.

- `virtualtimeunshare` is essentially the `unshare` system call with time dilation inputs. It is used by container-based emulators, such as Mininet, to create emulated nodes. `virtualtimeunshare` creates a new process with a TDF in a different namespace of its parent process according to `flags`.

- `settimedilaitonfactor` offers an interface to change the TDF of a process. Note that a command executed in an emulated host is equivalent to a shell command executed by `bash`. Therefore, adjusting a process' TDF requires the change of the calling process' parent (e.g., host's `bash`), which occasionally would lead to tracing back to the root of the process tree, especially in the case of dynamic TDF adjustment.

We also modified the `do_fork` system call to initialize the virtual-time-related attributes of a process, such as using the variable `stack_size` to pass the TDF value. Functions in `timekeeping.c` were modified to invoke `do_dilatetimeofday` in order to return the virtual time to system calls like `gettimeofday` and other kernel routines that request timing information.

4.1.3 Networking-related Kernel Modifications

In this work, we focus on capturing all the related system calls and kernel routings to support virtual time in Linux container with the application of Mininet. One particular case related to Mininet is the usage of `tc`, a network quality-of-service control module in Linux [17]. For instance, we can use `tc` to rate-limit a link to 100 Mbps using Hierarchic Token Bucket (HTB) `qdisc` in Mininet. If the TDF is set to 8, the link bandwidth would be approximately 800 Mbps from the emulated hosts' viewpoints as we observed from the time-dilated `iperf3` application.

As a network module in Linux, `tc` does not reference Linux kernel's time as the way user application does. Therefore, `tc` is transparent to our virtual time system. One way to solve

238

Algorithm 1 Time Dilation Algorithm

```
 1: function INIT_VIRTUAL_TIME(struct task_struct *tk, int dilation)
 2:     if dilation>0 then
 3:         tk→dilation=dilation
 4:         tk→virtual_start_nsec=0
 5:         struct timespec ts
 6:         getnstimeofday(&ts)
 7:         tk→virtual_start_nsec=timespec_to_ns(&ts)
 8:         tk→physical_past_nsec=0
 9:         tk→virtual_past_nsec=0
10:     end if
11: end function
12:
13: function DO_DILATETIMEOFDAY(struct timespec *ts)
14:     Let p denote the current process using virtual time
15:     if p→virtual_start_nsec > 0 and p→dilation > 0 then
16:         now = timespec_to_ns(ts)
17:         physical_past_nsec = now - p→virtual_start_nsec
18:         virtual_past_nsec = (physical_past_nsec - p→physical_past_nsec) / p→dilation +
    p→virtual_past_nsec          /* virtual time computation */
19:         dilated_now = virtual_past_nsec + p→virtual_start_nsec
20:         dilated_ts = ns_to_timespec(dilated_now)
21:         ts→tv_sec = dilated_ts.tv_sec
22:         ts→tv_nsec = dilated_ts.tv_nsec
23:         p→physical_past_nsec = physical_past_nsec     /* update process's physical time */
24:         p→virtual_past_nsec = virtual_past_nsec     /* update process's virtual time */
25:     end if
26: end function
```

this problem is to modify the network scheduling code in kernel to provide tc with a dilated traffic rate. In the earlier example with TDF set to 8, the experiment will run 8 times slower than the real time, and we can configure tc's rate limit as $rate/TDF = 12.5$ Mbps to emulate a 100 Mbps link. Note that we only tailored HTB in tc, which is the default qdisc used by Mininet. We will generalize the mechanism to other qdiscs including HFSC (Hierarchical Fair Service Curve) and TBF (Token Bucket Filter) in the future.

4.2 Network Emulator Modifications

4.2.1 Virtual-Time-Enabled Container

Containers allow groups of process running on the same kernel to have independent views of system resources, such as process IDs, file systems and network interfaces. We add the virtual time property to a container's namespace [7] so that every container can have its own virtual clock. We design our system in the way that minimal modifications of Mininet are needed for integration, so that the virtual time system can be easily extended to other Linux-container-based applications.

We modified the initialization procedure of Mininet, in particular, the mnexec program in Mininet, to process two additional parameters. When we create Nodes in Mininet (hosts, switches, and controllers are all inherited from Node), users can feed in a TDF argument with virtualtimeunshare (as a replacement of unshare) with -n option. This way, a system-wide TDF can be conveniently set for all the emulated hosts. We also provide the ability to dynamically adjust the TDF for every emulated host during runtime. To do that, we added a new option -t in mnexec to invoke the aforementioned system call settimedilaitonfactor to do

the actual TDF adjustment. The two modifications enable the integration of virtual time in Mininet, and also serve as the basis of the adaptive TDF management.

4.2.2 Adaptive TDF Scheduling

To optimize the performance of the virtual-time-enabled Mininet, we developed an adaptive TDF scheduler through two python modules MininetMonitor and DilationAdaptor (refer to Emulation Monitor and Time Dilation Adaptor in Figure 1) to accelerate the experiment speed while preserving high fidelity.

MininetMonitor is responsible to monitor the CPU usage of the entire emulation system, consisting of a group of processes including the Mininet emulator, the Open vSwitch module, and emulated nodes (e.g., SDN controllers, hosts and switches). Also, applications are dynamically created, executed and destroyed within containers, in the form of child processes of their parent containers. MininetMonitor utilizes the ps command to collect the group's aggregate CPU percentage and periodically computes and passes the average CPU load statistics to DilationAdaptor. The core of DilationAdaptor is an adaptive algorithm to calculate an appropriate *TDF*. Global *TDF* updating was achieved by invoking the mnexec -t tdf program for every running host.

Our adaptive virtual time scheduling design is similar to the one used in [21] in spirit with two major differences. First, both techniques target on different platforms. Our technique is applied to Linux-container-based network emulation to support scalable SDN experiments, and theirs uses virtual routing and executes OpenVZ instances inside Xen. Second, their solution needs be deployed on a cluster to emulate a medium-scale network, which results in much higher communication overhead in two types: (1) every VM's monitor needs to report the CPU usage, and (2) the adaptor needs to send new TDF to every VM. Therefore, the message transmission delay in LAN and the processing delay in protocol stacks contributes to the overall communication delay. In contrast, `MininetMonitor` runs as a lightweight background thread in Mininet, and `DilationAdaptor` is simply a python object that Mininet has a reference to. The communication in our system is through synchronized queues and method invocations, which is much faster.

4.3 Virtual Time Support for Applications in Containers

Network applications running inside containers (e.g., `iperf3` [1] or `ping`) should also use virtual time. We do not need to modify the application code because they are running as child processes of Mininet's hosts. A child process always copies its parent's `task_struct` when it is forked including the same `dilation` and `virtual_start_nsec` values. Although `virtual_start_nsec` does not present the virtual starting time of the child process, our algorithm is designed to work with relative values. When applications inquire about the system time, the modified kernel knows that they are using virtual clock and return the virtual clock time instead of the system clock time.

One issue we notice is that the 64-bit Linux kernel running on Intel-based architectures provides the Virtual Dynamic Shared Object (vDSO) and the `vsyscall` mechanism to reduce the overhead of context switches caused by the frequently invoked system calls, for example, `gettimeofday` and `time` [8]. Therefore, applications may bypass our virtual-time-based system calls unless we explicitly use the `syscall` function. Our solution is to disable vDSO with respect to `__vdso_gettimeofday` in order to transparently offer virtual time to applications in the containers.

5. EVALUATION

All the experiments are conducted on a Dell XPS 8700 Desktop with one Intel Core i7-4790 CPU, 12 GB RAM and one gigabit Ethernet interface. The machine runs a 64-bit Ubuntu 14.04.1 LTS with our customized 3.16.3 Linux kernel. The benchmark scores of this machine's CPU and FPU are: 1.52 seconds for Blowfish, 1045.62 MiB/seconds for CryptoHash, 0.63 seconds for FFT and 2.56 seconds for Raytracing. Our virtual-time-enabled Mininet was built on the latest version of Mininet (2.1.0), also named Mininet-Hifi, at the time of development.

Fidelity. We first evaluate how our virtual time system improves Mininet's fidelity through a basic network scenario: a single TCP flow transmission through a chain of switches in an emulated SDN network. As shown in Figure 2a, the network topology consists of a client-server pair connected by a chain of Open vSwitch switches in Mininet. We setup the default OpenFlow controller to function as a learning switch. In this set of experiments, we connected two hosts through 40 switches in Mininet, and all the links are configured with 10 μs delay. We used `iperf3` [1] to generate a TCP flow between the client and the server. TDF was set to 1 (i.e., no virtual time) and 4 for comparison. We also setup a real testbed for "ground truth" throughput data collection. The testbed was composed of two machines connected by a 10 Gbps Ethernet link. We varied the bandwidth link from 100 Mbps to 10 Gbps and measured the throughput using `iperf3`. In the real testbed, we manually configured the link bandwidth and delay using `tc`, and the delay was set as the corresponding round trip times (RTTs) measured in the switch chain topology in Mininet, so that the networking settings were tightly coupled for comparison. Although we did not setup an exact network with SDN switches, the stabilized TCP throughputs generated by the physical testbed should reflect what occurs in a real SDN network. Each experiment was repeated 10 times and the results with bandwidth 4 Gbps, 8 Gbps and 10 Gbps were reported in Figure 3a.

We observe that when the bandwidth was no greater than 4 Gbps (we only displayed the 4 Gbps case in the figure), Mininet was able to accurately emulate the TCP flow with and without virtual time, as the average throughputs were very close to the ones collected from the physical testbed. However, when we continued to increase the bandwidth, Mininet was not able to produce the desired throughputs, e.g., 28% (8 Gbps) and 39% (10 Gbps) smaller than the physical testbed throughputs. With virtual time (TDF = 4), Mininet was capable to accurately emulate the TCP flow even at high bandwidth, and the results were nearly the same as the ones measured in the physical testbed.

The root cause is that the machine running Mininet does not have sufficient resources to emulate networks with bandwidth greater than 4 Gbps, which would lead to fidelity issues, e.g., low expected throughputs. Note that we only emulated a single flow, and the results could be much worse and unpredictable in complicated multi-flow scenarios. Results show that virtual time can significantly enhance the performance fidelity by "slowing down" the experiments so that the system has sufficient resources and time to correctly process the packets. We further illustrate the effect by plotting the time series of throughput changes for the 10 Gbps cases in Figure 3b. With virtual time, the throughputs measured in Mininet closely match the real testbed results; without virtual time (TDF = 1), the ramp up speed was much slower, in particular, 22 seconds (TDF = 1) rather than 4 seconds (TDF = 4), and the throughput was incorrectly stabilized below 6.1 Gbps.

Scalability. Virtual time also improves the scale of networks that one can emulate without losing fidelity. In this set of experiments, we used the same switch chain topology in Figure 2a, and set the link bandwidth to 4 Gbps. We want to investigate, with virtual time, how many switches Mininet is capable to emulate without losing fidelity, i.e., preserving nearly 4 Gbps throughput. This time we increased the number of switches with the following values {20, 40, 60, 80, 100}, and TDF was selected to be 1 (no virtual time) and 4. We ran `iperf3` for 25 seconds between the client and the server. Each experiment was repeated ten times, and the throughput measurement is reported in Figure 4a.

In the case of TDF = 1, the average throughput kept decreasing as the number of switches grew over 20. The throughput decreased dramatically when the number of switches was greater than 60 (e.g., decreased by 41% for 60 switches, 65% for 80 switches, and 83% for 100 switches). The standard deviation, indicated the undesired high disturbance, also grew as number of switches increased. When virtual time was applied with TDF = 4, the throughput was always around 3.8 Gbps with small standard derivations in all the experiments. It is clear that virtual time helps to

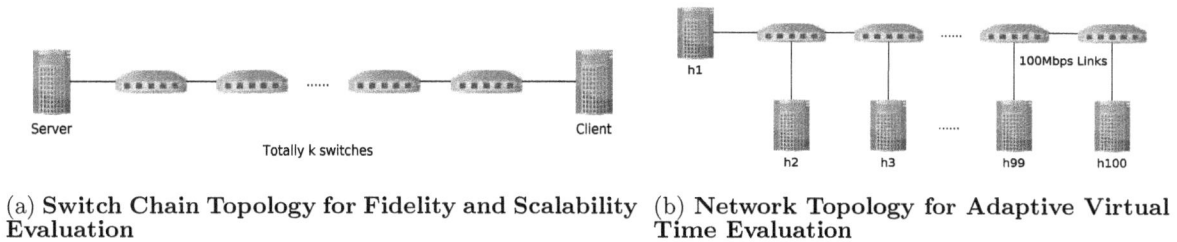

(a) Switch Chain Topology for Fidelity and Scalability Evaluation

(b) Network Topology for Adaptive Virtual Time Evaluation

Figure 2: **Network Topologies**

scale up the emulation. In this case, Mininet can emulate 100 switches with 4 Gbps links and still generate the accurate throughputs, rather than being saturated at 20 switches without virtual time.

We also recorded the running time in Figure 4b. Longer execution time is the tradeoff for the fidelity and scalability improvement. When $TDF = 4$, the execution time was about 4 times longer than the time required in the case of $TDF = 1$ in all the experiments. In fact, we have conducted extensive experiments with different TDF values on multiple network scenarios. The general observation is that a larger TDF allows an emulator to conduct accurate experiments with larger scale on the same physical machine, but typically requires longer execution time, approximately proportional to the TDF. This leads to the question on how to balance the speed and fidelity, and our approach is to explore the adaptive time dilation scheduling, whose evaluation is presented in the next section.

Adaptive TDF Scheduling. We design a set of emulation experiments consisting of multiple TCP flows to evaluate the adaptive TDF scheduling algorithm. The network topology has a simple linear structure as shown in Figure 2b and consists of 100 hosts and 99 switches. All the links are of 100 Mbps bandwidth and 1 ms delay. We selected 5 non-overlap client-server pairs: (h1, h20), (h21, h40), h(41, h60), h(61, h80), (h81, h100). The entire experiment was divided into three phases: (1) initially, transmit flow (h1,h20), (2) after 50 seconds, transmit all five flows, and (3) after 150 seconds, stop all the transmissions except for flow (h1,h20). The goal is to evaluate how our adaptive time dilation scheduler behaves under dynamic emulation workloads with the peak load exceeding Mininet's capability.

We ran the experiments in three cases. In case 1, TDF was set to 1 (i.e., no virtual time) and the adaptive virtual time scheduling was disabled. All flows' TCP throughputs measured by iperf3 over time are plotted in Figure 5a. In case 2, we enabled the adaptive time dilation management system with TDF initially set to 1, and conducted the same emulation experiments. Figure 5b plots the throughputs of all five flows. In case 3, we used a fixed TDF ($TDF = 11$) and disabled the adaptive virtual time scheduling. Results are shown in Figure 5c. We set $TDF = 11$ because 11 was the largest value observed in the TDF changing history in case 2. In addition, the entire trace of the dynamic TDF in case 2 is plotted in Figure 5d. We repeated each experiment for 5 times and observed very similar behaviors. All the time series reported in Figure 5 were based on the data collected from one run.

In phase 1, Mininet had sufficient system resources to emulate a single TCP flow (h1, h21). Therefore, we observe the close-to-line-rate throughput, i.e., 100 Mbps, in all three cases. In phase 2, there were five concurrent flows in the network and each case demonstrated different behaviors. Note that those flows were non-overlap flows because they did not share any links or switches. Therefore, all five flows should achieve close-to-line-rate throughputs, i.e., 100 Mbps, in physical world applications. In case 1, the throughputs of all five flows were very unstable as shown in Figure 5a, which reflected the heavy resource contention in Mininet. In contrast, in case 3, all five flows have stable, close-to-100-Mbps throughputs because of the virtual time. In case 2, we observed disturbances in throughput at the beginning of phase 2, but the five flows quickly converged to the stable close-to-line-rate throughput because the adaptive TDF scheduler managed to compute the optimal TDF value. The details of TDF adjustment are depicted in Figure 5d. In phase 3, the emulation returned back to a single flow (h1, h21), and the measured throughputs were accurate in all three cases. As indicated by Figure 5d, our scheduler decreased the TDF value accordingly in case 2 to save emulation time in phase 3 while still preserving the fidelity.

Table 1 summarizes the execution time, the average TDF, and the rate of execution time in wall clock to the emulation time (200 seconds) of all three cases. We can see that case 3 ($TDF = 11$) is around 10 times slower than case 1 ($TDF = 1$) in order to guarantee fidelity. Our adaptive time dilation scheduler managed to reduce 46% of the running time as compared to case 3 with little fidelity loss.

System Overhead. Our virtual time system introduces overhead with the following two reasons: (1) the computation cost in Algorithm 1 and (2) the pauses of emulation when changing containers' TDFs. We measured both types of overhead and report the results in Table 2.

First, we invoked both non-dilated and dilated gettimeofday 10,000,000 times from a user space application. The average overhead for one dilated gettimeofday is 0.013 microseconds. We then used strace to count the number of invocations for gettimeofday in a 60-second iperf3 run on both the server and the client. The total overhead is 18,145 microseconds after tracing 1,397,829 calls, which is about 0.03% of the 60-second experiment. Actually, iperf3 intensively invokes gettimeofday, because its timer is designed to exhaustively inquiry the OS time. The overhead amount will be even less for many other network applications. We also repeatedly changed a process's TDF 10,000,000 times using another test program. The average pause time was 0.063 microseconds, which is reasonably small. Since the number of TDF changes issued by the current adaptive TDF scheduling algorithm is a few orders of magnitude less than the number of calls to gettimeofday (e.g., only 14 TDF transitions occurred per host over the period of 1,332 seconds

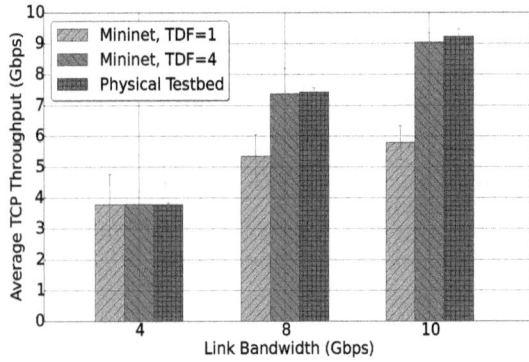

(a) TCP Throughput with Different Link Bandwidth

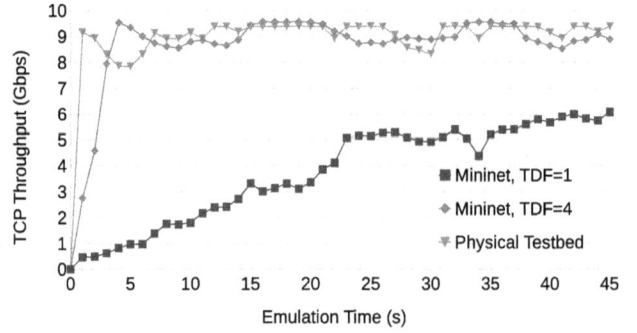

(b) TCP Throughput with 10 Gbps Links

Figure 3: Fidelity Evaluation Experimental Results

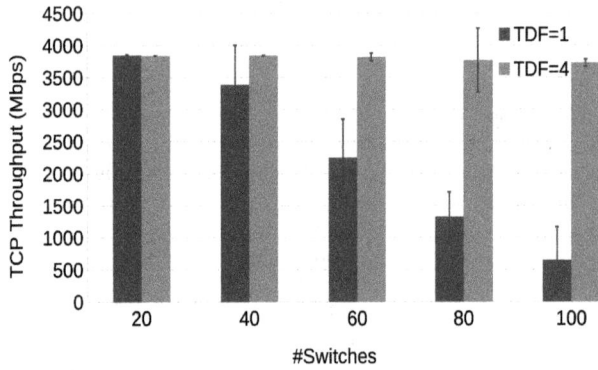

(a) TCP Throughput

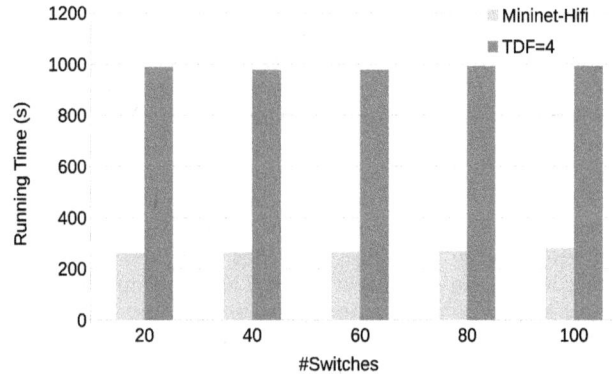

(b) Emulation Running Time

Figure 4: Scalability Evaluation Experimental Results

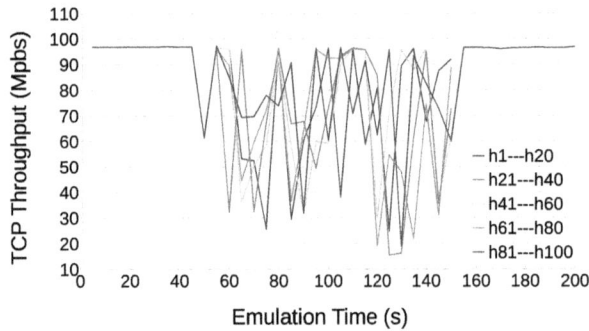

(a) TCP Throughput without Virtual Time

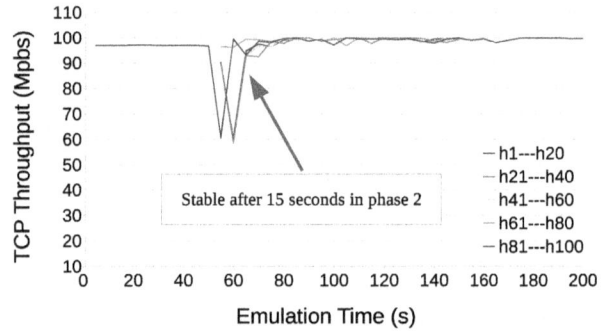

(b) TCP Throughput with Adaptive Time Dilation

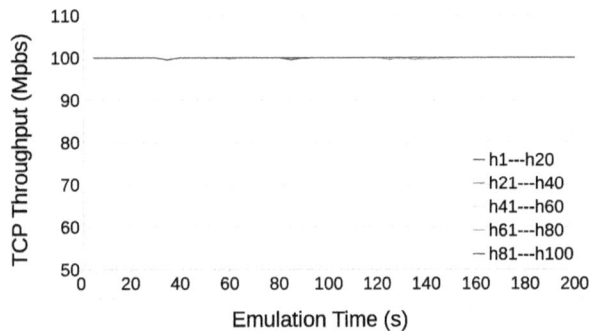

(c) TCP Throughput with Fixed Time Dilation (11)

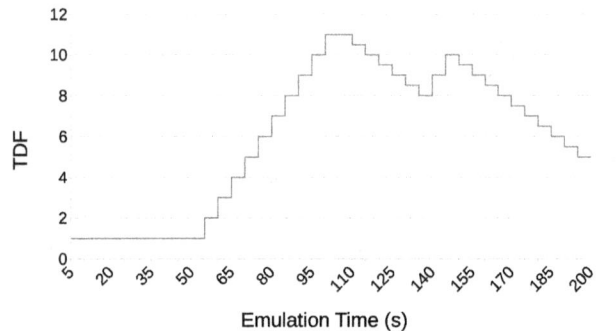

(d) TDF Trace: Adaptive Virtual Time Scheduling

Figure 5: Experimental Results: Adaptive Virtual Time Scheduling Evaluation

in the earlier adaptive TDF experiment), that overhead is negligible.

6. CASE STUDY: EVALUATION OF ECMP IN DATA CENTER NETWORKS

Network emulation testbeds are widely used to test and evaluate designs of network applications and protocols with the goal of discovering design limitations and implementation faults before the real system deployment. In this section, we present a case study to demonstrate how our virtual-time-enabled Mininet has been utilized to reproduce and validate the limitations of the equal-cost multi-path (ECMP) routing strategy in a data center network.

Many modern data center networks employ multi-rooted hierarchical tree topologies, and therefore ECMP-based protocols [6] are commonly used in data center networks for load-balancing traffic over multiple paths. When an ECMP-enabled switch has multiple next-hops on the best paths to a single destination, it selects the forwarding path by performing a modulo-N hash over the selected fields of a packet's header to ensure per-flow consistency. The key limitation of ECMP is that the communication bottleneck would occur when several large and long-lived flows collide on their hash and being forwarded to the same output port [16]. We borrowed the experiment scenario on a physical testbed described in [16], and created a set of emulation experiments in Mininet to demonstrate the limitation of ECMP. We built a fat-tree topology in Mininet as shown in Figure 6, and generated stride-style traffic patterns. Note that stride(i) means that a host with index x sends to the host with index $(x + i)$ mod n, where n is the number of hosts [16]. The hash-based ECMP mechanism is provided by the RipL-POX SDN controller [12]. The Mininet code was developed with reference to [11]. In all the following experiments, we set up 8 sender-receiver pairs transmitting stride-pattern traffic flows using step 1 and 4.

We first set all the link bandwidth (switch-to-switch and switch-to-host) to 100 Mbps, and conducted each experiment over three independent runs. The average throughput of 8 TCP flows was plotted in Figure 7a, and each individual flow's throughput (24 in total) was plotted in Figure 7b. The limitation of ECMP presented in [16] was clearly observed. When many conflicting flows occurred with stride-4 flow patterns, the average throughput in the fat-tree network dramatically fell below 30 Mbps with up to 75% throughput drop. As shown in Figure 7b, every flow's throughput was largely affected by the hash collision limitation of ECMP in the stride-4 scenario.

However, the link bandwidth configuration in the previous experiments are not realistic. As early as in 2009, links connecting edge hosts to top of rack switches (ToR), ToR to edge of rank switches (EoR), and EoR to Core switches in a data center had been already above gigabit, in particular, 10 Gbps switch-to-switch links and 1 Gbps host-to-switch links [38]. Can Mininet still show us the limitation of ECMP with such high link bandwidth? If not, can virtual time help to overcome the issue? Using the same configurations except that links were set to 10 Gbps, we re-ran the experiments in Mininet without virtual time ($TDF = 1$) and with virtual time ($TDF = 4$). We plotted the average flow throughput in Figure 8a and individual flow throughput in Figure 8b.

In the case of stride-1, there were very few collisions among flows. Hence, the network performance ought to be close to the ideal throughput, i.e., 160 Gbps bisection bandwidth and 10 Gbps average bandwidth between each pair. In the experiments that $TDF = 4$, the average throughput is above 9.0 Gbps, which is close to the theoretical value, and also match well with the results obtained from the physical testbed built upon 37 machines [16]. In the experiments that $TDF = 1$, however, the throughput barely reaches 3.8 Gbps because of the limited system resources that Mininet can utilize. In addition, as shown in Figure 8b, we observe that the variation of throughput is large among flows when $TDF = 1$. This is incorrect because no flow shares the same link in the case of stride-1. In contrast, when $TDF = 4$, the throughput of all 8 flows are close with little variation, which implies the desired networking behaviors.

In the case of stride-4, flows may collide both on the upstream and the downstream paths, thus using ECMP could undergo a significant throughput drop, e.g., up to 61% as experimentally evaluated in [16]. The virtual-time-enabled Mininet ($TDF = 4$) has successfully captured such throughput drop phenomenon. We can see that average throughput dropped about 80% when RipL-Pox controller used ECMP to handle multi-path flows. Large deviation (more than 55% of average throughput value) also indicates that the flows were not properly scheduled with ECMP. When $TDF = 1$ (no virtual time), Mininet also reported plummeted TCP throughput in the case of stride-4. However, we cannot use the result to experimentally demonstrate the limitation of ECMP. It is hard to distinguish whether the throughput drop was caused by insufficient resources to handle 10 Gbps or the limitation of ECMP, given the fact that the throughput was already too low in the collision-free case. Without a correct baseline (benchmark for the collision-free scenario), it is difficult to perform further analysis and qualify the limitation.

7. CONCLUSION AND FUTURE WORKS

In this paper, we present a Linux-container-based virtual time system and integrated it to a widely used SDN emulator, Mininet. The lightweight system uses a time-dilation-based design to offer virtual time to the containers, as well as the applications running inside the containers with no code modification. Experimental results show the promising fidelity and scalability improvement of Mininet with virtual time, particularly for high workload network scenarios. We have also used the platform to precisely evaluate the limitations of the ECMP routing in a realistic data center network with the results being validated by a physical testbed. Future works include the investigation of other effective control algorithms to further improve the adaptive TDF scheduler, and the integration to network simulators based on virtual time for large-scale network analysis.

8. ACKNOWLEDGMENTS

This material is based upon work supported by the Maryland Procurement Office under Contract No. H98230-14-C-

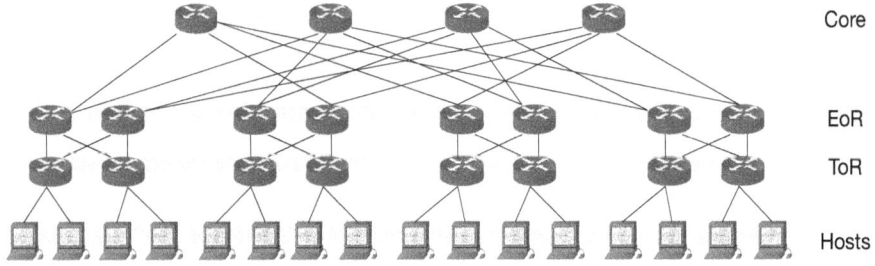

Figure 6: **A Data Center Network with a Degree-4 Fat Tree Topology**

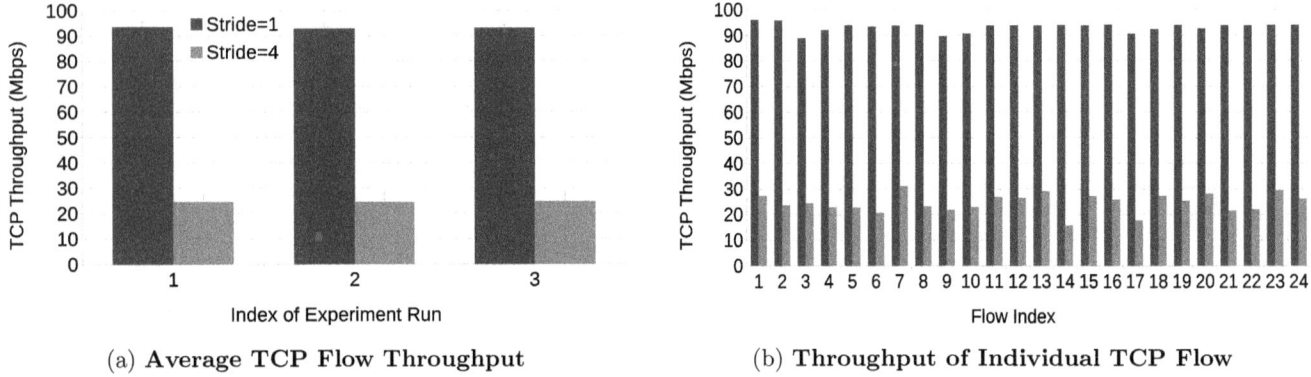

(a) **Average TCP Flow Throughput**

(b) **Throughput of Individual TCP Flow**

Figure 7: **Mininet Emulation Results: ECMP Limitation in a Fat-tree-based Data Center Network with 100 Mbps Link Bandwidth**

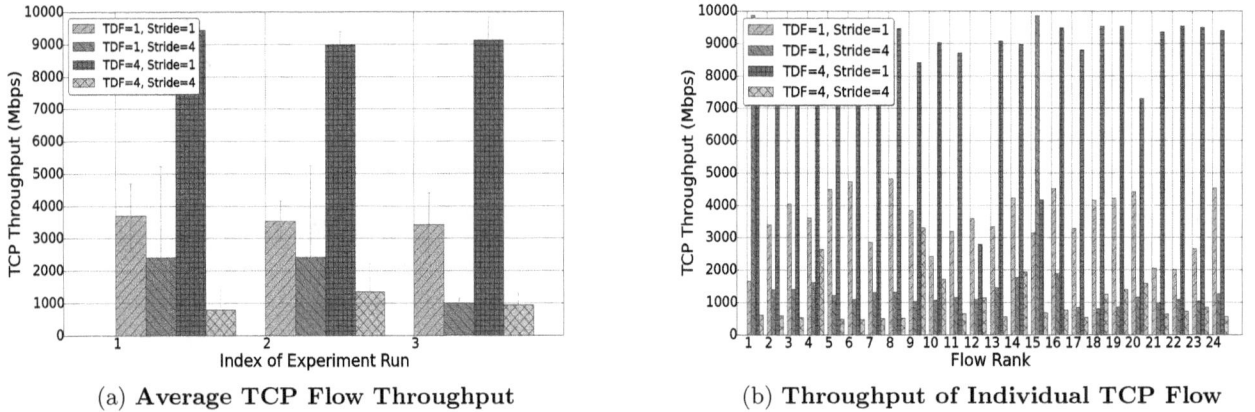

(a) **Average TCP Flow Throughput**

(b) **Throughput of Individual TCP Flow**

Figure 8: **Mininet Emulation Results with Virtual Time: ECMP Limitation in a Fat-tree-based Data Center Network with 10 Gbps Link Bandwidth**

Table 1: **Comparison of Emulation Execution Time**

	No Virtual Time	Adaptive Virtual Time	Fixed Virtual Time
Running Time (s)	240.730	1332.242	2434.910
Average TDF	1.000	5.900	11.000
Slow Down Ratio	1.000	5.534	10.115

Table 2: **Lightweight Virtual Time System: Overhead of System Calls**

	No Virtual Time	Virtual Time	Avg Overhead Per System Call
`gettimeofday`	0.0532 μs	0.0661 μs	0.0129 μs
`settimedilationfactor`	0	0.0628 μs	0.0628 μs

0141.[1] The authors are grateful to Jeremy Lamps for sharing the code base of TimeKeeper.

9. REFERENCES

[1] iperf3. http://software.es.net/iperf. [Last accessed December 2014].

[2] Jails under FreeBSD 6. http://www.freebsddiary.org/jail-6.php. [Last accessed December 2014].

[3] Link modeling using ns 3. https://github.com/mininet/mininet/wiki. [Last accessed April 2015].

[4] Linux containers. https://linuxcontainers.org. [Last accessed December 2014].

[5] Mininet: An instant virtual network on your laptop (or other PC). http://mininet.org/. [Last accessed Noverber, 2014].

[6] Multipath issues in unicast and multicast next-hop selection. https://tools.ietf.org/html/rfc2991. [Last accessed March 2015].

[7] Namespaces in operation, part 1: namespaces overview. http://lwn.net/Articles/531114. [Last accessed December 2014].

[8] On vsyscalls and the vDSO. http://lwn.net/Articles/446528/. [Last accessed March 2015].

[9] Open vSwitch. http://openvswitch.org. [Last accessed Noverber 2014].

[10] OpenVZ linux container. http://openvz.org/Main_Page. [Last accessed October 2014].

[11] Reproducing network research. https://reproducingnetworkresearch.wordpress.com. [Last accessed March 2015].

[12] RipL-POX (Ripcord-Lite for POX): a simple network controller for OpenFlow-based data centers. https://github.com/brandonheller/riplpox. [Last accessed March 2015].

[13] S3F/S3FNet: Simpler scalable simulation framework. University of Illinois at Urbana-Champaign. https://s3f.iti.illinois.edu/. [Last accessed Noverber 2014].

[14] The Xen project. http://www.xenproject.org. [Last accessed Noverber 2014].

[15] J. Ahrenholz, C. Danilov, T. Henderson, and J. Kim. Core: A real-time network emulator. In *Proceedings of the 2008 IEEE Military Communications Conference*, pages 1–7, Washington, DC, USA, Nov 2008. IEEE Computer Society.

[16] M. Al-Fares, S. Radhakrishnan, B. Raghavan, N. Huang, and A. Vahdat. Hedera: Dynamic flow scheduling for data center networks. In *Proceedings of the 7th USENIX Conference on Networked Systems Design and Implementation*, pages 19–33, Berkeley, CA, USA, April 2010. USENIX Association.

[17] W. Almesberger. Linux traffic control: implementation overview. In *Proceedings of 5th Annual Linux Expo*, pages 153–164, April 1999.

[18] C. Bergstrom, S. Varadarajan, and G. Back. The distributed open network emulator: Using relativistic time for distributed scalable simulation. In *Proceedings of the 20th Workshop on Principles of Advanced and Distributed Simulation*, pages 19–28, Washington, DC, USA, May 2006. IEEE Computer Society.

[19] M. Erazo, Y. Li, and J. Liu. Sveet! a scalable virtualized evaluation environment for tcp. In *Proceedings of the 2009 Testbeds and Research Infrastructures for the Development of Networks Communities and Workshops*, pages 1–10, Washington, DC, USA, April 2009. IEEE Computer Society.

[20] N. Foster, R. Harrison, M. J. Freedman, C. Monsanto, J. Rexford, A. Story, and D. Walker. Frenetic: A network programming language. In *Proceedings of the 16th ACM SIGPLAN International Conference on Functional Programming*, pages 279–291, New York, NY, USA, September 2011. ACM.

[21] A. Grau, K. Herrmann, and K. Rothermel. Efficient and scalable network emulation using adaptive virtual time. In *Proceedings of the 18th International Conference on Computer Communications and Networks*, pages 1–6, Washington, DC, USA, August 2009. IEEE Computer Society.

[22] A. Grau, K. Herrmann, and K. Rothermel. Netbalance: Reducing the runtime of network emulation using live migration. In *Proceedings of the 20th International Conference on Computer Communications and Networks*, pages 1–6, Washington, DC, USA, July 2011. IEEE Computer Society.

[23] A. Grau, S. Maier, K. Herrmann, and K. Rothermel. Time jails: A hybrid approach to scalable network emulation. In *Proceedings of the 22nd Workshop on Principles of Advanced and Distributed Simulation*, pages 7–14, Washington, DC, USA, June 2008. IEEE Computer Society.

[24] D. Gupta, K. V. Vishwanath, M. McNett, A. Vahdat, K. Yocum, A. Snoeren, and G. M. Voelker. Diecast: Testing distributed systems with an accurate scale model. *ACM Transactions on Computer Systems*, 29(2):1–48, may 2011.

[25] D. Gupta, K. Yocum, M. McNett, A. C. Snoeren, A. Vahdat, and G. M. Voelker. To infinity and beyond: Time warped network emulation. In *Proceedings of the 20th ACM Symposium on Operating Systems Principles*, pages 1–2, New York, NY, USA, October 2005. ACM.

[26] N. Handigol, B. Heller, V. Jeyakumar, B. Lantz, and N. McKeown. Reproducible network experiments using container-based emulation. In *Proceedings of the 8th International Conference on Emerging Networking Experiments and Technologies*, pages 253–264, New York, NY, USA, December 2012. ACM.

[27] T. R. Henderson, M. Lacage, G. F. Riley, C. Dowell, and J. Kopena. Network simulations with the ns-3 simulator. *SIGCOMM Demonstration*, 15:17, August 2008.

---

[1]Disclaimer: Any opinions, findings and conclusions or recommendations expressed in this material are those of the author(s) and do not necessarily reflect the views of the Maryland Procurement Office.

[28] M. Hibler, R. Ricci, L. Stoller, J. Duerig, S. Guruprasad, T. Stack, K. Webb, and J. Lepreau. Large-scale virtualization in the emulab network testbed. In *Proceedings of the USENIX 2008 Annual Technical Conference*, pages 113–128, Berkeley, CA, USA, June 2008. USENIX Association.

[29] D. Jin and D. M. Nicol. Parallel simulation of software defined networks. In *Proceedings of the 2013 ACM SIGSIM Conference on Principles of Advanced Discrete Simulation*, pages 91–102, New York, NY, USA, May 2013. ACM.

[30] D. Jin, Y. Zheng, H. Zhu, D. M. Nicol, and L. Winterrowd. Virtual time integration of emulation and parallel simulation. In *Proceedings of the 2012 ACM/IEEE/SCS 26th Workshop on Principles of Advanced and Distributed Simulation*, pages 201–210, Washington, DC, USA, May 2012. IEEE Computer Society.

[31] E. Keller, S. Ghorbani, M. Caesar, and J. Rexford. Live migration of an entire network (and its hosts). In *Proceedings of the 11th ACM Workshop on Hot Topics in Networks*, pages 109–114, New York, NY, USA, October 2012. ACM.

[32] J. Lamps, D. M. Nicol, and M. Caesar. Timekeeper: A lightweight virtual time system for linux. In *Proceedings of the 2nd ACM SIGSIM/PADS Conference on Principles of Advanced Discrete Simulation*, pages 179–186, New York, NY, USA, May 2014. ACM.

[33] B. Lantz, B. Heller, and N. McKeown. A network in a laptop: Rapid prototyping for software-defined networks. In *Proceedings of the 9th ACM SIGCOMM Workshop on Hot Topics in Networks*, pages 1–6, New York, NY, USA, May 2010. ACM.

[34] J. Liu, R. Rangaswami, and M. Zhao. Model-driven network emulation with virtual time machine. In *Proceedings of the Winter Simulation Conference*, pages 688–696, Washington, DC, USA, December 2010. IEEE Computer Society.

[35] S. Maier, A. Grau, H. Weinschrott, and K. Rothermel. Scalable network emulation: A comparison of virtual routing and virtual machines. In *Proceedings of 12th IEEE Symposium on Computers and Communications*, pages 395–402, Washington, DC, USA, July 2007. IEEE Computer Society.

[36] N. McKeown, T. Anderson, H. Balakrishnan, G. Parulkar, L. Peterson, J. Rexford, S. Shenker, and J. Turner. Openflow: enabling innovation in campus networks. *ACM SIGCOMM Computer Communication Review*, 38(2):69–74, April 2008.

[37] M. Reitblatt, N. Foster, J. Rexford, C. Schlesinger, and D. Walker. Abstractions for network update. *ACM SIGCOMM Computer Communication Review*, 42(4):323–334, August 2012.

[38] A. Vahdat. Scale and efficiency in data center networks. Technical report, UC San Diego, 2009.

[39] S.-Y. Wang, C.-L. Chou, and C.-M. Yang. Estinet openflow network simulator and emulator. *Communications Magazine, IEEE*, 51(9):110–117, September 2013.

[40] E. Weingärtner, F. Schmidt, H. V. Lehn, T. Heer, and K. Wehrle. Slicetime: A platform for scalable and accurate network emulation. In *Proceedings of the 8th USENIX Conference on Networked Systems Design and Implementation*, pages 253–266, Berkeley, CA, USA, March 2011. USENIX Association.

[41] Y. Zheng and D. M. Nicol. A virtual time system for openvz-based network emulations. In *Proceedings of the 2011 IEEE Workshop on Principles of Advanced and Distributed Simulation*, pages 1–10, Washington, DC, USA, June 2011. IEEE Computer Society.

Verification of Petri Nets based Simulation Models using Coverage Metrics

Markus Rabe, Maik Deininger, Anne Antonia Scheidler
Department of IT in Production and Logistics
TU Dortmund University
Leonhard-Euler-Str. 5 Dortmund, Germany
{markus.rabe, maik.deininger, anne-antonia.scheidler}@tu-dortmund.de

ABSTRACT

Through the wast growth of information technologies, verification is of high importance in many research fields. Most of the models describing modelling procedures include verification and validation as a single step or as an accompanying activity. Unfortunately, most of these models do not give more detailed operation guidelines. In this context, it is common that verification is necessary, but in real life projects there is often no time nor men power for verification, particularly, if verifying is an accompanying activity as in simulation projects. The complexity of simulation projects complicates a proper implementation of verification. Therefore, it is a common method to tailor the procedure models. In this paper we concentrate on modelling and introduce an approach for automated verification. Petri nets are widely used as modelling method. Petri nets are well defined and based on graphs. Thus, this paper introduces an approach for mapping petri-net-based models to control flow graphs. Then it is shown, how this mapping can be utilised for applying coverage metrics. This enables projects to use software testing methods of coverage for verifying petri-net-based simulation models. As a benefit, project time and personnel can be saved.

Categories and Subject Descriptors

K.5.1.1 [**Computing methodologies**]: Modeling methodologies; K.5.1.2 [**Computing methodologies**]: Model verification and validation; E.3.4.3 [**Software and its engineering**]: Software verification and validation

General Terms

Verification, Standardization, Theory

Keywords

Verification; Coverage metrics; Graphs; Petri nets; Software testing; Modelling

SIGSIM-PADS'15, June 10–12, 2015, London, United Kingdom.
Copyright is held by the owner/author(s). Publication rights licensed to ACM.
ACM 978-1-4503-3583-6/15/06 ...$15.00.
DOI: http://dx.doi.org/10.1145/2769458.2769460.

1. INTRODUCTION

Today, information technologies become more and more important and spread over all research fields. As a consequence, the implementation of procedure models as well as verification and validation (V&V) are supported by information technologies. But, verification is still an expensive and time-consuming activity where most procedure models give no proper operation guideline. As Kleijnen stated, "There is no standard theory on V&V" [15]. But, verification and also validation are becoming more and more relevant in industrial projects, as demonstrated by the focus of Arbeitsgemeinschaft Simulation (ASIM, German simulation society) on related procedure models [25]. Therefore, project leaders are focusing more on V&V activities and the related costs are getting more visible. With transparent costs, V&V is a target of cost savings. This paper applies common software verification techniques to simulation modelling using petri nets and enables reducing costs of verification. In particular modellers using petri nets for simulation in production and logistics are focused.

In computer science, techniques for automated verification of software code are well established [30]. Some of them are based on representing the software code as graphs and applying coverage metrics on it. Also, techniques for verification of simulation models do exist, but they lack a potential of automation. Most of these techniques require business knowledge and manual support. An overview of established techniques for verification of simulation models is given by Balci [3].

One of the techniques for automated verification is whitebox testing which can be based on representing the software code as a graph. This enables the project for supporting the functional quality assurance in an efficient manner. Defects regarding the functional behaviour can be found in relation to the used input data. This way defects within statements, conditions, and their connection can be found. But, no defects according to non-functional behaviour as performance or run-time or defects not covered by the data are detectable.

Most software tools do not completely include automated verification of simulation models [2]. Simulation models in production and logistics use stations, that may represent warehouses or machines, and relations between them represent the transport processes. These may be interpreted as nodes and edges of a graph. In this manner software code and simulation models have an assimilable representation.

A common technique in simulation modelling are Petri nets (PNs) [22]. PNs have been used to model business processes [1], manufacturing systems [8, 27], logistics [35] and many more. This paper shows how to map PNs to Control Flow Graphs (CFGs) with the aim of applying coverage metrics from software development to simulation model development. This may be a first step for a new automated verification of simulation models.

The application of coverage metrics on Petri nets enables the modeller for fast and efficient V&V of simulation models. Thus the costs and time of V&V within simulation projects can be reduced and made more transparent to project members. Additionally, this approach may lead to an automated V&V using coverage metrics which are rarely exist in current software tools.

This paper is structured as follows: Section 2 gives a short overview of coverage metrics and PNs. Section 3 introduces the approach for mapping PNs to CFGs, which builds up the basis for verification using coverage metrics. Section 4 gives an example for a manufacturing system and a distribution supply chain and how the approach is applied. The paper is closed with a short conclusion and outlook.

2. STATE OF THE ART

"Assuring total quality in a modeling and simulation (M&S) effort involves the measurement and assessment of a variety of quality characteristics such as accuracy, execution efficiency, maintainability, portability, reusability, and usability (human-computer interface)" [2]. This shows how widely verification and validation is spread. By applying coverage metrics to petri nets, this paper gives an approach for measuring the accuracy of a simulation model. Therefore, coverage and their requirements to graphs are introduced next followed by PNs that are examined according to them.

2.1 Coverage

Software testing is a very important discipline in computer science and it is widely used in industry for quality assurance. Testing is a process with the intent of finding errors in an application [20]. Many procedure models integrate software testing [10, 36, 23]. There are various software tests, depending on the project level to be used, project constraints, the technical abilities of the project, the know-how of the user, and the testing goals. It can be distinguished between the test strategy and category. Strategies are black-box and white-box testing and the categories are static and dynamic testing [32]. Depending on the decision, whether or not the source code is exploited in driving the testing, testing can be differentiated into two main classes of software tests [5]. White-box tests (also known as glass box or structural testing) are depending on the internal structures of the program code or data definitions and references [37]. The opposite is black-box test, where the functionality of an application is tested without looking at the code [4]. Static testing is a form of software testing, where the software is not actually used. Dynamic testing is based on the compiled software at runtime [19]. Combinations of the testing strategies and test categories are always possible. This paper concentrates on white-box static testing, where the internal structure of the program code has to be modelled. The internal structure may be modelled as generic concepts or language-specific concepts. The methods can be divided into two categories: textual and graphical. The most common graphical methods are data flow methods and control flow methods. Software validation metrics which are based on the control flow methods are called coverage metrics. There are different coverage metrics, which differ in complexity and testing aim. Today, the most commonly used software validation metrics are based on code coverage [34] using CFGs.

A CFG is a directed graph $G = (N, E, n_{root}, n_{final})$. N is a finite set of nodes and $E \subseteq N \times N$ is a finite set of directed edges which connects the nodes. n_{root} is a dedicated root node and n_{final} is a dedicated end node. Additionally, a path connecting n_{root} with each $v \in N$ must exist [19, 11, 30]. The International Software Testing Qualifications Board (ISTQB) defines a control flow graph as "an abstract representation of all possible sequences of events (paths) in the execution through a component or system" [14]. A path is a finite sequence of nodes $(n_1, \ldots, n_k) \forall k > 2$, such that there is an edge from n_i to n_{i+1} for each $i = 1, \ldots, k - 1$. Paths can have different features e.g. simple, loop-free or complete [26]. Coverage metrics in software

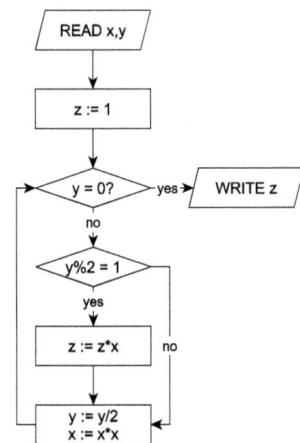

Figure 1: Example control flow graph

testing are based on the execution of statements, branches or sequences of statements [9]. Coverage metrics can be differentiated into multiple categories [38]. This paper addresses the most common coverage categories (C0, C1, C2). For additional tests and subcategories as boundary interior, LC-SAJ (Linear Code Sequence and Jumps), Primitive Branch Coverage, and different Condition Coverages see Riedemann [30].

- Statement Coverage (C0): Each node of a given graph should be executed at least once. Statement coverage is also known as segment coverage. Through statement coverage it can be identified which code is executed and which is not. This method is limited because empty branches cannot be detected and data dependencies within control elements are not taken into consideration. For example, an if-statement which isn't executed for one branch because of an invalid boolean condition cannot be detected. This may lead to a coverage less than 100%. Liggesmeyer stated that statement coverage, as independent testing method, plays only a subordinate role and most tools for software testing do not include statement coverage [19].

- Branch Coverage (C1): Each branch of a given graph should be executed at least once. ISTQB stated that branch coverage is closely related to decision coverage, where decision coverage measures the coverage of condi-

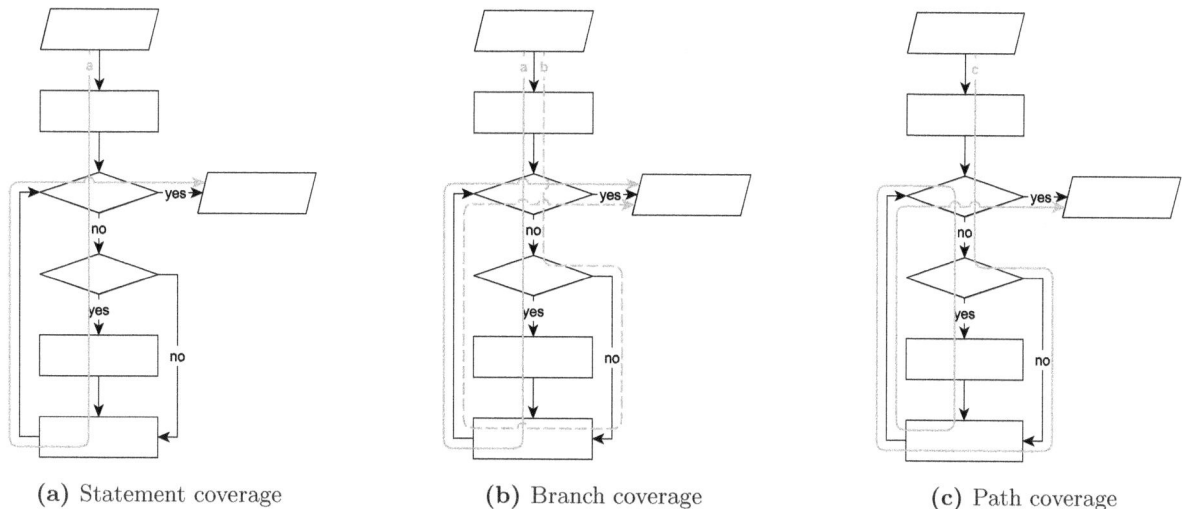

(a) Statement coverage   **(b)** Branch coverage   **(c)** Path coverage

Figure 2: Coverage categories

tional branches; with branch coverage, both, the coverage of conditional and unconditional branches are measured [14, 32]. Through branch coverage it can be verified that all the branches in the code are executed, in particular empty branches which are not detected by Statement Coverage. However, there are also disadvantages because loops are not tested in a satisfactory manner and dependencies between different conditions are not tested.

- Path Coverage (C2): Within a given graph, every possible route should be executed. A path represents the flow of execution from the start of a graph to its end. A graph which contains a loop may have an infinite number of paths. There are different subcategories of path coverage. The previous statement is listed as C2a [30]. Because of the infinite number of paths there are some relaxations of the C2 category, e.g. C2b (called boundary interior test) where every loop is maximum executed twice. For more special path features and its impact for software testing see Rapps and Weyuker [26].

The figures 2a - 2c depict the difference between C0, C1, and C2 coverage on the control flow graph shown in figure 1. For well-formed graphs all paths (C2) subsume all branches (C1) which subsume all nodes (C0) [7].

There are different tools for test automation of software coverage metrics. The tools are related to programming language, e.g. Pascal or C. An overview is given in Horgna [12] and Hyoung et al. [13].

2.2 Petri Nets

Petri nets (PNs) are used to model various systems [8, 16, 21, 35]. A PN is a directed graph $PN = (T, P, E)$, where T and P are a disjoint finite number of transitions and places and $E \subseteq (P \times T) \cup (T \times P)$ is a finite set of directed arcs that connect a transition with a place [28, 24].

As stated in section 2.1, coverage is based on CFGs. Thus, applying coverage to PNs, the following constraints need to be fulfilled:

1. PNs need to consist of nodes and edges,

2. the arcs need to be directed,

3. a dedicated root node must exist,

4. a dedicated end node must exist, and

5. all nodes need to be reachable from the root node.

According to the definition, PNs consist of two types of nodes (1): places and transitions. Places are used to save the state of the net through tokens and transitions consume those tokens and may produce new ones when firing. Transitions and places are set in relation by directed arcs, which fulfils 2. Some PN types define undirected arcs, but to comply with standard PN definitions those are treated as bidirectional or directed arcs that are not interpreted by transitions [31]. Simulating a PN starts with creating an initial mark-up, where tokens are placed on selected places. This initial mark-up activates at least one transition. As a consequence, there is no single root node, which violates 3. A simulation run stops when no transition is activated nor will be activated with ongoing simulation time (cp. [24]). This means, in PN there is also no end node and, therefore, 4 is not fulfilled. Reachability in PNs is examined by creating reachability graphs. Since those graphs may be infinite, they are converted into coverage graphs [28]. Having a reachability graph or a coverage graph, it can be investigated under which circumstance a transition is activated. But creating those graphs can be very time consuming. In order to apply coverage metrics, it only needs to be shown that a transition will be activated with a distinct input. Therefore, creating a complete reachability or coverage graph is not necessary and point 5 can be ensured. Concluding: PNs, by default, do not meet three conditions (root node, end node and reachability) of CFGs. But reachability can be examined using reachability or coverage graphs.

In order to still apply coverage, higher PNs are needed that enable the modeller to comply with the requirements of coverage. Higher PNs in general combine concepts of time constraints and object orientation. Both can be used to create dedicated root and end nodes.

Time constraints may be applied to all elements of a Place-Transition net, tokens, places, transitions, and arcs and can be one of two types: duration d with $0 \leq d < \infty$ or interval

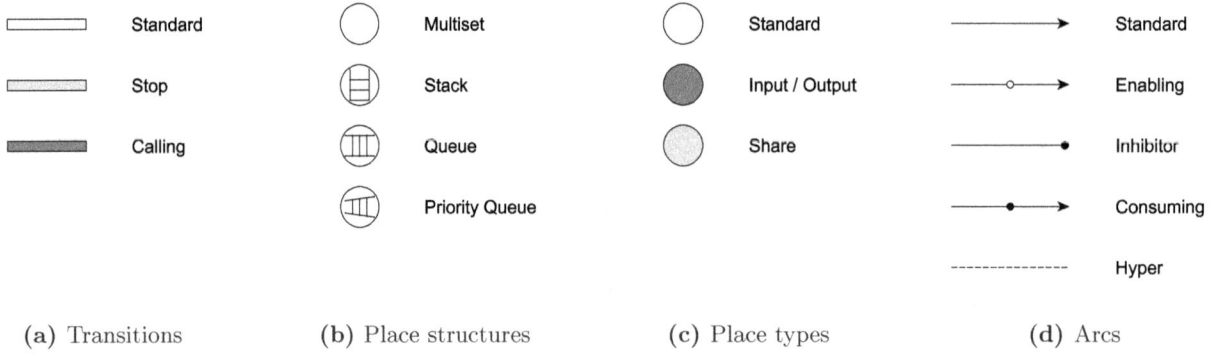

| (a) Transitions | (b) Place structures | (c) Place types | (d) Arcs |

Figure 3: Elements of THORNs

$[a, b]$ with $0 \le a \le b \le \infty, a \neq b$ [33]. To apply time to tokens, a clock with time τ is introduced for each token, that is set to 0 when it is born. Based on τ, a token can be valid or invalid. Starke named four types of time for tokens:

Duration of validity: The token is valid as long as $\tau \le d$.

Duration of invalidity: The token is invalid as long as $\tau < d$.

Window of validity: The token is valid as long as $a \le \tau \le b$.

Window of invalidity: The token is invalid as long as $a \le \tau \le b$.

It is stated that time constraints applied to places basically is the same as for tokens with the same four types. The difference is that all tokens on the same place have the same constraint applied, no matter which transition created them.

Starke [33] differentiates arcs into input ($E_{T,in} \subseteq P \times T$) and output ($E_{T,out} \subseteq T \times P$) arcs of transitions, when applying time to them. **Duration** is only applied to $E_{T,out}$ and delays the tokens movement by d units of time. **Window** is only applied to $E_{T,in}$. Here two types exist:

Flow window: The arc is open for a token, iff. $a \le \tau \le b$.

Lock window: The arc is blocked for a token, iff. $a < \tau < b$.

To apply time constraints to transitions, a clock with time ϑ is introduced for each transition. It is set to 0 at the moment the transition becomes activated. Starke gives four types of time constraints for transitions:

Duration of firing: The input tokens are removed immediately and output tokens produced at time $d + \vartheta$.

Duration of relaxation: After firing, a transition may not be activated before $d + \vartheta$.

Window of concession: The transition may fire, iff. $a \le \vartheta \le b$.

Window of invalidity: A transition may not fire, iff. $a < \vartheta < b$.

The concept of object orientation was introduced to PNs based on the concepts used in programming (cp. [29]). There are different approaches for using object orientation in PNs [6, 17, 8]. The most common is to treat tokens as instances of classes having member variables and function. Using this approach, tokens contain the data that are manipulated through transitions they pass.

Another approach is introduced with Object Oriented Petri Nets (OOPN), where PNs are organized in classes consisting of an object net and a set of method nets [17]. OOPNs supports inheritance. Subclasses may redefine or add transitions and places and new methods can be added. A token can either be a trivial object, e.g. a number, or an instance of an OOPN.

The PN type used in this paper is a Timed Hierarchical Object-Related Net (THORN) [8]. As Language for Object Oriented Petri Nets [18], a THORN uses four different types of place structures that are depicted in figure 3b. A multiset place contains an unordered set of tokens that may be used in any order through transitions. A stack place is ordered. The last token added is the first one to be used by transitions, whereas in queue places the first arriving token is the first one to be used. Priority queue places work in the same way as queue places, except that tokens are ordered through a priority function.

A transition contains several main functions. One is the action, that describes the functionality. The next one is a condition function that in addition to standard activation rules defines whether a transition may be activated or not. At last there are two functions describing time. One computes how long it takes to fire (duration of firing) and the other one describes how long a transition has to be activated before it is allowed to fire (window of invalidity with $a = 0$). All those functions can depend on the tokens lying on the places in the pre area. These functionalities are described by C++-functions.

In figure 3a the three types of transitions are depicted that differ in their functionality. The standard transition performs actions on the consumed tokens and may produce new ones. The calling transition creates a new THORN, where tokens from the pre area are used to create the initial marking of the new net. The last transition is a stop transition that only exist in sub nets. If this transition fires, the subnet will be stopped and destroyed.

Additionally, places can be differentiated into three types (fig. 3c) that may be of one of the four structures. A standard place contains tokens that can be consumed or created by transitions. An input/output place connects a THORN and its sub net. Whenever a sub net is created, tokens from an input place are moved to the sub net. If the sub net is destroyed, the tokens placed on output places are moved to the parent net. This way every input and output place has a connection to a place in the sub net. The last type of places are share places that can be part of multiple THORNs. Thus it has a representation in all nets it belongs to. Where tokens on input/ output places can only be used by a single net, tokens on share places can be used in all nets.

Figure 3d shows the different types of arcs. The standard arc equals traditional directed arcs in PNs. It can have weights and names for the tokens transferred. Is a transition connected to a place using an inhibitor arcs, the transition may not be activated if the place contains tokens. A test arc works in the same way as standard arcs, except that no token is consumed if the transition is activated. The last arc is a consuming arc, consuming all tokens from a place if the transition is activated. Inhibitor arcs, test arcs and consuming arcs can only be directed from place to transition. Standard arcs can be directed from place to transition (input arc) or from transition to place (output arc). A hyper arc is undirected, but may be treated as bidirectional, and only connects places with calling transitions. It illustrates that the place is used as a share place within the subnet created by the transition.

A THORN uses instances of objects as tokens that are described through C++-classes. Tokens consist of member variables and member functions that may be used and changed within transitions.

3. APPLYING COVERAGE METRICS TO PETRI NET MODELS

As shown in section 2.2, there are three aspects of CFGs that PNs do not fulfil. This section shows how the modeller can comply with these constraints using THORNs. First,

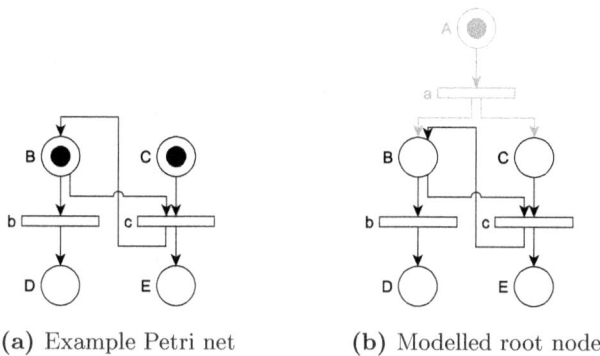

(a) Example Petri net   (b) Modelled root node

Figure 4: Petri net with and without root node

a distinguished root node needs to be introduced without changing the behaviour of the underlying net. If the initial marking only consists of one token to be placed on one place, this place will be treated as root node. This obviously does not work if the initial marking contains multiple tokens. In this case an additional place and transition can be added to the PN. The pre area of the new transition only

contains the new place, as root node, and its post area consists of all places included in the initial marking. The initial marking can be a set of tokens that are moved through the first transition to the places of the initial marking. This can be modelled using a consuming arc and depending on the properties of the tokens, the transition decides where to move them. Another option is to use a single token that contains all necessary information, so that the original initial marking can be created through the transition. Figure 4b shows an example where the second solution is used.

Since the simulation of a PN can stop with 'any' marking, a transition would need to be connected with all places that identify the final marking. Generating the reachability graph, all markings can be found where the simulation may stop. Figure 5a depicts the reachability graph for the example and shows two possible final markings. One has tokens at places C and D, the other one at places D and E. Knowing that there are only these two final states, it is possible to model a dedicated end node F, as figure 5b shows. Having a closer look at all possible markings it can be seen that place D only is marked within both final markings. D could be defined as end node, but for illustration purposes, a new end node is created for this example. Adding an end node afterwards is only possible for nets with all final markings known. As a consequence, it can not be ensured that an end node exists nor can be added. Section 2.2 showed that PNs

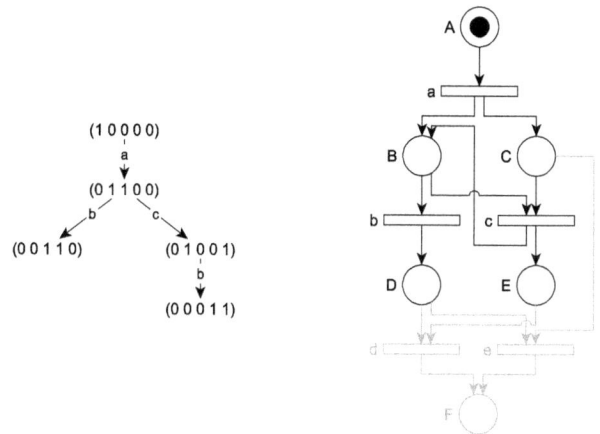

(a) Reachability graph of fig. 4b   (b) Modelled end node

Figure 5: Petri net end node

in general can not be treated as CFGs. In this section it is depicted how a PN has to be modelled to comply with the requirements of a CFG. For the rest of this paper, only PNs with dedicated root and end node are examined where all nodes can be reached from the root node.

After modelling a PN to comply with CFGs, the PN needs to be converted into a CFG in order to apply coverage metrics. As figure 6 shows, the above mentioned root place becomes the start node of the CFG. If the end place has multiple input arcs, it is converted into a conditional node followed by the stop node. Otherwise the conditional node may be omitted. All other places are transformed into a statement node with the action to store tokens. A transition is transformed into a conditional node, having only

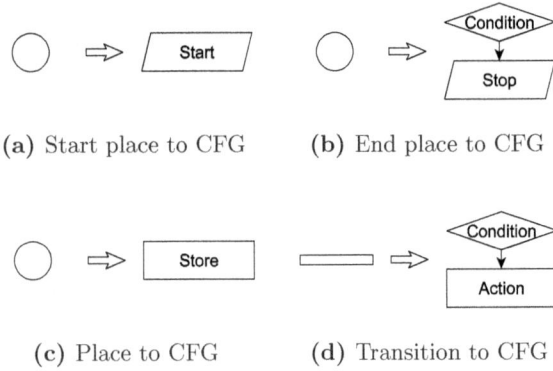

(a) Start place to CFG   **(b)** End place to CFG

(c) Place to CFG   **(d)** Transition to CFG

Figure 6: Mapping PN to CFG

one output arc that tests the firing condition followed by a statement node that performs the action of the transition. Additionally, the conditional node is connected to each store node resulting from the post area of the transition. The different arc types result in different conditions for the transitions' conditional nodes. Having mapped the PN enables to refine the complex node with the CFG for the action to be performed. Now, not only the PN can be verified, but also each action in detail of the transitions. Figure 7 depicts the transformed PN from figure 4a.

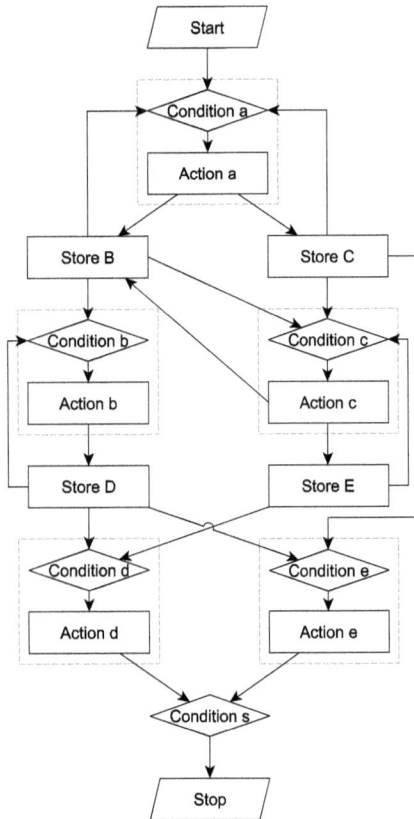

Figure 7: Generated CFG

4. EXAMPLES

Having shown that PNs can be modelled to meet the requirements for applying coverage metrics, two examples will illustrate how THORNs can be verified. Therefore, a production line and a supply chain are used for illustration.

4.1 Production Line

Figure 8 shows a small example for handling orders in a production system that produces two products (A, B). Product A is manufactured at machine $M1$ and product B needs two manufacturing steps, one at machine $M1$ followed by a finalization at machine $M2$. Each manufacturing step is managed by an order and may use additional resources. After all ordered products produced, they are commissioned and prepared for delivery.

Once a customer order is created on place O, it is divided into production orders for product A and B and a commission order through transition s. The production is regulated by the transitions pA, $pB1$ and $pB2$. Transition pA and $pB1$ both require machine $M1$ and need additional resources from place PAr respectively place PBr. Resources are assumed as infinite. After $pB1$ finished, transition $pB2$ can finalise product B using machine $M2$. Transition c commissions the order and creates a delivery order on place OD and the packed products at place PD.

In order to comply with the requirements of coverage metrics, a dedicated end node is created by adding transition e that has place OD and PD as pre area and place E as post area. Even though the final marking also contains places $M1$ and $M2$, the final state is uniquely defined through places OD and PD. Additionally, a dedicated root node had to be introduced. Therefore, transition i and place R are added. Place R contains a single token that contains all customer orders, resources and machines. Transition i then creates tokens on places O, PAr, PBr, $M1$ and $M2$. Before applying coverage metrics to the example, the conditions and actions of the transitions need to be known. In this example, no special conditions are defined. So, each transition may fire, if their pre and post area conditions are fulfilled.

The action of transition s analyses the customer order and creates three orders depending on it. If the customer order contains orders for products A and B, orders for A and B including the number of products to be produced and the commissioning order are generated. If one of the product is not ordered, a respective order with the amount of zero products is created. Figure 9 depicts the algorithm. Transitions pA, $pB1$ and $pB2$ basically have the same action. After consuming the order, machine, and resources, the transition produces a new product (places PA, $PB1$ or PB). $pB1$ additionally creates an order at place $OB2$ for the finalization step of product B.

Transition c consumes the products and the commissioning order to create two new tokens. Knowing the behaviour of each transition, input data can be generated for achieving maximum statement coverage, branch coverage, and path coverage.

- Statement Coverage: As the reachability graph (see figure 10) shows, each valid input on place R results in activating each of the transitions. Since transition s varies in the creation of orders for products A and B, input needs to be generated that triggers all cases. This can be achieved by customer orders that once only contain an

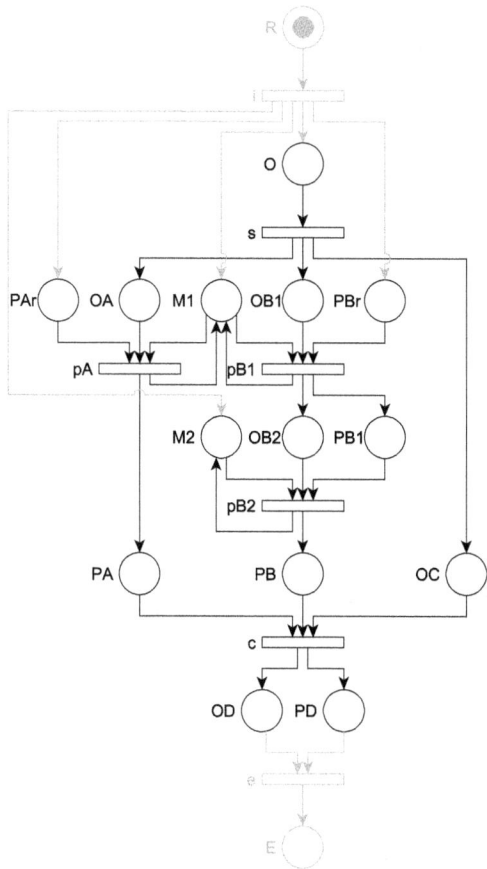

Figure 8: Production example

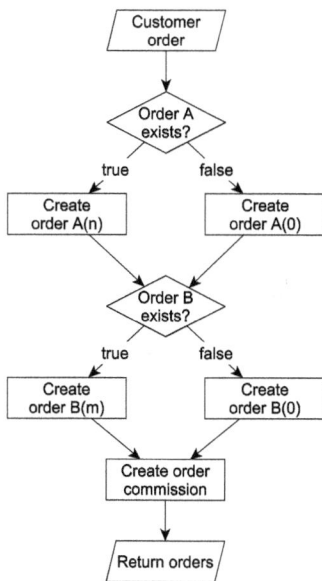

Figure 9: Action definition for transition s

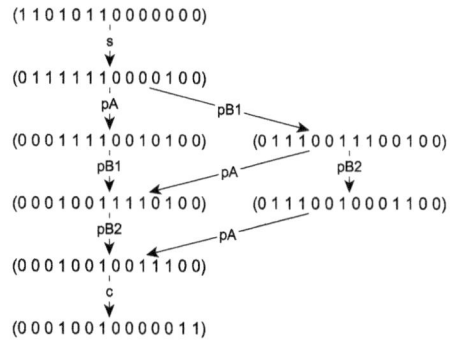

Figure 10: Reachability graph for fig. 8

order for product A and another one that only contains an order for product B. All other transitions do not include conditional paths, so a 100% statement coverage can be achieved with two input datasets.

- Branch Coverage: In order to achieve 100% branch coverage, each conditional statement needs to be evaluated as true and false. This is not possible in the given example. The condition of transition s will always be true. This is because it will only be triggered if all orders within the production systems are processed. Also the condition of transition e and $pB2$ will always be evaluated as true, since all requirements are fulfilled after the upstream transition is processed and no other path leads to an activation. All of the other conditions can be tested for both cases. Independent of the input data, the conditions of transitions pA, $pB1$, and c will automatically be evaluated true and false with a single input dataset. Calling the store statement resulting from place $M1$ triggers the conditions of transitions pA and $pB1$. No matter which is processed first, the other will be processed afterwards by calling the store statement again. After the second one is processed, the store statement is triggered again, and this time both conditions will be evaluated as false. As a result it needs to be concentrated on the action of transition s. Here, the two conditions need also to be evaluated as true and false, which can be achieved with the same input datasets as for statement coverage.

- Path Coverage: Since the example does not contain loops, path coverage equals branch coverage.

As a result, maximum coverage can be achieved with two input datasets to verify the example.

4.2 Distribution Supply Chain

The example in figure 11 illustrates a distribution supply chain. A manufacturer produces products using a make-to-stock strategy. These products are distributed from a central warehouse, which is located at the manufacturer's production site, to the retailers through an individual reorder point procedure with fixed purchase order quantity. Finally the products are consumed by customers. Starting with transition m, a manufacturer produces products that are stored at place W representing the central warehouse with capacity c_w. m has a time constraint type of duration of firing to represent the duration of the production (t_m). The total number of products (n) produced is limited through the tokens placed on place S. The manufacturer delivers products to

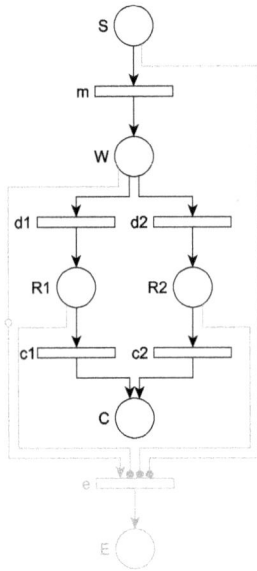

Figure 11: Distribution supply chain example

the warehouse as long as it has free capacity. Based on a delivery plan, the products are distributed to the two retailers warehouses (places $R1$ and $R2$ with capacities c_{R1} and c_{R2}) which is controlled through the condition of transitions $d1$ and $d2$. The purchase order quantities q_{R1} and q_{R2} are represented through edge weights attached to both the output arcs and input arcs of transitions $d1$ and $d2$. Additionally, both transitions use a duration of relaxiation constraint to model the transportation times (t_{R1} and t_{R2}). Henceforth, the products can be consumed through customers, which is represented by transitions $c1$ and $c2$. Both use a duration of relaxiation constraint to model the shopping behaviour of the customers with random relaxiation times. Place C collects all products consumed and has infinity capacity.

In the example the activation of transition $d1$ and $d2$ strongly depends on the selected parameters. Depending on the parameters, all products could be delivered through a single retailer. To ensure that both transition will be able to fire, the following constraints will be applied:

$$t_m < \frac{\min\left(t_{R1}, t_{R2}\right)}{q_{R1} + q_{R2}} \qquad (1)$$

$$c_W \geq q_{R1} + q_{R2} \qquad (2)$$

$$q_{R1} < q_{R2} \qquad (3)$$

These constraints ensure that after one of these transitions has fired, the other may fire while the first one is relaxing. Equation 3 is used for easier explaining the behaviour of the PN.

To comply with the requirements for coverage metrics, a root node needs to be defined. In this example, place S can be defined as root node and instead of a single token, the input data is a set of tokens that define how often m can fire. As a next step, a dedicated end node is needed. The final marking for this example is achieved when the places $R1$ and $R2$ are empty and the sum of tokens at place W and S are less than the minimum of q_{R1} and q_{R2}. Therefore, a new transition e is connected to the places $R1$ and $R2$ using inhibitor arcs and to S and W using test arcs.

- Statement Coverage: 100% statement coverage can be achieved by placing at least $q_{R1} + q_{R2}$ tokens on place S. Transition m will repeat to fire until the number of tokens at place W equal q_{R1}, which will activate transition $d1$ with m also still being active. Now, m may continue to fire until c_W is reached, which will also activate transition $d2$. Once $d1$ or $d2$ fired and is relaxing, the other one will fire next. This ensures the activation transitions $c1$ and $c2$. Once place S runs out of tokens, place W will not contain enough tokens to activate transition $d1$ nor $d2$. From this point, $c1$ and $c2$ will consume tokens from places $R1$ respectively $R2$ until those are empty, which will activate transition e and a token is placed at the end node. Thus 100% statement coverage is achieved.

- Branch Coverage: In this example 100% branch coverage can be achieved using the same input data as for statement coverage. After placing tokens at place S, the condition of transition m is evaluated as true. It will be evaluated as false, if S is empty or W reaches its capacity. Place S will be empty at the end. The conditions of transitions $d1$ and $d2$ will also be evaluated true and false. Equations 1 and 2 ensure that both transitions will be activated. In the end, place W will not contain enough tokens to activate one of these transitions, so their condition is evaluated as false. With transitions $d1$ and $d2$ firing, the conditions of $c1$ respectively $c2$ will be evaluated as true. After firing, their conditions will be triggered again. If the places $R1$ respectively $R2$ are empty, what will happen at the end of the PN simulation, the conditions of $c1$ and $c2$ will be evaluated as false. By placing tokens at W, $R1$, or $R2$, the condition of transition e will be triggered and always be evaluated as false except once, which will be the case if S, $R1$, and $R2$ are empty and W contains less tokens than q_{R1}.

- Path Coverage: As for the first example, no loops are included and path coverage equals branch coverage.

5. CONCLUSION

This paper outlined an approach for verifying PNs based on coverage metrics. It has been shown how PN models have to be designed or extended to meet the requirements of coverage metrics. The approach has been demonstrated using simple models of a production system and a supply chain. The expected benefit is that this approach does not need the complete reachability or coverage graph to be constructed and still allows for verifying the model. Additionally, it is possible to create input data that does not only cover the transition and places of the PN, but also the inner structure of the conditions and actions of transitions in higher PNs like THORNs.

Additionally, this approach may become a base for developing standardisation of verification in simulation modelling. Coverage metrics are part of ISTQB standard software testing certification. This standard may be adopted to simulation modelling verification based on PNs. Another research topic could be not using the PN model but the reachability graph as a basis for the analysis.

6. REFERENCES

[1] Aalst, W. M. P. v. d. 2014.
Geschäftsprozessmodellierung: Die killer-applikation für petrinetze. *Informatik-Spektrum*, 37(3), 191–198.

[2] Balci, O. 1998. Verification, validation, and accreditation. In Proceedings of Winter Simulation Conference (Washington, D.C, USA, December 13-16, 1998). ACM, Madison, WS, 41–44.

[3] Balci, O. 1995. Principles and techniques of simulation validation, verification, and testing. In Proceedings of Winter Simulation Conference (Arlington, VA, USA, December 3-6, 1995). IEEE Computer Society Washington, DC, USA, 147–154.

[4] Beizer, B. 1995. *Black-box testing: Techniques for functional testing of software and systems*. Wiley, New York.

[5] Bertolino, A. 2007. Software testing research: Achievements, challenges, dreams. In L. C. Briand and A. L. Wolf, editors, *Future of Software Engineering*, 85–103, Los Alamitos, CA, USA, IEEE Computer Society.

[6] Ceska, M., Janousek, V., and Vojnar, T. 1998. Object-oriented petri nets, their simulation, and analysis. In Proceedings of IEEE International Conference on Systems, Man, and Cybernetics (San Diego, CA, USA, 11-14 October, 1998). IEEE, 262–267.

[7] Clarke, L. A., Podgurski, A., Richardson, D. J., and Zeil, S. J. 1989. A formal evaluation of data flow path selection criteria. *IEEE Transactions on Software Engineering*, 15(11), 1318–1332.

[8] Dahms, M. and Schmidt, M. 2005. Modeling of dispatching-rules for job shop scheduling in manufacturing systems - a petri net approach. In Proceedings of IEEE International Conference on Systems, Man and Cybernetics (Waikoloa Hilton Village, Waikoloa, Hawaii, USA, October 10-12, 2005). IEEE, Piscataway, NY, USA, 2025–2030.

[9] Devadas, S., Ghosh, A., and Keutzer, K. 1996. An observability-based code coverage metric for functional simulation. In Proceedings of International Conference on Computer Aided Design (San Jose, CA, USA, 10-14 November, 1996). IEEE, 418–425.

[10] Friedrich, J. 2009. *Das V-Modell XT: Für Projektleiter und QS-Verantwortliche kompakt und übersichtlich*. Informatik im Fokus. Springer, Berlin.

[11] Gold, R. 2010. Control flow graphs and code coverage. *International Journal of Applied Mathematics and Computer Science*, 20(4), 739–749.

[12] Horgan, J. R. and London, S. 1991. Data flow coverage and the c language. In W. Howden, editor, *Proceedings of the symposium on Testing, analysis, and verification*, 87–97, New York and NY. ACM.

[13] Hyoung, S. H., Sung, D. C.,Insup, L., Sokolsky, O., and Ural, H. 2003. Data flow testing as model checking. In Proceedings of 25th International Conference on Software Engineering (3-10 May, 2003). IEEE, Los Alamitos and Piscataway, 232–242.

[14] International Software Testing Qualification Board. Standard glossary of terms used in software testing: Version 2.4. URL=http://www.istqb.org/downloads/glossary.html, last access Jan. 2015.

[15] Kleijnen, J. P. C. 1005. Verification and validation of simulation models. *European Journal of Operational Research*, 82(1), 145–162.

[16] Koch, I. 2014. Petrinetze in der Systembiologie. *Informatik-Spektrum*, 37(3), 211–219, 2014.

[17] Koci, R., Janousek, V., and Zboril, F. J. 2008. Object oriented petri nets modelling techniques case study. In D. Al-Dabass, A. Nagar, H. Tawfik, A. Abraham, and R. Zobel, editors, *European Modelling Symposium*, volume 2008, 165–170, Los Alamitos and Calif.. IEEE.

[18] Lakos, C. A. and Keen, C. D. 1991. Loopn - language for object-oriented petri nets. In Proceedings of Proceedings of the SCS Multiconference on Object Oriented Simulation (Anaheim, CA, USA). Society for Computer Simulation, San Diego, USA, 22–30.

[19] Liggesmeyer, P. 2009. *Software-Qualität: Testen, Analysieren und Verifizieren von Software*. Spektrum Akademischer Verlag, Heidelberg, 2nd edition.

[20] Myers, G. J., Sandler, C., and Badgett, T. 2012. *The art of software testing*. John Wiley & Sons, Hoboken and N.J., 3rd edition.

[21] Pawlewski, P. 2010. Using petri nets to model and simulation production systems in process reengineering (case study). In P. Pawlewski, editor, *Petri Nets Applications*, 422–445. InTech, Rijek and HR.

[22] Petri, C. A. 1962. *Kommunikation mit Automaten*. PhD thesis, Technische Hochschlue Darmstadt, Darmstadt.

[23] Pichler, R. 2008. *Scrum - agiles Projektmanagement erfolgreich einsetzen*. Dpunkt-Verl., Heidelberg.

[24] Priese, L. and Wimmel, H. 2008. *Petri-Netze*. Springer, Berlin and Heidelberg, 2. edition.

[25] Rabe, M., Speickermann, S., and Wenzel, S. 2008. *Verifikation und Validierung für die Simulation in Produktion und Logistik: Vorgehensmodelle und Techniken*. VDI-Buch. Springer, Berlin and Heidelberg.

[26] Rapps, S. and Weyuker, E. J. 1982. Data flow analysis techniques for test data selection. In Proceedings of the 6th International Conference on Software Engineering (Tokyo, Japan, 1982). IEEE Computer Society Press, Los Alamitos, CA, USA, 272–278.

[27] Recalde, L., Silva, M., Ezpeleta, J., and Teruel, E. 2003. Petri nets and manufacturing systems: An examples-driven tour. In *Lectures on Concurrency and Petri Nets'03*, volume 3098, 742–788.

[28] Reisig, W. 2010. *Petrinetze: Modellierungstechnik, Analysemethoden, Fallstudien*. Vieweg + Teubner, Wiesbaden.

[29] Reisig, W. and Desel, J. 2014. Konzepte der petrinetze. *Informatik-Spektrum*, 37(3), 172–190.

[30] Riedemann, E. H. 1997. *Testmethoden für sequentielle und nebenläufige Software-Systeme*. Leitfäden der Informatik. Teubner, Stuttgart.

[31] Schöf, S., Wieting, R., and Sonnenschein, M. 1997. *Abschlussbericht des Projekts DNS (Distributed Net Simulation)*. Report, OFFIS, Oldenburger Forschungs- und Entwicklungsinst. für Informatik-Werkzeuge und -Systeme, Forschungsbereich 4, Systemmodellierung.

[32] Spillner, A. and Linz, T. 2012. *Basiswissen Softwaretest: Aus- und Weiterbildung zum Certified Tester - Foundation Level nach ISTQB-Standard*. ISQL-Reihe. dpunkt.verlag.

[33] Starke, P. H. 1995. A memo on time constraints in petri nets. Informatik-Bericht Nr. 46, HU Berlin.

[34] Vanoverberghe, D., Halleux, J. d., Tillmann, N., and Piessens, F. 2011. Code coverage - extended version.

[35] Viswanadham, N. and Raghavan, S. N. R. 2000. Performance analysis and design of supply chains: a petri net approach. *Journal of the Operational Research Society*, 51(10), 1158–1169.

[36] Wagner, R. and Grau, N. 2014. *Basiswissen Projektmanagement: Prozesse und Vorgehensmodelle.* Symposion Publishing, Düsseldorf.

[37] Weiser, M. D., Gannon, J. D., and McMullin, P. R. 1985. Comparison of structural test coverage metrics. *IEEE Software*, 2(2), 80–85.

[38] Zhu, H., Hall, P. A. V., and May, J. H. R. 1997. Software unit test coverage and adequacy. *ACM Computing Survey*, 29(4), 366–427.

Big Data Decision Making Based on Predictive Data Analysis Using DEVS Simulations

Natacha Ellul
University of Corsica
SPE UMR CNRS 6134
Campus Grimaldi, 20250
Corte (France)
natacha.ellul@gmail.com

Laurent Capocchi
University of Corsica
SPE UMR CNRS 6134
Campus Grimaldi, 20250
Corte (France)
capocchi@univ-corse.fr

Jean-François Santucci
University of Corsica
SPE UMR CNRS 6134
Campus Grimaldi, 20250
Corte (France)
santucci@univ-corse.fr

ABSTRACT

Methods of processing and analyzing traditional data does not answer to the emergence of Big Data (BD) stemming from social networks and mobile applications. One of the best ways to bring the perspective of the customers to business decisions is by using data analysis to allow a company to deal with the customer experience for improved management and better profits. The work in progress presented in this paper concerns the development of an approach integrating discrete-event Modeling and Simulation (M&S) and statistical learning methods in order to perform both customer understanding through data classification and predictive modeling through data prediction. This work involves the integration of statistical learning algorithms in the DEVS formalism.

Categories and Subject Descriptors

I.6.8 [**Simulation and Modeling**]: Types of Simulation—
Discrete event

Keywords

Discrete event modeling, Simulation, Big Data, DEVSimPy, Artificial neural network

1. INTRODUCTION

Methods of processing and analyzing traditional data does not answer to the emergence of big data stemming from social networks and mobile applications. For years, data processing allows to ask questions and find answers through analytics. With the emergence of big data, larger amounts of data coming this time from a variety of sources has to be handled and it happens to see the emergence of issues that we did not suspect. The subject of this work in progress belongs to this previous context. The goal is the development of concepts and computer tools for predictive analysis of massive data. Predictive analysis will be conducted using modeling and discrete-event simulation coupled with techniques of artificial intelligence (neural networks [1], SVM

SIGSIM-PADS'15, June 10–12, 2015, London, United Kingdom.
ACM 978-1-4503-3583-6/15/06.
http://dx.doi.org/10.1145/2769458.2769491.

(Support Vector Machines) [3], etc.). In particular several predictive analysis models will be implemented and integrated into a library in a M&S environment based on the DEVS formalism (Discrete EVent system Specification) [7]. The innovative character of the work is highlighted by the close collaboration between the world of enterprise (Joint Venture Corsican CampusPlex Compagny including Good Barber enterprise) and the world of research (SPE lab.) on future issues around the treatment of massive data. Indeed the developed concepts and tools are been validated on a set of data provided by the Good Barber enterprise working on the development of mobile application. This enterprise has more than 2100 of customers worldwide and a marketing strategy will be developed from the results of the presented work. The rest of the paper is organized as follows: the background and problematic involved in the presented work is given in the next section. In section 3 a case study stemming from the Good Barber involving Big Data and DEVS Simulations is presented while the perspectives are pointed out in the final section.

2. BACKGROUND AND PROBLEMATICS

One of the best ways to bring the perspective of the customers to business decisions is by using data analysis to allow a company to deal with the customer experience for improved management and better profits. We point out the two main reasons to integrate big data analytics into the management of company information: (i) better customer understanding: Big Data analytics can be conducted in order to group customers according to their behaviors. (ii) predictive modeling: Predictive analytics will allow a company to forecast how customers are going to respond in the future based on their past behaviors.

In this paper we point out how the DEVS formalism has been combined with neural networks in order to perform classification in the framework of a real case study concerning customers understanding for the Good Barber enterprise implemented with the DEVSimPy environment. DEVS (Discrete EVent system Specification) has been introduced as an abstract formalism for the modeling of discrete-event systems, and allows a complete independence from the simulator using the notion of abstract simulator. DEVSimPy [2] is an open Source project supported by the SPE team of the University of Corsica.

From a M&S perspectives the following tasks have been performed: (i) Development of a DEVSimPy Neural Network (NN) components library for manipulating neural nets by extending the work already presented in [6] in order to deal with the problematics raised by the Good Barber application; (ii) Development of a set of DEVSimPy plug-in allowing to facilitate the design of NN configuration, training and validation when dealing with the Big Data.

3. CASE STUDY

3.1 Description

The case study concerns the classification of the customer behaviors in terms of period of subscription to a mobile application from customers. The collection of the data has been realized in closed collaboration with the Good Barber enterprise . From an analysis of the collected data, we have defined a set of feature types which should allow to characterize the behavior of a customer: country income level of the customer, number of connections per day to the back-office for the first month, number of exchanged threads with the support for the first month, number of exchanged messages with the support for the first month, number of downloads IOS for the first month, number of downloads Android for the first month, costumer language, pricing, number of application launches for the first month, Option GB_submit (yes or no), publish the first month (yes or no). In order to classify a given customer, two kinds of subscription are used: subscription less than three months and subscription more than three months. The DEVSimPy Neural Network library allows to build a back-propagation gradient network which is the most frequently used. A DEVSimPy plug-in (learning-algo) allows to select between the following learning algorithms: simple gradient descent [5], Levenberg-Marquardt [4].

3.2 Initial Results

Figure 1 depicts the four quadratic errors obtained after simulations with 1000 cycles, 80 vectors for the learning phase and 50 other vectors for validation phase.

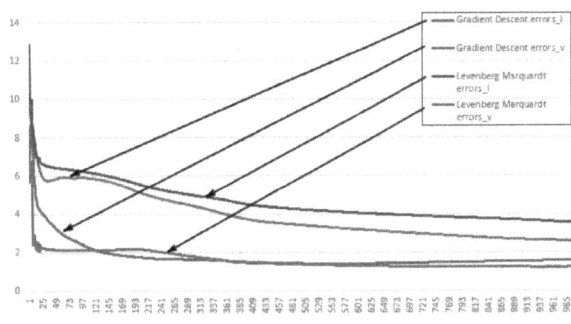

Figure 1: Quadratic errors with gradient descent and Levenberg-Marquardt algorithms.

The results obtained using the simple gradient descent learning algorithm on the training data highlight a slow evolution of the quadratic error. The Levenberg-Marquardt algorithm allows to improve the convergence.

4. FUTURE WORK

The first results are encouraging and we already initiate the second step consisting in developing a prediction process based on neural networks. The goal is now to predict the behavior of a given customer in terms of subscription actions. We also plan a long-term research work towards the development of concepts and tools allowing to integrate in the framework of the DEVS formalism and tools a set of statistical learning methods in order to deal with both classification or prediction problems associated with big data.

5. CONCLUSIONS

This paper deals with big data decision-making based on predictive data analysis using DEVS simulations. The background and problematics of this work in progress have been pointed out: the overall goal of the work is to offer a company - working in the Mobile applications design - a tool allowing to analysis and predict the behaviors of customers in terms of subscription period. The analysis leans on a set of data stemming from more than three millions customers of the company. This work involves the integration of statistical learning algorithms in the framework of the DEVS formalism. The implementation leans on the definition of a library of DEVSimPy components and plug-in allowing to efficiently manage neural network features as pre-processing, network configuration and learning algorithm selection.

6. REFERENCES

[1] Bishop, C. M. 1995. *Neural Networks for Pattern Recognition.* Oxford University Press, Inc., New York, NY, USA.

[2] Capocchi, L., Santucci, J.-F., Poggi, B. and Nicolai, C. 2011. DEVSimPy: A Collaborative Python Software for Modeling and Simulation of DEVS Systems, In *Proc. of 20th IEEE International Workshops on Enabling Technologies: Infrastructure for Collaborative Enterprises* (Paris, France, 27-29 June, 2011). IEEE, 170-175. DOI=10.1109/WETICE.2011.31.

[3] Hearst, M.A., Dumais, S.T., Osman, E., Platt, J. and Scholkopf, B. 1998. Support vector machines, *Intelligent Systems and their Applications*, IEEE, vol.13, no.4, 18-28. DOI=10.1109/5254.708428.

[4] Marquardt, D. W. 1963. An Algorithm for Least-Squares Estimation of Nonlinear Parameters, *Journal of the Society for Industrial and Applied Mathematics*, 11:2, 431-441. DOI=10.1137/0111030.

[5] Rumelhart, D.E., McClelland, J.L, and CORPORATE PDP Research Group (Eds.). 1986. *Parallel Distributed Processing: Explorations in the Microstructure of Cognition, Vol. 1: Foundations.* MIT Press, Cambridge, MA, USA. ISBN=0-262-68053-X.

[6] Toma, S., Capocchi, L., and Capolino, G.-A. 2013. Wound-rotor induction generator inter-turn short-circuits diagnosis using a new digital neural network. *Industrial Electronics, IEEE Transactions on*, 60, 9 (Sept 2013), 4043-4052. DOI=10.1109/TIE.2012.2229675.

[7] Zeigler, B., Praehofer, H. and Kim, T.G. 2000. *Theory of Modeling and Simulation, Second Edition.* Academic Press, Inc., Orlando, FL, USA.

An Asynchronous Synchronization Strategy for Parallel Large-scale Agent-based Traffic Simulations

Yadong Xu
School of Computer
Engineering
Nanyang Technological
University
Singapore 639798
xuya0006@ntu.edu.sg

Wentong Cai
School of Computer
Engineering
Nanyang Technological
University
Singapore 639798
aswtcai@ntu.edu.sg

Heiko Aydt
TUM CREATE Ltd.
CREATE Tower
1 Create Way
Singapore 138602
heiko.aydt@tum-
create.edu.sg

Michael Lees
Informatics Institute
University of Amsterdam
Amsterdam 1098 XH, The
Netherlands
m.h.lees@uva.nl

Daniel Zehe
TUM CREATE Ltd.
CREATE Tower 1 Create Way
Singapore 138602
daniel.zehe@tum-
create.edu.sg

ABSTRACT

Large-scale agent-based traffic simulation is a promising tool to study the road traffic and help solving traffic problems, such as congestion and high emission in megacities. Such simulation requires high computational resource which triggers the need for parallel computing. The parallelization of agent-based traffic simulations is generally performed by decomposing the simulation space into spatial subregions. The agent models contained by each subregion are executed by Logical Processes (LPs). As the simulated system evolves over the simulation time in individual LPs, synchronization among LPs is required due to data dependencies. Existing work has used global barriers for synchronization which is a type of synchronous synchronization method. However, global barriers have very low efficiency due to the waiting of processes at barriers. High synchronization overhead is still one of the major performance issues in parallel large-scale agent-based traffic simulations. In this paper, we proposed a novel asynchronous conservative synchronization strategy named Mutual Appointment (MA) to address this issue. MA removes global barriers and allows LPs to communicate individually. Since the efficiency of conservative synchronization relies on the lookahead of the simulated system, a heuristic was developed to increase the lookahead in agent-based traffic simulations. It takes advantage of the intrinsic uncertainties in traffic simulations. MA together with the lookahead heuristic forms the Relaxed Mutual Appointment (RMA) strategy. Its efficiency was investigated in the parallel agent-based traffic simulator SEMSim Traffic using real world traffic data. Experiment results showed that the MA

strategy improved the speed-up of the parallel simulation compared to the barrier method, and the RMA strategy further improved the MA strategy by reducing the number of synchronization messages significantly.

Categories and Subject Descriptors

I.6.8 [**Simulation and Modeling**]: Types of Simulation—*Parallel, Discrete event*; I.6.3 [**Simulation and Modeling**]: Applications

General Terms

Algorithms, Performance

Keywords

Agent-based traffic simulation, Asynchronous conservative synchronization, Relaxation

1. INTRODUCTION

With the fast urbanization of our modern society, road traffic in large cities and mega-cities are facing problems such as congestion and high emission which negatively impact the comfort and health of urban inhabitants. To study road traffic and solve urban traffic problems, the modeling and simulation of road traffic has been a useful tool. The modeling and simulation of road traffic can be approached in various ways, depending on the level of abstraction necessary. The levels of abstraction are commonly known as macroscopic [16, 23], mesoscopic [22], microscopic [9], and nanoscopic (a.k.a., sub-microscopic) [18]. Road traffic is a complex system whose behavior is difficult to predict. As a complex system, the behaviors of constituent components have an impact on the whole system. From this perspective, the modeling of the behaviors of individual components, i.e., driver-vehicle-units falls within the scope of the microscopic and nanoscopic levels of detail. Both microscopic and nanoscopic simulations can be conducted in an agent-based approach where driver-vehicle-units are agents that have certain behaviors and try to reach certain goals in the simulation. Large-scale agent-based traffic simulation is a promising method for studying the road traffic, for instance, the impact of various driving behaviors on the traffic and the influence of adopting electric vehicles (EVs) or automatic vehicles in the transportation system. SEMSim Traffic is a nanoscopic traffic simulator that is able to capture this level of detail [28]. It is designed to study how different vehicle designs and different infrastructures will influence the transportation system when EVs are introduced at a large-scale in mega-cities. However, one of the challenges to conduct a simulation at a large-scale, e.g., the whole city, is the requirement of high computational resource. To make large-scale agent-based traffic simulations computationally feasible, certain computing techniques should be deployed. To harness more computational resource, parallel computing can be used. There are many critical aspects of considerations on developing a parallel simulation, for example, time synchronization [7], partitioning and load balancing [28], and interest management [14]. The problem of time synchronization is addressed in this study. The focus is to reduce the overhead of the time synchronization in agent-based traffic simulation.

Existing microscopic and nanoscopic traffic simulations are conventionally executed in a time-stepped fashion [1–3, 17, 26]. In parallel microscopic and nanoscopic traffic simulations, the decomposition of the simulation is usually achieved by decomposing the simulation space into multiple spatial subregions. The agent models contained by each subregion are executed by Logical Processes (LPs). The LPs are usually assigned to different physical processing units. Due to the interaction of agents, there are usually data read and write dependencies between LPs. When read or write dependency happens between two LPs at a certain simulation time, the LPs should not progress over the simulation time until the dependency is fulfilled by the LPs exchanging necessary data. This operation to fulfill the dependencies is referred as a *synchronization* operation. The simulation analyzed in this work is a discrete-event simulation, where agents schedule time-stamped events which are ordered by their time-stamps and the simulation progresses by executing the events. Synchronization strategies have been well studied in the parallel discrete-event simulation community. Synchronization strategies can be broadly categorized into conservative and optimistic [7, 20]. Conservative strategies prohibits any causality error from occurring, whereas optimistic strategies uses a detection and recover approach: causality errors are detected, and a rollback mechanism is invoked to recover [7]. In existing work, synchronization in the traffic simulations is generally achieved using global barriers either in a shared memory environment [1, 2] or distributed memory environment [3, 17, 26]. This method is straightforward to use. Global barriers can be deployed at the end of time steps. This is equivalent to a *synchronous* conservative synchronization strategy where all LPs participate in a synchronization at the same time and usually global reduction is used. The limitation of this synchronization method is that all processes have to wait in front of a global barrier during the synchronization. This may decrease the parallel efficiency. Another type of conservative synchronization strategy is *asynchronous*. LPs do not wait at a global barrier when synchronizing in an asynchronous strategy. To the best of our knowledge, asynchronous conservative synchronization has not been used in parallel agent-based traffic simulations.

In this study, we have developed a novel asynchronous conservative synchronization strategy for agent-based traffic simulations named Mutual Appointment (MA). It considered the characteristics of the behavioral models of agents. In MA, LPs synchronize with each other using appointments. An appointment is an event scheduled at a specific simulation time where two processes exchange data by sending messages and whose time stamp is mutually made by the two communicating partners according to their *lookaheads*. Lookahead of an LP_1 towards another LP_2 at simulation time t is a time interval Δt in the simulated future within which LP_1 will not have data read and write dependency with LP_2. The lookahead values represent the ability of an LP predicting its future behavior that may affect other LPs. The larger the lookahead values, the less the synchronization operations. Due to the characteristic of behavioral models of agents, agent-based traffic simulations have inherently low lookahead. Low lookahead limits the efficiency of conservative synchronization strategies, therefore, a way to increase the lookahead is required. Therefore, we developed a heuristic to increase the lookahead. The lookahead heuristic takes advantage of the intrinsic *uncertainties* of traffic simulations. We claim that as long as the parallelization does not increase the uncertainty of the simulation, certain dependencies between the processes of the parallel simulation can be violated. The heuristic allows a certain amount of violation of dependency but keeps the output of the simulation statistically unaltered. It uses the traffic flow information at run-time to exploit the lookahead. This heuristic together with MA forms Relaxed Mutual Appointment (RMA) strategy. Statistical tests were performed to ensure that the output of the parallel and sequential simulations are statistically indistinguishable. The synchronization strategies are experimented in the traffic simulator SEMSim Traffic. Our contribution to the literature is

- an asynchronous conservative synchronization strategy for parallel agent-based traffic simulations (Section 3); and

- a heuristic to solve the problem of low lookahead of agent-based traffic simulations taking advantage of the uncertainties in traffic simulations (Section 4.2)

Examples of potential usage of the proposed methods are: enable large-scale traffic simulations to operate at or faster than real-time; let agent-based traffic simulations generate results faster when used as a forecasting tool in time critical decision making situations; and reduce the running time of scientific experiments which requires repeated runs of traffic simulations.

The remainder of the paper is organized as follows: The agent models and the partitioning of the traffic simulation that our algorithm operates on is described in Section 2. Terminology and more detail on the background are presented. Then we introduce the MA synchronization strategy in Section 3, and the RMA strategy in Section 4. These two sections are the main contribution of this work. Following that, experiments and results are presented in Section 5. Subsequently, related work is presented in Section 6. In the end, the conclusions and future work are presented in Section 7.

2. PARALLEL AGENTED-BASED TRAFFIC SIMULATION

The synchronization strategies are fundamentally determined by the behavior of the simulated models and partitioning of the simulation. Agent models, the partitioning of the simulation, and more review on conservative synchronization are introduced in this section.

2.1 Models and Model Execution

The simulation space of our agent-based traffic simulation is a road network which is a *spatial network*. The spatial network consists links and nodes. Links are containers/placeholders of agents. A link may have one or more lanes. Nodes contain the connectivity information of links and lanes. A small road network is illustrated in Figure 1. For simplicity, lanes are not shown.

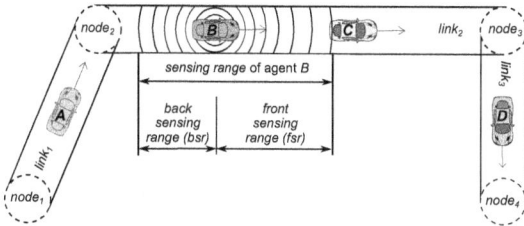

Figure 1: Agents with sensing ranges in a road network.

The *agent* in the simulation is a driver-vehicle-unit that contains driver behavior models and vehicle component models. Examples of driver behavior models are the acceleration model and the lane-changing model, and examples of vehicle component models are the motor model and the battery model for EVs. An agent has a *state* at a certain instant of the simulation time. The state contains multiple state variables which are classified into two groups according to there visibility: agent-based state variables and component-based variables. Agent-based state variables belong to the agent and are visible to other agents, e.g., velocity and position. The component-based variables belong to a specific model and are usually not visible to other agents, e.g., a state-of-charge state variable in the battery model. The state of an agent changes as the simulation evolves with the execution of timestamped *events* which contain certain update functions. Events are ordered in ascending order of their time stamp in an *event list*. There is one event list per LP. An LP repeatedly executes a three-step cycle: advance the simulation time to the time stamp of first event in the event list, execute the event (and schedule future events triggered by this event if any), and remove the event from the event list. Events are scheduled by driver behavior models and vehicle models [28]. This event-based execution enables the models to be executed with suitable temporal resolution individually. An agent has a *sensing range* which is the area around the agent within which the states of other agents may have an effect on the agent's behavior. An illustration is shown in Figure 1. Even though the traveling direction of the agent is unidirectional in the road network, the sensing range is omni-directional, since the agent needs to examine the area in front to decide appropriate accelerations, and the area both in front and behind to decide safe lane-changes.

The models that form the main computational components are currently the driving behavior models, i.e., the acceleration and lane-changing models. Examples are Gipps'

acceleration model [9] and Intelligent Driver Model (IDM) [27], and their corresponding lane-changing models [10, 13]. Acceleration models generates the actual velocity or acceleration in the next time-step based on the current surrounding information and characteristics of the driver and the vehicle. Similarly, lane-changing models decides if a lane change should be performed. The models schedule *move events*. A move event contains both acceleration and lane-changing and are scheduled periodically with a fixed interval. We refer to this fixed interval as a *move interval* in the rest of this paper. Move events change the dependency between agents since they change the positions of agents in the road network.

2.2 Partitioning and Dependency of Logical Processes

The road network is partitioned into multiple spatial sub-regions. A partitioning of Singapore into four partitions is shown in Figure 2. Different intensities of gray represent different partitions. An LP is responsible for executing the events of the agents in one partition, and only has access to the agents in the local space. The cutting of the network is performed on links. The links that are cut and spanning two partitions are named *boundary links*. A boundary link is evenly divided between two partitions. For instance, in Figure 3a, $link_2$ is a boundary link. The left half belongs to LP_1, and the right half belongs to LP_2. Since the driving direction of $link_2$ is from LP_1 to LP_2, we say $link_2$ is an *outgoing boundary link* of LP_1, and an *incoming boundary link* of LP_2. LP_1 and LP_2 are *neighboring processes*.

Figure 2: Singapore road network with four partitions.

As the simulation progresses, *migration* of an agent happens when the agent moves beyond the boundary of one partition and enters the space of another. For example, in Figure 3a, suppose agent B in LP_1 continues moving on $link_2$ and its new position falls within LP_2 at time t, it should be migrated to LP_2, and LP_2 would be responsible for executing future events of agent B. In this case, there is a *write dependency* between LP_1 and LP_2 at time t. If the position of agent C in LP_2 is inside the sensing range of agent B in LP_1, the state variables of agent C that may affect the behavior of agent B should be sent over to LP_1 and kept updated to maintain the correctness of the simulation. In this case, there is a *read dependency* between LP_1 and LP_2. These state variables of agent C are referred as *shared states*. To help determining where shared states are, *buffered regions* are defined. They are the areas along the boundary cut of partitions with the size equal to the sensing range of agents. The states of the agents that are inside buffered regions and directly next to the boundary cut are

261

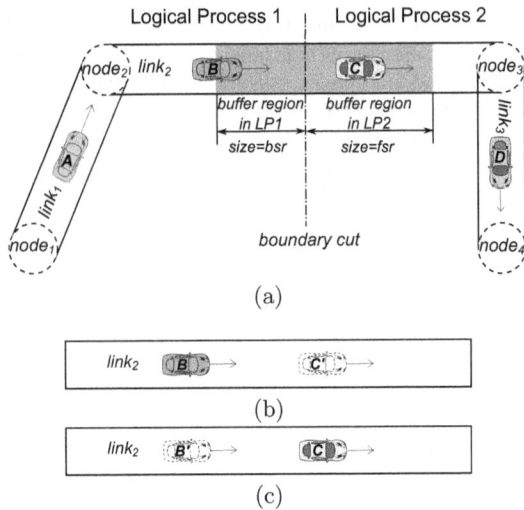

Figure 3: Road network partitioning: (a) illustration of boundary cut and buffer regions; (b) view of $link_2$ from LP_1; and (c) view of $link_2$ from LP_2.

considered as shared states. For example, in Figure 3a, the shaded area on $link_2$ are two buffered regions, with the left side inside $LP1$ and right side inside LP_2. The size of the buffer region inside LP_1 equals to the back sensing range of agents, and the size inside LP_2 equals to the front sensing range of agents. Since agent B and C are both inside the buffer region, shared states of agent B are sent to LP_2 and those of agent C to LP_1.

In addition, the LPs that receive shared states use the shared states to create non-local *proxy agents*. Proxy agents act as representatives of the *real agents* in other LPs, so that the agents can see the shared states as agents. For example, there is a proxy agent C' in LP_1 of real agent C (Figure 3b), and a proxy agent B' in LP_2 of real agent B (Figure 3c). This is for managing the shared states more easily and simplifying the implementation of the simulator.

2.3 Synchronization of Logical Processes

The need for synchronization originates from the read and write dependencies between LPs. An LP should not progress the simulation over the point when read or write dependency happens until the dependency is fulfilled by exchanging information with the relevant LPs. Synchronization here means the management of the sending and receiving of migrating agents and shared states. Synchronization strategies can be broadly categorized into conservative and optimistic [7,20]. Conservative strategies prohibits any causality error from occurring, whereas optimistic strategies allows causality errors to occur, and a rollback mechanism is invoked to recover the errors [7]. This study only deals with the conservative approach. A synchronization strategy is *synchronous* if global synchronization points are used, i.e., a barrier or a global reduction, where all LPs participate in the communication. *All* LPs are blocked until the communication is finished. In contrast, in an *asynchronous* strategy, blocking does not happen globally. When LP_2 is specially told by LP_1 that it might be affected by LP_1 at time t, only LP_2 is blocked at time t [20]. All other irrelevant LPs are free to proceed their execution without participating in this synchronization operation. Asynchronous strategy has the potential advantage over synchronous strategy that it

may reduce the waiting of LPs and decrease the number of synchronization messages.

A key ingredient of an conservative synchronization strategy is the *lookahead*. Lookahead defines the ability of an LP predicting its behavior that might affect other LPs. The lookahead in our simulation can be defined as follows: if an LP_1 is at simulation time t, and it predicts that it does not have any read and write dependency with LP_2 until simulation time $t + \Delta t$, then LP_1 has a lookahead of Δt towards LP_2. To determine the lookahead values is to predict when the read and write dependencies change in the simulated future. Determining the lookahead is a critical component of a conservative synchronization strategy.

3. MUTUAL APPOINTMENT STRATEGY

This section presents the MA strategy and the lookahead determination algorithm.

3.1 Mutual Appointment

The basic idea of MA is that an LP communicates with other LPs by making *appointments* individually with them at certain mutually agreed time points of the simulation. The execution of the LP will be blocked at an appointment until the appointment is fulfilled. This blocking only happens between this LP pair. An MA contains two tasks: exchange information of current dependency and make the next appointment. The MAs are scheduled as synchronization events. The logic of an MA synchronization event is shown in Algorithm 1.

Algorithm 1: MA Synchronization Event

Definitions:

t	time stamp of the synchronization event in LP_i
$A_{i,t}$	set of agents in LP_i at t
$C_{i,t}$	set of LPs having appointments with LP_i at t
$M_{ij,t}$	set of agents migrating from LP_i to LP_j at t
$S_{ij,t}$	set of shared states sent by LP_i to LP_j at t
$l_{ij,t}$	lookahead of LP_i towards LP_j at t
$\Delta t_{ij,t}$	time interval until next appointment between LP_i and LP_j at t

foreach $LP_j \in C_{i,t}$ **do**

    // 1. prepare the content of the message
    determine $M_{ij,t}$, $S_{ij,t}$, and $l_{ij,t}$;

    // 2. exchange messages
    send $M_{ij,t}$, $S_{ij,t}$, and $l_{ij,t}$ to LP_j;
    receive $M_{ji,t}$, $S_{ji,t}$, and $l_{ji,t}$ from LP_j;

    // 3. update the set of local agents
    $A_{i,t} \leftarrow A_{i,t} \cup M_{ji,t} \setminus M_{ij,t}$;
    // 4. update proxy agents with shared
        states
    update proxy agents with $S_{ji,t}$;
    // 5. make a new appointment
    $\Delta t_{ij,t} \leftarrow \min(l_{ij,t}, l_{ji,t})$;
    make an appointment with LP_j at time $t + \Delta t_{ij,t}$;

end

The event is in LP_i with the time stamp t. In the synchronization event, there is a set of LPs that currently have appointments with LP_i, denoted as $C_{i,t}$. An LP only synchronizes with its direct neighbors, therefore, $C_{i,t}$ only contains neighboring LPs. Note that $C_{i,t}$ may *not* include all the neighboring LPs of LP_i and can be empty. For each LP_j in the set $C_{i,t}$, LP_i performs the following five steps. The first step is to prepare the data for fulfilling the read and write dependency, and calculate lookahead for the next appointment. Migrating agents $M_{ij,t}$ and shared states $S_{ij,t}$ are determined by scanning the boundary links between LP_i and LP_j. Then in the second step, LP_i sends all that information to LP_j. A point-to-point communication is used. To reduce the number of messages, a single compound synchronization message is used which contains three parts of information: migrating agents (write dependency), shared states (read dependency), and lookahead (predicted time interval until the next MA event). At the same time, it receives a message from LP_j which contains the migrating agents $M_{ji,t}$, shared states $S_{ji,t}$, and lookahead $l_{ji,t}$. The partner LP_j is inside an MA event with the time stamp t as well. After receiving the message, the third step is to update the local agents. The local agent set $A_{i,t}$ is updated by removing the agents in $M_{ij,t}$, and adding the agents in $M_{ji,t}$. Then the next step is to update the proxy agents in LP_i with the latest shared state $S_{ji,t}$. Unnecessary proxy agents are removed, and new proxy agents are created if necessary. The last step is to schedule the next synchronization event. LP_i determines the time interval until the next appointment with LP_j as $\Delta t_{ij,t} = min(l_{ij,t}, l_{ji,t})$, and the next synchronization event with LP_j will be scheduled at time $t + \Delta t_{ij,t}$. If there is no synchronization event scheduled at the simulation time $t + \Delta t_{ij,t}$ yet, a new synchronization event is scheduled. Otherwise, the id of LP_j will be added to the set $C_{i,(t+\Delta t_{ij,t})}$ of the synchronization event that already scheduled at time $t + \Delta t_{ij,t}$ instead of scheduling a new event.

The initial MAs are scheduled at the beginning of the simulation for all LPs. The targets of the initial MAs of an LP are all of its neighboring LPs. All subsequent MAs are made based on lookaheads.

3.2 Lookahead Determination

The lookahead in the MA synchronization strategy is *directed*, which means that an LP may have different lookahead values towards each neighboring LPs at a certain simulation time. The lookahead values are used to make individual appointments. There are three cases considered according to different traffic conditions.

The first case is that no agents exist in the local space. This usually happens when the simulation just starts up. The lookahead should be the minimum time for any newly created agent to travel into buffer regions on outgoing boundary links. Suppose the set of agents to be created locally in LP_i is $NA = \{na_1, na_2, ..., na_{|NA|}\}$; agent na_k ($1 \le k \le |NA|$) is scheduled to be created nat_k later in the future, and requires minimum traveling time tt_k to travel from the point of creation to the buffer region connecting to LP_j on its route (if the agent does not pass by LP_j, $tt_k = \infty$), then the earliest time for newly created agents to possibly affect LP_j is $min(nat_k + tt_k)$ later from the current time. Thus the current lookahead towards LP_j should be $min(nat_k + tt_k)$. If the schedule to create new agents is not available, the effect of new agents should be considered in another way. Suppose the set of outgoing boundary links towards LP_j is OL_{ij}, the minimum traveling time from the start of a link l ($l \in OL_{ij}$) to the buffer region of that link is obt_l, then the minimum time for any new agent to travel to a buffer region is $min(obt_l)$. An example of obt_l is shown in Figure

4a. The lookahead should be $min(obt_l)$. Note that all the estimation of traveling time here is a lower bound. The actual traveling time is usually longer, since the actual velocities of agents are usually smaller than the speed limit, in other words, since agents usually do not travel with speed-limit, tt_k and $min(obt_l)$ are rather conservative estimations.

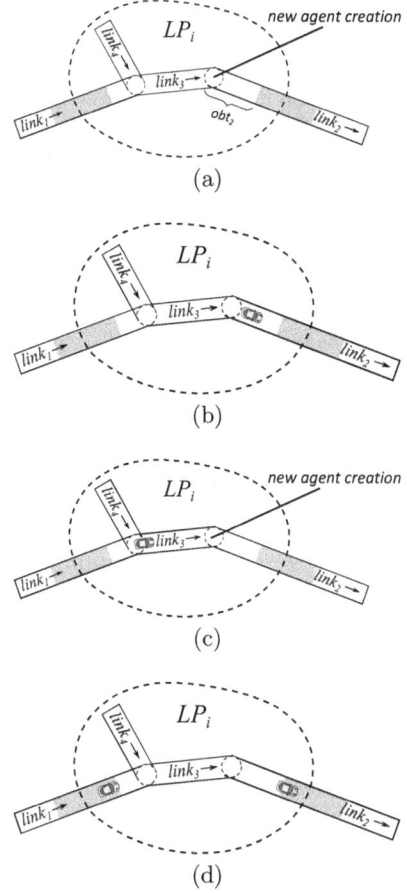

Figure 4: Scenarios of MA lookahead calculation: (a) no local agents exist, a new agent is being created in a network node; (b) buffer regions are empty and no migrating agents; (c) same with (b) with agents being created; and (d) buffer regions are not empty.

The second case is that there are local agents, but there are no agents inside buffer regions or migrating before the next move event, as depicted in Figures 4b and 4c. The lookahead is the minimum time for a local agent to travel to a buffer region. Migration of local agents only happens on outgoing links, therefore, the agents whose routes pass through outgoing boundary links should be examined. Note that new agents may be created on an outgoing link (Figure 4c). This case should also be considered. Suppose the minimum traveling time of any existing agent to a buffer region connecting to LP_j on its route is at_j, considering the agents to be created NA, the lookahead in this case is $min(at_j, min(nat_k + tt_k))$. If the schedule to create new agents is not available, similar to the first case, $min(obt_l)$ should be used instead of $min(nat_k + tt_k)$. Then, the lookahead is $min(at_j, min(obt_l))$.

The third case is that there are agents inside local buffer regions or to be migrated before the next move event. Lookahead can only be as big as one move interval, since the shared

Algorithm 2: MA lookahead determination

Definitions:

A_i	set of agents in LP_i
L_{ij}	set of boundary links between LP_i and LP_j
M_l	set of agents migrating on link l, $l \in L_{ij}$
S_l	set of shared states on link l in LP_i, $l \in L_{ij}$
nat_k	time interval before new agent k is created
tt_k	minimum time for new agent k to travel to any outgoing boundary link towards LP_j on its route
obt_l	traveling time from the start of link l to the buffer region of l, l is an outgoing link towards LP_j
at_j	minimum time for any agent in A_i to travel from its current position to the buffer region of any outgoing boundary link towards LP_j on its route
sa	boolean - if the schedule to create agents available

Result: lookahead towards LP_j

Initialize $lookahead \leftarrow maximum\ double$;
// the first case
if $A_i = \emptyset$ **then**
$\quad$ **if** sa **then**
$\quad\quad$ $lookahead \leftarrow min(nat_k + tt_k)$;
$\quad$ **else**
$\quad\quad$ $lookahead \leftarrow min(obt_l)$;
$\quad$ **end**
// the second case
else if $\forall l \in L_{ij}: M_l = \emptyset \wedge S_l = \emptyset$ **then**
$\quad$ **if** sa **then**
$\quad\quad$ $lookahead \leftarrow min(at_j, min(nat_k + tt_k))$;
$\quad$ **else**
$\quad\quad$ $lookahead \leftarrow min(at_j, min(obt_l))$;
$\quad$ **end**
// the third case
else
$\quad$ $lookahead \leftarrow one\ move\ interval$;
end
$lookahead \leftarrow max(lookahead,\ one\ move\ interval)$;

states must be updated before the next move event takes place. An example is shown in Figure 4d. There is an agent inside the buffer region of an incoming boundary link $link_1$ of LP_i and another inside the buffer region of an outgoing boundary link $link_2$.

The minimum value of a lookahead is one move interval, because one move interval is the assumed period of time in which no states of the agents that may affect other agents are updated. After estimating the lookahead, if the lookahead value is smaller than one move interval, its value is set to one move interval. An illustration of process of determining the MA lookahead is shown in Algorithm 2. The worse case of this lookahead determination algorithm happens when there are always migrating agents or shared states, in which case the lookahead always equals to one move interval.

4. RELAXED MUTUAL APPOINTMENT STRATEGY

The lookahead described in Section 3.2 approaches to one move interval when the traffic is always dense along the boundary of LPs and there are often migrating agents and shared states. In this case, MA may hardly have advantage over a global barrier synchronization. This section presents a method to increase the lookahead by exploiting the uncer-

tainty in the simulation and potentially trading-off certain accuracy of the simulation.

4.1 Uncertainties in the Simulation

Error and uncertainty exist throughout the process of modeling and simulation [11,21]. This is also true for traffic simulation. Traffic simulation mimics the behavior of the real world traffic but can never duplicate the real world. There are always uncertainties in a traffic simulation [5]. Uncertainty is categorized into two types in literature. The first category is *aleatory uncertainty*, a.k.a., stochastic uncertainty, irreducible uncertainty, inherent uncertainty, and variability. It is the inherent variation associated with the physical system, in this context, real road traffic. Aleatory uncertainty is represented as a number of streams of random variables drawn from specified probability distributions in a computer simulation, for example, the distribution of the trips starting time of agents in traffic simulation. Aleatory uncertainty can be quantified by repeated simulation runs with different random variable streams. In scientific studies, simulations are usually run multiple times to get statistically meaningful results. The second category of uncertainty is *epistemic uncertainty*, a.k.a., reducible uncertainty, subjective uncertainty, and cognitive uncertainty. It results from a lack of knowledge about the simulated system. For example, the input for traffic simulation, such as traffic demand, is usually estimated from real world observed data or forecast, and *input uncertainty* arises from the estimation and forecast process. Models used in the traffic simulation are the abstraction of the real world, and *model uncertainty* exists in both the model equation (e.g., certain assumption on the function form and omitted variables) and the values of model coefficients (usually estimated by calibration) [5]. Uncertainty in traffic simulation may be utilized to improve the synchronization of parallel traffic simulation, which is presented in the following subsection.

4.2 Lookahead in RMA

Consider a situation where the traffic is jammed on a boundary link, and all agents are hardly moving, the states of the agents do not change much, but the synchronization is performed once per move interval according to the MA lookahead algorithm. This frequent synchronization may not be necessary because skipping some synchronization events here may not have much influence on the output of the simulation. As discussed, traffic simulations have inherent stochastic uncertainties. The output of the simulations has certain variability and there is no single correct output of the simulation. This indicates that the parallel simulation does not necessarily produce the exact output as the sequential simulation; instead, a statistically equivalent output is sufficient. Thus, a relaxed lookahead algorithm can be developed, as long as the algorithm does not distort the output of the simulation statistically. This is a similar idea to Fujimoto's work in [8], where the temporal uncertainty of models are exploited to improve the synchronization of parallel and distributed simulations.

When the lookahead is relaxed, the migration of agents may not be achieved in time and the shared states may not be updated in time. The direct consequence is that agents use the obsolete states of proxy agents until the next synchronization. To reduce the discrepancy between the real agents and proxy agents, dead-reckoning is used to update the proxy agents. An illustration of possible discrepancy between a strict synchronization and a relaxed synchronization is shown in Figure 5. Suppose agent B is a local agent

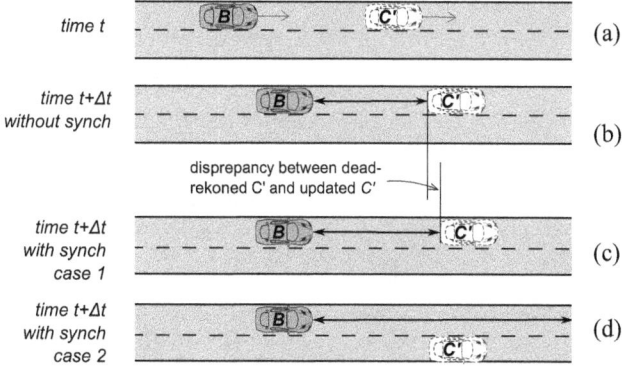

Figure 5: The effect of relaxed synchronization: (a) agent B and proxy agent C' at time t; (b) proxy agent C' at time $t+\Delta t$ calculated by dead-reckoning; (c) proxy agent C' at time $t+\Delta t$ updated by synchronization; (d) same with (c), but agent C performed lane-changing.

and agent C' is a proxy agent in the LP at time t (Figure 5a). The real agent of C', C, resides in another LP. As the simulation progresses to time $t + \Delta t$ (Δt is a move interval), agent B and C calculate their new states. The proxy agent C' should be updated with the shared states of agent C at time $t + \Delta t$ by a synchronization operation. When a synchronization is not performed, C' is updated by dead-reckoning. Discrepancy of the state of C' may occur here due to the difference between the real update function and the dead-reckoning function. Figure 5b and 5c show a case where there is discrepancy of positions between the updated C' and the dead-reckoned C'. Another case where the real agent C has performed lane-change is shown in Figure 5d. The discrepancy of proxy agent C' may or may not lead to discrepancy on agent B in the simulated future depending on their relative position, relative speed, and the sensitivity of the driver's behavior models. Further more, even if there is discrepancy on agent B, the discrepancy may or may not affect the final output of the simulation.

Two factors may influence the allowed relaxation of lookahead: dead-reckoning function and traffic condition. A simple dead-reckoning function can just assume that agents move in a constant speed until the next synchronization. It keeps the velocity of the proxy agents constant and updates the positions accordingly. In this case, the discrepancy is correlated with how much the velocities of the real agents change. Therefore the potential discrepancy in different traffic conditions can be estimated by investigating how the velocities of agents change. Lookahead can be lengthened in the traffic conditions where the discrepancy is potentially insignificant. Traffic condition is typically characterized by traffic density, speed, and flow. *Density* is the number of vehicles per unit length of a roadway. *Speed* is the average distance that vehicles travel per unit time. *Flow* is the number of vehicles passing a reference point per unit time. An experiment studying the relationships between the average change of velocities and these three metrics is shown in Figure 6. A road network with two connecting links l_1 and l_2 were used. The traffic direction is from l_1 to l_2. Agents are created on link l_1, and they travel through both links.

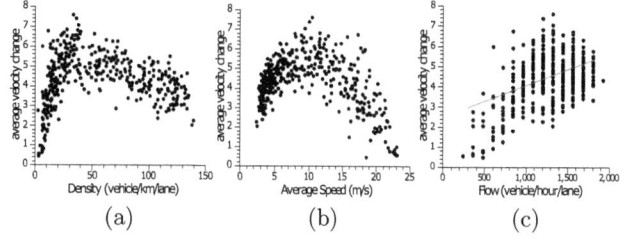

Figure 6: The change of velocities with respect to: (a) density; (b) speed; and (c) flow (the line here is a linear regression line).

Traffic flow, density, average speed, and the average velocity change on a segment of l_1 were recorded every move interval. To create different traffic conditions on l_1, we varied the inter-arrival time of agents, the speed limit of l_1, and the number of lanes in l_2. The average velocity change is calculated with $\sqrt{\frac{\sum_{a=1}^{N}[v_{(a,t+\Delta t)}-v_{(a,t)}]^2}{N}}$, where N is the number of agents on the road segment, and $v_{(a,\ t)}$ is the velocity of agent a at time t, and Δt is the move interval. The result in Figure 6 shows that there is a linear correlation between the change of velocities and traffic flow. The correlation between the change of velocities and density or velocity is not linear. This indicates that if the synchronization is relaxed, the discrepancy is more likely to be greater when traffic flow is higher. A lookahead model can be developed using traffic flow.

We firstly define a time window $window_{l,t}$ of a boundary link l at time t as the longest time period within which synchronizations can be skipped without altering the simulation output. The window is calculated using

$$window_{l,t} = \alpha \cdot \frac{1}{flow_{l,t}} \qquad (1)$$

where α is a sensitive factor, and $flow_l$ is the traffic flow on link l at time t. When $flow_{l,t} = 0$, $window_{l,t} = mw_l$, where mw_l is the maximum window. In fact, the physical meaning of $\frac{1}{flow_{l,t}}$ is the *time headway* which is the time difference between two consecutive vehicles passing a reference point on the road. Thus, this equation can also be interpreted as the time window on a link is proportional to the time headway on the link. The lookahead between two LPs should be the minimum of the time windows of all boundary links between them. Since the appointments are negotiated by both of the synchronizing partners, it is sufficient to consider only outgoing boundary links. Let OL_{ij} be the set of outgoing boundary links from LP_i and LP_j, then the lookahead from LP_i to LP_j at time t is

$$lookahead_{ij,t} = min(window_{l,t}), \ l \in OL_{ij} \qquad (2)$$

The value of α controls the amount of relaxation introduced. The optimal value of α is the one that can maximize lookahead and do not distort the statistical output of the simulation. It may be influenced by the models used in the traffic simulation, the road network, and partitioning. The discrepancy on boundary links may propagate to the upper stream and the lower stream of the link. Therefore, it may be not possible to obtain the optimal α value. A proper α value can be gained with testing experiments.

The lookahead determination algorithm for RMA is shown in Algorithm 3. The algorithm begins with checking the

Algorithm 3: RMA lookahead determination

Definitions:

A_i set of agents in LP_i
OL_{ij} set of outgoing boundary links from LP_i to LP_j
$flow_l$ current traffic flow on link l, $l \in OL_{ij}$
mw_l maximum window of link l, $l \in OL_{ij}$
Result: lookahead towards LP_j

Initialize $lookahead \leftarrow maximum\ double$;
if $A_i = \emptyset$ **then**
   | $lookahead \leftarrow \min(mw_l)$, $l \in OL_{ij}$;
else
   | **foreach** $l \in OL_{ij}$ **do**
   | | **if** $flow_l = 0$ **then**
   | | | $lookahead \leftarrow \min(lookahead,\ mw_l)$;
   | | **else**
   | | | $lookahead \leftarrow \min(lookahead,\ \alpha \cdot \frac{1}{flow_l})$;
   | | **end**
   | **end**
end
$lookahead \leftarrow max(lookahead,\ one\ move\ interval)$;

local agent population: if the local agent set is empty, the lookahead is set to the minimum value of maximum windows directly; if not, the outgoing boundary links are checked one by one and the minimum value of time windows is taken as the lookahead. If the value is less than one move interval, set the lookahead to one move interval. The maximum window of l is calculated using the minimum traveling time of l (length divided by speed limit).

4.3 Output Measurement

It is necessary to ensure that the output of the parallel simulation with the RMA synchronization strategy has no more uncertainty than the sequential simulation. If we treat the sequential simulation as the reference, we should make sure that the output of the parallel simulation is statistically identical to the output of the sequential simulation. For statistical test of equivalence, the Kolmogorov-Smirnov two-sample test or the Bootstrap method [6] can be used. They do not make assumptions on the probability distribution of the tested variable, thus fit for our study. The output variables measured may be different for different studies, for example, some studies are interested in trip durations of agents, and some studies are interested in traffic flows on roads [5].

5. EXPERIMENTS

We conducted experiments to investigate the performance of the MA method and the RMA method in terms of the average lookahead, total synchronization messages sent, and overall speed-up of the simulation. Comparison with the conventional barrier synchronization method was made. In the MA lookahead algorithm, the schedule of creating new agents was not used. The simulation is implemented using C++, and the communications are realized using OpenMPI.

5.1 Set-up

Real world data were used in the traffic simulation of our experiments, including the road network and trips of agents. The experiments were set up as follows: The road network is the network of whole Singapore that consists of 43,392 nodes and 84,343 links (124,589 lanes). The trip distribution was derived from the data of the Household Interview and Travel Survey (HITS). The acceleration model used was the IDM model. Due to the lack of real data on the traffic flow, the agent models are not calibrated, thus, only approximate values of the input parameters of models were used. Therefore, the simulated traffic may not accurately reflect the real world. The maximum number of agents during the peak traffic hours of the day was approximately 75,000, which is presumably smaller than the real traffic. The models were collision-free, therefore, no accidents or emergencies occurred in the simulation. The traffic of 24 hours from the midnight of one day to the midnight of the next day was simulated. The simulation warm-up period was from the midnight to 5 am of which the statistics was excluded. The size of a move interval was 0.5 second. The parallel simulation was partitioned using METIS [12]. Partitioning was only performed once at the beginning of the simulation, and no dynamic load-balancing was performed. Partitioning was performed in a way that the boundary links between LPs tended to be the long road links.

The experiments were run on a cluster that is composed of 4 compute nodes each of which has the following hardware configurations: 2 Octa-core $Intel(R)\ Xeon(R)\ CPU\ E5-26700\ @2.60GHz$, 192GB of RAM. The compute nodes are connected via 56Gbps InfiniBand.

5.2 Output Equivalence to Sequential Simulation

We expect the suitable values of α vary with different partitioning on the network. The number of links cut usually increases as the number of partitions increases, thus, the same α may have higher impact on the accuracy of the simulation with more LPs. We experimented on a range of α values to find out the effect. The sequential simulation was firstly run twelve times with different random seeds, as the referential output group. Then the parallel simulation was run with different α values and different number of LPs. For each α value and each number of LPs, the parallel simulation was run twelve times as one group using the same twelve random seeds as the sequential group. Statistical tests of equivalence were performed between each parallel group and the sequential referential group. The output variable investigated was the *average trip duration* of agents throughout the simulation. The statistical test of equivalence used was the *Bootstrap method*. The null hypothesis H_0 of the test was that there is no difference between the average trip duration of agents in the sequential simulation and that in the parallel simulation. The alternative hypothesis H_1 was that the average trip durations are different. Suppose the current sequential group is $A=\{a_1, a_2, \ldots, a_{12}\}$, and the parallel group is $B=\{b_1, b_2, \ldots, b_{12}\}$. The first step of the Bootstrap method is resampling. In each resampling, two new sample groups $A'=\{a'_1, a'_2, \ldots, a'_{12}\}$ and $B'=\{b'_1, b'_2, \ldots, b'_{12}\}$ were obtained, where $a'_i \in A$ and $b'_i \in B$. Then the difference of the means of the two resampled groups was calculated by $d=\overline{A'}-\overline{B'}$. We performed resampling 1000 times. Thus, we obtained 1000 values of the difference of means. The 1000 values formed the distribution of the difference of means. Using a 95% confidence interval, H_0 would be rejected if zero falls outside of the percentile range between 2.5% and 97.5%. Otherwise, H_0 could not be rejected. The testing result is shown in Table 1. For some α values, data were

Table 1: Acceptance of the null hypothesis using the Bootstrap method

	4 LPs	8 LPs	16 LPs	32 LPs
$\alpha = 0.2$	accepted	accepted	accepted	accepted
$\alpha = 0.4$	*	*	*	accepted
$\alpha = 0.5$	accepted	accepted	accepted	rejected
$\alpha = 1.0$	accepted	rejected	rejected	rejected
$\alpha = 1.5$	rejected	*	*	*

* data not collected

not collected since they were not necessary. For example, if H_0 could not be rejected when $\alpha=0.5$, H_0 must not be rejected when $\alpha<0.5$ either. This is because a smaller sensitivity factor results in a smaller average lookahead which means a more frequent synchronization, and it should lead to less discrepancy between the parallel simulation and the sequential simulation.

From Table 1, we can take 1.0 as a suitable α value for 4 LPs, 0.5 for 8 LPs and 16 LPs, and 0.4 for 32 LPs. The values may not be the optimum; however, the optimum value cannot be gained without traversing through all possible α values, which is not practical. Judging by the values we obtained, we noticed that the suitable α value decreased as the number of LPs increased. Experiments were not conducted for more than 32 LPs due to hardware constrains. If the RMA synchronization strategy would be used in practice, certain prediction model for α value should be developed to reduce the effort of obtaining α instead of running the simulation itself. The value of α using more than 32 LPs may also be estimated. Developing a model for α can be a piece of future work.

5.3 Lookahead and Synchronization Messages

The direct impact of different sensitivity factor α values is the lookahead and the number of synchronization messages. The average lookahead values of the simulation using the MA method and the RMA method with suitable α values (1.0 for 4 LPs; 0.5 for 8 LPs and 16 LPs; and 0.4 for 32 LPs) are shown in Figure 7, and the total numbers of synchronization messages are shown in Figure 8. The lookahead

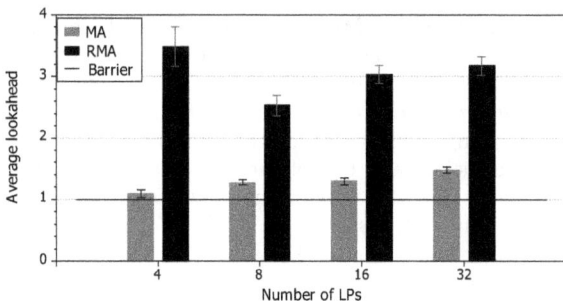

Figure 7: Average lookahead with the MA and RMS methods.

was measured in terms of move intervals. Figure 7 shows that the lookahead values in the MA method were slightly larger than one move interval. This indicates that the worse case, in which the lookahead is one move interval, did not al-

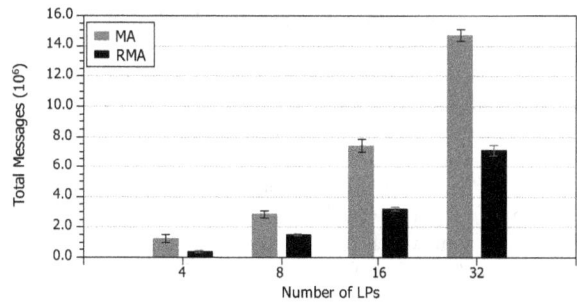

Figure 8: Total synchronization messages with the MA and RMS methods.

ways happen. The lookahead values were larger in the RMA method. When the average lookahead was larger, the total synchronization messages sent in the simulation were less (with the same number of LPs), as shown in Figure 8. The number of total messages was reduced by a large proportion in the RMA method compared to the MA method. The message count in the barrier method is not shown in Figure 8 because the barrier method uses an *all-to-all* MPI communication every move interval to determine the neighboring processes to communicate. The all-to-all communications acts as barriers. The message count is not comparable to the MA and RMA methods.

5.4 Speed-up

We investigated whether there was improvement on the overall speed-up of the parallel simulation using the MA and RMA methods over the conventional barrier method. We again used $\alpha=1.0$ for 4 LPs, 0.5 for 8 LPs and 16 LPs, and 0.4 32 LPs in the RMA method. The speed-ups are shown in Figure 9. The speed-up was calculated using the

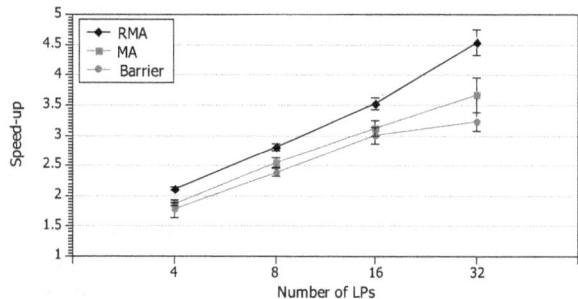

Figure 9: Speed-up of the three synchronization methods.

running time of the sequential simulation divided by the running time of the parallel simulation. Each configuration was run multiple times and the average was taken. The sequential simulation took approximately 4 hours to simulate the whole day's traffic. The parallel simulations using 32 LPs took around 50 to 70 minutes. The simulation time might be much longer if a full city-scale traffic was simulated. We observed that the MA method always performed better than the barrier method, and the RMA method always performed better than the MA method. The speed-up improvement of the MA method over the barrier method was in the range of 2.1% (4 LPs) to 13.6% (32 LPs), and the RMA method over the barrier method was in the range of 17.2% (8 LPs) to 40.7% (32 LPs). The advantage of the MA method over the barrier method has two sources: less waiting time of LPs since global barriers do not exist; and less communication overhead due to the omission of global all-to-all communications. The RMA method has even less synchronization overhead than the MA method. The reduction of the synchronization overhead comes mainly from two sources: the total size of data sent over is reduced since less shared states are sent over (despite that the number of migrated agents are the same); data are packed into larger messages and less messages are sent which reduces the overall message passing time (less start-up time for message passing).

6. RELATED WORK

The closest related work is the synchronization strategies in other parallel agent-based traffic simulations [17,26]. The simulation time in agent-based traffic simulations are conventionally progressed in a time-stepped fashion. Synchronization is performed synchronously among all LPs at the end of time-steps. To date, we have not encountered any literature studying asynchronous conservative synchronization in agent-based traffic simulations.

There is work on improving the synchronization of general agent-based simulations. One attempt is to use optimistic synchronization [15]. With an optimistic approach strategy, dependencies between LPs can be temporarily violated, and rollback is performed if any violation is detected. However, the method needs to save simulation states and perform rollbacks which are extra overheads and require more effort to implement. The optimistic approach might be not beneficial when the dependencies among agents are heavy along the boundary. Another attempt to reduce the synchronization is through asynchronous agent scheduling [25]. The dependencies between agents are analyzed every update cycle and the agents can be in different update cycles if they are not dependent on each other. In [25], synchronization was done by a central server that keeps the states of all agents. Processes only communicate with the server when proxy agents need to be updated.

Asynchronous conservative synchronization strategies have been well studied in the parallel discrete-event simulation community [4,8,20]. The performance is good in applications where lookahead can be well exploited such as queuing networks [19]. Our MA strategy is very similar to the appointment protocol in [19] which was used in a queuing network simulation. The difference is that in our simulation the appointments between LPs should be mutually agreed due to the characteristic of agent-based simulations.

Another related area of work is about relaxing the synchronization among LPs. An approximate time causal order were proposed in [8] which relaxes the conventional strict time stamp order of events. It took advantage of the fact that temporal uncertainty of events always exists in simulations. Events can be executed in an approximate order and more events could be executed concurrently. Our relaxed synchronization strategy focuses on improving the lookahead of LPs without affecting the accuracy of the simulation. We considered the characteristics of the agent-based models in traffic simulation and analyzed the discrepancy between the sequential simulation and the relaxed parallel simulation. A study on the impact of relaxing the barrier synchronization in distributed agent-based simulations was presented in [24], however, asynchronous synchronization was not mentioned and it was not studied how to maintain the accuracy of a distributed simulation.

7. CONCLUSIONS AND FUTURE WORK

We have proposed a new asynchronous conservative synchronization strategy for parallel agent-based traffic simulations. Its asynchronous nature reduces the waiting of processes at barriers compared to the conventional global barrier synchronization method. To address the low lookahead issue in agent-based traffic simulations, we have also developed a relaxed lookahead heuristic which improves the lookahead by taking advantage of the uncertainty in traffic simulations. Experiments have shown that it has improved the parallel speed-up to a certain degree when keeping the outputs of the parallel simulation statistically indistinguishable to the sequential simulation.

Future work may include: firstly, developing a prediction model for the suitable value of α to reduce the effort of obtaining α, which makes the lookahead model in the RMA method easier for practical use; the characteristics of the road traffic should be considered; and secondly, investigating more intelligent dead-reckoning functions under different traffic conditions which may improve the relaxation of lookahead.

8. ACKNOWLEDGMENT

This work was financially supported by the Singapore National Research Foundation under its Campus for Research Excellence And Technological Enterprise (CREATE) programme. M.L. acknowledges the support of the Russian Scientific Foundation, Project #14-21-00137.

9. REFERENCES

[1] H. Aydt, Y. Xu, M. Lees, and A. Knoll. A multi-threaded execution model for the agent-based semsim traffic simulation. In *Proceedings of the 13th International Conference on Systems Simulation*, pages 1–12, Singapore, November 06–08, 2013. Springer Berlin Heidelberg.

[2] J. Barceló, J. Ferrer, D. García, M. Florian, and E. Saux. Parallelization of microscopic traffic simulation for att systems analysis. In P. Marcotte and S. Nguyen, editors, *Equilibrium and Advanced Transportation Modelling*, pages 1–26. Springer US, 1998.

[3] G. D. Cameron. PARAMICS–Parallel Microscopic Simulation of Road Traffic. *The Journal of Supercomputing*, 53(1):25–53, 1996.

[4] K. Chandy and J. Misra. Distributed simulation: A case study in design and verification of distributed programs. *IEEE Transactions on Software Engineering*, SE-5(5):440–452, 1979.

[5] G. de Jong, A. Daly, M. Pieters, S. Miller, R. Plasmeijer, and F. Hofman. Uncertainty in traffic forecasts: literature review and new results for The Netherlands. *Transportation*, 34(4):375–395, 2006.

[6] B. Efron. Bootstrap methods: another look at the jackknife. *The Annals of Statistics*, 7(1):1–26, 1979.

[7] R. Fujimoto. Parallel Discrete Event Simulation. *Communications of the ACM*, 33(10):30–52, 1990.

[8] R. Fujimoto. Exploiting temporal uncertainty in parallel and distributed simulations. In *Proceedings of the 13th Workshop on Parallel and Distributed Simulation*, pages 46–53, Atlanta, GA, USA, May 01-04, 1999. IEEE.

[9] P. Gipps. A behavioural car-following model for computer simulation. *Transportation Research Part B: Methodological*, 15(2):105–111, 1981.

[10] P. Gipps. A model for the structure of lane-changing decisions. *Transportation Research Part B: Methodological*, 20(5):403–414, 1986.

[11] J. Helton. Uncertainty and sensitivity analysis in the presence of stochastic and subjective uncertainty. *Journal of Statistical Computation and Simulation*, 57(1-4):3–76, 1997.

[12] G. Karypis and V. Kumar. A Fast and High Quality Multilevel Scheme for Partitioning Irregular Graphs. *SIAM Journal on Scientific Computing*, 20(1):359–392, 1999.

[13] A. Kesting, M. Treiber, and D. Helbing. General Lane-Changing Model MOBIL for Car-Following Models. *Transportation Research Record: Journal of Transportation Research Record*, 1999(1):86–94, 2007.

[14] M. Lees, B. Logan, R. Minson, T. Oguara, and G. Theodoropoulos. Modelling environments for distributed simulation. In D. Weyns, H. Van Dyke Parunak, and F. Michel, editors, *Environments for Multi-Agent Systems*, volume 3374 of *Lecture Notes in Computer Science*, pages 150–167. Springer Berlin Heidelberg, 2005.

[15] M. Lees, B. Logan, and G. Theodoropoulos. Adaptive optimistic synchronisation for multi-agent distributed simulation. In *Proceedings of the 17th European Simulation Multiconference*, pages 77–82, Nottingham, UK, June 09-11, 2003. Society for Modelling and Simulation International.

[16] M. Lighthill and G. Whitham. On Kinematic Waves. II. A Theory of Traffic Flow on Long Crowded Roads. *Proceedings of the Royal Society A: Mathematical, Physical and Engineering Sciences*, 229(1178):317–345, 1955.

[17] K. Nagel and M. Rickert. Parallel implementation of the TRANSIMS. *Parallel Computing*, 27(12): 1611–1639, 2001.

[18] D. Ni. 2DSIM: a prototype of nanoscopic traffic simulation. In *Proceedings of the 2003 Intelligent Vehicles Symposium*, pages 47–52, Columbus, OH, USA, June 09-11, 2003. IEEE.

[19] D. M. Nicol. Parallel discrete-event simulation of fcfs stochastic queueing networks. In *Proceedings of the ACM/SIGPLAN Conference on Parallel Programming: Experience with Applications, Languages and Systems*, pages 124–137, New Haven, CT, USA, July 19-21, 1988. ACM.

[20] D. M. Nicol. Principles of conservative parallel simulation. In *Proceedings of the 1996 Winter Simulation Conference*, pages 128–135, Coronado, CA, USA, December 08-11, 1996. IEEE.

[21] W. L. Oberkampf, S. M. DeLand, B. M. Rutherford, K. V. Diegert, and K. F. Alvin. Error and uncertainty in modeling and simulation. *Reliability Engineering & System Safety*, 75(3):333–357, 2002.

[22] S. Paveri-Fontana. On Boltzmann-like treatments for traffic flow: a critical review of the basic model and an alternative proposal for dilute traffic analysis. *Transportation Research*, 9(4):225–235, 1975.

[23] P. Richards. Shock Waves on the Highway. *Operations Research*, 4(1):42–51, 1956.

[24] O. Rihawi, Y. Secq, and P. Mathieu. Relaxing Synchronization Constraints in Distributed Agent-based Simulations. *Jurnal Teknologi*, 63(3):65–76, 2013.

[25] M. Scheutz and J. Harris. Adaptive scheduling algorithms for the dynamic distribution and parallel execution of spatial agent-based models. In F. de Vega and E. Cantú-Paz, editors, *Parallel and Distributed Computational Intelligence*, volume 269 of *Studies in Computational Intelligence*, pages 207–233. Springer Berlin Heidelberg, 2010.

[26] T. Suzumura and H. Kanezashi. Highly Scalable X10-Based Agent Simulation Platform and Its Application to Large-Scale Traffic Simulation. In *Proceedings of the 2012 IEEE/ACM 16th International Symposium on Distributed Simulation and Real Time Applications*, pages 243–250, Dublin, Ireland, October 25-27, 2012. IEEE.

[27] M. Treiber, A. Hennecke, and D. Helbing. Congested traffic states in empirical observations and microscopic simulations. *Physical Review E (Statistical Physics, Plasmas, Fluids, and Related Interdisciplinary Topics)*, 62(2):1805–1824, 2000.

[28] Y. Xu, H. Aydt, and M. Lees. SEMSim: A Distributed Architecture for Multi-scale Traffic Simulation. In *Proceedings of the 2012 ACM/IEEE/SCS 26th Workshop on Principles of Advanced and Distributed Simulation*, pages 178–180, Zhangjiajie, China, July 15-19, 2012. IEEE.

Exact-Differential Large-Scale Traffic Simulation

Masatoshi Hanai
Tokyo Institute of Technology
/ Durham University
Tokyo, Japan
mhanai@acm.org

Toyotaro Suzumura
IBM T.J. Watson Research Center
/ University College Dublin / JST
Yorktown Heights, New York, USA
suzumura@acm.org

Georgios Theodoropoulos
Durham University
Durham, UK
georgios.theodoropoulos@durham.ac.uk

Kalyan S. Perumalla
Oak Ridge National Laboratory
Oak Ridge, Tennessee, USA
perumallaks@ornl.gov

ABSTRACT

Analyzing large-scale traffics by simulation needs repeating execution many times with various patterns of scenarios or parameters. Such repeating execution brings about big redundancy because the change from a prior scenario to a later scenario is very minor in most cases, for example, blocking only one of roads or changing the speed limit of several roads. In this paper, we propose a new redundancy reduction technique, called exact-differential simulation, which enables to simulate only changing scenarios in later execution while keeping exactly same results as in the case of whole simulation. The paper consists of two main efforts: (i) a key idea and algorithm of the exact-differential simulation, (ii) a method to build large-scale traffic simulation on the top of the exact-differential simulation. In experiments of Tokyo traffic simulation, the exact-differential simulation shows 7.26 times as much elapsed time improvement in average and 2.26 times improvement even in the worst case as the whole simulation.

Categories and Subject Descriptors

I.6.8 [**Simulation and Modeling**]: Types of Simulation—*parallel, distributed, discrete event*

General Terms

Algorithms, Performance

Keywords

Large-scale traffic simulation; parallel discrete event simulation; redundancy reduction

1. INTRODUCTION

Large-scale microscopic traffic simulation has been a beneficial way to research on areas such as prediction of traffic congestion, planning of urban developments, citizen's behavior in emergencies. Unlike other statistical and mathematical ways, such approaches can give detail analysis results of the individual vehicles and other entities like junctions and roads because it actually emulates the vehicles' behavior and interactions with each other.

To analyse by such simulation, it needs to repeat execution many times with different scenarios and parameters. In Tokyo traffic simulation [13, 14, 16, 6], for example, we need to execute 770K times simulation when we simulate what happens if one of the roads is blocked because there are 770K junctions in Tokyo. When we simulate multiple blocks of the roads, we need to execute 2^{770K} times (the sum of combination from 770K choosing 0 to 770K). Also, it often needs to execute a lot of times for parameter tuning (e.g. road speed limit, a time interval of signals) to imitate a realistic situation.

However, previous simulating methods and simulators have a big overhead and a lot of redundancy when repeating the simulation, especially when very small part of scenarios are changed. For example, if only one of all roads is changed in later repeating execution, almost all of simulating results are same as prior execution and the change affects only small part but we have to simulate whole scenarios from the beginning. The reason why the previous simulators have to simulate whole scenarios from the beginning is that a naive spatial partial way (separating simulation space in advance and only simulating the separated part) brings about inconsistency of simulating results from the whole simulating results because it cannot simulate an influence from outside of the separated part and such influence cannot be fixed in advance.

In this paper, we propose a novel technique to simulate only a part of all scenarios and states keeping exact same simulating results as whole execution, called *exact-differential simulation*. The "exact" implies that the output result will be identical. The "differential" implies that only affected events will be reprocessed.

The main idea of the exact-differential simulation is that, in initial whole execution, the simulator stores all events and intermediate states before reprocessing only changing events in later repeating executions by using the stored events and states. There are 3 main contributions in this paper: (i) we describe a way to store processed events and intermediate states and a way to reuse them. (ii) we illustrate implementation of the simulator, which meets requirements of the exact-differential simulation. (iii) we evaluate an efficiency and performance of the exact-differential simulation by Tokyo traffic simulation.

The rest of paper is organized as follows. In Section 2, we give the main idea of the exact-differential simulation. We also discuss about static analysis of performance. In Section 3, we illustrate the system implementation. In Section 4, we show modeling of large-scale traffics. In Section 5, we evaluate the exact-differential simulation with the Tokyo traffic simulation. In Section 6, we illustrate related work to our research before conclude in Section 7.

2. EXACT-DIFFERENTIAL SIMULATION

In this section, we describe the processing flow of the exact-differential simulation and its static performance analysis.

2.1 Processing Flow

The simulation flow basically consists of two parts: initial whole execution and repeating execution. In the initial whole execution, the simulator stores all processed events and intermediate states. After the initial whole execution, the simulator starts the repeating execution from a changing point and reprocesses only affected events using the stored events and states.

2.1.1 Initial Whole Execution

In the initial whole execution, events are processed in the almost same way as the optimistic PDES [10], where unlike the normal optimistic PDES, events, cancel events and stored states are never released by the global synchronization (or GVT, $global\ virtual\ time$). Instead, such events, cancel events and states are stored to storage for reusing in later repeating execution. Thus, in full, each LP processes events in parallel with a time-sorted event queue and exchanges new generated events with other LPs. When a LP receives the new event with earlier time stamp than its own local time, the LP rollbacks its local time and sends cancel events to neighbors. In the other case that the new received event is older than its local time, the new event is just inserted to its event queue. Cancel events and states are stored whenever a new event is generated. In the global synchronization, older events, cancel events and states than the global time are stored to storage instead of releasing as usual.

2.1.2 Exact-Differential Simulation in Repeating Execution

In the repeating execution, the simulator, at first, inputs a what-if query, which defines changing time and place (LP) and a query's type: ADD or DELETE. Algorithm 1 shows the what-if query processing. In the case of ADD (line 3 – 7), a new event generated from the ADD query is inserted to the event queue and the local time is rollbacked to the new event's time before cancel events are sent to all affected LPs. In the case of DELETE (line 8 – 13), an old event generated from the DELETE query is removed before a cancel event related to the old event is sent. The local time is rollbacked to the old event's time. And finally, cancel events are send to affected LPs. After finishing processing what-if queries, the simulation starts from the rollbacked time in the same way as the optimistic PDES. In the repeating execution,

---

Algorithm 1 Query Processing Flow

1: **while** $hasWhatIfQuery()$ **do**
2: $\quad query \leftarrow getWhatIfQuery()$
3: $\quad$ **if** $query.type = ADD$ **then**
4: $\quad\quad newEvent \leftarrow query.event$
5: $\quad\quad insert(newEvent)$
6: $\quad\quad rollback(newEvent.time)$
7: $\quad\quad sendCancelsToNeighbors()$
8: $\quad$ **else if** $query.type = DELETE$ **then**
9: $\quad\quad oldEvent \leftarrow query.event$
10: $\quad\quad delete(oldEvent)$
11: $\quad\quad sendCancel(oldEvent)$
12: $\quad\quad rollback(oldEvent.time)$
13: $\quad\quad sendCancelsToNeighbors()$
14: $\quad$ **end if**
15: **end while**
16: **while** $getGlobalTime() < TIME\_TO\_FINISH$ **do**
17: $\quad reprocess\ unprocessed\ events\ with\ optimistic\ PDES$
18: **end while**

---

events, cancel events and states are sometimes required to load from storage unlike the usual optimistic PDES. Algorithm 2 shows a mechanism to load the events, cancel events and states during receiving events. We extend the optimistic PDES as showed in algorithm 2 (line 3 – 24). In the exact-differential simulation, received events from other LPs are once buffered before they are inserted to event queues (line 1). If a new received event has less received time than minimum loaded time, which is initialized as infinity, then the stored events, cancel events and states are loaded from the storage (line 7 – 9) before they are inserted to the queues (line 14 – 21). After that, the minimum loaded time is updated to the new received time (line 22), and then the new received event is inserted to the event queue as usual (line 25).

2.2 Static Analysis

In this part, we illustrate efficiency of the repeating execution compered to a naive way. In the repeating execution, a main factor of its performance is how often redundancy events are skipped to process. To clarify the performance improvement, we first define speed up based on the number of processing events and redundancy reduction rate. After that, we discuss detail on the redundancy reduction rate in the repeating execution.

2.2.1 Speed Up

Let E be a set of events; E_{all} be a set of all events; $t_{sim}(\cdot)$ be execution time of processing events; and $t_{init}(\cdot) = t_{init\_local}(\cdot) + t_{init\_global}$ be execution time of initiation, where $t_{init\_local}(\cdot)$ is initializing events time and t_{init_global} is initializing time including state initialization and other initialization independent of events.

The execution time of whole simulation t_{whole} is represented as following.

$$
\begin{aligned}
t_{whole} &= t_{sim}(E_{all}) + t_{init}(E_{all}) \\
&= t_{sim}(E_{all}) + t_{init\_local}(E_{all}) + t_{init\_global}
\end{aligned}
$$

We represent T_{n_diff} as execution time of n times repeating exact-differential simulation.

$$
T_{n\_diff} = \sum^{n} t_{sim}(E_{re}) + t'_{init}
$$

272

Algorithm 2 Receive Event Processing Flow

```
1: while receiveEventBuffer.isEmpty() do
2:     newEvent ← receiveEventBuffer.dequeue()
3:     /* Extended Part */
4:     if newEvent.time < store.minLoadedTime then
5:         from ← newEvent.time
6:         to ← store.minLoadedTime
7:         oldEvents ← store.getEvent(from, to)
8:         oldCancels ← store.getCancel(from, to)
9:         oldStates ← store.getState(from, to)
10:        while oldEvents.isEmpty() do
11:            loadedEvent ← oldEvens.dequeue()
12:            eventQueue.insert(loadedEvent)
13:        end while
14:        while oldCancels.isEmpty() do
15:            loadedCancel ← oldCancels.dequeue()
16:            cancelQueue.insert(loadedCancel)
17:        end while
18:        while oldStates.isEmpty() do
19:            loadedState ← oldStates.dequeue()
20:            stateQueue.insert(loadedState)
21:        end while
22:        store.minLoadedTime ← from
23:    end if
24:    /* Extended Part End */
25:    eventQueue.insert(newEvent)
26: end while
```

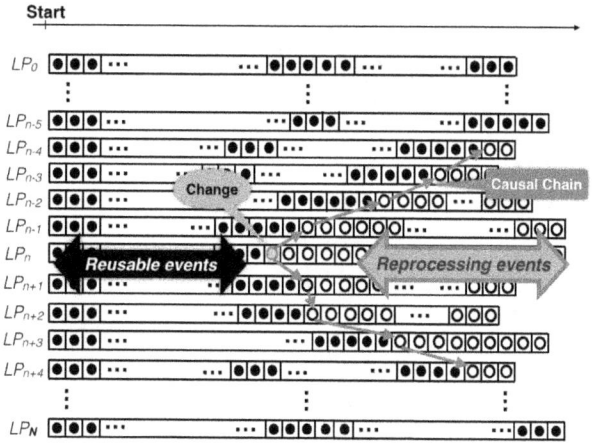

Figure 1: Reusable Events and Reprocessing Events.

We define speed up as the division of naive way's execution time ($T_{n\_whole} := \sum^{n} t_{whole}$) by our proposal one ($T_{n\_diff}$). The speed up is represented as follows.

$$
\begin{aligned}
(Speed\ Up) &= \frac{T_{n\_whole}}{T_{n\_diff}} \\
&= \frac{\sum^{n}\{t_{sim}(E_{all}) + t_{init\_local}(E_{all}) + t_{init\_global}\}}{\sum^{n}\{t_{sim}(E_{re}) + t_{init\_local}(E_{re})\} + t_{init\_global}} \\
&= \frac{n\{|E_{all}|t_{ev} + |E_{all}|t_{init\_ev} + t_{init\_global}\}}{n\{|E_{re}|t_{ev} + |E_{re}|t_{init\_ev}\} + t_{init\_global}} \\
&= \frac{n\{|E_{all}|t_{ev} + |E_{all}|t_{init\_ev} + t_{init\_global}\}}{n\{r|E_{all}|t_{ev} + r|E_{all}|t_{init\_ev}\} + t_{init\_global}} \\
&= \frac{|E_{all}|t_{ev} + |E_{all}|t_{init\_ev} + t_{init\_global}}{r|E_{all}|t_{ev} + r|E_{all}|t_{init\_ev} + t_{init\_global}/n}
\end{aligned}
$$

, where r is *redundancy reduction rate* defined as $r := |E_{re}|/|E_{all}|$. In the case that the execution is repeated enough much times, t_{init_global}/n can be ignored.

$$
\begin{aligned}
(Speed\ Up) &\sim \frac{|E_{all}|t_{ev} + |E_{all}|t_{init\_ev} + t_{init\_global}}{r|E_{all}|t_{ev} + r|E_{all}|t_{init\_ev}} \\
&= \frac{1}{r} \cdot \left(1 + \frac{t_{init\_global}}{|E_{all}|(t_{ev} + t_{init\_ev})}\right) \quad (*)
\end{aligned}
$$

This result means that in the case that the global initialization time is much shorter than the event processing and initialization time, or in the case that there are many events to be processed, the speed up is nearly proportional to $1/r$. The more redundancy is reduced, the more speed up it is. On the other hand, in the case that the global initialization cannot be ignored compared to the event processing and initializing time, the speed up depends on the ratio of the global initialization time by the event processing and initializing time, and on the number of all events.

2.2.2 Redundancy Reduction Rate

The rest of the section focuses on the redundancy reduction rate, namely parameter r as stated above. Let lp_i be

, where $E_{re}(\subseteq E_{all})$ is a set of reprocessing events and t'_{init} is initialization execution time in the exact-differential simulation. Actually, the global initialization is required to execute only one time. Thus, we can represent t'_{init} as follows.

$$
t'_{init} = \sum^{n} t_{init\_local}(E_{re}) + t_{init\_global}
$$

As the result, T_{n_diff} is represented as following.

$$
\begin{aligned}
T_{n\_diff} &= \sum^{n} t_{sim}(E_{re}) + t'_{init} \\
&= \sum^{n} t_{sim}(E_{re}) + \sum^{n} t_{init\_local}(E_{re}) + t_{init\_global} \\
&= \sum^{n}\{t_{sim}(E_{re}) + t_{init\_local}(E_{re})\} + t_{init\_global}
\end{aligned}
$$

We assume processing and initializing time per event is constant. Then, we can represent the execution time by one event processing time t_{ev} as follows.

$$
\begin{aligned}
t_{sim}(E) &= |E| \cdot t_{ev} \\
t_{init\_local}(E) &= |E| \cdot t_{init\_ev}
\end{aligned}
$$

, where $|E|$ is the number of elements in E and $t_{ev} = t_{sim}(\{e\})$, $t_{init\_ev} = t_{init\_local}(\{e\})$ ($e \in E$).

To simplify the discussion, we also assume the number of whole events (E_{all}) and reprocessing events (E_{re}) is constant even if scenarios are changed. Then, the sum of events processing time is represented as following.

$$
\begin{aligned}
\sum^{n} t_{sim}(E_{all,re}) &= n \cdot |E_{all,re}| \cdot t_{ev} \\
\sum^{n} t_{init\_local}(E_{all,re}) &= n \cdot |E_{all,re}| \cdot t_{init\_ev}
\end{aligned}
$$

a logical process and LP be a set of logical processes. We assume there are l logical processes in simulation. The LP is represented as following.

$$LP := \{lp_i | i = 0, 1, 2, ..., l-1\}$$

We define a function that makes a causal chain from one event as $f : E \to E^l$.

$$f(e) := \{f_0(e), f_1(e), f_2(e), ..., f_{l-1}(e)\}$$

, where $f_i(e)$ is a function from an event to the earliest affecting event in lp_i. Also, let Ei_{re} be an event after $f_i(e)$.

$$Ei_{re} := \{e | e \geq f_i(e)\}$$

The parameter r is represented like that (Figure1).

$$r = \frac{|E_{re}|}{|E_{all}|} = \frac{\sum_{i=0}^{l-1} Ei_{re}}{|E_{all}|}$$

3. IMPLEMENTATION

In this section, we show system implementation. For implementation, there are two requirements to be satisfied. First, our proposal is for actual city-scale or country-scale traffic simulation. Its implementation needs to be scalable to large-scale and to be run in parallel. Second, as we showed in Section 2, our proposal needs to store all processed events and intermediate states in the initial whole simulation. To meet these requirements, our system is designed as the extension of an optimistic parallel traffic simulator.

3.1 Overview

Figure 2 shows the system overview. Our simulator is executed on distributed environment and includes three modules for traffic simulation and one module for storing events and states: application, Time Warp layer, communicator and local storage.

In application, actual simulation logic and algorithms are constructed. The exact-differential simulation mechanism is fully independent of the application code such as modeling of traffic simulation or logic of a vehicles' behavior. The application gets an event and simulation state (namely the state of junction and roads) from Time Warp layer before processing the event based on the vehicles' behavior algorithm, and then returns a new event and a changed state because of the processing event.

The Time Warp layer, which is a core module of our system, consists of a LP manager, LPs and a local storage. Each LP has an event queue, a cancel queue and a state queue just the same way as optimistic PDES. The LPs are managed by a thread pool in LP manager because there are some load imbalances between LPs in the traffic simulation. For example, such load imbalance is happened when in some roads there are a lot of vehicles to be process while in other roads there are few vehicles to be processed. The LP manager also manage the partition of the simulation, that is, the meta-data of each LP. Also, the LP manager controls the access to the local storage, where all processing events and intermediate states are stored in the initial whole execution.

The communicator controls node to node communication using MPI as well as inner process communication between LPs in the same node.

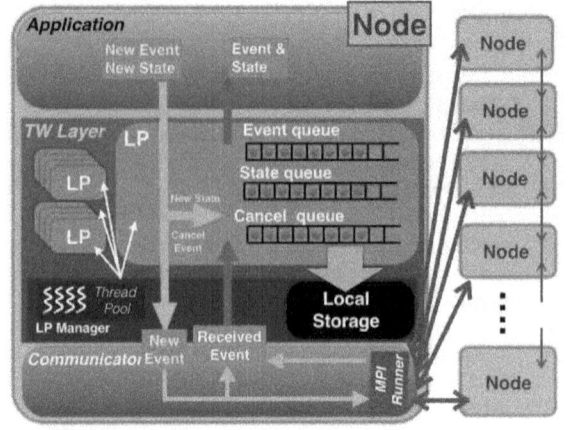

Figure 2: System Overview and Initial Whole Simulation.

3.2 Initial Whole Execution

Figure 2 also shows the flow of initial execution per node. In the initial execution, the simulator at first inputs states and scenarios before simulation. The states data are deployed to each node based on the defined partitioning. After inputting, the simulation starts and processes events (Figure 2). In the initial execution, the LP manager allots a free thread to a LP to process events. The LP passes the earliest unprocessed event to the application before the event is processed in the application. After that, the LP gets a new generated event and a changed state from the application. The new event is sent to a new destination LP via communicator according to a partition discussed later. Also a new cancel event is stored in the cancel queue. If the event has to be sent to other node, the event is communicated via MPI. On the other hand, if the new destination LP is in the same node, the event is sent as inner process communication. Such new sending event is received in the communicator and passed to the destination LP.

Unlike usual optimistic PDES system, events with smaller time stamp than global time are not released after global synchronization. Instead, such events are stored in the local storage for later exact-differential execution.

3.3 Exact-Differential Simulation in Repeating Execution

In repeating exact-differential execution (showed in Figure 3), the system first inputs a changing query and then distributes to a destination LP. The query is received in the LP via communication layer before accessing the local storage to load the changing event and all events affected by the changing event. These events (the changing event and the affected events) are inserted to an event queue to process again. After that, the LP passes the earliest unprocessed event to the application before gets the new generated event and changed state by the application. The new generated event is sent to the destination LP via communicator and the new state is stored to a state queue. After communicator receives the new event, the new event's received time is checked and the affected events are loaded if the time is less than minimum loaded time as discussed in Section 2.

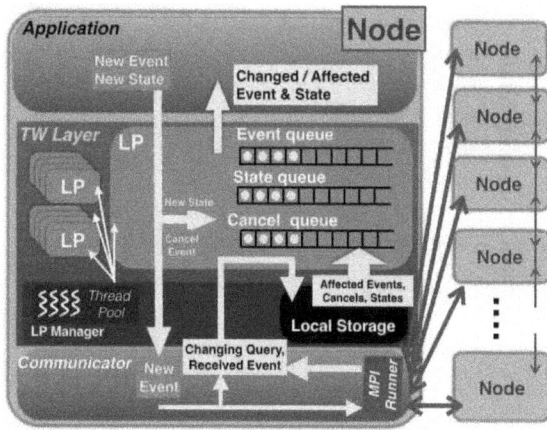

Figure 3: Exact-Differential Simulation.

4. LARGE-SCALE TRAFFIC SIMULATION

In this section, we describe the modeling of traffic system. In a first half of this section, we illustrate how to simulate local vehicles' behavior, that is, how to decide their route at junctions and vehicles' speed on a road. In the other half, we show the model of the global interaction with each other on the road map.

There are two requirement in the modeling way like the system requirement discussed in Section 3. First, the traffic simulation needs to be scalable to city-scale or country-scale. Second, the traffic simulation is required to be modeled on the top of optimistic PDES since the exact-differential simulation is totally based on the optimistic PDES as we discussed in Section 2. To meet such requirement, the model of our traffic simulation is based on IBM Megaffic [13, 14, 17] and SCATTER [15, 18].

4.1 Individual Vehicle's Behavior

The individual vehicle's behavior is based on Megaffic, where it optimises drivers' decisions by estimating some of the parameters of the model from probe-car data before actual simulation execution, differentiating Megaffic from many other traffic simulators which need to calibrate these parameters during the simulation. In short, Megaffic pre-computes some of the simulation data, such as, road segments and lanes chosen by the drivers on their route, speed of the vehicles on the road. This is because in large-scale traffic simulation, the processing time of individual vehicles becomes the main bottleneck of the simulation and has to be reduced as much as possible.

In the same way as Megaffic, a vehicle's track of junctions from origin to destination is all fixed before execution by estimation with some defined behavior model, for example, shortest path or minimum hops of junctions. After that, in the execution, the vehicle's speed, traveling time to next junction and selection of a lane are calculated based on some defined behavior models. Finally when the vehicle reaches its destination, it is removed from the simulation.

4.2 Interaction of Vehicles on the Road Map

The global interaction of vehicles around the road map is based on SCATTER. Thus, we mainly use the optimistic PDES technique for parallelization including synchroniza-

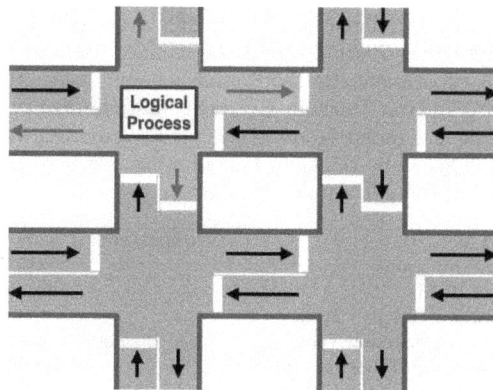

Figure 4: Road Map and a Logical Process Unit.

tion. As SCATTER, we represent a vehicle's track as a sequence of events. One event is represented as vehicle's moving from one junction to a next junction. A unit of a logical process in the optimistic PDES is a set of a junction and its outgoing roads (Figure 4). The arrival timing to junctions and synchronization with other junctions are fully controlled by the optimistic PDES.

Also, the road map is partitioned in advance by the k-ways graph partitioning algorithm [12] with METIS [11], which is the software including the k-ways algorithm implementation.

5. EVALUATION

In this section, we describe evaluation of the exact-differential simulation with Tokyo traffic scenarios.

There are two topics to evaluate: efficiency and performance. In the efficiency evaluation, we evaluate how the exact-differential simulation can reduce the number of redundant events in repeating execution. We experiment with two types of changing scenarios. The first one is the case to change vehicle's scenarios. We change a vehicle's track in repeating execution. The second one is the case to change the road map. We change the parameter of one of LPs (one junction and its out-going roads) in repeating execution. The efficiency evaluation shows, in high level, how the exact-differential simulation "potentially" can improve the performance. On the other hand, in performance evaluation, we show the "actual" performance improvement in our implementation, where we evaluate the elapsed time compared to the whole simulation as well as the scalability and parallelization of the simulator.

5.1 Efficiency Evaluation

In this part, we illustrate the efficiency of the exact-differential simulation with Tokyo traffics in 3 hours. Table 1 shows the simulation scenario. We simulate the traffic in Tokyo bay area with 161,364 junctions and 203,363 roads (Figure 5). Based on the Tokyo's statistical data collected by the MLIT (Ministry of Land, Infrastructure, Transport and Tourism) in 2011, totally 5000 vehicles depart from their origin in 3 hours. Each vehicle has a trip pattern which has randomly generated origin/destination. In total, this scenario generates 798,177 events to be outputted, where we use the term "outputted event" as a processed event which is fixed and never canceled in Time Warp layer. Thus, actually in Time Warp layer, over 798,177 events are handled and canceled.

In this experiment, we use Hamilton4 supercomputer (10 MPI processes) in Durham University but the result of efficiency here is independent of the cluster environment. A result influenced by the environment (thus, elapsed time) is discussed in the performance evaluation.

Road Map	Tokyo Bay Area (Figure 5)
– # of Junctions	161,364
– # of Roads	203,363
Scenario of Tokyo's Traffic	
– Sum of Departing Vehicles	5,000 (3 hours)
– Trips Origin/Destination	Random
Result of Whole Simulation	
– Total Outputted Events	798,177

Table 1: Traffic Scenario.

Figure 5: Road Map of Tokyo Bay Area.

5.1.1 Evaluation with Changing a Vehicle's Track

Here, we study the impact of changing vehicles on repeating execution. In this evaluation, we change one of the 5000 vehicles' track paths and then execute the exact-differential simulation. The new track path is generated randomly so that the number of hops is unchanged. We totally change all 5000 vehicles' track path respectively and count the number of events affected by the change, which need to be outputted in the exact-differential simulation.

Figure 8 shows the number of outputted events in the changes. We plot the results in departing time order, but as you can see, we cannot find the impact of departing time in the exact-differential simulation. In Figure 6, we compare the worst case and average case to the whole simulation. In average, the number of outputted events in the exact-differential simulation is 44,261, which is only 5.5 % of the whole simulation. Even in the worst case, the number of outputted events is 233,749, which is 29.2 % of the outputted events in the whole simulation.

5.1.2 Evaluation with Changing a Road Parameter

In this evaluation, we show the efficiency of the exact-differential simulation with changing a speed limit parameter of the road map. We change the speed limit of one LP

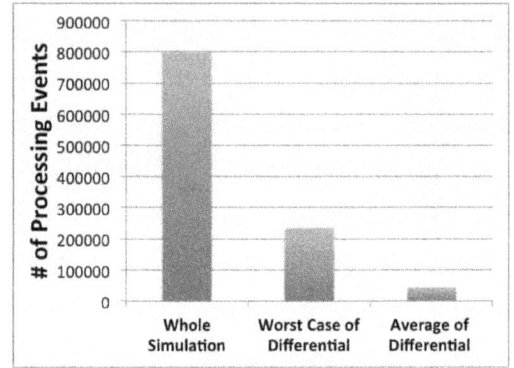

Figure 6: Number of Differential Outputted Events in a Vehicle Change.

and execute the exact-differential simulation from the beginning, where we randomly pick up about 1 % of all 161,364 LPs (1,600 LPs).

Figure 9 shows the number of outputted events in each LP ordered by junction ID, where close numbers are roughly located near points in the actual road map. As you can see, the number of outputted events in the differential simulation has a big gap, that is, some junctions affect the large number of events while the others bring about few events. This is because in Tokyo there are two types of junctions; the first one is the hub, where a lot of vehicles cross over and the other one is a junction, where only few vehicles enter. In Figure 7, we compare the worst case and average case to the whole simulation. In average, the number of outputted event is 61,206. Thus, the events to be outputted are only 7.6 % of whole simulation. Even in the worst case, the number of outputted events in the differential simulation is 297,181, which are 37.2 % of the outputted events in whole simulation.

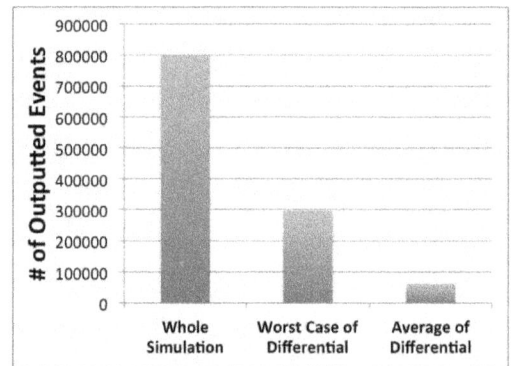

Figure 7: Number of Differential Outputted Events in a Road Change.

To sum up the efficiency evaluation, the exact-differential can reduce over 90% of whole events in average (94.5% in vehicle changes, 92.4% in road changes), and even in the worst case it can reduce over 60% of whole events (70.8 % in a vehicle change, 62.8% in a road change).

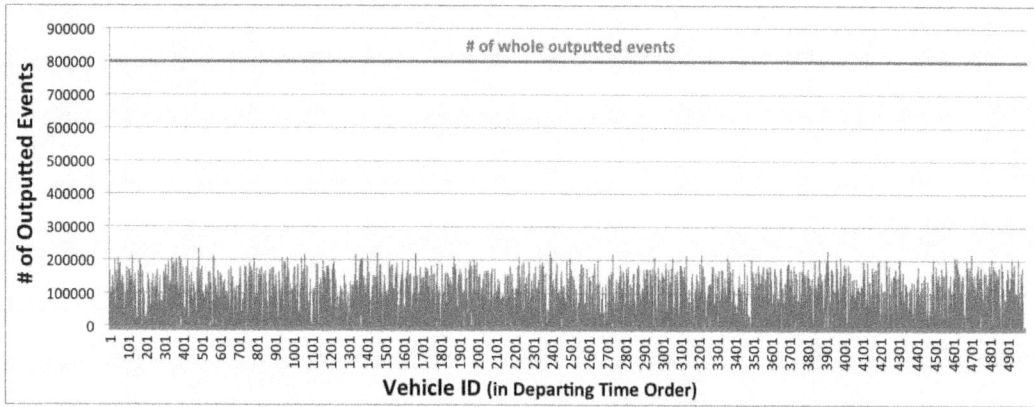

Figure 8: Number of Differential Outputted Events in a Vehicle Change.

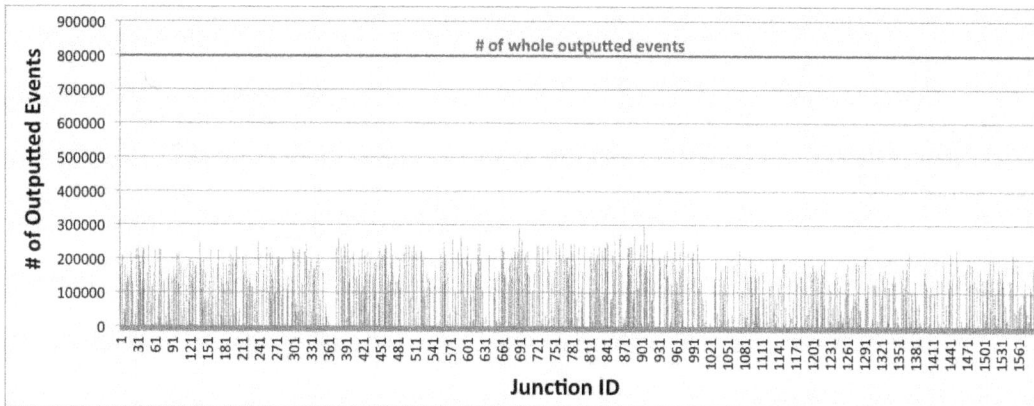

Figure 9: Number of Differential Outputted Events in a Road Change.

5.2 Performance Evaluation

In this part, we show the actual performance of the exact-differential simulation with our simulator. We use the worst and average cases of road changing scenarios as we evaluated above.

Table 2 shows a summary of the evaluation environment. Our simulator is implemented by C++ and MPI with a hybrid parallel architecture, where each MPI process includes multiple threads. We run the simulator with TSUBAME 2.5 Supercomputer in Tokyo Institute of Technology, where there are 12 processors per node with 54GB memory and connected by QDR InfiniBand.

Service	TSUBAME 2.5 in Tokyo Tech.
CPU	Intel Xeon X5670/2.93GHz × 2
Memory	54GB per Node
Network	QDR InfiniBand Interconnect
OS	SLES 11 SP3
MPI	Open MPI 1.6.5

Table 2: Cluster's Configurations.

We change the number of processors according to the table 3. In the simulator, it needs 2 processors per node at minimum because MPI thread and event processing thread are separated in our simulator. Also, it needs 2 MPI process at minimum because of the implementation. Thus, we start from 4 processors and increase the number of cores to 192 (including 16 nodes with 12 threads per node).

Nodes	Threads per Node		Processors
1	4	(2 MPI threads)	4
1	6	(2 MPI threads)	12
2	12	(2 MPI threads)	24
4	12	(4 MPI threads)	48
8	12	(8 MPI threads)	96
16	12	(16 MPI threads)	192

Table 3: Number of Nodes, Threads and Processors.

According to the efficiency result, we pick up the worst case of a road changing scenario needed to be outputted 297,181 events and the average case needed to be outputted 61,530 events, and then evaluate the elapsed time respectively.

Figure 10 shows a strong scaling of the simulator. From 12 processors to 24 processors, the performance becomes once worse because from 24 processors, node to node communication occurs, which is higher cost than a inner node communication. From 24 processors, the performance becomes better according to the number of processors. In the whole simulation, the elapsed time is improved to be 21.7 % of 4 processors elapsed time. In the exact-differential simulation of the worst case scenario (297,181 outputted events), the elapsed time is improved to be 33.6 % of 4 processors elapsed time. Also, in the exact-differential simulation of the average case scenario (61,530 outputted events), the elapsed time is improved to be 49.7 % of 4 processors elapsed time.

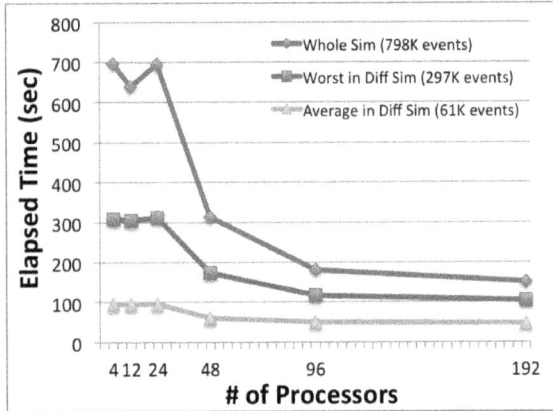

Figure 10: Strong Scaling of Simulation.

Figure 11 shows a speed up from the whole simulation, defined as follows.

$$\frac{(Elapsed\ Time\ in\ Whole\ Sim.\ )}{(Elapsed\ Time\ in\ Exact\text{-}Differential\ Sim.)}$$

The exact-differential simulation achieves at most 7.26 times as much speed up in average case and 2.26 times speed up in the worst case as the whole simulation (4 processors). The speed up decreases according to the number of processors. There are still gaps from ideal cases (showed dotted line in Figure 11), calculated by (*) in Section 2, where we assume $(Speed\ Up) = 1/r$ because $|E_{all}|$ is enough bigger than t_{init_global}. This is because the overhead of the processing events increases according to the number of processors as discussed later.

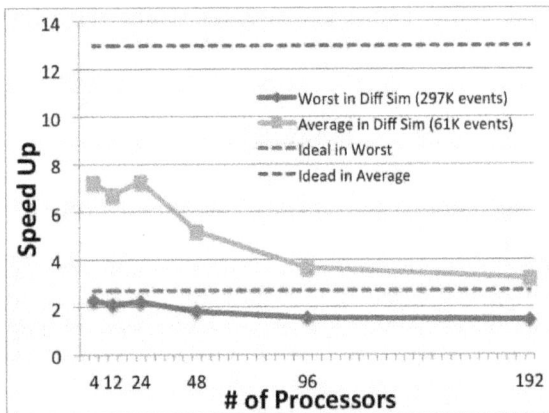

Figure 11: Speed Up from Whole Simulation.

Figure 12 shows elapsed time per outputted event. The elapsed time becomes worse if the number of outputted events decreases in the same number of processors, because the effect of parallel processing decreases in smaller input size.

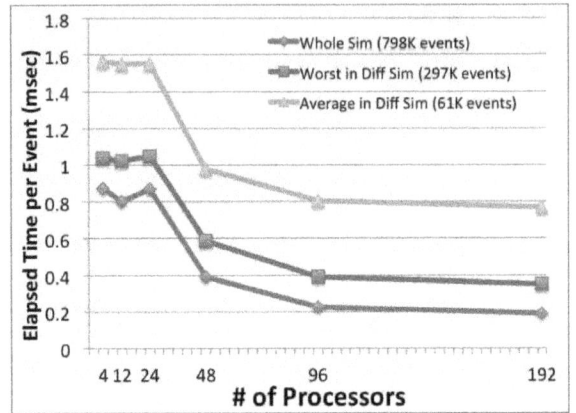

Figure 12: Elapsed Time per Outputted Event.

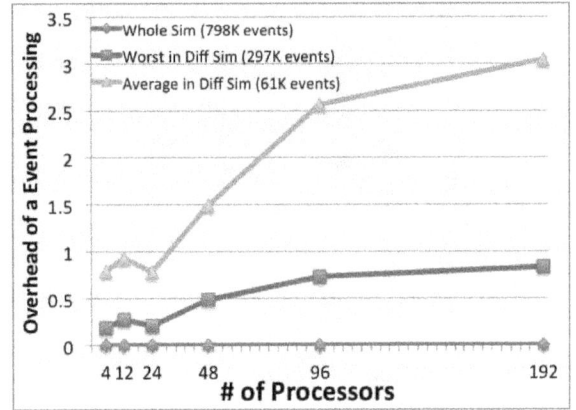

Figure 13: Overhead of Differential Simulation Compared to Whole Simulation.

Figure 13 shows the overhead of repeating execution compared to the whole simulation. The overhead of a differential simulation becomes worse according to the number of processors, where the overhead is defined as follows.

$$\frac{(Time\ per\ Event\ in\ Whole\ Sim) - (Time\ per\ Event\ )}{(Time\ per\ Event\ in\ Whole\ Simulation)}$$

This is because if the more processors there are, the more events are needed to be processed for synchronization, namely, the number of cancel events and the frequency of rollback increase because of the increasing of processors. Also, the overhead increases in the fewer events because the ratio of overhead increases because the elapsed time becomes faster itself in more processors.

To sum up, our simulator with the exact-differential simulation achieves a good performance improvement from the whole simulation. It achieves 7.26 times as much performance improvement in average and 2.26 times improvement even in the worst case as the whole simulation with a road changing scenario. Also, it achieves a good strong scaling till 48 processors in the worst case. Although the strong scaling in the average case is still limited and it has much overhead compared to the whole simulation, the exact-differential simulation can achieve better elapsed time even with fewer processors than the whole simulation.

6. RELATED WORK

Updateable simulation [5] is highly related in our work. In this research, they propose the technique to simulate a part of events and states in repeating execution by canceling and reprocessing events in the similar way as optimistic PDES technique. In the proposal, they define the *reuse function*, which estimate the number of reprocessing events in repeating simulation and it enables to reprocess part of simulation efficiently. Not only the target domain of application, there are also mainly two differences between the proposal and our approach. First, our approach always achieves the exactly same results as the original whole simulation. This is possible by assuming the separated state (LP) and storing all of intermediate states instead of using the reuse function, which is too general to always ensure the exactly same results. Second, in our proposal, we evaluate the simulator on much larger scale than their proposal. This is one of the main contributions in our research.

Cloning techniques [8, 9, 7, 4, 19] are also ways to reuse the intermediate simulation states and events for efficient repeating simulation. In the cloning of simulation, the simulation states in some decided time is copied and from the decided time the simulation is branched with different parameters or scenarios. The difference from our proposal is that such technique does not have "differential" feature, namely, the cloning technique cannot simulate a part of whole state but they can only simulate wholly from intermediate time.

Reducing the scenario patterns or parameter spaces is the direct and general way to speed up the repeating execution. There have been previous researches with such techniques, illustrated in [1, 2, 3]. For example in [2], the all patterns of scenarios are filtered by random sampling and clustering algorithm before simulation for getting the optimum scenario pattern. In [3], they use GA (genetic algorithm) to pick up the appropriate scenario patterns to be simulated in agent-based simulation.

7. CONCLUSION

In this paper, we proposed the exact-differential simulation for large scale agent-based traffic simulation, which enables to reduce the redundant events in repeating the simulation. In our evaluation, we illustrated how many events are required to be processed in the exact-differential simulation and show a big improvement in reducing the number of processing events. Actually, in the case of vehicles' path changes, we can reduce 94.5 % of processing events in average and even in the worst case, we can reduce 70.8 % of processing events compared to a naive way. In the case to change the parameter of one LP, we can reduce 92.4 % in average and 62.8 % in the worst case. Also with our traffic simulator, we show 7.26 times as much performance improvement in average and 2.26 times improvement even in the worst case as the whole simulation with changing a road's speed limit.

For future works, the implementation should be sophisticated. In Time Warp layer, we should adopt some Time Warp's optimizations like lazy cancellation to reduce the overhead of synchronization. Such optimizations are effective not only to the simulation execution itself but also to the exact-differential simulation since the exact-differential simulation uses directly the mechanism of Time Warp. In local storage layer, to achieve larger traffic simulation, we should expand the size with secondary storage to store vast amount of intermediate state and processed events. Also, we should evaluate various patterns of scenarios with different traffic characteristics to show comprehensive effects of our proposal.

8. ACKNOWLEDGMENTS

This research was partly supported by JST CREST (Japan Science and Technology Agency, Core Research for Evolutional Science and Technology).

9. REFERENCES

[1] S.A. Brueckner and H. Van Dyke Parunak. Resource-aware exploration of the emergent dynamics of simulated systems. In *Proceedings of the 2nd international joint conference on Autonomous agents and multiagent systems (Melbourne, Australia, 14–18 Jul. 2003)*, AAMAS'03, pages 781–788. ACM, 2003.

[2] E. Cabrera, E. Luque, M. Taboada, F. Epelde, and L. Ma Iglesias. Abms optimization for emergency departments. In *Proceedings of the 2012 Winter Simulation Conference (Berlin, Germany, 9–12 Dec. 2012)*, WSC'12, pages 1–12. IEEE, 2012.

[3] B. Calvez and G. Hutzler. Automatic tuning of agent-based models using genetic algorithms. In *Proceedings of the 6th international conference on Multi-Agent-Based Simulation (Utrecht, Netherlands, 25 Jul. 2005)*, MABS'05, pages 41–57. Springer, 2005.

[4] D. Chen, S.J. Turner, W. Cai, B.P. Gan, and M.Y.H. Low. Algorithms for HLA-based distributed simulation cloning. *ACM Transactions on Modeling and Computer Simulation (TOMACS)*, 15(4):316–345, 2005.

[5] S.L. Ferenci, R.M. Fujimoto, M.H. Ammar, K.S. Perumalla, and G.F. Riley. Updateable simulation of communication networks. In *Proceedings of the 16th ACM/IEEE/SCS Workshop on Parallel and Distributed Simulation (Washington, D.C., USA, 12–15 May 2002)*, PADS'02, pages 107–114. IEEE, 2002.

[6] M. Hanai, T. Suzumura, A. Ventresque, and K. Shudo. An adaptive vm provisioning method for large-scale agent-based traffic simulations on the cloud. In *Proceedings of IEEE 6th International Conference on Cloud Computing Technology and Science (Singapore, 15–18 Dec. 2014)*, CloudCom'14, pages 130–137. IEEE, 2014.

[7] M. Hybinette. Just-in-time cloning. In *Proceedings of the 22nd ACM/IEEE/SCS Workshop on Principles of Advanced and Distributed Simulation (Kufstein, Austria, 16–19 May 2004)*, PADS'04, pages 45–51. IEEE, 2004.

[8] M. Hybinette and R.M. Fujimoto. Cloning parallel simulations. *ACM Transactions on Modeling and*

Computer Simulation (TOMACS), 11(4):378–407, 2001.

[9] M. Hybinette and R.M. Fujimoto. Scalability of parallel simulation cloning. In *Proceedings of the 35th Annual Simulation Symposium (San Deigo, CA, USA, 14–18 Apr. 2002)*, SS'02, pages 275–282. IEEE, 2002.

[10] D.R. Jefferson. Virtual time. *ACM Transaction Programming Languages and Systems (TOPLAS)*, 7(3):404–425, 1985.

[11] G. Karypis and V. Kumar. METIS - a software package for partitioning unstructured graphs, meshes, and computing fill-reducing orderings of sparse matrices-version 5.1.0. http://glaros.dtc.umn.edu/gkhome/metis/metis/overview (Last access data: 10 May 2015).

[12] G. Karypis and V. Kumar. Multilevel *k*-way partitioning scheme for irregular graph. *Journal of Parallel and Distributed Computing*, 48(1):96–129, 1998.

[13] T. Osogami, T. Imamichi, H. Mizuta, T. Morimura, R. Raymond, T. Suzumura, R. Takahashi, and T. Ide. IBM Mega Traffic Simulator. Technical report, Technical Report RT0896, IBM Research–Tokyo, 2012.

[14] T. Osogami, T. Imamichi, H. Mizuta, T. Suzumura, and T. Ide. Toward simulating entire cities with behavioral models of traffic. *IBM Journal of Research and Development*, 57(5):6:1–6:10, 2013.

[15] K.S. Perumalla. A systems approach to scalable transportation network modeling. In *Proceedings of the 2006 Winter Simulation Conference (Monterey, CA, USA, 3–6 Dec. 2006)*, WSC'06, pages 1500–1507. IEEE, 2006.

[16] T. Suzumura and H. Kanezashi. Accelerating large-scale distributed traffic simulation with adaptive synchronization method. In *Proceedings of the 20th ITS World Congress (Tokyo, Japan, 14–18 Oct. 2013)*. ITS Japan, 2013. Paper No.4083.

[17] T. Suzumura, S. Kato, T. Imamichi, M. Takeuchi, H. Kanezashi, T. Ide, and T. Onodera. X10-based massive parallel large-scale traffic flow simulation. In *Proceedings of the 2012 ACM SIGPLAN X10 Workshop (Beijing, China, 11–16 Jun. 2012)*, X10'12, pages 3:1–3:4. ACM, 2012.

[18] S.B. Yoginath and K.S. Perumalla. Parallel vehicular traffic simulation using reverse computation-based optimistic execution. In *Proceedings of the 22nd ACM/IEEE/SCS Workshop on Principles of Advanced and Distributed Simulation (Rome, Italy, 3–6 Jun. 2008)*, PADS'08, pages 33–42. IEEE, 2008.

[19] G. Zhang, M. Fang, M. Qian, and S. Xu. Parallel cloning simulation of flood mitigation operations in the upper-middle reach of huaihe river. In *Proceedings of the 2012 International Conference on Cyber-Enabled Distributed Computing and Knowledge Discovery (Sanya, China, 10–12 Oct. 2012)*, CyberC'12, pages 73–80. IEEE, 2012.

Traffic Simulation Performance Optimization through Multi-Resolution Modeling of Road Segments

Daniel Zehe, David Grotzky, Heiko Aydt
TUM CREATE
1 CREATE Way
138602 Singapore
+6566014015
{daniel.zehe,david.grotzky,heiko.aydt}@tum-create.edu.sg

Wentong Cai
Nanyang Technological University
639798 Singapore
+657904600
aswtcai@ntu.edu.sg

Alois Knoll
Technische Universität München (TUM)
85748 Munich Germany
+498928918104
knoll@in.tum.de

ABSTRACT

In an agent-based traffic simulation the level of detail is crucial to the system's runtime performance as well as the fidelity of the results. Therefore, different model abstractions have been used throughout literature. Macroscopic, mesoscopic and microscopic models have their use-cases and benefits. Microscopic traffic simulations have a high level of detail but at the same time require a large amount of computational resources. In a large traffic network of a mega-city or an entire country, the use of a complete microscopic simulation is just not feasible. The resource required to do so are for most use-cases in no relation to the actual outcome. We propose a hybrid traffic simulation model that uses both, a high-resolution agent-based microscopic simulation alongside a lower resolution flow-based macroscopic simulation for specific road segments. The problem with using different simulation models is the fidelity at the boundary between such simulation models. This fidelity discrepancy is caused by the difficulties with aggregation and disaggregation passing through the boundary. We show, in this paper, that the computational performance (simulation time) can be improved by 20% while maintaining a relative high accuracy of below 5% deviation from a pure microscopic simulation.

Categories and Subject Descriptors

I.6.8 [**Simulation and Modeling**]: Types of Simulation—*Discrete event*; I.6.3 [**Simulation and Modeling**]: Applications; I.6.5 [**Simulation and Modeling**]: Model Development—*Modeling methodologies*

SIGSIM-PADS'15, June 10–12, 2015, London, United Kingdom.
ACM 978-1-4503-3557-7/15/06.
http://dx.doi.org/10.1145/2769458.2769475.

General Terms

Performance

Keywords

Multi-Resolution Modeling; Macroscopic Modeling; Microscopic Modeling; Traffic Simulation; Aggregation; Disaggregation

1. INTRODUCTION

When simulating traffic, a fine grained view of the given problem is beneficial in many cases; especially when assessing the fragile interactions between driving behavior and the consequences on the vehicle models. For large traffic simulations with several (hundred-) thousand agents the processing power required is rather large. High performance computing is a viable option to decrease the computing time of a given simulation; however, access to such systems is not available to everyone.

There might be regions of a road network of an entire city or country where a lower level of detail is sufficient and computing resources can be saved. In such cases, a multi-resolution model may offer a means to improve processing efficiency while only marginally affecting the overall simulation's fidelity. Such regions could be a highway between different on and off-ramps or long country roads connecting cities or villages.

The purpose of this paper is to present a prototypical design of a multi-resolution agent-based traffic simulation and evaluate its performance with regards to computational performance (decrease in execution time) and fidelity (deviation from the highest resolution). We present model switching between microscopically and macroscopically modeled road segments. We asses the performance gains and fidelity losses of the multi-resolution models at different microscopic to macroscopic ratios for a stretch of road between two intersections.

2. RELATED WORK

There have been several approaches to multi-resolution modeling of traffic. Two main approaches towards the topic have been (1) the use aggregation and disaggregation at runtime and (2) the use multi-resolution entities.

The first approach, which aggregates a high resolution model at runtime to a lower resolution and then disaggregates from the low resolution to a high resolutio, is trivial on the aggregation side. This is because there is usually sufficient data to average over the existing high resolution agents' states. The disaggregation algorithm on the other hand has to interpolate or create/reconstruct information from the low resolution model in order to obtain the state information for the high resolution model. It has been shown that a frequent transition between high and low resolution models through aggregation and disaggregation is not good practice [12]. One problem is the *thrashing effect*, where agents cross between resolution boundaries often, can create a large overhead in computation; especially when running a distributed simulation.

This method of aggregation and disaggregation was initially developed for military simulations [13, 1], since it conforms very well with the command security structure in the military. Battalions, for example, are disaggregated divisions and allow manageable view on certain battlefield scenarios for different key personnel in the chain of command, whereas a disaggregated view of individual fighters is necessary for group leaders.

An approach to multi-resolution traffic modeling was discussed by Burghout [3, 2], where a *ghosting* method was used to ease the transition between microscopic and macroscopic boundaries in the aggregation based approach.

In order to avoid the trashing effects of frequent model switching, Natrajan et al. [11] propose the concept of *Multi-Resolution entities* (MRE). A MRE consolidates the properties of several resolutions in one object. Those properties are then kept consistent by design. This requires a larger memory footprint and individual operations require mode computing cycles for each of the resolutions, but there is no consistency problem.

Another approach to mitigate the trashing effects, especially for traffic simulations, while avoiding the use of MRE has been presented by Chua and Low [5], proposing a set of predictive algorithms. These algorithms are used to project an agent's future position on a road segment.

The multi-fidelity modeling approach presented by Choi et al. [4] describes generally how to convert an existing model into a multi-resolution model. This methodology can be used to increase the simulation speed for a given simulation as well as give measures for fidelity derivation. While their approach generalizes a methodology, this paper focuses on using multi-resolution modeling to investigate its potential in regard to a use in high performance traffic simulations.

3. MODEL DESCRIPTION

The multi-resolution model is comprised of a microscopic car-following model with lane changes and a macroscopic flow model. These models are executed simultaneously and are connected through a model-switching strategy to form a multi-resolution model of traffic on road segments. This section will begin with a detailed description of the two model types independently, followed by a description of the con-

necting boundaries between two joining road segment zones. Such connections require aggregation agent states at the microscopic-macroscopic boundary and a disaggregation at the macroscopic-microscopic boundary.

The model uses a discrete time model for advancing the time in the microscopic and also macroscopic model at the same rate with fixed time intervals. The multi-resolution model has to function as a drop-in replacement for either macroscopic or microscopic simulations. This requires the two different models to have no knowledge of the respective other model and be fully self-sufficient traffic simulations.

3.1 Microscopic Model

For the microscopic traffic simulation models, a car-following model that determines acceleration and gap calculation between agents is important to express the traffic behavior correctly. The Intelligent Driver Model (IDM) developed by Triber et. al. [14] is widely used in agent-based traffic simulations. Together with the Minimal Overall Breaking Induced by Lane Change (MOBIL) [9] algorithms that extend the capabilities of IDM, this model is sufficient to model the driving behavior on a road segment. The acceleration for each agent is given by Equation 1;

$$a_{cur} = a \cdot \left(1 - \left(\frac{v_\alpha}{v_0^\alpha} \right)^\sigma - \left(\frac{s^*(v_\alpha, \Delta v_\alpha)}{s_\alpha} \right)^2 \right) \quad (1)$$

it uses the maximum acceleration of the agent (α) along with the current velocity of the agent as well as the position, derived using Equation 2

$$s^*(v_\alpha, \Delta v_\alpha) = s_0 + v_\alpha \cdot T + \frac{v_\alpha \cdot \Delta v_\alpha}{2\sqrt{a \cdot b}} \quad (2)$$

as well as $s_\alpha = x_{\alpha-1} - x_\alpha - l_{\alpha-1}$, and the velocity of the leading agent. Where s_0 denotes the minimum distance between two agents on one lane, T is the time headway in seconds between agents in normal traffic conditions, and a and b are the comfortable acceleration and deceleration of the agent.

In addition to the IDM and MOBIL features, the underlying microscopic model is augmented to support arbitrary obstacles. Intersections, standing and moving vehicles are considered obstacles. An agent has to assess whether to adjust the acceleration or to change lanes in order to avoid collision with the obstacle. Intersections are a special type of obstacle that span the entire width of the road and have a transparency state. If the state is set to transparent, agents can pass through and normal car following models apply. Otherwise, agents will adjust their speed to come to a full stop. This allows for manipulation of the traffic simulation without violating any IDM or MOBILE rules.

3.2 Macroscopic Model

The macroscopic metrics described by Hoogendoorn and Bovy [7] are one way of expressing a macroscopic view on a road segment. They assume the traffic density k can be derived, as in fluid dynamics, from the number of vehicles that pass through a certain section of road (vc) in a given time and the length (l) of that road segment (Eq. 3).

$$k = \frac{vc}{l} \quad (3)$$

This density, together with the average velocity ($\overline{v}$) of all agents within the given time frame, produces the traffic flow

q (Eq. 4).

$$q = \overline{v} \cdot k \qquad (4)$$

Since the macroscopic model is not aware of individual agents within the segment, the model uses *detectors* at the boundaries to gain knowledge about entering and leaving agents. A front detector senses a microscopic agent entering the macroscopic zone and saves its ID as well as the cycle number (simulation time). The information gathered by the front-detector is used to calculate the vehicle's velocity at the end of the macroscopic zone and when a single vehicle should be passed to a connecting model. This model can either be a macroscopic, microscopic or even a multi-resolution model. The front and back-detectors are illustrated in Figure 1. The three important metrics for macro-

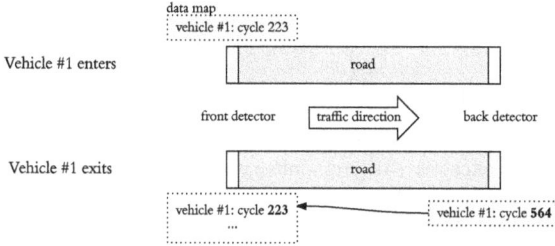

Figure 1: Using detectors to record entering and exiting vehicles

scopic traffic state are average velocity ($\overline{v}$), density (k) and traffic flow (q). The average velocity ($\overline{v}$) can be determined solely by the information gathered from the traffic detectors.

$$\overline{v} = \frac{vc \cdot \overline{v}_{old} + v}{vc + 1} \qquad (5)$$

An update to $\overline{v}$ is done whenever the back detector records a vehicle leaving the macro zone. This will implicitly decrease the vehicle count (vc) by one, since the vehicle is not present in the data structure map assigned to this macroscopic zone. Because the number of vehicles on the road segment has changed, k and q values (Eq. 3 and 4) have to be updated as well.

3.3 Multi-Resolution Model Extensions

The microscopic and macroscopic simulations can be run independently in separate simulations. In a multi-resolution simulation they are executed simultaneously and have to exchange data. The points on a road segment at which data has to be exchanged are the front and back detectors discussed in Section 3.2. In our model we use two approaches for aggregation and disaggregation at the boundaries of the different zones. On the boundary between the microscopic and macroscopic zone (front detector), a *position-triggered aggregation* is used. The back-detector's boundary between the macroscopic and microscopic zone uses a *cycle-based disaggregation* scheme.

There are three different categories in which overall traffic can be categorized, they are dependent on the current traffic density (k). Since they can be observed and/or calculated in macroscopic as well as microscopic zones, they are a good indicator for comparing macroscopic and microscopic road segments.

- **Free Flow Traffic** $k \leq k_c$: The vehicles on the road segment are able to achieve their desired velocity by accelerating normally. This critical density (k_c) has been described by Hoogendoorn and Bovy [7] and is the density at which congestion starts.

- **Congested Traffic** $k_c \leq k \leq k_j$: Since traffic density that exceeds k_c leads to congestions, vehicles can not accelerate as freely as before and might not reach their desired velocity. The vehicles also have not yet come to a full stop that k would be reaching the jam density k_j. Intermittent breaking of agents can be observed. This traffic state has been described by Helbing et. al [6].

- **Jammed Traffic** $k = k_j$: When the density of a road segment reaches k_j as described by Hoogendoorn and Knoop [8]. All vehicles come to a full stop and no movement is possible.

3.3.1 Aggregation

In the microscopic area before the aggregation boundary (micro-zone) the simulation checks during each simulation cycle what agents traverse though the defined position where the micro-zone ends and the macro-zone starts. For estimating the projected cycle time for disaggregating the vehicle back into the micro-zone, two operation modes are possible. One is the single-lane mode where overtaking is not possible and the other one is the multi-lane mode.

In the single-lane case, the vehicle's velocity (v) before passing into the macro-zone is taken, together with the length of the macro-zone (l_{macro}), to determine the number of simulation cycles that have to pass before the vehicle is disaggregated back into the micro-zone at the back detector.

$$\Delta cycles = \frac{l_{macro}}{v \cdot t_{cycle}} \qquad (6)$$

When looking at the model for a multi-lane road segment, the aggregation and cycle prediction gets more complicated. Since overtaking is possible, a vehicle's maximum velocity is not restricted by the leading vehicle on the same lane but also by the vehicle furthest away on any of the parallel lanes. Therefore, the projection takes the traffic density (k) immediately after the macro-zone into account as well. The three cases of traffic state as discussed above have to be regarded.

For the free flow traffic case, the acceleration (a) is regarded for the entire length of the macro-zone. The total travel time through the macro-zone is determined using Equations 7, 8 and 9.

$$l = \frac{a}{2}\Delta t^2 + v \cdot \Delta t \qquad (7)$$

$$\Delta t = \frac{-v + \sqrt{v^2 + 2 \cdot a \cdot l}}{a} \qquad (8)$$

$$\Delta cycles = \frac{\Delta t}{t_{cycle}} \qquad (9)$$

Should the velocity at the end of the macro-zone ($v_{end} = a\Delta t + v$) exceed the desired velocity v_0, the total travel time has to be recalculated by having an acceleration time (Δt_a) and a constant velocity phase (Δt_{v0}).

$$\Delta t_a = \Delta t - \frac{v_{end} - v_0}{a} \qquad (10)$$

$$l_a = \frac{a(\Delta t_a)^2}{2} + v\Delta t_a \qquad (11)$$

The constant velocity phase is calculated using Equation 12.

$$\Delta t_{v0} = \frac{l - l_a}{v_0} \qquad (12)$$

Where t_{v0} is the time spend in constant velocity v_0. l and l_a represent the total distance of the macro-zone and the distance traveled while accelerating respectively.

The cycle count when the vehicle exits the macro-zone is then determined by Equation 13.

$$\Delta\text{cycles} = \frac{\Delta t_a + \Delta t_{v0}}{t_{cycle}} \qquad (13)$$

For the congested traffic state, the acceleration is determined as in the free flow case (Eq. 7,8,9), but then multiplied with a density proportion factor p_{dens} which leads to an adjusted acceleration value a'. This is necessary to cope for very slow moving traffic and to counteract unrealistic acceleration and breaking behaviors. The density proportion factor is calculated using Equation 14 with the densities from above.

$$p_{dens} = \frac{k - k_c}{k_j - k_c} \qquad (14)$$

The cycle count is then determined as it would in the free flow case, except the acceleration is adjusted.

In the traffic jam case, the velocity at the back detector boundary is 0 and the projection is performed using the vehicle's velocity and zero acceleration.

Since both, the single and multi-lane calculation of Δcycles, calculate the time a vehicle spends in the macroscopic simulation, the returned position ($x_{ret} = x + l_{macro}$) is equal with the back detector's position. The absolute cycle in which the vehicle is put back into the microscopic simulation, after removing it, is determined using Equation 15.

$$\text{cycle}_{ret} = \text{cycle}_{now} + \Delta\text{cycles} \qquad (15)$$

IDM car-following model relies very much on a leading vehicle to determine the new acceleration. When there is no vehicle leading, a free-flow mode is chosen. The free-flow mode in the IDM model is much simpler and assumes the maximum acceleration. However, once an agent is removed from the microscopic model, a following vehicle loses its leading vehicle to base its acceleration algorithms on (Eq 1). Free-Flow traffic mode is not applicable to the following vehicle, since it could lead to unwanted acceleration. Therefore, we introduce *ghost vehicles* to mitigate this problem [3]. A ghost vehicle contains only a subset of a true microscopic agent and is used to approximate a microscopic model. A ghost vehicle is spawned as soon as

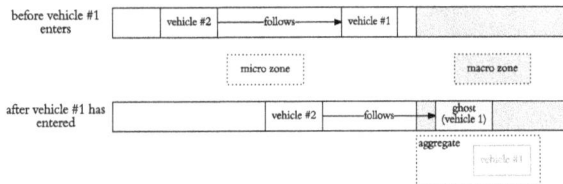

Figure 2: Ghost vehicle generation at micro-macro boundary

a vehicle traverses through the micro-macro boundary. At

this point the ghost's length, position and velocity are set to the properties of the removed agent's. Each cycle, the ghost's microscopic model states are updated by the multi-resolution component. This tricks the subsequent agent into following into the macro-zone. A ghost moves along the macro-zone until another vehicle enters the macro-zone. At that point the ghost is discarded and replaced by a new one. The movement of a ghost is dependent on the number of lanes (single or multi-lane mode) and the traffic state behind the macro-zone. In single lane mode, the ghost moves along the macro-zone at a constant velocity it had when it was created. In a multi-lane scenario, the traffic state in the microscopic zone behind the macro-zone is used to modify the ghost's velocity. The new velocity $v' = (1 - \text{visc}) \cdot v$ uses a viscosity metric that is derived from the traffic density behind the macro-zone and given by Equation 16 (similar to the density proportion factor p_{dense}).

$$\text{visc} = \begin{cases} \frac{k - k_c}{k_j - k_c} & k_c \le k \le k_j \\ 1 & k > k_j \end{cases} \qquad (16)$$

At each cycle the density inside the macro zone is queried and if it exceeds the jam density k_j the ghost is stopped. This leads to agents reducing their speed when entering the macro-zone and eventually stopping agents before entering the macro-zone. Since the macro density is updated whenever a vehicle is disaggregated back into the microscopic model, movement of the ghost continues when k_{macro} falls below k_j. Should a vehicle reach the end of the macro-zone before being replaced, it is discarded.

3.3.2 Disaggregation

When vehicles are returned to the macroscopic-microscopic boundary disaggregation, has to be performed. There are 3 steps involved to ensure the model integrity is not violated.

1. Depending on the current cycle time, the internal data structure holding all agents currently in the macro-zone is checked, and all agents that have a lower return cycle number (cycle_{ret}) are prepared to be returned to the microscopic zone. The data structure is depicted in Figure 3

2. If there is a vehicle that is supposed to be returned at the current cycle, the lane(s) are checked for enough free space to insert the vehicle safely.

3. Once a vehicle is supposed to be returned at a specific location, the IDM calculation is executed. It is then checked if an emergency breaking situation would occur. If this is the case, insertion is suspended. This check is not executed when the average velocity of the micro-zone is below 10% of the roads recommended speed, in order to allow for insertion when the traffic state is strongly congested.

For a multi-lane scenario, all lanes are checked against the free-space and emergency breaking conditions. Should the checks fail for every single lane, the disaggregation is postponed. Vehicles stay in the data structure and are checked again on the next cycle. On a successful disaggregation the vehicles are removed from the data structure and the back-detector is notified.

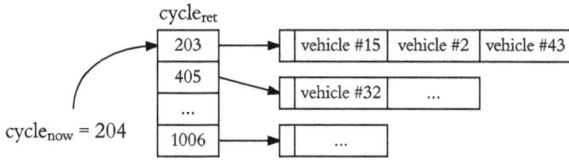

Figure 3: Microcscopic vehicle date holding data structure

4. MODEL EVALUATION

Since the aim of the proposed multi-resolution model is tc increase the performance while affecting the model fidelity as little as possible, we compare the multi-resolution performance against a pure microscopic simulation.

4.1 Design of Experiments

We design three experiments with the following setup in order to establish a microscopic base line for comparison and experiments for evaluating performance and fidelity respectively.

- The **Microscopic Mode** simulates the entire road segment using only the microscopic model. There is no need for model switching and it serves as the base-line implementation we are going to compare the performance and fidelity against (compare Figure 4a).

- The **Multi-resolution Mode** simulates a road segment as discussed in Section 3. Both microscopic and macroscopic models are used and model-switching at the boundaries is executed (compare Figure 4b). This is done to gain the performance measures that are later compared to the base-line microscopic model experiment.

- The **Dual-Simulation Mode** runs the previous modes simultaneously with identical starting conditions. The mode is used to evaluate the fidelity effects of multi-resolution execution (compare Figure 4c).

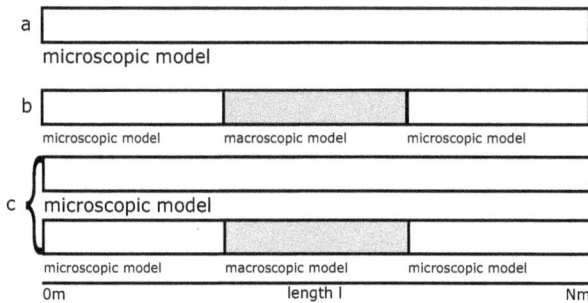

Figure 4: Simulation experiment setups

We have chosen 4 different driver-vehicle unit configurations for the microscopic road segments. They are normal, timid and aggressive driver as well as trucks. Each of the configurations have different values for the preferred maximum speed, the time headway, the acceleration and deceleration for normal traffic conditions. These values for different types have been identified by Kesting et al. [10]. In order

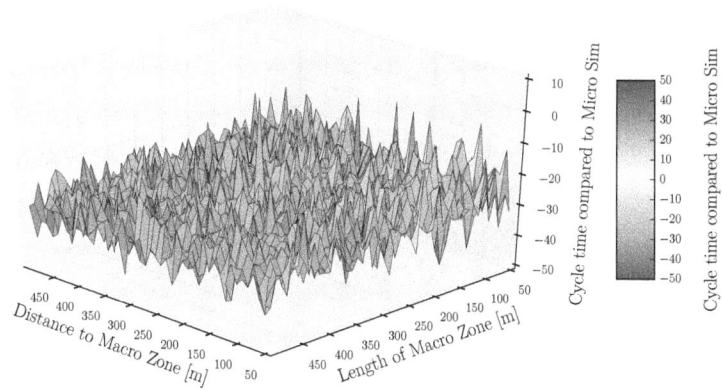

Figure 5: Single lane performance comparison: Relative performance between microscopic and multi-resolution mode. Cycle time up to 40% reduced for long macro-zones and long distance to macro-zone.

to generate a heterogeneous agent population, the properties are uniformly distributed around the values identified by Kestig et al. with a margin of ±20%.

4.2 Model Performance

The goal of this paper is to evaluate the performance increase when using multi-resolution models for traffic simulations. Therefore, we compare the average processing of one processing cycle in the simulation for a pure microscopic simulation ($\bar{t}_{micro}$) and a multi-resolution simulation ($\bar{t}_{mrs}$). The performance difference (Δp) was then calculated using Equation 17.

$$\Delta p = \frac{\bar{t}_{mrs}}{\bar{t}_{micro}} - 1 \qquad (17)$$

A close-to-zero The experiment run several (> 20) simulations in microscopic mode (Figure 4 a) as well as multi-resolution mode (Figure 4 b). Each simulation created 15 agents and stopped them at the same location within each simulation with a non-transparent obstacle. Once all agents fully stop, the obstacle are made transparent. This allows the IDM to accelerate the agents and move along the road segment. For each simulation cycle the exection time is recorded and then averaged over the entire simulation until all agents reach the end of the road segment.

value of Δp indicates that the performance of both simulations is equal, whereas negative values indicates less processing time is spend on a cycle in the multi-resolution simulation. The performances for single- and multi-lane simulations are shown in Figues 5 and 6. It shows that for the single-lane mode the performance increases when the macrozone becomes longer. An increase in model performance is also seen, even though not so prominently visible, when the distance to the macro-zone gets longer. The same general shape can be seen in the multi-lane mode. There, the overall performance increase is, averaged over all configurations, bigger(+30% compared to +25%). Nevertheless, the individual data-points can show a higher performance increase. It also shows that there is a larger deviation from the mean value. The performance increase is bigger due to the more complex model in the pure microscopic simulation. There is of course an overhead due to the model switching mechanism. The mechanism includes the aggregation of the agent

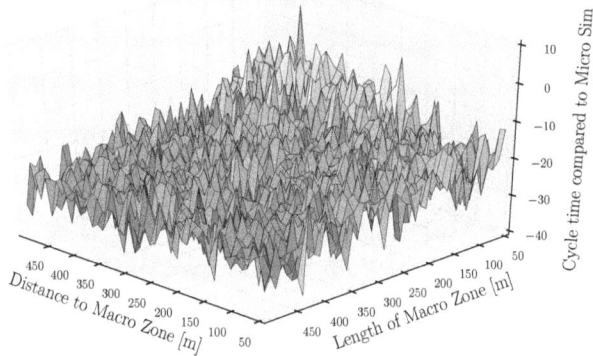

Figure 6: Dual lane performance comparison: Relative performance between microscopic and multi-resolution mode. Cycle time reduction lessens when decreasing the length of the macro-zone.

at the front-detector, where the agent is removed from the microscopic simulation, the estimated re-entry cycle is calculated and a ghost vehicle is created; and the disaggregation, where the agents is put back into the microscopic simulation (see Sections 3.3.1 and 3.3.2). This overhead with regard to the entires simulation run is shown in Table 1.

	min%	max%	mean%	σ
single-lane	9.3	14.5	9.4	$\pm\,0.39$
multi-lane	6.5	10.8	7.6	$\pm\,0.74$

Table 1: Model switching overhead

4.3 Model Fidelity

The model fidelity is determined between the multi-resolution simulation and the pure-microscopic simulation using the experimental setup *Dual-Simulation Mode*. In order to quantify the differences we have to execute both simulations with the exact same starting parameters and settings. This leads to each agent in the microscopic simulation having an exact counterpart in the multi-resolution simulation. We are evaluating two types of deviations that occurs from the switching and the macroscopic model:

- **Agent State Deviation** describes the difference between the interval state variables.

- **Differences in Traffic Flow** is a more statistical assessment of the influence of the multi-resolution simulation. It is a macroscopic metric used instead of the individual state based agents fidelity.

4.3.1 Agent State Deviation

In order to determined the agent state deviation by the proposed multi-resolution model, we use the dual-simulation mode simulation with a road length of 5000 meters and 100 vehicles. Vehicles are spawned with a distribution of $3:3:3:1$ of the vehicles classes discussed previously. Both simulations contain a non-transparent obstacle at the exact same position and are only opened when all agents have come to a full stop. This obstacle will mimic an intersection, where a defined number of vehicles are release at

the same time. This intersection is always placed before the macroscopic zone (front detector). In the multi-resolution simulation model a macroscopic zone is placed at the 2000 meter mark. This is not present in the pure microscopic simulation. The dual simulation mode setup is illustrated in Figure 7. Once a vehicles leaves the macroscopic zone,

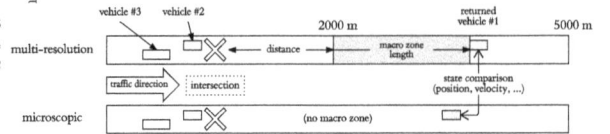

Figure 7: Dual-Simulation setup for agent stat deviation experiment

its state is logged in each of the simulations and analyzed after the simulation finishes. The root-mean-square for the position (x_{rms}) and velocity (v_{rms}) deviation are calculated.

$$y_{rms} \in \{x_{rms}, v_{rms}\} \qquad (18)$$

$$y_{rms} = \sqrt{\frac{\sum_{i=1}^{N}(y_{mrs}^i - y_{micro}^i)^2}{N}} \qquad (19)$$

Since the rms value grows with positive and negative value differences, it only gives absolute discrepancy information. A more fitting estimate for over- and underestimation of the agent state variables is the root mean square of the ratio ($y_{rms}^{\%}$) between multi-resolution simulation and pure microscopic simulation.

$$y_{rms}^{\%} = \sqrt{\frac{\sum_{i=1}^{N}\left(\frac{y_{mrs}^i}{y_{micro}^i}\right)^2}{N} - 1} \qquad (20)$$

If the root-mean-square ratio is 0.0 then there is no significant difference between the microscopic and multi-resolution simulation, but if the value is negative, the multi-resolution vehicles have a smaller value (e.g. position behind microscopic simulation). This means they were underestimated when aggregating. Should the value be positive the multi-resolution vehicles overestimated their projection values. These experiments were repeated 20 times and the standard deviation (σ) to all values was calculated.

$$\sigma_y = \sqrt{\frac{\sum_{i=1}^{20}(y_{rms}^i - \overline{y}_{rms})}{20 - 1}} \qquad (21)$$

The experiments were conducted with different ratios of microscopic and macroscopic regions. This was done by changing the length of the macro-zones without changing the overall road segment length constant. This leads to an increasing proportion of the road segment being handled by the macroscopic model. We choose macro-zones length between 50 and 500 meters with 10 meter increments (45 configurations). Additionally, we varied the distance from the intersection to the beginning of the macro-zone. The same 50 to 500 meter and 10 meter increment was applied there (45 configurations). This lead to a total number of 40,500 simulation runs ($45 \cdot 45 \cdot 20$) in single lane mode and the same amount in multi-lane mode.

The two parameters discussed previously are shown on the x an y-axis of Figure 8. The z-axis shows the positional deviation in percent between the microscopic and

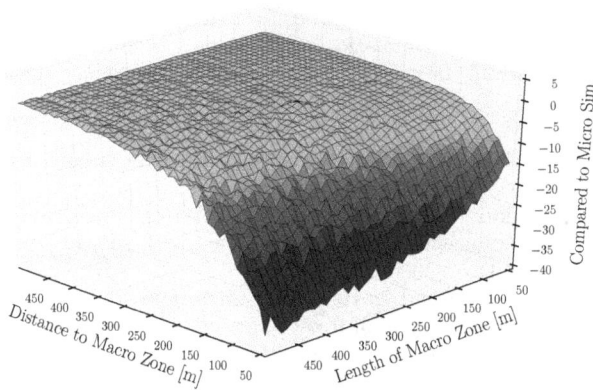

Figure 8: Position deviation in percent on single-lane mode: Longer macro-zones and short distances to the macro-zone show the highest positional difference. Small deviation visible for longer distance to the macro-zone regardless of the length of the macro-zone.

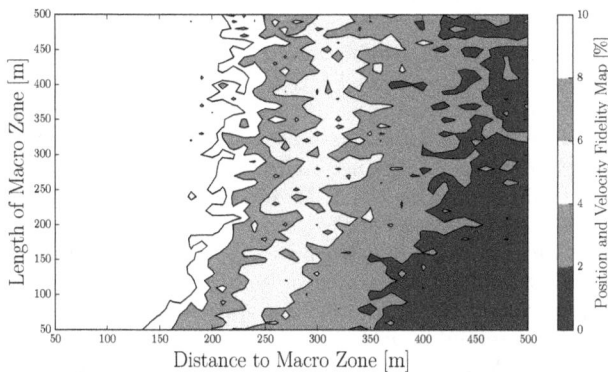

Figure 9: Position and velocity deviation map for single-lane mode: Maximum percent deviation for either velocity or position dependent on the distance to macro-zone and the length of the macro-zone. Distance to macro-zone bigger influence than the length.

multi-resolution simulation. A negative value stands for an underestimation of the projected position after disaggregation.

In the single-lane scenario the distance to the macro-zone is more important than the length of the macro-zone itself. This can be observed since the graph falls down when the distance to the macro zone is below 200 meters for the distance to the macro-zone but not when the length is changed. This only has a significant effect when the distance to the macro-zone is already low.

For the multi-lane mode (number of lanes between 2 and 5) the results are similar. It also shows that the distance to the macro-zone has a smaller influence than the length. Short macro-zones and long distance to the macro-zone have the least influence on the deviation of position.

The map in Figure 9 shows the absolute maximum deviation from either position or velocity (worst case for deviation) for the single-lane mode. It can be seen that the distance to the macro-zone has a bigger influence and is more

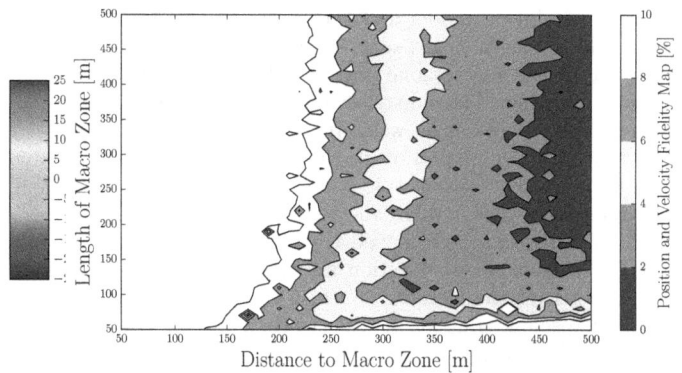

Figure 10: Position and velocity deviation map for multi-lane mode with three lanes: Maximum percent deviation for either velocity or position dependent on the distance to macro-zone and the length of the macro-zone. Distance to macro-zone has bigger influence than length, except for very short macro-zones.

volatile. For road segments that are at least 200 m the deviation is below 10%. The same is shown in Figure 10, except that there are fewer areas with less than 2% deviation and more configurations lead to a higher than 10% deviation. Also it can be seen that the distance to macro-zone is of influence since the fidelity gets worse when the length of the macro-zone is really short.

4.3.2 Traffic Flow Deviation

After looking at the agents' state deviation, the comparison of the traffic flow gives a more statistical approach to the influence of the multi-resolution simulation. Therefore, the region behind the macro-zone is examined. The tested scenario is depicted in Figure 11, where the observed area in both simulations is shown. We logged the traffic flow in both simulations from the cycle when the first vehicle enters the zone in either simulation until the simulation run ended. A student's-t test, to disprove the hypothesis

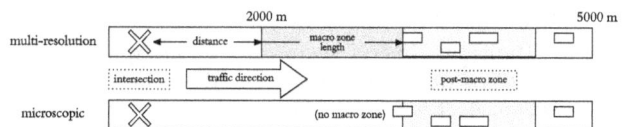

Figure 11: Post macro zone flow comparison

that there is no significant difference between the two zones, has been conducted. This test shows that for a single-lane ($p \leq 0.773$) and a dual-lane ($p \leq 0.879$) the null-hypothesis cannot be discarded and therefore the traffic flow in both simulation shows no significant difference by introducing the multi-resolution model.

5. CONCLUSION

The evaluation shows that a more than 20% performance increase compared to a pure microscopic model can be achieved. The main factors that influence the relative performance (pure microscopic vs. multi-resolution) is the complexity of the high resolution model and the length of the road segment. The longer the road segment, the more time that can be spent in the macro-zone and therefore less computing needs to be done. The side-effect of this is that the fidelity of the result decreases as well. It also shows that a lower than 6% fidelity deviation on single-lane roads can be kept. This is given the macroscopic zone is at least 150m from an intersection. For a dual-lane road segment, a deviation of less then 6% can be achieved when the macro-zone is at least 300m from an intersection and 200m long. We have also shown that the introduction of a macroscopic element into a microscopic simulation does not change the traffic flow behind a macroscopic zone modeled.

In this paper we have shown that a simple multi-resolution approach to agent-based traffic simulations can have a great improvement in the performance of the simulation. Nevertheless, the performance improvement comes at a price of model fidelity. We have shown that with macroscopic metric there is no significant difference between a multi-resolution simulation and a pure-microscopic. With microscopic measures a loss in fidelity is observed; however, depending on the road configuration, this can be reduced to a minimum. For a city scale scenario we have statically analyzed the potential performance gain and fidelity loss.

Future research should look into the dynamic creation of multi-resolution road segments depending on the road conditions. Also, the static analysis for an entire country could lead to an even bigger performance increases, since connecting highways or country roads are longer and offer more macroscopic zones that are easier to predict.

6. ACKNOWLEDGMENTS

This work was financially supported by the Singapore National Research Foundation under its Campus for Research Excellence And Technological Enterprise (CREATE) programme.

7. REFERENCES

[1] M. Adelantado and P. Siron. Multiresolution Modeling and Simulation of an Air-Ground Combat Application. In *proceedings of the 2001 Spring Simulation Interoperability Workshop*, Orlando, USA, 25-30 Mar., 2001. IEEE.

[2] W. Burghout. *Hybrid microscopic-mesoscopic traffic simulation*. Doctoral dissertation, Royal Institute of Technology, Stockholm, 2004.

[3] W. Burghout and H. Koutsopoulos. Hybrid Traffic Simulation Models: Vehicle Loading at Meso–Micro Boundaries. In *proceeding of the International Symposium of Transport Simulation*, Lausanne, Switzerland, 04-06 Sep., 2006.

[4] S. H. Choi, S. J. Lee, and T. G. Kim. Multi-fidelity modeling & simulation methodology for simulation speed up. In *proceedings of SIGSIM-PADS '14*, pages 139–150, New York, New York, USA, 18-21 May, 2014. ACM.

[5] B. Chua and M. Low. Predictive algorithms for aggregation and disaggregation in mixed mode simulation. In *proceeding of the Winter Simulation Conference*, pages 1356–1365, Austin, Texas, USA, 13-16 Dec., 2009. IEEE.

[6] D. Helbing and A. Hennecke. Micro-and macro-simulation of freeway traffic. *Mathematical and computer modelling*, 35(5):517–547, 2002.

[7] S. Hoogendoorn and P. Bovy. State-of-the-art of vehicular traffic flow modelling. *Proceedings of the Institution of Mechanical Engineers, Part I: Journal of Systems and Control Engineering*, 215(4):283–303, 2001.

[8] S. Hoogendoorn and V. Knoop. Traffic flow theory and modelling. In D. Banister, B. Van Wee, and J. A. Annema, editors, *The Transport System and Transport Policy: An Introduction*, pages 125–159. Edward Elgar Publishing Ltd, Cheltenham, United Kingdom, 2012.

[9] A. Kesting, M. Treiber, and D. Helbing. General Lane-Changing Model MOBIL for Car-Following Models. *Transportation Research Record: Journal of the Transportation Research Board*, 1999:86–94, 2007.

[10] A. Kesting, M. Treiber, and D. Helbing. Agents for traffic simulation. In A. M. Uhrmacher and D. Weyns, editors, *Multi-Agent Systems: Simulation and Applications*, pages 325–356. CRC Press, Boca Raton, Florida, USA, 2008.

[11] A. Natrajan. MRE: a flexible approach to multi-resolution modeling. In *proceedings of the 11th Workshop on Parallel and Distributed Simulation*, pages 156–163, Lockenhaus, Austria, 10-13 June, 1997. IEEE.

[12] P. F. ReynoldsJr, A. Natrajan, and S. Srinivasan. Consistency maintenance in multiresolution simulation. *Transactions on Modeling and Computer Simulation (TOMACS)*, pages 368–392, 1997.

[13] G. Tan, W. Ng, and F. Moradi. Aggregation/disaggregation in HLA multi-resolution distributed simulation. In *proceedings of the IEEE/ACM International Symposium on Distributed Simulation and Real Time Applications*, pages 76–83, Cincinnati, Ohio, USA, 13-15 Aug., 2001. IEEE.

[14] M. Treiber, A. Hennecke, and D. Helbing. Congested traffic states in empirical observations and microscopic simulations. *Physical Review E*, 62:1805–1824, Aug. 2000.

Author Index